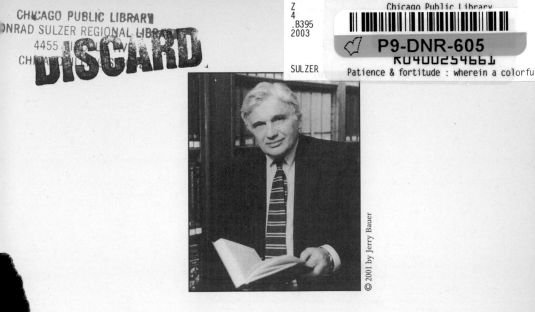

© 2001 by Jerry Bauer

About the Author

NICHOLAS A. BASBANES was born in Lowell, Massachusetts, in 1943, graduated from Bates College in 1965, and received a master of arts degree from Pennsylvania State University while serving as a naval officer aboard the aircraft carrier *Oriskany* in the Tonkin Gulf in 1969. An award-winning investigative reporter during the early 1970s, Basbanes was literary editor of the Worcester *Sunday Telegram* from 1978 to 1991, and for the next eight years wrote a nationally syndicated column on books and authors. He is a former president of the Friends of the Robert H. Goddard Library of Clark University, which has established a student book-collecting competition in his honor. His first book, *A Gentle Madness*, was a finalist for the National Book Critics Circle Award in nonfiction and was named a *New York Times* Notable Book of the Year.

ALSO BY NICHOLAS A. BASBANES

A Gentle Madness:
Bibliophiles, Bibliomanes, and
the Eternal Passion for Books

Perennial

An Imprint of HarperCollins*Publishers*

PATIENCE

&

FORTITUDE

Wherein a Colorful Cast of Determined Book Collectors, ~~Dealers~~, and Librarians Go About the Quixotic Task of Preserving a Legacy

NICHOLAS A. BASBANES

A hardcover edition of this book was published in 2001 by HarperCollins Publishers.

HarperCollins books may be purchased for educational, business, or sales promotional use. For information please write: Special Markets Department, HarperCollins Publishers Inc., 10 East 53rd Street, New York, NY 10022.

First Perennial edition published 2003.

Designed by Claire Naylon Vaccaro

The Library of Congress has catalogued the hardcover edition as follows:
Basbanes, Nicholas A.
Patience & fortitude : a roving chronicle of book people, book places, and book culture
/ Nicholas A. Basbanes.—1st ed.
p.   cm.
Includes bibliographical references (p.).
ISBN 0-06-019695-5
1. Books—History.   2. Books and reading—History.   3. Book collecting—History.
4. Libraries—History.   I. Title: Patience & fortitude.   II. Title.
Z4 .B395 2001
002'.09—dc21   2001016935

ISBN 0-06-051446-9 (pbk.)

03   04   05   06   07   ❖/RRD   10   9   8   7   6   5   4   3   2   1

For CVB and the next quarter-century

ACKNOWLEDGMENTS

Primary research for this book was carried out over a period of five years in many places, and I am indebted to those individuals listed in the general bibliography who gave generously of their time, and whose insights enliven these pages. I regret being unable to use all the material they so graciously provided, though I profited enormously from their willingness to share their knowledge with me, and thank them for their contributions to this work.

I am equally beholden to the librarians, curators, and staff of the many libraries, repositories, and museums I visited. All were unfailingly forthcoming and generous with their time and expertise; they are a dedicated lot, and I commend them for their service to books and to the great community of appreciative readers.

Special mention must be made of Kenneth E. Carpenter of Harvard University, Martin Antonetti of Smith College, Robert W. Allison of Bates College, Dr. Graham Speake of Oxford University, Ray English of Oberlin College, Alan Bell of the London Library, Andrea Immel of Princeton University, and the booksellers William S. Reese and Fred Schreiber, each of whom read portions of the book in manuscript, and offered advice that improved the work measurably. All conclusions, opinions, and findings, of course, remain my own.

For leads, suggestions, contacts, and help in obtaining research materials, I am grateful to individuals throughout the book world, and wish to cite in particular the courtesies extended by William P. Stoneman and Roger E. Stoddard of the Houghton Library at Harvard University; Paul LeClerc and Edward J. Kasinec of the New York Public Library; András J. Riedlemayer and Jeffrey B. Spurr at the Fine Arts Library of Harvard University; Tania Vitvitsky of the Sabre Foundation in Boston; Robert K. O'Neill of Boston College; Bernard A. Margolis and Katherine Dibble at the Boston Public Library; David H. Stam of Syracuse University; John Y. Cole of the Library of Congress; James E. Hogan and Jayne M. Fox at the Dinand Library of the College of the Holy Cross; Susan Baughman, Mary Hartman, and Irene Walch at the Goddard Library of Clark University; Joel Silver at the Lilly Library of Indiana University; William A. Gosling at the University of Michigan; Alice Prochaska at the British Library; Alice D. Schreyer at the University of Chicago; Jean W. Ashton at Columbia University; Joanne Schneider at Middlebury College; Robert L. Byrd at Duke University; Ellen S. Dunlap at the American Antiquarian Society; Terry Belanger at the University of Virginia, Charlottesville; Charles A. Schwartz at the University of Massachusetts, Boston; Eric Holzenberg and Carol Z. Rothkopf at the Grolier Club in New York; Richard Landon at the Fisher Rare Book Library of the University of Toronto; Richard W. Oram at the Harry Ransom Humanities Research Center, University of Texas, Austin; Peter E. Hanff and Anthony S. Bliss at the Bancroft Library, University of California, Berkeley; Kurt Nowak and Erica Dieter at Die Deutsche Bibliothek in Frankfurt; Thierry Grillet, Yannick Maignien, Daniel Renoult, and Alix Chevallier at the Bibliothèque Nationale de France in Paris; Carola Sjögren de Hauke of the Bernadotte Library at the Royal Palace in Stockholm; Kai-Michael Sprenger at the Gutenberg Museum in Mainz; Trevor Joy Johnson at the Boston Athenæum; Rebecca Chetley at the British Museum; Andrea Grimes at the San Francisco Public Library; Priscilla Juvelis in Cambridge, Massachusetts; Justin Schiller in New York City; Walter Biller in San Francisco; Bernard M. Rosenthal and William P. Wreden Jr. in Berkeley, California; Philip D. Leighton in Portolo Valley,

California; Judith Lowry in New York City; Steven J. Schuyler in North Reading, Massachusetts; Carol Grossman in Boulder, Colorado; Irwin T. Holtzman in Detroit; and Edgar Rose in Chicago.

In Washington, I express my deepest appreciation to Elias N. Galanis at the Greek embassy, Basma Mahmoud at the Egyptian embassy, Carlos Rey at the Spanish embassy, Sensu Remisci at the Turkish embassy, and Michael Giacalone at the Italian embassy for their assistance in helping make my research trips to their countries productive; in Vatican City, Mirella Giacalone of the U.S. embassy to the Holy See took steps to ensure that everything went smoothly.

Niclas Samuel Wallin was tireless in his determination to introduce me to the bibliophilic high spots of Sweden, a bravura performance that he matched several months later during an unforgettable walking tour of Rome; Theodore Korres, professor of Byzantine history at Aristotle University in Thessaloniki, Luis Escobar de la Serna of the University of Madrid in Spain, Konstantinos Sp. Staikos in Athens, and Lucy Gordon Rastelli in Rome were most hospitable during my visits to their cities.

Minor portions of chapters 2, 3, 4, 5, and 6 appeared in substantially different form in *Gazette of the Grolier Club*. I am grateful to the editors of those publications for giving me an opportunity to develop some of the ideas for *Patience & Fortitude* in their pages.

For encouragement and sage advice, my deepest thanks to George J. Basbanes, attorney and brother, and Everett M. Skehan, Brian A. Higgins, and Robert Bradbury, my longtime friends and confidants. My literary agents, Glen Hartley and Lynn T. Chu, have been rock-solid in their support of my endeavors over the years, and I am pleased once again to record the high regard I have for the care and attention they apply to the task.

At HarperCollins, I am grateful for the excellent support extended by Jane Beirn, the director of publicity; David Semanki, the assistant to my editor; David Koral, the senior production editor; copyeditor Miranda Ottewell; and Elaine Luthy, for a meticulously prepared index.

For all the vicissitudes endemic to the publishing industry—I have had eight editors come and go over the past dozen years—I count my blessings that I began my career as a published author with Allen H. Peacock at Holt, and that I am now at HarperCollins in the welcoming hands of Hugh Van Dusen, a consummate professional whose support and enthusiasm have been a source of great satisfaction to me.

My father, John G. Basbanes, ninety years old this year, remains the greatest storyteller I have ever known, and my mother, Georgia Koumoutseas Basbanes, the most steadfast champion of my work, and I recognize them yet again for the examples they set in my life, and for the direction they provided. I note with great affection as well the gentleness, humanity, and sweetness of soul of Louis G. Valentzas, my father-in-law.

My daughters, Barbara Georgia Basbanes and Nicole Stella Basbanes, gave me love and inspiration the first time around; this time they added their creative skills to the mix, Barbara with her elegant translations from the French, Nicole with her exquisite feel for narrative and her simpatico sense of humor that unfailingly helped keep the ship on an even keel.

Expressing proper credit for the contributions of my wife, Constance V. Basbanes, continues to be an exercise in futility, but I will offer a few heartfelt words all the same. She is my alter ego, my sounding board, my most perceptive critic, my beloved travel companion, and my resourceful research associate, but above all else she is a model of strength, sanity, and civility in an uncertain world. For all this and so much more, she has, as always, my deepest love and admiration.

CONTENTS

CONTENTS

PART THREE: BOOK PLACES

LIST OF ILLUSTRATIONS

Like all the men of the Library, in my younger days I traveled; I have journeyed in quest of a book, perhaps the catalog of catalogs. Now that my eyes can hardly make out what I myself have written, I am preparing to die, a few leagues from the hexagon where I was born. When I am dead, compassionate hands will throw me over the railing; my tomb will be the unfathomable air, my body will sink for ages, and will decay and dissolve in the wind engendered by my fall, which shall be infinite. I declare that the Library is endless.

JORGE LUIS BORGES
(1899–1986)

PROLOGUE

D r. Otto Bettmann had been talking for several hours about the past, recalling in poignant detail his escape from Adolf Hitler's monstrous fury in 1935, and how he had fashioned a new life in America as one of the great innovators in modern communications, but now it was noon, and time to take a break. "Come," the ninety-two-year-old legend known for decades as the "Picture Man" said cheerfully, clapping his hands with crisp finality, "You must be starved. Let's go have some lunch."

Internationally respected as the creator of a vast archive of photographic material that he had furnished to book designers, magazine publishers, newspaper editors, advertising agents, and television producers, Dr. Bettmann was a man of many interests, and a superior conversationalist to boot; the author of numerous books on a variety of consuming subjects, he was particularly eloquent about the power and majesty of the written word. A skilled musician as well, he was devoted to the compositions of Johann Sebastian Bach, and as we walked out of his study, I asked if he would play something for me and my wife on the small organ in his living room. Without any hesitation, he sat at the keyboard and proceeded directly into a lovely minuet from one of the master's piano suites.

Later, at a seafood restaurant near his retirement home in Deerfield Beach, Florida, Dr. Bettmann explained his passion for Bach, a native, like himself, of Leipzig. "Bach always brings us back to the beginning. It is my conviction that this man was sent here to make a little order out of chaos. Beethoven doesn't do that at all; he starts out, then shoots off into outer space. Bach, on the other hand, is confined, small in his melodic inventions, but then he gets hold of a theme, and everything is in such wonderful order."

We sat for a while, enjoying our lunch and indulging the demands of some brazen songbirds that had stopped by our outdoor table to scrounge for bread crumbs. Presently, Dr. Bettmann picked up the conversation from where he had left off a few minutes earlier. "What did God do when he started the world? He made order out of chaos. I get this wonderful feeling of *order* in everything Bach writes. He starts with a theme and develops it. It must always be in the same tonality and in the same spirit. The theme is carried forth, it goes up, up into forms of variation, but it always comes back to where it started."

My meeting with Otto Bettmann had been occasioned by a lavish story on the front page of the *New York Times* in October 1995. "Huge Photo Archive Bought by Software Billionaire Gates," the headline had announced, trumpeting yet another coup pulled off by William H. Gates III, the chairman of Microsoft Corp. and owner of Corbis Corp., the private company based in Bellevue, Washington, that had negotiated the acquisition. With his purchase of the Bettmann Archive, said to be a "multi-million-dollar transaction," the world's principal provider of the software used to operate computer systems had secured sufficient raw material to become a major supplier of electronic content as well, and he would continue to add other materials to his inventory. By 2000 Corbis was claiming access to more than 60 million images.

A sampling of the pictures Gates had acquired in the transaction, including 11.5 million news photographs that the Bettmann Archive had bought from United Press International and Reuters in 1990, was printed alongside the article: baseball great Joe DiMaggio kissing Marilyn Monroe; a dapper Winston Churchill flashing his trademark "V for Victory" sign; and the classic drawing of a floppy-eared dog cocking his head toward an RCA Victor record player. In time, the pictures would be scanned, converted into the "zeroes and ones" of digital imagery, and offered to a wide range of commercial clients over the Internet.

In all the excitement surrounding the huge sale, marginal attention had been paid to Otto Ludwig Bettmann, the Jewish emigré to America who started to create the archive in the 1930s, a man whose life had touched every decade of the twentieth century, a pioneer whose worldview had been influenced just as profoundly by the events of his times. A sidebar to the *Times* story appeared inside the newspaper under the headline "From One Vision to Sixteen Million Images," and showed how the world's largest photo archive originated with the private collection of one person: "That collector, Otto L. Bettmann, was born into a prosperous family in Leipzig, in 1903. His father was an orthopedic surgeon who transmitted his love of books to his son. As early as age twelve, Otto began rooting through the family's wastebaskets and stockpiling medical illustrations."

Though briefly sketched in this compact profile, Dr. Bettmann's life experiences clearly involved some of the themes I was developing for this work, among them the transmission and preservation of knowledge, sweeping changes in the way information is amassed and stored, and, above all, an abiding reverence for reading and the printed word. Trained as a historian, Dr. Bettmann had worked as a curator of rare books at the Prussian State Art Library in Berlin, where he began using a new invention—the 35-millimeter Leica camera—to photograph manuscripts in the German national collections. When the National Socialists assumed control and began removing Jews from influential positions, he fled to the United States, carrying with him two steamer trunks packed with 25,000 photographic images, many of them on film negatives he had made himself. Notwithstanding the many thousands of pictures he amassed in his lifetime, Dr. Bettmann remained firmly committed to the primacy of books in civilized society, and the best news of all in the *Times* story, as far as I was concerned, was the disclosure that he was alive and well, articulate as ever, and living in Florida. We made our introductions by telephone and met several weeks later for two days of memorable conversation.

"The Chinese have a saying that one picture is worth a thousand words, but I disagree," he said toward the end of our second interview. "I believe that one word can be worth a thousand pictures. Pictures come to us as messages from the past, but there are no pictures that I really, definitely, can say that I love or find fulfilling, because they aren't quite substantial enough. It's all surface stuff, very superficial, and only reading allows you to penetrate the world. That is the power of the book."

A little more than two years later, on the very day that I was beginning work on this prologue, word came from Florida, again by way of an article in the *New York Times,* that Dr. Otto L. Bettmann, the founder of a "treasure house of pictorial material that percolated into American culture," had died at ninety-four of kidney failure in a Boca Raton hospital. We had exchanged letters a few weeks earlier, making plans to get together once again in Florida; "a happy reunion of kindred spirits," he had written, to my everlasting joy. That meeting would never take place, but the thoughts this gentle man had expressed to me in 1996 about Bach—a thinker who made order out of chaos, an artistic genius who always returned to where he started—were as resonant as ever.

From the beginning of my research, I have tried to illumine a continuum in the chronicles of book people, book places, and book culture, a tableau of constant change and variation, to be sure, but one that inevitably returns to its philosophical origins. My explorations in these areas began fifteen years ago with an attempt to document the passion people have exhibited through the centuries to possess and pass on the objects we call books, and to demonstrate the myriad ways that they have managed to preserve the fragments of our history, heritage, and literature. *A Gentle Madness,* the first fruit of those efforts, concerned itself primarily with the impulse to collect. While *Patience & Fortitude* also esteems the book as symbol and vessel for what Richard de Bury in his *Philobiblon* called "the heavenly food of the mind," it goes on to consider the more comprehensive concept of book culture, with emphasis on the experiences and thoughts of all dedicated people—be they librarians, readers, writers, scholars, bookmakers, booksellers, bibliographers, conservators, archivists, or collectors—and the continuing relevance of these objects in their lives. Questions of just what constitutes books—be they chiseled slabs of granite, baked clay tablets inscribed with cuneiform scrawlings, papyrus scrolls, palm-leaf manuscripts, words etched on parchment with a honed stylus, texts printed on paper with metal type, compact disks scanned by laser beams, or minuscule bits of data embedded in microchips and displayed on a glass screen—form part of my examination as well, but with the focus always trained on their timeless function of conveying knowledge.

During the bleakest days of the Great Depression, the always-chipper mayor of New York City, Fiorello La Guardia, closed his Sunday-night radio addresses with a stirring phrase meant to sustain his listeners through the gloomy ordeal that still lay ahead. The uplifting words the

tude," struck a hopeful chord among his constituents, so much so that they became the unofficial names of the two lions carved from Tennessee pink marble that have stood majestically outside the New York Public Library on Fifth Avenue since 1911. The image of lions at the gates of knowledge, be they guardians facing outward or predators poised to strike inward, seemed an apt way for me to suggest the thrust of this book.

In the course of my travels I assembled a wealth of pertinent information, and as my manuscript went well past the thousand-page mark, it became increasingly clear that the subject I had chosen demanded two books, not one. Thus it is that *Patience & Fortitude* pays particular attention to the endlessly fascinating tales of the individuals and the places that I encountered, while the work to follow, *A Splendor of Letters: The Perma-*

nence of Books in an Impermanent World, deals more pointedly with the issues involved, and the stories that clarify them.

"There are two meanings of the word 'book,' " the poet Archibald MacLeish wrote in 1940 during his five-year tenure as Librarian of Congress, the most basic of which, he made clear, identifies an artifact "made of certain physical materials." But the far more consequential connotation, he continued, is one that signifies an "intellectual object made of all materials or of no materials and standing in as many shapes as there are forms and balances and structures" in people's minds. The physical book, MacLeish stressed, "is never more than an ingenious cipher by which the intellectual book is communicated from one mind to another, and the intellectual book is always a structure in the imagination which may hang for a time above a folio page in ten-point type with a half-calf binding only to be found thereafter on a different page above a different type and even in another language." That sentiment, expressed long before the word *computer* entered the realm of daily discourse, has greater relevance today than it did when it was written more than half a century ago and has guided me in my various investigations. Beyond the form of books to come is the far more pressing issue of safeguarding the volumes we already have. One of the most challenging dilemmas we face today involves saving millions of "brittle books" printed on acidic paper that are decaying at an accelerating pace. More paradoxical is the matter of ensuring the longevity of electronic data, the production of which is an unqualified wonder of our age, yet one that is proving to be a far more transitory medium than printed books.

If there are heroes to be encountered in these pages, they are the purveyors and custodians of books, and the sanctuaries they stock and oversee. "What's past is prologue," Shakespeare maintained in *The Tempest,* a refrain that fortified *A Gentle Madness* and now structures *Patience & Fortitude.* It was impossible for me to visit every significant book repository that has graced the planet since the dawn of recorded time—indeed, a good many of them no longer exist—but it certainly was feasible for me to pay my respects to a select few that have played pivotal roles through the centuries, and to tell the stories of some remarkable people who have inhabited them.

For documentary material, the heavy work was done once again in the stacks of Widener Library at Harvard University, the Boston Athenæum, the Boston Public Library, the Dinand Library of the College of the Holy Cross in Worcester, Massachusetts, the Goddard Library of Clark University in Worcester, and the American Antiquarian Society, also in Worcester, all places where serendipity still rules, and where the discovery of unexpected treasures remains a common occurrence. My research was assisted by access to a number of computer services that were not available to me ten years ago, though for all the time-saving wonders of modern technology, my narrative technique still demands that I see the places and things I write about, and that I conduct face-to-face interviews with my primary subjects.

Of all the personal experiences that have driven this project, one above all others shaped what became a major theme of the work. Fittingly, this defining moment—and I can honestly describe it as an epiphany—came in April 1995 while I was typing, up to the final minutes of hanging on *A Gentle Madness*. During the frenetic rush to answer every question put to me by an exacting copy editor and still get the book published on schedule, it happened that I needed to corroborate a minor detail in Frank Sidgwick's three-volume edition of *A Descriptive Catalogue of the Pepys Library*, issued in England in 1914. My use of material from that book—specifically the introduction to volume 2 discussing the codicils to Samuel Pepys's 1703 will, which created one of the most unusual library bequests in history—had been furnished to me as a photocopy by Dr. Richard Luckett, the Pepys Librarian at Magdalene College at Cambridge University in England. I had never handled the actual book, and I needed more publishing information from the copyright page. It was a simple enough bibliographical matter to ascertain, but if this edition of a significant compilation was going to appear in my bibliography—and I very much wanted it there—then I needed to verify a few facts. Widener Library at Harvard University, which had never failed me before, and which has not failed me since, had an 1829 edition of the Pepys catalog, and another published in 1978, but not the Frank Sidgwick edition from 1914 that I needed; I had no luck at my next stop, the Boston Public Library, either. Finally, before attempting another desperate telephone call to Dr. Luckett in England, who had been away on holiday, I decided to make a last stop at the Boston Athenæum, one of America's great book places and home of a magnificent research library that itself has been a work in progress since 1807.

There, I not only turned up the three elegantly printed volumes on a remote shelf in a basement storeroom, but found them in remarkably pristine condition, with pages that had remained uncut, and presumably unread, after all this time. As I was signing the books out at the front desk—the Athenæum did not yet use a scanning device to record loans to its members, although that quaint practice was about to change as well—I confirmed by the blank cards tucked inside the rear pastedowns my assumption that they were, in fact, leaving the library for the first time. "Eighty-one years," I said aloud, shaking my head with amused gratitude. "You wonder who they bought these books for anyway." James P. Feeney, the silver-haired circulation librarian who was checking me out, paused momentarily and fastened his unblinking eyes on mine. "We got them for *you,* Mr. Basbanes," he replied evenly, and resumed his work.

What Feeney did not say—what he did not have to say—was that the books had been set aside by his predecessors for the better part of a century on the off chance that one day somebody in need might want to see them. Fortunately, the fact that nobody had requested the titles before me was not considered sufficient grounds for discarding them, a practice employed by so many other libraries in these days of reduced storage space, stretched operating budgets, and shifting paradigms. It was as if the collective hands of Aristophanes of Byzantium, Petrarch, Robert Cotton, Christina of Sweden, Thomas Jefferson, Arthur Alfonso

Schomburg—every temporary custodian of the world's gathered wisdom—had reached out through the swirling eddy of the ages and placed in my hands the precious gift of a book. It was an act of faith fulfilled, and we, their heirs, owe no less a compact to the readers of the third millennium.

PART ONE

OVERTURE

1.

ETERNAL LIFE

Almost without exception every great library, from the days of classical Athens to the Age of Reason, has been built on holy ground. The reason is plain. Of all the devices of magic by which a king maintains his sway over his subjects, the magic of the written word is the most potent.

—*Raymond Irwin*, The Origins of the English Library

WHILE probing the murky bottom of Alexandria's Eastern Harbor for fragments of Queen Cleopatra's sunken palace, French divers came across an ancient stele that had been shielded from the sunlight for sixteen centuries. After making an underwater cast of the stone inscriptions with a silicone-rubber mold, archaeologists translated the hieroglyphics to mean "Eternal Life," a fitting tribute to a city that began as an idea from a book and perpetuates its legacy today through the wonder of literature.

Plutarch tells us that Alexander the Great carried his copy of the *Iliad* with him on his eleven-year campaign to conquer the world, and that he stored it in a richly wrought jeweled casket taken from the personal collection of King Darius III, by common consent the most exquisite trophy seized from the Persian royal treasury by the Greek forces. The story, as handed down from generation to generation, is that the blind poet Homer appeared to Alexander one night in a dream at a time when the Macedonian was considering where among his recent triumphs to build a new

Greek colony. Here, in John Dryden's seventeenth-century translation of Plutarch's *Lives*, is the advice Alexander received from his favorite author:

> *An island lies, where loud the billows roar,*
> *Pharos they call it, on the Egyptian shore.*

Jolted awake by the vision, Alexander proceeded directly to the small island that Homer had described in the *Odyssey* as having a "snug harbor" with a "good landing beach where crews pull in, draw water from the dark wells, then push their vessels off for passage out," and determined straightaway that he had found exactly what he was looking for, a strategic outpost on the Mediterranean Sea through which Greek culture could pass to Africa and Asia. He then sketched out on the bare ground what he conceived as the basic layout for his glittering namesake, indicating precisely where temples, ornamental gardens, fountains, and public buildings should be erected. The architect Dinocrates, who had accompanied Alexander's army on its campaign eastward, set about creating a city of rectangular shape with broad streets intersecting at right angles and an efficient hydraulic system that would bring fresh water in from outlying areas to be stored in underground cisterns. In time the little island just offshore would be connected to the mainland by a narrow causeway called the Heptastadion, so called because it was seven stades, or furlongs, in length, creating the oval enclosure known today as the Eastern Harbor.

To guide sailors along the tricky coastline, a three-tiered lighthouse was erected on the outermost tip of the breakwater; called the Pharos in honor of the island, it cost eight hundred gold talents to build, according to Pliny the Elder. The 385-foot-tall beacon—about 80 feet taller than the Statue of Liberty in New York Harbor—assisted mariners well into the fourteenth century, and was esteemed in its time as one of the Seven Wonders of the World, the only ancient wonder that had a totally practical function. The lighthouse inspired such awe that likenesses were reproduced on Roman coins, and a brisk business was to be had in the sale of souvenir models to tourists, precursors to the Eiffel Tower and Empire State Building replicas that are hawked about by street vendors in Paris and New York today. Examples of the popular ancient clay trinkets still turn up from time to time in various reaches of the region. The dimensions of the lighthouse are fairly well known, thanks in part to an Arab traveler, Abu el-Haggag el Andaloussi, who carefully measured them in 1166. At the summit stood the statue of a deity, thought by some to have been Poseidon, believed by others to have been Zeus. On the façade was a formal inscription that is reported by Lucian of Samosata to have read, "Sostratus of Knidos, son of Dexiphanes, has dedicated this monument to the gods for the protection of sailors."

All of this bustling activity got under way in the winter of 331 B.C., when Alexander was twenty-four years old. The tempestuous monarch never saw the city he willed into being, although his mortal remains were brought there from the ancient Egyptian capital of Memphis fifty years later. Embalmed by skilled Egyptian and Chaldean morticians, his body was wrapped in sheets of gold leaf, immersed in honey, and placed in the heart of the royal quarter in an elaborate mausoleum known as the Brucheum, where it attracted throngs of tourists for seven hundred years.

Unlike Athens and Rome, where architectural ruins endure in glorious profusion, modern-day Alexandria offers little visible evidence of its noble heritage, and the original city exists only as a glittering memory. Whatever graceful edifice was not pillaged over the centuries was toppled by earthquakes or leveled in modern times by indifferent developers. A tidal wave that swamped the city in A.D. 365 also inflicted devastating damage, burying much of the waterfront beneath twenty feet of water. Two spectacular red-granite obelisks that had survived the tribulations intact were dismantled in the nineteenth century and sent abroad as gifts to England and the United States. Although called Cleopatra's Needles, the spires have no known connection with the famous queen; dating from 1500 B.C., they were erected at Heliopolis by King Thothmes III, and moved to Alexandria in 12 B.C. by the Romans. Centuries later, one was shipped to London in recognition of Admiral Horatio Nelson's victory over the French fleet at the Battle of the Nile in 1798, and stands today on the Victoria Embankment by the Thames River. The other went to New York in 1881 with the hope of stimulating American investment in Egypt, and was given a prominent berth in Central Park near the Metropolitan Museum of Art. It is only in recent years that archaeologists, aided by satellite positioning devices, have begun to locate and identify some of the submerged landmarks, including a palace on the island of Antirhodos that was the home of Cleopatra.

In its heyday, Alexandria served as a true crossroads to the world, a cosmopolitan, sophisticated, prosperous, and active city that was home to a widely diverse population. The founding Greeks and native Egyptians were joined early on by an influential Jewish minority. With the death of Cleopatra in 30 B.C. and the assumption of control by Octavian of Rome, three hundred years of Ptolemaic rule came to an abrupt end. The establishment of a new Egyptian capital at Cairo in 969 by the Arabs helped nudge Alexandria into further obscurity. During the long occupation by the Ottoman Turks that followed, the city groped along as little more than a dreary fishing village. A modest reversal of fortune began in the 1870s when the newly completed Suez Canal created a direct shipping route to the Red Sea that required a modern seaport on the Mediterranean. Today, with close to 4 million residents, Alexandria is the third largest city in Africa, smaller only than Lagos, Nigeria, and Cairo to the southeast, although it has a long way to go before it can hope to reclaim anything approaching the political, economic, and cultural dominance it once enjoyed in the region.

One project aimed at stimulating a resurgence has been construction of a twenty-first-century research center known as the Bibliotheca Alexandrina. Funded principally with support from the United Nations and built in the heart of the old royal quarter, the ambitious project can never replicate the original library, but organizers hope it might recall the universal spirit the ancient institution embodied, and revive a tradition that made the city synonymous with the noblest principles of intellectual inquiry. After ten years of construction and repeated delays, the inaugural of the $200 million center was scheduled to take place on April 23, 2002—International Book Day.

Twenty-three hundred years earlier, the glorious predecessor of the Bibliotheca Alexandrina, the Alexandrian Library and Museum, was founded by Ptolemy I Soter on the daring assumption that all of human knowledge could be gathered in one place, creating what in essence was the world's first university with its own college of scholars. To assist the eminent thinkers in their noble pursuits, a nexus of incomparable research materials was assembled for their use. Books from a multitude of cultures were aggressively sought out and acquired, and authoritative translations were commissioned, including the first rendering into Greek of the Bible, a text still known as the Septuagint in honor of the seventy-
____ _____ _____ work. Using the vast resources placed at their disposal, resident scholars were ____ __ _____ and correct important literary texts, a practice that led to the writing of critical commentaries.

The many mathematicians, astronomers, physicians, philosophers, engineers, poets, geographers, historians, musicians, and critics whose work was nurtured at Alexandria—Archimedes, Callimachus, Ctesibius, Diophantus, Eratosthenes, Euclid, Herophilius, Hypatia, Ptolemy, Theocritus, Zenodotus, are some of their names—left legacies that have enriched all of civilization. Some early accounts estimate that at the height of its activity the library held up to 700,000 papyrus scrolls, many of them unique copies of works long since lost. This vast assemblage was acquired by purchase on the open market, and also by the confiscation of books from ships that came calling on the busy seaport. Then, too, the scholars lured to Alexandria by its collections, as well as by guarantees of generous stipends and agreeable accommodations, produced entirely new works that enhanced the collections.

For years it was fashionable to blame the destruction of the library on Julius Caesar's decision in 47 B.C. to set ships in the harbor on fire to protect his Roman garrison against rebellious Macedonians, although no contemporary accounts support that claim, and voluminous evidence indicates that the library functioned for decades afterward. Some historians contend that it was a Christian mob intent on eradicating all pagan rituals at the behest of the emperor Theodosius I that destroyed the library and its contents in A.D. 391; others believe that the scrolls were ordered burned by the caliph Omar in 640, purportedly because any book that did not support the teachings of the Koran was considered irrelevant, and thus disposable. Because there were at least two libraries known to have operated in Alexandria in antiquity—the "mother" library situated in the Mouseion (Museum), and the "daughter" library, founded later, and probably located in another section of the city known as the Serapeum, or Temple of Serapis—it is entirely possible that each of these accounts bears some measure of truth. "What seems indisputable," Jon Thiem has written in a carefully reasoned essay on the subject, "is that at some point in history, the Alexandrian library, center and symbol of Hellenistic culture, burned."

Regardless of who delivered the final blow, the likelihood is remote that the library would have survived much longer in any case, since very little of ancient Alexandria has made it safely to our times. Of the library itself, there is only the hint of a few traces. One historian has suggested that two stone relics found buried fifteen hundred feet from the waterfront near the intersection of al Horreya Avenue and Nabi Daniel Street—the dead center of where the original repository may well have stood—functioned as fixtures in the old library. One of the items, a granite block with a hollowed-out center ten inches wide by eight inches long by three inches high, bears the carved inscription "Dioskourides 3 Volumes." It is thought that the stone receptacle, possibly a bin for storing papyrus scrolls, might have contained texts written by any one of four classical scholars named Dioskourides. It was unearthed in the garden of the Prussian consulate general in 1847, and the shape of the opening at the top suggests that it may have been fitted with a protective lid. Another artifact found in 1890 has been identified as the base of a statue dedicated by one Flavius Hierax to Aelius Demetrios, a master of rhetoric, with the additional notation that it was erected on behalf of the dedicatee's colleagues, "the philosophers dining in common," a probable reference to the scholars early historians tell us quite explicitly took their meals together in the museum commissary. Because statues were used to ornament Greek libraries—the nameplates of several writers were found inside the ruins of the Royal Library at Pergamum—the strong possibility exists that this pediment once performed that function in Alexandria. Aside from these two curiosities, no other objects that might have been associated with the library are known to survive.

My journey to Alexandria began one afternoon in the backseat of an old Mercedes being driven at breakneck speed across the Great Desert Highway by a chauffeur named Hassan. About ninety minutes outside Cairo, we came within several screeching inches of ramming a flatbed truck filled to the gunnels with pomegranates, a decidedly surreal experience that left me in a reflective mood for the rest of my visit. Later that night, I relaxed with a double Dewar's on a tiny balcony outside my room at the Metropole Hotel, determined to indulge a frequent amusement of mine when traveling to exotic places, especially those I have researched in advance. I had been told beforehand that these charming accommodations rose on ground once occupied by the Caesareum, an ornate temple begun by Cleopatra in honor of Mark Antony and completed by Octavian after the couple's dual suicide; the obelisks known as Cleopatra's Needles once stood on the site as well. From this vantage point, I had a sweeping view of the oval harbor and what was once the Royal Quarter. On my right, about a quarter-mile off to the northeast, a small ship stood calmly at anchor, its night lights twinkling red and white in the loom of the modern city. The following day I would watch from the shore as a crew of divers and deckhands under the direction of the

French explorer Franck Goddio winched an 825-pound dark gray granite sphinx—a lion with a human head—aboard this vessel. Dating to 50 B.C., the sculpture was determined to be a likeness of Ptolemy XII, Cleopatra's father.

Setting the scene for my excursion back in time, I layered the outlines of the ancient landmarks I knew from my books over the modern city spread out before me, visualizing them as if they were drawings etched on a sheet of clear acetate. Off to my left, on the outer flank of a narrow promontory now occupied by a fourteenth-century Muslim fort built with rubble from the Pharos lighthouse, I pictured a spire of roaring flame, its seething light being beamed thirty-five miles into the busy sea lanes by a giant copper mirror; I could almost smell a waft of acrid smoke drifting my way in the onshore breeze.

Unwilling to wait any longer, I gazed next toward a cluster of plain urban buildings two hundred yards or so to my immediate right, the general area where the Great Library and Museum is believed to have stood. The first-century geographer Strabo gave us a description of the ancient repository with just enough detail to tease the imagination: "It has a colonnade, a lecture-room, and a vast establishment where the men of letters who share the use of the Museum take their meals together." At that point I summoned forth an image of a graceful building bursting at the seams with the gathered wisdom of the classical world, and like some seductive song of Circe, it was inviting me down for an interlude of eager examination.

Altogether a thrilling rumination, but you had to be there to appreciate it, I suppose, and as I listen now to the exuberant impressions I dictated that night into my tape recorder, what I hear most of all is the ambient clamor of a busy city. Police whistles pierce the air, horns honk without letup, taxicabs in need of tune-ups speed along the famed Corniche that traces the waterfront, streetcars brake to a squealing stop, and gleeful children run around a floodlit fountain in the crowded plaza beneath my feet—all of them impatient instruments in an urban symphony. "You must close your eyes in Alexandria and block out the sounds," the Chicago bibliophile, philanthropist, restaurateur, and veteran world traveler Louis Szathmary had advised me a few weeks before his death in 1996. "Only then will you feel the magic of the books rising up to capture your soul." Chef Louis, I remind myself often, was a very wise man.

On June 13, 1894, an international authority on the history and design of libraries gave a prestigious Rede Lecture at Cambridge University on what was then, as most assuredly it is now, a seemingly esoteric subject—the evolution of book storage during the Medieval and Renaissance periods. Like all sound thinkers who are passionate about their work, John Willis Clark had amassed his material with a sure hand, and he rose confidently to the occasion. The professor began by stressing his belief that for all their transcendent qualities, books exist primarily as tools, and he placed firmly on the record his unqualified enthusiasm for the expanding technology he could see taking shape on the horizon. He urged his audience to consider a repository of books from two perspectives—as a workshop for the mind, and as a museum filled with precious objects. If a library is to function as a place where insight and wisdom are pursued by every means possible—if it is to be, in other words, a true laboratory for scholars—then "common sense urges" that "mechanical ingenuity, which has done so much in other directions, should be employed in making the acquisition of knowledge less cumbrous and less tedious; that as we travel by steam, so we should also read by steam, and be helped in our studies by the varied resources of modern invention."

To underscore the point, Clark made special mention of a *Handbook of Library Appliances* recently arrived on his office desk, a supplier's sales catalog, apparently, "in which fifty-three closely printed pages are devoted to this interesting subject, with illustrations of various contrivances by which the working of a large library is to be facilitated and brought up to date. In fact, from this point of view a library may be described as a gigantic mincing-machine into which the labours of the past are flung, to be turned out again in a slightly altered form as the literature of the present."

Clark then turned to the primary focus of his lecture, the appealing image of a "gigantic mincing-machine" for the intellect notwithstanding. Gadgetry aside, his primary purpose was to explore the concept of a library as a museum, and as a working definition he invoked the earliest Greek usage of the word that identified a "temple or haunt of the Muses." Using that model, a library assumes a dimension that goes well beyond providing adequate storage space for collections. Clark explained what he was driving at:

> *What I may call the personal element as affecting the treasures there assembled is brought prominently forward. The development of printing, as the result of individual effort; the art of bookbinding, as practised by different persons in different countries; the history of the books themselves, the libraries in which they have found a home, the hands that have turned the pages, are there taken note of. Modern literature is fully represented, but the men of past days are not thrust out of sight; their footsteps seem to linger in the rooms where once they walked—their shades seem to protect the books they once handled.*

A prefatory note to the printed version of Clark's remarks states that the Rede Lecture for 1894 was "illustrated by lantern-slides," an innovative feat accomplished, we can safely assume, with one of the "various contrivances" listed in his handbook of library devices. From the tenor of Clark's remarks, it is apparent that he had great fun showing off its varied applications. "It is unnecessary to describe," he quipped at one point, declining to put into words the design characteristics of an early book press, "for it is exactly like a still later example which I am about to shew you." Photographs of interior fittings at the Vatican Library and the north walk of the cloister at Durham Cathedral were projected in due course. "I will next shew you two bird's-eye views of the Benedictine House of St. Germain des Près, Paris," he announced presently, then offered yet another bird's-eye view of Citeaux, the parent house of the Cistercian order.

How the Cambridge University students reacted to this bold use of a primitive visual aid is anyone's guess, but we do know that Clark was encouraged to continue his inquiries, and that they led to other well-attended lectures and to the writing of *The Care of Books*, a firsthand inventory of old libraries and their fittings published in 1901, and still regarded as a standard reference in the field. To research that project, Clark embarked on a grand tour of important book places in Europe and Asia Minor, armed only with a measuring tape, pencils, and ample pads of paper. The meticulous academic took particular pride in pointing out that with the single exception of the Escorial Palace Library in Spain, "I personally examined and measured every building which I have had occasion to describe; and many of the illustrations are from my own sketches.

As much as he would have liked to include Alexandria on ary, Clark bypassed Egypt altogether, explaining that surviving accounts offered very little information about the vanished library's "position" and nothing whatsoever about the "arrangement" of its interior appointments. Clark began his consideration of Hellenistic times instead in northwest Turkey at Pergamum, site of the "other" great library of the period, and a place where he could study position and arrangement to his heart's content. After leaving Alexandria, I made a pilgrimage of my own to Pergamum, carrying photocopied pages from *The Care of Books* with me as if they were a Michelin Guide, all the while respectful of the fact that one border away in Iraq were the oldest known library sites of them all, the Mesopotamian repositories of Ur, Ninevah, and Sumer.

For visitors approaching Pergamum through the modern city of Bergama, the regal cluster of white marble temples and red andasite ramparts appears in profile at the crest of a narrow saddle of uneven hills, looking for all the world like a giant snake slithering its way through the lowlands of the Caïcus River Valley. Travelers arriving from the west are greeted by the far more dramatic sight of a seemingly vertical amphitheater carved from the face of a thousand-foot cliff, a primary landmark for those keen on fixing the coordinates of the ancient library from afar. Just above the top row of spectator seats, at the outer edge of the acropolis, lie the trunks of a fallen colonnade arranged in a long, neat line. Several hundred feet back, in the heart of the Royal District, these marble stumps join up with another walkway to form a spacious compound—the Sanctuary of Athena—that was consecrated in ancient times to venerate the virtue of wisdom. To enter this sacred area, worshipers had to pass through a two-story monumental gate that is now a greatly admired showpiece in the Berlin Museum, removed from Pergamum in the 1870s and reassembled there by German archaeologists. Flanking this majestic vista to the northwest are the remains of another temple known during its brief history as the Royal Library of the Attalid Kingdom. Its stone walls shelter no books today, of course, and philosophers no longer gather in small groups within them, but their spirit endures in meaningful ways, and the dimensions have not changed since Professor Clark marked them off with his tape measure more than a century ago:

The enclosure, paved with slabs of marble, was entered at the southeast corner. It was open to the west and to the south, where the ground falls away precipitously, but on the east and north it was bounded by a cloister in two floors. The pillars of this cloister were Doric on the ground-floor, Ionic above. The height of those in the lower range, measured from base to top of capital, was about 16 feet, of those in the upper range about 9 feet. The enclosure had a mean length of about 240 feet, with a mean breadth of 162 feet. The north cloister was 37 feet broad, and was divided down the centre by a row of columns. The east cloister was of about half this width, and was undivided.

At least seven rooms were part of the library compound, several of which could only have been entered from an upper foyer near the Temple of Trajan. Today, clusters of prickly bushes known as *devedikeni*—camel thorns—grow wildly where long reading desks once stood. Two horizontal rows of holes are clearly visible in the stone walls, drilled there to hold brackets that secured the wooden bookshelves. The library was encircled by a second stone barrier set eighteen inches back from the interior walls, put there, presumably, to protect the scrolls from humidity. Panels bearing the names of Herodotus, Alcaeus, Sappho, Balacrus, Apollonius of Rhodes, and Timotheous of Miletes, each the likely recipient of portrait busts in the various library chambers, were uncovered by German archaeologists in the nineteenth century. Another panel, inscribed with twenty lines of poetry, was dedicated to Homer. A narrow platform, thought to be the foundation stones of a long bench, runs along the fringe of a large chamber that opens to the east colonnade. A marble statue of Athena believed to have been modeled after a sculpture carved by Phidias and found in the main reading hall is now in the Berlin Museum with other relics.

Like Alexandria, Pergamum was a planned city, and because property was at a premium on the summit, one of its most prominent features was the creative use of leveled terraces and retaining walls. At the bottom of the steep western slope are the ruins of the Sanctuary of Asclepion, a Roman spa famous in its time for the mineral waters of its springs and the therapeutic wonders concocted by its pharmaceutical staff; notable on the periphery of that complex are the remains of a medical library used in the first century A.D. by Galen, a native of Pergamum who later served as personal physician to the emperor Marcus Aurelius in Rome. Tracing the horizon sixteen miles farther to the west, across a narrow channel in the Aegean Sea, is the faint outline of Lesbos, home in the seventh century B.C. of the poet Sappho. An open basin to the southwest is where historians believe a large force of Greek mercenaries, returning home from an unsuccessful campaign in the service of Cyrus the Younger of Persia, camped out in the final bivouac of what became known as the Retreat of the Ten Thousand. Once back in Athens, the commander of the force, Xenophon, became a prolific author whose works included several discourses about Socrates, most notably the *Memorabilia*, *Apology*, and *Symposium*. His mention of Pergamum in the closing pages of the *Anabasis* is the earliest known reference to the kingdom to reach our time in any work of history.

The first Greeks to occupy Pergamum—the name itself derives from *pergamos*, "inner citadel"— arrived in the twelfth century B.C. during a period of settlement known as the Aeolian. Many centuries later, the hilltop functioned as the refuge of Heracles, the son of Alexander the Great by the Persian princess Barsine. Believing the elevated fortress to be impregnable, Alexander sent the youngster and his mother there when he set out on his military campaigns. After Alexander's death, Heracles was lured down from the hill by a wily rival who offered to help him succeed his father as king; the naive lad was promptly imprisoned and put to death. Strabo records that the rapacious Macedonian general Lysimachus picked the outpost as an ideal place to store the vast cache of loot that he had gathered during a gainful sweep of Asia Minor, which may explain why so many of the ruins have been identified as watchtowers, arsenals, magazines, and troop barracks. At the highest terrace on the hilltop, in the most secure precinct of the citadel, is a capacious stone-lined cistern believed to have been one of the treasure vaults. Impatient to gather greater spoils, Lysimachus embarked on another campaign, leaving Philetaerus, a capable subordinate, behind to oversee his interests. Philetaerus wasted little time securing control of the hill and taking possession of the nine thousand gold talents left in his care, a huge fortune that would in time underwrite a series of great cultural projects and allow him to endow a dynasty that would retain power for the next century and a half. Said by Strabo to be a eunuch from boyhood, Philetaerus had no direct heirs and was succeeded by his nephew Eumenes I, who expanded the territory and ruled for twenty-two years, often at odds with his neighbors in Alexandria, three hundred miles to the southwest. The Royal

Library established during his reign came to symbolize the high-stakes rivalry that simmered between the two cities, both ruled by the descendants of Macedonians, and both distinguished for the refined splendor of their courts and the richness of their book collections.

Attalus I, the king for whom the Attalid dynasty is named, began his reign with a resounding victory over the "barbarian" Galatians, a previously unvanquished band of nomadic predators who exacted enormous duty from everyone they encountered. This remarkable accomplishment was consecrated in the form of an extraordinary frieze of sculptures that is housed today in the Pergamon Museum in Berlin, a building erected exclusively in its honor. Known as the Great Altar of Zeus, the monument was conceived as an allegorical narrative of the victory, and built around 190 B.C. on a solitary bluff abutting the citadel; dedicated to "King Attalus the Savior," it measured 120 yards around its base. The frieze sculptures are considered second in importance only to the Parthenon marbles that were removed from Athens to London in 1806 by Lord Elgin. Buried for centuries under dirt and rubble, the panels were recovered in the 1870s by Carl Humann (1839–1896), a German engineer and archaeologist commissioned by the Berlin museum to gather artifacts on a scale that would compare favorably with those being accumulated at the British Museum. Humann was inspired to dig at the Turkish site by the Roman author Lucius Ampelius, who had written admiringly in his fourth-century compendium of wondrous things, *Liber memorialis,* of "a great marble altar" at Pergamum, "forty feet high, with the most marvelous sculptures," and so grandly executed that it "reflects a certain megalomania." Humann uncovered 132 panels chiseled from marble believed to have been brought over from Lesbos, and his team turned up another 2,000 fragments. In a transaction that was perfectly legal at the time, Humann paid the Ottoman sultan 20,000 German marks for the right to remove the treasures to Berlin. In their place, by the altar he had stripped of its exquisite veneer, Humann planted two saplings; today the plants are fully grown fir trees, beautiful to behold on the terraced hillside, but small compensation for the artifacts they replaced. In keeping with his final wishes, Humann's body was buried beneath a rough-hewn granite marker in a hollow near the pedestal.

Although Attalus I gave his name to the kingdom, it was his successor, Eumenes II, who raised it "to the level of the largest dynasties of his day," according to the historian Polybius, and he did it by allying himself with Rome. This maneuver allowed Eumenes to gain control of the largest kingdom in Asia Minor without raising an army. At the height of its influence, Pergamum controlled 66,750 square miles, an area slightly larger than the six New England states, with a total population of about 5.5 million people. This impressive accomplishment—brought about in the course of just a decade—enabled Eumenes to acquire tremendous wealth and transform Pergamum into one of the great centers of Hellenistic art and learning, a program that included establishment of the Royal Library.

The Roman architectural commentator Vitruvius—to whom we owe the apocryphal story of Archimedes running naked through the streets of Syracuse shouting "Eureka!" after discovering the mysteries of water displacement in his bathtub—reported that the library was conceived from the beginning as a worthy rival to Alexandria. Of particular significance was his assertion that it was meant by its founders to be for the "delight of the world at large"—*in communem delectationem*—a clear indication that the collections were regarded as an accessible resource, and not for the exclusive use of the privileged few. The rivalry between Alexandria and Pergamum was anything but cordial, and at one point Egypt shut off all shipments of papyrus to the rival kingdom, paralyzing its ability to produce scrolls. Undeterred, the Pergamese turned to producing writing materials fabricated from the skins of sheep and goats. Though the process was not invented there, it was employed to such an extent that the word *parchment*, derived from a medieval Latin phrase meaning "from Pergamum," came into common usage.

Among the writers and philosophers to have studied at Pergamum, the most famous is Crates, the first scholar, according to Strabo, to illustrate his theories of geography with a globe, and the leader of what became known as the Pergamene school. Other prominent thinkers made comfortable there by royal patronage included the art critic, biographer, and sculptor Antigonus; Artemon of Pergamum, the author of an influential commentary on the odes of Pindar; the historian Menecrates; the didactic poet, grammarian, and physician Nicander of Colophon; and the critics Carystius of Pergamum and Polemon the Periegete.

In his *Natural History,* Gaius Plinius Secundus, known today as Pliny the Elder, declared Pergamum to be "by far the noblest city in Asia Minor," and given Pliny's unabashed love of scholarship, he undoubtedly had personal knowledge of the magnificent collection that had been assembled in the precincts of its marble citadel. A tireless intellect who routinely disdained sleep for reading, Pliny lived by the credo "To be alive means to be awake." Pliny the Younger, the scholar's nephew and ward, wrote that on trips away from Rome his uncle "seemed to throw aside all other interests and used the opportunity for study only: he had a secretary at his side . . . his hands in winter protected by mittens so that even the inclemency of the weather might . . . time from his studies; and with this object he used to go about in a chair even in Rome." Pliny took pleasure in citing "the names of my authorities" in the text of his encyclopedia, giving explicit credit, in other words, where credit was due, a system of scholarly attribution virtually unheard of at the time. "There is a marvelous neatness in the titles given to books among the Greeks," he wrote admiringly at one point, "titles that might tempt a man to forfeit his bail."

And where did Pliny say he found all this material? "As Domitus Piso says, it is not books but store-houses that are needed; consequently by perusing about 2,000 volumes, very few of which, owing to the abstruseness of their contents, are ever handled by students, we have collected in 36 volumes 20,000 noteworthy facts obtained from one hundred authors that we have explored, with a great number of other facts in addition that were either ignored by our predecessors or have been discovered by subsequent experience."

When Pliny wrote his encyclopedia in the latter half of the first century A.D., the 200,000-volume "store-house" at Pergamum—one of the greatest of the age—was already a memory; it had been dispatched to Alexandria a century earlier by Mark Antony as a gift to Queen Cleopatra in a summary imposition of Roman will that effectively ended a remarkable chapter in the chronicles of Western civilization. As a center of learning, Pergamum had enjoyed a fairly brief exposure in the limelight, and all that remains of it today are some white marble ruins atop a hill in western Turkey.

I n an engaging book of historical deliberation audaciously titled *How the Irish Saved Civilization*, Thomas Cahill paid homage to a band of Celtic missionaries who founded a string of Christian settlements in Europe during a crucial hinge period of cultural inertia sometimes called the Dark Ages, and set in motion a tradition of textual preservation that has left every succeeding generation in their debt. It was a "moment of unblemished glory" for the itinerant monks, Cahill wrote, and the case he made, though often ignored by mainstream historians, is briskly argued: "For, as the Roman Empire fell, as all through Europe matted, unwashed barbarians descended on the Roman cities, looting artifacts and burning books, the Irish, who were just learning to read and write, took up the great labor of copying all of Western literature—everything they could lay their hands on. These scribes then served as conduits through which the Greco-Roman and Judeo-Christian cultures were transmitted to the tribes of Europe, newly settled amid the rubble and ruined vineyards of the civilization they had overwhelmed."

The unqualified hero of Cahill's book is the Romanized Celtic Briton who called himself Patricius, the onetime slave turned evangelist known universally today as Saint Patrick (c. 390–461). Patrick brought Christianity to Ireland, and was the first Western historical figure of note to oppose the institution of human bondage. Given a generous supply of books by Pope Sixtus to take with him on his evangelical mission, Patrick carried the Roman alphabet and a knowledge of Latin culture with him on his journey. During a later visit to Rome he acquired additional copies of the Scriptures and presented them to various chieftains when he returned to Ireland. Presumably the books were copied for further distribution, and were used to instruct others in the ways of the calling.

One of the faithful who followed in Patrick's footsteps, Saint Columba (521–597), emerged from profoundly different social circumstances. Born a prince of Ulster in Donegal, Columba was given to the church by his parents, destined, they believed, for great things. Also known to the Irish as Columcille, Columba founded dozens of monasteries, including key settlements at Derry, Durrow, Iona, and Kells, and is known to have written many books, including a number of Celtic poems that survive to this day. Rigorously educated by the most prominent _____ _____ Columba developed a fondness for beautifully inscribed and illuminated books ____ _____ _____ remarkably proficient as a scribe. Every hour of Columba's spare time—indeed, up to the day of his death—was spent making elegant copies of the Psalms and Gospels that he passed on to the various abbeys and churches he had founded. Stories about the miraculous quality of books "written by the holy fingers of Saint Columba" were circulated among the faithful, and recorded by his first biographer, the eighth-century abbot of Iona, Adomnan. Columba is described as a man of strong will, particularly in his passion for books. Adomnan tells of one instance when he visited a holy and learned recluse named Longarad to see the man's greatly prized personal library. When the suspicious old man refused to let anyone near his collection, an exasperated Columba is reported to have uttered a curse: "May the books be of no use to you, nor to anyone after you, since you withhold them." An examination of the books after Longarad's death showed them to be filled with gibberish, impossible to read.

Columba is said to have transcribed more than three hundred copies of the Gospels and Psalters during his lifetime, but it was his obsession with one volume in particular that brought about a vital change in his life's mission. Columba suffered from a chronic case of what I have elsewhere called the gentle madness of bibliomania, with symptoms of such severity as to occasion a not-so-gentle visitation of "bloody madness." As told by several chroniclers, the notorious episode had its genesis during a courtesy call the future saint made on the abbot of Moville, a future saint in his own right named Finnian and a former mentor to Columba. While showing his protégé around the abbey, Finnian brought out an exquisitely decorated psalter encased in silver and gold that he had recently acquired. Overwhelmed by the book's beauty, Columba immediately informed his entourage that they would be extending their stay at Moville. Later that evening, after everyone had gone to sleep, Columba gathered his scribal tools and made his way into the sacristy where the book was stored, repeating the routine over the next several nights until he had made a painstakingly faithful facsimile of the book. When Finnian discovered what had happened, he declared that since the original manuscript was his, the unauthorized copy, or "son-book," belonged to him as well. Columba's refusal to turn the duplicate over prompted the outraged abbot to seek relief from Diarmuid, king of Meath.

When a royal judgment was announced, it was delivered in the form of a proverb: "To every cow belongs her calf, to every book belongs its son-book." Some say the king's smug ruling was meant to humiliate a possible rival; whatever the motivation, his declaration amounted to history's first adjudicated case of copyright infringement and left Columba seething with anger. Mobilizing a force of clansmen—the O'Neills of Ulster—Columba engaged Diarmuid's soldiers at Cul Dreimne in 561, the provocation being that one of his followers had been killed on the king's orders. He won decisively, leaving three thousand of the king's men dead on the battlefield. Flush with victory, Columba promptly retrieved the "son-book," which became known as the Cathach, a word variously translated to mean "chief relic" or "battle book." Housed today in the Royal Irish Academy in Dublin, the Cathach is considered one of the earliest surviving examples of a script known as Irish majuscule, and is the earliest known instance of an Irish scribe using the Roman alphabet.

Although victorious in combat, Columba still had penance to pay for having taken up arms, and in 563, as an act of contrition, he chose to leave Ireland forever. Accompanied by a dozen followers, he boarded a skin-covered boat known as a coracle and headed for an island in the Inner Hebrides off the west coast of Scotland known as Iona, bringing the gospel to the British Isles a full generation before Augustine arrived in Canterbury on a mission from Rome to convert the English. Barely three and a half miles long by one and a half miles wide, the tiny island was the center of Celtic Christianity for 150 years, and the springboard for Irish monasticism to the continent. Iona's cemetery, Reilig Odhrain—"the burial place of kings," in Gaelic—contains the remains of sixty Scottish, Irish, and Norse monarchs, including Macbeth, who was slain by Malcolm in 1057, and Duncan, the man murdered by Shakespeare's thane of Cawdor in 1040 to usurp the throne. Traveling to Iona with James Boswell in 1773, Samuel Johnson described the island as a sacred spot "whence savage clans and roving barbarians derived the benefits of knowledge, and the blessings of religion." It is still revered as one of the holiest places in Europe.

For students of illuminated manuscripts, Iona is where one of the most splendid productions of the early Middle Ages, a volume containing the four gospels of the New Testament in Latin known as the Book of Kells, is believed to have been produced around the year 800. Identified at one time as the Gospels of Columcille in honor of the founding saint—the name, in fact, under which the book was first recorded at Trinity College in Dublin, where it now resides in the East Pavilion of the Old Library—the book consists of 680 pages, lavishly decorated and illuminated on vellum in a flourish of colors. Here are the opening sentences of

Françoise Henry's bibliographic description of the book: "Its Gospel text is interspersed with large illuminated pages covered with an incredibly fine maze of brilliantly coloured ornaments and with strange, hieratic figures wrapped in the near geometric folds of their draperies. Through the text pages runs the constant coloured arabesque of animated initials made of the bent bodies of fantastic elongated beasts. The student engrossed in the exploration of all these unexpected patterns is soon overpowered by a feeling of both strength and mystery."

According to some estimates, the skins of 185 calves, culled from a herd of more than 1,200 animals, were used to produce the vellum for the folio pages. "By the known standards of the day the Book of Kells is an extraordinarily ambitious and splendid work," George Henderson has written in a detailed monograph of the "Insular Gospel-books" of the seventh and eighth centuries. "The precondition for its manufacture was obviously a mature scriptorium, lavishly equipped with technical expertise." In the early ninth century, after repeated Viking invasions, Columba's followers left Iona for Kells in County Meath northwest of Dublin, taking the precious book with them. It remained at Kells for the next seven hundred years—thence the accepted name of the book—and was presented to Trinity College in 1661.

In succeeding decades, other itinerant monks carried their Celtic spirituality and passion for books deeper and deeper into Europe. According to one contemporary account, Irish wanderers living "in exile from their country" and "visiting holy places" became a common sight on the continent. Standard equipment on these transcontinental travels was a distinctive style of leather satchel fitted with shoulder straps, known as the *polari*, that the missionaries used to transport books from abbey to abbey; several examples survive to this day. Most prominent among these early wayfarers was Saint Columban (543–615)—known also as Columbanus—who left Bangor in Ireland for Burgundy on the continent to shore up what was anxiously being reported as lapsing piety among the West Franks. Arriving there around 590, he vigorously applied himself to the task for twenty years before carrying the mission elsewhere.

Sometime around 610, Columban stopped at the former Roman town of Bregenz near Lake Constance. Two years after that, he established a monastery and a scriptorium south of the Alps in northern Italy at Bobbio, on the road to Rome. An inventory of library holdings commissioned in the tenth century recorded close to seven hundred manuscripts, an enormous number for an abbey of that period. Several volumes from Bobbio later made their way to the Biblioteca Ambrosiana in Milan, where they remain today as outstanding examples of Irish scribal craftsmanship. One of the most famous books to pass through the abbey, an eighth-century manuscript of the Vulgate Bible written at the twin monasteries of Monkwearmouth and Jarrow in Northumbria, is now at the Biblioteca Medicea Laurenziana, the Laurentian Library, in Florence. Known today as the Codex Amiatinus, the large folio includes a famous illustration of a monk seated by a cupboard containing nine books, and writing into a volume. It is believed to be a portrait of Cassiodorus (c. 490–c.585), founder in 550 of a monastery at Vivarium in the south of Italy where many important classical works were copied.

When Columban left Bregenz for Italy in 612, an Irish follower named Gallus remained behind and built a hermitage in an elevated valley some 2,200 feet above sea level near the Steinach River known as the Arbon Forest. People in search of spiritual counsel visited the monk over the next forty years, and the area, named Saint Gall after his death, became a place of holy pilgrimage. In 719 the Alemannic abbot Otmar founded a monastery on the site, and it rose rapidly to prominence, with deeds from the 730s and 740s recording transfers of real estate. The activities of a monk named Winithar, the dean charged with supervising the scriptorium, can be dated to 760. Documents show that he had fourteen men assigned to help him in the making of books. Paper not being used yet in the West, materials needed for copying were scarce, and were fabricated from animal hides, as Winithar wrote in the colophon of a copy of the Pauline epistles: "If then it seems to you useful that so insignificant a person as I should write something for you, give me your vellum."

When Saint Gall adopted the Rule of Saint Benedict in 747, a new monastic work ethic was adopted that allowed for the production of secular manuscripts in addition to theological tracts. In 816 the abbey entered its golden age of book production with the election of the abbot Gozbert. Modern analysis of manuscripts produced during his twenty-one-year tenure has identified the handwriting of one hundred different scribes, a convincing indication that the scriptorium was anything but a marginal enterprise, something more on the order of a cottage industry. Gozbert assumed leadership at a time when morale was low among the brotherhood, when land owned by the abbey had been taken over by secular neighbors, and when the aging buildings were in great need of refurbishment. By pursuing litigation in the courts, he recovered many of the monastery's properties, revived its sagging fortunes, and initiated a program of new construction. To further these goals, he requested guidance from his superiors, headquartered at the time on the island monastery of Reichenau in Lake Constance.

Sometime before 825, Gozbert received a document drawn in red and black ink on vellum that outlined in precise detail how the expansion should proceed. Copied from an original now lost, the manuscript—the oldest building plan of any kind preserved in Europe—depicts a monastic community fashioned to accommodate the work, study, and prayer activities of about 270 people. By showing exactly where various buildings, walls, doors, and courtyards were to be located, it set forth guidelines for constructing the ideal ninth-century Benedictine abbey. Known today as the Plan of Saint Gall, the layout offers unparalleled insight into the organization of secular and religious life during the time of Charlemagne (742–814), the great king of France who was crowned Holy Roman Emperor by Pope Leo III on Christmas Day 800. Though unable to write himself, Charlemagne was a great admirer of learning who encouraged the refinement of a fine, clear script that came to be known as

Carolingian minuscule. Charlemagne learned to read in his declining years under the tutelage of Alcuin of York (732–804), an Anglo-Saxon theologian and educator of enormous intellect who in 781 became scholar in residence at Aachen, the emperor's magnificent palace in western Germany that served as capital of the Holy Roman Empire. The fact that literacy in the eighth century was a luxury restricted to a select few is underscored by one claim, even if apocryphal—that Alcuin personally knew everyone in Europe who could read and write. Whether this was true or not, of far greater moment is that Alcuin enjoyed the unqualified respect of Charlemagne. His sway on the emperor's deliberations was enormous, comparable to the influence Aristotle exercised on the worldview of his most eminent pupil, Alexander the Great, only in this instance the impact came later in life, not in the bloom of adolescence. According to Charlemagne's biographer Einhard, the aging king kept a notebook under his pillow so that he could practice his writing lessons while he rested, and his favorite subjects were rhetoric, didactics, grammar, astrology, and mathematics.

During his tour as director of the Palace School, Alcuin taught the seven liberal arts and supervised the collecting and copying of many Latin classics, a number of which are the earliest surviving Roman texts. Because he combined a study of the humanities with Christian writings, his academy became widely known as a center of intellectual inquiry, and was visited by Irish, English, German, and Italian scholars. Under Alcuin's guidance, Charlemagne commissioned the construction of religious centers that promoted learning and culture, with libraries and schools central to the design. It is within this framework that the Plan of Saint Gall is best appreciated, since it represents an attempt to standardize monastic practice in the Christian world. At the center of its grand scheme was a great church three hundred feet long, the length of an American football field. Strategically placed around the compound were numerous buildings, each designed for specific functions. Significantly, there were provisions for two schools, one for the training of monks, the other—the *domus communis scolae,* or general schoolhouse—intended for secular studies. The plan also located facilities for medical treatment, horticulture, barrel making, grain storage, animal husbandry, cooking, and, not least, a place for the copying and storage of books.

Recommended as the ideal site for the library was the north corner of the church between the east choir and the transept of the basilica. This choice location, immediately adjoining the spiritual nexus of the monastery and given optimum exposure for sunlight, indicates just how highly esteemed books, and the people who made them, had become in monastic life. The plan calls for a rectangular room with two floors. The lower area, marked *infra sedes scribentium,* is where the scribes would gather to do their copying and illuminating. Pictured at the center of the room is a large table, with seven smaller work stations arranged by the windows along the two exterior walls. Finished books were to be shelved in the room above, identified as *supra bibliotheca.* A corridor leads directly into the great choir of the church. "Thus a liturgically significant location in the abbey layout is assigned to the production and preservation of the book," the Swiss historian Christoph Eggenberger emphasizes. "The measure of such importance in the Middle Ages is always the distance from whatever space to the altar." A similar configuration was set aside on the south side of the church for the sacristy, where holy vessels, monastic relics, and vestments were to be stored, a revered sanctuary, like the library, placed alongside the core of the church.

Although no physical evidence proves that this specific arrangement was ever adopted at Saint Gall, a scriptorium, quite possibly the greatest of the age, was active at the abbey during this period. Of that there is no doubt. The eleventh-century chronicler and poet Ekkehart IV, described by one commentator as "one of the best narrators of the Middle Ages," specifically praised the scribes and illuminators of the scriptorium there—he used that word—in *Casus sancti galli* ("Happenings at the Abbey of Saint Gall"), written about 1040. He also used the word *armarium,* a medieval Latin term used to identify a storage chest or wall recess where books and sacramental objects were kept. But the most persuasive evidence of all that the Plan of Saint Gall was used as a model for the abbey comes in the form of a greeting inscribed on the document itself. The identity of the person who wrote the salutation is not indicated in the message, but the tone clearly suggests someone of very high rank: "For thee, my sweetest son Gozbertus, have I drawn out this briefly annotated copy of the layout of the monastic buildings, with which you may exercise your ingenuity and recognize my devotion, whereby I trust you do not find me slow to satisfy your wishes."

Superbly executed and fully annotated, the plan is an instructive example of the various ways that knowledge has been transmitted over the centuries, and also an illustration of how much historic material has been lost. Once the drawing's original purpose had been served, it was deemed unimportant, and thus disposable. Measuring 113 centimeters high by 78 centimeters wide, the plan survives through a succession of highly unlikely incidents. In 926 it was evacuated temporarily to Reichenau when the fear of being sacked by Magyars was rampant in the region, but otherwise it has spent the eleven centuries of its existence in Saint Gall, most of that time entirely unknown to the outside world. About three hundred years after it had served its original purpose, a scribe whose name is lost to history set about writing a life of Saint Martin, and chose this swatch of crisp parchment stitched together from five sheets of animal skin for the task at hand. Instead of cutting up the fabric, as was the custom at the time, and scraping off the original information to make a layered document known as a palimpsest, he devised a way to preserve the original contents. He folded the single sheet into a sequence of fourteen pages so that the unused sections faced outward in the form of a conventional book, then wrote his biography on the verso, or reverse, side of the plan. Needing one additional page to complete his text, the scribe erased the outlines of a building in the northwest corner of the monastic complex and wrote the final words there.

In 1461 the document—to all intents and purposes now just another book in the abbey's inventory—was entered in the library catalog as a *Life of Saint Martin,* with the erroneous notation that it included "a depiction of the houses of his monastery," obscuring the context of the original document for another 143 years. In 1604 the scholar Henricus Canisius determined that the plan derived from the period of Abbot Gozbert, and he published it as a literary curiosity. The first monographic study of its significance was issued in 1844 by Ferdinand Keller of Zurich.

As a center of monastic activity, Saint Gall acquired additional land through donations and developed into one of the few centers of scholarship, teaching, and artistic achievement to thrive during the early Middle Ages. Here, again, is Christoph Eggenberger's interpretation: "Saint Gall together with its abbey library and archives has become a mythos primarily because of the book and documents. The book is at the center of medieval culture; the church, monastery, state, and school revolve around the book." Prayer was central to daily life at Saint Gall, but the monks also studied and taught Latin, rhetoric, logic, mathematics, music, medicine, astronomy, and the liberal arts in the two schools they operated on the grounds—the very subjects they were copying so assiduously from books being brought to them by pilgrims and itinerant brothers.

Gozbert's successor as abbot, Grimald, institutionalized the position of librarian and ordered preparation of the first detailed catalog of the abbey's holdings. Compiled between 850 and 880, the list identifies 316 volumes, and categorizes them as biblical, patristic, monastic, hagiographical, historical, poetic, legal, and grammatical texts, with a few works of medicine, astronomy, and geography included. Thirty volumes are listed under the heading *Libri scottice scripti,* "Books written in Irish script," a respectful acknowledgment of the work done by the earliest copyists. Other entries are classified by subject and author. Subsequent catalogs prepared over the next six hundred years reflect numerous additions and gifts to the collections.

With the approach of the Renaissance and the emergence of universities as centers of intellectual inquiry, the influence of Saint Gall declined abruptly. The scriptorium was abandoned, and books were scattered about the monastery, some of them stored in the basement of a tower built in the ninth century. When the humanist book hunter Poggio Bracciolini arrived on a scouting mission in the summer of 1416, the glory days of the abbey were a distant memory. His prowlings through a "most foul and obscure dungeon at the very bottom of a tower, a place into which condemned criminals would hardly have been thrust," and the discoveries he made there—most spectacularly a manuscript containing the only known copy of the *Institutio oratorio* ("Education of an Orator") by Quintilian (Marcus Fabius Quintilianus), a *Commentary* by Asconius on five of Cicero's speeches, and a manuscript containing four books of the *Argonautica* of Valerius Flaccus—are the stuff of legend.

For all the material that vanished from the abbey, however—the collections have remained fairly intact since the sixteenth century—the enduring wonder is that so much extraordinary material remains on site, in the very place where a good deal of it was produced. The German philologist Walter Berschin has written that "nowhere else in the world are there as many Carolingian documents as in the Abbey Archives of St. Gall or as many handwritten books on the early Middle Ages preserved at or near their point of origin as in the Abbey Library of St. Gall." A renewed interest in the library coincided with the invention of movable type in the mid-fifteenth century and the ready availability of inexpensive printed books, setting off a new wave of acquisitions that has continued modestly since then. Of the present collection, totaling about 100,000 volumes, 2,000 are manuscripts from the seventh to sixteenth centuries, and 1,650 others are incunabula from the "cradle period" of printing, books issued between 1450 and 1501, and great rarities in their own right.

In 1755 all monastic buildings at Saint Gall, including a surrounding wall, were razed, and a majestic Baroque church was built on the original foundations. The Swiss government closed the monastery in 1805 and confiscated the property. Today, every vestige of a medieval community is gone. Apart from the books produced there, only the Plan of Saint Gall endures as a visible reminder of how high a place the scriptorium occupied in the abbey's life. For the modern visitor, a trip to Saint Gallen in eastern Switzerland takes an hour by train from Zurich, two hours and twenty minutes from Munich. The old quarter of the town, known as the Altstadt, is set among narrow, winding roads, some of them reserved exclusively for pedestrians. Beautifully restored buildings outfitted with turrets, bay windows, and carved wooden balconies line the immaculate sidewalks, but the most popular tourist attraction by far is the church precinct, a majestic sight with its twin towers, embodying architecture of such importance that UNESCO has included the building among its list of the world's most important cultural monuments. Equally impressive is the building known in German as the Stiftsbibliothek, the ornate library designed by the master Swiss builder Peter Thumb and his son, also named Peter, in the mid-eighteenth century. Completed in 1767, it has one of the most beautiful rococo interiors to be found anywhere, a "work of art of the highest order," the architecture critic Peter Meyer has written, "the most opulent and the purest profane baroque room in Switzerland," according to Johannes Duft. Vigorously painted frescoes of the first four Ecumenical Councils adorn the ceiling; a floor of inlaid walnut, fir, and cherry wood gleams in the natural light that streams in through thirty-four windows. It is not an enormous library—94 feet long, 32 feet wide, 24 feet high—but it teems on two levels with books and manuscripts of remarkable importance, many of them decorated with breathtaking illuminations, others clad in intricately tooled bindings of leather, gold, and ivory, and on permanent display at the back of the hall is the Plan of Saint Gall. It is an extraordinary bookroom to behold, and all visitors are required to slip large floppy slippers over their shoes before being allowed to walk inside. Above the main entrance has been inscribed the oldest known library motto in the world, a saying Diodoros Siculus reported seeing outside the chamber where books were stored by King Ramses II of Egypt about 1350 B.C.:

ΨΥΧΗΣ ΙΑΤΡΕΙΟΝ

Translated from the Greek: "House of Healing for the Soul."

. . .

Louis Sullivan, the American architect regarded in some quarters as the father of modernism, lived by the dictum "Form follows function," a principle that has been especially evident in the design of libraries for the better part of five thousand years. In *The Care of Books*, John Willis Clark showed how various repositories had facilitated the pursuit of scholarship through history, and he outlined the methods "adopted by man in different ages and countries to preserve, to use, and to make accessible to others, those objects, of whatever material, on which he has recorded his thoughts." When Clark got to Gloucester Cathedral in west-central England, his first order of business was to measure twenty compact cubicles in the south cloister built between 1370 and 1412 as places of study and reflection. "Each carrel is 4 ft. wide, 19 in. deep, and 6 ft. 9 in. high, lighted by a small window," he reported, using the formal term *carrel* to describe the reading spaces used by monks; "but as figures do not give a very vivid idea of size, and as I could not find any one else to do what I wanted, I borrowed a chair from the church and a folio from the library, and sat down to read, as one of the monks might have done six centuries ago."

What Clark was really doing in these years before dustjackets and author photographs became commonplace in publishing, though he was much too proper a gentleman to say so, was setting up a photo shoot of himself that he could use as an illustration in his book. Given the degree of preparation necessary to set up a formal portrait in the late nineteenth century, the sitting must have been a far less casual procedure to arrange than Clark makes it sound. But we are fortunate he made the effort; the appealing scene shows the white-bearded scholar impeccably attired in a three-piece suit seated with a sturdy volume opened in his lap. Because fire, as William Blades made clear in *The Enemies of Books*, has destroyed millions of volumes over the centuries, libraries built before the advent of electricity took full advantage of natural light. Thus it happens that the book in Clark's lap is richly illumined by rays of sunshine streaming in through the windowpanes above his left shoulder.

In France and England alone, Clark's inquiries took him to Bayeux, Saint Germain l'Auxerrois, Citeaux, Clairvaux, Noyon, Rouen, Obazine, Gloucester, Worcester, Durham, Hereford, Saint Albans, Lincoln, Canterbury, Wells, and Westminster. As enjoyable as these forays must have been, the meticulous don was the first to acknowledge that he did not have to visit every surviving cathedral and monastery to appreciate how books were copied, stored, and read during the Middle Ages: "The uniformity which governed monastic usage was so strict that the practice of almost any large monastery may be taken as a type of what was done elsewhere."

The strict tradition that governed the making of books applied just as severely to how they were handled. "Idleness is the enemy of the soul," Saint Benedict wrote in the forty-eighth chapter of the famous monastic code that bears his name, "hence brethren ought, at certain seasons, to occupy themselves with manual labor, and again, at certain hours, with holy reading." Times assigned for mental exercise changed from season to season according to the availability of daylight. "During Lent," Benedict wrote, "let them apply themselves to reading from morning until the end of the third hour," instructing further that they "receive a book apiece from the library, and read it straight through." Since Benedict's Rule dates from the sixth century, this clearly suggests that books were available in sufficient numbers at this time to supply every monk with at least one volume.

In a decree governing the custody of books by English Benedictines issued in 1070, Archbishop Lanfranc—recently arrived in Britain with the Norman conquerors—directed that every monastic librarian in the realm convoke an annual meeting in which "a document setting forth the names of the brethren who have had books during the past year" would be disclosed at an assembly: "and let each brother, when he hears his own name pronounced, return the book which had been entrusted to him for reading; and let him who is conscious of not having read the book through which he had received, fall down on his face, confess his fault, and pray forgiveness."

Ruins of the Royal Library of Pergamum, the great rival to Alexandria, and the only library from the Hellenistic period to survive in any form.

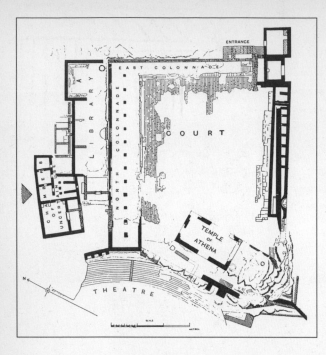

A plan of the temple and precinct of Athena at Pergamum, with a sketch of the ruins of the Royal Library and adjacent buildings, made by John Willis Clark in the 1890s for The Care of Books.

Restored façade of the Celsus Library at Ephesus in Turkey, built in A.D. 110 by the Roman consul Galius Julius Aquila in memory of his father, Gaius Julius Celsus Polemaeanus.

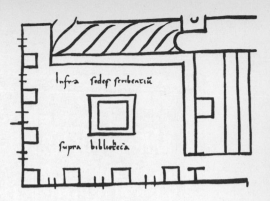

Detail of Plan of Saint Gall, c. 820, showing the layout for the library and scriptorium of a typical ninth-century Benedictine monastery. Scribes and illuminators would work at the eight tables arranged on the ground floor (infra sedes scribentium), *and books would be stored on the level above* (supra bibliotheca).

North Cloister, Durham Cathedral, where medieval scribes copied manuscripts.

John Willis Clark (1833–1910) seated in a work carrel at Gloucester Cathedral (from The Care of Books*).*

An accomplished architectural
historian, *John Willis Clark* made
many detailed sketches during his
nineteenth-century tour of old
libraries. Pictured here is one of
several chained bookcases in the
Chapter Library at Hereford
Cathedral, with detailed views of
a single volume standing on a shelf,
and a hasp used to lock a restraining
bar in place. The other drawing
illustrates a wall press, or armarium,
in the twelfth-century Cistercian
abbey of Fossa Nuova in central
Italy (*from* The Care of Books).

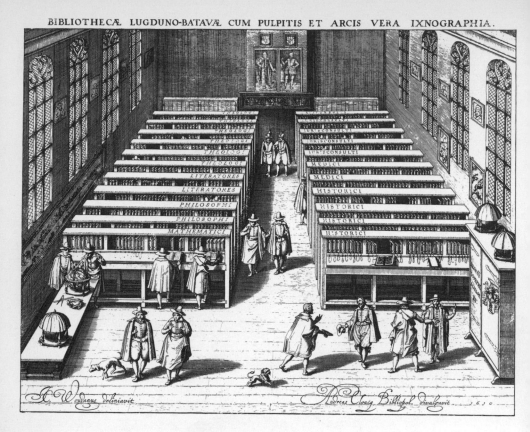

Interior of the library of the University of Leiden, dated 1610.

*Sir Thomas Bodley (1545–1613),
engraving made from a contemporary
portrait and used as frontispiece for a
biographical sketch of the library founder
"written by himselfe," first printed in
1647, reissued in 1894.*

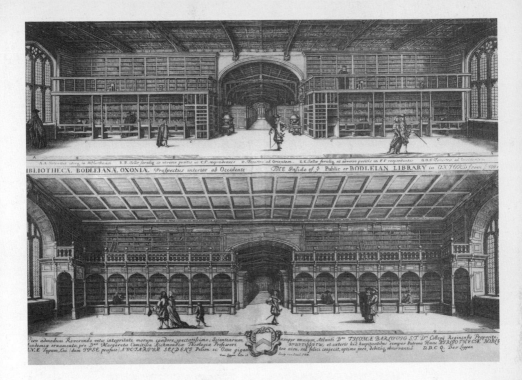

*Two early views of Duke Humfrey's
Reading Room in the Bodleian Library
at Oxford University, from engravings
made by David Loggon and printed as
one plate in* Oxonia illustrata, *1675.
Above, looking westward down the length
of Duke Humfrey's Library from Art's
End; the latter of the two wings to be
built, Selden's End, pictured below.*

*A thousand-year-old cypress tree planted at the
Great Lavra Monastery on Mount Athos by the
founder, Saint Athanasios.*

*Main entryway to the restored abbey of Monte Cassino,
established in southern Italy in the sixth century.*

*A statue of Saint Benedict, founder of the monastery at
Monte Cassino, overlooks the main courtyard.*

A tenth-century copy of the Rule of Benedict, in the abbey of Monte Cassino.

*Looking up the stairway from the cell of Saint Benedict,
where the Rule is believed to have been written in the
sixth century.*

Interior of the Biblioteca Malatestiana in Cesena, built in the fifteenth century, and the oldest library in the world still housed in its original building.

BELOW LEFT: *The Vatican Library; the decorated cases pictured here were once used to store rare books and manuscripts.*

BELOW RIGHT: *Interior view of the Biblioteca Medicea Laurenziana in Florence, begun in 1525 by Michelangelo for Pope Clement VII.*

Monumental door at the entrance to the library of the abbey of Saint Gall in Switzerland, with an inscription that reads, in Greek, "House of Healing for the Soul."

Biblioteca Columbina, Seville.

The London Library.

Biblioteca Ambrosiana, Milan, with bust of Cardinal Federico Borromeo above the doorway.

The British Library, London.

Die Deutsche Bücherei, Leipzig.

*Bibliothèque Polonaise
(Biblioteka Polska), Paris.*

*Biblioteca Nazionale Marciana,
Venice.*

GALLERY

OF

BOOK

PLACES

Biblioteca Capitolare, Verona.

Dr. Otto L. Bettmann (1903–1998), the émigré who fled Nazi Germany to create an internationally renowned photo archive in the United States, plays a Bach piece at his retirement home in Florida.

Carlo Alberto Chiesa (1926–1998) of Milan, one of the great book-sellers of his generation.

The Rev. Leonard E. Boyle (1923–1999), internationally renowned paleographer and director of the Vatican Library from 1984 to 1997.

Don Fabrizio Massimo in the archive storage room of Rome's Palazzo Massimo, which contains records documenting more than five centuries of family history; the bookcase in the background was designed for the Massimo family by Giovanni Lorenzo Bernini (1598–1680), a leading exponent of the Baroque style in Italy.

Jay Fliegelman, collector of association copies, in the Council Room of the American Antiquarian Society, Worcester, Massachusetts.

Diana Korzenik prepares to ship her book-arts collection from Massachusetts to the Huntington Library in California.

The earliest Christian library on record was assembled in Jerusalem by Bishop Alexander, who died in A.D. 250. Without being specific, Saint Jerome (c. 342–420) advised a friend in a letter to make full use of church libraries, the clear suggestion being that religious book collections were readily available, and by no means uncommon. During the eleventh century, armariums were being built into recesses in the cloisters of churches to contain books, but as Clark pointed out in example after example in *The Care of Books*, no scriptorium from the Middle Ages survives with its fittings intact. Durham Cathedral in northern England is no exception to this, although many of the books made there do remain safely stored on the very grounds where they were produced hundreds of years ago, and the cathedral itself, begun in the eleventh century during the reign of William the Conqueror and said to be the finest example of early Norman architecture in existence, remains largely intact.

"The main appeal of Durham Abbey lies in its simplicity," James Wall wrote in an architectural history of the cathedral in the early years of the twentieth century. One reason usually given for its survival in the aftermath of the Dissolution of the Monasteries is its remote location in the northern Highlands near the Scottish border, and the shrewd decision of its principals to mind their business during particularly difficult times. When King Henry VIII "reconstituted" the cathedral in 1541, he appointed a dean and twelve canons to replace the prior and the governing monks. Significantly, the last Catholic prior, Hugh Whitehead, became the first Anglican dean, and the new canons were the same men who had served under him so loyally as friars. The life of the ecclesiastical community at Durham, as a consequence, went on without the kind of devastating interruptions so apparent at other religious centers throughout England. Between 1536 and 1539, eight hundred monasteries were seized, closed, and torn down, taking with them a corresponding number of libraries, and most of the books they contained. Some abbeys, like Christ Church and Canterbury, had collections numbering upwards of two thousand volumes, though most were considerably smaller. About a hundred miles west of London among the softly rounded hills of Somerset stood the most beautiful English abbey of them all, Glastonbury Cathedral, home of the nation's greatest medieval library. It was in this gloriously verdant countryside that Joseph of Arimathea, the patron saint of the cathedral, is purported by the twelfth-century historian William of Malmesbury to have come from the Near East thirty years after the Crucifixion and buried the Holy Grail, and here the mythical King Arthur and his knights are said to have held court in the fifth century while mounting a futile search to find the sacred cup of Christ. When John Leland, keeper of books and official antiquarian for Henry VIII, visited the cathedral library in 1534, he was overwhelmed by the spectacle of so much knowledge gathered together in one place:

> *I straightaway went to the library, which is not freely open to all, in order to examine with great care all the remains of most sacred antiquity, of which there is here so great a number that it is not easily paralleled anywhere else in Britain. Scarcely had I crossed the threshold when the mere sight of the most ancient books took over my mind with an awe or stupor of some kind, and for a while literally stopped me in my tracks. Then, having paid my respects to the deity of the place, I examined all the book cases for several days with the greatest interest.*

Leland wrote that he was given free run of the Glastonbury library through the "goodwill of the abbot Richard Whiting," and he described in some detail forty-four manuscripts he was able to examine during his stay. Leland could not have known at the time the awful fate that lay in store for his host or what would become of the magnificent books. Five years later, on September 19, 1539, Abbot Whiting—a member, also, of the House of Lords—was summarily arrested and hauled back to London by a detachment of the king's agents. The king's officers—the historian Ernest A. Savage called them "myrmidons," a particularly descriptive word the *Oxford English Dictionary* defines as "unscrupulously faithful followers" or "hired ruffians"—arrested the abbot, charging him with having harbored in his quarters a "written book of arguments against the divorce of the King's majesty and the lady dowager," undoubtedly a trumped-up charge. Any question as to whether or not the old man was given due process is clarified by an entry that survives in the personal diary of Thomas Cromwell, a member of the king's privy council and the principal force in implementing the Act of Supremacy: "Item. The Abbot of Glaston to be tried at Glaston and executed there." Convicted and condemned with frightful alacrity, Whiting was dragged on a sled to the top of the five-hundred-foot hill known as Glastonbury Tor and put to death horribly. The abbot's quartered remains were distributed between Wells, Bath, Ilchester, and Bridgewater for public display, and his head was mounted above the Glastonbury gate, leaving no doubt that a new order had taken hold throughout the realm.

The cathedral was ransacked and ravaged, with its crushed walls used for roadstone, but enough of the magnificent edifice survives to suggest its grandeur, including the gatehouse, a huge kitchen, and the immense piers of chancel crossing, perhaps the "bare ruin'd choirs where late the sweet birds sang" that Shakespeare had in mind when he was writing his sonnets half a century later. "It is impossible to step within the shrunken precincts without submitting to the spell they weave," Ralph Adams Cram wrote in *The Ruined Abbeys of Great Britain*. "Here facts fall and dissolve: the instant one stands in the shadow of these mighty crags of riven masonry, all the inheritance of a thousand years come back, and we know that here also walked St. Joseph of Arimathea, St. Patrick, King Arthur and his Queen, and that beneath the vanished vaults once rested the Holy Grail." Like the great library at Alexandria, nothing whatever of the book repository remains, and where, precisely, the scriptorium may have stood is not known either.

The passage in 1550 of the Act against Superstitious Books and Images by the king's commissioners continued the same obtuse policy. By the middle of the sixteenth century, the only libraries of any importance remaining in England were at Oxford and Cambridge Universities, and in the few fortunate cathedrals that had given unswerving support to the new religious order, with Durham especially prominent among the latter.

"This was a healthy, wealthy, and well behaved cathedral," Roger C. Norris, the deputy librarian at Durham Cathedral, explained as he introduced me to some of the treasures entrusted to his care. "I think it was acknowledged that those cathedrals which were not corrupt, that were not impoverished—those that had not put their foot in it, so to speak, and otherwise kept their noses clean—managed to survive. So here at Durham there was a strong continuity and no disruption of buildings, or anything like that which you will find elsewhere." Norris and I made our introductions in the eleventh-century refectory off the South Cloister of the cathedral, a large room now known as the Old Library and used as a repository for about twenty thousand books printed between 1500 and 1800. Another thirty thousand volumes are kept just off the West Cloister in a huge hall overlooking an impeccably manicured garden. That spacious room, just over two hundred feet long and latticed with the original ceiling beams, once served as sleeping quarters for seventy of the abbey's monks, and is still known as the Dormitory; it was built between 1398 and 1406 with oak hewn from the woods surrounding the prior's summer residence at Beaupaire. Directly beneath the Dormitory is a cavelike bower of two rooms dating from Norman times, which has functioned as the cathedral's treasury for many hundreds of years; it is called the Spendiment, and Norris would take me to see that sanctuary in due course. "What you are sitting on right now is a bench from the fifteenth century," he said, "and you are sitting at a monastic table from the medieval refectory on its original trestles." With the photograph of John Willis Clark seated in a Gloucester carrel dancing in the back of my mind, I wondered aloud if we could assume that some copyists worked at these thick planks of solid English wood six or seven centuries earlier. Norris smiled benevolently at the suggestion. "You certainly can assume that some copyists *ate* at this table six or seven centuries ago," he said cheerfully, then led the way to the ancient cellar where the abbey's rarest treasures have been kept for more than nine hundred years.

Inside the cathedral, a plain marble slab at the front of the nave marks the final resting place of Saint Cuthbert, the former shepherd boy from Scotland who is remembered today for having preached the gospel, fed the hungry, clothed the naked, and delivered the poor from oppression, but it took four centuries from the time of his death in 687 to when his followers were able to erect an enduring shrine to his memory. The result of their perseverance, however, is a triumph of medieval engineering that remains the finest example of early Norman architecture in England. For more than two hundred years Cuthbert's cult had lived on Lindisfarne, a sandy spit of land off the Northumberland coast also known as the Holy Island. Repeatedly attacked by Danish raiders, the monks finally abandoned the island in 875, carrying with them an exquisitely carved casket containing the saint's remains and some precious relics. After years of fitful wandering around what Sir Walter Scott described as the rugged "mountain, marsh, and moor" terrain of the north country, taking up residence variously at Crayke, Norham on Tweed, and Chester le Street, the brothers finally chose a high rock plateau in Northumbria surrounded on three sides by the river Wear to build a permanent memorial. Their first shrine, known as the White Church, was dedicated to Saint Cuthbert in 998; it was dismantled ninety-four years later when work on a three-towered edifice of carved sandstone—the building that dominates the landscape today—was begun on the orders of William the Conqueror. Durham Cathedral was meant to serve God, of course, but its virtual impregnability as a fortress—it was called a *propugnaculum*—provided a formidable line of defense against Scottish incursions from the north.

Throughout their long history as a brotherhood—even while they were casting about for a permanent home—the monks continued a Celtic tradition of making exquisite manuscripts, including among their triumphs one masterpiece that is esteemed today as the most precious book in the United Kingdom. Produced on the Holy Island in the seventh century by illuminators and calligraphers as a tribute to Cuthbert, the incomparable folio aptly known as the Lindisfarne Gospels lay open on the altar by the saint's tomb for six hundred years; the vellum manuscript was confiscated and brought to London by Henry's agents in 1537. On the occasion of the thirteen-hundredth anniversary of Saint Cuthbert's death in 1987, it returned north for a brief period to be laid open once again on the altar by his tomb. Despite occasional demands for repatriation of the book to Northumberland, it remains a prime attraction in the new British Library and the subject of a digital facsimile that allows visitors to "turn the pages" of national heirlooms.

As Roger Norris led the way out of the refectory, he paused to point out places where copying would have been done in medieval times. "As you can see, we get lovely lighting there," he said, indicating an enclosed arcade on our left, where a series of carrels once were located. "If you look closely over there in the North Cloister, you can see some pegmarks halfway up on the wall where the armariums would have been secured. There would have been a series of desks there as well. In northern Europe, the north cloister is the one that gets the great proportion of the sun, and that's where the writing would have been done. In southern Europe, it doesn't really matter where you had your scriptorium, because the light in that part of the world is gorgeous everywhere."

A description of exactly what the carrels on the north side looked like here was provided sometime around 1590 in *The Rites of Durham:*

[The] pewes or carrells was all fynely wainscotted and verie close, all but the forepart, which carved wourke that gave light in at ther carrell doures of wainscott. And in every carrell was a deske to lye there bookes on. And the carrells was no greater then from one stanchell of the wyndow to another. And over against the carrells against the church wall did stande certaine great almeries of waynscott all full of bookes, wherein did lye as well the old auncyent written Doctors of the Church as other prophane authors with dyverse other holie mens

wourks, so that every one dyd studye what Doctor pleased them best, havinge the Librarie all tymes to goe studie in besydes there carrells.

Because the light was so good in the North Cloister, that area was reserved for full-fledged monks; novices were assigned similar spaces on the west walkway, where the entry to the Spendiment is located. The author of *The Rites of Durham* tells us how the treasury got its name: "In 1391 it was Cancellaria, from the grate, or 'le Spendement,' from the paying of wages and other money through the iron bars, 'cancelli.' " Upon entering the room, the first sight is a recess in the far wall in the shape of a shouldered arch, closed off by a grated door. A modern security system protects the contents, but the chamber itself goes back to the earliest years of the cathedral, and looks not much different, presumably, from other cathedral depositories of the period. Cassiodorus, it is known, had the books of his monastery stored in armaria similar to this, and the manuscripts of Abbot Simon of Saint Albans were kept in "the painted aumbry of the church." An aumbry, like an armarium, was a recess lined with wood for protection against moisture from the masonry.

"Although we have some books which are beautifully decorated, you could still reasonably conclude that this is a very austere library," Norris said by way of introduction to the codices lying on the shelves behind the bars. About three hundred titles are kept here, along with a selection of precious medieval crosses, seals, and rings, and some vestments embroidered by nuns a thousand years ago. "Durham was a scholarly community, and that may be why, ultimately, the books you see here survived the Dissolution, because the monks had a very strong connection with secular learning." Oxford and Cambridge are home to the oldest universities in the United Kingdom, but Durham College, which occupies the same fortified area as the cathedral, ranks third in the hierarchy. What is known today as Trinity College at Oxford was established in the thirteenth century by monks from the cathedral, and was known then as Durham College.

At the time of my visit, a major restoration of public viewing areas was in progress, and a number of objects normally on display were being kept in the treasure room. "That's Saint Cuthbert's coffin right there behind you," Norris said, pointing to a decorated wooden casket made in 698. Attached to the sides of the casket are wooden panels inscribed with sequences of figurative art similar to designs that appear on the pages of the Lindisfarne Gospels, leading some scholars to believe they were executed in the seventh century by the same monks. Norris then retrieved from a strongbox the pectoral cross of garnet stones and gold cloisonné found draped around the saint's neck when the casket was opened in 1827. Tucked under his head was a perfectly preserved copy of the Gospel of John bound in goatskin on boards, now on deposit in the British Library in London.

Norris then selected three books from the Spendiment to bring back upstairs for closer study. I was assigned the glorious task of carrying an eighth-century gospel written in uncial script on calfskin. "Anglo-Saxon vellum is very stiff and hard," Norris said as we carefully opened this volume for examination first. "As you can see, it's been done in two columns. The ruling is done blind; there was a blunt instrument which ruled on the page and created a plane where the text goes. You can see at the end here that somebody else has finished what another scribe started, the handwriting is so obviously different. So we know that at least two different scribes worked on this book." We looked next at an eleventh-century work called the *Chronicles of Martin Polonus,* and then moved on to "a very late" twelfth-century copy of *The Church History of the English People,* written by an English historian known today as the Venerable Bede. "The Venerable Bede had a very wide circulation, and his works were internationally known," Norris said. "The earliest copies of Bede are from the eighth century, and you will see in this one a bit of progression from Anglo-Saxon script to the twelfth century, which is much more Gothic in appearance."

Earlier, I had asked Norris why books had never been chained at

Durham the way they were at other church libraries in England, most famously at Hereford Cathedral to the southwest, which my wife and I would be visiting the next day. "Our house has never been chained because the books here were never available to the public," he answered. "These were for the exclusive use of the brothers." As we browsed further through the Bede folio, I was struck by a kind of paradox. Extraordinary illuminations were everywhere apparent, and the pages themselves were breathtaking works of art. "You can see that the whole plan of the page, the design, is to enable you to understand the beauty of the book, and if it was a scholarly text that needed annotations, they provided places where you could write within the margins," Norris had pointed out. But if nobody from outside the cathedral was meant to see these books, why, I wondered, did the monks take such pains to make them so beautiful? Who were they trying to impress, if the readership, by design, was to be so severely restricted?

"Well, they were made for God," Norris said after a perfectly nuanced pause. "That was part of their offering. They gave their lives in prayer, chastity, and obedience, and they obviously wanted to make the very best of whatever it was they did. I believe that was the motivation. They were wonderful artists, as you can readily see, and they had a great facility for doing this kind of work. And that was part of their offering as well. This does not mean the illuminations were not intended for human eyes, because these were practical people. They weren't going to make the books if they weren't going to use them. But they wanted them to be beautiful. Everything was to be praiseworthy. And I must say that the materials they used seem to last forever."

The opportunity I had to handle Durham's copy of *The Church History of the English People* seemed especially appropriate since the bones of the author lie buried inside the cathedral on the south side of what is called the Galilee Chapel. A man of encyclopedic learning, Saint Bede (c. 673–735) left forty-five scholarly works at his death and is credited with beginning the practice of dating Western history in relation to the birth of Christ. "He was the first English historian, in the sense of a narrator who carefully weighs his sources rather than transcribes mere stories just as they come to him, the first English theologian, and the first English man of letters," James Wall wrote in his exhaustive history of Durham Cathedral. The Venerable Bede spent most of his life at the nearby monastery of Jarrow, but his remains were spirited to Durham in 1022 under questionable circumstances by Ælfred the Sacrist, a monk Wall described as a "curious man who combined a touch of piety with a keen collecting instinct" for various holy relics. Whether Ælfred actually was responding to a "command" given to him in a "vision," as he later insisted, is suspect, but the end result is that Bede's bones have rested peacefully in Durham since the eleventh century, and not at Jarrow. Bibliophiles who make the trip here are able also to pay passing respect to Richard de Bury (1287–1345), the former bishop of Durham who wrote history's first great valentine to bibliomania, *The Philobiblon*. He is buried in the western angle of the cathedral before the altar of Saint Mary Magdalene. Perhaps the most famous tribute to this worthy bastion was offered by Sir Walter Scott:

> *Grey towers of Durham,*
> *Yet well I love thy mixed and massive piles*
> *Half church of God, half castle 'gainst the Scot*

For the better part of seven hundred years books had been confined to the sacristies and armariums of monasteries and cathedrals, revered as precious objects and restricted to the scrutiny of a privileged few. Manuscripts frequently were exchanged for the purpose of making copies, giving credence to John Willis Clark's claim that abbeys were the "public libraries of the Middle Ages." When books were loaned out, substantial security deposits had to be pledged as guarantees against their safe return. "In some abbeys the purchase of books, and the copying of them for sale, became just as much a business as the manufacture of Chartreuse,"

Ernest A. Savage notes in a lively study of medieval book culture. Monasteries, as a consequence, were the principal source for what Richard de Bury called the "heavenly food of the mind" and "vessels of sacred wisdom."

The situation began to change dramatically in the thirteenth century with the emergence of colleges and universities as principal centers of intellectual inquiry, creating an unprecedented demand for access to knowledge. When librarians began to chain their treasures to wooden cabinets, it meant that people from outside the cloistered walls were finally being allowed inside to read, and as more and more ideas were considered appropriate for mature contemplation, a greater variety of books forced them to develop new ways of maximizing storage space. Readers no longer focused their efforts exclusively on theology; some studied civil and canon law, others concentrated on medicine, music, mathematics, and philosophy. In the years before Johannes Gutenberg introduced the printing press to Europe, a single volume in manuscript could cost as much as a farm, but unlike real estate, which is fixed in place forever, books are highly mobile pieces of property, and tempting targets for opportunists.

"In the Middle Ages books were rare, and so was honesty," Burnett Streeter wrote in a 1931 monograph on chained libraries. Because curses threatening everything from excommunication to eternal damnation did little to deter thieves and vandals, more pragmatic steps were developed to safeguard books. Once chains became a basic component in the layout of libraries, it followed that the buildings themselves would be shaped in very specific ways as well. Since folios fastened to shelves could not be carried to a light source, windows had to be installed nearby. Chaining, as a consequence, is considerably more than an "interesting irrelevance" for cultural historians, Streeter pointed out, especially since the practice "conditioned the structure and development" of libraries from the beginning of the fourteenth century to the end of the seventeenth, a period that embraces the full sweep of the Renaissance in Europe.

John Willis Clark identified three general stages of book shelving during these years, innovations that he christened the "lectern-system," the "stall-system," and the "wall-system," each of which followed hard on the heels of the "carrel-system" employed when far fewer books were maintained in less space. The transition to chains is believed to have taken place sometime around 1300. Where, specifically, they made their debut remains open to speculation, since so many early abbeys have long since disappeared. But it is known that in 1320 Thomas Cobham, bishop of Worcester, offered to underwrite construction of a chained library on the second floor of St. Mary's Church at Oxford, a clear indication that the fashion was already in vogue. Fifty-three years later funds were provided to build a similar facility at Queen's College, and six years after that instructions for the installation of another were included in the Founder's Plan for New College.

In England, monastic colleges were established at both Oxford and Cambridge, and the first libraries in those institutions were of the "lectern" variety. In this layout, rows of wooden desks with peaked tops were placed at right angles to the outside walls of a compact gallery, positioned so as to bathe each reading position in as much sunlight as possible. Slanted planes on both sides of the lectern facilitated reading, with all volumes chained to bars running along the front of the cabinets. Books not in use would lie flat on shelves underneath. Some stands were designed low to the floor so that people could sit as they read, though the French were partial to "standing" lecterns that required readers to remain on their feet.

Despite the general abandonment of the practice several hundred years ago, there are still a few chained libraries left in Europe, and they are all worth a visit. By far the most complete example is in the city of Hereford, the administrative center of a lush farm region 135 miles northwest of London in a borderland area called the Marches. Well known for a breed of beef cattle that bears its name, Hereford is three hours by train from Paddington Station, with stops along the way in Oxford and Worcester. Just across the border in Wales is Hay-on-Wye, a tidy country town that has become a fixture among itinerant bibliophiles for its rich concentration of secondhand bookstores—about forty, all told—and for a literary festival mounted each summer that brings authors in from all over the world to participate in various symposiums and conferences.

The Cathedral Library at Hereford is home to the largest collection of chained books still maintained anywhere in the world. There, some 1,500 books stand upright in a series of seventeenth-century bookcases, each volume firmly secured to an iron rod by a strand of chain links attached to the front edge of the binding. Book titles are posted on placards attached to the outer end of each press. As far as substance goes, a number of important items reside here, consisting mostly of theological treatises and canon law, but the greater relevance lies in the circumstance of their shelving, not the uniqueness of their content. Still, seventy of the books are incunables, two of them exceedingly scarce titles by William Caxton, and fully three thousand books in the entire library—including a goodly number that are not chained—were printed before 1800. Though regarded as an historical curiosity, the bookcases—known as presses—remain part of a working library that has operated continuously since the twelfth century, with some books and manuscripts that are much older than that. Foremost among the cathedral's earliest treasures is a volume known as the Hereford Gospels, believed to have been made somewhere nearby in the eighth century.

For book historians, the Hereford library is a "unique and intriguing" story of survival, according to the current librarian, Joan Williams, primarily because precious little is known about how a large portion of this magnificent time capsule came together in the first place. A detailed catalog of the 229 manuscripts in the collection begins with this caveat: "Any estimate of the Cathedral's medieval Library, of its history and holdings, is hampered by the lack of documentation." Indeed, the paucity of information is such that the See of Hereford "is opaque to the modern historian until the late eleventh century," or roughly the first three hundred years of its existence. But the books have survived—through the Norman Conquest of 1066, through the religious upheaval of the sixteenth century, through the civil war that followed—and many of them are several hundred years older than the seventeenth-century shelves that embrace them. Because Hereford never had any monastic ties, it was not subject to suppression by the agents of King Henry VIII, so the library made it through that perilous passage unscathed as well.

That there was reading furniture for some time at Hereford is known by virtue of the cathedral statutes, drafted in 1583, which require the master of the library to affix a list of titles at the end of each desk. These units were probably made between 1482 and 1490, when Thomas Chaundler— formerly the chancellor of Oxford—was dean of Hereford, and they were likely modeled after those formerly in Duke Humfrey's Library at the university. The earliest books were probably kept in chests, of which an excellent example from the fourteenth century, fitted with three locks, is still in the library. Oddly enough, the cathedral archives offer more detailed information on the construction of the presses than on how some of the books entered the collection. For 250 years, the chained library was kept in a beautiful early English Gothic room above the crypt of Saint Thomas of Hereford known as the Lady Chapel. The shelves were built to the specifications of Dr. Thomas Thornton, a canon of Christ Church, Oxford, tutor to Sir Philip Sidney, and master of the Library at Hereford from 1595 to 1597 and 1610 to 1617. Dr. Thornton supervised installation of the first four shelving units in 1611, with the others assembled shortly thereafter. The carpentry was carried out by a local craftsman, with chains and locking mechanisms provided by an Oxford ironsmith. Each piece was provided with three tiers, or "stalls," as Clark called them, to contain the books. The chains have swivels to prevent twisting, and every strand has a ring that runs horizontally on a rod secured at the upright edge of each case. Whenever a new volume was added, two hasps were unlocked to release the bar from its mooring at the end of the cabinet. The wood used is unplaned oak, still rough after all these years. What furnishings these pieces replaced is not known for certain. In the original layout, six double-sided and two single-sided cases were set perpendicular to the north and south walls, with a spacious aisle running down the center of the chapel that enabled readers to move about unimpeded. Benches were provided at each lectern.

A number of the older books were once fitted with chains that made it impossible for them to have been kept other than flat on their sides, compelling evidence of an earlier shelving method. With the invention of movable type in the fifteenth century came the production of books in greater numbers, a development that undoubtedly precipitated the adoption of upright storage. Since 1996, the eight bookcases at Hereford have been installed in a £2.7 million structure described by one writer as a "high-tech medieval building." It was underwritten substantially with a £1 million gift from John Paul Getty Jr., the American-born philanthropist knighted in 1998 by Queen Elizabeth II in recognition of his many benefactions to the arts in Britain. The new library was built close to the Southwest Cloister, where the first church repository was located, and allows for the seventeenth-century bookcases to be arranged as they were originally; it also provides for public viewing of a thirteenth-century artifact that enjoys as much fame as the chained library, a large map of the world on vellum with Jerusalem at the center. Known as the Mappa Mundi, the chart is believed to have been made between 1290 and 1300 by a man named Richard of Haldingham. As with many of the cathedral's older books, there is no record of how, why, or when this curious artifact came to Hereford. The oldest known reference to the map appears in a description of Herefordshire antiquities published in 1682, with the unmistakable implication that it had been there for a long time when the guide was written.

The Mappa Mundi became the center of controversy in 1988 when officials of the financially strapped cathedral announced that they would repair the crumbling building and enhance their public ministry by selling the treasure at public auction. When its consignment to Sotheby's was announced, the auction house's resident expert on Western manuscripts, the noted paleographer Christopher de Hamel, described the Mappa Mundi as being "without parallel" and arguably "the most important and most celebrated medieval map in any form, the most remarkable illustrated manuscript of any kind." Fueled by fears that yet another national treasure was in jeopardy of being removed from the United Kingdom by some wealthy foreign bidder, a spirited public outcry followed. The Mappa Mundi was expected to bring at least £7 million on the open market, although for insurance purposes its value has since been estimated at £13 million to £20 million. Several frantic strategies were proposed, including the sale of individual shares to the general public at £1,000 each, but in the end a number of substantial grants—including another £1 million from John Paul Getty Jr.—rescued the map from the auctioneer's hammer, and transferred ownership in perpetuity to a nonprofit trust.

The glory of the Mappa Mundi is that it is based on literary sources, not geographical soundings. Unlike most maps, which exist as navigational devices to help wayfarers find their way from one place to another, the Mappa Mundi is a window into the way people of a particular time and place believed the world existed. More than a network of roads and signposts, it suggests where a segment of humanity believed it had been, and where its destiny was lying in wait. The continuing mystery of how this magnificent chart of the imagination got to Hereford makes it all the more fascinating. Like most medieval maps, the Mappa Mundi is drawn as a circle, with east at the top, where the sun rises and a trail leads to the door of heaven. At the apex, a figure of Christ sits in judgment among clouds of glory. For pilgrims who have followed the true path, an angel stands at the right with a trumpet, summoning the blessed to joy; another angel at the left pronounces damnation for the sinful. At the center are Jerusalem and the Holy Land, with the Mediterranean Sea plunging westward at the bottom to the Pillars of Hercules and the Straits of Gibraltar. What the chart lacks most is an itinerary, and the reason is that Richard of

Haldingham relied on geographical knowledge that had gone unchallenged for a thousand years. Most of his material came from ancient texts, and was intended as a statement about the world and its wonders, making the map a revealing guide to its own era.

A statement, prepared by Haldingham, inscribed at the lower left-hand corner, uses a word, now archaic, to describe the concept he employed. The Mappa Mundi, he declared—and the actual title of the map appears above the head of a horseman in the bottom right corner—is an *estoire*, a designation that carried the dual connotation of "story" and "description" in the sense that stories are offered in proximity to their associations. Alongside the island of Crete, for instance, is the depiction of a labyrinth, where the mythical Minotaur roamed. The track of the Israelites to the Promised Land passes through the parted waters of the Red Sea, and in Italy a personification of Rome holds the reins of the planet. Moving away from the center of the inhabited world, the outer sea is populated by images of fearsome creatures. The considerable size of the map, sixty-four by fifty-four inches, leaves no doubt that it was intended for display, perhaps as an altarpiece at first, but hidden away later during the Reformation, which would explain the dearth of information on its whereabouts during that period of its history. Because Haldingham's intention was to provide a visual narrative, not a navigational fix, the Mappa Mundi retains the magic to make minds soar with wonder.

Just about every library history of any depth reproduces an old woodcut by Jan Cornelis Woudanus showing the library of Leiden University as it appeared in 1610, executed about the same time that chained presses were being installed in Hereford. Like the Mappa Mundi, the drawing delineates a finite space—in this case within the four corners of a room, not a sphere of the imagination—and it was this illustration as much as anything else that persuaded me to make a day trip to the charming Dutch city. My primary reason for being in the Netherlands on this occasion was to interview the booksellers Nico and Max Israel, both survivors of the Nazi occupation during World War II, but with the famous university town less than an hour away by train—and with an image of that famous engraving in the back of my mind—the prospect of seeing yet another sensational library proved irresistible.

The Woudanus print pictures a working library, and from the refined elegance of the men pictured, it is apparent that it functioned during a time of great prosperity. It is also obvious that the planners failed to think vertically; the room is high and spacious, yet each of the bookcases is single-tiered. There are eleven presses on either side of a central aisle, each containing forty to forty-eight volumes, with two cupboards at the far end that probably contained manuscripts. John Willis Clark was unsure how, exactly, he should classify this odd shelving scheme in the evolution of book storage. "I therefore submit that they may be looked at here as transitional specimens," he concluded tentatively, "bridging over the interval between the desks we have lately been considering." But he chose nonetheless to reproduce the picture over two full pages of *The Care of Books*, probably because it depicts a late Renaissance library teeming with activity.

According to the terms of its charter, the library belonged to the people of Leiden, but since most of the books were printed in Latin—and since most of the population spoke only Dutch—access was limited to those skilled in the tongue of the educated. The room was intended nonetheless to be attractive and filled with "adornments," a place of beauty for everyone to enjoy. A famous sepia drawing of Constantinople, donated in 1598 by the treasurer of the university, can be seen on the northern wall. Various coats of arms and paintings, including portraits of Erasmus, Raphelengius, and Janus Secundus, treasures still owned by the university today, are visible as well. For me, the human traffic and the purposeful bustle are most endearing. There are fifteen well-dressed men moving about in the picture, twelve of them at the front of the long room. Several are engaged in animated conversation, the two at the left are absorbed in the study of a globe; two others read at a bench marked "Mathematici," while a single browser enters a bay marked "Medici." Books, manuscripts, globes, and a long mural print occupy the left wall. Clearly, it is a house of learning in the truest sense, a place where a universe of knowledge is freely available, but relaxed enough to allow two playful dogs to saunter around the room untethered. Modern-day Leiden is a resplendent city, with canals, windmills, cobblestone streets, tidy brick houses, museums, friendly people, and bicycles to be seen everywhere, and though the building that lodged the old library still stands, the interior has long since been put to other uses. When I arrived on campus, I went directly to the modern repository in use today, an efficient facility teeming with students, and was treated to a guided tour of the extensive collection of rare books, maps, atlases, and globes that are maintained in the lower levels. But I ended up at the old brick building by the banks of an ancient canal, peering through the arched windows of the old library.

Leiden University was chartered in 1575 by William the Silent, Prince of Orange, as a reward to the people for supporting his campaign to end Spanish rule, and came along at a time when the Dutch Republic was entering its great golden age. The first library opened in 1587 in what was known as the Vaulted Room, but a steady flow of new purchases necessitated a move to larger quarters eight years later. Within a decade the library had achieved such sophistication, according to one contemporary account, that it had the capacity to provide "the theologian knowledge, the lawyer exercise, the physician instruction, and the antiquarian pleasure." A bibliography of the university's holdings, the *Catalogus Principum*, prepared in 1595 by Petrus Bertius and arranged by location, became the world's first library catalog to appear in print. A telling touch was the inclusion of blank pages at the back, leaving sufficient room to list new acquisitions. In 1607 the librarian Paullus Merula drafted a catalog of *Rariora*, a category that he defined as all Latin and Greek manuscripts, any books with handwritten notes or collations, most old editions, and the many maps, atlases, globes, and "books bought from distant lands" by Dutch explorers that had been presented to the university. Thus was born the common practice known today as maintaining "special collections." Merula included important information on where the rare books were bought or who gave them, and distributed lists to wealthy alumni as inducements to be considered when preparing wills, yet another fund-raising strategy widely employed by universities today. The gift of a stuffed alligator is mentioned in the *Catalogus Principum*, prompting the librarian at the time to ask his curators if the toothy reptile belonged in storage, or displayed on top of a bookcase. Whatever they decided, the animal is nowhere to be seen in the Woudanus print.

Throughout its history, Leiden has maintained what is arguably the most important intellectual virtue of all—an open mind. For twelve years in the seventeenth century, the city was home to a group of English dissenters from Calvinism known as the Pilgrims. Unable to secure tolerance in their home country, the separatists found refuge in Holland, where they were free to worship as they pleased. As it happened, the locals were just a bit too relaxed in temperament to suit their expatriate guests, persuading the Pilgrims in 1620 to weigh anchor and set sail for North America. Failing to convert the Dutch to their austere way of life, they tried their hand with the Wampanoag Indians, although they carried a number of Dutch traditions with them, including a judicial code that was incorporated in the Mayflower Compact, and a custom that was improvised into the distinctive American holiday known as Thanksgiving. After deciding to call their new settlement Plymouth, the settlers honored the Dutch city that had given them refuge by designating the first street they laid out Leyden, using a variant spelling of the name.

The Pilgrims were biding their time in Leiden when the famous engraving of the library was drawn, and the artist Rembrandt van Rijn (1606–1669), the city's most renowned native son, was living there as well. In addition to nurturing a bustling university, Leiden had become a great book-making center with the stunning success of the Elsevir family printing firm.

It was also during this period that an important British visitor to Holland, the diplomat Sir Thomas Bodley (1545–1613), was thinking about ways to revitalize a library at Oxford University that had gone derelict over the previous half century, and in all likelihood he received a few helpful pointers from the people at Leiden. No conclusive evidence survives to document that Bodley was influenced directly by the Dutch model, but as one Amsterdam scholar wrote at length in a learned journal on the subject, circumstantial evidence "seems too plentiful to preclude all conjecture as to the existence of some link."

From 1585 to 1596 Bodley led important missions to Denmark, Germany, France, Spain, and the Netherlands on behalf of Elizabeth I, and spent the final seven years of that tour as the queen's permanent representative at The Hague. Bodley lived abroad as a child with his family, devout Protestants from Exeter who were fleeing Papist persecutions, and studied at Geneva, learned Hebrew under Chevalerius, Greek under Constantinus, and Divinity under John Calvin. Following the death of Queen Mary and the ascension of Elizabeth, the Bodleys returned to England, and young Thomas enrolled at Magdalen College.

The Leiden collections had been moved into their new quarters just two years before Bodley arrived, and he had to have been impressed by the enlightened acquisitions policy he would have seen at work there. What must have rankled him more than anything was the knowledge that the institution he sought to reconstitute into a center shaped "by scholars for scholars" had a history that extended back several hundred years. Not long after Oxford was formed as a confederation of independent colleges in the mid-twelfth century, its elders saw wisdom in establishing a central place where common, or "public," interests could be managed, and for many years the University Church of St. Mary on High Street served as a central library, storing books in chests and loaning them out to scholars upon receipt of a sufficient security pledge.

In 1320 Thomas Cobham, the bishop of Worcester, provided funds for construction of an upper gallery at the church for use as a chained library. After repeated delays, the space opened in 1410, fitted with lecterns and benches, and functioned in that capacity for another sixty-five years. The gift in 1459 of 280 manuscripts, including Latin translations of Plato, Aristotle, and Plutarch and works by Dante, Petrarch, and Boccaccio, occasioned the construction of a commodious gallery above the Divinity School to house them; it was named in honor of Humfrey, duke of Gloucester, the benefactor. But as the various colleges strengthened their individual holdings over the next century, fewer resources were committed to the communal collections, with the result that Duke Humfrey's Library fell into disuse, and was abandoned outright in 1556. The books were dispersed, many of them turned over to local bookbinders for the value of their vellum, and the furnishings were sold to Oriel College.

By the time Thomas Bodley matriculated at Magdalen College in 1559, Duke Humfrey's Library had been empty for four years. Bodley earned two degrees, a B.A. in 1563 and an M.A. in 1566, and in 1564 was named a fellow at Merton College, where he taught courses in Greek and natural philosophy. He became a university proctor in 1569 and assumed a number of high administrative positions. To further his knowledge of the world, he spent 1576 to 1580 in Europe, becoming proficient in Italian, French, and Spanish. In 1584 he took a seat in Parliament, and he went abroad the following year on his first diplomatic assignment. Although Bodley devoted the next dozen years to government service, it is clear that he remained an academic at heart. In a short memoir written toward the end of his life, he recalled that an image of the abandoned library had remained with him years after he left Oxford, and that it filled him with a sense of purpose that occupied the remainder of his days. "I concluded at the last to set up my staffe at the Librarie-dore in Oxon; being throwghly perswaded that, in my solitude and surcease from the commonwealth-affayers, I coulde not busie myselfe to better purpose then by redusing that place (which then in every part lay runined and wast) to the publique use of students."

On February 23, 1597—less than a year after returning to England from The Hague—Bodley wrote a letter to the vice chancellor of the university with a proposition that would prove irresistible: "There hath bin heretofore a publike library in Oxford, which, you know, is apparent by the roome itself remayning, and by your statute records, I will take the charge and cost upon me, to reduce it again to his former use." Given an enthusiastic go-ahead, Bodley immediately began repairing Duke Humfrey's Library and fitting it up with shelves, desks, and chairs. During the four years that work was being done in the gallery rooms, he directed an ambitious acquisitions program, buying some material on his own and soliciting several collections of medieval manuscripts and printed books from what he called his "store of honourable friends," notables who included Robert Devereux, second earl of Essex, and Sir Walter Raleigh.

In 1606 Bodley wrote a notation in the flyleaf of a recently acquired title indicating that the volume had been purchased with funds provided by the earl of Northumberland. What makes the entry interesting today is that it was written at the back of the text of the volume, not the front. The book—believed to have been bought from a sailor returning from the Far East—was printed in Chinese, a language that nobody at Oxford could read at the time. Another eighty-three years would pass before a visiting orientalist determined that the book was part of a text of the Analects of Confucius.

To further his goal of creating a truly universal collection, Bodley retained the services of two London booksellers to seek out important books published on the Continent in various foreign languages. A first edition of *Don Quixote* was bought by an agent in Spain in 1605, the year of publication, and remains shelved today in its original press. That same year the first printed catalog of the Bodleian Library was issued, listing nearly ten thousand titles. In 1608 Bodley wrote the English counsel in the Syrian city of Aleppo, requesting that he be on the lookout for "bookes in the Syriacke, Arabicke, Turkise and Persian tongues, or in any other language of those Esterne nations, bycause I make no doubt but in process of time, by the extraordinary diligence of some one or other student they may be readily understoode." Three years later the counsel turned over to Bodley twenty choice manuscripts in several of the requested languages.

Bodley appreciated that if he was going to assemble what is today called a "critical mass" of material, he would draw no distinction between manuscripts and printed books. He wanted everything. With the backing of King James I, Bodley negotiated an agreement with the London stationers that required every English publisher to supply, unbound and free of charge, one example of "all new books and copies never printed before" to the university library on condition that they might borrow the books if needed for reprinting. The agreement made the Bodleian Library the unofficial national library of England, a distinction it maintained until the founding of the British Museum in 1753.

To accommodate all the material that was arriving, Bodley set about building a new wing across the east side of Duke Humfrey's Library, called Art's End once books from the arts faculty were brought over in 1612. It remains one of the most significant transitional library rooms to be seen anywhere in the world, combining in one sweeping layout medieval and Renaissance styles. Instead of being chained to lecterns and laid flat on individual shelves, books were placed upright on presses secured flat on the walls, and rose in tiers to the rafters. To reach the upper levels, lattice staircases were attached to the galleries, and books were retrieved by staff members and delivered to readers at their tables.

Bodley was knighted for his efforts in 1604, and his achievement was acclaimed throughout the realm. During a visit to Oxford the following year, King James I paused to examine a handsome marble bust of the founder commissioned by the chancellor of the university that today still occupies an ornamental niche on the south side under a great archway. Reading the extravagant inscription chiseled at its base, the king wondered aloud if the founder ought not to be called "Sir Thomas Godly instead of Bodley." As he left the gallery, James is said to have remarked that if he were not the monarch, he would choose to be a university man, "and that, were it his fate at any time to be a captive, he would wish to be shut up, could he but have the choice, in this place, as his prison, to be bound with its chains, and to consume his days amongst its books as his fellows in captivity."

At his death, Bodley directed that most of his estate go toward building the west wing of the library, completed in 1640 and known as Selden's End, and the third story of the quadrangle. He left virtually nothing to his brothers, or to his faithful servants or his closest friends, and hardly anything at all to the children of his deceased wife, Ann Ball, by whom he had acquired the greater portion of his wealth. One advocate for the ignored family members accused Bodley of being "so drunk with the applause and vanitie of his librarie that he made no conscience to rob Peter to pay Paul." A close friend, John Chamberlain, complained in a letter of "having been acquainted with him almost forty years, and observed and respected him so much, I should not be remembered with the value of a spoon or a mourning garment."

Outside of this disgruntled inner circle, however, Bodley's library was uniformly hailed. The poet Samuel Daniel spoke for many writers and researchers when he dedicated a "newly augmented" edition of his *Works* of 1601 to "Sir Thomas Bodley, Knight," and opened with some lines penned for the occasion:

> *Heere in this goodly Magazine of witte,*
> *This Storehouse of the choisest furniture*
> *The world doth yeelde, heere in this exquisite*
> *And most rare monument, that dooth immure*
> *The glorious reliques of the best of men;*

Thou, part imperfect work, voutsafed art
A little roome, by him whose care hath beene
To gather all what ever might impart
Delight or Profite to Posteritie.

In 1605 Sir Francis Bacon sent Bodley a copy of his newly published *Advancement of Learning,* in which he championed a program of education meant to "illuminate the border regions" of knowledge. In a covering letter, Bacon praised Bodley for the library, and used a biblical metaphor appropriate to the moment: "You, having built an ark to save learning from deluge, deserve propriety in any new instrument or engine whereby learning should be improved or advanced." The notion of a beamed ark lashed together to rescue learning from a torrent of indifference is an appealing image to consider while walking through the Bodleian Library, not only for the dark timbers and coats of arms that predominate brilliantly on the ceiling but for the echoes of constancy that seem to ring so crisply through the elegant woodwork. It is a tribute that applies to every great temple of learning, every haunt of the muses. Wherever John Willis Clark went in his inspired quest to see the great libraries of the world, he always paused to consider the floors he was walking on, to marvel that they might once have been "trodden by the feet of the great scholars of the past; that Erasmus may have sat at that window on that bench, and read the very book which we are ourselves about to borrow." As a person who had dedicated his life to the long-term "care of books," the nineteenth-century bibliophile looked forward with hope and optimism:

On all sides we see progress; the lecterns and the stalls are still in use
and keep green the memory of old fashions; while near them the plain
shelving of the twentieth century bears witness to the ever-present
need for more space to hold the invading hordes of books that repre-
sent the literature of to-day. On the one hand, we see the past; on the
other the present; and both are animated by full, vigorous life.

2.

GODSPEED

What a place to be in is an old library! It seems as though all the
souls of all the writers, that have bequeathed their labours to these
Bodleians, were reposing here, as in some dormitory, or middle state.
I do not want to handle, to profane the leaves, their winding sheets. I
could as soon dislodge a shade. I seem to inhale learning, walking
amid their foliage; and the odor of their old moth-scented coverings
is fragrant as the first bloom of those sciential apples which grew
amid the happy orchard.

—*Charles Lamb, "Oxford in the Vacation"*

The signal to wake up on the narrow promontory in the Aegean
Sea known as Mount Athos had been sounded at 3 A.M. by the
periodic ringing of bells in the towers and by the rhythmic beat-
ing of a large wooden beam called a *semantron*. Thirty minutes later can-
tors were reading from their psalters by the glow of flickering candles,
casting long silhouettes on inlaid marble floors worn smooth by centuries
of use. At the Great and Holy Monastery of Vatopedi, bearded men in
black robes moved deliberately about their rituals, chanting hymns from
ancient texts, blessing cherished relics, burning incense, crossing themselves repeatedly, all the while praying for the salvation of humanity and
the safe deliverance of their souls. Another three hours would pass before
the brotherhood gathered silently in the refectory for a breakfast of

braised vegetables, freshly baked bread, thick slices of feta cheese, tangy black olives, water from the nearby springs, and a few sips of red wine.

When daybreak finally did arrive, narrow sunbeams had entered the thousand-year-old *katholikon* through clear glass windows in the nave, appearing at a juncture in the liturgy where the faithful celebrate dawn and the coming of light into the world. No longer hidden in the shadows, delicately wrought chandeliers and chalices began to glimmer as if on fire, and on every exposed wall surface—the decorated dome, the arches, the curved ceiling, the lateral choirs, the apse, the exonarthex—narrative paintings depicting scenes from the life of Christ emerged in richly colored detail.

As this drama was unfolding at Vatopedi, similar services were under way at numerous other spiritual enclaves scattered about the 223-square-mile monastic republic on the upper Greek seaboard, and in each instance exquisitely crafted artworks figured prominently in the rites. Thousands of holy objects not selected for use on this crisp November morning—an unrivaled inventory of woodcarvings, jewel-encrusted boxes, medallions, illuminated manuscripts, pectoral pendants, votive lamps, liturgical fans, candlesticks, crosses, all of them icons in one fashion or another—remained safely locked in sacristies, treasure rooms, and libraries. Just a few months earlier, fifteen hundred of these artifacts, a mere sampling of the total holdings, had been displayed eighty miles away in the Museum of Byzantine Culture in Thessaloniki, marking the first time the monks had allowed any of their sacred possessions to leave the Holy Mountain. Attracted by the rare opportunity to appreciate a way of life normally masked from casual scrutiny, 750,000 people thronged the *Treasures of Mount Athos* exhibition in Greece's second largest city.

An icon, by definition, is a painted panel of a subject intended for veneration, but the term can be applied to any hallowed image, whether in smaller, personal objects such as ivories and enamels or in larger mural decorations. Since the ninth-century resolution of the iconoclasm controversy that had bitterly divided the church over the use of images in holy ceremonies, Orthodox Christians have revered their icons as windows into another world, reflections of the subjects they represent. It is largely for this reason, the historian John Meyendorff has written, that of all the cultural families of Christianity, the Byzantine tradition is "the only one in which art became inseparable from theology." On Mount Athos, where it is said that "every stone breathes prayers," successive generations of monks have gathered twenty thousand of these delicately crafted objects. Fifteen thousand manuscripts are preserved there as well, many of them brilliantly illuminated parchments that are hundreds of years old, and inside the churches and refectories, which are architectural triumphs in their own right, frescoes cover 100,000 square meters of total wall surface.

Occupying the easternmost of three promontories attached to the Chalkidiki Peninsula, Agion Oros, the Holy Mountain, pokes its slender mass thirty-five miles into the Aegean Sea on a line pointing toward the island of Lemnos and Asia Minor. It begins on ground that is low and flat, but quickly rises into a chain of rugged peaks and ravines that end abruptly with Mount Athos itself, a sheer formation of marble and limestone that slopes dramatically down to the sea from a summit of 6,660 feet. Although it is connected to the Greek mainland by a narrow isthmus, there is no direct access to the territory by road, and visitors must travel two hours by ferry from Ouranoupolis to the port of Daphne to get there. The all-male theocracy is a union of twenty sovereign monasteries, a dozen smaller dependencies known as *sketae*, scores of hermetic caves burrowed into the sides of mountains reachable only by chain ladders or treacherous pathways, and many isolated huts that are home to the most solitary souls of all. A semi-autonomous state, the community of two thousand monks is self-governed under an administrator appointed by the Greek government. Its special status was reaffirmed by the Greek constitution of 1927 and later by a vote of the European Union, which paved the way for the *Treasures of Mount Athos* exhibition by designating Thessaloniki the "cultural capital of Europe" for 1997.

Together, the Greek government and the EU have committed 50 billion drachmas, about $180 million, to finance long-needed restoration projects at the monasteries.

Mount Athos gets its name from a mythological giant who is said to have thrown a mass of stone at the god Poseidon during a cosmic brawl, creating the imposing landmark that we see today; another version has Poseidon emerging victorious from the duel and burying his impudent opponent beneath a pyramid of pulverized rock. In the *Iliad*, Homer follows the goddess Hera as she passes over Athos on a trip from Mount Olympus to Mount Ida, and in the play *Agamemnon*, Aeschylus proclaimed the site sacred to Zeus. In 492 B.C., a Persian fleet attempting to make the perilous passage around the outer tip of the land mass was destroyed by a storm, prompting King Xerxes to build a canal on the narrowest section of the isthmus. One hundred and sixty years after that, the architect Dinocrates proposed carving the mountain into a monumental likeness of his patron, Alexander the Great, holding a new city in his left hand, and a huge bowl to collect water in his right. Alexander declined the audacious offer, choosing instead to have Dinocrates design a Greek outpost on the Mediterranean Sea in Egypt, the metropolis we know today as Alexandria.

One of the reasons Alexander gave for rejecting a Mount Athos settlement was the difficult terrain. "I think that if someone were to set up a colony there," the Roman architectural historian Vitruvius reported the young king as saying, "their judgment might be held at fault." These proved to be prescient words; there is evidence of a few settlements during pagan times, and monks and hermits are known to have lived on the mountain in the eighth century, but nothing permanent was established until the arrival in the year 963 of the onetime schoolteacher—later to be saint—Athanasius, who chose a rocky outcrop at the base of the mountain to establish the Great Lavra monastery partly because of its remoteness and inaccessibility. With funds provided initially by the Byzantine emperor Nikephoros Phocas, Lavra has enjoyed the backing of affluent patrons through much of its existence, even during the years of the Ottoman occupation (1424–1912), when it received support from Eastern Orthodox countries in the Danube basin and from the czars of Russia.

Prevailing Orthodox doctrine holds that Mount Athos is not part of this world but separate from it, "a heaven on earth," which is why every man who moves there takes a new name and eschews discussing his past. Christian monasticism dates from the fourth century and involves a retreat into solitary life to achieve communion with God; "He who is a monk keeps himself apart from the world and walks forever with God alone," is how Symeon the Theologian (c. 949–1022) characterized the calling. Archimandrite Ephraim, the current abbot of Vatopedi, offered a contemporary description: "On Mount Athos, men are not born; here they die. They pray and die, but the preparation for death, like death itself, is full of life." The ultimate goal of every monk, as Saint Paul put it, is to "pray without ceasing," even during times of rest. "I sleep," goes one injunction, "but my heart is awake."

Two flags fly in tandem on the Holy Mountain. One bears the familiar blue-and-white colors of Greece; the other, a bright yellow banner emblazoned at the center with a two-headed Byzantine eagle, perpetuates the symbol of a Christian empire that collapsed more than five centuries ago with the loss of Constantinople to the Muslim Turks. Signifying the union of church and state, the crest is used frequently by the Athonite government. It appears on the license plates of the four-wheel-drive vehicles that snake their way through the precipitous terrain, and on all official documents. But to suggest that Mount Athos is little more than a curious anachronism on the periphery of modern civilization is to miss the point of its existence entirely. The artworks and manuscripts safeguarded there were produced by a long succession of craftsmen, scribes, and illuminators to express their deepest devotion and, in a powerfully palpable way, to perpetuate a heritage that in the fifteenth century was threatened with what seemed to be certain annihilation. "When the Turks breached the walls of Constantinople on 29 May 1453, they extinguished the longest-lived political entity in Europe, the Byzantine state," Thomas F. Mathews has written. "The disappearance of this ancient Christian polity from the living family of nations reduced its civilization to a study for historians and archaeologists."

Although the Byzantine nation was lost forever, its ideals were kept alive some three hundred miles west of the fallen capital on Mount Athos. Many monks fled there in haste, taking along whatever icons and manuscripts they could gather, and added them to the treasures already assembled over the previous five hundred years. Painters and artisans made their way there as well, and produced work that became stylistically distinctive in its own right. Always a resourceful lot, the monks had already made their peace with the Ottoman overlords, who had seized Thessaloniki twenty-nine years earlier. To underwrite the heavy tribute demanded by the Turks, the monasteries relied on properties given to them over the years by various emperors and benefactors, and maintained a delicate détente with the sultans during most of the occupation.

For all the artistic wonders it has preserved, the Holy Mountain is not a museum, and the idea of playing host to sightseers is anathema to the monks. Male visitors of all faiths are welcome, but they come as pilgrims, not tourists, and only 110 "residence permits" are issued each day by patristic officials in Ouranoupolis. Of these, ten are allotted to non-Orthodox applicants. This document, known as a *diamonitirion*, entitles visitors to four days of full hospitality—beds with fresh sheets, clean towels, and two meals a day.

The sensation of stepping back in time begins during the two-and-a-half-hour bus ride through the Macedonian mountains from Thessaloniki to the port of Ouranoupolis ("City of Heaven"); looking out on the broad plains below, it is easy to visualize Alexander the Great and his army marching eastward on the first leg of their quest to conquer the world. Most of the men on the ferry I took were Greek, some of them obviously fathers and sons traveling together. Many had cameras slung around their necks, and a large number had mobile telephones tucked into their jacket pockets, an incongruous lifeline to be maintained with the world they were leaving behind. Built to carry supply vehicles as well as passengers, the sturdy vessel hugged the craggy shore at about eight knots. Before long, a succession of huddled buildings began to appear off the port bow, some with formidable walls and medieval towers erected centuries ago to ward off raids by Saracens, Crusaders, Catalans, and Latins. In measured succession, the vessel passed the monasteries of Docheiariou, Xenophontos, Saint Panteleimon, and Xeropotamou, each an imposing bastion built near the shore, and each an arresting sight to behold.

Distinctive for their green onion-shaped domes, the multistory buildings of Saint Panteleimon at one time provided refuge for more than a thousand monks; they now shelter about thirty full-time residents. As it is the only Russian Orthodox monastery on Mount Athos, Saint Panteleimon's library of 20,000 printed books and 1,920 manuscripts is especially rich in Slavonic religious material, and is regarded as one of the best resources in the world for primary research in this field. Similar circumstances apply at Zographou, the Bulgarian monastery, and Chelandari, a Serbian enclave. There also are several Romanian *sketae*, and Iveron, now a Greek monastery, was founded by a Georgian in the tenth century and includes in its magnificent library about a hundred important texts on parchment in the Georgian language.

Once docked at Daphne, the visitor quickly realizes that Mount Athos is a place where even the calendar and the clock, as Shakespeare would put it, are "out of joint." Dates are measured in the Julian tradition, thirteen days behind the rest of the world, and days, which end at sunset, are divided into three eight-hour segments, portioned equally for prayer, work, and sleep. A few of the *sketae* still practice what is called idiorhythmic monasticism, a somewhat relaxed system that allows monks to live either in small groups or entirely by themselves, and to retain the use of private property. The word *idiorhythmic* itself translates as "living by one's own life patterns," a perfect description for the wealthy men and nobles who wanted the piety of monasticism but also the accoutrements, including servants, that their personal resources could provide. In the mid-1960s nine of the monasteries were still idiorhythmic, but today all twenty are cenobitic, meaning that each monk is part of a community of men who live, eat, and work together, and accept the unquestioned authority of an abbot. Jobs are assigned each year on the first day of January; there are cooks, gatekeepers, librarians, farmers, housekeepers, beekeepers, and four-by-four drivers as well. "Everyone works," one monk told me. "But first they must pray."

The thirty-minute bus ride up the mountainside from Daphne to the administrative capital Karyes marks the only time any of the pilgrims will travel on a surfaced road. After that, it is long footpaths through heavily forested hills or pitted dirt trails wide enough for just one vehicle to navigate at a time, with frequent hairpin turns made high above the water's edge. Distances are computed in kilometers, but are measured mostly by the time it takes to walk from one monastery to another. To the continuing displeasure of feminists worldwide, women are not allowed on Mount Athos, having been formally banned in 1045 when Emperor Constantine IX Monomachus decreed that the Holy Mountain be set aside for the exclusive adoration of the Virgin Mary. According to one tradition, Mary was on her way to Cyprus to see Lazarus when a sudden storm forced her ship to land near the present site of Iveron. Overwhelmed by the beauty of the land, she is said to have asked for, and received from her son, the Holy Mountain as her "inheritance and . . . garden." The prohibition imposed against all other females, known as the *avaton*, extends to various domestic animals as well; there are no grazing cows, sheep, or goats, and no hens on the Holy Mountain. There are numerous mules, to be sure, and cats of both sexes do roam the territory—recently born kittens can be seen sauntering about everywhere—tolerated because they keep the rodent and snake populations under control.

A central thrust of my explorations has been to witness and write about the dynamic that makes possible the long-term documentation of a threatened cultural legacy, and for that reason I wanted to visit monasteries on Mount Athos with the strongest libraries. Although precise figures are not available, the Greek archaeologist Sotiris Kadas has estimated that the combined holdings on Mount Athos total 204,500 printed books and 15,830 manuscripts. I was granted access to two of the most extensive collections on the Holy Mountain, those maintained at Vatopedi and Iveron, which rank second and third in the hierarchy. "You are about to enter a medieval village," Father Iakavos, a gray-bearded monk at Iveron, told me as I set off early one morning to visit the Great Lavra, the oldest and largest monastery of them all. "The Holy Mountain," he said, "stands beyond time." To a great extent, Iakavos was absolutely correct; Mount Athos is a place that defies time as most people know it, which is one of the reasons, historians agree, that so many books, traditions, and art treasures could survive the forces gathered to destroy them.

In the months preceding the outbreak of World War I, Frederick A. Hasluck, formerly fellow of King's College, Cambridge, and librarian of the British School at Athens, wrote with awe about the trips he had made to the Holy Mountain in his youth, recording his observations in *Athos and Its Monasteries,* published posthumously in 1924. "Much of the difficulty and not a little of the romance of a pilgrimage to Mount Athos has vanished with the coming of steam," he noted wistfully; but once landed at Daphne, he quickly added, "you are quit of modernity. There are few reminders at all of the outside world, and those few are for the most part confined to the shops—such as they are—at the port and the village capital."

A good deal of what Hasluck described still applies today, although he probably would be shocked by some of the concessions that have been made to changing times. "If you wish," he wrote, "a mule is provided by your hosts for your next stage; if you prefer a lay mule, it also and its master are lodged and fed during your stay." Today Land Rover, Mitsubishi, and Mercedes four-wheel-drive vehicles have taken the place of animals. Construction equipment and scaffolding is everywhere apparent, with restoration in progress at sites in desperate need of repair. To generate income, the monasteries now allow loggers to harvest trees on parts of their land in cycles that provide for carefully managed regrowth. And outside labor is plainly in evidence; about a thousand men, many of them from Albania and other onetime Iron Curtain countries, have been hired to ease the massive workload in the fields and vineyards. Monasteries have electricity and running water, and monks assigned to office work have telephones, personal computers, xerographic copiers, and fax machines at their disposal, with Internet access on the way. At Dionysiou Monastery, Father Gabriel, a graduate of Athens Economic University, is creating a digital archive of eleven hundred manuscripts installed in a new wing of the library—quite a turnabout for a way of life that almost did not make it to the twenty-first century.

During its most active periods, as many as 20,000 monks are said to have lived on the Holy Mountain, but by 1959 the resident population had fallen to 1,641, and as Mount Athos approached the end of its first millennium as a Christian sanctuary in 1963, few were optimistic about its future. "Huge monastic complexes that had once pulsated with life now stood derelict and deserted," Georgios I. Mantzaridis, a professor of theology at Aristotle University, has written. "Everything betokened decline and decay." Even more ominous, he added, were rumors that "on the fringes of the millennial celebrations, it was being said that the festivities were in fact the 'funeral service' or even the 'requiem' for Athonite monasticism." A 1971 census recorded a total of 1,145 monks living on Mount Athos. The following year, there were 1,146—an increase of one—and for reasons that are still not fully understood, a steady resurgence has continued ever since. By 1996, 1,036 more men had taken monastic vows, 609 of them arriving since 1987 alone. Bishop Kallistos of Diokleia, also known as Dr. Timothy Ware, a lecturer at Oxford University and the author of *The Orthodox Church*, a standard work, believes that the more severe system has actually contributed to the dramatic renewal of interest in monasticism over the past three decades. "Young Orthodox today who turn to the Holy Mountain," he wrote in a 1983 article, "are looking for the monastic life in its full integrity." Further figures show that the new residents are not only younger—the average age is now under forty—but better educated than ever before. Only three men who moved to Mount Athos between 1960 and 1964 had attended college, while 27 percent of those who have arrived since then have received university degrees.

These figures are pertinent, since one of the justifications over the years for the removal of artifacts from monasteries has been the presumed incompetence of the people charged with their safekeeping. As recently as 1965—when conditions were at their bleakest—many of the old slanders were repeated by Leo Deuel, a Swiss-born writer and teacher of history at City College in New York who expressed irritated dismay at the reluctance of the fathers to share their manuscripts. "Like some negligent but perversely possessive parent, they could not tolerate an outsider's attention to their abused children," he wrote in *Testaments of Time,* a popular history of the worldwide search for lost documents. "At one point these half-literate monks would be entirely oblivious of the hoary, rotting manuscripts, and at the next, when the foreign visitor expressed the slightest interest, they declared them to be of extravagant value." Deuel was delighted to relate how such nineteenth-century opportunists as Lobegott Friedrich Constantin von Tischendorf of Germany, "a seeker after the ancient verities," and the Englishman Robert Curzon, the fourteenth baron of Zouche, were able to "outwit the monks and clergy" and return home with many exciting finds. "Tischendorf, although often exasperated and disgusted, and sometimes deceived, eventually acquired a measure of equanimity, together with a much needed proficiency in Levantine diplomacy which enabled him to carry away manuscripts from places adjudged by his colleagues to be barren or out of reach." By far Tischendorf's most spectacular triumph was his acquisition of the book known today as the Codex Sinaiticus, 347 pages of manuscript removed from the rich library of the monastery of Saint Catherine at the foot of Mount Sinai in Egypt, after pledging to return it once a facsimile had been made. Produced in the fourth century, it is one of the oldest surviving texts of the Bible in existence, and is now in England, sold to the British Museum Library in 1931 for £100,000 by a cash-starved Soviet Union; reneging on his promise, Tischendorf had presented the codex to Czar Alexander II of Russia at the Winter Palace in St. Petersburg in 1859 as a gesture of thanks for supporting his expedition, a gift he had no authority whatsoever to give.

In his memoirs, Robert Curzon recalled the travels he made to Egypt, the Holy Land, Syria, and Greece in the early 1800s with the express purpose of finding "literary treasures." Though not a sportsman in any conventional sense of the word, his journey was inspired by a hunt for what he called "venerable game." At a time when the tusks of elephants, the skins of tigers, and the mounted heads of gazelles were brought back to "civilization" as "trophies" tracked and dressed in the open field, Curzon's prey, "collected by myself, in various out of the way places, in different parts of the world," formed the core holdings of Coptic manuscripts now held in the British Library, and even his harshest critics recognize that he performed a valuable service by rescuing many materials that might otherwise have been lost forever. For all its stuffy posturing, Curzon's account of his parchment-scouting forays, *Visits to Monasteries in the Levant,* is considered a valid cautionary tale on the neglect and ruin of books.

Describing his first visit to the Great Lavra, Curzon wrote that before he was allowed to enter the monastic library, he had been required to join the abbot in a breakfast of garlic cloves "pounded down, with a certain quantity of sugar," into a white paste mixed with shreds of cheese. "Who could have expected so dreadful a martyrdom as this?" he asked. "Was ever an unfortunate bibliomaniac doused with such a medicine before? It would have been enough to have cured the whole Roxburghe Club from meddling with libraries and books for ever and ever. I made every endeavor to escape this honour." But if Curzon wanted to see the books, then he had to eat the concoction, and eat it he did, even though "the taste of that ladleful stuck to me for days." Given the key to the library, and left alone to poke around at will for hours, he was overwhelmed by what he saw, and decided to bide his time. "I did not attempt to purchase anything, as it was not advisable to excite the curiosity of the monks upon the subject; nor did I wish that the report should be circulated in other convents that I was come to Mount Athos for the purpose of rifling their libraries." Small wonder that today the monks exercise great caution about who they allow in to see their books, why they require scholars to explain the nature of their research in advance, and why at least one monk is always in attendance when books are being consulted.

Robert W. Allison, a professor of religion and philosophy at Bates College in Lewiston, Maine, and a Byzantine scholar, has been traveling to Mount Athos regularly since 1977 under the sponsorship of the Patriarchal Institute for Patristic Studies in Thessaloniki, supervising a project to microfilm all the manuscripts maintained at Philotheou, one of the smaller monasteries, and to prepare a descriptive catalog of its holdings. Allison also is North American secretary for the Friends of Mount Athos, a charitable foundation based in England.

"There are a great many treasures on Mount Athos, but what is really exciting is that I have had the opportunity to see a library in its totality," Allison told me. Although considerably smaller than Lavra, Vatopedi, and Iveron, Philotheou has suffered no major depredations in more than eight hundred years, and enables scholars to relate the contents of the library with the life of the monastery itself. "This is a library that has remained intact since 1141," Allison said. "It is much more than the sum of its parts; it reveals themes that are lost when the books are scattered. There are only four hundred manuscripts or so at Philotheou, but what that means from my standpoint is that I have been able to see them all, and see how the different parts relate to each other. I can see patterns, note names that recur, and I can associate them with other events and other people. I have been able to identify the work of a scriptorium which functioned in distinctly different periods of time, and I have learned to recognize the hands of the various scribes who worked there. Most of them are anonymous, but recognizing their hands has helped me find manuscripts elsewhere. It is always emotional for me, every time I go up to the Holy Mountain. I feel the presence of the ages when I'm there."

Approaching from Karyes, Vatopedi appears as a triangular cluster of fortified buildings at the base of a lush valley. Set on a gentle slope above a sweeping inlet to the Aegean Sea, the enormous complex was once home to eight hundred monks. Today some ninety men, most of them youthful members of a "new brotherhood" that moved in from a hermitage known as New Skete in 1990, have infused the monastery with their vigor and enthusiasm. It was my good fortune to be greeted when I arrived on a Sunday morning by Father Isidore, a native of Cyprus who studied in the United States at the University of New Orleans in the early 1980s. His English is impeccable, his insights keen, and his job as a librarian at the monastery made him an interesting person for me to know.

"This is the aristocrat of monasteries," he said during one of several conversations we had over the next twenty-four hours, an observation borne out by historians who have documented the support of numerous royal patrons over the years, and validated just a few months earlier when Prince Charles of England—an honorary member of the Friends of Mount Athos—made his second trip in four years to the monastery; he would return again in the spring of 2000 for another three days, and again in 2001.

Vatopedi maintains two libraries; the New Library curated by Father Isidore gets its name from the content of its holdings, not the date of its construction. "Everything in here is pretty much 1900 and after," he explained during a walking tour. Modern books are collected in most European languages to support a Vatopedi tradition of education that reached its height in the eighteenth century with establishment of the Athonite Academy, a college that in its few decades of existence made generous use of the monastery's unique manuscripts and turned out some of the most important Greek scholars of the period; the majestic ruins, with an arched stone aqueduct still intact, overlook Vatopedi from a nearby hill.

After evening services had concluded, Father Isidore took me to the Tower of Our Lady, an imposing stone bulwark built on the northeast corner of the monastic precinct in the sixteenth century to defend against pirate attacks, but since 1867 the repository of rare books and manuscripts. The Athonite collections are regarded as preeminent among extant Byzantine materials from the ninth to fifteenth centuries, with the Vatopedi holdings regarded among the most significant of them all. This collection of 2,050 manuscripts, some brilliantly illuminated on parchment with gold and lapis lazuli, is kept on the top floor. We began our inspection on the lower levels with maps and archives, moved our way up to books, many of them dating from the earliest years of printing, and concluded with a memorable hour spent among the manuscripts. "By preserving the knowledge, and especially the faith, we keep our identity," Father Isidore reminded me as he was securing the building for the night. "We know who we are."

From Vatopedi, I took a small launch along the rocky northern coast, pausing briefly at various monasteries along the way. We stopped at Pantokrator, established in 1357 by two Byzantine noblemen with an endowment from the Byzantine emperor John V Paleologos, followed by a call on Stavronikita, a fortified complex built on a leveled headland in 1541, the only monastery on the peninsula established after the fall of Constantinople. We pulled into Iveron at a time in the morning when there was a decided lull in the daily routine. The librarian, Father Theologis, was resting, and would see me later in the day, offering a stimulating introduction to the books entrusted to his care. They are kept in a refurbished building that once served as the bakery for the monastery.

After partaking of the traditional welcome offered to newly arrived visitors—a glass of cold water, a cube of the sweet confection *loukoumi*, and a bracing shot of the potent drink *raki*—I started walking. I made one leisurely pass around the gray stone buildings, wandered briefly into the vegetable garden, then headed up a well-worn trail toward Karyes. The higher I climbed, the more breathtaking the sight became. Filling the pristine sky to the southeast was Mount Athos, below on my left was the peaceful monastery, and spread out on the horizon beyond were the mesmerizing waters of the Aegean Sea. Birds were chirping in the trees, and a stream that I could not see was rustling somewhere nearby; otherwise, the silence was total and glorious. I had a camera, and I fired away repeatedly, knowing with every exposure that I could never do justice to the panorama laid out before me, but I snapped and snapped until I ran out of film.

During my hike up that hill—and again the next day when I spent the final hours of my journey strolling about the Great Lavra at the foot of Mount Athos itself—I had a profound sense of what it means to be a pilgrim in a sacred place, all the while reminding myself that a pilgrim is nothing more than a transient, a person passing through. As splendidly unspoiled as this land might be, I sailed out of Daphne thinking about the men who spend their lives on the Holy Mountain cut off entirely from the outside world, perpetuating a tradition and cherishing artifacts through an overwhelming sense of spirituality, an unbending force of will, and a fervent determination to always "know who we are."

With the flowering of humanism and the triumph of the Renaissance came the creation of the modern library, making a visit to Italy and its dazzling assortment of book repositories vital in any grand tour of literary landmarks. The richness and variety of Italy's collections parallel in many ways the unfolding of the national saga itself, aptly described by the nineteenth-century scholar John Addington Symonds as an enormous puzzle that is nearly impossible to decipher. "After a first glance into Italian history," he wrote, "the student recoils as from a chaos of inscrutable confusion." Unlike France or England, where distinctive ethnic cultures took shape over a span of centuries, or the United States, where a "melting pot" of many immigrant groups worked synergistically to produce a unique American identity, there was no uniform emergence of a national persona in Italy. Venice, Milan, Genoa, Florence, Bologna,

Siena, Perugia, Amalfi, Lucca, and Pisa, for example, had periods when they existed as republics; Sicily, Sardinia, and Naples at one time were kingdoms; Ferrara, Modena, Mantua, and Savoy were duchies. Some areas were loyal to the Vatican, others stood resolutely aloof. From 754 to 1870, parts of Italy known as the Papal States were governed under the temporal rule of the popes, with the boundaries constantly varying as allegiances shifted back and forth. "Democracies, oligarchies, aristocracies spring into being by laws of natural selection within the limits of a single province," Symonds observed with bemusement. "To treat of them collectively is almost impossible."

The example of Federigo da Montefeltro, second duke of Urbino (1422–1482) and one of the most powerful men of the fifteenth century, is instructive. A cunning military tactician, Montefeltro shrewdly deployed his army of mercenaries in support of various factions in return for large sums of money; occasionally, if the price was right, he withheld his forces from the fray altogether. A classic opportunist with a profound respect for historical precedent, Montefeltro sometimes provided support for both sides of an issue, although he was respected as a man who unfailingly kept his word. His success was such that the region of Urbino in northern Italy became, to all intents and purposes, a territorial fiefdom in its own right. In 1474 Pope Sixtus IV made him Papal Duke of Urbino and commander of the Papal Army, the first of many honors tendered with the hope of securing his support in a constantly changing political landscape. A liberally educated man with a great love of the classics, Montefeltro built an exceptional library of magnificently bound manuscripts that was famous in its time for excluding printed books as inferior substitutes whose very presence would have made him "ashamed." The treasures are now among the choice holdings of the Vatican Library.

An ever-present threat from all the quarrels, squabbles, and conflicts among neighbors was that they invited foreign intervention. From 1494 to 1559 France and Spain jousted for supremacy during a prolonged conflict known as the Italian Wars, and many prominent observers concluded that the only way to avoid outside domination was to achieve internal unity. The final chapter of Niccolò Machiavelli's *The Prince*, written in 1513 in the midst of the turmoil, pleads for the eventual liberation of Italy from foreign rule; the "ideal" prince of the classic work, modeled on Cesare Borgia, whom Machiavelli met twice, is an amoral and calculating tyrant whose great success is in creating a unified state. But not until 1861, during a period of cultural nationalism known as the Risorgimento, would most of the nation finally agree to confederation. Rome did not come into the fold until 1870, and two tiny states within Italy's boundaries, Vatican City and San Marino, continue to function independently. Even today, there is periodic grumbling from conservative factions in northern Italy about breaking away from the less affluent districts in the south and forming a new country. Most Italians are vehemently opposed to the secessionist movement, but it has generated sufficient support to send thousands of people into the streets of Milan and Venice to demonstrate vigorously in opposition.

Not surprisingly, different regions in Italy evolved different dialects, developing significant speech variations that persist to this day. In literature, Dante, Petrarch, and Boccaccio wrote in a form of Florentine considered to be the noblest mode of expression. "Not many of the languages were ever very close to each other," Dr. Marino Zorzi, a native Venetian who is director of the Biblioteca Nazionale Marciana in Venice, told me during a visit to the magnificent library he oversees on the Piazzetta San Marco. "Even now, if you go to Lombardy, you can't make out a word of what they are saying unless you are a native." As an amusing example of continuing linguistic anomalies, Zorzi cited the curiosity of a 1948 film by the noted director Luchino Visconti, *La Terra Trema*, which used subtitles in standard Italian so that viewers in the rest of the country could understand the regional dialect being spoken by Sicilian peasants.

From this lively mix of cultural diversity has emerged a magnificent array of book repositories. Unlike other countries that get along nicely with one national library, Italy maintains seven with that designation, although only those located in Rome and Florence serve as legal depositories for materials published within the nation's borders; the others specialize in the histories of their respective regions. Operating apart from these repositories are eleven hundred ecclesiastical libraries, which maintain more than 27 million books among them, and entirely independent of these collections is the Vatican Library, custodian of "the richest collection of Western manuscripts and printed books in the world," according to the distinguished Renaissance scholar Anthony Grafton.

Although libraries proliferated during the Renaissance, they had their origins during classical times, with twenty-eight public libraries known to have been operating in Rome in the fourth century. Private collections among the privileged elite were fashionable as well, as the barbed jibes of Seneca about pretentious people who stockpile books they cannot read make humorously clear. As more and more Italians embraced Christianity in the second, third, and fourth centuries, libraries took on the responsibility of preserving sacred texts, an essential role for a religion that ranks the Bible second only to the Crucifix as an object of veneration. Professor Symonds identified three stages in the history of modern scholarship, beginning with what he called an age of "passionate desire" in which everything from the past was seductively new and mysterious. He invited his readers to visualize a scene in which Francesco Petrarca (1304–1374), the archetypal humanist known as Petrarch, can be seen "poring over a Homer he could not understand," while his devoted protégé, Giovanni Boccaccio (1313–1375), author of the *Decameron,* is slavishly learning Greek so that "he might drink from the well-head of poetic inspiration" and translate it for his mentor. From this rich cauldron of endless curiosity bubbled forth a phase of "acquisition and of libraries," a dynamic period in which an enlightened populace set out in all directions to gather fragments of wisdom that had been preserved in old documents. "Manuscripts were worshiped by these men, just as the reliques of the Holy Land had been adored by their great-grandfathers," Symonds marveled, and the yearning for discoveries gripped every social class, with popes, princes, entrepreneurs, and peasants consumed with the hunt. "The ultimate effect of this recovery of classic literature was, once and for all, to liberate the intellect," and front and center in the process, at every step along the way, was the library.

To stock these burgeoning collections, Renaissance book hunters scoured the monasteries of Europe for manuscripts. Cosimo de' Medici spent immense sums on priceless treasures, and lavished his patronage on writers and scholars with commissions to produce entirely new works for his amusement, many of which are housed today in a building of great opulence designed by Michelangelo Buonarroti at the behest of Pope Clement VII. "The Biblioteca Laurenziana must be reckoned as the most important and influential Italian secular building of the sixteenth century," R. Wittkower concluded in a trenchant evaluation of Michelangelo's design, and he just as easily could have added that it is also one of the most beautiful libraries to be seen anywhere in the world.

Shortly after completing a tour of Italy's most spectacular libraries with members of the Grolier Club of New York in 1962, the club's librarian, Gabriel Austin, wrote that the "history of the Laurenziana is almost the history of humanism and the revival of classical learning." During that three-week trip, 140 of America's most prominent book people were treated to a bibliophilic tour of uncommon splendor. The travelers included the renowned collectors Donald and Mary Hyde, William H. Scheide, Clifton Waller Barrett, Norman H. Strouse, and H. Bradley Martin, and the internationally prominent booksellers Hans P. Kraus, Michael Papantonio, William P. Wreden, and George Goodspeed. In his published account of the trip, Donald Hyde wrote that the group did not travel to Italy as tourists, but as de facto emissaries of the United States of America. "We were to be received by its Foreign Minister, by the heads of government of its major cities, by members of the great Italian families and by our own Ambassador." The agenda was not all illuminated manuscripts, incunables, and exquisite bindings, of course; there were black-tie dinners and memorable outings to La Scala in Milan, the Uffizi in Florence, the Duomo di San Giorgio in Ferrara, and the frozen-in-time ruins of Pompeii and Herculaneum. But the unifying focus at every stop was books and the esteemed institutions that contain them. That "wildly, incredibly successful" adventure came thirty-five years before I was offered membership in the Grolier Club, yet it provided the conceptual framework for a lengthy research trip that my wife and I undertook in 1997 to gather material for this book.

Our selective tour of Italian book places began with a flight into Milan for a visit to the Biblioteca Ambrosiana and substantive interviews with the author Umberto Eco and the bookseller Carlo Alberto Chiesa. From there we ventured across the upper neck of the peninsula to the Biblioteca Capitolare in Verona, then on to Venice for calls on the Biblioteca Nazionale Marciana and the Mekhitarian Monastery on San Lazzaro Island, traveling as the cities appear on the map, one whistle-stop after another. A swing through Bologna to Cesena and an appreciation of the Biblioteca Malatestiana came next, followed by visits to the Biblioteca Medicea Laurenziana and the Biblioteca Nazionale Centrale in Florence. A straight shot down the fast track to Rome beckoned presently, climaxed by a rendezvous with the incomparable riches of the Vatican Library. While in the Eternal City, we spent a memorable afternoon in conversation with the Reverend Leonard E. Boyle, the former prefect of the Vatican Library.

In Rome we also were shown an extraordinary family archive stored in one of the most storied private residences in the city, the Palazzo Massimo. Our host was the eldest son of Prince Fabrizio Massimo, by a family custom of many centuries also named Fabrizio, and heir to a noble title with roots that have been traced back to the early days of Rome. Massimo's lineage boasts statesmen, diplomats, cardinals, and two popes, one of them the fifth-century martyr Anastasius I. The family claims further that it descends directly from Quintus Fabius Maximus, a Roman general from the third century B.C. who is credited with defeating Hannibal in the

Second Punic War. "We say that our family is twenty-seven hundred years old," Don Fabrizio said. "Maximus is Massimo in Italian, and Fabius Maximus was one of the leading patrician families of Rome. They went back to the founding of the city—and they believed that they were descended from the god Hercules."

Indeed, an elegant emblem designed for the Palazzo Massimo by the famed architect of the High Renaissance Baldassare Peruzzi (1481–1556) features an image of the infant Hercules grappling with a pair of snakes, and appears on a rounded ceiling just inside the front entrance. Located along the Corso Vittorio Emanuele between Piazza di Sant'Andrea della Valle and Piazza San Pantaleo, the elegant building was restored under Peruzzi's direction after the Sack of Rome by the French in 1527. Called alle Colonne for the Doric columns on the convex façade that curve along the front of the building, the landmark is notable for having housed the first printing press set up in Rome by the Germans Conrad Sweynheym and Arnold Pannartz in 1467, clear evidence of the Massimo family's long-standing support of cultural activities. A plaque marks the presumed location of the press behind an interior courtyard at the rear of the building.

Although the family's history goes back many hundreds of years, the papers filed in numerous containers embossed with the Massimo coat of arms—and stacked on a large Italian Baroque bookcase designed in the seventeenth century by the great sculptor Gianlorenzi Bernini (1598–1680)—contain no material from before 1527. "There were records here that we know went back to the tenth century, but everything in the house was burned by the French in the Sack of Rome," Massimo explained. Even with that grievous loss, what has been preserved since then is formidable. The Archivo Casa Massimo—Archive of the Most Excellent House of Massimo—is family records, to be sure, but family records that include deeds, documents, and exchanges with the likes of Peruzzi, Bernini, and the painters Caravaggio (1573–1610), Velázquez (1599–1660), and Nicolas Poussin (1594–1665), each of whom did work for the Massimo family, "and letters from all the important royalty of Europe." The larger significance of the Massimo archive is that while quite extraordinary, it is by no means unique. Though not a library in any formal sense, or a readily accessible public resource for that matter, it is a cogent example of the passion Italians through history have demonstrated for documenting their lives and experiences, a predilection apparent to scholars who are repeatedly amazed at the quantity of correspondence, records, journals, and scrapbooks kept by people from all social strata, surviving the passage of so many centuries.

Because the order of our Italian itinerary was determined by the quirks of location, not chronology, it happened that our final destination, the mountaintop abbey of Monte Cassino, turned out to be the one place where a consideration of Italian book culture properly begins, not ends. A trip to Monte Cassino is an act of homage as much as a celebration of treasures. It was on these grounds in the early years of the sixth century that Saint Benedict, an ascetic visionary from Nursia by way of Subiaco, compiled a code of monastic conduct that permitted a regimen of textual replication to take root throughout Europe, leaving all of Western civilization forever in his debt. "Though it was not part of St. Benedict's design that his spiritual descendants should make a figure in the world as authors or statesmen, as preservers of pagan literature, as pioneers of civilization, as revivers of agriculture, or as builders of castles and cathedrals, yet circumstances brought them into all these spheres," G. Cyprian Alston has written in an authoritative commentary on the code of monasticism known as the Rule of Benedict. "His sole idea was the moral and spiritual training of his disciples, and yet in carrying this out he made the cloister a school of useful workers, a real refuge for society, and a solid bulwark of the Church." Whether deliberate or unintended, the consequences of the Rule of Benedict are beyond calculation. "For a period of more than six centuries, the safety of the literary heritage of Europe, one may say of the world, depended upon the scribes of a few dozen scattered monasteries," George Haven Putnam declared in a comprehensive history of medieval book production. "It is not too much to say that it was St. Benedict who provided the 'copy' which a thousand years later was to supply the presses of Gutenberg, Aldus, Froben, and Stephanus."

Located eighty-seven miles south of Rome off the main highway to Naples, the stout complex of pale mountain limestone and bright orange roof tiles appears with striking suddenness several miles to the east, and if the skies are as bright and clear as they were on the morning of our visit, the monastery's bone-white façade glints like a beacon in the brilliant sunshine. The roadway to the abbey curls seventeen hundred feet up a steep ridge, a spiraling drive that rises above the orbits of soaring hawks, above the flight patterns of helicopters on final approach to the city below. Painted in bright red letters over a thick wooden door outside the arched gateway is the word *Pax*, a hopeful motto for a monastery that has been reduced to rubble on four occasions over the past fifteen centuries by a variety of calamities, the first coming around 585 at the hands of plundering Lombards. Rebuilt and reconsecrated after an extended interval, Monte Cassino was leveled again in 883 by Saracen invaders and in 1349 by an earthquake.

But the most crushing blow of all was delivered on February 15, 1944, by two waves of American warplanes attached to the Ninety-sixth Bombardment Group during the European campaign to secure what Winston Churchill had called the "soft underbelly of Europe." A great deal has been written about the bombing of Monte Cassino, and opinions remain sharply divided to this day over whether such a devastating attack on a sanctuary of such enormous cultural importance was necessary to defeat the Germans. Beyond dispute is the long-standing conviction that the army that controls Monte Cassino controls the road to Rome, and before Allied forces could capture the Italian capital, they had to neutralize the German defense in the south known as the Gustav Line. As a gesture of solidarity to its Axis ally, the Germans never occupied the abbey while it was still functioning, although they did place troops and gun emplacements outside the enclosure and station artillery spotters immediately below the towering walls. According to a report released by the Vatican in 1993, the Germans also stockpiled ammunition in a cave that runs underneath the monastery, strengthening the Allied argument that it was a legitimate military target.

British and American generals had committed themselves to sparing the abbey as well, but in the first battle for Monte Cassino, General Mark Clark's Fifth Army suffered 14,375 dead and wounded, more casualties than his forces had recorded at El Alamein in North Africa, and more than double the German losses. Those sobering figures, along with the virtual annihilation of two brigades of the U.S. Thirty-sixth Division that were attempting to cross the Rapido River at the base of the Aurunci Mountains, followed by heavy casualties among the U.S. Thirty-fourth Division as it moved along Snakeshead Ridge toward the monastery, brought about a change in plans. The decision to bomb was explained by General Dwight D. Eisenhower. "If we have to choose between destroying a famous building and sacrificing our own men," the Supreme Allied Commander declared a few weeks before authorizing the operation, "then our men's lives count infinitely more and the buildings must go."

Thousands of leaflets were scattered in the area announcing that an attack was imminent and that the site should be abandoned. Most people left, though 250 peasants who sought refuge in the cellars died in the raid that followed. The operation was carried out by B-17 Flying Fortresses and B-26 medium-range bombers carrying a lethal combination of 500-pound bombs, 100-pound incendiaries, and half-ton "blockbusters." Before the smoke had cleared, the Germans moved their ground forces inside the toppled walls, and another three months would pass before Monte Cassino finally came under Allied control, and only then after a heroic assault was carried out by Polish rangers, a thousand of whom are buried on Monte Calviro facing the northwest wall of the rebuilt abbey. A month after the mountain was declared secure, Rome became the first Axis capital to be captured in the war.

Writing within weeks of the bombing, William Dana Orcutt, an

American scholar, author, and printer who had been honored in 1924 by the Italian government "for interpreting Italy to America in the sister arts of literature and typography," wrote poignantly about the fate of the "sleepy little hamlet" of Cassino by the Rapido River, and the abbey on the mountain where he had spent many rewarding hours doing research.

> *I have worked in many libraries the world over; I have studied in buildings of infinitely greater architectural beauty; I have been surrounded by collections of greater value; I have always received the utmost courtesy from those in charge. I ask myself why it is that I look back on Monte Cassino with such particular affection. Perhaps it was the sincerity and the earnestness of that little band of educators, who had set themselves apart from the allure of the world outside— not as a religious fetish, but as a tribute to learning. They belonged to a religious order, truly, but they gave the impression of being incited by a desire to give something out to the world, through those whose studies they assisted. Each time I left Monte Cassino, I felt myself filled with a new urge for personal accomplishment.*

Orcutt expressed relief that the abbey's paintings, books, and archives had been saved, and pointedly used the present tense when celebrating the "Humanistic creed this old library exemplifies," even though at the moment he was writing the monastery was in ruins. "Even its ashes will continue to give out that message until the walls again rise to prove its everlasting permanence," he concluded. A few days after the mountain was declared secure, a crew of thirty-five priests, aided by a working party of one hundred German prisoners, began sifting through the fallen walls, applying an edict handed down by church and government officials that every stone should be placed "where it was, as it was." Twenty years after the bombardment, Monte Cassino was reconsecrated by Pope Paul VI, who declared Benedict to be the patron saint of all of Europe, and the books, which had been removed in October 1943 and stored in Vatican

City, returned in glory. Today the statues of Saint Benedict and his sister, Saint Scholastica, cobbled together from pummeled fragments, look out on the courtyard.

To modern visitors, the seven-acre complex has the unmistakable look and feel of a medieval abbey. When it is viewed alongside photographs taken before the war, the similarities are impressive. The arching cloisters, the observatory overlooking the central courtyard, the basilica, the sacristy, the crypt where Benedict and Scholastica are buried, the capitular hall, the great southeastern corridor where the main library is located, have been painstakingly rebuilt, and Saint Benedict's cell, the very place where the great rule is presumed to have been written fifteen centuries ago, survives intact.

Of primary consequence is that the most fragile artifacts of all—the precious books and manuscripts—are shelved once again in their original surroundings. Christopher de Hamel has perceived a pattern to this circumstance and concluded that a number of important books throughout history have had "a knack of surviving," despite all odds. He cited the example of Saint Augustine's Abbey in Canterbury, established in the sixth century as the first monastery in England, and "an utter ruin for centuries"—yet 250 books originally gathered there still exist, passed on from custodian to custodian down to the present day. "What private possessions still survive from the great figures of European history, such as St. Boniface, Charlemagne, Otto III, Thomas Becket, St. Louis, Boccaccio, and Erasmus?" he asked. "Their books survive, handled and read by all of them." Perhaps the greatest example of this phenomenon is the forty-eight Bibles produced in Mainz, Germany, by Johannes Gutenberg in the 1450s, which live on while the printing press, the type, and the shop used by the man who produced them have vanished entirely, along with most of the documentary record confirming his own existence. "All we have is the book," Dr. Eva Hannebut-Benz, director of the Gutenberg Museum in Mainz, Germany, told me, "and that is more than enough."

In *The Scriptorium and Library at Monte Cassino, 1058–1105*, the

American paleographer Francis Newton emphasized that his reconstruction of bookmaking at the abbey and the development of a distinctive script known as Cassinese would have been impossible without the availability of the manuscripts that were rescued, and he gratefully acknowledged the initiative taken by two German officers to remove them from the site four months before the Allied bombing. Fully three hundred of the codices they saved were produced in the monastery's scriptorium between the end of the eleventh century and the beginning of the twelfth, when the abbey was governed by Desiderius, the "bibliophile abbot," and his successor, Oderisius I. For a characterization of this particularly fruitful juncture in the late Middle Ages, Newton deferred to the British scholar E. A. Lowe, who declared the abbey to be "the greatest centre of light and learning" in Italy. "Any investigation of the Monte Cassino scriptorium and library is aided by several resources," Newton wrote. "The principal one is that in spite of the grave losses suffered over the centuries, the abbey still possesses a sizable part of its medieval library. There are only a handful of ancient monastic centers in Europe of which this can be said."

My visit to Monte Cassino began in the Archivio, where the abbey's fourteen hundred manuscripts are kept, and moved on to the forty-thousand-volume library of printed books, which includes several fifteenth-century titles printed at Subiaco, where Sweynheym and Pannartz operated before moving on to the Palazzo Massimo in Rome. Displayed by itself on a Bible stand in a conference room is the abbey's own copy of the Rule of Benedict, copied and illuminated at the monastery in the tenth century. The original draft, believed to have been in Benedict's hand, was carried to Rome in 581 when the abbey was sacked by the Lombards, and returned by Pope Zachary after completion of the first reconstruction. At the direction of Charlemagne, it was reproduced toward the end of the eighth century in numerous copies for distribution throughout Europe. By the time the original was destroyed in a fire in 896, the rule had achieved widespread influence. Significantly, Monte Cassino has a coat of arms that is displayed throughout the complex, and was pointed out to me repeatedly by our gracious host, Dom Faustino Avagliano, the archivist and prior of the abbey. It pictures a fallen oak tree sprouting a new shoot from a prone trunk. Emblazoned on the crest is the motto of Monte Cassino, *Succisa virescit*—"Struck down, it comes to new life."

A short walk from the twelfth-century courtyard where a fanciful statue of Juliet Capulet lures thousands of sentimental tourists to Verona each year is a landmark of enormous bibliographic interest, known as the Biblioteca Capitolare di Verona. The venerable library, which faces a sharp bend in the river Adige, does not come close to attracting as many visitors as the monument erected to celebrate Shakespeare's star-crossed lover, yet it does claim international distinction on a number of significant levels, most notably that it continues an institutional history of close to sixteen hundred years. Because the collections have been housed in several structures over the centuries, it is not the world's oldest library building still in use in its original form—that distinction goes to the Biblioteca Malatestiana a few hours away in Cesena—but it is believed to be the oldest working collection. One reason cited for this unparalleled record of survival is that the books and manuscripts went unnoticed during much of the region's turbulent history. "The central treasures of the Biblioteca Capitolare survive largely because nobody ever thought very much about them during critical times," the late librarian, medieval scholar, and great admirer of the Verona holdings the Reverend Leonard E. Boyle told me. "People simply forgot the library was there; the stuff laid untouched for several hundred years. Nobody was interested in it until the Middle Ages."

A noted fourteenth-century scholar, Giovanni de Matociis, also known as Giovanni Mansionario, made extensive use of the holdings in pursuit of his work, most notably an immense biographical compilation of Italy beginning with the emperor Augustus known as *Historia Imperi-*

ali. Between 1339 and 1341, Pietro Alighieri used the resources of the library to write a commentary on the *Divine Comedy,* written thirty years earlier by his father, Dante Alighieri. In 1345 Petrarch visited Verona while scouring ecclesiastical libraries for lost literary treasures, and discovered the only surviving copies of Cicero's letters to Atticus and Brutus.

In an exacting study of medieval texts, E. A. Lowe declared the Biblioteca Capitolare to be the "queen of ecclesiastical libraries" for its exquisite collections; "It is difficult to speak in measured terms, so numerous are its ancient manuscripts and so venerable the oldest among them." There is some evidence that a library may have been in existence as early as the fourth century during the time of Saint Zeno, when a scriptorium is believed to have been making texts for use in the church. The earliest document in the collection that bears a date is a life of Saint Martin of Tours by Sulpicius Severus, transcribed by Ursicinus, who is identified on the manuscript as "Lector of the Church of Verona." It is dated August 1, 517. Among the Capitolare's most celebrated treasures are five codices produced during the fifth century in the scriptorium of the Duomo, the cathedral of Verona, which stands a few yards away from the library in the piazza. In 1630 the library's ninety-nine most precious manuscripts were stored for safekeeping in a recess on top of an ornamental cupboard; in the mass confusion brought about by the onset of the plague, they lay forgotten and gathering dust for eighty-two years. Their recovery in 1712 by the playwright Scipione Francesco Maffei (1675–1755) caused a minor sensation when announced. Committed to writing an authoritative history of his native city, Maffei had read repeated references to important codices once known to have been kept in the cathedral library, and he was determined to turn the place upside down until he found them. "With a ladder Maffei examined this space and found it filled with a veritable treasure-trove of manuscripts—the finest, oldest, and in some respects the most important collection of Latin codices in existence," James Westfall Thompson wrote in a major history of medieval libraries. Their discovery resulted in a period of book bene-factions that strengthened the collections measurably.

Like so many of the world's outstanding libraries, this quiet enclave is closely identified with the contributions of one towering personality, in this instance a ninth-century archdeacon known as Pacificus (776–844), whom Anthony Hobson called "one of those exceptionally able and ener-getic men whose careers have often been decisive in the transmission of a text or the history of a library." Pacificus has been variously described as a man of letters, a theologian, a historian, an astronomer, an architect, and a prime mover in the copying of manuscripts. A memorial tablet erected in the cathedral praises the archdeacon as a man "outstanding in wisdom and of conspicuous appearance; no such man has been known in our time, or we believe ever."

In diverting contrast to the ecclesiastical collection assembled in Verona, including a good many manuscripts that were prepared hundreds of years ago on the very site where they remain to this day, are the Malat-estiana and Laurenziana libraries, each bearing the name of a mighty lay patron. Although by far the grander and more significant of the two, the Laurenziana defers seniority to its counterpart in Cesena, a rural region in northern Italy south of Ravenna, near Rimini, where the Apennines meet the Adriatic Sea. It was undertaken in 1445 with the intention of supporting a fledgling university at the monastery of San Francisco; con-struction costs were assumed by Novello Malatesta, lord of Cesena and member of a family dynasty that ruled much of the territory for two and a half centuries.

The Malatesta name earned a degree of immortality in 1289 when Paolo Malatesta made the mortal mistake of being caught in flagrante delicto with Francesca da Polenta, the gorgeous wife of his spiteful older brother, Gianciotto, who had the pair put to death. Touched by their tragic story, Dante installed the young sinners in the second circle of hell and doomed them to be whisked about forever by stormy winds. Though not by any means the most severe punishment meted out in the *Inferno*, the couple's agony was too much for Dante to bear, all the same. When Francesca tells the poet during his tour through the netherworld that it was a book—a "single passage" describing the forbidden love of Lancelot and Guinevere read aloud with Paolo in her garden—that "caused our eyes to meet" and for their passions to become hopelessly aroused, he is overcome with emotion and faints at the feet of Virgil.

If it was a book read aloud in a garden that caused one Malatesta to burn in infamy, it would be the erection of a grand library that emblazoned the name of another in glory. For his architect, Novello chose a family friend, Matteo Nuti, who paid careful attention to the plans prepared in 1440 by Michelozzo di Bartolommeo for the library of San Marco in Florence, the original repository for the Medici family books. Construction of the Malatestiana was begun in 1447 on the second floor of a new wing at the Franciscan friary and completed in 1452, with another two years spent on installing the decorations and crafting the furniture. The accommodations include two aisles of parallel desks arranged so they can be entered from the outside of each row near the exterior walls, and also from a wide corridor that runs down the center of the long rectangular room. There are twenty-nine lecterns in each aisle, fifty-eight altogether. Illumination is provided by the numerous arched windows that line the side walls, and by a circular window at the front. Even distribution of the soft natural light is made possible by a vaulted ceiling supported in the center aisle by two rows of white columns, each bearing a different capital, and a floor of brownish red reflective tiles. On a pediment above the double wooden door at the entrance is the Malatesta family device, a carving of an elephant, inscribed with the enigmatic motto *Elephas Indicus culices non timet*—"The Indian elephant does not fear mosquitoes." Another inscription on the pediment, also in Latin, translates: "Novella Malatesta, son of Pandolfo, gave this work." Inside, all the fittings and pearwood furnishings are original, including the wrought-iron chains that are still used to attach manuscripts to the desks.

Always a bit off the beaten path from the major metropolitan centers of Florence, Venice, and Milan, Cesena never enjoyed ready access to the producers and purveyors of books, a circumstance of geography that persuaded Novello Malatesta to set up his own in-house scriptorium and bindery to make copies of books that he was unable to buy on the open market, but could borrow from other libraries. The content generally followed the list drawn up in 1439–40 for Cosimo de' Medici by Tommaso Parentucelli, later to be Pope Nicholas V. Most of the Malatestiana books are works of the church fathers, although there are some notable exceptions. Fourteen codices are Greek, including copies of Homer's *Odyssey* and the *Republic* and *Dialogues* of Plato, which may have been bought from a dealer in one lot; a small collection of Hebrew codices was acquired from the Cesena city council. Fifteen manuscripts, including Pliny's *Natural History*, were written out by Jacopo da Pergola, the first copyist retained by Novello. Almost all of the two hundred codices produced in the scriptorium are illuminated, thirty of them embellished by an artist who signed himself "F.Z.," believed to be Frater Zuane. Novello's library gained appreciative notice quickly; the fifteenth-century humanist Flavio Biondo judged it as being "on a par with the best in Italy."

When Novello died in 1465 at the age of forty-seven, a systematic program of collection development ended abruptly, and his early death probably explains why humanistic literature and poetry are not represented in any great depth. The scriptorium was closed, and outside of a major donation of manuscripts in 1474 from Novello's physician, the inventory was basically complete. One reason cited for the library's long record of survival is the circumstance of its being subsequently enclosed within a much larger building that today maintains three separate municipal collections. More consequential, however, was the perceptive decision of Novello to give the people of Cesena joint custody of the Biblioteca Malatestiana with the Franciscan friars then in residence, an arrangement that proved critical during the periods of monastic abolition that swept through Italy many years later, which could well have led to the dispersal of the collections.

·   ·   ·

It is said that the zeal to create a great library in Venice took root in the fourteenth century when the great poet and scholar Petrarch reneged on a promise to give his books to the city fathers, choosing instead to place them in Milan, where many remain to this day. Another two hundred years would pass before a gift of comparable importance would come along and provide the core collection for what is today the Biblioteca Nazionale Marciana, the Library of Saint Mark, patron saint of Venice, but the end result, it turned out, proved to be well worth the wait. The generous benefactor was not a native Italian but a Greek scholar and priest who chose Venice as the ideal place to deposit a trove of intellectual treasures that he had taken heroic steps to gather during unusually uncertain times. Bessarion, whose baptismal name was Vasilios—Basil in English—was born in Trebizond, a Greek city in Asia Minor on the Black Sea, in 1400. Ordained a deacon of the Eastern Orthodox Church when he was twenty-six years old, Bessarion had received a liberal education in Constantinople and developed a profound passion for the achievements of his forebears. He continued his studies after becoming a priest, learning mathematics, astronomy, philosophy, and rhetoric under several prominent teachers, all the while forming a balanced approach to Christian beliefs that was deeply influenced by Platonic principles.

After a period of international travel on church business, Bessarion was named archbishop of Nicaea in 1437. A year later he accompanied the Orthodox patriarch to the Council of Ferrara-Florence, which had been convened by Pope Eugene IV and Emperor John VIII of Byzantium with hopes of repairing the Great Schism, which had divided the western and eastern branches of the church since 1054. Bessarion was praised as a unifying voice at the conference, and it was largely through his efforts that a tentative union was announced in 1439. When the agreement was rejected by the Greeks, Bessarion left Constantinople for Rome and was named a cardinal of the Catholic Church, convinced that it was only with the full support of the Western powers that a credible force could be mounted against the Ottoman Turks who were systematically bringing about the collapse of the once mighty Byzantine Empire. When Constantinople finally did fall to Mehmed II, the Ottoman sultan, in 1453, and when it was apparent to Bessarion that his constant pleas for a holy crusade had fallen on deaf ears, he turned his energy to gathering and copying ancient Greek writings, concluding that textual transmission was the only way to protect his heritage.

A man of towering intelligence, Bessarion rose rapidly within the Vatican hierarchy. With the elevation of Nicholas V to the papacy in 1447, Bessarion found a kindred spirit who shared his enthusiasm for classical writings, and when Nicholas died in 1455 Bessarion was considered a leading candidate to replace him. A bibliophile of the first rank, it was Nicholas who established the Vatican Library as a true center of humanistic learning. An illuminated manuscript in the library's collection of Giovanni Tortelli's *De Orthographia* (1450) celebrates the pope's patronage of scholarship, praising him for having commissioned the translation of classical texts into Latin from the Greek and for creating "the most splendid" library "that ever existed." It is no coincidence that these were the same virtues valued by Bessarion, who transformed his elegant villa on the Quirinal Hill in Rome into an academy for the study of the humanities, and used the power and prestige of his position to acquire manuscripts. He hired agents to locate obscure books, and those he could not buy outright he had copied at a scriptorium he established in his residence. Years later, he explained the rationale that had shaped his acquisition strategy: "I tried, to the best of my ability, to collect books for their quality rather than their quantity, and to find single volumes of single works; and so I assembled almost all the works of the wise men of Greece, especially those which were rare and difficult to find."

The great literary works were represented in his collection, covering the full range of classical Greek philosophy, rhetoric, drama, geography, astronomy, medicine, and history, but also among the contents were many scientific treatises, including copies of the ancient mathematical works of Archimedes, Apollonius, and Ptolemy. In addition to Plato and Aristotle, authors represented included Theophrastus, Alexander of Aphrodisias, Simplicius, Plotinus, Hierocles, and Plethon. Determined to fashion a form of scholarship that combined Byzantine and Latin traditions into one discipline, Bessarion was constantly on the lookout for intellectuals who could help his cause. While on a lengthy diplomatic mission to Germany in 1461, he recruited the services of Johannes Müller (1436–1476), a young mathematician and astronomer who would achieve world renown by the name of Regiomontanus. Persuading the German to return with him to Italy, Bessarion arranged for the brilliant scholar to learn Greek so that he could examine the mathematical manuscripts in his collection. It was from these investigations that Regiomontanus developed the studies of algebra and trigonometry. The *Ephemerides* he published in 1473 was put to good use nineteen years later by Christopher Columbus on his voyage to the New World. In 1471 Guillaume Fichet, the rector of the Sorbonne and with Johann Henlin founder of the first printing press in Paris, recognized Bessarion's efforts in the spread of Platonism by dedicating his own *Rhetorica* to the cardinal. "Throughout his life, Bessarion worked as a kind of scholarly catalyst," Lisa Jardine wrote in a recent history of the Renaissance, "bringing the contents of his book collection to life by connecting them with the right readers, patrons and interpreters."

When it came time to pick a home for his collection, Bessarion looked north of Rome toward Venice. Given the enlightened attitude that prevailed at the Vatican Library, it would have been a simple task to deposit his legacy there, but the aging cardinal was moved profoundly by the reception the Venetians had extended to the Greek emigrés who had been arriving in droves from Asia Minor since the fall of Constantinople. Not only had four thousand of Bessarion's countrymen been welcomed in the city, they had become prosperous members of the cosmopolitan community, and in 1470 were given a wing of the church of San Biagio, where they could worship in their own language. In 1514 they began building San Giorgio dei Greci, which was completed in 1573 and continues to hold Greek Orthodox services to this day. In the 1468 deed that formalized his extraordinary gift, Bessarion explained why he chose Venice over Florence, another option he had considered: "I could not select a place more suitable and convenient to men of my own Greek background," he wrote. "So I have given and granted all my books, both in Latin and Greek, to the most holy shrine of the Blessed Mark in your glorious city, sure in the knowledge that this is a duty owed to your generosity, to my gratitude, and to the country which you wanted me to share." A firm believer in the civilizing power of literature, Bessarion was adamant on the matter of supporting scholarship, and imposed a condition of "free access to all who want to read and study" the books.

Bessarion's gift of 746 manuscripts—482 in Greek, 264 in Latin—was gratefully accepted, but ten years after his death the precious codices still remained in the presentation boxes in which they had arrived from Rome, stored in the Sala di Scrutinio of the Palazzo Ducale, and unavailable to the scholarly community. In 1537 Jacopo Sansovino (1486–1570), the High Renaissance architect and sculptor who had worked with Michelangelo, was commissioned to design a suitable repository on the Piazza San Marco. The ornate building he created finally received the books in 1560, twenty-three years after work began, and ninety-two years after Bessarion announced his gift. Praised by Andrea Palladio as the "most magnificent and ornate structure built since ancient times," the library stands directly across the piazzetta from the ducal palace. A few hundred feet away are the 325-foot-high brick tower known as the Campanile and the five-domed Basilica San Marco, where the bones of Saint Mark are enshrined, and where long lines of tourists line up each summer to view the forty thousand square feet of spectacular mosaics that decorate the interior.

In the half millennium that has elapsed since Bessarion gave his library to the Venetian Republic, the Biblioteca Marciana has built around it a choice collection of 1 million books—preeminent in the history and culture of Venice, as one might expect, but so strong in the classics that the great publisher Aldus Manutius (1450–1515), producer of the first printed editions of so many Greek works, the *editio princeps* of Aristotle among them, chose to set up his legendary Aldine press close to where so many of the earliest versions were located, and where a large colony of educated Greeks was in place to help him prepare Greek type fonts and to proofread the galleys. That was the lure, in any case; the difficulties involved in consulting the Bessarion manuscripts were notorious during this period, and Aldus had to rely on flawed texts for his earliest editions. Venice nonetheless became the headquarters for Greek printing, and until the end of the nineteenth century most Orthodox ecclesiastical books were printed there. This was just part of a much larger print culture that got under way in 1469, a year after Bessarion's gift was announced. "Venice may not have been even the first city in Italy to establish a printing industry," Martin Lowry noted in a learned biography of Aldus, "but the amazing expansion of that industry, once established, leaves no doubt that Venice was the first city in the world to feel the full impact of printing."

Dr. Marino Zorzi's corner office on the second floor of the library commands a dramatic view of the waterfront, but when I sat down to talk with him about the collections he supervises, he directed my attention to a portrait in oil on an opposite wall. "Cardinal Bessarion," he said, needing to say no more, and then led the way into the Sala Sansovino, where the expatriate benefactor's books are shelved. The unqualified highlight came when Zorzi invited me to hold in my hands a manuscript from the tenth century known as the Venetus A, the oldest known copy of the *Iliad* in existence, and primary source of Homer's timeless text.

When Michelangelo agreed to design a library for the Medici family of Florence in 1523, the understanding was that he would create a temple that would glorify the majesty of books. The collection it would house had already been assembled, and had a value beyond calculation. Had storage been the single motivation for such a grand enterprise, a perfectly adequate repository designed by Michelozzo di Bartolommeo was functioning next door to the chosen site in the Convento di San Marco, and could have served the purpose admirably. The nucleus of the great collection was gathered by Cosimo de' Medici (1389–1464) with help from some of the great scholars and book hunters of the period, Niccolò Niccoli, Poggio Bracciolini, Leonardo Bruno, and Vespasiano da Bisticci most prominent among them. Cosimo's willingness to spend whatever was necessary to form a great collection was legendary. Vespasiano once recalled being asked directly by the grand duke how he would go about building an unrivaled collection. "I answered that to buy the books would be impossible, since they could not be purchased," he replied. "I told him that they must be copied." Agreeing immediately to such a scheme, Cosimo gave Vespasiano carte blanche to make it happen. "After beginning the collection, since it was his will that it should be finished with all speed possible, and money was not lacking, I soon engaged forty-five copyists, and in twenty-two months provided two hundred volumes, following the admirable list furnished by Pope Nicholas V." The collections were expanded appreciably by Cosimo's grandson, Lorenzo de' Medici (1449–1492), known as "the Magnificent." As he lay on his deathbed, Lorenzo confided to Angelo Poliziano, an esteemed poet and frequent user of his books who at one time had thirty-five manuscripts out on loan, "I wish that death would have at least waited to come until I had finished putting together *your* library."

Two years after Lorenzo died, however, the Medici family was banished from Florence in a political upheaval exacerbated by the indecisiveness of his inept son Pietro, aptly nicknamed "the Unfortunate," and any plans to build a great library were sidetracked indefinitely. In the turmoil that followed, the palace was ransacked by the army of Charles VIII of France, and some of the Medici books were lost, including one rarity that turned up four hundred years later in the United States, to be returned to

Florence by a thoughtful donor. The 1,039 treasures that did survive the onslaught were transferred to the convent library in San Marco and the uneasy care of the obsessed friar Girolamo Savonarola; that the books were not destroyed in the chaos brought on by his excommunication and execution in 1498 is a miracle of circumstance. Ten years after that unsettling denouement, the books that had been spared—about two-thirds of the original collection—were returned to the custody of Giovanni de' Medici, a younger son of Lorenzo the Magnificent renowned for his support of literature and the arts. When Giovanni became Pope Leo X in 1513, he had the books shipped to Rome and installed for safekeeping in the Villa Medici, where the literati of the day were welcome to come and study them. Leo's death in 1521 was followed by the fourteen-month papacy of Adrian VI; Adrian was succeeded by the first cousin of Leo X, Giulio de' Medici, who took the name of Clement VII. The family, meanwhile, had regained power in Florence, setting the stage for a true celebration of Medicean glory and a triumphant return of the priceless books to the city.

Barely three weeks after Giulio was elected pontiff on November 19, 1523, Michelangelo arrived in Rome to discuss plans for the new library, which everyone understood would be named for Clement's uncle, Lorenzo the Magnificent. Many detailed letters would be exchanged between the artist and the pope's representatives over the succeeding months, touching on every conceivable aspect of the enterprise. Nothing was overlooked. A choice location that would ensure optimal exposures for exterior lighting was essential, as were separate shelving areas for Greek and Latin manuscripts. Michelangelo sketched out his ideas for such elements as a grand stairway at the entrance and a groin-vaulted ceiling, and he indicated precisely where the thirty-six pilasters with capitals and bases would be placed in the reading room, never failing to submit detailed drawings to the papal court for review. Determined to use nothing but the finest materials for the project, he personally chose the high-quality marble and fine-grained Apennine sandstone known as *magico* for the interiors at various quarries outside of Florence. He selected the walnut for the desks, benches, and interior ceiling, and supervised the seasoning process. Before leaving for Rome in 1533, he hired two master woodcarvers to craft the reading desks he had designed nine years earlier, "not simply as furniture but as necessary elements integrated with the architecture," and he retained five stonecarvers to make the cornices for the doors and the large staircase.

Although empowered to create a work of art that celebrated the wonder of the human intellect—"Spare no expense," he was told—Michelangelo had very specific marching orders all the same. "At the back of the library," he was informed in one letter, the pope wanted "two small studies on either side of the window which faces the library entrance. And in these studies he wishes to place certain very secret books, and he wants to employ these again on either side of the door." That was in March of 1524; thirteen months later the pope's representatives informed Michelangelo that His Holiness did not want a chapel "at the end of the library, but he wants instead a secret library to hold certain books more precious than the others." Seven months after that, Clement made known his disapproval of having windows installed over the vestibule to the reading room "with those glass oculi in the ceiling." The pontiff readily conceded that allowing for sunlight to enter from above was a "new and beautiful" feature, but might prove so difficult to maintain that "it would be necessary to marshall two Jesuit brothers who would do nothing else but clean off the dust."

Because Michelangelo was involved in a number of other important family projects at the same time—most notably some marble sculpture for the New Sacristy, or Medici Chapel, in the same San Lorenzo complex—a man named Bartolommeo di Giovanni di Leppo, known as Baccio Bigio, supervised construction of the substructures, but the incomparable sculptor-artist-architect remained in total charge of the operation, as the pope had insisted. Copious correspondence and numerous sketches survive to document the evolution of the laborious process, including instructions issued in 1526 directing Michelangelo to reduce monthly expenses by two-thirds, a sudden regimen of austerity brought on by economic "stresses" experienced at the time by the pope. The foundations for the library were laid in August 1524; the walls and roof were finished by April 1527. The grand staircase, designed by Georgio Vasari, was completed long after Michelangelo left permanently for Rome, but conformed with the master's exacting guidelines all the same. The exquisite ceiling, terra-cotta floor, and decorative fittings came later, and were "a secondary problem that occupied Michelangelo far less than it has modern scholars," William E. Wallace has wryly noted in a recent monograph. To enter the library by way of the monumental staircase, Wallace concluded, "is to feel like a prince and to experience the grandeur of the Medici," and to sit at one of the desks "is to become, as in the vestibule, part of the building."

Like the Medici of Florence, who counted several cardinals and two popes in their lineage, the Borromeo family of Milan saw wisdom in maintaining close ties with Saint Peter's in Rome. Their direct connection with the Vatican was temporarily interrupted in 1584 by the unexpected death of the cardinal of Saint Praxides and archbishop of Milan, a beloved figure who in time would be canonized as Saint Charles. Heeding the urgent advice of family and friends, Count Federico Borromeo, the revered prelate's young cousin, accepted the role and became deeply involved in the affairs of the church. Giulo Cesare Borromeo, Federico's father, descended from a family that traced its roots back to the sixth century, and included among its members Frederick Barbarossa, Holy Roman Emperor from 1152 to 1190; Federico's mother, Margherita Trivulzio, had a similarly impressive Milanese heritage.

Federico was twenty-two years old when he went to Rome in 1586; the following year, Pope Sixtus V made him a cardinal, a rapid advancement up the hierarchical ladder for such a young man, but he was a Borromeo, after all, and that mattered a great deal. The thirteen years he spent in Rome came at a time when the new Vatican Library was being constructed and the Vatican Press established, two events that would influence his own plans for the future. Anticipating a return to Milan, where he would be named archbishop of the diocese, Borromeo confided in a letter to a friend how he intended to protect his native region from outside influences. "In this corner of Italy, on her frontiers, at the foot of the Alps and of mountains once hard to cross, we shall try to keep the fine arts with us, however much they want to escape over the mountains or beyond the sea."

Toward the end of his first year at the Vatican, Borromeo received some advice from Cardinal Augustin Valier, an older colleague and a close friend of his sainted cousin. Valier counseled the young idealist on some productive ways to commit his youthful energy and focus his considerable resources: "Good books do not waste our time as most people do; books are friends which enrich us as much as we desire. You should, then, Cardinal Borromeo, collect a great quantity of books, build a library worthy of your noble soul, and spend without stint all the money necessary for it." Acting on this sage advice, Borromeo began collecting books years before he had a permanent library in place to house them, and he referred to them throughout his life as close "friends." By 1601, using the vast resources of the family treasury, he was dispatching agents all over Europe and the Near East in search of material. Giacomo Grozi, his secretary, scouted for him in Italy; Antonio Olgiati, his first librarian, negotiated choice acquisitions in Germany; others traveled to Spain, Greece, Albania, Lebanon, Jerusalem, Flanders, Syria, and Alexandria on his behalf. In Corfu alone, Antonio Salmazia acquired 113 codices, and bought the entire library of Michele Sofiano in Chios. Book-hunting missions to churches and monasteries yielded many valuable items, and enlisted for the cause were bishops, missionaries, businessmen, and ship captains, anyone who was traveling abroad.

At an auction in Naples in June 1608, the cardinal paid 3,050 ducats for five hundred codices from the library of Gian Vincenzo Pinelli (1535–1601), acquiring in one transaction the remnants of what is said to have been the finest private library in Italy in the second half of the sixteenth century. Pinelli was a passionate reader who not only collected books and manuscripts with great enthusiasm but put them at the disposal of others. At his death the library passed to a nephew, who died about two years after that. Some of the materials were lost at sea while being shipped to Naples for sale, not by an act of nature but through the petulance of a band of pirates who, disappointed at finding only books on board, threw eight crates over the side. Nonetheless, many remarkable materials were saved, and were sold at what is the earliest recorded book auction in Italy. According to the surviving accounts, the contest began with the lighting of a candle; when the flame burned out, the contents were hammered down to the highest bidder. Borromeo's agents were opposed by a group of Neapolitan Jesuits. Among the items they secured for the Ambrosiana were an exceptional illustrated Homer, precious texts of Plautus, Cicero, and Horace, and the correspondence of Bembo and Lucrezia Borgia, including a famous lock of hair that two hundred years later transported Lord Byron into dizzying flights of romantic fancy. Packed in seventy crates, the volumes were transported to Milan in nine wagons under heavy security, and only after false rumors about their destination had been circulated.

Unlike the Medici and Malatesta families, who named their elegant libraries after themselves, Cardinal Borromeo chose to honor Saint Ambrose, the fourth-century bishop and patron saint of Milan. Founded in 1603, the Biblioteca Ambrosiana was inaugurated on December 7, 1609, the Feast of Saint Ambrose. On the day the Ambrosiana opened its doors, the cardinal had gathered thirty thousand printed books—seven times as many contained in a 1608 inventory at the Vatican Library—and fifteen thousand manuscripts, two hundred of them illuminated.

Influenced by a scheme developed two decades earlier at the Escorial Palace Library in Spain, Borromeo's architects designed a room that made every wall surface available for storage. At each corner of the 74-by-29-foot hall was a staircase leading to a gallery, where more books could be stored. The roof, a barrel vault, was covered with white stucco, which reflected light entering from two large windows at either end. Recently restored to its original brilliance during a $50 million renovation, the main room reveals a chamber latticed with shelves firmly secured to the walls. There are no chains and no columns, and to maximize storage space even more, the volumes are stored according to size. The cardinal did not order prohibited books destroyed but kept them in a basement repository where they could be consulted by scholars intent on finding their way to the "truth," however rocky the path. To facilitate the widest circulation of knowledge, Borromeo installed a printing press in the library. It operated from 1617 to 1650 and again from 1747 to 1753, reproducing works in Italian, Latin, Hebrew, Chaldaic, Arabic, Persian, and Armenian. In 1621 he established an art academy within the Ambrosiana, with the painter Giovan Battista Crespi, known as Cerano, as its first chairman; it functioned for 155 years.

In his *Italian Voyages* of 1698, the English traveler Richard Lassels declared the Ambrosiana to be "one of the best libraries in Italy, because it is not so coy as the others, which scarce let themselves be seen; whereas this opens its dores publikly to all comers and goers, and suffers them to read what book they please." What Lassels was describing, in a crude fashion, was the world's first library that could truly be called public. Just twenty years after the Ambrosiana admitted its first readers, Gabriel Naudé, the brilliant young Frenchman who served as librarian to Cardinal Mazarin of Paris and Queen Christina of Sweden, expressed similar incredulity in his seminal bibliographical handbook, *Advice on the Building of a Library*. Naudé ranked the Ambrosiana superior to the Bodleian Library at Oxford, the collection installed in Venice by Cardinal Bessarion, and the Vatican Library in Rome, claiming that it "surpasses all in grandeur and magnificence." Like Lassels before him, Naudé was struck by the ease with which so much precious material could be consulted:

There is nothing more extraordinary [than the fact] that anyone may enter it at nearly any convenient hour and remain there as long as he pleases, to look, to read, and to extract whatever author's works he finds agreeable. . . . And without further difficulty he may go there on ordinary days at regular hours, and sit in one of the chairs put there for his use, and ask the Librarian or one of his three assistants for the books he would like to peruse.

Most visitors who call on the Ambrosiana today go there to view the twenty-four rooms of exquisite paintings that grace the walls of the adjoining Pinacoteca, or gallery—further evidence that Borromeo was just as keen on acquiring exceptional artworks as assembling a premier book collection. Shortly after opening the library, he undertook a program of integrating the written legacy with a gallery of visual masterpieces, and in this endeavor as well he demonstrated great taste. During his years in Rome he was a patron of several artists, and provided housing for a number of them, including Joseph Breughel and Paul Brill. Included in Borromeo's deed of gift of April 28, 1618, were 250 paintings, including Caravaggio's *Basket of Fruit*, Barocci's *Nativity*, Titian's *Adoration of the Magi*, Botticelli's *Madonna of the Pavilion*, and works by Giovanni Bellini, Giulio Romano, and Perugino. Included in the Pinacoteca collection, but not on public view, is the Codex Atlanticus by Leonardo da Vinci, including 1,750 scientific and technical drawings.

Borromeo's library, museum, printing press, and academy were a response to the religious upheavals set in motion by Martin Luther a century earlier, and for all the Ambrosiana's enlightened rules supporting access to materials, it remained very much a library of the Counter-Reformation. It reflected the humanistic interests of the cardinal, but its motivating function first and foremost was to defend and promulgate the faith. The stakes were high, and the opposition strong. Just across the Alps in Lower Saxony was a comprehensive library that approached the upheaval from the other side of the issue. It was formed by Duke

August the Younger of Brunswick-Wolfenbüttel (1579–1666), and it too was regarded as a resource for scholarship, but there was an underlying agenda as well. Like Cardinal Borromeo, Duke August was wealthy, well educated, and well connected. When August was thirteen, his library possessed sufficient depth to justify his having his own binding stamp; by the time he was thirty, he had agents scouring the continent for interesting material, and every item that was admitted to his shelves passed through his hands first. Employing a cataloging system of his own invention, the duke arranged all of human knowledge into twenty categories and assigned codes in a way that anticipated the Dewey decimal system by two hundred years. He designed a "book wheel" made of oak that could hold the six hefty volumes of his catalog, and revolved at the turn of a crank to simplify access; it remains a functioning tool in Wolfenbüttel today.

"His library in its time was one of the greatest collections of modern Europe, and he conceived of it from the start as a public institution," Dr. Werner Arnold, curator and cataloger of the Wolfenbüttel Library, told me in New York on the day that an exhibition of fifty-eight rarities from the collection was about to open at the Grolier Club, marking the first time any materials from the repository had been allowed to cross the Atlantic. "The duke referred to his library in his will as 'one of the inestimable treasures of our land,' " Arnold said. "The leading discipline of the library very definitely was theology, but he was strong on history, philosophy, and music. What is of singular importance to us today is that he collected the books of his time, which was the period of the Thirty Years' War, 1618 to 1648. That was quite a departure then; instead of focusing exclusively on the past, current events were of principal importance to him." Remembered as a man of peace, Duke August had specific religious and philosophical views, and many of the books he acquired supported those reformist convictions. "But he took special care to find writings from the other side," Arnold said. "He wanted the balance. And you can see that he held every book in the library in his hands; he signed off on everything that came in, and he paid the invoices himself."

In his will, the duke directed that the library "should as one entity forever be, remain and be kept in this our residence as long as our princely dynasty shall continue and survive," and he made provisions for the hiring of "qualified and learned" people to run it. Librarians over the years have included the philosopher Gottfried Wilhelm Leibniz and the critic and dramatist Gotthold Ephraim Lessing. At his death in 1666, the 135,000 titles the duke had gathered constituted the largest European library north of the Alps, and formed the nucleus of a resource that today totals about 800,000 volumes, 450,000 of them published before 1850. There also are 12,000 manuscripts, a thousand of them dating from medieval times. The core collection of 150,000 books published in the seventeenth century serves as the German national collection for that period, an accomplishment perhaps unique among private collectors.

The Grolier exhibition included a copy of Martin Luther's 1522 translation of the New Testament, known as the September Testament and illustrated with colored woodblocks from the workshop of Lucas Cranach, which was opened to an image of a personification of Babylon in the form of a regal woman in a crown and red dress riding a seven-headed dragon. Brought over from Germany and displayed in the first-floor gallery was a wooden plaque crafted in 1636, stating in Latin the three golden rules of Duke August's library. These are summarized in the elegant catalog of the exhibition as follows: "The visitor should not upset the order of the books, he should not steal any of them, and he should show respect for their contents."

Seeking relief from the kidney stones that had caused him excruciating pain through much of his life, and determined to gratify a life-long dream to visit the magical city of his imagination, Michel Eyquem de Montaigne (1533–1592) set out from France on June 22, 1580, aboard a horse-drawn wagon filled with a variety of medical preparations to ease his physical discomfort, and a mixed selection of books to nourish his spirit during the arduous journey. Over the next seventeen months the man who gave the word *essay* to the world would visit a series of mineral spas in Austria, Germany, and Switzerland, then proceed south to Italy. When he arrived outside the gates of Rome on November 30, 1580, after a pleasant interlude in Venice, Montaigne's portable library, including several volumes of his own recently published magnum opus, was inspected by customs agents, a routine practice at the time but one that unsettled the famous author all the same, as he confided in a travel journal he kept throughout the trip. The censorship rules "were so extraordinary," Montaigne wrote, that a Book of Hours was questioned simply because it had been printed in Paris, not Rome. Books by "certain German doctors of theology" that were critical of "the heretics" raised suspicion as well, not for the positions they argued but "because in combating them," the authors made "mention of their errors" all the same. After what seemed an interminable wait, Montaigne was told that he carried "no forbidden book in the lot," but the examiners did retain custody of a few titles for further scrutiny—including a copy of his own *Essays.*

Four months later the chief Vatican censor returned the book to Montaigne, noting that the contents had been "corrected according to the opinion of the learned monks." The man who delivered the essays to the visitor from Paris, known as the Master of the Sacred Palace, allowed that he "had been able to judge them only by the report of some French friar, since he did not understand our language at all; and he was so content with the excuses I offered on each objection that this Frenchman had left him that he referred it to my conscience to redress what I should see was in bad taste." It turned out that what had bothered the "learned monks" in particular about Montaigne's compositions was his use of the word *fortune* where *heaven* would have been more appropriate, and his having cited a number of "heretic poets" whose very names were taboo. The chief censor—Montaigne judged him to be an "able" man—"wanted me to realize that he was not very sympathetic to these revisions; and he pleaded very ingeniously for me, in my presence, against another man, also an Italian, who was opposing me." The censors held on to a history of the Swiss translated into French, "solely because the translator" was another heretic; "but it is a marvel how well they know the men of our countries. And the best part was that they told me that the preface was condemned."

Having navigated his way through one disturbing book experience, Montaigne had another of far greater satisfaction to record. On March 6, 1581, he went to the Vatican Library, which had already earned renown for a humanistic collection that went well beyond theological matters, and described with great enthusiasm the materials he was allowed to see: "There are a large number of books attached onto several rows of desks; there are also some in coffers, which were all opened to me; lots of books written by hand, and especially a Seneca and the *Moral Essays* of Plutarch. Among the remarkable things I saw there were the statue of the good Aristides with a handsome bald head, a thick beard, a big forehead, a look full of gentleness and majesty; his name is written on the very ancient pedestal; a book from China, in strange characters, the leaves made of some material much softer and more pellucid than our paper; and because they cannot endure the stain of ink, the writing is on only one side of the sheet, and the sheets are all doubled and folded at the outside edges, by which they hold together."

Montaigne was enthralled as he moved from treasure to treasure, and the mere memory of the visit made him giddy. He made special mention of a "handwritten Virgil in extremely large lettering" known as the Codex Romanus that he enjoyed, and a book by Saint Thomas Aquinas "in which there are corrections in the hand of the author himself, who wrote badly." There also was a Bible on parchment presented to Pope Gregory XIII by Philip II of Spain that he handled, and a "bit of papyrus on which there were unknown characters." Specific mention was also made of an Acts of the Apostles "written in very beautiful gold Greek lettering, as fresh and recent as if it were of today," and a book sent by Henry VIII of England fifty years earlier to Pope Leo X inscribed in the king's own hand, and composed against Martin Luther. "I saw the library without any difficulty; anyone can see it thus, and can make whatever extracts he wants; and it is open almost every morning. I was guided all through it and invited by a gentleman to use it whenever I wanted."

Montaigne could not resist mentioning the frustration of the French ambassador, who had been denied the privilege of handling a "handwritten Seneca, as he had hugely desired to do," during the diplomat's earlier visit to the library. "Fortune brought me to it," Montaigne wrote of his own good luck in seeing the very manuscript that had eluded his distinguished countryman. The smug satisfaction he felt in having scored such a coup is lightly touched upon, though tangible all the same. "Opportunity and opportuneness have their privileges, and often offer to the common people what they refuse to kings. Curiosity often gets in its own way, as also do greatness and power."

These two experiences from Montaigne's journal are particularly revealing in that they demonstrate two opposing attitudes involving the power of books in the course of everyday life in sixteenth-century Rome. For all the great variety of content made available to a privileged few in the Vatican Library, books were still very much a controlled substance for the rest of society, and reading material was carefully monitored. Guidelines governing "acceptable" literature were established at the Council of Trent just thirty-five years earlier, and the practice of maintaining an Index of Forbidden Books was enforced well into the twentieth century, as Paul LeClerc, the president of the New York Public Library and a graduate of the College of the Holy Cross in Worcester, Massachusetts, emphasized during one of several interviews we had in his spacious office overlooking Fifth Avenue. LeClerc, formerly the president of Hunter College in Manhattan, has a doctorate in French literature and has written authoritatively on the works of Voltaire.

"I was introduced to Voltaire by a Jesuit in my freshman year at Holy

Cross in 1959, and I have often wondered how my life would have turned out if I had a different instructor for French that semester, or if I had failed to go to class that particular day," LeClerc recalled. "I thought the little scene he discussed in class that day was immensely seductive, and I wanted more. My appetite was whetted. But in those days, for people like me who accepted current religious practice as dogma, it was a mortal sin to read a book that was on the Roman Index of Forbidden Books, and all of Voltaire's books were on the index." So before he dared to proceed any further with his new literary interest, LeClerc wrote a letter to the bishop of Worcester requesting authorization to read Voltaire's *Candide,* and while he was at it, Stendhal's *Red and the Black* and Gustave Flaubert's *Madame Bovary,* which also were on the list. "I got a letter back giving me permission to read all three, with the titles enumerated." Before he could discuss the books with his teacher in class, the instructor, a priest, also was required to obtain permission. "I could have read them without asking, I suppose, but that would have been a sin, and I would have had to confess it. And I would have confessed it, too. I was confessing everything else then, why not confess that? But what I did was the right thing to do. That's what you did if you believed church teaching, because your soul could be in jeopardy. Your soul supposedly was threatened by contact with the thoughts invented in these texts. They were dangerous."

Specific procedures governing the condemnation of pernicious books and the excommunication of offenders drawn up at the Council of Trent in 1546 included works that extended well beyond the realm of faith to any "lascivious or obscene" subject that might corrupt a person's morals. On the matter of "ancient books written by heathens," the council allowed that some works "by reason of their elegance and quality of style" might be permitted, "but may by no means be read to children." The assembly was convened in response to Martin Luther's challenge to the papacy with the nailing of his Ninety-five Theses on the church door at Wittenberg in 1517. The pamphlets, commentaries, catechisms, sermons, and hymns Luther wrote for general distribution traveled throughout Europe by way of the printing press, setting in motion the Counter-Reformation.

The first Roman list of forbidden books to bear the title *Index Librorum Prohibitorum* was issued by Pope Paul IV in 1559. Major revisions followed in 1596, 1664, 1753, and 1757, with many individual titles added intermittently. Twentieth-century modifications came in 1900, 1917, and 1948, when the last edition of the index was issued. By the time it was discontinued in 1966, the number of books that had been condemned totaled 4,126 titles. In addition to Voltaire, authors whose complete works had been prohibited included Anatole France, André Gide, Thomas Hobbes, David Hume, Jean-Paul Sartre, and Emile Zola. Philosophers, economists, political scientists, and historians selectively condemned have included Francis Bacon, Honoré de Balzac, Auguste Comte, Denis Diderot, Edward Gibbon, Oliver Goldsmith, Immanuel Kant, John Locke, John Stuart Mill, Virginia Paganini, and Jean-Jacques Rousseau. In a decree of January 28, 1676, *Les Essais de Michel de Montaigne* was placed on the index as well.

There had been a papal library of theological works in Rome since the sixth century, but the Biblioteca Apostolica Vaticana we see today emerged in the 1450s at the height of the Renaissance under the guidance of Pope Nicholas V, the same man who as Cardinal Tommaso Parentucelli (1397–1455) advised Cosimo de' Medici on the books he should acquire for his library in Florence. Young Tommaso was a great lover of the classics, his worldview shaped by some of the great humanists of the age. When he assumed the papacy in 1447, there were 340 books in the collections, just 2 of them in Greek. He wasted no time dispatching agents abroad with instructions to buy all the manuscripts they could find. Before long, there were 1,200 codices in the library, fully a third of them in Greek. Nicholas invited numerous Byzantine scholars to his court, paid them to translate the great works of their ancestors into Latin, and commissioned the leading calligraphers and illuminators of the day to transform them into works of art.

The Biblioteca Apostolica Vaticana came into being, Anthony

Grafton has written, at a time "when scribes, illuminators, binders, and printers prided themselves on creating books as physically splendid as they were substantially illuminating." In a catalog issued to mark a landmark exhibition of Vatican treasures at the Library of Congress in 1993, James H. Billington, the Librarian of Congress, expressed surprise that the Vatican Library's collections "are not primarily theological," and that it has "consciously pursued an acquisitions policy that focused upon the liberal arts and sciences." What this policy reflected, he continued, was "the conscious determination of the Renaissance papacy to place knowledge systematically at the service of governance," creating in the process "the prototypical modern research library of western culture."

The elaborate library we admire today, a spacious complex of lavishly decorated rooms overlooking the Cortile del Belvedere, was erected during the papacy of Sixtus V. The collections now number some two million printed books, eight thousand of them produced before 1501, and an astonishing collection of seventy-five thousand Latin, Greek, Arabic, Hebrew, Persian, Ethiopian, and Syriac manuscripts. There also are one hundred thousand prints, engravings, maps, and drawings. "In number alone, these materials make the library something more than an ordinary repository of valuable books," Grafton wrote. "Aesthetically and historically, moreover, they belong to the treasures of humanity."

Few books embody the volatile nature of Italian history more forcefully than *The Prince*, a fascinating study of practical politics that has lost none of its relevance as a shockingly frank evaluation of human nature. The "little volume," as Niccolò Machiavelli (1469–1527) described the work that would make a variation of his surname an adjective known to generations of people, was written in 1513, shortly after his dismissal as head of the Second Chancery and secretary to the Council of Ten in the Florentine Republic. When he wrote it, the Medici family had recently regained power after spending eighteen years in exile. Arrested on fabricated charges of having conspired against the new regime, Machiavelli was tortured and humiliated during a brief imprisonment. Once released, he was stripped of all honors and deprived of everything except the precious books that he had carefully protected from confiscation. Declared an outcast, the probing intellectual withdrew to a small farm in Percussina near San Casciano. It was in this bare retreat that he began to write, focusing at first on a series of discourses on Livy and then on *The Prince,* driven by the faint hope that his years of having dealt first-hand with such figures as Cesare Borgia, Louis XII of France, Pope Julius II, and the emperor Maximilian I would ingratiate him with the Medici if presented as a compendium of practical advice. Machiavelli dedicated the completed manuscript to Lorenzo de' Medici II, grandson of Lorenzo the Magnificent, and drafted a letter of transmittal, in which he offered the work as a token of humble esteem: "Take then, Your Magnificence, this little gift in the spirit in which I send it; written, if it be diligently read and considered by you, you will learn my extreme desire that you should attain that greatness which fortune and your other attributes promise. And if Your Magnificence from the summit of your greatness will sometimes turn your eyes to these lower regions, you will see how unmeritedly I suffer a great and continued malignity of fortune." Machiavelli's pathetic entreaty was ignored, and *The Prince* remained unpublished during his lifetime. A small edition was finally printed in 1532, and condemned by the Vatican twenty-seven years later in its first list of forbidden books.

Stung mightily by his banishment to obscurity, Machiavelli spent his final years immersed in the teachings of ancient historians and philosophers, but he continued with his writing. He composed three comic plays, several works of fiction, a history of Florence in verse, and a number of long poems, all the while maintaining a rich correspondence with old acquaintances, a great deal of which has been preserved. In a famous letter to his close friend Francesco Vettori, at that time the Florentine ambassador to the Vatican—the same letter in which he disclosed that he has just written a "short study" discussing "the categories of prince-dom"—he described his crude and rustic life among the peasants of San Casciano. Forever removed from the bustle and intrigue of high office, he now spent his days hunting thrushes and cutting wood and, for tempo-rary amusement, playing penny-ante games of backgammon with his crude neighbors at the local inn. "Thus, having been cooped up among these lice, I get the mold out of my brain and let out the malice of my fate, content to be ridden over roughshod in this fashion if only to dis-cover whether or not my fate is ashamed of treating me so." But he still had his books, and it was among them that he found final solace:

> *When evening comes, I return home and enter my study; on the threshold I take off my workday clothes, covered with mud and dirt, and put on the garments of court and palace. Fitted out appropri-ately, I step inside the venerable courts of the ancients, where, solici-tously received by them, I nourish myself on that food that* alone *is mine and for which I was born; where I am unashamed to converse with them and to question them about the motives for their actions, and they, out of human kindness, answer me. And for four hours at a time I feel no boredom, I forget all my troubles, I do not dread poverty, and I am not terrified by death. I absorb myself unto them completely.*

At a time in the late fifteenth century when exciting innovations were redefining how people would entertain, instruct, and inform them-selves for centuries to come, the German physician and Renaissance scholar Hartmann Schedel (1440–1514) offered a modest gift to the world between the hard covers of a book. Known today as the Nuremberg Chronicle, the elegant folio Schedel proudly chose to call *Liber Chroni-carum* was compiled from dozens of works he had assembled with consummate taste and care, and was a decade in the making. His stated purpose was nothing less than a fully illustrated account of "all happenings that are worthy of note from the beginning of the world" to the present, and to produce the monumental undertaking, Schedel had engaged the services of Anton Koberger, an esteemed publisher who brought out 236 books between 1473 and 1513, "most of them of the first importance, in the best possible format," according to Lucien Febvre and Henri-Jean Martin. The Nuremberg artists Michael Wolgemut and Wilhelm Pleydenwurff were commissioned to prepare 645 wood engravings, many of which were used repeatedly in the lavishly illustrated text; Albrecht Dürer, just beginning his career as a young apprentice in Pleydenwurff's shop, was among the contributors.

To allow for what today might be described as "breaking developments," Schedel had instructed Koberger to include a few blank leaves of paper in the back of each volume. He explained the logic of this unorthodox feature in his colophon: "Several pages have been left at this point on which to record further history or future events." What factors may have persuaded the fifty-three-year-old humanist described by his friends as a "bibliophage"—a person who devours books—to introduce what could well be the earliest deliberate application of an interactive book device are open to speculation, but it turned out to be a sagacious move, as news of momentous events worthy of inclusion began to move rapidly through Europe.

We know a lot about Hartmann Schedel today because the window into his soul—his library—has passed through the centuries fairly intact. The son of a prosperous merchant, he studied law and the classics at the University of Leipzig, followed by courses in medicine and Greek at the University of Padua. A book collector of relentless enthusiasm, his library was inherited by a grandson whose own predilection for rare books forced him into bankruptcy, a fortuitous turn of events, as matters turned out, since the young man sold his grandfather's books to Duke Albrecht V of Bavaria in 1571, who made sure that the library stayed together as an unbroken collection. About 370 manuscripts and 600 printed works remain preserved today in the Bayerische Staatsbibliothek in Munich.

"Schedel's library reveals that he was a resourceful and prodigious collector as well as a versatile scholar and bibliophile," the German historian Peter Zahn has written. His principal interests were medicine, philosophy, history, and geography, and he particularly enjoyed reading the works of Latin writers. Included in his library were the works of Cicero, Virgil, Horace, Livy, Saint Jerome, and Saint Augustine, and he reserved ample space on his shelves for the writings of the Italian Renaissance. "To these," Zahn noted, "he added the literature of his time which makes his collection so valuable today." He was celebrated for his willingness to share this wealth with friends and colleagues. "The most splendid example of his bibliomania is the hand-colored copy of his own *Liber Chronicarum* into which are inserted many extra pages including nine broadsides, all rarities, among them a copy of the Chronicle's advertisement."

When Schedel wrote the prospectus for his history in the summer of 1493, the book had just appeared in a Latin edition of fifteen hundred copies, with a German version of a thousand more about to enter production. Printed on one side of a single sheet of paper, the advertisement consists of an introductory paragraph, followed by twenty-four lines of verse, both written in Latin. It is a straightforward marketing pitch—a hard sell, in today's parlance—with rich intellectual rewards guaranteed to prospective customers:

> *I venture to promise you, reader, so great delight in reading it that you will think you are not reading a series of stories, but looking at them with your own eyes. For you will see there not only portraits of emperors, popes, philosophers, poets, and other famous men each shown in the proper dress of his time, but also views of the most famous cities and places throughout Europe, as each one rose, prospered, and continued. When you look upon all these histories, deeds,*

*and wise sayings you will think them all alive. Farewell, and do not
let this book slip through your hands.*

The twenty-four lines of verse that followed opened with similar
ebullience:

*Speed now, Book, and make yourself known wherever the winds blow
   free.
Never before has your like been printed.
A thousand hands will grasp you with warm desire
And read you with great attention.
The affairs of both gods and men you systematically relate,
Aglow with charming illustrations by accomplished artists.
The beginning of things and the world from its start you present,
Recounting everything that has occurred in the passage of time.*

Although the Nuremberg Chronicle was published in 1493, Schedel
had signed off on the content well before three Spanish caravels named
Niña, Pinta, and *Santa María* had set sail on the first leg of a voyage that
would take them from one side of the Atlantic Ocean to the other, and as
the ambitious production was being readied for the marketplace, an
obscure printer in Barcelona was setting into metal type the text of a letter addressed by Christopher Columbus to his patrons in Spain. Dated
February 15, 1493, the document was composed while the master mariner
was still on the high seas, making his way back home. Known today as the
Columbus Letter, it was sent by courier from Portugal to Spain, and
appeared in April as a rather shabbily produced four-page pamphlet, as
an examination of the sole surviving copy at the New York Public
Library makes readily clear. But it attracted sufficient notice in Spain to
occasion production of a Latin translation, which by the end of 1494 had
passed through nine editions. Over the next four years, copies were sold
in Valladolid, Spain; Basel, Switzerland; Antwerp, Belgium; and Paris

and Strasbourg in France, with French and German renderings produced to augment the Latin and Spanish versions already in print. Before long, a fanciful treatment set in verse was being sold in Florence, along with two other Italian editions. A number of other hastily assembled productions were illustrated with woodcuts plucked from books that had no relation at all to Columbus or to his ships. By 1500 no fewer than seventeen editions of the Columbus Letter had been printed. The discovery of a New World was being proclaimed throughout Europe in a medium that was still in its infancy. Print, a paradigm shift of monumental proportions, was serving as midwife to the mother of all paradigm shifts. And even the most sanguine of modern journalists would have to agree that Columbus wrote a memorable lead paragraph:

> *Since I know that you will be pleased at the great victory with which Our Lord has crowned my voyage, I write this to you, from which you will learn how in thirty-three days I passed from the Canary Islands to the Indies, with the fleet which the most illustrious King and Queen, our Sovereigns, gave to me. There I found very many islands, filled with innumerable people, and I have taken possession of them all for their Highnesses, done by proclamation and with the royal standard unfurled, and no opposition was offered to me.*

A peripheral consequence of Spain's far-flung adventures abroad was a bureaucratic obsession for documentation, a predilection most strikingly evident during the reign of Philip II (1556–98), which the historian J. H. Elliott has described as a period of "government by paper." On one day alone the king, builder of the great Escorial Palace Library, is said to have read and signed four hundred documents. "No wonder his eyes grew red with the strain, or that his face acquired the parchment colour of a man who had come to live among, and for, his papers," Elliott writes. In 1785 Charles III established the Archive of the Indies in Seville to serve as a central repository for the mass of materials relating to the country's foreign adventures that up to that time had been haphazardly stored all over Spain. The move was a response to the frustration experienced six years earlier by José de Gálves, marquis of Sonora, who had been commissioned to write a general history of the Indies based on "irrefutable documents." Gálves discovered early on that much of what he needed was "widely scattered" among many government offices. One example of the bureaucratic quagmire he encountered involved the daily logbook kept by Columbus during his first voyage to the Americas and presented to King Ferdinand and Queen Isabella on his return. Two copies were made, with the original ordered kept in the palace. At some point, it disappeared, and the only text to survive was a severely truncated abstract of a flawed copy.

The Archive of the Indies documents close to half a millennium of history, certifying in 80 million pages of material the exploration, conquest, pacification, settlement, defense, and charting by Spain of an area extending from what is now the southern United States to the lower tip of South America, with materials detailing adventures in the Philippines and the Spanish Far East as well. The papers are housed in a sixteenth-century building that once served as headquarters for a consortium of merchants doing business overseas, in the heart of a district dominated by the magnificent Gothic Cathedral of Seville. Adjoining the cathedral is the Alcázar, an exotic palace-fortress built in the fourteenth century on a site that still reflects the layering of many cultures, including Roman, Paleochristian, Visigoth, and Arabic.

The interior features spacious rooms, arched ceilings, thick mahogany shelves, and translucent floors inset with polished slabs of Málaga marble. Some 43,000 bulky *legacos*, or bundles, containing about a thousand sheets of manuscript each, comprise the archive, with 10 percent of the papers now accessible by computer. Storage boxes that fill the shelves upstairs are largely decorative, with the documents now maintained in environmentally sound areas in the basement. About 7,000 maps, and a support library of 25,000 books, are part of the collection. Pedro

González García described the scope of the collection in a beautifully illustrated history of the archive, *Discovering the Americas*: "The Catholic Kings and Christopher Columbus, the conquistadors and the discoverers, missionaries and *encomenderos*, masters and slaves, viceroys and natives, seamen and merchants, elite officialdom and emigrants, judges and protectors of Indians in the New World, treasures and shipwrecked galleons, city-building and silver and gold mining, printing works and universities leap from the time-worn pages."

Just a five-minute walk from the Archives of the Indies, on the second floor of a rear annex to the great cathedral, is the Biblioteca Columbina, a collection of six thousand books gathered with consummate taste by Hernando Colón (1488–1539), the illegitimate son of Christopher Columbus known to English writers as Ferdinand Columbus. As a book place, this tiny library has a quiet majesty, a transcendence that suggests Christopher Marlowe's wonderful phrase, "infinite riches in a little room." Here, in sixteen glazed cases, reside what remains of a library gathered between 1509 and 1539 to honor a father whose horizons were measured by the length and breadth of the earth.

Ferdinand was just four years old when his father set sail on his first voyage to the New World. Beatriz Enríquez de Arana, his mother, was the sister of Pedro de Arana, a Spaniard who commanded a ship on the explorer's third voyage. In his memoirs, Ferdinand provided an eyewitness account of the departure of the second voyage, consisting of seventeen vessels and carrying fifteen hundred colonists: "Wednesday, on the 25th of September of the year 1493, an hour before sunrise, my brother and I being present, the Admiral raised anchors in the Port of Cadiz." When he was ten years old, Ferdinand became a page at court, and four years after that his father took him along on the fourth voyage to America.

Ferdinand spent a good deal of time and most of his income assembling a library that would add luster to his father's legacy. Among his published works were a dictionary of Latin definitions and a treatise on the colonization of the Indies. After the death of his father in 1506, the lifelong bachelor used his inheritance to indulge his enduring passion, traveling throughout Europe and acquiring books at every stop. In 1509 he embarked on an official mission to establish churches and monasteries in Santo Domingo, and accompanied Charles V on three journeys abroad. A skilled cartographer, he headed an official commission charged with updating navigational charts and developing a globe of the earth that would incorporate Spain's dramatic new discoveries.

Above all else, Ferdinand's driving ambition was to honor his father's accomplishments, and this he pursued by writing a biography, which was completed shortly before his death in 1539. Its title is so lengthy that it usually is referred to simply by the first word, *Historie*. The sole surviving text is the Italian translation by Alfonso Ulloa, printed in Venice in 1571. Because the original manuscript has long since disappeared, and because the earliest source is not in Spanish, the biography's authenticity has been attacked by some critics, although most Columbus scholars, Samuel Eliot Morison among them, accept it as genuine. In his three-volume life of Columbus, the American man-of-letters Washington Irving called Ferdinand's biography an "invaluable document, entitled to great faith," declaring it to be "the cornerstone of the history of the American Continent."

In the dedication to the 1571 Italian edition, Giuseppe Moleto evaluated the importance of Ferdinand's personal book collection: "Don Ferdinand was no less meritorious than his father, but was much more learned, and left to the Cathedral of Seville, where he had honorable burial, a library that was not only very large but rich, full of rarest works in all the sciences and regarded by all who have seen it as one of the most remarkable things in all of Europe." The historian John Boyd Thacher, whose own collection of fifteenth-century books is now owned by the Library of Congress, used superlatives in his description of Ferdinand's library: "Here were gathered no less than 15,370 books and manuscripts, representing the classics, the gems of incunabula, the first fruits of the fecund press, the rarest editions of the poets and of those who had written prose; the sermons and the teachings of the fathers of the Church, the works of the philosophers, the printed fabrics of countless dreams."

Among Ferdinand's surviving books are a number of items once owned by the admiral himself. Foremost among them is a copy of Marco Polo's account of the East, with annotations in the margins by Columbus. A copy of Martin Waldseemüller's *Cosmographiae Introductio* (Strasbourg, 1509) just may have been the most reviled book in the founder's library; the edition published in 1507 included a map that proposed naming the recently discovered continent after Amerigo Vespucci. Ferdinand's copy of *Antibarbarorum Liber Unus* contains a handwritten inscription from the author, Erasmus of Rotterdam, along with a few words of glee from the ecstatic collector: "Erasmus gave it to me in Louvain on October 7, Sunday, in 1520; Erasmus himself wrote here, with his own hand, the first two lines." In another volume he has written, "This book was read while I ate, in Seville in February, 1538." Ferdinand wrote inside all of his books, including notations on how much he spent for each volume, in what currency he paid, and the rate of exchange in Castilian money. With this kind of detail at their disposal, scholars can track his activity as a book hunter. It can be determined, for instance, which books he bought during trips to Italy in 1512–13 and 1515–16, in Flanders, Germany, and England between 1520 and 1522, and the order in which these titles entered his library.

By the time Ferdinand began building an elegant manor near a bend in the Guadalquivir River in 1526, Seville had become the center of the American trade, an enterprise in which he had valuable interests, and planted on the grounds were some five thousand trees and bushes brought home from the New World. A woodcut picturing the estate, made twenty-five years after Ferdinand's death, is now at the Huntington Library in California. To help organize his books and to supervise their installation in the new villa, Ferdinand brought a full-time librarian over from the Netherlands. In 1536 he proposed using the proceeds of an annual grant given to him by Charles V to underwrite the "conservation" of his books and to create what would have been in effect a national library. He wanted books "of every branch of knowledge" to be acquired as they were issued, and preserved forever in a central repository. Had Ferdinand's ambitious project been enacted—it was doomed the moment he suggested that Charles V earmark the stipend "in perpetuity"—it would have established procedures for conducting the kind of research that is taken for granted today. He called for the formation of an alphabetical catalog listing all important authors and their works, cross-referenced by title and subject, a system he had already introduced in his own library. He further recommended preparing concise summaries of important books, "so that whoever reads this digest may know whether it satisfies his need of hunting for it and reading all of it or whether the digest is sufficient, as it is impossible to read the multitude of books written in each branch of knowledge." Since there are always people who "may wish for guidance, or have matters presented for their consideration of which they hope to read and have no knowledge of the places where such are to be found," he recommended that another book—a kind of encyclopedia, apparently—"be made of subjects arranged alphabetically according to the matter treated."

The admiral's son died three years after making this request, and his proposals were forgotten, along with his dream of attaching an Imperial College to his house for the study of mathematics and navigation. But he did take meticulous steps to maintain the integrity of his library. He left the books and a sum of money to Luis Colón, his nephew. A key clause stipulated that if the young man failed to care for the books precisely as directed, custody would transfer to the Cathedral Council in Seville. This strict clause so impressed Samuel Pepys when he visited Seville two hundred years later that he incorporated a similar provision in his own will, requiring Magdalene College at Cambridge University to keep his library intact, or turn it over to Trinity College.

Although Ferdinand supported the principles of scholarship, he believed that his primary function as a collector was to preserve books. In the perfect world he envisioned, readers would satisfy themselves with access to the summaries and abstracts he wanted prepared of his holdings, not the artifacts themselves. "It is impossible to keep books even if tied up with one hundred chains," he complained after visiting a number of libraries in Italy, but he was determined to do everything possible to forestall the inevitable. To shield the books from human contact, he directed that a network of iron screens be placed parallel to every case, each positioned six feet out from the shelves. So that readers could sit in front of what amounted to a kind of isolation cell, benches would be positioned in the middle of the room. From there, they would be able to reach through an opening where a special desk, positioned literally at arm's length, would allow just enough space for a single page to be turned at a time.

As happens so often with a library bequest, Ferdinand's nephew was indifferent to books and proved himself an unworthy heir, neglecting the collection and not adding any new titles. The library was moved around from place to place, and finally became the subject of a court action entered to invoke the punitive clause of the will. After a long process, the Cathedral Council gained title to the books, and in 1552 moved them to a room off the Patio of the Orange Trees known as the Nave of the Lizard. They have been there ever since, although not always under the most agreeable of conditions. For many years the books "suffered a shameful neglect and dilapidation," Samuel Eliot Morison lamented, with the result that only 5,500 titles, about a third of the original collection, have survived: "Yet this Biblioteca Columbina, adjoining the great cathedral where the Admiral worshiped and where his sons lie buried, is today an inspiration for every American scholar; an alembic as it were where a new civilization was distilled from classical scholarship, medieval piety and modern science."

In his 1970 survey of great libraries, Anthony Hobson hailed the admiral's son as "unique among early library founders in placing the emphasis in his collection on the contemporary and the ephemeral." He also credited him with storing books in wall cases alphabetically and by number, fore edges facing outward, several decades before the practice was adopted by Philip II at the Escorial in New Castile. Although Ferdinand had some manuscripts, he concentrated mostly on printed books, perhaps the first bibliophile of consequence to do so, and his tastes were eclectic. "He bought romances of chivalry and *chansons de geste,* ballads, carols and poetry of all kinds, moral tales and love stories, saints' lives, accounts of miracles, prodigies and funerals, relations of current events, mystery plays, prognostications, chapbooks and jestbooks," Hobson wrote. "He bought his books to read." During my visit to the Biblioteca Columbina, the director, Dr. Nuria Casquete de Prado Sagrera, showed me the one item she feels is the "jewel of jewels of the collection." It is a copy of the Roman dramatist Seneca's *Tragedies,* printed in Venice in 1510. These words appear in the play *Medea:*

> *The age will come in the late years*
> *When ocean will unlock its chains*
> *And a great land lie open;*
> *Typhis shall reveal new worlds,*
> *And Thule will no longer be*
> *Earth's Boundary.*

In keeping with his fondness for annotation, Ferdinand had a personal comment to offer here: "This prophecy was fulfilled by my father the Admiral in the year 1492." Every volume in the Biblioteca Columbina contains a dedicatory bookplate, each one bearing the same words of godspeed: "Ferdinand Columbus, son of Christopher Columbus, First Admiral who discovered the Indies, left this book for the use and benefit of all his fellow men. Say a prayer for him."

PART TWO

BOOK PEOPLE

3.

MADNESS REDUX

If we think of it, all that a University, or final highest School can do for us, is still but what the first school began doing,—teach us to read. We learn to read, in various languages, in various sciences; we learn the alphabet and letters of all manner of Books. But the place where we are to get knowledge, even theoretic knowledge, is the Books themselves! It depends on what we read, after all the manner of Professors have done their best for us. The true University of these days is a Collection of Books.

— *Thomas Carlyle, "The Hero as Man of Letters"*

We were seated in the Council Room of the American Antiquarian Society on a bracing winter morning in New England, a good 3,300 miles from the sun-drenched campus of Stanford University in Palo Alto, California, where Jay Fliegelman, a professor of English and the author of several important historical monographs, normally makes his home. It was snowing outside when we met, a circumstance that only sharpened an incongruity that went well beyond the weather. Twenty-five items of uncommon historical interest—choice selections from Fliegelman's personal library—had just been brought from the stacks downstairs on a steel trolley and arranged on a long conference table for us to examine. "When I want to see any of my own books," he said, deadpan, "I have to put in a request slip like everybody else."

Fliegelman was in no way complaining about the accommodations or the resources, merely amused by the paradox of the moment; if anything, he was thrilled that an internationally renowned research library had given him the opportunity and the wherewithal to tackle a project that represented a first in American scholarship. "It was an irresistible offer," he said of the invitation he received to spend a year in Worcester, Massachusetts, and it came to him from "totally out of the blue." He had been lured east to be the Mellon Distinguished Scholar in Residence at the AAS, and the "irresistible offer" was such that in addition to a generous stipend, he received the institutional support he needed to learn more about a unique library that had been thirty years in the making—his own—and be given an opportunity to write a book about it.

All this was made possible by the fact that Fliegelman owns "association copies," books that in a very real sense have context apart from the words they contain. Indeed, what makes them so unusual is not the text at all—reading versions of these titles are available in research libraries throughout the United States—but their remarkable significance as physical objects. Fliegelman has acquired about five hundred association copies over the years, and what every title in his collection has in common is that each was the property at one time or other of a person significant in the making of American history, or someone who had a profound impact on the life of an important figure. The AAS arranged to ship the books across the continent to Massachusetts from California, cared for them, and guaranteed their security. As an even more seductive inducement—the clincher, really—the society promised Fliegelman unlimited access to holdings that are preeminent in the early history of North America, stronger in some areas than the Library of Congress.

"What I am doing here is writing a kind of cultural history of America, disguised as a fully illustrated catalog of my own library," Fliegelman said. "It's from the artifact up. I'm telling stories about individual books, and linking them in a way so that they can be read as a continuous narrative." The scope of his collection—and thus the scope of the book he is writing—is from the 1660s to the beginning of the Civil War, two hundred years precisely. "I am writing a book about my library, and the book I am writing is going to be a kind of artifactual tour of cultural and intellectual history in America. But in every case, the story is tied to a specific book, with specific signatures, annotations, and inscriptions inside, sometimes deeply moving inscriptions. Each of these books stands as a kind of witness to something, or it sheds light on something." The title of the work in progress is *Belongings: Dramas of American Book Ownership, 1660–1860*.

Most of Fliegelman's books have been purchased out of dealers' catalogs or secured by him directly at auction. A few he has cajoled from friends and acquaintances: others he bought after conducting indefatigable detective work, following trails that oftentimes led him to the descendants of people he is collecting. Every volume he brought to the conference table for me to see—indeed, every volume that has entered his collection—required a setup story before proceeding with an examination. Because he is a man who places a high value on order and symmetry, Fliegelman suggested that we start with a consideration of the beginning and the end poles of his continuum—the chronological bookends, as it were—and amble around from there to what were undeniably some of the high spots.

At the "beginning" are several books, one of them a theological work written by a man named John Goodwin titled *Imputatio Fidei,* and published in England in 1642. Fliegelman's copy bears the ownership signature of Simon Bradstreet (1603–1697), a Puritan minister, colonial statesman, onetime governor of Massachusetts, and husband of Anne Bradstreet (1612–1672), generally regarded as the first English poet in America. One of Anne Bradstreet's best-known verses is called "Upon the Burning of My House," and reflects on the loss of her home in 1666 by fire. Fliegelman picks up the story from there:

"Anne writes about how she needs to wean her affections from the things of this world, the kitchen table and the chairs that she used to sit in, for instance, all these objects that were meaningful to her, in order to recognize that they were God's, and he can take them back at will, and that the eternal things are awaiting her arrival in heaven." Simon Bradstreet, meanwhile, was not nearly as composed as his wife. "Simon has just lost one of New England's largest libraries, and instead of writing a poem trying to reconcile the disaster with his religious faith, he desperately tries to replace the books that he has lost, which in 1666 is pretty hard to do. He wants the same books back. So what I have here to show you is a book that he bought ten days after the fire from his son-in-law, Seaborne Cotton, and he has recorded all of this in the book."

Jumping abruptly ahead to the end, Fliegelman then picked up an early edition of Ralph Waldo Emerson's *Conduct of Life*, published in Boston in 1860. "This book is a kind of text of Christian consolation, and this copy was given by one of Emerson's sons, Edward Emerson, to Oliver Wendell Holmes Jr., who goes on to become a famous Supreme Court Justice. They are friends, and something they have in common is that they are both the sons of famous men. But Holmes, meanwhile, goes off to fight in the Civil War. He's wounded, he's in a military hospital, and he has this copy of Emerson's book brought to him for consolation." Fliegelman then showed me the book, which is in a desperately fragile state. "This was handed around in the hospital from wounded solider to wounded soldier. In a sense, emotionally, this is a wounded book, and I connect it with the wounded body of Holmes. You can see that the spine is partially off, you can even see the guts of the book inside here. The book is battered, but it survives." The copy bears an 1860 Christmas inscription from Edward Emerson to Holmes, and a lengthy inscription from Holmes to a wounded friend, George Abbot James, eloquently discussing the nature of valor; it also has the bookplates of two later owners.

As this volume readily affirms, the time-honored concept of demanding good condition goes entirely out the window in a library of association copies. "There are book collectors whose fantasy is the pristine copy, exactly as it came out from the presses," Fliegelman said. "I like to see the thumbprint where somebody has turned the page over and over again. In fact, the more a book is read, if it's read to death even, that's what I love. What moves me beyond words is that there have been people here before me, and now I am joining their company." Fliegelman acknowledged that occasionally there is very little material within the hard covers of a book—outside of the printed text itself, of course—to help him "triangulate" the factual detail he needs to nail down the facts of a particular association. In these cases, he has to do research that will flesh out the stories. "I have to make inferences sometimes, based on the evidence I find," he said, and turned to another book as an example of what he meant.

"Thomas Jefferson did not like to write in his margins, but he did keep a commonplace book in which he transcribed passages from his reading, and in that commonplace book are many passages he copied from this very book," Fliegelman said, picking up a copy of John Milton's *Paradise Lost* that Jefferson had in his possession as a young man. On the title page, the copy bears the full ownership signature of Jefferson. It also bears, in four places, the signature of James Madison, Jefferson's Virginia neighbor, and his successor as president of the United States. "This is the only book, so far as anyone knows, that has the signatures of both Jefferson and Madison in it. But that is by no means the most interesting part of the story here." What happened, apparently, is that Madison borrowed the book from Jefferson, took it to his home in nearby Montpelier, kept it there during the four-year period that Jefferson served as American envoy to France, and signed his name on the title page—but not before scrawling three practice versions on the other side.

"At some point the book comes back to Jefferson," Fliegelman said. "And if you look closely here," he continued, indicating a smudged area of the title page, "someone—presumably Jefferson—has attempted to erase Madison's signature. Being unable to remove the name entirely, he then signs his full name here at the bottom. Jefferson, as you probably know, used a clever system of initialing most of his books. I have one of those here to show you as well, in fact; but there are only a handful of instances like this, where Jefferson is known to have signed his full name into a book." Five of those other books are at the Library of Congress, and what Fliegelman has learned is that in each instance there is a failed attempt to erase another person's name. "Once somebody had defaced one of Jefferson's books, and once he failed to completely get rid of it, then he had to write his own name in there to acknowledge his ownership."

One of the most poignant items in Fliegelman's pantheon of favorites is a book of psalms formerly owned by Catherine Sedgwick (1789–1867), the nineteenth-century American novelist. "She writes in here that 'this book has seen me through forty years of the vicissitudes of life.' So the book becomes an important relationship, as important as the relationship with a family member. This is her life's companion, with which she had a physical intimacy."

When he is buying books, Fliegelman is always looking for connections beyond the obvious. "There are dealers out there who have an idea of what I'm looking for, and they work very hard to make a case for their books. That's what good booksellers do, they create value, and they do that by being able to tell a story about it. Why is this book important? Why was it important that this person owned it? And in a sense, that's what I am doing. But I've got to be convinced there's a story to tell before I buy the book." The ultimate appeal for Fliegelman is the opportunity he has to move around in time. "I'm interested in looking over the shoulders of previous readers, and understanding what a book means emotionally to somebody, not just intellectually. The book has to be brought to life. It's a dead object until you open it and read it. And in a sense, the participation of reading extends to the participation of writing comments inside the books."

A number of books in Fliegelman's library combine all of these elements, and they do it in powerfully revealing ways. "Let me show you now what many people consider the best book in my collection," he said, then laid before me a protective box containing two volumes, *Narrative of the Life of Frederick Douglass, an American Slave, Written by Himself* (1845), and *My Bondage and My Freedom* (1855), also by Douglass (1818–1895). Both books were once the property of Ellen Richardson, the Englishwoman who met Douglass in 1846 after hearing him speak, and raised the money to purchase his freedom from a southern slave owner. Douglass discusses Richardson's efforts on his behalf in the second book. The inscription he wrote in this copy says everything a modern reader needs to know about the copy's value as an artifact: "To Miss Ellen Richardson, with the respect, esteem and most grateful regards of the author, and as a token of his sentiments toward her, as the friend and benefactress through whose active benevolence he was ransomed from American slavery. 1860."

How Fliegelman acquired these books is a story in itself, though it is worth noting that the two volumes spent a number of years as virtual outcasts. They were bought in a Paris bookstall by the Seine for a few francs in the 1930s by a French university professor, who sent them to the United States as a gift to an American colleague. The American colleague—a former professor at Stanford—had them on his shelves for many years. Fliegelman spotted them there not long after he had received his Ph.D. in English and American literature in 1978, and started work as an assistant professor at the university. "I totally flipped out when I read this inscription," Fliegelman said, recalling that he asked immediately if he could buy the books. The man refused, but allowed him to use them in his teaching. "I use all of these books in my teaching, incidentally," he said. A few years went by, circumstances changed in the man's life, and Fliegelman made another, more substantial offer, which was accepted.

As a child growing up in New York City, his hometown, Fliegelman suffered from a chronic disease that required frequent hospitalization. It was during this period that he began buying secondhand books from Fourth Avenue bookstores in lower Manhattan. "I was a very sick kid with a lot of surgery, even through high school, with a lot of painful procedures, and I was worried about dying, to tell you the truth. I saw these books that had survived a couple of hundred years. These were powerful moments in my life. There was something comforting in buying those books. They had survived, and in a way, I could kind of play doctor, reverse the roles. They were my patients, and I was going to take care of them the way that I'm taking care of all these books now. I have a deeply intimate relationship with them. They are, in a sense, my only child."

Fliegelman did not just collect books when he was young, he read them as well, and for a time he was considered something of a prodigy. "In 1957, when I was eight years old, I was invited to be a contestant on the *$64,000 Question* television show. I knew everything there was to know about astronomy—I lived a couple blocks from the Hayden Planetarium—and that was my specialty." A few weeks before his scheduled appearance, the scandal dramatized in the 1997 movie *Quiz Show* broke, and he never got on the program. When Fliegelman was thirteen, he got a job as a copy boy for *Look* magazine, and before long he was writing some stories: "When I was seventeen, I got a job as a stringer for the *London Daily Telegraph*, and covered Mick Jagger's drug trial in the summer of 1967." After graduating magna cum laude from Wesleyan University in 1971, he headed west and has been in California pretty much ever since. His published works include *Declaring Independence: Jefferson, Natural Language, and the Culture of Performance,* and *Prodigals and Pilgrims: The American Revolution against Patriarchal Authority, 1750–1800.*

Fliegelman is a savvy collector who firmly believes in selling material that is no longer relevant to his interests in order to finance new acquisitions, and he is constantly examining the relationships between the books that he owns. "I wake up sometimes and I will go to my library and move a book from one shelf to another, because in the middle of the night I thought about certain connections between the two. I am wondering, does this author belong with this author? If so, I want them to commune with one another, physically, right now. It's a matter of what becomes visible when I bring these two things together that's not visible when they're kept apart." He paused before offering a concluding thought. "All of these books," he said, "are about the presence of the past in the present."

On April 10, 1997, a group of authors, illustrators, editors, librarians, booksellers, and bibliophiles gathered at the James Madison Memorial Building in Washington, D.C., for a national conference mounted to celebrate the sixtieth anniversary of a literary enterprise unique in the history of American publishing. Sponsored by the Center for the Book at the Library of Congress, the two-day symposium paid tribute to the Rivers of America series of books, a bold venture that illuminated the formative history of the United States by focusing on its vast network of waterways. Sixty-five books were published between 1937 and 1974, an impressive output that included works by such noted authors as Henry Beston, Branch Cabell, Henry Seidel Canby, Marjory Stoneman Douglas, and Edgar Lee Masters. John O'Hara Cosgrave, Lynd Ward, and Andrew Wyeth were among the fifty-five artists who contributed original illustrations to the series. By all accounts, the Rivers of America project was a smashing success, with one-third of the titles still in print. Yet remarkably enough, no comprehensive history of the series had ever been published. In fact, until the arrival on the scene eleven years earlier of a Florida collector, very little was known about the origins of the series or about the people who were responsible for making it a reality.

"It's a miracle we are here today, and the credit belongs to Carol Fitzgerald," Pace Barnes, a former series editor and one of the participants in the conference, declared in her remarks. John Y. Cole, director of the Center for the Book and organizer of the event, stressed that a central objective of the symposium was "to further Carol's research into the Rivers of America," and one immediate benefit, he announced formally, was the creation of a four-year educational project that aimed to highlight the literary, historical, and environmental heritage of America's waterways. Another goal of the effort would be to develop ideas for other books on the nation's rivers, each to be conceived in the same spirit as the original sixty-five. Among the guests at the Washington conference were six of the nine surviving authors to write books in the series. They included Thomas D. Clark, author of *The Kentucky* (1942) and, at ninety-four, the oldest participant; James Taylor Dunn, *The St. Croix: Midwest Border River* (1965); Wilma Dykeman, *The French Broad* (1955); William D. Ellis, *The Cuyahoga* (1965); Richard Mathews, *The Yukon* (1968); and Margaret Sanborn, *The American: River of El Dorado* (1974), who traveled to Washington for the conference by train from her home in Mill Valley, California. Unable to attend were Lew Dietz, author of *The Allagash* (1968), and Frank Ellis Smith, author of *The Yazoo* (1954), both of whom died later that year, and Marjory Stoneman Douglas, author of *The Everglades: River of Grass* (1947), who died in 1998 at the age of 108. The artists present were Gerald Hazzard, *The St. Croix*; Harry Heim, *The Minnesota: Forgotten River* (1962); Aaron Kessler, *The Merrimack* (1958); and George Loh, *The Allagash*.

"Carol united us," Kessler said in his remarks. "Until she came along, I don't think any of us had any idea at all what this series involved. Working on *The Merrimack* was something I took very seriously, but it was just one project for me, and because it had pretty much been forgotten by everyone, I had no idea how extensive this really was until now." Fitzgerald's passion for the Rivers of America series began in a curious way. In 1984 her husband, Jean Fitzgerald, a retired Navy captain and onetime commander of a destroyer squadron, donated an extensive collection of Federal Writers Project books produced during the Great Depression to the Broward County Library in Fort Lauderdale, where the couple lives. Two years later, the Florida Center for the Book and the Library of Congress sponsored a symposium to announce the gift. "It was the same weekend as the Miami Book Fair, so

Jean and I went over to take a look," Fitzgerald told me during an interview in her home. While poking around from booth to booth, she picked up a copy of *The St. John's River: A Parade of Diversities* (1943) by Branch Cabell and A. J. Hanna. "It was in pretty good shape, it had a nice dustjacket, and I thought this would make a nice Christmas gift for my sister Jeannie, who lives on the St. John's River in Jacksonville. Bill Hale, a book dealer from Washington and an old friend of ours, said in passing, 'You know, the Rivers of America would make a very nice collection for someone.' So when I brought the book home, it turned out that I didn't give it to my sister after all; I decided to keep it and look for some others."

During a trip to San Francisco the following year, Fitzgerald found two more books, one of which, *The Brandywine* (1941), by Henry Seidel Canby, featured illustrations by a young Andrew Wyeth. "I paid sixty-five dollars for that book," she said. "The other one I got, *The Arkansas,* was twenty-five dollars; but more importantly, I now had three books in the series." It was at that point that an interesting dynamic came into play. "I looked around and asked for information, but I still had nothing to tell me how many titles there were in the series. I went to the library, I looked at *Books in Print* to see if the Rivers of America was listed. Some were there, but it was all very confusing, because if a book was out of print, obviously it wasn't listed. I still had no idea of what I was looking for, and my curiosity was getting the better of me. So I decided to take a very aggressive approach."

She started by writing letters to antiquarian and secondhand booksellers all over the country. "I got many responses," she said. "My initial goal was to get a first edition in very good or better condition in dustjacket; before long, they were arriving in boxes, and I was putting them on my shelves." The key phrase in that sentence, of course, is "initial goal," since mere ownership of all the published books did not satisfy Fitzgerald's innate sense of completeness. She wanted to know about the authors and the artists, why certain rivers were picked and why others were not, how many printings had been ordered for each title, and how well they sold. The early books in the series included an essay by Constance Lindsay Skinner called "Rivers and American Folk," believed written in 1935 or early 1936, that articulated the premise in general terms. "There are several reasons for telling the great saga along the rivers," Skinner, an accomplished playwright, wrote. "We began to be Americans on the rivers. By the rivers the explorers and fur traders entered America. The pioneers, who followed them, built their homes and raised their grain and stock generally at, or near, the mouths of rivers." What truly distinguished Skinner's approach was her inspired conviction that the books be written by "novelists and poets" and illustrated by professional artists. "This is to be a literary and not an historical series," she made clear. "The special function of literature is to diffuse enchantment without which men's minds become shrunken and cold." The first title to be published was *Kennebec: Cradle of Americans* (1937), by the poet Robert P. Tristram Coffin, with illustrations by Maitland de Gogorza. A publisher's note included in this eloquent study of the Kennebec River in Maine elaborated on Skinner's dream a bit further:

> In the valleys of the Kennebec, the Connecticut, the Hudson, and later the Ohio, the Mississippi, and the Sacramento, the early pioneers found rich land to farm and a path of waters to as yet unsettled portions of the country. The folk along the rivers were bound each to his neighbor by the very shape of the valleys in which they lived. So a treatment of our country's past in terms of the men and women who peopled it and the rivers which united them is a natural, effective way of recasting the great American romance to living drama for America today.

Constance Lindsay Skinner died unexpectedly in 1939, at her desk, pen in hand, while editing one of the books, it was said at the Washington conference. By that time four additional books had been issued: Walter

Havighurst's *Upper Mississippi: A Wilderness Saga* (1937); Cecile Hulse Matschat's *Suwannee River: Strange Green Land* (1938); Struthers Burt's *Powder River: Let 'Er Buck* (1938); and Blair Niles's *The James* (1939). Carl Carmer's *Hudson* and Julian Dana's *Sacramento: River of Gold* were published shortly after Skinner died. She had projected twenty-four books, but when the project was finally discontinued in 1974, sixty-five volumes had been published. Before long Fitzgerald had made contact with three booksellers who deal knowledgeably in the series—Timothy B. Wuchter of Pelkie, Michigan, Gordon Beckhorn of Hastings-on-Hudson, New York, and John Townsend of Deep River, Connecticut— each of whom participated in the Washington conference. They furnished her with many of the copies she was looking for, and pointed her toward others.

Through diligent book hunting, Fitzgerald wasted little time assembling a complete collection of first-edition copies. By then she wanted to know more about what she had, and what kinds of supplemental items remained to be acquired, particularly copies of all subsequent editions, so she could determine whatever textual changes may have been made between printings. Her husband explained what he saw emerging in Carol's attitude: "At the beginning, I don't think there was any scholarly impulse at work, I just think it was Carol's own passion for order that was driving her to get things organized. It started out with a simple question: How many books are there in the series? Well, nobody knew. And then that led to all sorts of ideas about variant editions, special editions, commemorative editions, foreign editions, Armed Services editions, and the like. Carol was relentless. She wanted to know, What were the Rivers of America? Where are they? Who wrote them? Why hasn't anyone documented all of this?"

There is little in Fitzgerald's background to indicate a bent for bibliography and scholarly research. Born in Pittsburgh, Pennsylvania, in 1942, she received a bachelor of arts degree in political science and Spanish from the University of Mississippi, with a minor in English and psychology. "I am administrative assistant to a county commissioner, and my office is directly across the street from the library," she said. "I began to spend every lunch hour over there looking for leads, looking for needles in a haystack, and sometimes I came up with wonderful, wonderful information. I found some addresses in various reference books, and in May 1991 I started writing letters to authors. I wasn't sure what I was going to get, but it seemed like a good way to proceed." To her pleasant surprise, some of the writers began writing back, and from these correspondents Fitzgerald got the names of editors, agents, and publishing executives. In cases where principals were deceased, she made contact with relatives and associates, all the while filing what she had compiled in her home computer and preserving the original material in acid-free notebooks. Before long, she began writing a book titled *The Rivers of America: A Descriptive Bibliography* that went well beyond details of titles issued in the series to include concise biographies of the authors, illustrators, and editors; the book was acquired for publication in 2001 by Oak Knoll Press of New Castle, Delaware.

"As time goes on, there will be a lot of interest in the literature of the 1930s and 1940s," she said. "All these documents will be as perfect for the next historian as they were for me. This will give people a chance to read what the authors and illustrators had to say. I confess that I have not read every book in the series through from cover to cover. But I do familiarize myself with the content, and with the authors. My energy has been in collecting, and in being sure that I preserve and pass on what I can."

Where her collection of 450 books and hundreds of pieces of correspondence will be deposited has not been decided. With virtually all of the books now in hand—only the German editions of two titles still elude her grasp—Fitzgerald has started a collection of original prints done by illustrators in the series. "Everything will go to an institution, of that I am certain," she said. "Which one, I can't say, but it has to be a place that will guarantee that everything will remain together, books and papers. Nothing must be broken up. I just don't think that I could do what I have done again. Not only are people passing on, but the books simply don't exist anymore. So I have an obligation to future scholars to preserve all this. And believe me, I will."

What was immediately noticeable about the breathtaking books in Abel E. Berland's compact library of enduring literary treasures—it was my first reaction, in fact—was that none of the five hundred precious volumes gathered over the previous five decades were kept behind glass like museum objects, dazzling trophies to be seen but never touched. Instead, they remained within their owner's easy reach, there to be consulted and enjoyed on a daily basis. Sharing shelf space in the alcove of the Illinois collector's spacious house were some of the towering monuments of Western literature, including early copies of Shakespeare that passed through the hands of John Dryden and Samuel Johnson. "You are about to meet my dearest friends," the affable bibliophile said with utter conviction during my first visit with him in 1996, and I had no doubt whatsoever that this was to be the case.

We had just spent two hours in Berland's study, a room quite distinct and apart from his library. It was in this room that the Ohio native explained why he collected the things he kept in the other room, and how reading the books he had gathered with such taste and discrimination figured prominently into his bibliographic equation. "This room is where all the work is done," he said. "I want to know something about the historical circumstances that produced the books I have in the other room. When I read John Milton's poems in the 1645 issue over there, I want to know the social, the economic, the political circumstances, and the climate of opinion that existed during the time in which he wrote. I am not interested in a single author, a single period, or a single subject. I buy books that I want to make a part of my life."

There were more volumes shelved in Berland's study than there were in his library. They included bibliographies, biographies, histories, and reference works, along with auction catalogs of other recent collectors, familiar names like Carl H. Pforzheimer, H. Bradley Martin, Estelle Doheny, Harrison Horblit, and Thomas W. Streeter. "I am not in their league by any means," Berland said with a modest chuckle. "But some of my books are certainly comparable to what they had, and their catalogs are excellent sources of information for me." Of the five hundred titles in Berland's library, sixty-three were works printed between 1455 and 1501, and known as incunabula. They made up one of four categories in his general scheme, the others being scientific texts, English literature in general, and the works of William Shakespeare in particular. "Most are books of paramount importance, and exceedingly uncommon."

Noteworthy among manuscript items were a draft on vellum of the Magna Carta, copied about 1310, and formerly owned by Sir Thomas Phillipps; a 1430 Book of Hours with gorgeous illuminations; and the only known holographic copy of John Keats's eight-stanza poem "To Hope," written in 1815. "The book is a living thing for me, and every book I buy has to be something more than an icon or an artifact," Berland stressed. "Otherwise, I might just as well go to a great university or institutional library and look at the books they have on display there." As a sideline, Berland said he had begun to relearn Latin, a diversion of his youth, because most of his incunabula were printed in that language.

"So," he said after a meaningful pause, "do you have any other questions at this point?"

"Just one," I replied. "Is it time now to see some books?"

"After you, sir," he said formally, waving the way into an adjoining room, and motioning me to sit down at a large horseshoe-shaped hunt table he uses as a reading desk.

"I think perhaps we should start with some things from the fifteenth century," he began, and promptly set before me a copy of a world history known as the Cologne Chronicle, printed in 1499 by Johann Koelhoff the Younger, a remarkable specimen in its original pigskin binding, fitted with metal clasps and bosses, which were intact. So that I would fully appreciate the illuminations, he encouraged me to fan the pages. "This book has survived for over five hundred years," he said. "You aren't going to hurt it." Next out from the shelves came his copy of Dante Alighieri's *Divine Comedy,* printed in Florence in 1481, with two illustrations after Botticelli. "Here's another one which I really love," he said, offering as a worthy encore a two-volume edition of Plutarch's *Lives,* printed in 1478 in Venice by Nicholas Jenson, "a typographic monument" in every respect, with marbled edges and gold fillets on the sides.

This measured presentation, carefully structured to suggest the rich sweep of Western history, literature, philosophy, early printing, and scientific triumph, continued with an examination of Berland's copy of the Jenson 1475 edition of Saint Augustine's *Civitate Dei,* and Thomas Aquinas's *Summa Theologica* (1478). Among his three Cicero items, the 1467 *Laelius de Amitita* is the *editio princeps,* the first printed edition; his *De Oratore* (1468) was one of two copies in the United States (the other is owned by the Pierpont Morgan Library in New York). There was one book produced by William Caxton, England's first printer, in Berland's library, *Cordyal* (1479), one of eleven copies in the world, and the only one in private hands.

"My incunables were selected for their basic importance, not simply because any one of them might be beautiful," he made clear, explaining why only twenty of his fifteenth-century books were illustrated. Cornerstones of science, medicine, economics, and philosophy in his library included these examples: William Gilbert's *De Magnete* (1600); Francis Bacon's *Advancement of Learning* (1605); Galileo Galilei's *Dialogo* (1632); William Harvey's *Anatomical Exercises* (1653); Isaac Newton's *Principia Mathematica* (1687); Adam Smith's *Wealth of Nations* (1776); Thomas R. Malthus's *Essay on the Principle of Population,* published anonymously in 1798, which Berland owns uncut and in original boards; and Charles Darwin's *On the Origin of Species* (1859).

There was not enough time, of course, to see every book in Berland's library in this introductory visit. About halfway into the session, he shifted from fifteenth-century books and scientific landmarks to English literature, this time reversing the process by beginning in more recent years and moving back in time to what we both knew would be the pièce de résistance. Berland placed his inscribed copy of Percy Bysshe Shelley's *Adonais* (1821) on the reading table ahead of his exquisite copy of *Songs of Innocence,* written, engraved, and hand-colored in 1789 by William Blake, Copy J in the G. E. Bentley Jr. bibliography and census. Then came the Kilmarnock edition of Robert Burns's *Poems* (1786), originally from the library of the poet's patron, followed by a first issue, first state of Jonathan Swift's *Gulliver's Travels* (1726), an "immaculate copy." The Holford copy of Izaak Walton's *Compleat Angler* (1653), in its original sheets, was placed before me next, along with the second, third, fourth, and fifth editions of the book, all printed during the author's lifetime.

At that point Berland turned to seventeenth-century poetry. He began by showing me a copy of John Donne's *Poems* (1633), with additional verses written inside in a contemporary hand, a detail of great interest to literary scholars. Then came a trio of John Milton titles, beginning with a copy of the 1645 *Poems,* inscribed warmly by the author to Philip Heimbeck in Latin, which Berland translated to read, "To an erudite scholar and a dear friend." Bright copies of the first edition of *Paradise Lost* (1667) and *Paradise Regained* (1671) were brought forth next as a pair. "We're almost there," Berland said, but first he thought it important for me to see his copies of Edmund Spenser's *Faerie Queene* (1590), and Thomas More's *Utopia* (1516). "I get around to each of these books at least once a year. It is important for me to visit with them frequently. Every finger on this hand is important to me, and that's the way I feel about these books, they are all equal in my eyes."

But when pressed to cite a favorite among his "dearest friends," he singled out the first four editions of the *Comedies, Histories, and Tragedies* of William Shakespeare, known as the Four Folios. It is no exaggeration to suggest that Berland's copy of the 1623 First Folio represented the finest copy in private hands. Only six copies in the United States are owned by individuals, and only three of these are complete, meaning they have no missing leaves or facsimile pages inserted. The Berland copy is complete, in excellent condition, and has a binding from the early seventeenth century. Beyond the physical details is the ownership signature on the back pastedown of the first known owner, Alan Puleston, and of the poet John Dryden, whose family had the book until 1913, when it was bought by Bernard Quaritch of London. From Quaritch it went to the great Philadelphia bookseller, Dr. A. S. W. Rosenbach, and from Rosenbach it passed through several important owners before becoming the property of the bookseller John Fleming in 1961. "This was John's personal copy, and I nagged him year after year to sell it to me," Berland said. "I already had a First Folio, but this was the one I felt I just had to have. It happened that he needed to raise some capital, and I came by one Friday afternoon in 1970 at precisely the right time." Along with the First Folio, Fleming sold Berland a Second Folio (1632), a Third Folio (1663), and a Fourth Folio (1685), all in original bindings, as well. And as impressive as the Dryden association is for the First Folio, the names attached to the Third Folio fare pretty well in their own right; formerly the property of the Cambridge Shakespeare scholar Richard Farmer, the Berland copy is believed to have been consulted by Samuel Johnson when he was preparing his eight-volume edition of Shakespeare in the 1760s.

Berland was adamant about working with established booksellers, and he did most of his business with Fleming, who died in 1987. "I want to deal with someone who is responsible. I want the books to be collated. I want to be able to return the book if it is not right, and what you pay for this service is worth every penny." Only once did Berland ever buy a book at auction without using a dealer as his agent, and that is a classic collecting story in its own right. "What happened is that I heard at the very last minute that a copy of a book known as *Schatzbahalter* was about to be sold at Christie's in New York," he said, and retrieved the incunable for my examination. It is a book of Christ, printed in Germany in 1493 by

Anton Koberger, and illustrated with splendid woodcuts. "I had been looking for it for years, and I just had to have it."

Berland called Fleming's office, only to learn that the bookseller was out of town, and not expected back before the sale. In a "mild panic," he thereupon called Stephen Massey, for many years the head of Christie's book department in New York, and gave what is known as an "open bid" on the lot, meaning that he agreed in advance to pay whatever it would take to acquire the book. As the bidding progressed, it was apparent that another buyer in the gallery was intent on securing the lot, but in the end Massey knocked the book down to Berland, as he had been authorized to do on his behalf. "What I soon learned, to my great horror, was that John Fleming had rushed back to New York to bid on the book for me, knowing that it was something I desperately wanted to have," Berland said. "He hadn't had time to let me know he would be there. When the numbers got too high, he dropped out. So what it comes down to is that I got the book by bidding against myself."

When Berland tells the story, there is a strained smile, but at least he had the satisfaction of having owned the book. Another instance of where he acted against his better judgment had a far different consequence, one that continues to rankle him to this day. It involved a perfect copy of John Bunyan's *Pilgrim's Progress* (1678), one of six known complete copies in the world, and one Berland bought in the early 1970s from the late Warren Howell of San Francisco. Only one other copy is in private hands, the William Scheide copy, which is now on deposit at Princeton University. During a 1974 visit to the Lilly Library at Indiana University in Bloomington, Berland remembers being "besieged" by the director of special collections, the late David A. Randall, to sell the book to the library. A former rare-books dealer with Scribner's in New York and author of an excellent memoir of forty years in the trade, *Dukedom Large Enough* (1969), Randall was reputed to be relentless when he set his mind to anything, and he acted true to form with Berland. "He begged and pleaded with me to sell him the book," Berland said, "but I turned him down."

Toward the end of the year, Randall visited Berland in his home and made the plea with renewed vigor, telling him how he dearly wanted to include the book in an exhibition of world masterpieces he was planning for the American Bicentennial. "I never intended to sell at any price, but I was overcome by David's sincerity and desire to share the book with the world, so in what can only have been a moment of temporary insanity, I agreed to let him have my wonderful copy of this precious book." Berland has never forgiven himself for being so "weak," and in the years that followed made several concerted attempts to buy the book back, in one instance offering the university what he conceded to have been a "humongous" figure to reclaim it. In 1994 he received a letter from William R. Cagle, Randall's successor at the Lilly Library, now retired, informing him that the Bunyan is "one of the true jewels in our crown," and a book he would never let go, even if it were in his power to do so. It did not make Berland feel much better to learn that Cagle ranked *Pilgrim's Progress* as one of the "greatest treasures of the Lilly Library."

As much as he respects institutional research collections, Berland agrees with Robert Hoe (1839–1909), builder of what is generally acknowledged to be the greatest private library ever assembled by an American, who explained in one sentence why he wanted his estate to sell his treasures at auction: "If the great collections of the past had not been sold, where would I have found my books?" Berland said he could not agree more. "I owe it to the next generation," he said of the decision he made for the future of his books. "Does the Folger Shakespeare Library in Washington need another First Folio? They have seventy-nine already. Someone has to replenish the supply; if not me, then who?" Berland reflected on that for a moment, then nodded toward his shelves. "The most important thing I can say to you about these books is that I never take them for granted. I am nothing more than their temporary keeper. It is my privilege to visit with them every day, and to be in their company."

Given this sense of responsibility for the next wave of collectors, it came as no great surprise when Berland informed me in May 2001 that he had just consigned his precious library to Christie's for sale in the fall. The retired real estate developer gave me the news two days after movers had packed the books, some 530 of them all told, into fifty crates and taken them from his home outside Chicago to New York, where an elegant catalog would be prepared for the auction, and where they would be put on exhibit before going on the block. "There were many reasons why I decided to sell now," he told me, not least among them the sobering realization that time marches on, and that nothing is forever. "Mostly, I wanted to have the satisfaction of seeing the books find good homes with people who will love them as much as I do." Berland said he had hopes of witnessing the transfer in person, "though it will not be easy—and I don't want to be tempted to buy them all back. The truth is that I don't think I can take it. It will just hurt too much."

On a hot afternoon in July, a prominent Harvard educator who had spent twenty-five years forming a unique collection of nineteenth-century art instruction books and artifacts by rummaging through flea markets and antiques barns all over New England welcomed seven people into her Victorian home a few miles outside Boston to appreciate the fruits of her labors. Although most of Diana Korzenik's visitors knew her work on a professional basis, none had ever seen her personal collection before, and none had any idea how extensive it was until that memorable summer day. Later that week, movers would come to crate everything in boxes for shipment across the continent to San Marino, California, where they would find a new home at the remarkable research library, art museum, and botanical gardens established by Henry E. Huntington in the early years of the twentieth century.

Korzenik had recently retired as professor and chair of the Art Education Department at Massachusetts College of Art in Boston, and was no longer teaching the course in the history of art education at Harvard University in which her collection had been used as a primary tool. Before sending the cherished objects on their way to the West Coast, she had decided to enjoy them in her home one more time. It also gave her a chance to elucidate for some colleagues the vision that had shaped her collecting focus over such a long period. For me, it was a rare opportunity to be with an eloquent collector as the reality of divestiture—the moment of reckoning that is inevitable for everyone who cherishes books—finally arrives.

"It is time for the collection to have a new life, and I want people to understand exactly what the collection is," Korzenik explained while waiting for the others. "I didn't want this in my will. What I have done is far better than a will. This way, I am available to guide people through it, and I will be going out to California to show them what they have. I will have a series of meetings with their curators to discuss what research possibilities they have for the future. They already know that they have tremendous opportunities, but they don't know yet the significance of the individual pieces."

Amy Myers, curator of American art at the Huntington, said she couldn't agree more. "What is extraordinary is that Diana's collection was created for the purpose of teaching. Diana wanted to bring into the discourse about the history of American culture a discussion of the role of art education from the late eighteenth century to the early twentieth century. What she wanted—and what she found in all those trips of hers to the New England flea markets—were various authentic texts and materials that she could use in her classroom. Once she had gathered the materials, she interpreted them and brought them alive for her students. By giving context, perspective, and meaning to these objects, Diana, in a very real sense, is herself the text of the collection."

Alan Jutzi, curator of rare books on the library side of the Huntington, works with many priceless treasures, the fabled Ellesmere Manuscript of Chaucer's *Canterbury Tales* of the early 1400s and a vellum copy of the Gutenberg Bible in its original binding among them. He called

Korzenik's gift of 450 books and about 1,000 ephemeral objects and artifacts such as paint boxes, stencil kits, sketchbooks, crayons, porcelain mixing trays, and teacher manuals "one of the more interesting collections we've received in the last several decades. I have no doubt that it will have more popular interest than many of the English literary collections we have acquired, because there is a visual aspect to it, there is a demonstrative aspect to it. The best part is that it all comes with Diana's knowledge. When she comes out here next year, she will organize the collection for us and tell us how it will be used. We just may videotape her doing all this so we can have a permanent visual record."

For the general collector, lessons to be learned from Korzenik's example are numerous and worth noticing. Most notable is the necessity of defining a clear plan at the outset and sticking to it, remembering all the while that the true value of a collection lies in the wisdom and scope of the objects as a whole, not in the price tag of individual items. Korzenik chose to give the collection to the Huntington, but it was professionally appraised for $200,000, a considerable sum for materials that she acquired, for the most part, for $5, $10, and $20 each during what she likes to call her countless "ferreting excursions" in the countryside. What kinds of things did she find? A few titles are instructive: *The Child's Palette Painting Book* (1897); *Bail's Drawing System* (1859); *Coe's Drawing Cards for Schools* (1858); *The Eye and the Hand* (1827); *Progressive Lessons in Landscape Drawing* (1840); *Free Hand Drawing* (1897); *How to Draw: The Right and Wrong Way* (1871); *Child's Own Drawing Book* (1846).

"These were in junk boxes in all the flea markets," Korzenik said. "What you see here are art supply catalogs, pattern books, pasting books, drawing cards, glass slates, which were a way children learned to draw. I'd like to say that condition was always important to me, but it really wasn't. These are things I had never seen before, and things I have never seen anywhere since. We're talking in many cases about ephemeral items, so when I saw them, I got them, and I'm thrilled that I did." Whenever she brought home something she had just found, a firm and fast rule she applied was to document the items immediately. "Everything that came into the house had to be cataloged then and there, and then researched thoroughly."

Despite Korzenik's willingness to accept less than mint condition, a good many of her books and artifacts are in fine shape anyway, a circumstance she credits to the lucky discovery of a cache of material gathered many years ago by a onetime art director in the seaport community of Gloucester, Massachusetts, a woman named Mabel Spofford. "One of my former students at the Massachusetts Institute of Art is married to a bookseller; it was through this woman's knowledge of my collection that I found out about Mabel Spofford, who herself had attended Massachusetts Art in the class of 1902. When I took one look at what she had done, I bought out the entire apartment from her estate." For some unexplained reason, Spofford, unmarried and living alone, saved every manner of art item that came her way, including dealer samples of crayons, boxes of lead pencils, jars of paper paste, art instruction magazines, and manuals.

"Maybe I'm reading too much into this, but it is clear to me that Mabel had this sense of the objects as documents. She also collected World War I posters, and was a wonderful artist in her own right. She clearly loved visual material. The more I look at this stuff, the more I ask, 'What was this maiden lady up there on the North Shore doing?' I discovered that she took a cartooning course in the 1920s, and she didn't take it just to teach kids how to draw cartoons. She took it to learn how to be a cartoonist herself. It's a very interesting insight into female aspiration, I think, because this woman had to be very ambitious to have saved all these things and to have taken such careful notes the way she did. I think she was brilliant. I never knew her, but I feel more and more that Mabel Spofford is my soul mate, my partner, in this enterprise, and very much a part of the collection."

Korzenik believes the principal reason the materials she found at flea markets were priced so low is not because they are abundant—in fact they are quite scarce—but because so few people understand the circumstances in which they were produced, or how much a part they were of nineteenth-century American culture. "That puzzled me for a while, why these things were treated so indifferently, and why they were so cheap, and I think the reason is that the history of American taste in art, and certainly in art education, has been to have a disdain for one's benefactors. In a way, it's a kind of automatic disrespect, the idea that, 'It's old stuff, and we're on to new stuff, and who cares about art education anyway?' "

A central concern for Korzenik, then, was to evaluate the materials she had found, and to place them in the context of their times. "I love looking at things, and I have always been endlessly interested in objects. I actually had myself tested recently, because I figure I am old enough to find out what the truth is. They found out that I am mildly dyslexic, and what is really incredible is that I have written books. The secret is, I walk from object to object, and learn from the object. And then, if I need to understand something, I find a book on the subject."

A native of Brooklyn, New York, Korzenik attended Vassar College before transferring to Oberlin College in 1959, where she graduated magna cum laude with a bachelor of arts degree in art history. After spending a year at Columbia University under a Woodrow Wilson fellowship, she taught in Harlem for five years before entering the Harvard Graduate School of Education to study under Rudolf Arnheim, the noted author of numerous scholarly books and articles, *Art and Visual Perception: A Psychology of the Creative Eye* (1954) most prominent among them. "Rudolf made the whole field of what people get out of artmaking come alive. That whole thing I had been missing in art history, I got from him. He is an incredible man."

Shortly after receiving her Ed.D. from Harvard in 1972, Korzenik began teaching at the Massachusetts College of Art. Once settled in the Boston area, she began visiting the remarkable variety of flea markets and antiques shops that New England is so famous for, and started finding "for peanuts" the materials that now, at the Huntington, comprise the

Korzenik Collection of the History of American Art Education, an endowed collection that will not only be augmented with more material but provide the basis of an exhibition, a symposium, and, in all likelihood, the publication of a book comprised of the presented papers.

Essential to Korzenik's interpretation of art instruction in nineteenth-century America was an understanding of a law passed in Massachusetts known as the Drawing Act of 1870, and the consequences it entailed. This legislation mandated a program of free drawing instruction in every city and town in the state with a population of more than 10,000. Within three years of its passage, Massachusetts had created a new public college—now the Massachusetts Institute of Art—to train the teachers who would implement the law. By 1872 art exhibitions were annual affairs, attended by thousands of people.

Korzenik contends that this sudden burst of art fever can be traced to the success of New England's textile mills. "What I like to say about these books is how dependent all this material was on what was then new technology. The growth of photography and the mass production of images made it possible for art instruction to become an industry, and it became a huge industry," she said. "If Americans could be taught how to draw, they could design patterned ribbons, colorful aprons, and ornamental pottery, and even rethink and improve the machines that fabricated them," she wrote in her 1985 book *Drawn to Art: A Nineteenth Century American Dream*. Soon, she pointed out, art became "a commodity appreciated as a sign of luxury, and perhaps even of education and culture."

Drawn to Art was written on the strength of yet another treasure trove Korzenik had acquired in 1981; the letters, journals, sketchbooks, watercolors, drawings, prints, engravings, and proof sheets of three nineteenth-century children from one Merrimack, New Hampshire, family who became professional artists. Embracing the years 1850 to 1900, the materials are now installed at the American Antiquarian Society, where it is known as the Cross Family Art Archive. Korzenik's gift of the

Cross family material occasioned a 1993 exhibition and symposium and the publication of a book, *The Cultivation of Artists in Nineteenth-Century America* (1997). "That was a discrete collection, complete in and of itself, and the AAS seemed the proper home for it," Korzenik said. With that gift—like the gift she made to the Huntington—Korzenik committed herself to sharing her vision of the materials with a new generation of scholars.

In 1912, when Henry E. Huntington bought a superb collection of early English poetry for $230,000, the California railroad magnate confided that he would gladly have paid twice that amount, if only the knowledge of the man who had built the collection so tastefully over several decades, New York City banker Beverly Chew, could have been worked into the transaction. For Henry Huntington, the Chew acquisition was one of 112 en bloc purchases negotiated between 1904—the year he embarked on a frenetic effort to build one of the world's finest private libraries in the shortest time—and 1927, when he died at the age of seventy-seven. "It cannot be stated too often," Professor George Sherburn of the University of Chicago wrote in 1931, "that the Huntington Library is essentially a 'library of libraries or a collection of collections.' " Still, as Huntington's comment to Chew made clear, the wisdom, experience, and insight that goes into the shaping of individual libraries and collections would remain tantalizingly unattainable, at least during his lifetime. But that was then, and this is now, as witness the happy circumstance of Korzenik's decision to give not only her collection but a good deal of her vision and knowledge to the institution where the materials will reside.

Parting with the collection was difficult, and a month after it had left her house in thirty-six carefully packed boxes, Korzenik had trouble talking about it. Indeed, when the movers arrived in July, she could not bear to supervise them as they went about their business, leaving that chore instead to her domestic partner of many years, Andrew Dibner. "They were here from nine in the morning to seven at night, and I stayed the whole time in my bedroom," she said. "I am thrilled about where the collection has gone, and I'm much happier giving it than having sold it, because it feels much better this way. But for all that, I think I'm still in mourning."

For most people who collect books, the goal is to acquire and possess the elusive titles of one's dreams, a worthwhile pursuit driven by a passion for the object. But there are others who refuse to rest until they add their favorite authors to what bird-watchers call a "life list"; among this species of bibliophile, building a library is just the beginning of the process.

In my case, the exercise involved a kind of mantric ritual: Whenever I interviewed an author for the literary column I wrote every week for twenty-two years, I asked for an inscription in my review copy of the book being discussed, oftentimes bringing along first-edition copies of other books these people had written that I had acquired in the antiquarian market. Thus it was that certain authors became "my" authors, accounting for well over a thousand inscribed books on my shelves, books that I not only had read critically, but had discussed face-to-face with their creators. Imagine, then, my reaction when I read a feature story in the *Washington Post* detailing the activities of a country lawyer who lives on a forty-five-acre estate in the Missouri Ozarks just outside of Springfield and travels thousands of miles every year to get books signed by his favorite writers. "One for the Books," proclaimed the main headline to the *Washington Post* story, followed by this teasing subhead: "Missouri Bibliophile Rolland Comstock Goes to Great Lengths to Indulge His Passion."

The passion being indulged by the Missouri bibliophile, as it happens, is one collector's ambition to make the authors he admires "a part" of himself. To accomplish this, Rolland Comstock spends a third of every month—about 120 days a year—traveling from his rural home thirty-five miles north of the Arkansas border to larger metropolitan cities where major authors routinely give readings and sign copies of their books. More often than not, Comstock finds what he is looking for in Washington, San Francisco, New York, Boston, Los Angeles, and Chicago in the United States, and London in Great Britain. On each trip he takes with him as many as thirty different items, not just books the authors have previously written but uncorrected proofs, broadsides, magazine excerpts, ephemeral pamphlets, and publicity photos he has obtained through a variety of sources he has aggressively networked—all with the hope that the authors will sign them all for him, which they usually do.

The funny thing about all this is that I actually had heard about the quixotic Mr. Comstock a few months prior to the *Post* piece during an interview with A. S. Byatt, the author of *Possession,* a magnificent novel that is must reading for all bibliophiles. "You would not believe this man Rolland Comstock," Byatt said with an amused sigh. "He flies halfway across North America in every direction for the single purpose of attending author signings, and he brings with him a satchel full of books. It is unique to my experience." Indeed, the reporter for the *Washington Post,* David Streitfeld, was introduced to Comstock at just such a function in the nation's capital, a reading and signing at Chapters Bookstore arranged for Richard Russo, the author of *Mohawk, Risk Pool,* and *Nobody's Fool.* Streitfeld had this to say of Comstock's technique: "He is very patient and very polite, always waiting around until the writer is done with everyone else and has time to sign his stuff. Then he takes his box and flies home." As luck would have it, I had business scheduled in Kansas City a few weeks after that article appeared, making possible a side trip to Springfield and a meeting with Comstock. "I have one little problem with your book," he said good-naturedly about *A Gentle Madness* after we shook hands in the long driveway of his estate. "Collecting is very definitely a madness, but there is nothing gentle about it at all. This is hand-to-hand combat."

An overstatement to be sure, but this is not the home of any ordinary collector, either. Comstock estimates he has fifty thousand books in his library, with the heart of the collection maintained in a two-floor annex he and his wife, Alberta, added on to their house five years earlier when he finally decided to "get serious" and take his show on the road. "That new room cost $200,000 to build, and it probably devalued the place by $300,000," he said, explaining that the demand for houses with huge libraries in his part of Missouri is not especially intense. "That's the one problem with this collection; I have nobody around here I can show it to."

Having said all that, Comstock's library, thirty-two by thirty-five feet, is quite a sight to behold, with wood-paneled alcoves jutting out from the exterior walls toward the center on both floors of the room. All of the books have been encased in acetate wrappers, and all have color-coded stickers on their spines, red for signed or inscribed books, blue for unsigned American editions, green for unsigned English editions. "What I am working toward is a sea of red stickers," Comstock said. If there is to be an ocean of red, though, it will be confined to the lower level, as I quickly learned from the succinct designations Comstock has for the two sections of his library. "They're all dead up there, so that's the 'dead authors floor,' " he said with a smile, pointing to the second story.

"I have loved books all my life," Comstock said during a break for cocktails, and offered as proof the yellowed clipping of an old newspaper story from 1953 that reported how sixteen-year-old Rolland Comstock, at that time a high school senior, had just opened up his own secondhand bookstore in downtown Springfield. How in the world did that come about? This is what the article in the local newspaper, the *Springfield News and Leader,* had to say then: "With a tremendous number of novels, biographies and the like in his personal library, Rolland conceived the idea of ridding himself of some of them while perhaps picking up new literature he wanted to read, by opening up a bookstore." Looking back, Comstock laughs at the innocence of it all. "I find it ironic that the only way I was ever going to be able to get all the books I wanted was to forget about being a bookseller or a teacher—which is what I really wanted to do—and become a lawyer." But the calling has served him admirably. "I handle more probate cases by far than any other law office in Spring-field," he said. "The nature of my practice is that all my clients are either dead or crazy."

When he turned sixty in 1997, Comstock began assigning most of the work in his office to a junior partner, leaving him ample time to pursue books and authors with renewed vigor. The Comstocks have five adult children, all living away from home; their former bedrooms are used now for books. This sudden increase in gross weight caused the upper rooms to sag a few years ago, requiring some expensive modifications to the structure. "The big dramatic shift in my collecting came around 1990 when a bookseller I did a lot of business with, Bev Chaney, told me I would really enhance my copies by getting them signed. Only problem there was that everyone I was collecting to that point was dead. So it was then that I started hitting the road as a literary groupie, going after the writers who were very much alive." Comstock began by ordering Sun-day newspapers in all the major cities around the country and reading the book review sections for notices of upcoming author appearances. As he became known at various stores, he was placed on mailing lists. "I have managers calling me all the time now, telling me Edna O'Brien is going to be in Los Angeles or Paul Auster is going to be in New York. I even get invited to private receptions." Wherever he goes, Comstock brings his own copies of older material for the authors to sign, and he always buys numerous copies of the new releases from the stores he visits.

A dedicated reader, Comstock has his favorites, though he is always alert to emerging voices. "I buy *Publishers Weekly* to read the forecasts, and I pay attention to what the important critics have to say. What I'm emphasizing now is young writers nobody ever even heard of. Once I adopt new writers and go searching for their signatures, I never give up. There's an old saying out here in this part of the country, 'A terrapin will bite you and won't let go until it thunders.' That's the way I am with my authors." Comstock has about twenty authors he collects as an "unrepen-tant completist," meaning that nothing—even childhood scribblings and

Abel Berland in his library, among his "closest friends."

Rolland Comstock on the second level of his Springfield, Missouri, literary collection, the tier devoted to deceased authors; all "living" writers are shelved on the ground floor.

Fort Lauderdale, Florida, collector and bibliographer of the Rivers of America series, Carol Fitzgerald.

Minor Myers Jr., president of Illinois Wesleyan University, and collector of "anything pertaining to the eighteenth century."

The Strand Book Store at Broadway and Twelfth Street, New York City.

Prominent critics of the San Francisco Public Library project included the best-selling novelist and "library activist" Nicholson Baker, and the noted short-story writer and essayist Tillie Olsen.

Nancy Bass and Fred Bass, owners of the Strand Book Store.

Louis Cohen (1903–1991) and the original Argosy Book Store on Fourth Avenue, circa 1928.

Louis Cohen with his daughters (from left) Naomi Hample, Judith Lowry, and Adina Cohen, and his wife, Ruth Shevin.

Peter B. Howard,
Berkeley, California, bookseller.

Serendipity Books, Berkeley, California, where
the owner, Peter B. Howard, maintains that he
"distrusts bookstores that are neat as a pin."

Novelist, semiotician, and bibliophile Umberto Eco
among the thirty thousand books in his Milan apartment,
and the book that inspired him to write The Name of
the Rose.

Barry Moser, a self-portrait, 2000.

Maurice Sendak receives a National Medal of the Arts from President Clinton and Hillary Rodham Clinton in 1996.

Author Penelope Fitzgerald (1916–2000) in her North London home.

Author and champion of hypertext, Robert Coover.

Marguerite Goldschmidt and her husband, Lucien Goldschmidt (1912–1992), in their Madison Avenue bookstore-gallery, 1986.

Dutch booksellers Nico Israel and his brother, Max Israel, both survivors of the Holocaust, in Amsterdam.

Booksellers Madeleine Stern and Leona Rostenberg in their New York apartment, with Bettina, their dachshund.

German bookseller Heribert Tenschert among treasures in the vault of his Swiss headquarters.

Priscilla Juvelis and her mentor, John Fleming (1910–1987); the portrait is of Fleming's mentor, Dr. A. S. W. Rosenbach (1876–1952).

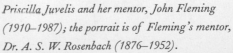

Bookseller William S. Reese in his New Haven, Connecticut, office.

Philanthropist Lloyd N. Cotsen with one of several hundred Noah's Ark sculptures gathered in memory of his late son.

A view through the keyhole into the Giant Book at the Children's Library Cotsen established at Princeton University.

The British Library.

*Two of four "open-book" glass towers of the French
National Library in the Tolbiac section of Paris.*

Flood damage in the basement of Boston Public Library, August 1998.

One of the lions ("Patience") at the Fifth Avenue entrance of the
New York Public Library.

A cross-sectional view of the seven levels of stacks serving the Main Reading Room of the New York Public Library as it appeared in Scientific American *on May 27, 1911, shortly after the building opened.*

The San Francisco Public library, known as the New Main, which opened in 1996.

Overflow books being stored in Brooks Hall, beneath the new San Francisco Public Library, where there was insufficient room to shelve the entire collection.

Kenneth E. Carpenter on his rounds at Harvard College's Widener Library, selecting books for off-site storage.

A book-storage module at the Harvard Depository in Southborough, Massachusetts.

The disc-shaped roof of the new Bibliotheca Alexandrina takes shape in 1998; after many delays, formal dedication was scheduled by the Egyptian government for April 23, 2002.

Prof. Dr. Mohsen Zahran, project director of the Bibliotheca Alexandrina.

juvenilia whenever he can find it—is excluded, and he has stories about flying off to meet with them all. "I don't follow the flag," he said, indicating shelves full of books written by such writers as the Canadian Margaret Atwood, the Italian Umberto Eco, and the Irishman Patrick McCabe to go along with the many American and British writers who occupy most of his attention. He flies about 50,000 miles a year and has "worn out" several travel agents with his unending requests for arrangements on extremely short notice. Authors he will travel "just about anywhere" to see include Martin Amis, Madison Smartt Bell, Julian Barnes, Kate Braverman, Maya Angelou, T. C. Boyle, John Banville, Rick Bass, Larry Brown, and Charles Baxter.

The idea of "embracing" an author is very much one of Comstock's goals, but like every abstraction, this one has several layers of meaning. There is the matter of duplicates, for example. Most collectors believe that one fine copy of a particular book is sufficient; not so with Comstock. "I have decided that I can have as many copies as I want of a writer's first hardcover book—sometimes I have fifteen—but of all subsequent books I can have only two. Unfortunately, that's a rule I violate about ninety percent of the time."

The most notable example of that rule involves the British author Jim Crace, who in 1986 won the Whitbread First Novel Prize, the Guardian Prize for fiction, and the David Hingham Prize for *Continent*, a heady brace of honors for a young writer just starting out. Despite its strong critical reception, however, the book recorded disappointing sales and failed to sell its first printing. When Comstock heard that *Continent* was about to be remaindered, he bought all 1,085 unsold copies at bargain prices and had them shipped from England to his house in Missouri, where most lie neatly shelved in a third-floor storage area. His numerous encounters with Crace since then have led to a transatlantic friendship and the use of the name "Comstock" for characters in two of Crace's works. Further validation of Comstock's long-standing confidence in the novelist's talent came in 2001, when Crace's most recent effort, *Being Dead*, won the

National Book Critics Circle Award for fiction in the United States. While the 1,085 copies of *Continent* holds the record in Comstock's house, he has bought 800 copies of another author's book, 400 of yet another, and scores of numerous others as well.

"I do not buy these books as any kind of investment or a scheme to make money. If a book is good, I want a lot of them, and one of my other goals is to promote the author. I want to give these books away to people who really want them, and by the time I die, I hope all of them are gone. It offends me to see the first editions of significant writers selling for peanuts on remainder tables." He thought about that for a while and offered one more thought: "I get a kick out of possessing ten copies of a great book. If one copy is great, it stands to reason that having ten copies is going to be ten times as great."

One of the cornerstone precepts of book collecting is the need to establish a focus; a person who gathers indiscriminately and without direction, this premise holds, is little more than an accumulator. A focus can be as finely defined as the works of one author, or even the various editions of a single book. One enterprising collector in the Midwest, Jon Lindseth, has put together a formidable collection of *Alice in Wonderland,* more than a thousand copies in numerous editions and languages of Lewis Carroll's timeless tale of childhood whimsy. He has gone so far as to commission a translation of the book into Yiddish, since none in the language has appeared thus far in print. The capstone to Lindseth's collection came when, after years of trying, he persuaded the Hollywood producer William Self to part with his exceedingly scarce 1865 copy of *Alice,* the "suppressed" copy, of which only one—this one—is known to be in private hands; Lindseth was so pleased by the exciting turn of events that he dedicated the catalog of a Grolier Club exhibition of his collection to Self.

What matters most in the exercise is a lively imagination and an open mind. Dr. Minor Myers Jr., president of Illinois Wesleyan University in

Bloomington, Illinois, provides an interesting case study in how a collector's focus can represent a certain attitude, and how it can work in many exciting ways to preserve the creative wisdom of another time. Myers has many interests, a good deal of them befitting both a teacher and an administrator at a liberal arts institution of two thousand students. Among his personal pastimes—*hobby* is far too tame a word—is being intellectually engaged by eighteenth-century music and thought, and finding materials printed during that period to illumine them. An amateur harpsichordist, he has collected what he likes to call an "orchestra with no players," an ensemble of "fourteen violins, three violas, two cellos and a bunch of other stuff," all made before 1820. His dream is to form a group of like-minded musicians who will play the forgotten pieces he has rescued, in some cases from the scrap heap, on these instruments, and give them new life.

"Antiquarian music is just a part of what I collect," Myers said one snowy night over cocktails and dinner at the University Club in Chicago. Our first meeting was arranged by a mutual friend and great champion of books and higher education, Chef Louis Szathmary, a few weeks before his death in 1996. "The one area I pursue with unbridled enthusiasm is the eighteenth century, and that means the whole of it," Myers made clear. "Anything I can find. Everything I can find. I am interested in music, and I have a special fascination for early violins, but I am fascinated by material from the eighteenth century just for itself. It doesn't have to mean anything or be anything. My motto boils down to this: Anything I can find eighteenth-century, and cheap, I will buy. Anything. Anywhere. Japan, China, Europe, it doesn't matter. I want to have it."

But why, I asked, does he covet the eighteenth century, and not something closer to our own time, like the nineteenth, or something more remote, such as the seventeenth? "Why do some people like vanilla and not chocolate?" he answered with a shrug. "I don't know. I suppose, probably, because it's a lot closer than the seventeenth century, which means the likelihood of finding more material is greater. But the larger reality is that as a child I formed a fascination for that whole period of Colonial America and the American Revolution, and that grew into a fascination for not only the history but the music, the art, the architecture, and virtually every aspect of what seems still to be the classic taste."

A native of Akron, Ohio, Myers received a bachelor's degree from Carleton College in Northfield, Minnesota, in 1964. After spending a year at Duke University in Durham, North Carolina, he transferred to Princeton University in Princeton, New Jersey, where he earned master's and doctorate degrees in politics and political philosophy. Before assuming the presidency of Illinois Wesleyan University, he held a variety of teaching and administrative positions at Connecticut College in New London, Connecticut, and Hobart and William Smith Colleges in Geneva, New York.

The impulse to collect began at an early age. Every place Myers has studied, every place he has worked, and every place he has visited has afforded him an opportunity to seek out material, be it a flea market in New England, a yard sale or library sale in the Midwest, a secondhand bookstore on the West Coast, or an antiquarian bookstore in New York City. When he was a student at Princeton in the 1960s, he used to go into Manhattan and call on David Kirschenbaum, the founder of Carnegie Bookstore, who remained active in the business to his death in 1994 at the age of ninety-nine, and who I had the great pleasure of profiling in *A Gentle Madness*.

"On a whim, I went in to see him just a few months before he died— I had no idea, in fact, that he was still in business until I found him by chance in the phone book—and bought all kinds of wondrous things. These were obscure items that undoubtedly had been gathering dust for years—an autographed letter by John Stuart Mill, not eighteenth-century but certainly worthwhile all the same, something else by an English admiral, neither one in the best of shape, but for five dollars each, I wasn't going to quibble. There was a wonderful ink drawing of Paganini dancing on a violin, ten dollars, and an English copybook of eighteenth-century poems and letters. It was a memorable day of picking up things I least expected to find, and Dave was clearly interested in parking them someplace where somebody wanted to have them."

Myers takes special pleasure in finding music composed in the eighteenth century by people largely forgotten by historians, and seeing what it sounds like when brought to life on his own 1787 harpsichord. Among a stack of miscellaneous pieces he bought in France were some concerti composed in the mid-1700s by Richard Mudge, an English clergyman and graduate of Pembroke College, Oxford University. "Mudge's father was a friend of Samuel Johnson's, and I knew of him slightly as one of the lesser-known British composers, someone who had heard Handel on many occasions. When I called Pembroke College, they knew next to nothing about him; he was lost, in other words, even to people at his own college, and it happens that his work is very interesting. What I'm hoping is that we can put on a performance of some of his music at Illinois Wesleyan. He may have been lost, but now he's been found."

Myers is equally enthusiastic about works by two eighteenth-century composers of African descent: Joseph de Boulogne, a man born in the Caribbean who became known as the Chevalier St. Georges in France; and Ignatius Sancho, a son of slaves who made his way from Jamaica to England, where he wrote a number of minuets and dances that were popular in their time but are unknown today. "They both have strong links to the Caribbean, where they remain little known. They can offer a whole depth to Caribbean culture as it explores its roots."

Other composers represented in Myers's collection include William Hamilton Bird, a Scottish military officer whose travels to India enabled him to transcribe native music so it could be played on the harpsichord, and Sir William Herschel, a German-born British astronomer who discovered the planet Uranus and spent a good deal of time composing music. Another item in Myers's collection, something, in fact, he hopes the university's music and drama departments will mount as a production, is *Lord of the Manor,* a ballad opera written in 1781 by John Burgoyne, the British Army general who fought at Bunker Hill, took Ticonderoga, and surrendered to General Horatio Gates at Saratoga. By admitting the full scope of the eighteenth century into his domain, Myers has found himself learning about such things as the layout of ornamental gardens, the design of country houses, ornithology, theories of mathematics, and the preparation of food. "Essentially, my cookery collection is an attempt to understand English cookery in the time of Handel and Haydn," he said.

"In the eighteenth century, the basic outline for music and for food preparation was the same: Add such ornaments as you will to make the piece the way you like it. When the eighteenth-century cookery writers produced their books, they told you to add salt, pepper, or nutmeg. They didn't say anything about how much to put in—that was left to the judgment of the artist. Creating early music and creating eighteenth-century cuisine are absolutely parallel in every way. There's a wonderful line from Sherlock Holmes that applies here, I think. Watson says, 'Well, Holmes, I was with you the entire time, how did you see all this?' And Holmes says, 'My dear Watson, we saw the same things, I simply observed them differently.' So, the more you see things in a different way, the more observations you are likely to make."

As consuming as the eighteenth century may be for Myers, it has not stopped him from nurturing other interests. A recent area of activity involves what he calls his "Music Theater in Chicago" collection. "We have a program at Illinois Wesleyan in music theater in the School of Art and the School of Drama, and so far the library hasn't had too much of a collection of music theater material. So one day I'm at a flea market, and I say, 'I wonder how many examples of music theater I can get in piles of sheet music that are real cheap.' I then proceeded to find a show from Chicago with music by Gustav Luddens and words by Frank Pixley, who it turns out worked with my great-grandfather in the newspaper business in Akron back in the 1880s. I later learned that on the side he used to write the words for musicals. This led me to get interested in Chicago theater. I just started doing this because I was finding the stuff and nobody else had it. I pay about fifty cents to a dollar for the items I buy; it may well be true that I'm the only person alive who is collecting them."

So far, Myers has gathered the music of about 120 shows that originated in Chicago during the late nineteenth and early twentieth centuries, and has researched their performance histories. A few, like *Babes in Toy-land* (1903), with music by Victor Herbert and lyrics by Glen MacDon-ough, have familiar names, but most, like *Fun in a School Room* (1907) and *The Flirting Princess* (1909), have dimmed with the passage of time. "There was a show called *The Winning Mists* that I think is a very good subset for Chicago musical theater. It was great out here, but it kind of missed when it got to New York." Meanwhile, a colleague at the university is making plans to stage student productions of some of these musicals.

While every collector covets completeness and perfect condition, Myers said the age and scarcity of the material he collects very often pre-clude the acquisition of complete copies, and that he is grateful for what he is able to find. He recalled a discovery in London of "miscellaneous parts" of some eighteenth-century compositions at a secondhand book-store. He explained what these are: "Let's say you have an orchestra, and you've got a couple of violins, a couple of violas, cellos, bases, horns, and flutes. What you find may be the music for the flute part, and the rest of the piece is missing. You still buy it anyway. You don't ignore it because it is incomplete. If you look at the catalogs of institutions that collect music like the British Museum, you sometimes will see how thrilled they are just to have the viola part, for example, or the cello part. They don't have anything else from a particular symphony; yet they're happy to have whatever fragment they've got."

The beauty of collecting like this is that it stresses intuition while imposing no restrictions whatsoever on how the hunt is to be conducted. "That's the most exciting aspect of bringing home a pile of miscellaneous stuff. You don't really know what it is you have until you've had a chance to sort through it all and see what is actually there. I've been very lucky. I buy these things—and it is at that point that I start to get curious."

4.

SPLENDID ANACHRONISMS

From this slender beginning I have gradually formed a numerous and Select library, the foundation of my works and the best comfort of my life both at home and abroad. On the receipt of the first quarter a large share of my allowance was appropriated to my literary wants: I cannot forget the joy with which I exchanged a bank-note of twenty pounds for the twenty volumes of the Memoirs of the Academy of Inscriptions; nor would it have been easy by any other expenditure of the same sum to have procured so large and lasting a fund of rational amusement.

—*Edward Gibbon*, Memoirs of My Life

Whenever any of the two hundred or so people who work at the Strand Book Store in Lower Manhattan thirst for a café latte or a foaming cup of cappuccino, they send a colleague off on a coffee run to one of the Marquet Patisserie or Dean & DeLuca takeout shops located in the neighborhood nearby. If any of the six thousand customers who pass through the front door each day in search of great book values have similar cravings, the unspoken understanding is that they can always make a side trip to the Barnes & Noble superstore six blocks to the north, or to another a few blocks south, where refreshments are available, and where the marketing strategy is geared to shoppers' creature comforts.

Aside from the colorfully emblazoned T-shirts, chic canvas tote bags, and bibliophilic-themed neckties and scarves available for sale at the front desk, the only commodity offered for purchase in the venerable Strand is books, and that, apparently, is enough to satisfy its legions of hard-core admirers; an inventory of 3 million volumes makes the family-owned business by far the largest secondhand bookstore in the world. "My favorite place in America," the Italian novelist and admitted bibliomane Umberto Eco told me during an interview, and all I needed was one look at the thirty thousand volumes he has shelved in his massive apartment in Milan to know why. "I always see something different in there, something I never expect to find," he said, which is why most people who visit the store return again and again.

"What we're all about here is what you see piled up all around you," Fred Bass, the second-generation owner, made clear to me one steamy August morning during an exhaustive tour of the premises, though I hardly required proof; I have been a grateful dawdler at the Greenwich Village landmark myself for the better part of three decades, and located many of the obscure titles I needed for *A Gentle Madness* scattered among the nooks and crannies of this onetime manufacturing plant at Broadway and Twelfth Street. For all my familiarity with the place, Bass still thought it prudent that we begin our conversation with a walk through the bulging storerooms he maintains on the fifth and tenth floors of the old building. "Most everything you see in this area is pretty much under control," he reassured me, indicating aisle after aisle of previously owned books and remainder copies that occupy 10,500 square feet of the fifth floor. "I say 'pretty much under control,' because we can readily retrieve what we have in the middle of the room, it's either in the computer or on a list; but I don't even want to take you down there, it's impossible." He was nodding toward a clanky old elevator at the back where an inchoate heap of bulging cardboard boxes was stacked from floor to ceiling in dozens of teetering spires.

"The books multiply at night, it really has nothing to do with us," joked Nancy Bass, Fred's daughter and partner in the business. She was perpetuating a bit of in-house folklore that contends that more books come into the Strand each day than go out. "My father's particular obsession is that he has to have everything, and he never passes up an opportunity for a bargain." Indeed, in the mid-1990s Fred and Nancy Bass opened a satellite store, the fifteen-thousand-square-foot Strand annex at 95 Fulton Street, three blocks east of Broadway between the South Street Seaport and the World Trade Center, primarily to take some pressure off the tenth floor of the main building, which was the next stop on our walking tour, and an even more unruly situation than the fifth floor, if that is at all possible. "Just the other day I bought a library of thirty thousand volumes from a former customer of mine, all handpicked by him," Fred Bass said. "That's all right here. Everything in here is mostly individual libraries and estate purchases, and a lot of it is things I haven't gotten around to yet, and maybe never will. I would say there are two thousand boxes up here for the Rare Book Department alone that we may never get to. And there are two big rooms back there that are just as full as this."

Named for the famous publishing and bookselling district in London, the Strand was founded in 1927 by Benjamin Bass, the father of Fred Bass, as a small storefront operation on Fourth Avenue, in the heart of New York's celebrated Book Row. Like so many of his competitors, the elder Bass featured daily book bargains on sidewalk tables, a practice that his son and granddaughter continue today, with white-on-red stenciled signs offering specials of five books for two dollars. At its height in the late 1940s and mid-1950s, the Book Row area between Eighth Street and Fourteenth Street, roughly from Union Square to Astor Place, was packed with four dozen secondhand operations. Today all of them are gone; only the Strand, which moved a few blocks west to its current quarters in 1956, remains in business.

Opinions vary on what caused their disappearance, although spiraling rents certainly had a great deal to do with it. "We lost our lease, and we were one of the first stores to move off Fourth Avenue," Fred Bass said. "We went from 81 Fourth Avenue, where we were paying $110 a month rent, to Broadway and Twelfth, where it immediately went up to $400 a month. We were scared, and everybody down there thought we were crazy. Before I bought the building here in 1997, my landlord was getting a check from me for $55,000 every month." Despite staggering increases in the cost of doing business, Bass does not agree that higher rents were solely responsible for the death of Book Row. "The real reason Fourth Avenue disappeared is because the forty-odd booksellers who were there were all very strong, self-centered people who kept all their knowledge to themselves. They didn't teach anybody. Most of them came out of the Depression, and they played everything pretty close to the vest. It's true that they couldn't deal with the increase in the rents, but they also got older, they got tired, and they just faded away. That is my theory of what happened."

A computer search of newspaper and magazine articles published since the mid-1970s, using "New York" and "Book Row" as keywords, bears that observation out rather poignantly. A depressing litany of obituaries shows up, each one noting the passing of yet another secondhand bookseller. A 1981 article in the *New York Times* profiled one of the last survivors, Walter Goldwater, owner of the University Place Book Shop at 821 Broadway, who had opened his store in 1932 with $600 and the help of "a Communist uncle by marriage." Goldwater bemoaned the disappearance of a tradition that had consumed not only his entire adult life, but that of his second wife, Eleanor Lowenstein, owner of the Corner Book Shop at 102 Fourth Avenue for more than forty years. When she died in 1980, the *Times* praised her 1972 compilation, *Bibliography of American Cookery Books,* as an "exhaustive, definitive listing of American recipe-collections dating back to 1742" and cited her own collection of cookbooks—now a prize archive at the Arthur and Elizabeth Schlesinger Library on the History of Women in America at Radcliffe College—as being among the best assembled on the subject to be found anywhere. When someone once suggested that perhaps Lowenstein should move the ten thousand books shelved in her shop and the thousands more kept in an upstairs apartment so that painters could get inside and brighten up the premises, she immediately refused. "I'd rather live in squalor," she said. "Books and paint don't mix. Only book lovers would appreciate this shop. Housekeepers would be horrified."

Sheldon M. Wool, a senior executive with CBS during the late 1970s and a determined bibliophile who made regular visits to the Fourth Avenue bookshops, became friendly with both Lowenstein and Goldwater toward the end of the Book Row era, and he placed both dealers "high among the most unforgettable characters" he had ever met. "Eleanor frequently said that she preferred to sell her most valuable books to collectors over seventy years of age," recalled Wool, who now lives in Concord, Massachusetts, where his wife, Jacqueline Wool, operates a small secondhand bookstore, Books with a Past. "That way she would have a reasonable chance of getting them back at some point for herself." Goldwater's specialty was African-American literature, and he was instrumental in building research collections at many universities during the 1960s when black studies programs were just starting to be developed. He also featured a strong selection of avant-garde literature, incunabula, and works about Russia, where he had traveled extensively. A lifelong chess player, he served as president of the famed Marshall Chess Club in Greenwich Village for fifteen years. Founded in 1915, the elite organization was visited by many of the world's greatest masters, including the reclusive Bobby Fischer, who played a tournament by Teletype from the group's back room in 1965 when denied a visa by the U.S. State Department to visit Havana, Cuba. "Walter and Eleanor were booksellers, but they were scholars of the first rank," Wool said in tribute. "I firmly believe they knew their specialty subjects as well as anyone in academe, probably a lot better."

Goldwater and Lowenstein also understood that they were part of an ephemeral culture. "As a book center, the street is gone," Goldwater said in the 1981 *Times* profile, a view shared in the same piece by Jack Biblo, a partner in Biblo and Tannen of 63 Fourth Avenue from 1928 to 1975, and seventy-five years old at the time of the interview. "You can't even compare bookselling today with what we did. When I started, you had an old Russian revolutionary down the street who kept a wood-burning stove in the middle of the store. If he liked you, he gave you a cup of tea. If he didn't like you, he threw you out. If he told you a price and you said you'd think about it, he'd double the price." What was particularly distressing for Goldwater was that "there aren't many young people entering the field. There isn't anybody to take over." The next time Goldwater's name appeared in print was on June 28, 1985, with news of his death four days earlier at the age of seventy-nine.

Marvin Mondlin, executive vice president in charge of estate purchases for the Strand and director of the fifty-thousand-volume rare-book department on the third floor, has been with the company since 1951, beginning with Benjamin Bass on Fourth Avenue, and moving over to Broadway with the founder and his son five years later. The author of *Appraisals: A Guide for Bookmen,* Mondlin is widely respected for his expertise on the finer points of book evaluation and appraises, by his own reckoning, about a million volumes a year, although most of them, he readily acknowledges, are summary judgments made in bulk lots. For the better part of two decades Mondlin has been writing a book tentatively titled *Book Row America: An Anecdotal and Pictorial History of the Fourth Avenue Antiquarian Book Trade,* basing much of it on his own observations.

Mondlin said he basically agrees with Fred Bass's theory on the decline of Book Row, with the notable exception of Fred Bass himself, who began working in the old Strand when he was thirteen years old, went into business with his father in the early 1950s after graduating from Brooklyn College, and made the operation the tremendous success it is today. "I saw his father, and I have seen Fred, and I have the greatest respect for each of them. Both of them liked working out in the open, and Ben was out there right up until the day before he died in 1978. To describe his temperament, I would say he was a collector at heart, while Fred is a much better businessman. There's a quality of toughness and shrewdness with Fred. He has a great feel for the potential value of a book, and he is a very good gambler when he finds that he has to gamble. Ben was the founder, but Fred really made the Strand what it is today."

Still, attempting to fathom why the Strand thrives as an open shop while so many of its competitors have fallen by the wayside remains one of life's great imponderables. The Strand is not part of any chain; it has no off-street parking, no air-conditioning, no author readings, no signings, no coffee bar, a pair of shabby one-stall rest-room facilities, peeling paint on the walls, crumbling tiles on the floors—yet it continues to prosper. Only in the fall of 2000 did the store finally organize an active website, and even then with the greatest of reluctance on the part of Fred Bass, and primarily at the urging of his daughter.

It is a matter of family pride that both owners are constantly on the floor, and that neither has an office. "I had an office upstairs for all of two months about twenty-five years ago, but I turned it over to the accountant," Fred Bass said. "I belong out here." More often than not, he is standing behind the horseshoe-shaped desk near the center of the main floor making offers on the used books that are continuously being brought in for sale; with his neatly trimmed beard, no-nonsense demeanor, and acutely attuned eyes, he looks for all the world like a salty sea captain at the helm of a three-masted schooner. Nancy Bass, also the store manager, is frequently occupied in handling the book rental and bulk sales side of the business. The employees, many of them moonlighting artists, musicians, writers, and actors who live in the culturally vibrant neighborhood, are unfailingly knowledgeable and courteous. "Whenever I go to the apartments of any of the employees or the managers, it's exactly like being in the Strand, with books piled everywhere on the floors and the shelves," Nancy Bass said.

"For years our slogan has been eight miles of books, but we recently figured it's probably a lot closer to thirteen miles," she continued. "We believe we have the best prices and the best quality, and the only way to maintain that is to keep the volume up, and to always offer fresh inventory. We work very hard at keeping our edge on the competition." The Basses do not keep precise figures on how many volumes they sell every week, but the annual gross during the late 1990s was above $20 million, which is a pretty fair indication that they must be doing something right. "We're surrounded by superstores, and our sales are still increasing," Fred Bass said. Even though the Strand is primarily a secondhand bookstore, it does offer a selected "front list" of items bought directly from publishers, and thousands of newly released books known as review copies. These, for the most part, are complimentary volumes that publishers have sent to newspaper, magazine, radio, and television critics around the country in the hope of getting favorable notices. Because virtually every major American trade publisher is headquartered in Manhattan, new books come into the Strand from a variety of sources, not just reviewers.

While Fred Bass did not introduce the practice of offering review copies for sale to the general public, he is credited with having refined it to a high art. His willingness to pay cash for every recently published title reviewers bring in, "provided they don't cream the good stuff off the top," guarantees the steady volume he covets. Bass buys these books at 25 percent of the dustjacket price, and sells them at half the listed price in the basement known as "Strand Underground," where they are clearly marked as review copies. Since authors and publishers receive no royalties from these sales, the practice is controversial in some segments of the industry, but legal all the same.

The prospect of acquiring newly issued books at half the suggested retail price appeals not only to customers coming in off the street or buying from catalogs that the Strand periodically issues but to "hundreds" of public and academic libraries everywhere. "You can't prove by me that libraries have cut back on their book purchases," Fred Bass said, though he declined to identify any of the institutions he does business with. "I will say that they include some of the most prestigious names in the world. Quite a few librarians come here regularly when they're in New York. They have their want lists, and before they order from the publishers, they'll check with us to see if we have the titles they're looking for."

The Strand's inventory is so extensive it has inspired creation of a book rental and collection development division, managed by Nancy Bass. "Books," the English novelist Anthony Powell observed, "do furnish a room," an aesthetic reality not lost on savvy decorators keen on creating a mood of studied elegance. Clients in dire need of a literary look can rent or buy vintage volumes, all priced by the linear foot. "The prices vary from ten dollars a foot to two hundred dollars a foot," Nancy Bass said. "Some people want old books, just new books, or a mixture; if they want full leather bindings, or very specific subject categories, then it's going to be more expensive. I did an order for some people in Miami Beach a while back, and they told me 'hot pink,' 'yellow,' 'magenta,' things like that. Whatever it is they want, it's always right now, yesterday if possible. I have book emergencies happening all the time, especially with people having elegant uptown parties. The movie industry is in New York now in full force, and we are forever getting directors who change their minds about what they need at the last minute." She was pleased to note that Strand books decorate the studio for the *Today* show at Rockefeller Center, and have been used as props in such films as *The Horse Whisperer*, *You've Got Mail*, *Sleepers*, and *The First Wives Club*, for soap operas that include *As the World Turns*, the television series *Law and Order*, *Saturday Night Live*, and *The Cosby Show*, and theatrical productions on and off Broadway too numerous to enumerate.

Customers with needs that go well beyond decor—those who are interested in content but have neither the time nor the inclination to ferret out books on their own—also have options available to them. For Hollywood film magnate Steven Spielberg, Nancy Bass and her staff assembled a choice collection of four thousand books on art, theater, film, literature, and history, and were given a budget of $30,000. "It was a lot of fun putting that collection together. We made sure he had a great library, the very best of what we had."

Of all the words that have been used over the years to characterize the Strand, the most colorful appeared in a Dutch tourist magazine, which called it *De Boekenjungle*. Other writers have called the store "messy," "dingy," "disheveled," and "chaotic." In a front-page article published on August 21, 1986, the *Wall Street Journal* remarked incredulously on the continuing resilience of the business, and offered the following physical description: "To the uninitiated, entering the Strand can be intimidating. Books are piled to the ceiling on shelves and in boxes on three large floors. Dozens of large fans hanging from Doric-style columns blow musty air. Downstairs, the sprawl of volumes extends beneath Broadway."

As 2000 became 2001, very little had changed at the Strand, although some thought was being given to opening up the second floor to customers, installing an escalator, and allowing easier access to the third floor, where the rare-book and antiquarian department is located. "If I make any changes at all, it will be something that gives the customers easier movement and provides us with more space for books," Fred Bass said, but in no way would he consider tinkering with a winning formula. "I absolutely insist on keeping the same crummy look. Every time I make the place too neat, business goes down."

As the lone surviving heir to the Book Row tradition still operating in the old neighborhood, the Strand recalls a particular time and place with its own blend of style and spirit, but it is by no means the only secondhand book emporium in New York City that has become a legend in its own time. Boasting an upscale zip code of 10022, the Argosy Book Store at 116 East Fifty-ninth Street between Lexington and Park Avenues is an urban anomaly that occupies a piece of prime real estate in Midtown Manhattan. Every floor of the six-story brownstone, moreover, bulges with piles of used books and prints. Like the Strand, the Argosy has a Fourth Avenue provenance and is independently owned and operated.

When the guiding spirit of the enterprise, Louis Cohen, died in 1991 at the age of eighty-seven, Nicolas Barker eulogized him in the *Independent* of London as an American original, the proprietor of "the last bookstore of its kind in New York, as vigorous as ever, and a notable tribute to its founder." What pleased Barker in particular was the fact that the Argosy—named for the mighty Spanish galleons that once ferried cargoes of gold bullion across the Atlantic Ocean—remained firmly in the hands of Cohen's widow, Ruth Shevin, who observed her ninety-fourth birthday in 2001, and their three adult daughters, Judith Lowry, Naomi Hample, and Adina Cohen. A casual visit to the store finds the four women tending to the needs of their customers, Shevin minding the front desk for a few hours each day near the entrance, Lowry specializing in modern first editions on the fifth floor, Hample overseeing autographs on the sixth, and Cohen supervising the sale of prints on the second. In striking contrast to the controlled chaos of the Strand, the Argosy retains a quiet formality, "an oasis of calm and mustiness, amid the skyscrapers and bustle," Dinitia Smith marveled in the *New York Times*.

Like their father before them, the Cohen sisters sell nothing that is new, and because they own the building, they do not have to worry about escalating rents in an impossibly expensive Midtown neighborhood. "Real estate put a lot of book people like us out of business," Hample acknowledged in an interview, a conviction readily affirmed by her sisters. They have been able to avoid that fate because their father had the foresight to buy the building in 1964 for $100,000. "He saw where the rents were going," Lowry said, "and it happened that a lot of buildings on the street were for sale. To tell you the truth, I dearly wish he had bought four or five more."

As circumstance would have it, Louis Cohen bought just the one building, but that was more than enough to secure his family's future. "My sisters and I are constantly being approached by people who tell us to just name our price, and we are constantly telling them what our father said when he started getting these offers forty years ago, that we enjoy being booksellers, bookselling is in our blood," said Lowry, whose husband, George Lowry, owns and operates Swann Galleries, an auction house in Lower Manhattan that specializes in rare books and prints. Their sons are in the business as well, Nicholas working with his father at Swann, Benjamin, trained as a computer graphics designer, in charge of Internet sales at Argosy. Judith Lowry said that when some developers were planning to build a skyscraper next door during the late 1960s, they offered her father $1 million for the building. "Father turned that down, and they came right back with an offer of $1.1 million. This kept going on and on, back and forth; they would make a higher offer, he would refuse. 'Tell us what you want, name your price,' they said. 'We will give you what you want. We will rent you space in the new building.' They just wouldn't believe him when he said, 'I am not in the real estate business, I am in the book business, and because I like the book business, I have no price.' We still get these offers all the time, and for a lot more money too. If money was what we wanted, believe me, we could sell our building today, throw all the books in the Dumpster, and come out way ahead, or we could sell the building, stay at home, and do all our selling on the Internet. But our father taught us that being in the book business means having contact with people. We believe in that, and the fact of the matter is that we love what we are doing. If we were leasing this space today, our rent would be something like $200,000 a month, probably a lot more, so it would be impossible for us to do what we're doing."

Shortly after observing his eighty-fifth birthday in 1989, Louis Cohen began writing an informal memoir of his experiences in the book business as a gift for his three grandchildren. "It's a first draft which he meant to revise, but he died before he had a chance to get back to it," Lowry said when she allowed me to make a copy of the typescript, and to quote from it in this book. Whatever the narrative may lack in polish, it more than compensates for with charm and honesty. The son of poor

Jewish immigrants to the United States, Cohen was born in New York in 1903 on the Lower East Side, and moved to the Bronx as a child. When he was eighteen, Cohen got a part-time job working for Alexander A. Salop at the Madison Bookstore on Fifty-ninth Street, a few doors away from where he would set up his own business in 1933. "There were moments when I thought how exciting it would be to have a shop of my own," he wrote of the experience. "It was an intoxicating thought."

After high school, Cohen entered City College of New York, "headed for a Bachelor of Business Administration degree, in which I had no interest." With just one semester left before graduation, he cashed in a five-hundred-dollar insurance policy his family had bought for him when he was a child, borrowed another five hundred from his mother's brother, and began buying books at regional auctions and country fairs, storing them in the homes of his relatives. "Buying books was wonderful. Exciting. Even though I wasn't selling anything, it was thrilling." When Cohen's relatives ran out of space, he began looking for a shop, "where else but on Fourth Avenue—old Book Row." He found the perfect place on Ninth Street and Astor Place, a large storefront with a high ceiling and a dry basement with a double window in front. Searching for a name for the business, he chose Argosy, not only for the "romance attached to it," but also because it began with the letter A, which would position his enterprise "foremost on any list of bookstores."

Astutely choosing to stay open until ten o'clock every night, Cohen began to attract a steady clientele of librarians, out-of-town book scouts, and other dealers. Every nickel of profit he earned was invested in the purchase of more books. Determined to develop strategies for finding fresh stock, he sent every member of the Social Register a postcard on the assumption that wealthy people had excellent libraries, and he managed to cultivate some worthwhile contacts. He wrote how he "loved making calls for the purchase of private collections within a radius of one hundred and fifty miles," always trying to arrive at his destination by nine in the morning. "Later, my daughters very obligingly grew older and relieved me of the pressure of early-morning calls." Frequently accompanying him on these trips was his wife, who became "a veritable space engineer" in learning how to utilize every inch of room in their station wagon. During one return trip to the city, Cohen stopped the car suddenly, "with the result that there was a cascade and shower of books that fell on our shoulders, into our laps, and heaped on the front floor of the car, causing us to be wedged into our positions in an almost immovable state." A tenuous book-by-book extraction at the side of the road left them "none the worse for our experience, topped by much laughter."

Cohen's willingness to travel anywhere to acquire "fresh stock" inevitably elevated the level of his business, and before long it was time to move. "I didn't like Fourth Avenue anymore," he admits. "My stock was getting better, and I lovingly thought of Fifty-ninth Street," where he had served his apprenticeship. He moved uptown in 1933, claiming as a trademark an outdoor "arcade" at the entrance to his store. "I had it built so I could have shelves of books outside my front door, housing over a thousand volumes, racks of prints and the like, with an iron gate coming down to protect it at night. It worked out very well. Nobody in New York had this, and to my knowledge nobody has it today." Books are still displayed on one side of the entrance, about six hundred volumes.

In 1935 Cohen bought a collection of "miscellaneous books of no special merit," only to discover while pricing them that thirty children's books from the 1880s had been signed on the front flyleaf by Sarah Delano, whose son, Franklin Delano Roosevelt, was halfway through his first term in the White House. "I thought President Roosevelt would be pleased to have them and sent the lot along to him" at the White House. An appreciative bookman in his own right—FDR was a member of the Grolier Club in New York—Roosevelt quickly responded with "a warm two-page letter in which among other things he recollected being bounced on his mother's knee when quite young."

Of what Cohen calls his "galloping bibliomania," he set down a number of diverting anecdotes. Once he and A. B. Shiffrin, a former mentor at Madison Books, had been invited to the home of an elderly man who was ready to part with an outstanding library of three thousand volumes, including many scarce first editions of important books, and many files of autograph letters. Instead of bidding against each other for the collection as the owner clearly had hoped would happen, the two men agreed to offer one reasonable price and then resolve final disposition of the material among themselves. "My colleague was as eager to have the books as I, and when the truck was loaded we were confronted with a problem. It was all but impossible to divide such a varied collection of books, autographs, prints, and broadsides into two parts of equal value. So we decided to toss a coin—the winner to get the entire library at the price paid. The thought of a single toss for such stakes was unnerving. I suggested two tosses out of three. Mr. Shiffrin won the first toss, I the second, so it really amounted to a single toss after all. Mr. Shiffrin won." But then Cohen's true passion for the material kicked in. "I felt I had to have the collection. I offered Abe a handsome profit, and the truckman drove the books to the Argosy instead."

In what had to be the riskiest acquisition of his career, Cohen and another New York bookseller were invited to make an offer on a medical library assembled by a small-town Illinois physician who had recently died. Impressed by the 100-page catalog they were sent to examine, the men offered $15,000. A telegram of acceptance was received, and the two men were on a sleeper train to Illinois the next day. When they arrived, they were shown to an enormous room on the third floor of a building that was packed with material far better than anything they had imagined would be there. The only problem was that the estate lawyer who had enthusiastically accepted their price the day before now informed them that the deal was off. "We repeated that we had his telegram accepting our offer, we made the trip, and we were ready to fulfill our part of the deal." But the lawyer was adamant.

"We finally decided to wait for the evening, leave our check on the table in the anteroom, break the door lock, and take the books, which we considered ours. I called my lawyer early that night at home and explained our plight. 'Lou,' he said, 'you're on your own.' " Choosing to proceed with their bold plan, Cohen and his colleague "made arrangements to have two large trucks with six men arrive at the loft building at 9 P.M. We had previously forced the door, which was tenuously held by a simple latch." Working rapidly over the next three hours, they filled the trucks, "and made a dash for New York." Cohen expected to receive an outraged phone call the next day, possibly even a visit from the police, but nothing happened; in due course the check was cashed, and "I never heard from the man again." The new books, in the meantime, "set Argosy up in the front rank of the medical history field," a development that led directly to yet another transaction involving similar verve and daring, a caper he called "The House in Bridgeport."

During World War II, Cohen was asked if he would be interested in seeing a collection of "many old medical books" owned by Dr. Benjamin Hart, an elderly physician in Bridgeport, Connecticut. "I recalled Dr. Hart as one who used to haunt the outside bookstalls of Book Row on Fourth Avenue," he wrote. "I had a clear image of him with his spectacles perched high on his forehead, rapidly skimming pages in the hope of finding material he was after." Driving up to Bridgeport, Cohen was taken "to an old inconspicuous brownstone on State Street," where "the books literally came out to greet us. The hall walls and stairway steps were perilously piled up with well-balanced books way above hand's reach. As we edged into the hall, made narrow by stacks of books on each side, we got glimpses of rooms with all walls completely shelved," and every shelf was stacked with two rows of books. This pattern continued throughout the spacious triple-decker. "Dust was everywhere. The closets had not been shelved but were solidly packed with books from floor to ceiling." Bathrooms has been converted to miniature libraries, aisles were clogged, and the doctor knew, or so his wife claimed, "just where to put his hands on anything he wants."

The building, it turned out, was once a combination home and office where Dr. Hart had conducted his medical practice, and the growing book collection had forced him to buy another house. Conducting a quick inventory, Cohen found much more than a "simple collection of old medical books," but a comprehensive library in many scientific fields. "The doctor simply had to buy any book he considered interesting and worthwhile, and his range was wide, embracing the sciences and humanities. Books on curious subjects abounded. Tattooing, beards, Rosicrucianism, Atlantis, zoology, cosmology, hypnotism, Arthurian legend, Egyptian magic, Greek philosophy, animal husbandry, folklore, and many others." Dr. Hart's principal concern was to get the books "into the hands of students, collectors, libraries, and book lovers who needed them for research and reference. He was also assured that if Argosy were the successful bidder, the books would be gone over with great care and all hurt books would be mended, all odd volumes brought together, and the ravages of time would be coped with by proper restoration."

Cohen decided straightaway that he "wanted the collection desperately and was determined to purchase it, regardless of the financial haggling it would surely entail." The problem was not money, since Dr. Hart found Cohen's offer for the 75,000 books attractive, but logistical. "The Argosy is not unlike many old bookshops. Books are double-shelved and crammed into every available space, under the tables, on the ledges, and occasionally on the chairs and ladders," a situation that pretty much describes the ambience today. It was agreed that Cohen would buy the books, and that he would be allowed to remove them over some time. Hoping to assimilate the books into his New York inventory in an orderly fashion, Cohen began making one trip a week to Bridgeport with his station wagon. "It was after the seventh or eighth trip that a calamity befell us." Mrs. Hart, the doctor's wife, informed Cohen that she had received an offer to sell the house and intended to accept it. All remaining books had to be removed immediately. "It was like the clap of doom. I had visions of moving those thousands of books to a warehouse, and then moving them again piecemeal to the store as we could absorb them."

Although he found the prospect of becoming a property owner in Bridgeport "appalling," Cohen wasted no time asking Mrs. Hart how much she had been offered, "exceeded it slightly" with an offer of his own, and the house was his. For the next two years, Cohen and his helpers removed the books at their leisure, "truckload after truckload, room after room." There were still fifteen tons of discarded books, about twenty thousand volumes, to deal with; he sold these for fifty cents per hundred pounds to "one ingenious dealer," who removed the volumes by throwing them out the windows into a "big open truck" parked on the sidewalk. The house was then offered for sale, and sold "within a few weeks at about the price I paid."

Cohen's daughters stress that there was never any pressure put upon them to enter the business, and that they all gravitated toward it in different ways. Judith, the oldest, and Adina, the youngest, both graduated from Cornell University in Ithaca, New York, with degrees in English, and Naomi majored in psychology at Simmons College in Boston. "I never really thought about my future," Adina said. "When I got out of college, Judy and Naomi were already working here. So I just kind of drifted in. It really wasn't thought out that thoroughly. Back in the 1950s and 1960s, a woman graduating from college had the choice of being a schoolteacher or a nurse. The three of us had the book business as an option, and it was something that we had all learned to love growing up. The conversation at home was always about the book business."

In his memoir, Cohen confessed to being elated at the path his daughters chose to follow, and that once involved in the business, he "conducted classes in the bookstore by going over new acquisitions with them. This daily occurrence has been going on for over fifteen years, and still goes on as a daily routine." These sessions generally involved discussions on determining value, and how certain books—many totally unknown to them—should be priced. "The purchasing of old books is the most difficult and exciting part of the book business," Cohen wrote. "The diversity of book titles and subjects, the different editions, bindings, issue points, color plate books, fine press books, sets, books printed on vellum, antiphonals, miniature books, presentation copies, early medical books, Americana, old atlases, antique maps, old prints, extra-illustrated books, books in black letter, incunabula, STC books [*Short Title Catalogue*, a standard British guide to works published in England, Scotland, and Ireland between 1475 and 1640], suggest a good variety of the material we handle." This "exposure to every conceivable kind of book," he maintained, gave his daughters "rich experience" and "enabled all three to buy expertly. Now they often correct me, and justifiably so."

Cohen's wife Ruth joined him at Argosy with far less fanfare than their three daughters. "Mother was originally a schoolteacher and came into the business kind of late," Lowry said. "She started coming in when my father bought Harry Stone's art gallery on Madison Avenue in 1955. Harry was getting on in years, and he decided to sell everything to us. We always had prints, but my father didn't know anything about American primitive paintings. So he called my mother and asked her, 'Can you come down right now? I have a job for you.' She came down from Washington Heights, where we lived. He told her, 'I just bought this gallery, and you're going to run it.' That's what she did, and she educated herself marvelously in the process."

As committed as the Cohen sisters are to maintaining their father's legacy, they are realistic when they consider the future, and the direction they choose to pursue will have nothing to do with the market value of their property. "What is changing the nature of the secondhand book business worldwide—and this has all happened in what seems like an instant—is the Internet," Lowry said in the spring of 2000. "We used to get a lot of accidental people coming in the store, people just walking by, and that has slacked off quite a bit. Our Internet business, on the other hand, is booming, and accounts for about 50 percent of our sales."

For years Argosy has maintained a stock of about 200,000 books, keeping the overflow in a Brooklyn warehouse. "Now we're gradually decreasing the inventory and concentrating more on higher-end material," Lowry said. "The problem is that we have fewer people calling with libraries for sale these days, and there is more competition among booksellers for the good stuff. Our advertisement in the Yellow Pages is still the best way to find people who are moving and want to get rid of their books. Overall we are buying fewer ordinary books these days, just good books. A good book is a book that we would price over a hundred dollars. On the other hand, books that have been on the shelf for thirty years, suddenly we are getting orders for them from all over the world, and that has been the delightful part of the Internet."

Despite the slowdown of foot traffic, Lowry said she and her sisters remain committed to serving their regular customers. "Why don't we just close and move to Brooklyn and operate a website from there? We can't do that. That wouldn't be fun. That would be like selling cans of peas. For us, it's not selling books if you don't have the contact with the customer. What keeps us going is the people who come in and look around and say, 'Thank God you're still here.' These are people who still want to touch the books."

The first known usage of the word *serendipity*—its provenance, in antiquarian terms—can be dated precisely to January 28, 1754. On that day Horace Walpole, a prolific eighteenth-century author remembered mostly now for the letters he posted to a wide range of interesting people, characterized an unexpectedly pleasant occurrence to one of his correspondents as typical "of that kind which I call Serendipity." Walpole cited his source for the coinage as *The Three Princes of Serendip*, an old Persian fairy tale in which the central characters are "always making discoveries, by accidents and sagacity, of things they were not in quest of."

Used as a noun, the word describes an experience that is not uncommon to people who pride themselves in being veteran book hunters. As a proper name, it captures with style and panache the spirit of a cavernous bookstore located at 1201 University Avenue in Berkeley, California, which has earned itself legendary status. Built in the 1960s as the head-quarters for a company that distributed wine-making equipment, the utilitarian building that is home today to Serendipity Books, Inc., was never meant to contain the 300,000 volumes that today occupy every inch of available floor space, but when viewed in one sweeping panorama from a catwalk on the second level, it is apparent just how triumphantly it serves the bold purpose of its owner, Peter B. Howard.

Ian Jackson, a friend and colleague of Howard's who lives a few blocks from his store in Berkeley, devoted the contents of two erudite guidebooks, both titled *The Key to Serendipity*, with advice on how to shop in the store, not all of it tongue-in-cheek. The subtitle to volume 1 is *How to Buy Books from Peter B. Howard*; to volume 2, *How to Find Books in Spite of Peter B. Howard*. The epigraph to the latter consists of an "interchange overheard at Serendipity Books" by Jackson:

> *Puzzled customer: Is there any rhyme or reason to this place?*
> *Peter B. Howard: Yes! My rhyme! My reason!*

"I am extremely mistrustful of bookstores that are neat as a pin," Howard told me one Friday morning while he was preparing to leave on a book-scouting foray to the East Coast that would include three days manning a booth at the Washington, D.C., International Antiquarian Book Fair. "There are numerous booksellers I know, people in fact who are my good friends, who keep their stores neat as a pin. What that means is that I may not like their bookstores as much as I like them. I like to see booksellers who are in the habit of having new arrivals. The books you see all around on the floor here are new arrivals, and new arrivals, as far as I am concerned, are the essence of the antiquarian book trade."

Howard has owned the freestanding building on University Avenue since 1986, and in that time he has secured warehouse space at three other locations sufficient to accommodate 100,000 additional books, giving him a general stock of some 400,000 volumes. During the 1990s Howard's gross sales averaged $1.75 million, most of it consummated by telephone, through the mails, on the Internet, and in person with dealers and private collectors. Despite all the sophisticated strategies required by the modern economy, Serendipity still is very much an open shop where customers are welcome to wander through bulging cases and cabinets arranged in rows, corners, cubbyholes, crossing angles, and improvised alcoves. They can even crank their way through a string of compact shelves installed against an outside wall, or climb ladders positioned among some of the taller stacks. During my most recent visit, three visitors from Japan took turns photographing each other among the books.

"Anyone is allowed to come in here during normal business hours and browse to their heart's content, so long as they leave us alone," Howard said. "If they seek our assistance, we will offer it to them. Otherwise, we have work to do. I do regard myself as a bookstore for the community, but the community itself does not provide a sufficiency of dollars by which I can keep my doors open. I have to keep all this going on an overhead of $40,000 a month or so, and it has been that way for a long time. My only desire is to continue. I don't have any goals other than to continue with dignity."

Because Serendipity is open to the public, there is an apparent scheme to everything. Howard invites visitors to determine what is available for themselves, although he will ask newcomers to identify their interests. "I have a sifting mechanism by which I do challenge anyone new who comes through the door to be interested in Serendipity, and the potential that is here for me to serve them." Pressed to characterize his holdings, Howard reluctantly offered the following summary, although severely compressed at best: "Everything is in perfect good order on shelves and it is alphabetical according to subject. I have a classics section. I have an American fiction since the war section, I have an Ernest Hemingway section, a Henry James section, a bibliography for sale section. I have a western Americana section, I have a broadside section, I have a Grace Livingston Hill section, I have a Faith Baldwin section, I have an American books in wrappers section, I have a Coleridge, Keats, and Shelley section, I have a Shakespeare section, a theater section, a film section, a poetry section, an anthology section, a literature in translation section; I have South American literature, Scandinavian, German, French, I have an Australian section along with New Zealand, I have a North Point Press section, I have a proof section." But since Howard abhors signs of any kind, none of these sections are labeled as such, a factor that contributes mightily to the serendipitous nature of an afternoon spent poking among his stacks.

In addition to the categories he rattled off to me, Howard also has literary manuscripts, screenplays, magazines, ephemera, archives, playbills, correspondence, fine printing, eighteen thousand volumes of American fiction from the library of the late Carter Burden—but before he could mention any of them, or any of the myriad others he has in storage, a prospective customer walked into the store and asked about a book that Howard knew instantly that he did not have. "I do not have a metaphysical section," he explained after the person had left. "It is not an area in which I have any particular knowledge or any deep interest. And those people have not been customers in the past that I have proven I could nurture."

On the matter of the scheme Howard applies to the science of selecting and shelving books, Ian Jackson offered this: "Mr. Howard's 'Logic' appears at best to mean no more than that two adjacent books are likely to be linked by some common element beyond their paper and type, but that this element may be indeterminate and ever-varying. This is one of the many reasons why one of the adjectives occasionally applied to Mr. Howard by friend and enemy is 'crazy.' In fact, in the course of the long and arduous researches required to prepare this book, I have encountered very few informants who have failed to use the word, if given time." Jackson quickly added his conviction that Howard probably is eccentric, but by no means "crazy."

When I asked Howard what most prepared him to be a bookseller, he immediately cited his education. "I was determined from early in high school to become a student of literature in American and English, to teach it." After graduating from Haverford College in Pennsylvania with a double major in biblical literature and English literature, he entered the University of California at Berkeley in 1960, earning an M.A. and continuing toward his doctorate. "I passed my tests in German, Old English, Middle English, Latin; I had French yet to go, and I had been advanced to candidacy. But in fact I was being wooed by the antiquarian book trade in ways that probably were unique to me. So I left school without a Ph.D."

Howard recalled that he had collected D. H. Lawrence while in college, so he knew his way around secondhand bookstores from an early age. As a graduate student, he found himself deriving a certain pleasure helping other students build their personal libraries: "I took greater joy in finding books for my colleagues than I did for myself." A defining year, he now believes, was in 1963, when he got his resale number from the state of California, proof positive that he had embarked on a lasting career.

Widely known for the candor with which he describes the quirky life of antiquarian booksellers, Howard insists that he is not an intellectual, his academic credentials notwithstanding. "The truth is that I am not preoccupied with ideas, and ideas do not monopolize my head time. I am preoccupied with the emotions associated with professional baseball, and the emotions associated with beginning, forming, shaping, and continuing to direct an evolving business." Howard's passion for baseball is made evident by the San Francisco Giants cap he wears at book fairs, and by the antique catcher's mask hanging among all the bookish relics and photographs in Serendipity. His feeling for the game is such that he was the subject of a feature article published in the *Wall Street Journal* on August 8, 1993, under the headline, "The Ninth Row's Happy Fan." In the article, Jane Vandenburgh wrote that Howard had owned the same season tickets on the third-base line at Candlestick Park "for as long as he can remember," and that he had "developed an articulate and elegant view of the game that continues to buoy him." Baseball, Vandenburgh wrote, gives Howard "everything—an understandable past, rules, reason, magic, beauty, a sense of justice and a complete world view, including an acquaintanceship with heaven and one with hell. It offers whatever a person might need: 'Even fun,' he adds sardonically, if 'fun' is what a person finds himself requiring."

Howard is served by a small staff of three assistants, and he buys all the books himself. "I know them all, I like to believe I do, yes," he said when asked if he has a sense of the 400,000 volumes in stock. "How well I know them is a measure of how good a bookseller I am. Others would say that I know them superficially, and often I will admit to that. That's not a question the bookseller usually welcomes; 'Have you read this book, do you know what this book is?' But I think I have a sufficient understanding of the books that I deal in. Sometimes I sell books before they get collated, but that's at the behest of the buyer, and when these books come back, I welcome them back with open arms. I am a servant of the community and have the responsibility to honor all of the opportunities that come about. I have always been willing to deal with the opportunity rather than saying no, and I have always learned to take them all rather than to take only the one."

Because he typically will "take them all," Howard often finds himself in possession of some books that he does not especially want or cannot sell. Those items he places outside in cardboard boxes in front of his store, where students from the University of California and street people from the community are free to help themselves.

The idea to call his business Serendipity was suggested by a friend of Howard's more than thirty years ago, "and it became a happy choice because of its obvious connotations. In fact, it mirrors the way I run the business in that I allow the books to choose me more than I allow myself the right to choose only the books I think I know. I certainly am governed by circumstance and opportunity and the needs of others more than by any wish of mine to prove that I can get the finest copies in the world of these particular books in order to offer them at the highest possible prices."

Two acquisitions dramatize just how much the book business depends on circumstance and opportunity. In 1991 Howard was offered an archive of materials that documented the activities of the California chapter of the National Association for the Advancement of Colored People (NAACP) from 1910 to 1940. The archive included 3.3 linear feet of correspondence, operational files, legal documents, and financial records maintained by Thomas M. Jackson, an Oakland grocer and recording secretary of the chapter for many years; he died in 1963. For Howard, the material represented "documentary history of the formation of consciousness in the African-American community in California," and he sold it to the Bancroft Library of the University of California, where it carries the designation BANC MSS 92/97. What makes the transference of this material particularly unusual is that it had been sent to the Berkeley landfill for disposal, and was rescued from certain oblivion by people who spotted it among the debris and offered it to Howard on consignment.

Similarly, he took possession in the late 1990s of 946 letters exchanged over a two-and-a-half-year period between Tamaki Tsubokura and David Hisato Yamate, a Japanese-American couple who met as teenagers at an internment camp in Utah in 1943 and then were separated, but maintained contact through the mail. They married in 1945 after their release. The letters document their relationship, and include other ephemeral items such as mimeographed leaflets for camp dances and immunization cards. "He immediately joined the American army, and they again wrote each other every day," Howard said.

"I am not aware that they had any children, but at the end of their lives the archive was thrown into the dump. It is a wonderful epistolary document of a moment in American history that has not generated a lot of glory for our country. They were kids in high school when they met. I can actually chart the day they met and how many times he danced with her. I believe it is the largest single internment-camp correspondence extant and that it has enormous historical and physical importance. It has its own integrity, and now I have the responsibility for making sure that it finds a proper home, since I split the profits with the source organization, to which I advanced some money." Howard finally placed the archive at the University of Utah, a "perfect fit" for the material, it turned out, since the Japanese internment camp where the couple met was located in that state, and the subject is of particular regional interest there.

A past president of the Antiquarian Booksellers Association of America (ABAA), Howard takes pride in having strengthened the practice of buying important private libraries in partnership with other dealers, a strategy he used with great success in 1989 to acquire for $445,000 the Carl Petersen Collection of William Faulkner material. His partners in that enterprise were Jeffrey H. Marks Rare Books of Rochester, New York; Transition Books of San Francisco; a colleague, Burton Weiss; and Howard's attorney, Gary Lepper. Howard wrote the 643-page catalog, which was intended to serve as both a price catalog and a temporary bibliography, based upon existing scholarship. More recently, he teamed up with Waiting for Godot Books of Hadley, Massachusetts, to acquire books from the library of Cleanth Brooks, the late professor of rhetoric at Yale University and a major proponent of New Criticism. Some of Brooks's books are listed on Howard's website.

Having observed his sixty-third birthday in 2001, Howard said he thinks often about the future of Serendipity, but he has no plans to stop or to slow down. He has two adult daughters, both nurses and neither interested in the antiquarian book trade. Ultimately he would like to see the business pass on to a trusted colleague, but if that possibility does not develop, then he is confident that "the books will be liquidated in ways customary to the book business, and the building will be sold for the benefit of my heirs." Bookstores, he said, "are extremely fragile things, and are almost always one-generational, at least in the United States. They reflect the personality of the founder. I have made my business so big and so complex that no one in their right mind but me would ever want to take the responsibility for it."

"Having said that," he quickly added, "if the availability of some library walks through the door right now, I'm very likely to be out the door in hot pursuit. All of the satisfaction for me is being part of a continuum in which books move from one place to another. My job is to orchestrate the continuum, to do so honorably, and to bring some pleasure to all parties. I am in the business of continuing to go on." And regardless of how dramatically buying-by-computer has changed the nature of the business, an essential factor in the equation, Howard stressed, is that he continue to maintain an open shop. "Book buying, book collecting, good reading, all together are an extraordinary element in self-education, in continuing education. An open shop provides the most wonderful—and the most endangered—venue by which I may be informed by my customers and my friends, and by which they may, perhaps, be touched by me."

The London Library at 14 St. James's Square enjoys a rich heritage that is best suggested by some portraits that decorate the Victorian staircase of its converted eighteenth-century town house. Most prominently displayed on the dark green wall is an image of Thomas Carlyle (1795–1881), the tempestuous sage, man of letters, and founding spirit of what is today the largest independent membership library in the world. Nearby are the likenesses of John Stuart Mill, Thomas H. Huxley, Rebecca West, T. S. Eliot, Herbert Spencer, Alfred, Lord Tennyson, Rudyard Kipling, William Makepeace Thackeray, Dame Veronica Wedgwood, and the prime ministers William Gladstone and Arthur Balfour, all former members.

The principle articulated so passionately by these notables, that the library devote itself to collecting and making readily available "the best that has been thought and said" through history to its corps of subscribing members, remains intact to this day. "A good friend does not change, nor does the London Library," Lord David Cecil (1902–1986), the Oxford professor of English literature and author of a magisterial biography of Lord Melbourne, asserted. The writer John Wells paid tribute to the institution and its enduring principles in a discursive history he called *Rude Words*. When the library was celebrating its 150th anniversary in 1991, the eminent diarist Frances Partridge, the last survivor of the Bloomsbury circle, placed her judgment clearly on the record. "Nothing has changed," she told Wells—and she had known the library at that point for seventy years—"absolutely nothing. The same smell, the same atmosphere, the same clanking noise as you walk through those long passages at the back, and you always seem to meet someone you want to meet."

With the creation of a website and the inevitable transition to an electronic catalog undertaken in the late 1990s, the library is keeping pace with the times, but members have been assured that the distinctively quirky scheme for placement of the books will remain intact. "The truth is that many changes have taken place," the current librarian, Alan Bell, acknowledged in an interview, "but they have been so discreet as to be almost imperceptible." Membership, for one thing, is far more democratic now than it was in the early years, although a mildly liberal bent is part of the library's tradition; women have always been welcomed as equals. Today, a candidate for admission does not have to be proposed by a member and vetted by a selection committee, although character references are still required. "We've got to satisfy ourselves of people's bona fides," Bell said. "But we are very much open in that way, because we are a recognized charity." Dues are £150 a year, or about $220; currently, there are 8,400 members.

Several independent institutions in the United States can claim counterpart status to the London Library, most notably the Library Company of Philadelphia, founded in 1731 by Benjamin Franklin; the Redwood

Library, established in 1747 in Newport, Rhode Island, and still housed in the original building; the New York Society Library, established in 1754; and the Boston Athenæum, founded in 1807 on Beacon Hill and located in one of the most beautiful neo-Palladian buildings in the United States, made doubly beautiful by a $20 million face-lift expected to be completed in 2002.

Sir Leslie Stephen, editor of the monumental reference work *Dictionary of National Biography*, was president of the London Library from 1898 to 1902. Although his daughter, Virginia Woolf, was a member for forty years, she expressed ambivalence about the clubbish atmosphere and declined E. M. Forster's offer to nominate her for membership on the governing committee. A number of famous authors have used the library as props in their books over the years. Arthur Conan Doyle dispatched Dr. Watson to its stacks once to brush up on Chinese pottery, and Ian Fleming sent James Bond there in *On Her Majesty's Secret Service* for some quick research. The Booker Prize–winning novelist A. S. Byatt, a recent member of the governing committee, set the opening scene of her 1991 novel *Possession* in the main reading room, where one of her principal characters, a young scholar named Roland Mitchell, begins his inquiries into the life of one Randolph Henry Ash, a fictional poet cut in the mold of Robert Browning.

"The London Library was Roland's favourite place," Byatt wrote, and then explained why, with reasons that in all likelihood parallel her own. "It was shabby but civilized, alive with history but inhabited also by living poets and thinkers who could be found squatting on the slotted metal floors of the stacks, or arguing pleasantly at the turning of the stair. Here Carlyle had come, here George Eliot had progressed through the bookshelves. Roland saw her black skirts, her velvet trains, sweeping compressed between the Fathers of the Church, and heard her firm foot ring on metal among the German poets." Byatt characterized the shelving arrangement of the library's books, which today number about a million volumes, as "felicitous alphabetical conjunctions" inserted in various subject groups like "Science and Miscellaneous," and then offered a few typical examples: "Dancing, Deaf and Dumb, Death, Dentistry, Devil and Demonology, Distribution, Dogs, Domestic Servants, Dreams." This agreeably eccentric system, she pointed out, once catalogued "Evolution" under "Pre-Adamite Man." But it is precisely these "felicitous alphabetical conjunctions" that make book-hunting in the London Library such an intellectual adventure. The scheme was elaborated and refined during the long tenure of Charles Hagberg Wright, librarian from 1892 until his death in 1940. In *Rude Words*, Wells described the morning in 1944 after a German bomb took the roof off the library, exposed a twisting cluster of steel girders to the sky, and ignited a fast-spreading fire that caused the destruction of sixteen thousand books. "We've lost our 'Religion,' " one library member is said to have reported sadly after examining the gutted top floor.

"What Carlyle was after in the 1840s," Bell told me, "was a library that would have 'serious literature,' as he put it, and not the same stock as the commercial circulating libraries popular at that time, which essentially were loan facilities for three-decker novels and entertaining literature. He was looking for more substantial material that would accommodate a great store of knowledge, which would be accessible to readers in the sense of being 'browseable' and 'borrowable.' These two aspects of the founder's wishes have been in our mind ever since."

Because books are assigned to broad subject groups, members can prowl through a seemingly endless cluster of shelves and indulge themselves in the joys and surprises of good fortune. "It is possible to do a great deal of what might be called associative browsing," Bell said. "A lot of people actually don't use our subject catalogs at all; they prefer to look on the shelves and see what they will find. You may go into the stacks looking for a single book by an English author on a particular theme, and then you might find alphabetically near it a French one that is more recent and more authoritative that you perhaps didn't know existed. That sort of browsing is very good. It is all part of the accessibility of the library."

Occasionally, minor but nonetheless nettlesome problems develop in matters of perceived impropriety. Bell cited the example of "Women," which is shelved in the creaky stacks with "Wine" and "Witchcraft, See also Occult Sciences" on one side, and "Wool" and "Yachting" on the other. "There are some people who think this is demeaning in some way, but it's not. The whole concept of what the Victorians regarded as the woman question—works of John Stuart Mill, for instance—is there, and it goes up to Susan Sontag and so forth, all in one alphabetical sequence." With such a grouping, Bell continued, readers are able to employ "a sort of mental cross-referencing, which is very good indeed. And 'Women,' let me add, is a subject that has been consistently kept up over the years. 'Wine,' for example, is not; we haven't collected systematically there, and of course wine is now a matter of scholarship rather than just miscellaneous information. So looking there, it's higgledy-piggledy, but under 'Women,' it's actually, historiographically, quite a major accumulation. And I think Carlyle would approve of that. I think his wife would too."

To truly appreciate why Carlyle would approve of such accessibility is to appreciate the circumstances under which the library was formed in 1841. Carlyle had been a regular reader at the library of the British Museum, now known as the British Library, from the time he moved to London from Scotland in 1831, and in particular a few years later when he began working on his biography of Oliver Cromwell. A meticulous researcher, he grew increasingly frustrated by the unwillingness of officials to provide him with what he considered an agreeable place to read, and the rule prohibiting him from taking books out on loan to study in his house. The famous domed reading room, which closed when the British Library moved from Russell Street to its new home in St. Pancras, was still more than twenty years away from completion, and Carlyle, as John Wells made clear, "was not a man to suffer with the common herd." He was not someone, in other words, who took much pleasure in sitting uncomfortably on the floor or perching himself on a ladder.

Support for an independent library came quickly, with shares selling at

£10 each. Carlyle determined he would need two hundred members to get started, each paying an annual subscription of £5, to keep the operation going. Charles Dickens was among the founder members. The earl of Clarendon was the first president, William Makepeace Thackeray the first auditor. Because the books are of a more serious nature and conducive to research, the library has always been popular with writers, especially those not affiliated with academic institutions. The quaint Reading Room, with its terra-cotta walls and its famous notice "Silence Is Requested," is a blessedly congenial place to pursue a line of thought, and the library is made even more accommodating by borrowing terms that allow members to take out up to ten books at a time, even more by special arrangement.

"We lend out books for quite considerable periods, so long as people renew them," Bell said. "They can have them out oftentimes for the duration of a biographical project, maybe the background reading essential for a historical novel or something like that. This lending policy is quite good for the encouragement of research or in-depth reading, by which I mean serious reading that is not geared by the requirements of academic research or the pursuit of degrees or for actual publication." But there is a disadvantage in that members sometimes "do get possessive" of certain books, and it can be difficult to extricate them from their homes.

"We are not a club," stressed Bell, who came to the London Library in 1993 from the Rhodes House Library at Oxford University, where he had been librarian. "We don't give lectures, we have no education program, we don't have afternoon tea, and there is an ancient notice in the Reading Room stating that silence is requested, and that admonition is normally obeyed. You can guarantee that you are not going to be disturbed there. Many of the people you see in that room come regularly, sometimes daily, and some do their writing there. They regard it in a way as their writing office. I'm not going to be naming names, but I can think of two novelists who came here and actually wrote their fictional works in the Reading Room, because it was very different from working in their faculty offices."

The day before I paid my first visit to the library, I interviewed the author Penelope Fitzgerald in her North London flat to discuss *The Blue Flower,* a widely praised novel based on the life of the German Romantic poet Friedrich Leopold von Hardenberg, known by the pseudonym Novalis. To get sufficient background for the project, Fitzgerald spent two years translating all of the poet's correspondence from German into English. She had found the letters in the London Library. "There never would have been a novel if they had asked me to return the books right away," she told me.

Simon Winchester, a noted travel writer and author of *The Professor and the Madman,* a marvelous book released in 1998 about the considerable contributions a murderer confined to a lunatic asylum in England made to the *Oxford English Dictionary,* told me how he once went into the London Library to find the third volume of a work he described as a Royal Navy intelligence survey of the Pacific. "I asked for the book at the front desk, and the chap there said, 'I think I do know who has it, a woman who lives in Devon, and she's had it since 1958. I'll ring her up.' This was in 1988; she had it out for thirty years."

Bell said stories like these are commonplace. "It is amazing what books people will want, however strange they may be to some sensibilities, however dull they may seem." Although not by definition a research facility, it is a library "that provides for research," he continued. And while a number of books in the collections are rare, they achieve that status simply by having been on the shelves for long periods of time.

"We have acquired books that have become rare over the years, and this occasionally leads to difficulties. It is possible, for example, to borrow Trollope first editions to read. We lend them out, but you've got to sign a guarantee form acknowledging that they are of special value." Because many of these books have been re-bound several times over the years, they have little desirability on the open market. "To a collector they have no commercial value at all, but they do have value to scholars as original texts, though by no means are they in their original condition," Bell said.

As popular as the London Library is among writers and scholars, Bell said a diverse cross section of people is represented. He indicated a bookcase in his office that contains every application for membership submitted since the mid-nineteenth century, all bound in cloth. "Anybody picking up those books and knowing something about British social and literary life in the last century and a half would be able to find something resonant just by turning the pages," he said. "But what I would like to do is find out the number of people that rely on us for reading. Reading for pleasure, reading for information, rather than for writing, and that is quite the distinction to make. That, unfortunately, is not something you can work out from membership applications."

Many members now use computers to locate information on the Internet, but they still must arrive early to be assured of a seat at one of the twenty tables in the Reading Room. Laptops are not allowed there, but they can be used in a smaller room where outlets have been installed, and where several terminals are available for computer searches. For those who worry about too much change taking place too quickly, closing time is still announced each afternoon by the ringing of a bell, and that is accomplished as it has always been—by hand.

As eccentrically Victorian as the London Library may be, it is a third-millennium dynamo when compared to Skokloster Slott, a baroque palace that contains a fourth-floor assemblage of books so totally untouched over the past three and a half centuries that its very existence remains virtually unknown outside Sweden. I heard about this extraordinary collection while visiting one of the most beautiful book rooms to be seen anywhere, the Bernadotte Library in the Swedish Royal Palace in Stockholm, and again while being shown through the 200,000-volume Nobel Library, the repository of every book gathered since 1901 to determine which author would receive the most prestigious award in all of literature. My hosts at both libraries told me I would be terribly remiss if I failed to spend a day in Skokloster, just thirty-five miles northwest of the capital, and were instrumental in arranging a guided introduction for me on very short notice.

Skokloster Slott—*slott* means "palace"—was built in the mid-1660s on an island on the Sko peninsula once occupied by a thirteenth-century nunnery that had been seized by the crown when Sweden converted to Lutheranism in the sixteenth century. In 1611 King Karl IX ceded the estate to Herman Wrangel, a twenty-four-year-old Estonian nobleman who had helped Sweden establish close ties with the Baltic states. Wrangel prospered under royal patronage, rising from governor of the district to the rank of field marshal. His son and heir, Carl Gustav Wrangel, distinguished himself in numerous foreign adventures, serving at one point as governor-general of Swedish Pomerania. These were prosperous times for Sweden, which had recently emerged from the Thirty Years' War as a victorious military power, and spoils of war were very much a way of life; the powerful were not at all shy about claiming exquisite materials for their own pleasure. "Send me the library and the curiosities," Queen Christina, one of the great bibliophiles of all time, wrote to her commander in Czechoslovakia when informed in 1648 that her army had taken Prague. "You know they are the only things I value."

Flush with wealth, and accustomed to entertaining in grand style, Carl Gustav Wrangel (1613–1676) spared no expense in building what has been described as the ultimate trophy for the Swedish nouveau riche. An amateur architect to boot, Wrangel closely supervised construction of the showplace, which began in 1654, the same year that Queen Christina abdicated her throne, moved to Rome, converted to Catholicism, and brought her fabulous library along with her in a sumptuous wagon train as a gift to the Vatican. Wrangel had some wonderful books too, and to go along with them he had huge collections of muskets, suits of armor, and countless curiosities gathered during his military travels, a good many of them brought home for deposit in what became a "curio cabinet of wonders" at Skokloster. Today the stone castle endures almost exactly as it was conceived, complete with original artworks, fixtures, gilded leather wall coverings, furnishings, kitchenware, domestic implements, tools, even the privies and camber stools. More than twenty thousand books and ten thousand prints accumulated by several generations of affluent occupants are stored in their original shelves in the upstairs library. Only the manuscripts have been removed; they have been kept in the National Record Office since 1980.

Skokloster Slott remained privately owned well into the twentieth century and was finally acquired by the Swedish government in 1967. Walls have been cleaned and lightly touched up where necessary, but everything remains the way it has always been. Among the highlights are the various armories kept by successive owners, most prominent among them a tower room installed in 1669 featuring dozens of seventeenth-century handguns and rifles. Equally fascinating is an unfinished banquet hall, left exactly the way it was when Carl Gustav Wrangel died in 1676, prompting workers fearful of not being paid their wages to walk off the job. Uncovered ceiling beams and untiled floorboards remain fully exposed, carpenter's ladders and scaffolding still climb up the walls, and antique lathes, hammers, and saws lie where they were left more than three hundred years ago, a unique collection.

An easy ride from Stockholm to the south and Uppsala to the west, Skokloster is popular among tourists, although the seven library rooms on the top floor, each bearing the name of a European city and each containing books and prints gathered by the castle's various occupants, are closed to the public. My guide was Elisabeth Westin Berg, curator of the collection since 1978. The gray October morning, crisp, cool, and drizzly, made the wearing of sweaters and coats mandatory, even while inside Skokloster, where there is no central heating, and no electricity in the library. The only light inside these rooms comes from the windows, all of which face the east. "The combination of cold air and good circulation has been surprisingly healthy for the books," Westin Berg said as she pulled out volume after volume for me to examine.

The most treasured item in the library is Saint Birgitta's (Saint Bridget's) *Revelations* (1492), one of only five known copies of the title printed on vellum. The collection includes books published between 1466 and 1840, most of them dated between 1550 and 1750. The oldest book in the library is a copy of Cicero's *De officiis,* printed in 1466 on vellum in Mainz by Johann Fust, a financial backer of Johannes Gutenberg and one of his successors. On the back pastedown, the resident-owner of Skokloster who acquired this book, Carl Gustav Bielke (1683–1754), wrote that the precious incunable was a gift, and that he had authorized a new binding. Bielke bought actively at auctions in Stockholm and Uppsala and took deliberate steps to maintain the integrity of the collection.

Westin Berg primarily concerns herself these days with determining provenance, and she expressed hope that in time a catalog of the library will be available on the World Wide Web. The collection covers subject areas ranging from theology, history, constitutional law, topography, and technology to architecture, astronomy, exploration, and philosophy. "The intellectual landscape of Sweden over a particular period of time is represented here," she said, noting that where books acquired by professors and educators were often dispersed when their owners died, books owned by the nobility generally were passed on from generation to generation. In the case of Skokloster, family ownership extended well into the twentieth century. "We can determine to a great extent the ideas and the thoughts available to these people and what kinds of things interested them by studying the books in this library. That is why the provenance is so important. By knowing which generation brought in which books, we can speculate about the reading interests of different people at different periods of time."

The rooms contain a number of marvelous maps, globes, and atlases, each one unmistakably a rarity. Books are shelved in cases latticed with wooden grids. Delicate paintings of various plants and animals decorate the walls. Ceiling beams are painted gaily with ribbons, flowers, and ornaments in many colors, and the pine floors date from the construction of the castle. One of Wrangel's seventeenth-century books, *Architectura Recreationis,* by the German Josef Furttenbach, stipulates an eastern exposure as best for a room that will store books—precisely the arrangement incorporated in the design of Skokloster.

As a total surprise, I also encountered a sixteenth-century painting known to book lovers the world over, a wacky construction of a librarian fashioned from books by Giuseppe Arcimboldo (1527–1593). The Italian painter's other bizarre compositions of human forms include portraits painted from arrangements of fruits, flowers, and vegetables. G. P. Harsdörfer's wood engraving based on the painting of the librarian appears on the back dustjacket of my book *A Gentle Madness.* How, I wondered, did the original of this famous painting enter the castle's collections, and where did it come from? Westin Berg shrugged, noting that the question applies to many of the materials entrusted to her care. "We simply don't know," she said. "Quite possibly it was war booty."

5.

PROFILES IN
BIBLIOPHAGIA

I began my life as I shall no doubt end it: amidst books. In my grand-father's study there were books everywhere. It was forbidden to dust them, except once a year, before the beginning of October term. Though I did not yet know how to read, I already revered those standing stones: upright or leaning over, close together like bricks on the book-shelves or spaced out nobly in lanes of menhirs. I felt that our family's prosperity depended on them. They all looked alike. I disported myself in a tiny sanctuary surrounded by ancient, heavy-set monuments which had seen me into the world, which would see me out of it, and whose permanence guaranteed me a future as calm as the past.

—Jean-Paul Sartre, The Words

Before taking up residence in a sprawling suite of rooms over-looking the historic Castello Sforzesco fortress in a picturesque district of Milan, Umberto Eco had twice been forced to give up comfortable quarters elsewhere because he owned too many books. "The floors were about to collapse," the world-renowned semiotician, medievalist, philosopher, essayist, educator, cultural critic, and author of three best-selling novels said as we walked about the beautifully appointed apartment where he and his wife, Renate, are surrounded by thirty thousand volumes, and where the concept of a personal library takes on an almost bewildering aspect. The floors in the stone-faced building Eco now calls home, once an elegant hotel, were constructed to bear considerable weight loads; the ceilings, moreover, are high, allowing the placement of shelves that can accommodate eleven tiers of books. To help him reach the highest levels, Eco had several ladders mounted on steel tracks that move effortlessly from room to room. His own writing is done at the rear of the apartment in a secluded cove surrounded by another complex of bookcases, arranged almost like a fantastical maze. Eco insisted that I note the depth of the shelves, which had been designed to his specifications. A quick examination indicated about nine inches of space, just enough room for one book per slot. "No more guessing," he said, arching his eyebrows for emphasis. "Never again will I have two books deep. Never. Now I can see every title I have at a glance. Everything is in a single line."

The day before Eco welcomed me and my wife into his home to talk about books, writing, and the passion for reading, we met with the greatly admired Italian bookseller Carlo Alberto Chiesa and his gracious wife, Elena. "Are you planning to see Umberto Eco?" Chiesa asked during a memorable Milanese lunch of pasta, sautéed medallions of veal with braised baby artichoke hearts, and a chestnut *torta* that can only be described as sublime. When told that such an appointment was scheduled for the next afternoon, Chiesa said simply, "You will be overwhelmed by what you see. This is a man who surrounds himself with books, and he does this for the knowledge they contain. He consumes them."

Eco smiled when I asked his reaction to that comment, then shrugged and nodded toward a softly illuminated glass exhibition case in his living room where a dozen rarities were on display, as much for his own pleasure as for visitors to his home. His rare-book collection, which includes several choice incunabula, a fully rubricated *De Civitate Dei*, and a splendid *Divine Comedy*, are kept in a small study apart from the working library that engulfs the rest of his residence. "I am not one of those collectors who keeps the books closed and in secret; when I need them, I open them, I handle them. Every fifteen days I make a selection that follows a certain theme, and I put them in that cabinet. You don't have to tell me that leaving them exposed to the light for fifteen days or more is not so good. I know that already, okay? Fine. But so what? I don't care."

As a collector, Eco's primary focus reflects his broad interests as scholar, educator, and probing intellectual. He has a name for his collection, which he wrote into my notebook, and which summarizes his antiquarian interests: "Biblioteca Semiologica, Curiosa, Lunatica, Magica et Pneumatica." The *semiologica*, he then explained, concerns science, symbols, and "strange" languages; the *curiosa* is there "because it must be curious"; *lunatica*, "because I don't collect serious science, only old science, alchemy, and things of a cabalistic nature"; and *pneumatica*, which, according to the *Oxford English Dictionary*, relates in an ancient Greek sense to inquiries of the spirit or to spiritual existence, and in gnostic theology to a spiritual being of higher order. In English universities during the seventeenth and eighteenth centuries, pneumatics was frequently presented in opposition to physics as a form of metaphysics, and was used to classify a "doctrine of spirits." The word also has been used to describe an early form of medicine, altogether a rich area to pursue as a collectible category.

A highlight of our afternoon visit with Eco was the guided tour he offered of his library, and the generous opportunity he allowed us to handle some of his choicest items. Of particular interest to me was a book Eco does not include among his most valuable possessions, but which he told me about in 1995 when we met for the first time in Boston to discuss his third novel, *The Island of the Day Before*, which had just been released in the United States. During that interview, our conversation inevitably turned to the writing of his first novel, *The Name of the Rose*, the medieval detective story set in a prosperous Italian abbey that transformed this highly respected professor of semiotics at the University of Bologna into an international celebrity. More than 9 million copies of the book have been sold in a spate of languages since then, and a film starring Sean Connery as the intrepid detective, Brother William of Baskerville, has entertained viewers worldwide. As Eco has explained in *Postscript to the Name of the Rose*, he began writing the novel in 1978 "prodded by a single idea: I felt like poisoning a monk. I believe a novel is always born of an idea like this: the rest is flesh that is added along the way. The idea must have originated even earlier."

Toward the end of *The Name of the Rose*, William of Baskerville points out that a solution to the deadly mystery "turns on the theft and possession of a book." The instrument of murder, we finally learn, is a poison cleverly implanted on the pages of a lost text of Aristotle's *Poetics*, placed there to be consumed by unwary readers foolish enough to lick their fingers while leafing through the mysterious volume. When examined finally by William of Baskerville—attentive readers should note the playful reference to Sherlock Holmes—the lethal book is described as having some pages "almost worn away, with a part of the margin consumed, spattered with pale stains, such as time and dampness usually produce on other books," while other pages toward the back are stuck together near the upper corner by a "kind of sticky paste."

In our first interview, Eco explained that when he and his wife were preparing to move from Bologna to Milan in 1990, he found in an upper shelf of their old apartment a sixteenth-century Italian translation of the *Poetics* of Aristotle. "As a collector, it has become my custom to write down the price, the size, and a physical description of every book I buy; I indicate if there are stains, wormholes, whatever. The point to be made here is that I didn't know I had this book. So I opened it, and here was written, in pencil, 1,000, which is one thousand lire, seventy cents. So probably twenty years before, I found this book someplace for seventy cents, and I bought it."

Eco decided at that point to write a bibliographic description of the book, and as he examined its contents, he discovered that in the last section the sixteenth-century Italian translator had attempted a reconstruction of the lost second book of the *Poetics*. "As I was writing my findings, I was obliged to say, 'Water stains, exaggeratedly soiled, the inferior margins are cropped, the pages are stuck together at the back.' It was *exactly* the book I had described in *Name of the Rose*! It was not a manuscript, it was a printed book, but the physical description was exactly the same, and the subject was the same. And the last two pages, really, it was disgusting to handle, as if they were poisoned. So it means that I bought this book for seventy cents, I realized it was too soiled and unpleasant to touch, and I put it away someplace and forgot all about it." As events turned out, of course, he had not forgotten about the book at all; he had "photographed" it with his eyes and subconsciously stored it away in his mind for future reference. "Twenty years later, I believed I had invented a manuscript for this novel, when in fact I was describing that ugly book in my own house." He tapped on his forehead, and smiled his jolliest of smiles. "I had it here all the time."

Yet ugly as this book may be—and when he withdrew it from a bottom shelf in his study, an examination did reveal a particularly unpleasant volume—it enjoys an honored place in Eco's inner sanctum. "Sometimes the forgotten book is the most important book you can have," he said. "At first glance, it is inexplicable that you have this book for twenty years, you have never read it, but when you pick it up and you open it, you understand that you know everything about that book you need to know." One explanation for this, he suggested halfheartedly, "is that there is some magnetic force by which, having touched the book so many times, you have sucked up this information. But the real explanation is that by picking it up and moving it around several times, you have opened it, and in the meantime you have read other books that are addressing the same subject; then you realize that you know the book without actually having read it. It is a phenomenon that happens to me all the time." After putting that volume away, Eco retrieved a totally "manufactured" volume of Aristotle, an impressive folio with wounded pages and unsightly stains that was used as a prop in the making of the 1986 film of *The Name of the*

Rose, and the only souvenir he has from the production set, where he served as technical adviser.

Not only did becoming a celebrated novelist occasion a dramatic change in Eco's life, it was the catalyst that enabled him to become a serious book collector. "I started to collect books late in my life for the simple reason that after *The Name of the Rose* was published, I had more money. Second, I felt that since I got money because of the book, it seemed morally correct to use some of it on books." Among his early acquisitions were about two thousand volumes dealing with such topics as occultism, alchemy, and invented languages. "I ransacked all the bookshops in at least ten cities in Italy, France, and America," he was pleased to report, and quickly noted that the material was put to good use in the development of *Foucault's Pendulum,* a mammoth novel of ideas published in 1989 that benefited enormously from these highly specialized acquisitions. "Even though it had nothing to do with my collection, I later bought certain things of geography, navigation, cartography, the formulation of longitude," resources he drew on when he wrote *The Island of the Day Before,* which is set in the Pacific Ocean on the international dateline.

The tons of other books in Eco's house, by contrast, are the everyday tools of his profession. "Most of them, I must tell you, I get for free," he said, offering a big grin. "In America, an author is entitled to send, what, twenty books out to his colleagues? Here in Europe you are allowed to send two hundred. So I receive an enormous quantity of books from people who want me to see their books for whatever reason. Of course I cannot keep all of them, and now I have a strict rule. There are thirty thousand books in this house, and thirty thousand it will remain. I have a transit area just for books in this category, and every six months I decide what stays, and what goes."

Those judged expendable, however, are not necessarily deaccessioned entirely. "Okay, so I still have an apartment in Bologna, and a lot of books go there, and I have a flat in Paris, and the French books I can send there." Then there is a summer house in the hills near Rimini, a seventeenth-century manor that once served as a Jesuit school, where other rejects from the Milan shelves are sent to find a new life; very few books, he acknowledged, are banished altogether from his custody. "It isn't easy," he allowed between deep drags from an ever-present cigarette. "But I did send some boxes the other day over to the local prison for their amusement."

In addition to his novels, Eco has written thirty other books on a variety of subjects, with titles that range from *The Aesthetics of Thomas Aquinas, Art and Beauty in the Middle Ages,* and *Apocalypse Postponed* to *A Theory of Semiotics, Travels in Hyper Reality,* and *The Search for the Perfect Language.* He has received honorary degrees from universities throughout the world, and he is in constant demand as a speaker and participant at scholarly symposiums.

When I asked Eco if he could give a painless definition of semiotics, he began by citing a book titled *How to Travel.* "Chapter eleven is how to travel with children, and the text is, 'Don't.' So how to explain semiotics in a few words, the answer is, 'Don't.' But let me offer this: semiotics is interested in all those devices we use in our everyday life to make something present which is not there. It deals with the activities by which we use something present—a word, an image, an object—in order to tell you something which is not there." When people speak of God, or parents, or Ireland, or Antarctica, for instance, "we can do it through words, or maps, or through a photograph—it is our common human activity to go continuously beyond the limits of crude physical presence. Semiotics is interested in all of this, and in trying to see if there is a unified set of intellectual instruments in order to analyze those phenomena. Today semiotics is interested in research in artificial intelligence, in computer science, with so-called cognitive studies. We frequently have meetings with neurologists, psychologists, and the like."

When Eco writes about these subjects, his audience—and the language he uses—is decidedly different from that for his fiction, or for essays and articles he submits to general-readership magazines and newspapers, as he does often. Here, for instance, is a typical paragraph from *The Role of the Reader: Explorations in the Semiotics of Texts,* in which he discusses his concept of the "model" reader:

> *A more reasonable picture of the whole semantico-pragmatic process would take the form (Figure 0.2) already proposed in* Theory, *where, even disregarding both the rightmost quarter of the square (all the 'aberrant' presuppositions) and the lower components (circumstances orienting or deviating the presuppositions), the notion of a crystal-like textual object is abundantly cast in doubt.*

Here, he discusses "the analysis of meaning":

> *According to the principles of compositional analysis, a semiotic expression (be it a verbal item or any type of physical utterance) conveys, according to linguistic conventions, an organized and analyzable content, formed by the aggregation (or hierarchy) of semantic features. These features constitute a system, either closed or open, and belong to different contents of different expressions in different arrangements. Compositional analysis should describe and define a virtually infinite number of contents by means of a possibly finite ensemble of features, but this exigency of economy gives rise to many aporias.*

Nobody could possibly confuse that prose with the style he has assumed in his novels. "In a book," he explained in our first interview, "you are building up your readers, you are designing a possible reader, and then the model reader is the one who plays your game." Writing fiction, he stressed, is a "duel" with the audience. "I also like to use the word 'seduction.' I am accustomed to lecturing as a university professor, this is my job. Every time I start a class with my students, I feel as if it were the first time, even though they are not a new audience by any means. Yet I feel every time that if I don't capture them in the first five minutes, I am lost."

Eco admits that one of the reasons he decided to try his hand at writing a mystery novel when he was almost fifty years old involved little more than a challenge to himself to see if he could do it, and to experiment with the "open text" concept he has developed that invites readers to formulate their own interpretations. "I had no expectations at all for *Name of the Rose*. My wildest dreams when writing it were, 'Let's see if I can sell ten thousand copies.' " It was a similar act of literary chutzpah that prompted Eco to open *Foucault's Pendulum* with a piece of Hebrew text, followed in due course by the narrator's keen interpretation. "I do not speak Hebrew, so it was a challenge to the reader: Do you want to play the game? If so, you must accept me this way. No? Then go. To stay, you must play the game."

As he approached his seventieth birthday in 1998, Maurice Sendak found himself reflecting often about art, the wellsprings of imagination, and the impulse to create beautiful things. On the afternoon that we met in his house in the Connecticut countryside, the celebrated author and artist of children's books was thinking about the death a few days earlier of the great Russian pianist Svyatoslav Richter, and the incalculable wealth of musical information stored in the maestro's mind that had perished with him. "Richter was legendary for having memorized a massive classical repertory, all the Haydn, Beethoven, Schubert, Prokofiev, Mozart sonatas and piano works," Sendak said. "And then he dies, and poof, all his brilliant thoughts go with him. The library in Richter's head is gone. That scares me. Where does all that knowledge go?"

The concept of creating a "cerebral catalog" is central to Sendak's outlook on life. Following the death of his brother, Jack, in 1996, he found himself being consumed more and more with the plays and sonnets of William Shakespeare and the exquisite poems of John Keats, two canonical figures of extraordinary depth he had shied away from confronting during a lifetime of voracious reading. "I had been intimidated from taking them on by the lack of a college education, by a presumption I had that my lack of formal instruction meant that these two great masters were beyond me. But since the traumatic loss of my brother, I find that I'm getting over that reticence, and I have been reading Shakespeare and Keats with a vengeance. The purpose in reading them is to find what I'm looking for in *myself*. That's how I've always done it. When I am illustrating, I look at William Blake, or Goya, always with the joy of looking at their work, but also with the motivation that I will find myself in *them*, that I will take what I find, and I will use it for my own purposes." To appreciate that quality in Sendak's artistic approach—that he searches for what is vital in himself by absorbing the essence of other artists and writers—is to understand the forces that make his creative juices flow so copiously. "I am a living sieve," he said. "Everything I touch, everything I see, smell, and hear, goes through me."

In a career that has spanned five decades, Sendak has produced illustrations for close to ninety books. For a dozen of these he also wrote the texts, elevating them to an elite category within his own corpus that he calls "picture books." Sendak classifies the other projects he illustrates as "story books," meaning that his responsibility is strictly one of "adding something" to narratives someone else has written. Sendak's best-known "picture books"—*Where the Wild Things Are* (1963), *In the Night Kitchen* (1970), and *Outside Over There* (1981)—are creations that he says are fused as tightly as an opera's libretto and its music, combining to produce a performance that is greater than the sum of its parts. Such musical imagery animates his conversations about his work. Although he writes his stories in silence, when drawing he always listens to music. "I find something uncanny in the way a musical phrase, a sensuous vocal line, or a patch of Wagnerian color will clarify an entire approach or style for a new work," he once wrote.

In 1970 Sendak became the first American to receive the Hans Christian Andersen Award, a prize given every two years by the International Board on Books for Young People, and considered the world's most prestigious prize in children's literature. Altogether, his work has appeared in sixteen languages and sold many millions of copies worldwide, 3 million alone for the English-language edition of *Where the Wild Things Are*. Not long after Sendak won the Caldecott Medal in 1964 for that book, Brian O'Doherty, the art critic for the *New York Times*, declared him to be "one of the most powerful men in the United States" in that he had the capacity to give "shape to the fantasies of millions of children—an awful responsibility." On January 10, 1997, President Bill Clinton echoed those sentiments when he presented Sendak with the National Medal of Arts. "His books have helped children to explore and resolve their feelings of anger, boredom, fear, frustration, and jealousy," the president said. Clinton joked that before the presentation ceremony began, Sendak had told him privately that "this is my first grown-up award," a wry comment on the tendency of some critics to categorize his work as "children's literature," suggesting, in a way, that the books he creates belong in a genre limited to young readers.

"I care about children a great deal," Sendak made clear in our interview. "But I can't say that I *write* for them, because there is no way to isolate what is meant for children from what is intended for everyone else. While I don't write with children specifically in mind, I do believe that they make the very best audience, and that they are, without question, the very best critics." Millions of children have been absorbed by the brazen experiences of Max, the mischievous boy who angers his mother and wills himself off to rule an imaginary land of wild and fangy beasts in *Where the Wild Things Are*, but they were not the only audience he had in mind. With 380 carefully chosen words, and an enchanting suite of closely integrated illustrations, Sendak probed abstractions once thought too complex for children to engage; today, the book is regarded as a twentieth-century classic.

"The book asks the question, 'How do children survive a particular moment of unexpected circumstance?' " Sendak explained. "How do children survive those few seconds where an experience occurs which is imprinted forever, either a hurt or a happiness, perhaps a colossal anxiety? The mother turns her back, and something has happened with the child. *Where the Wild Things Are* is about those few moments when a child who is totally trusting of his mother in an instant sees another face. He believes that she understands why he is in pain, and why he makes holes in the wall, why he screams, and that she always tolerates him. But one day, dramatically, she doesn't. The collision shocks him, and in the end, there is a coming to terms; she has frightened him, but he still trusts her, and when he finally comes home, his hot supper is waiting for him in his room."

The total seriousness with which that book was received, and the financial security it produced for the author-illustrator, allowed Sendak the freedom he had long coveted to stake out new territory. "I feel I am at the end of a long apprenticeship," he said in his acceptance address for the Caldecott Medal, and that he had reached "a critical stage" in his work. In recent years, he has been embarked on yet another critical stage of creative expression, designing sets for productions of Mozart's *Magic Flute* and *Idomeneo*, Prokofiev's *Love for Three Oranges*, and Tchaikovsky's *Nutcracker*, where his costumes and designs became the basis for a feature film. In 1990, working with Arthur Yorinks, also a critically acclaimed author of children's books, he established the Night Kitchen, a theater company devoted to developing quality arts productions for children and adults. Productions have included *Really Rosie*, a musical with music by Carole King and lyrics, design, and direction by Sendak, and *The Juniper Tree*, an opera based on a tale from the Brothers Grimm, with music by Philip Glass and Robert Moran, libretto by Arthur Yorinks, and design by Sendak. On the day I visited him, he was putting the finishing touches on his designs for the Houston Grand Opera's production of *Hansel and Gretel*, which opened two months later.

Sendak was born in Brooklyn, New York, on June 10, 1928—the same year Walt Disney introduced Mickey Mouse, he is quick to point out—the third and youngest child of Philip and Sarah Sendak, poor immigrants who moved to New York from a Jewish shtetl just outside Warsaw before the onset of World War I. A sickly child, Sendak recalls being constantly terrified of death. "I had measles, double pneumonia, scarlet fever, all by the age of four. I know my mother and father were afraid that I wouldn't survive, and their anxiety rubbed off on me; I rarely went outside to play, I had very few friends to speak of, I was a pretty miserable kid." But he did have the love and support of his parents and two older siblings, Jack and Natalie, who cared deeply about his welfare. "My passion for storytelling comes from my father," he said of Philip Sendak, a Manhattan dressmaker who died in 1970.

"My father only spoke in Yiddish. It was only years after he arrived in America that he began to teach himself English by reading Marvel comics and Superman comics. Then he went on to *Amazing* magazine, and then he graduated to books. When we were children, we would sit and he would make up stories, and they were mostly shtetl stories from the old country of how the Poles killed the Jews. This was all pre–World War II stuff, of course, nightmare stories, pogroms. These were the stories he told us before we went to bed. No wonder I'm an insomniac."

I asked Sendak if he remembered any of the tales, and he said he could recall only one in its entirety. We were having a delightful lunch in the sun-filled kitchen of his house when he began retelling it, a stark contrast to the setting he invited me to imagine. The story was about a game his father played with his friends when he was a boy growing up in Poland. "The rules were that you ran into the Jewish cemetery in the dark of the night as far as you could go, then you jammed a stick with your name on it in the ground and ran back out. In the morning, the stick that was the farthest in the cemetery was the winner. So one night they are all doing this, and as the boys are running out of the cemetery, they hear a bloodcurdling scream. In the morning—this is a story that has stayed with me and scared me to death—in the morning, they find one of their little friends dead."

Sendak paused here, taking a sip of iced tea before explaining that in his haste to get the deed done quickly, and in the pitch gloom of night, the doomed boy had unwittingly plunged the stick through his big overcoat, making him think "dead hands" were pulling him into the ground. "He died of heart failure, and that was the scream his friends had heard. My father must have told me thousands of stories, but that's the only one I remember in vivid detail because I *saw* it as he was telling me—this little boy in the dark—I *saw* him, someone was pulling him into the grave. I still get the chills when I think about it."

Just as his father had refused to tone down unhappy endings in the tales he told his children, Sendak has spent his career giving young readers the chills, not with images of ghosts and gore but with the real anxieties that plague all children: fear of abandonment, loneliness, jealousy. To compensate for his lack of outdoor skills as a child, Sendak began to draw pictures, developing in the process a remarkable memory for detail. "I retained everything I saw," he said, and everything he has absorbed with his eyes has had an influence on his work. His first color drawings were of Mickey Mouse, a character he still regards as a "best friend" from his early years, and whose first initial, the letter *M*, has inspired the naming of several important Sendak characters, most notably Max in *Where the Wild Things Are* and, in direct tribute, Mickey, the protagonist of *In the Night Kitchen*.

A dedicated reader for as long as he can remember, Sendak nonetheless detested school as a child, and considers his learning a product of his own intellectual curiosity. "I hated the confinement of school. There is a certain concern today for children who don't quite fit in or conform, but in my day you were just herded into a room and thrown into competition. The smart ones sat in front of the class and the dumb ones sat in the back, where I mostly sat, because I was numb with anxiety at the endless competition. So there was no pleasure at all for me, no fun at all. I took some night classes at the Art Students League to quiet my father, who so much wanted me to go to college. But I just wanted to work." Sendak's artistic talents were recognized at Lafayette High School in Brooklyn, where he contributed material to the yearbook and other literary projects. By the time he graduated, he had, as an after-school job, done background detailing for the comic strip *Mutt and Jeff* and provided the illustrations for a physics textbook titled *Atomics for the Millions*, written by one of his teachers, a job he did for a "tiny fee and a passing grade." After high school he moved to Manhattan and worked at a variety of jobs, including, fortuitously, FAO Schwarz, the famous Fifth Avenue toy store, where he designed window displays. He spent long hours in the children's book section, where he got to know the store's buyer. In 1950 she arranged an introduction to Ursula Nordstrom, who presided over the children's book division at Harper and Row from 1940 to 1973 and became one of the most innovative forces in American children's book publishing. Sendak's first project for Nordstrom was to illustrate *The Wonderful Farm*, a collection of tales written by Marcel Aymé; it was published in 1951, when he was twenty-three years old.

"Those were the days when publishers allowed artists and writers to grow. I was an apprentice to Ursula Nordstrom for ten years, and I did every book she told me to do. I had no taste, I had no definition of what I was doing. She said, 'Maurice, do this, and when you're done, I want you to do that,' and I said, 'I can't draw that,' and she said, 'Do it.' So I did it. I was trained by Ursula Nordstrom, and when you ask, Who was I trying to please during that time? I say Ursula Nordstrom, and Ursula Nordstrom alone." But perhaps the most liberating of his artistic exercises around that time were the fantasy sketches Sendak did while listening to classical music. These sequences—drawn so vividly they seem to move on the page—gave birth to many of his richest ideas. "By the time the 1950s were over, the beginning of the '60s, I was blooming into an artist. That was a fabulous time. The world was insane. Publishing was heaven. And you could do all the crazy books you wanted, not like today, where there is no more interest in nurturing talent, and where you are expected to make money with every book you do, or you are gone."

In the early 1970s Sendak moved a few miles across the New York State border to Ridgefield, Connecticut. His spacious, gray-frame house on an old country road is surrounded by dogwoods and flowering shrubbery and filled with various objects of personal importance, including an impressive collection of early Mickey Mouse memorabilia. Books are everywhere—the fragrance of old paper and leather bindings permeates the air of his private office—with particular prominence given to a tattered copy of Mark Twain's *Prince and the Pauper* that his sister gave him when he was a child. "My very first book," he said with a touch of quiet reverence.

"Natalie was nine years older than me, my brother Jack was five years older, and I was always very envious of their books. So when she gave me this book, I absolutely wept with joy. I took it to bed with me the way other kids go to bed with teddy bears; I sniffed it, I pressed it, I stroked it, I even tried to bite into it. Look at the beautiful red cloth and the gorgeous endpapers inside. It was several years before I actually read it, mind you; it was the object itself that moved me at first."

Fittingly, it is through objects—books and personal possessions—that Sendak has accomplished his quest for intense communion with his creative heroes. Books are more than containers of information for him; they are "love objects," and there is no question that the love he feels for them is total in every respect. When he creates material for a book, his attention to detail is all-encompassing. He concerns himself with the design, the binding, the typeface, the weight and texture of the paper, the ink, the dustjacket, everything that goes into the making of what we call a book.

For more than forty years Sendak has been a discriminating collector of first editions, letters, artifacts, engravings, and watercolors executed by his favorite authors, artists, illustrators, and composers. Among his prize possessions are Beatrix Potter's watercolor bats; etchings by

William Blake; a Thomas Rowlandson drawing of a tavern brawl; early editions of the Brothers Grimm, including an English translation with illustrations by George Cruikshank; a watercolor drawing by Randolph Caldecott of a fox hunter and his servant; and a letter regarding the publication of *Pierre*, signed by Herman Melville.

"I've gotten as close as a live person can get to a dead person—through imaginary means, through aesthetic means, through reading, through collecting first editions, through smelling letters and examining handwriting," he said. "I have letters Mozart wrote to his father, letters written with the same hand that wrote the concertos that I love, the symphonies that I love, the operas that I love—*the same hand!* His smell is on there. His palm, as he was writing, is on there. I'm not a mystical man, the fact is that I am a very pragmatic man. But something happens when I handle these things, and I don't know what it is. I'm not implying that some alien creatures come and kidnap me in the night and do weird things to my mind. I think, oddly, that this is a very pragmatic process. I can't really describe it any way other than that."

In 1995 the Rosenbach Museum & Library in Philadelphia mounted an exhibition that paid tribute to Sendak's distinctive form of artistic synergy by juxtaposing his illustrations with various items from his personal collection. In the catalog, *Sendak at the Rosenbach*, Sendak and curator Vincent Giroud wrote that "it is our hope that the visitor will recognize George Cruikshank in the Ruth Krauss and Little Bear books, Arthur Hughes and George Pinwell in *Higglety Pigglety Pop!* and the George MacDonald books, Rowlandson and Caldecott in *The Bee-Man of Orn*, Ludwig Grimm in *The Juniper Tree*, and, most admired and present of all, William Blake, from *Charlotte and the White Horse* and *Lullabies and Night Songs* to the newly conceived illustrations to Herman Melville's *Pierre*."

To truly absorb his greatest literary hero, Sendak has visited Arrowhead, the farm in western Massachusetts where Melville lived for thirteen years, reclined briefly in his bed, and sat in the chair where the author did much of his writing. He gazed out Melville's office window to feel what the author might have felt when he dedicated his novel *Pierre* to "the majestic mountain" that stands off in the distance, "my own more immediate sovereign lord and king," Mount Greylock. At the Rosenbach Museum & Library in Philadelphia, which includes among its holdings many literary treasures, Sendak has held and examined numerous precious objects, most notably the copy of *Moby-Dick* that Melville presented to the dedicatee, Nathaniel Hawthorne, "in token of my admiration for his genius."

A bachelor, Sendak has often said that his children are the books that he has created with love and affection and presented to the world. He was especially close to his brother Jack, to whose memory he dedicated the illustrations for a recent edition of *Pierre,* and the exhibition catalog for *Sendak at the Rosenbach.* Well known for his love of dogs, he also suffered the loss of his beloved German shepherd Runge in 1997. "I lost my brother, and then I lost Runge, my two major support systems. All my dogs are gone now, all dead, and the last one, I must admit, Runge, was my favorite. *Outside Over There* is an homage to the artist Philipp Otto Runge, and I named my dog after him; he is in that book as well. I took each of my dogs to the vet's and put them to sleep when they got really sick. I cradled them, watched them die, and I have made a vow, the next dog, I will give driving lessons to, and he or she will drive me to the vet and put *me* to sleep. If I could guarantee that, I would get another dog."

Not long after the death of his brother, Sendak committed himself to reading all of Shakespeare, and then moved on to Keats. "My brother taught me to love Herman Melville. He was the greatest influence in my life in every way, and when I illustrated *Pierre,* the sad irony is that he died just before the book was published. But my reading of Shakespeare came as the result of trying to pull myself out of an emotional nosedive. I did what Melville did when his depression set in over the disastrous public response to *Moby-Dick,* and after the failure of *Pierre*—he went to Shakespeare. The anxiety about whether or not I was smart enough to read Shakespeare went out the window. The Keats thing? I don't really know what flicked me on to him. But here I am with him now, thinking, how does this twenty-two-year-old poet know everything, and verbalize it so beautifully? You know what? To me, he's Mozart. He's Schubert. He's of the tiny cluster of perfection that has appeared on this earth. And I love this person beyond description."

Sendak expects a picture book to develop from this reading of Shakespeare and Keats, a book that will deal in some fashion with the life and death of his brother, but when it will appear, he was unable to say. "It will in some essential way be about my brother, but it won't be about my brother. It will be profoundly about something I'm scouring for, the kind of things which I'm always scouring for whenever I do a book. It takes years for me to start a book. I think I have found what I was looking for in Shakespeare, but I'm still working with Keats. I'm snuffling through everything, and when I find what I want, I'll move on to the next step."

In the meantime, he is content with continuing the search, and at peace with the company he keeps. "The only conversations I have these days are with William Blake, Herman Melville, William Shakespeare, and John Keats," he said. "That is the absolute truth. These are passionate conversations I have, intense conversations. And you know what? They don't talk back."

A drizzly Sunday afternoon in the North London district of Highgate provided the welcome opportunity for me to meet separately with Penelope Fitzgerald and Robert Coover, two novelists highly regarded on both sides of the Atlantic for their work, and for their disparate views on the act of writing fiction. My interview with Fitzgerald came just a week before the eighty-one-year-old author of nine novels won the National Book Critics Circle Award in the United States, an honor she later said left her "speechless." *The Blue Flower,* her winning effort, is a brilliantly conceived novel based on the early years of the German

Romantic poet Friedrich Leopold von Hardenberg (1772–1801), later known by the pseudonym Novalis. Fitzgerald was the first foreign author to receive the NBCC citation, a circumstance made possible by a new rule that allowed non-U.S. citizens to be considered by the 650 members of the organization. With Don DeLillo, Philip Roth, and Charles Frazier as her principal competition, she was considered a long shot at best for top honors, and her selection in 1998 was greeted with widespread approbation.

Widely respected as a consummate stylist with an exquisite sense of subtlety, a sharp eye for detail, and a perceptive grasp of the human soul, Fitzgerald had been a finalist four times for the Booker Prize in her native England, winning once in 1980 for *Offshore*. That novel was inspired by her own experience of having lived among a community of houseboat dwellers on a barge at Battersea Reach on the Thames River. The great enthusiasm critics developed for Fitzgerald's work was especially remarkable given that she wrote her first novel just after observing her sixtieth birthday. Over the next twenty-three years she published eleven more books, and was said to have been working on a new story collection up until the week of her death, on April 28, 2000.

We met at teatime in her small flat, a converted coach house that adjoins the Victorian home of a daughter and son-in-law. There were few adornments and fewer frills; books lined one wall, with more volumes tucked above the ceiling in the rafters, she confided, laughing. The spare ambience of the apartment paralleled in many ways the lean austerity of Fitzgerald's books, which were written to be read in one sitting. A stately, elegant woman of quiet demeanor who spoke in precisely phrased sentences, Fitzgerald did not disguise her conviction that writing is an extremely difficult and demanding exercise, something she enjoyed far more for having done than doing on a daily basis. "It would have been nice to be a young novelist, and to have developed my literary skills over a period of years, but that just wasn't something that was meant to be," she said.

"You start really from nothing, all writers do, and you simply hope for the best. I had an aunt who wrote all her life, mostly novels, and she finally had a nervous breakdown." Ultimately the aunt was placed in a nursing home, where she continued her literary aspirations undeterred. "She used to put the lights on in her room after the nurses had gone home for the night, and began writing a novel about a nursing home. She couldn't be stopped, and she wrote all of her life. I would rather have liked to have done that myself, write all my life, but that just wasn't possible in my case. I had a family to raise."

An omnivorous reader of the classics, Fitzgerald was a graduate of Somerville College at Oxford University, where she read English and was taught by J. R. R. Tolkien. The idea to write professionally was born not out of any compulsion harbored for decades toward self-expression but from the need to generate income during a difficult time in her life. "My husband was very ill, and I needed to make some money. I determined that there were only two ways by which I could do this, and that was either through teaching or writing." Since she had already taught at several private schools years earlier, she decided to try her hand at writing, and began with nonfiction.

Her first effort was a 1975 biography of the artist Edward Burne-Jones (1833–1898), friend and colleague of William Morris and Dante Gabriel Rossetti. This was followed two years later by *The Knox Brothers,* a group portrait of her father, Edmund V. Knox, for many years the editor of *Punch* magazine, and his three brothers: Dillyn, a classicist who played a vital role in decoding German communications during both world wars; Wilfred, a High Church Anglican priest and author of many theological works; and Ronald, a well-known Roman Catholic apologist. She also wrote a 1984 biography of the poet Charlotte Mew (1869–1928). Fitzgerald's move to fiction grew out of a wish to write "what I thought might be a thriller" to entertain her ailing husband, Desmond, who died in 1976. The result of that effort was *The Golden Child,* a witty murder mystery set in a museum that turns on the clever breaking of a code contained in an ancient artifact, a respectful nod to the exploits of her beloved uncle Dillyn Knox, the cryptographer. "My publisher thought it wasn't thrilling enough to call a thriller, so they cut the last eight chapters out and called it a mystery story. I think there were some ends left hanging as a result, but it did amuse my husband, for which I am grateful. It seems old-fashioned now, but there you are."

The five novels that followed continued to draw on personal experience. *The Bookshop* tells of the goodhearted widow Florence Green's doomed effort to open a bookstore in the damp seaside town of Hardborough, a community not unlike Southwold in Suffolk, where Fitzgerald attempted a similar undertaking. There is a moment in this taut novel of middle-aged chutzpah when Florence ponders the consequences that await her. Instead of turning away from an enterprise that is totally alien to her experience, the challenge infuses her with a "precious sense of beginning again which she could not expect too often at her age."

"I think most people draw from their own lives," Fitzgerald told me about her first books. "But when you get to the end of your experiences—or rather you get to the end of what you feel comfortable writing about—you go outside, and that is what I finally did." So as a change of pace, she set her next novel, *Innocence,* in Florence during the 1950s; *The Beginning of Spring* takes place in an English community in Moscow just prior to the outbreak of the Russian Revolution. Fitzgerald said she began work on *The Blue Flower* after coming across a set of Friedrich von Hardenberg's collected works and letters at the London Library in St. James's Square. She spent two years translating all of the correspondence from German into English, and getting the raw material for her book.

Novalis, whom Fitzgerald called by his nickname, "Fritz," in *The Blue Flower,* died at twenty-nine. The novel centers on his obsessive passion for a twelve-year-old girl named Sophie, who dies at fifteen, shortly after their engagement. "I write only in pen and ink, and I labor over every word," Fitzgerald said. "I have made a rule for myself: I don't start until I feel I have my title, my first paragraph, and my last paragraph. I can't choose the ending as I go along. I've got to have that before I can begin to write." Knowing what will happen to her characters in advance is an interesting admission, since all but one of Fitzgerald's nine novels have what everyone agrees are unhappy endings. Only *The Gate of Angels,* which drew sustenance from the years she spent doing research in Kings Library at Cambridge University, has a cheerful resolution. "I really had to work hard at making that one turn out that way," Fitzgerald said. "Why do most of my books end up unhappy? Because I take my cues from real life."

Following her death, the British novelist A. N. Wilson wrote in tribute that Penelope Fitzgerald maintained "the highest standards," and that there was "nothing false about her" at all. "The spare, brilliant novels she wrote, most of them in retirement after a lifetime of teaching, are a monument to her good taste. Perhaps she herself did not quite know how very good they were."

Unlike Fitzgerald, a late bloomer among authors if ever there was one, Robert Coover has been a professional writer all of his adult life, and is among the very few to have made an impact with his debut effort. A native of Iowa, he spent 1998 in England on sabbatical from Brown University, where he has taught creative writing since 1979. In 1966 Coover won the prestigious William Faulkner Award given for the best first novel of the year—he was thirty-two at the time—for *The Origin of the Brunist.* Michiko Kakutani of the *New York Times* wrote that "of all the postmodernist writers, Robert Coover is probably the funniest and most malicious, mixing up broad social satire with vaudeville turns, lewd pratfalls and clever word plays that make us rethink both the mechanics of the world and our relationship to it." Coover's books include the novels *The Universal Baseball Association, Inc., J. Henry Waugh, Prop., The Public Burning, A Political Fable, Spanking the Maid, Gerald's Party, Whatever Happened to Gloomy Gus of the Chicago Bears?, Pinocchio in Venice, John's Wife,* and *Briar Rose;* the story collections *Pricksongs and Descants* and *A Night at the Movies, or, You Must Remember This;* and a volume of dramatic works, *A Theological Position*. Coover's fourteenth book, *Ghost Town,* was described by his publisher as a "postmodern Western" featuring a forlorn horseman, "leathery and sunburnt and old as the hills," who drifts into an abandoned desert town where he must serve as both lawman and outlaw.

"What I write tends to be controversial," Coover admitted in an interview with the *New York Times,* noting that when *Gerald's Party* appeared in 1986, "one reviewer actually recommended that I be committed." The occasion for our meeting in London was not to discuss his conventionally published work, but to find out how this respected craftsman has become so identified with hypertext, and why he uses the digital medium as a tool in his creative writing classes. A huge essay of Coover's, published on June 21, 1992, on the front page of the *New York Times Book Review,* made it clear that this was a man who saw himself caught in the middle of a technology crisis. The headline on the essay—which has become a catchphrase for the computerized-fiction-versus-print-novel controversy—read, "The End of Books."

Hypertext, Coover explained in that piece, is not a system but a generic term coined more than thirty years ago by a computer populist named Ted Nelson to describe writing in the nonlinear or nonsequential space made possible by computer technology. "I must confess at this point that I am not myself an expert navigator of hyperspace, nor am I—as I am entering my seventh decade—likely to engage in any major hypertext fictions of my own," he wrote. But what better way to learn about it, he decided, than to teach a course in the subject? "Thus began the Brown University Hypertext Fiction Workshop," he continued, "a course devoted as much to the changing of reading habits as to the creation of new narratives." The standard text on the subject of hypertext was written by a Brown University colleague of Coover's, George P. Landow, and titled *Hypertext: The Convergence of Contemporary Critical Theory and Technology.* In that book, Landow wrote that electronic text writing "promises (or threatens) to produce effects on our culture, particularly on our literature, education, criticism, and scholarship, just as radical as those produced by Gutenberg's movable type." A similar theme has been advanced more recently by Janet H. Murray, senior research scientist in the Center for Educational Computing Initiatives at Massachusetts Institute of Technology, in *Hamlet on the Holodeck: The Future of Narrative in Cyberspace.*

Coover, whose flat was across Hampstead Heath in North London, suggested a comfortable pub called the Flask to talk about his experiments with this developing form, which he is convinced is the way fiction will one day be written. As an introduction to hyperfiction, he recommended that I look at several compact discs issued by Eastgate Systems of Watertown, Massachusetts. The company publishes what it calls "serious hypertext" works, and its backlist includes what is said to be the best known example of the genre to date, *Afternoon, A Story,* by Michael Joyce, which Coover himself described in a 1993 *New York Times* review of hyperfiction releases as "utterly essential to an understanding of this new art form." The most revolutionary departure hypertext makes from print is that it removes all linear boundaries from conventional narrative and offers a multiplicity of linking paths and alternate routes. By freeing readers and writers from the printed page, and by allowing them to construct, deconstruct, reconstruct, and basically tinker with fiction any way they wish by merely clicking choices on a computer screen with a mouse, hypertext is a dream come true for devoted postmodernists. (Let it be said that even Coover is not entirely sure exactly what *postmodernism* means, and prefers to leave the making of definitions for others.)

"There will always be libraries with valuable books and manuscripts in them, and there will always be a respect for the Gutenberg tradition, but it's a very cumbersome technology relative to the movement of light," Coover offered straightaway. "The inescapable fact is that we will eventually digitize everything—smells, tastes, and all of our sensual experiences can in some manner be digitized. But that only means you can put a code in, that there needs to be something on the other end that can translate it into the real thing. As with all digitized information, the problem is with reproduction. The hard part is not digitizing, but undigitizing, and long-term preservation of the technology."

Coover stressed that none of his books have been written in hypertext, and that his fundamental interest is in discerning how he can use it to help his students. "I like teaching hypertext. I like to see what happens in people's heads when they get into it. They become much better readers, much better writers, because it informs their perceptions. The whole idea is to help them understand narrative strategy." The goal, he continued, is to encourage aspiring writers to "see beyond the standard form." Barely a week after teaching his first hyperfiction workshop, Coover said, "there was a sudden awareness of form" among the students. "You start with nothing. So you have to build everything. The discovery of that, of how writing fed the reading, how the form dictated both, was suddenly transparent; the leap was almost instantaneous." With hypertext, Coover focuses on traditional concepts—which, he stresses, emerge from print. "So we talk about voice, for example, when voice seems to hold a hypertext together when nothing else does."

Coover emphasized that this is an emerging narrative technique, and readily offered his opinion that "there have been no great writers yet dealing with hyperfiction." But, he added, "there is some good writing being done, and it will take a while to get there. We don't have a James Joyce or a Cervantes yet. Remember that Cervantes arrived on the scene a hundred and fifty years after Gutenberg, so it may take a while before we find a committed writer who is so engaged and so understands the medium, and so loves it, that a work of pure genius will appear."

When I met with Coover again a year later in Providence, Rhode Island, the occasion was a three-day conference he had organized at Brown University called "Technological Platforms for Twenty-first Century Literature," devoted entirely to the writing of fiction and poetry on computer, and read by computer. A commonly heard concern during the conference about the concept of "hypertext as art form" was expressed best by Diane Greco, an author who openly worried about producing material that ultimately is "unreadable." By that she did not mean fiction that can be enjoyed by people unable to read and write, but material that has been rendered inaccessible by obsolete machinery or software.

For all the reservations expressed about longevity and access, Coover has no doubt that the new form ultimately will prevail. "Digitization, the minute I understood what it was all about, the minute I got a glimmering of it, oh yeah, it's so obvious," he said. "It is a little hard for me working pretty much in the old print media foreseeing exactly what great narrative art is going to look like thirty years from now. It may not be a revolution that is going to last for the next million years, but it certainly is going to last for a couple of hundred years at least. Of that I am sure."

When I first wrote about Barry Moser in the fall of 1986, I described the distinguished illustrator, engraver, designer, print-maker, and publisher of fine press editions as a "throwback" to old-fashioned traditions, a perfectionist who insisted on having a hand in every detail of the bookmaking process. The occasion for our first meeting was what I called an "embarrassment of riches," the forthcoming release at the time of nine new trade titles from five major publishing houses, one of them intended specifically for children, but the others meant for readers of all ages. "This is really unusual," Moser allowed then, agreeing that perhaps he might have been a bit too ambitious in taking on so many projects at once, but insisting that he had no doubts about his ability to handle the load. "What do you do," he asked with a shrug, "if you have unlimited energy and you have all these projects you are doing, and people want to buy them?"

That interview took place in the spacious house in western Massachusetts that Moser had used as a combination home, studio, and workshop, and the fruits of his labors were everywhere apparent. Engraved woodblocks were lying about in various stages of preparation, sketches and drawings hung on poster boards, the tools of his trade—pencils, pens, gravers, routers, brushes, sharpening stone, tri-square, a box of Kleenex—were arranged on a neatly organized workbench, and copies of the nine books about to be released nationwide had already been assigned slots in a cramped bookcase that occupied a full wall in Moser's studio. When we got together again thirteen years later to discuss his latest undertaking, he had moved to larger quarters, and the number of books he had worked on in one capacity or other over the previous thirty years now totaled 230 titles.

"Everything I've done, everything, has been a warmup for the main event," Moser said after we had sat down for coffee and corn muffins in his spacious kitchen. We faced each other across a long wooden table while Truman and Ike, a pair of English mastiffs the size of Harley-Davidsons, poked about amiably in search of stray treats; his daughter's rottweilers, Trooper and Charlie, were dozing on couches in the living room. A selection of recently pulled black-and-white prints was lying to Moser's right, and a dummy volume of what he had just described as the "main event" was at his left, bound in creamy white vellum; "The Holy Bible" had been stamped in twenty-four-carat gold leaf on the front cover of the mock folio. Finished books, due in a couple of months, were being printed in Austin, Texas, by Bradley Hutchinson of Digital Letterpress, Inc., on luxurious paper with a specially modified version of Matthew Carter's Galliard types, and stitched together by hand in two volumes by the noted binders Claudia Cohen and Sara Creighton. Produced in an edition of four hundred copies and priced at $10,000 a set, the undertaking represented one of the last major fine-press projects to be launched on such an ambitious scale in the twentieth century, and the first to be completed in time to greet the new millennium; an even more luxurious five-volume edition of fifty copies, each accompanied by an original engraved block and unique suites of first-state proofs pulled by master printer Harold McGrath on handmade Japanese Kitakata paper, was being priced at $30,000 a set. A single-volume offset edition for the general trade was published by Viking Studio Press in 1999.

The enterprise, christened the Pennyroyal Caxton Bible, had been four years in the making, and was being issued at a time when two other Bible projects were making news of their own. Out in San Francisco, Andrew Hoyem of the Arion Press, the veteran fine-press publisher for whom Moser illustrated a resplendent edition of *Moby-Dick* in 1979, was producing a one-volume large-folio Bible, projected for delivery in the year 2000. Grandly conceived as a hopeful successor to the magisterial Oxford Lectern Bible fashioned by the great American book and type designer Bruce Rogers in 1935, the Arion Bible, limited to four hundred copies, was being offered to subscribers in unbound sheets at $7,250 a set, although options such as cloth or leather bindings and illuminated initial letters could bring the total cost up to $11,000. Like the Bruce Rogers edition of six decades earlier, the Arion Bible was arranged in a two-column format to facilitate use during liturgical functions; unlike Rogers, who used the King James, or Authorized, version, of 1611 for his text, Hoyem selected the New Revised Standard Version, an ecumenical translation adopted in 1989 by the National Council of Churches, and popular among many mainline Christian denominations.

In Collegeville, Minnesota, meanwhile, the Benedictine monks of Saint John's Abbey and Saint John's University announced in the spring of 1999 that they had commissioned Donald Jackson, the official scribe to Queen Elizabeth II and one of the foremost calligraphers in the Western world, to create a seven-volume manuscript version of the Old Testament and New Testament entirely on vellum, complete with hand-painted illustrations and illuminations prepared by a team of artisans working in his scriptorium in Monmouth, England. Because it uses language that is gender inclusive and nonintrusive to contemporary sensibilities, and is "multicultural," "ecumenical," and "prophetic" in its approach, the monks also chose the New Standard Revised Version as their text. Executing every letter with goose-quill pens on calfskin sheets,

Jackson's group is expected to finish the $3 million project in 2004. When it is completed, the Saint John's Bible will be sent out on a worldwide exhibition tour and be made available to the general public on CD-ROM, over the Internet, and in a facsimile trade edition.

For all their differences in method and design, each of these efforts is notable for paying painstaking attention to the "Book of Books" as a physical artifact, a work of artistic expression to be admired in its own right. The Pennyroyal Caxton Bible boasts the further distinction of featuring 232 original engravings executed by Barry Moser, an artist I had no qualms about describing in my 1986 essay as "probably the most important book illustrator working in America today," an assessment openly shared by many connoisseurs of what are collectively known as the "book arts," and library curators throughout the world who have included examples of his work in their permanent collections. For his text Moser chose the King James version, by far the most poetic translation of the scriptures ever to appear in the English language, and arguably the only enduring work of literature ever produced by a committee.

By illustrating the King James text, Moser was paying tribute to the most lyrical and most literary of all English-language Bibles, an ideal vehicle for an artist who makes the most of narrative, character, and setting in his work, and whose goal was to make a book that would be used for generations to come. Just as there is no definitive version of Homer or Dante or Shakespeare, the Bible is a book that demands constant examination and interpretation, and an examination of Moser's haunting engravings reveals a sensibility that is decidedly of its time and place. Only an artist who came to maturity in the years following World War II, for instance, could have used the image of a burning cross, and all that implies, as background for an engraving in the Book of Zechariah captioned "Turn Ye Now from Your Evil Doings," or inserted a tight one-column image of barbed wire in Psalm 34 entitled "Many Are the Afflictions" to suggest the horror of a holocaust to come.

"This is the only instance in the twentieth century, so far as I can determine, where every book in the Old Testament and the New Testament has been illustrated throughout by a single artist," Moser said with no small measure of satisfaction, and the first ever, he could easily have added, to be done by an American. The last time such a comprehensive effort was seen through the press was in 1865, with release of the prolific French illustrator Gustave Doré's *La Sainte Bible*, and even that edition failed to illustrate four of the five books of poetry. Two works of fairly recent vintage that Moser said he particularly admires treated the subject selectively; he called Eric Gill's *Four Gospels of Our Lord Jesus Christ*, printed in 1931 by the Golden Cockerell Press, "one of the finest printed books of the century," and Marc Chagall's *Hebrew Bible*—begun in 1930 and published in 1957—"the single grand example" of recent illustration of the Jewish Tanakh, more familiarly known as the Old Testament.

Art history resonates with the names of artists who have interpreted the Bible visually, and Moser studied every one he could find when he was selecting scenes to illustrate. "I was constantly asking myself what an old country boy from Tennessee could possibly add to the iconography of the Holy Bible not already done by Michelangelo, Leonardo, or Caravaggio," Moser said, and those were just three names from the Italian Renaissance that popped immediately to his mind. Biblical renderings of the Spaniards Diego Rodríguez de Silva y Velázquez and Jusepe de Ribera, the Dutch master Rembrandt van Rijn, the great English mystic William Blake, and the American painter Henry O. Tanner were of keen interest to him as well, along with numerous other artists who have made their mark in the long history of biblical interpretation: James Tissot, Hieronymus Bosch, Peter Breughel the Elder, Jan Breughel the Elder, Hans Baldung Grien, Hans Memling, Andrea Mantegna, Bartolome Esteban Murillo, Giovanni Battista Tiepolo, Georges Rouault, Elihu Vedder, and Leonard Baskin.

To document the enterprise from conception to delivery—and he repeatedly used the image of a long gestation in our wide-ranging conversation—Moser kept a daily journal of his activities. Each day at six

A.M. he typed into a personal computer his thoughts of what had been accomplished the day before, using the exercise as a mental warmup for the twelve hours of effort ahead, "between the sixes," as he likes to describe his workday. As he approached publication in the spring of 1999, the diary numbered more than 250,000 words, a magnum opus in its own right that will prove invaluable to students of the book arts for many years to come. "I figured this is going to be the biggest thing I ever do, and I wanted a real good record of everything I did," he said. His first entry, dated August 11, 1995, reflects that attitude: "I have dreamed of doing a Bible ever since I learned how to set type and print books," he wrote. "I am old enough and experienced enough now. In fact, I think that everything I have done in my life has led me inexorably to this time and this project."

Born in 1940 in Chattanooga, Tennessee, Moser grew up in a part of the country known for its religious fundamentalism—the southern author Flannery O'Connor called the region of her birth "Christ-haunted"—but he did not consider himself "overly religious" until New Year's Eve 1958, when he was out crow-hunting with his brother Tom and a stray bullet from a stranger's rifle tore a hole in his jacket, leaving him unscathed. "I took that as a sign from God," Moser said, and for the next four years he worked his way through college as a licensed Methodist preacher, graduating from the University of Chattanooga in 1962 with a degree in education. While professing allegiance to no formal denomination now, Moser said he retains a deep sense of personal spiritualism that informs his outlook on life, and that influenced the images he created for the Bible.

Moser's career path took on sharper definition after he graduated from college and moved north to teach art at a private high school located in a section of western Massachusetts along the Connecticut River known as the Pioneer Valley. "I call myself a 'born-again' Yankee," Moser said of the four decades he has spent living in New England, "but I still consider myself a 'cultural Southerner.'" Roughly 90 miles west of Boston and 160 miles north of New York City, the scenic region boasts a number of outstanding liberal arts colleges located within a dozen miles of each other—Amherst, Smith, Mount Holyoke, Hampshire, and the University of Massachusetts—and is home to one of the most vibrant book arts communities in the United States.

Among the names from the area to achieve international prominence over the years, few are better known than Harry Duncan (1917–1997), founder in 1939 of the Cummington Press, and the fine-print publisher of Robert Lowell, Allen Tate, Wallace Stevens, Marianne Moore, William Carlos Williams, and Tennessee Williams. Among typographers, the legendary Bruce Rogers designed his Centaur types at Carl Purington Rollins's Dyke Mill Press in the town of Montague. Notable binders in the valley have included Arno Werner, who died in 1995 at the age of ninety-six after passing on a great deal of what he knew to a succession of grateful apprentices. "He was the master, and he was my mentor," David Bourbeau, the owner of Thistle Bindery in Northampton and unofficial historian of book arts in the area, offered in tribute.

At One Cottage Street, a converted textile mill in the town of East-hampton, no fewer than eight book arts workshops, including those of the binders Moser selected to work jointly on the Pennyroyal Caxton Bible, are in residence. Other tenants there include Carol Blinn, the founder and owner of the Warwick Press; Faith Harrison, a paper marbler; Greta Sibley, a graphic artist and book designer; and Daniel Kelm, an "alchemist" and binder who creates books that are "technical master-pieces of construction," according to one admiring bookseller. Occupying yet another corner of the spacious brick building is Alan James Robinson, an illustrator, engraver, book designer, and owner of Press of the Sea Turtle, formerly known as Cheloniidae Press. Robinson told me that he learned engraving from Barry Moser, and that he had relied heavily on the expert services of Harold McGrath, a towering figure in American printing who worked for years at Leonard Baskin's Gehenna Press, to usher many of his exquisitely crafted books through the publishing process.

It was an early introduction to McGrath, in fact, that inspired Moser to expand his creative horizons into the book arts. "I saw a printing press operated by a master," Moser wrote in an early autobiographical sketch. "I smelled the viscera of printing-oil, ink and solvents. I saw books the likes of which I had never seen before. That day I touched the pulse of both form and direction. Even though I've never been a great and voracious reader, I've always loved letters, pages of books, books, and book-filled rooms. I sensed in this place, and with this work, a potential for my own artistic activity."

At the same time that he was learning the subtleties of printing from McGrath, Moser was paying close attention to the varied artistic and technical skills of Leonard Baskin, the eminent sculptor, artist, author, printmaker, engraver, founder in 1942 of the Gehenna Press, and arguably the most consequential influence in the American book arts movement throughout the second half of the twentieth century. "The focus of a private press tends to be upon typography or illustration or text, but Gehenna has explored them all and excelled in each," the estimable Colin Franklin wrote in a 1992 appreciation of Baskin's achievement. When Baskin began teaching at Smith College in 1953, people from throughout the country came to learn under his tutelage, some to study art in his classes, others to be apprentices at the Gehenna Press, a few, like Moser, to observe and absorb the niceties of engraving. "I became an engraver out of imitation," Moser said, adding that Baskin—who died on June 3, 2000, at the age of seventy-seven—was the "poet laureate" of the craft. Five months after Baskin's death, the Pioneer Valley book arts community mourned the loss of master printer Harold McGrath.

In 1970 Moser established Pennyroyal Press, which he named for a plant associated with witches' gardens. "I found that image appealing, since witchcraft and printing both share the sobriquet of 'the black art,'" he told me. "I also found the built-in oxymoron of 'penny' and 'royal' ideal for what I knew I would always be doing: trying to make regal and beautiful things on a shoestring." Over the next eight years he designed and published twenty-four fine-press books, all the while expanding his mind with an intensive program of independent reading. "I had no intellectual curiosity whatsoever until I was twenty-five," he admitted in our first interview. "Before going off to college I spent six years in military school—1952 to 1958—and I never once read a book. All I did back then was play second-string football and make pictures of naked women. And the only book I later illustrated that I read while I was in college was *Frankenstein*." The upside to this youthful indifference to literature is that Moser has no trouble generating genuine enthusiasm for every assignment he chooses to accept. "I bring a freshness to what I do because just about every book I've decided to illustrate—with the notable exception of the Bible—I have just read for the first time."

Moser's drawings for Allen Mandelbaum's translations of Virgil's *Aeneid* and Dante's *Divine Comedy* led to a commission from Andrew Hoyem of the Arion Press to prepare a suite of wood engravings for *Moby-Dick*. That 250-copy edition—fully subscribed before the print run was completed in 1979, and an unqualified triumph—persuaded Moser to take his own press to a higher level, a realm "beyond the slender volume syndrome" he had been practicing up to that point. He produced lavish editions of *Alice's Adventures in Wonderland*, *The Wizard of Oz*, and *Adventures of Huckleberry Finn*. Although these larger efforts were enthusiastically received when released, and immediately snapped up by collectors, Moser found them tremendously expensive to finance on his own. "I nearly went bankrupt doing *Oz* and *Huck*," he said, and soon turned to illustrating and designing more projects for mainstream publishers, many of them children's books. He also found enormous satisfaction in illustrating the works of living authors, doing the kind of writer-artist collaborations that were quite common in the eighteenth and nineteenth centuries but are rarely done today outside children's literature.

"Working with my contemporaries is one of the greatest joys there is," he said. "Unfortunately, most authors today aren't willing to share their royalties with artists, and the publishers certainly aren't going to increase their royalty schedules to accommodate both contributors. The economics really don't work out except in the private-press world, and that is where I have experience." Among living authors, Moser has illustrated fine-press editions of books and stories written by Joyce Carol Oates, Willie Morris, Donald Hall, Eudora Welty, John Updike, Larry Brown, Kaye Gibbons, Virginia Hamilton, Ken Kesey, Robert Olen Butler, and Nobel Laureate Wole Soyinka. "The job of illustration, if it's done well, is not merely to mimic and repeat the text. The idea is to provoke the reader into thinking that something else is possible."

The long honor roll of artists whose illustrations have been carved into wood includes Albrecht Dürer, Hans Holbein, William Blake, Edward Burne-Jones, Eric Gill, and Winslow Homer. One of the qualities that unites their work, Douglas Percy Bliss wrote in a standard history of the craft first published in 1928, is that it has a quality of "woodiness" so recognizable that it is "obvious to even the most ignorant" that the images could not have been created in any other way.

The difference between woodcuts and wood engravings is subtle, but important. Woodcuts are made on a soft surface that is incised plankwise, and as an art form they predate the invention of metal type. To create an image, a design is drawn upon a block; the areas intended to appear as white are cut away with a knife or plowed out with an instrument known as a graver, leaving the surface in relief. Ink is then applied by a dabber or roller, and prints are pulled by rubbing the paper on the block, or by applying vertical pressure on a press. With the development of the printing press in the mid-fifteenth century, woodcuts found a natural application in textual illustration. The first complete English-language Bible, produced by Miles Coverdale, contained 150 woodblock prints, and was printed in 1535, either in Zurich or Cologne.

In the late eighteenth century, the woodblock method gave way to wood engraving, emerging first in England and achieving mastery in the work of Thomas Bewick, whose illustrations for *A History of British Birds* represented the first advanced use of the technique. To make an engraving, an instrument called the graver, or burin, is pushed forward on the end grain of a very hard surface, usually boxwood. By cutting across the ends of the grain instead of with it or against it, engravers were able to make much narrower lines and to create subtle effects of light, tone, and shade.

"It is generally agreed that no photographic processes can give just that element of intensity and sharpness that is obtained by engraving on wood," Bliss wrote. "The old reproductive craftsmen loved their work. How they must have caressed the beautiful pieces of smooth box, and held no labour too much to bestow upon anything, were it a reproduction after Raphael or an advertisement of a bath-tub!" Wood engraving, he continued, is a craft that demands "at least as much concentration" as any other, and because "good 'original' wood-engravers have always been and always will be few," the vast majority of artists who use the technique typically entrust the task to professional craftsmen.

A true traditionalist, Moser learned the craft on what he calls "real good" boxwood, and it remains his engraving surface of choice. "The problem is that the quality of boxwood these days is so bad I'd rather cut on maple, and my big concern with starting the Bible was that I didn't know if there would be engraving blocks of sufficient quality available to do a project of that magnitude. The last blocks I bought were really terrible. They looked beautiful, but when you started cutting into them, they were just too brittle, and they 'stuttered' under the graver."

A surprisingly viable option—one that Moser said he would never have dreamed was possible—came in the form of a synthetic material formulated by Richard Woodman, a chemical engineer who lives in California. "When this fellow retired, he decided he was going to go back to his childhood hobby, which was wood engraving, and like everyone else he discovered there was no good boxwood available, so he invented a substitute he calls Resingrave. It's a cast polymer resin, and for a good while I refused to put a knife to it. I was a very hard sell." Moser was so opposed to using synthetic blocks that he often brought the sample he had been given to various seminars he attended, and always held it up as an example of what he considered inadequate substitutes for the "real thing."

"The first time I cut a line into it, I was giving a lecture at Art Center School in Pasadena, California," he said. "I happened to have an engraving tool in my hand, and I impulsively cut across the surface of the thing while I was talking, while I was publicly demeaning the material. Well, I was stopped right in my tracks. I had stayed away from doing anything with the stuff because it just looked so ugly, but boy oh boy, it was so sweet. Then I said, 'You guys hold on a minute here, okay, I'll be right back to you.' I did five or six more cuts to make sure I wasn't imagining what I was seeing, and I was just stunned. I did a little dog's head, and darn it all if it didn't hold that line beautifully. Well, the short of all this is that I immediately got in touch with the guy who invented it, and I was in business. It's not perfect. I still prefer good boxwood. But it sure made this project possible." In time, Moser would call this process "relief engraving," to distinguish it from "wood engraving."

The most critical element in realizing the Bible, though, was not the substance or texture of the engraving blocks but the sudden appearance on the scene of an "angel" to finance it. That happy circumstance developed out of a casual conversation he had in 1985 with Bruce Kovner, a New York investment consultant who admired his work. Kovner's appreciation for beautiful books was such that he had named his investment management company the Caxton Corporation after William Caxton, the first English printer. During the course of their talk, Kovner asked a seemingly innocent question: If Moser had a choice of any book to design and illustrate, what would it be? "I didn't have to give it any thought at all, of course, it was the Bible," but little did he realize then that ten years later the man asking the question would underwrite the project to the tune of $2 million.

"The deal we made was that Bruce would put up the money and we would be partners, fifty-fifty all the way." As he said these words,

Moser—a stocky bear of a man with a full gray beard—was smiling broadly, clearly pleased to be liberated of the logistical pressures that inevitably come with entrepreneurship. "I feel today the way I would guess artists in the Renaissance must have felt when they were fortunate enough to get a patron. I get paid a salary every month that I work on the project. If I need something, anything at all, it's right there in the budget, and I just order it."

Armed with this uncommon gift of professional freedom, Moser concentrated on achieving his lifelong goal. His daily journal, as a result, was focused on the making of the drawings, the engraving of the blocks, the selection of the paper, the choice of a printing type—all the myriad details that are involved in the creation of a beautiful book—and not a hint of anxiety over being able to afford doing it. There is repetition to some of Moser's entries in the diary, but they reflect a comforting, almost exhilarating sense that progress is being made, and that the goal is clearly in sight.

People familiar with Moser's body of work know they can count on seeing at least one self-portrait somewhere within the pages of every book he has illustrated since 1979. Most of the time it is a cameo appearance in the spirit of the late filmmaker Alfred Hitchcock, a kind of signature walk-through, but the exercise involves more than self-indulgence, he steadfastly maintains. "If all you see is me," Moser once said to his daughter Cara, who had suggested that perhaps there was a bit too much ego involved in the ritual, "then you don't understand the self-portrait."

The first time Moser inserted a likeness of himself in a book was in the Arion Press edition of *Moby-Dick*. On page 438, he appears in profile as a lowly deckhand, "stowing down and clearing up." It is no secret in book-arts circles that Moser and Andrew Hoyem, owner of Arion Press, parted on less than amiable terms when that project was over, and the fact that they were both working on their own Bibles at the same time twenty years later has only exacerbated talk of lingering disquietude. Moser said he made that first image of himself as a statement of annoyance at being given a limited role in illustrating the book. "I felt my intellect wasn't being respected. I felt I was hired because nobody else could engrave the wood. I felt that I was hired for my hands, not my mind, and not my eye. So I did this self-portrait as a response to that, and I started doing it in all my books from that point on." For the Pennyroyal Caxton Bible, Moser appears four times: as Huram the Artisan in 2 Chronicles; as the decapitated head of Goliath the Hittite, in 1 Samuel; in costume and makeup as Saint Paul in prison, in 2 Timothy; and in the conversion of Saul of Tarsus, Acts 9:4.

Although he uses many professional models for his characters, Moser said he relies primarily on fortuity for inspiration. "I was sitting right there where you are here in the kitchen," he said, recalling the night he found one of the most important models of all for his Bible. "A friend of mine, Jane Dyer, had hired a chef from Amherst to come by and cook for a group of friends she was having for dinner. It happened that her kitchen was too small for a large group, so she asked if she could use mine. Anyway, all I had to do was sit around and watch this fellow do his work. What I saw was a man with a wonderfully sculptured face and black hair pulled back in a ponytail. After a few drinks and wine, I said, 'Hey, Lew!'—his name is Lewis Silver—'Would you take that rubber band out of your hair?' He looked at me kind of strange, said, 'Sure,' and the hair fell down to his shoulders. Then I said, 'Would you do me a favor and get almost naked and let me put a crown of thorns on you—and would you be my Jesus?' He was a little taken aback by that, but he said that he would, and that's how I got my Jesus."

Moser said he discovered his model for the Virgin Mary under similar circumstances one night while having dinner at the Green Street Café in Northampton. "There was a striking woman in there, a waitress, and she was working my table," he said. "What I liked about her immediately was that she did not possess the kind of dazzling beauty you usually associate with a movie star. What she had is a transcendent kind of beauty, a plainness in a sense, but a plainness that is infused with a very large pinch of the erotic; this was very important, because to my way of thinking the

Mother of God has got to be a little bit on the sensuous side. I am always looking for people like this who are not archetypical. They aren't what you expect, and that helps take me away from making cliché characters."

In addition to hiring professional models and recruiting strangers for his scenes, Moser just as often prevails on people he knows to pose for him. To cite just one example, the New Hampshire poet Donald Hall, for whom Moser has illustrated several books over the years, appears in the Pennyroyal Caxton Bible as Ecclesiastes the Preacher. In Exodus, a full-page engraving pictures a bearded man holding a huge mallet in his right hand and a chisel in his left. There is the suggestion of a smile, but most arresting of all are the probing, intelligent eyes. The caption reads: "And Moses hewed two tables of stone like unto the first." It is a regal likeness of Leonard Baskin, standing erect in the guise of Moses, but Leonard Baskin all the same.

"When I got to thinking about Moses having to go back up that mountain to cut out the second tablet with his own hands—he broke the first ones in a fit of rage when he found his people worshiping the golden calf—I immediately thought of my mentor and old friend Lennie Baskin," Moser said. "He is a little cantankerous and prone to showing less-than-saintlike traits of patience, but I chose him mostly because he is a sculptor. You have to admit that the mallet and chisel you see there fall into his hands quite nicely, and mingle with his features perfectly."

For scenes where he does not use live models, Moser has never had any compunction about borrowing bits and pieces of other people's work. A bank of file cabinets line the west wall of his studio, each drawer crammed with hundreds of photographs and illustrations, many of them seemingly mundane representations of swords or helmets or waterfalls or wild animals, but all grist for the graphic mill. As a further demonstration of his creative process, Moser sat down in front of a computer terminal with an enormous screen and called up an image that ultimately would become *Elijah Fed by the Ravens* in his Bible. "This process is called 'transformation,' " he explained while fiddling with the keyboard to alter the appearance of the picture. He moved the figures of five crows around, and adjusted the position of an old man who is pictured crouching on top of a stone mound. "Look at this," he said. "I can turn his head—I can put his head anywhere I want, I can put him anywhere I want. This astounds me what I can do." What we were looking at, he readily acknowledged, were photographs from his files, and he was "manipulating them, appropriating them" for his own purposes. "I can make birds peep over the top of that rock there like this if I want to; I can put this bird down here in the foreground and make it bigger. When I have what I want, I just 'command save' it to the hard disk; then I make a print, transfer it to the block, redraw the whole thing, then make my engraving."

While the computer represents a recent development in his technique, Moser said the process of gleaning ideas from other sources is something that he has always done. "I came across a word in *Time* magazine some time ago in an article about the sculptor David Smith. He was described by the writer as a 'gargantuan bricoleur,' meaning that he was a user-up of discarded things." Charmed by the word, Moser promptly wrote Jonathan Mandelbaum, the son of Allen Mandelbaum, the translator of the *Divine Comedy* and the *Aeneid* who also works as a translator in Paris, and asked for a fuller definition.

"Jonathan translated it to mean a 'putterer,' a person who putters around; it can be a 'do-it-yourself tinkerer,' a 'handyman.' It also means 'to cobble together,' 'to experiment with objects or concepts,' 'to construct objects with odds and ends.' Well, that's exactly what I do. It's what I've always done. I am a person who requires things. I need my crutches. My sources are anything that I find. If I need a Near Eastern costume, I will look in my files under 'costumes,' and chances are I'll have something there. You see, I don't consider anything I've ever done as original. I am not concerned about being perceived as an 'artist.' If I am an artist, that is for you to say, not for me to say. What I am trying to do is make interesting images, and I will make them interesting any way that I can."

It is for this reason that Moser prefers to be known for his individual skills—the printing, the engraving, the designing, the illustrating techniques he has perfected. "The book arts are more akin to theater, architecture, and filmmaking than they are to painting, sculpture, or performance art because it's all a matter of teamwork," he said. "I can do certain aspects of this myself, but I can't do the whole of it alone, because I'm not a paper-maker, I'm not a typographer, I'm not a punch-cutter, I'm not a type-designer. This kind of work depends on the efforts of so many people, and not least of all is that you need to have someone around to pay the bills. That is probably the number-one reason why something like this Bible has not been done in a long time, because it's too bloody expensive on the front end. It's costing $2 million to do this, and $1.7 million of that was gone before a single page came off the press. To give you one example, we are using the skins of two goats for every book we make; the bindings alone are costing us $2,000 a set."

Despite the hefty price tag of his Bible, Moser said he intends that it be read and handled, not kept under glass as a museum piece. "It is a precious object, and it is going to be kept as an artifact, but it is meant to be touched. The choice of the materials all have to do with things that actually get more beautiful the more they are used. This book is meant to be turned page by page. A little dog on a page, that's just fine, that's the way it ought to be. Like anything that strives to be a work of art, it is greater than the sum of its parts."

6.

HUNTERS AND GATHERERS

Please send the things you have got for my Academy as soon as possible. The very thought of the place, let alone the actual use of it, gives me enormous pleasure. Mind you don't hand over your books to anybody. Keep them for me, as you say you will. I am consumed with enthusiasm for them, as with disgust for all things else.

—*Cicero,* Letters to Atticus

Antiquarian bookselling has enjoyed a spirited run in the United States, but like so many other transplanted institutions, the tradition is not nearly as ingrained in America as it is in Europe, where a number of prestigious firms have operated continuously for decades, many of them passing on the craft from generation to generation, often as mentor to apprentice, sometimes as parent to child. Among the most prestigious is the London company founded in 1847 by Bernard Quaritch (1819–1899), a man described by Nicolas Barker as "the Colossus of the nineteenth-century book trade." Bernard Quaritch Ltd. staffs numerous divisions at its headquarters on Lower John Street in Golden Square, and was the focus of an entire issue of the *Book Collector* on the occasion of its 150th anniversary in 1997. No longer operated by members of the Quaritch family, the company is now owned by Milo Cripps, the fourth Baron Parmoor.

The London firm of Maggs Bros. Ltd., established in 1853 and since 1939 located in a splendid Georgian town house at 50 Berkeley Square, is in its fifth generation of family ownership, and includes among its prize customers John Paul Getty Jr. One of the company's principals, Bryan Maggs, worked closely with Sir Paul in forming the collection, and serves as librarian of his Wormsley Library, an apt testament to the confidence one important client has in the judgment of his principal agent in the book trade. In the United States, the prominent autograph and manuscript dealer Kenneth W. Rendell enjoys a similar relationship with William Gates III, having presided over the stocking of the Microsoft chairman's massive private library of rare books and reference works at his fifty-seven-room home on the eastern shore of Lake Washington, and flies into Seattle periodically to serve as curator of the collection he helped assemble.

Pierre Berès of Paris, the acknowledged dean of international booksellers, serves important clients all over the world and enjoys a reputation that assures him first look at prime collections as they come out of private ownership and into the marketplace. As he approached his seventieth anniversary in the book trade in 1997, Berès wrote a reflective essay for the *Book Collector* in which he put forth his conviction that all important collections "need the assistance of a professional," and that nothing "can replace the trusting, friendly relationship between the amateur and the bookseller: all collections have reached their highest degree of perfection thanks to the advice, the help, and somehow the complicity of great merchants." While having the means to buy magnificent material is certainly an advantage, Berès argued that all collections "become worthy of esteem from the moment they show a real concern for quality in the choice of copies and a coherence in their treatment of a subject, however minor." A charming man who shows little patience with subjects he considers irrelevant, Berès seems most comfortable when he is sharing the wisdom of his years.

"Every day I read two, three, four, five catalogs, and every day I look at anywhere between ten, twenty, two thousand books, sometimes perhaps a private library of twenty thousand books—all on the same day," he told me in his home after hosting a pleasant dinner at an elegant Paris restaurant overlooking the Eiffel Tower. He had poured tumblers of fine cognac for our get-together, and brought out a few books to ponder while he held forth on his unending passion for the trade. "I am never bored because there is always something new for me to learn," he said. "When I enter a room, and I do not mean a made-up, formal room, but let us say a room somewhere in an old attic, I find that I know exactly what is there. Sometimes the room has been untouched for thirty, forty, even two hundred years, and yet I feel I know exactly what the contents are. Then I go through every one of the books, and I proceed to discover something that is wonderful, or I may discover something that is very disappointing. But it is always an adventure."

More often than not the books Berès discovers will be titles he knows from his vast experience, but the greatest excitement comes when he encounters one he has never seen or heard of before, something he knows intuitively is important. "I am not a magician, but you still feel something that is magical. It is a recognition of sorts. In the amount of time it takes to form a simple sentence in your mind you are making an identification, and it is at that point that you gather all of your skills very quickly and you start working on the book." For Berès, the process of working with a book is as much a physical communion as it is intellectual, involving all the senses and all the emotions, and he used a common Anglo-Saxon verb to describe the interaction that takes place, declining my offer to substitute the phrase "make love" in its place, leaving no doubt that the feeling he has for books is more carnal than platonic. "An amateur book lover is a beginner, which is why it is good to be an amateur, since the amateur is also a lover," he said of his favorite kind of bibliophile. "Amateur comes from the Latin verb *amare,* which means to love, and a true bibliophile is a lover in every sense of the word. You have to sleep with the book, to live with the book. You must handle the book, you must not be afraid to have intimate contact with the book. It is like life, really; you look at the lady, you smile at the lady and make sure that you are not being rebuked.

Then you have to be humble, and then you have to be brave, and then you must not be afraid to proceed with the task at hand."

Berès has occupied the same building at 14, avenue de Friedland off the Champs Elysées near the Arc de Triomphe for more than half a century, and remained in business during World War II, even prospered during that time. He entered the book trade, he said, in 1926 at the age of thirteen as an apprentice, and discovered his calling. In 1952 he acquired the firm of Hermann Editeurs des Sciences et des Arts, publishing a wide variety of books in the sciences, humanities, philosophy, and the history of ideas. Periodic news stories such as those reporting him spending $1.1 million at auction in 1989 for a thirteenth-century prayer book reinforce his stature as a master of the high-end clientele, and ensure steady access to the choicest materials. His purchases at a Paris auction in 1990 brought this comment in the *Independent* of London: "Dealers took note of the keen interest shown by Pierre Berès, widely regarded as the doyen of the French book trade, and whose buying activities can affect the market." A New York sale at Sotheby's in 1998 was notable for the purchase of a large illuminated Book of Hours from 1470, known as *The Hours of Lo,* for $3.6 million, a record at the time, and more than $2 million above the high estimate. "All works at Tuesday's sale were from the collection of Jaime Ortiz-Patino," the Associated Press reported, "which was formed in close consultation over many years with the Parisian connoisseur-dealer Pierre Berès."

Although Berès has a staff of twenty people working for him, he insists that he writes all of his own catalogs, and he does so in a distinctively personal style well known to discriminating book buyers and librarians all over the world. "In my profession, everything ends with a description," he said with pointed emphasis. "A description can be very long sometimes, perhaps too long, but it is always thorough. Every one follows a certain line. Many people sell books by looking at the bibliographies. They look at books as objects. I never do that. I never look at bibliographies or reference books until after I have finished my tour, my promenade, of the book. I look at the book first, I enjoy looking at it, I may disagree with it, and after I make my tour of the book, then I make a collation, then I measure the height, examine the boards, and then I read it, perhaps not always all of it, but I do read it efficiently, because I also am a publisher, so I have a habit of reading quickly. I have the bad habit of giving the same amount of my time for a book that costs twenty pounds, sometimes perhaps more time than with a book that costs two hundred pounds. I am both a gardener and a curator. I have to weed the book, and also to read it. It is an exercise that never varies."

Roger E. Stoddard, an American librarian who buys important books on behalf of the Houghton Rare Books and Manuscripts Library at Harvard University, said that the catalogs of Pierre Berès are unique in his experience. "Most people of his seniority and stature, and with his budget for operating a business of that size, would delegate the task of writing those descriptions to other people, but it is obvious to me that he does them all by himself. I know this because every one of those descriptions is a personal take on the book, a concise essay. Most catalogs you see produce an amalgam of quotations from other sources about the importance of a particular title and its rarity. Pierre's amalgam comes out of his own wits, what he finds and sees. And I find this most refreshing, because the antiquarian bookseller's point of view is different from the scholar's point of view, different from the librarian's point of view, and different from the collector's. Not many people get to understand these distinctions because they don't pay attention. There's always a clever theme in Pierre's catalogs, and he's not simply copying things and retailing them as salable items, he's making novel observations, and the reason for that is because he's looking with a fresh eye. And you know what the best part is? You can still buy books from Pierre Berès. His prices are not all fifteen thousand dollars and more. A good many of them are in that range, to be sure, but you still find interesting things that you actually can afford to buy on a librarian's budget."

An examination of the catalogs prepared and published by Heribert

Tenschert, a German bookseller based in Ramsen, Switzerland, outside Basel, offers a telling point in contrast to Berès. His catalogs, frequently comprising more than five hundred pages of text and generously illustrated throughout with full-color plates, are marvels of scholarship, and worthy examples of the bookmaker's art in their own right. Discriminating librarians and bibliophiles throughout the world buy copies of these catalogs, not only for their obvious beauty but more importantly for the information they contain on precious materials that can be found nowhere else. Only a handful of people, however, will be in a position to buy any of the materials they offer, one reason why the prices are listed separately and inserted loosely inside the front cover.

Leuchtendes Mittelalter, Neue Folge III ("The Glowing Middle Ages, new series III"), a compendium of thirty-four French manuscripts from the Gothic, Renaissance, and Baroque periods of the late Middle Ages, includes exquisite examples that span the reigns of King Louis IX (1236–1270), known as Saint Louis, and Louis XIV (1643–1715), the monarch acclaimed as the Sun King. Copies of the catalog, which was issued in 2000, cost $200 each, and include descriptions of manuscripts that have never been evaluated in print before. A Book of Hours from Châlons-sur-Marne of about 1440 in French and Latin on vellum, with ten painted pages by a Reims artist known as the Master of Walter, each reproduced in the catalog, is described in twelve pages of commentary; the price, listed separately on an insert, is half a million Swiss francs, about $286,000. Another Book of Hours, believed to have been prepared in 1500 for Anne de Bretagne, receives forty-two pages of attention, beginning with this description: "One of the richest manuscript Books of Hours known, the true chef d'oeuvre of the Master of Antoine de Roche—an artist of Burgundian origin, working probably in Lyon and then in Paris, where he painted two walls in the Hotel de Cluny for the same clientele as the Grand Prior of La Charité-sur-Loire, one of the most important houses of the order of Cluny who has lent his name to the anonymous master." The book is "so spectacular," the description reads, "that we shall publish it in full facsimile." Its cost: 780,000 Swiss francs, or $446,199.

"I am nearly never selling to libraries," Tenschert, a former professor of Romance languages at the University of Cologne, told me in perfect English. "I like to sell to private individuals because then I can buy them back at some point in the future. Because I pay the fairest prices in the world, the same prices I would be paying in the auction rooms of Sotheby's and Christie's, that is a reasonable expectation. And that answers another question you asked: How do I find these books? The answer is that because I am so renowned in my field, people call me. They come to me. All of the great manuscripts in the last ten years, I have bought them all. Of the fifty manuscripts in my new catalog, forty I bought privately, the others I secured at auction."

Tenschert's gross sales are in eight figures every year, he told me, yet customers for his top-end material comprise no more than thirty people in the world, most of them private collectors buying directly for them-selves. The process often involves having the customer visit Tenschert's home outside Basel in Ramsen at what he calls the Antiquariat Biber-mühle, a restored eighteenth-century mill on the banks of the Biber, a tributary of the Rhine River near the German border, where he has lived with his family since 1993, and where he conducts his most important business. The illuminated manuscripts, the incunabula, important early printed books, and an imposing reference library of 30,000 bibliographic works and 100,000 catalogs are kept in Ramsen as well. Tenschert still operates his original shop in Rotthalmünster in Bavaria, where his gen-eral stock is maintained, although he expects in time to consolidate the entire operation in Switzerland.

The manuscripts are the centerpiece of his inventory, and all are kept in a spacious steel vault in his home. It was in this cubicle, nicely appointed with hand-carved wooden chairs and painted fire-engine red on the outside, that we conducted the first two hours of our interview, surrounded by these matchless treasures. "There are also eighty very fine incunabula in here as well, and I mean very fine, not just 'old' fifteenth-century books. I would never lay my hands on a normal incunabulum. This, for instance, is of the quality that I refer to." He picked up a book known as the *Gratianus* printed on vellum in Mainz in 1472 by Peter Schöffer, the successor to Johannes Gutenberg. "This is one of three copies in the world. The others are in Munich in the Bavarian State Library and the Duke August of Brunswick Library in Wolfenbüttel. This is one of three copies that has been extensively embellished, and the only one with thirty-eight miniatures painted in a workshop known as the Hausbuch Master. None of the other sixty known copies of this book have miniatures painted in, just three. And mine, one can say, is the finest of them all. It is unique, and it came to me out of a private collection in northern Europe."

The book was one of fifty that Tenschert was planning to include in a special catalog, his fortieth, to commemorate his first twenty years in the book business. Titled *Fünfzig Unica* ("Fifty Unique Books"), it appeared in 1998, with the *Gratianus* appearing first. All the other works Tenschert included in the catalog were in the vault that day as well, and we looked at many of them during the course of our conversation, each one an example of what he called a "Tenschert quality" book—a book that "is more than fine, more than outstanding—a book that is one of a kind." What would appear as Number 15 in the catalog, for instance, was described as a "miracle" of circumstance, "the only known copy" of a huge seventeenth-century Dutch atlas entirely printed on silk and colored by a contemporary hand, comprising 149 copperplate maps.

Even though his clients comprise some of the wealthiest people in the world, Tenschert said he never buys material with any of them in mind. "I have always been convinced that if I choose the right things for the right reasons, then the right customer will come to me. So I never buy books for certain customers, and I am certain that I am perhaps the only bookseller in the world who does business like that. I never have commissions in public auctions either. Most of my colleagues in the book trade live on their commissions. People who know me know they can trust everything I write about these books, and they know they can buy them on the strength of the descriptions. But most of them still like coming here and having the books laid out in front of them, and getting convinced by me. We are talking about serious sums here, sometimes six-figure sums, sometimes seven figures." Condition is the universal criterion that is applied in collecting, and it takes on a particular dimension at this level. "The whole market of medieval manuscripts consists of 230 or 240 manuscripts, that is all there are left right now in private circulation. H. P. Kraus in New York has perhaps fifteen, and I have two hundred, all acquired by me over the past fifteen years or so." Tenschert said he applies only one rule when acquiring books or manuscripts: "It has to be in a language that I can read." He said he is proficient in fourteen languages, and that he writes the catalogs himself, although he does retain the services of professional scholars as consultants.

For all the impressive prices these extraordinary artworks command, Tenschert insisted that "selling the book is only a small percentage of the work that I do around the book. When I get offered a book, I see it, I feel it, I browse through it. I smell it. I get in touch with it. And then I buy it. Or I don't buy it. Most of the time, if it is a prime book, I buy it, and if it is a very prime book, I always buy it. But I do not buy everything. Not at all. I used to buy everything in my first years as a bookseller, and I still have 80 percent of what I bought back then still on my shelves. What I shamelessly believe is that you have to fall in love with the book first. It is physical as well as emotional. You have to fall in love with the book, and then you have to develop this passion into a lasting love. And then you must convince other people that this is worth not only your love, but their love. And I am very successful in doing this."

Tenschert did not dispute the suggestion that he has to be a salesman in his line of business as much as a bibliophile. "If I am otherwise, you would not be here today, would you? We wouldn't be together in this room, because otherwise I would be in my little place in Bavaria selling books for two hundred marks and being happy to have a turnover of 200,000 marks a year, and in 1992 I made a turnover of nearly 30 million marks as a one-person company. I think I made the three or four most important deals in the history of bookselling. I recently made a deal selling to one man books for the value of 18.5 million German marks, which was then $13 million. I am not allowed to tell you who this person is, but it was an extraordinary transaction, and I was required to make my case for every one of these books. This is very important, because I think that you cannot ask one million dollars from a person for a very fine book without proving that this book is worth that amount of money. And to prove this, it is vital to convince this person in every aspect as to its unique qualities—its scholarly description, collation, provenance, condition, whatever—which is why these catalogs are so very important. You give the customers these treasures, one has to have a feeling of confidence that everything is all right." How Tenschert goes about pricing a particular book follows its own dynamic as well. "It depends on how much I cherish it. A book that is really close to my heart will be dearer, more expensive than another book that occurs from time to time."

As to whether or not he serves a vanishing breed of collector, Tenschert thinks not. "I think that they will never vanish, particularly at this level, because more and more people recognize that these things, these books that are objects in themselves, will only get more valuable as time goes on. And there will always be more people to collect them. The thirty people I deal with will always exist. If one dies, there will always be another."

The book business had been agreeable for Bernard Israel, providing him with the means to make a good living and an honorable trade to pass on to his four sons. He established his company in 1895 in Arnhem, a medium-size city on the lower Rhine River in the eastern Netherlands, the site of what would be a devastating defeat for British Airborne troops in September 1944. "My father was a well-educated man who came from a Jewish provincial family," Nico Israel said a few months after he had observed his seventy-eighth birthday in the fall of 1997. We met in his apartment in Amsterdam, and although he recently had retired from the antiquarian book trade and sold most of his stock, a small collection of his own books remained on the shelves. Several exquisite Dutch globes, remnants from one of his specialties, the history of cartography and exploration, and each several hundred years old, occupied a corner of the room he uses as an office. "I don't know why my father chose to become a bookseller, but he was devoted to books, and he was devoted to people who were interested in books. That is probably the most important quality he had, because books alone are not enough. You have to have some connection with people, and I think that was one of his great gifts."

At its height, the company had more than 150,000 books of general stock, many of them titles from the sixteenth, seventeenth, and eighteenth centuries acquired from numerous European owners, some of them German and French aristocrats. There were nine children in the Israel family, four sons who followed their father into the business, and five daughters. Salomon, born in 1900, was the oldest, and the one looked up to by Max, Bob, and Nico, the youngest of the brothers. "Had Salomon lived, he would have been recognized as one of the world's greatest booksellers, of this I have no doubt," Israel said with an admiring shake of the head. "Salomon had spent a good deal of time in Father's business before the war. He knew everything there was to know about a book before having seen it or heard of it. This is something you either have in your blood or you don't. He was nineteen years older than me, and I must say I looked upon him as an idol. In 1937, when I was eighteen, the family got a car and I got my driver's license. We would travel many places together in search of books, and I am convinced that he could smell a good book from a distance. And he was a highly self-educated person. He never stopped reading. He was what you would call an autodidact."

Salomon struck deals at every opportunity, always intent on building up the company's stock. "He had some very good book spies reporting to him in Germany, just before Hitler took over. He bought from many of those noble families who needed money during the depression, and he got some wonderful libraries out of old castles. Just a tremendous number of books. I remember when I was twelve or thirteen years old, I was helping to unload hundreds of books out of train wagons, and not one was later than 1750. Just thousands of books came in that way. At a certain moment we had several warehouses filled with books in Arnhem."

With the outbreak of World War II and growing anxiety over a German invasion of the Netherlands, the preoccupying concern among Jews was survival. Since its founding as a democratic kingdom in 1815 from the old Dutch republic, the Netherlands had never been at war with another state. Despite assurances from Hitler that Germany would respect its neutrality, the Wehrmacht invaded the country on May 10, 1940; three days later, Queen Wilhelmina left for England aboard a Royal Navy destroyer. Over the next five years, some 104,000 Dutch Jews were sent to concentration camps, the young diarist Anne Frank among them. Another 36,000 managed to save themselves, some through the help of neighbors and acquaintances, others by going into hiding.

"There was an escape route that was known to my brothers and my parents-in-law, and my wife and I were the last ones to make use of it," Israel said. The passage to safety for Nico and his wife Nanny ran through France and Belgium to Switzerland, where the couple took refuge in 1942. "We learned along the way that the line was going to be cut and that it was no longer safe. When we arrived in Switzerland, I sent a cable to a rare-book dealer who was friendly with my family: 'Books arrived well, but further shipments impossible.' Sadly, the message arrived too late. My brother Salomon, together with my wife's parents, tried the same route and were arrested by the Germans in Brussels. We never saw them again."

In 1944 Israel enlisted in the Canadian Army, and when the Dutch

Army organized units in England, he joined up with them and participated in the Allied invasion of Europe. "I came back over the Rhine, and when we landed in my region, I went directly to Arnhem, which had just been liberated. When I got there, you can believe me or not, I was the only person in town, absolutely the only one. Right away I looked for books, and I found some of our family's most important books, but the roof in the warehouse was destroyed. This was the Dutch spring, April of 1945, very damp, and there was one heap of wet paper, a mass of pulp. Everything was lost. First I cried. And then I decided never to stay in Arnhem again."

In addition to his brother Salomon and his wife's parents, Israel lost his own parents and three of his five sisters to the Holocaust. With his brother Max—who survived by hiding out for three years in dense woods fifteen miles outside of Arnhem in the cottage of a sympathetic forester—he started a modest business in Amsterdam, dealing at first in newly published books. Because their entire inventory had been lost, there was no thought of picking up the business where it had left off, but since he knew no other line of work, Nico entered the family trade. "I was brought up in a family where books were the daily bread and butter, but when I came back, I didn't know very much about the business. Max was three years older than me and had more experience, more knowledge, than I did at that point. But not having one book, and not one penny, we had very few options to choose from. The trade association of Dutch booksellers gave us some stock to get started, and the day we opened for business, there was a whole queue of people lined up outside our door. There was such a thirst for books after so many years of war."

One experience that influenced Israel's lifelong approach to the buying and selling of old and important books occurred when he was asked by the Dutch government to prepare a report on the availability of scientific textbooks in Switzerland, where he had just recently been a refugee. He traveled to Berne with his wife, met some publishers, compiled his data, and prepared to go home. "As I was going around the city, I saw in the window of a secondhand bookshop a fantastic book. Something I knew instantly was a really great book. So I went into the shop—you have to understand that we did not have one penny, just enough money for a simple room and a plain meal—but I was drawn into the shop anyway. There was an elderly lady there and I asked to see the book in the window. She showed it to me. Then I asked if she had any other books like this. And she went in the back and returned with three or four other really great books. She was asking two thousand Swiss francs altogether, not very much at all, but the problem was that I had no money. So I looked at the woman, and I said in German, 'Do you trust me?' Just like that. And she said, 'Yes, why not?' And I said, 'Would you trust me enough to let me take those books for twenty-four hours? I will return within that time, and I will either have the money you ask, or I will give you back your books.' "

The woman agreed, and within the hour Israel was on a train for Geneva, where he sold two of the titles—a 1511 edition of Claudius Ptolemy's *Geographia* and a first edition of Andreas Vesalius's *De Humani Corporis Fabrica* in English—to "a really great bookseller" there, William S. Kundig. From Geneva, he rushed off to Lausanne and placed "a large, very old, very beautiful book on astronomy with all kinds of movable figures" to Nicolas Rauch, another dealer he knew from before the war. "Then I went to Zurich to the firm of Erwin Rosenthal, and they bought the last book I had. This was all in cash, incidentally, I had to be paid by cash. I arrived back in Berne the next day, gave the woman her money, and made a profit of a few thousand francs. Then my wife and I went out to a fabulous restaurant and treated ourselves to the most fantastic dinner, with first-class wines, everything—not to be forgotten. And when we got back to Amsterdam, I decided that my future was in rare books, not the moderns." The most lasting lesson of all that Israel took from the experience was discernment. "I decided I could spend the little money I had on one good book instead of a lot of rubbish. So that is what I have always done. I would buy one good book, sell it at a profit, then spend the money I earned to buy another good book, and then get some more. I have always concentrated on getting a small number of the very best books, and cultivating clients who were only interested in having the very best."

Respected internationally for his conviction that certain books belong on certain shelves, Israel is credited with helping build many great collections in his native country. On the occasion of his seventieth birthday in 1989, thirty-eight colleagues from all over the world contributed essays to a commemorative book published in his honor known as a *Festschrift*. "Nico Israel has earned the gratitude of libraries, collectors and antiquarian booksellers in many ways," the publisher of the book stated in the foreword, "not the least of which is his constant campaign to keep important books and manuscripts in the Netherlands." That sentiment was echoed by numerous others in the book world. Lord Wardington, an English collector of atlases and the former chairman of the Friends of the British Library, noted that Israel's "greatest asset, besides a prodigious knowledge on all things, is his enormous sense of selectivity." Of the many books, manuscripts, charts, and atlases Israel steered toward national collections over the years, he chose to tell me about one particular book that got away, a 1523 copy of proverbs and sayings known as *Adagia,* compiled by the great Dutch humanist and scholar Desiderius Erasmus (1466–1536). Among the readily recognizable proverbs included were "God helps those who help themselves," "One swallow doesn't make a summer," "Looking a gift horse in the mouth," and "Blowing one's own trumpet," all of which Erasmus had tracked to their original sources in Greek and Latin. The first edition was published in 1500 with 818 entries; by the time of Erasmus's death thirty-six years later, the number had increased to more than four thousand in the tenth edition.

"This copy wasn't the first edition, it was much later, but it was full of annotations, many of them in Erasmus's own hand, others in the hand of one of his students, thousands of annotations that were used to supplement the subsequent editions," Israel said. "I was wild when I saw it, and

I called the Amsterdam University and tried to persuade them that this was a national treasure that belonged in the Netherlands. They agreed, they said they wanted it, but they weren't so sure about the money. Finally they came to me and asked if I would bid for them at a certain price." The amount the university was willing to pay was "embarrassingly low," Israel said, "so low that I knew it had no chance to succeed," and he declined to bid in the government's behalf. He then agreed to act as agent for a European collector who had approached him for representation at the sale, and secured the volume on November 20, 1990, for $975,000 at Sotheby's in London. But he would much rather have seen the book installed in a Dutch institutional collection all the same.

In 1950 Israel and his brother Max decided to go their separate ways. "Our characters were so different, and we agreed it would be better for both of us to have our own businesses. It has worked out well for both of us." Indeed, for years they have maintained their own operations in Amsterdam, Nico working out of his home and meeting with clients strictly by appointment, Max maintaining an open shop in a converted eighteenth-century town house a ten-minute walk from the Anne Frank attic annex in downtown Amsterdam. My interviews with the two men took place on the same October day in 1997, Nico in his apartment, Max in his shop.

"I stayed in the little house of a forester, a man my family knew who took care of the woods, and he saved my life," Max Israel recalled in halting English of his experiences during World War II. He remained in hiding for about three years, he said, biding away the hours by reading and teaching himself everything he could about medicine and science. "One of my former employees brought books out to me—these were the only subjects he had available—and that is how I became an expert in these areas." The long-term consequence of this regimen was the creation of his own firm, B. Israël, B. V., continuing the business name used by his father; dealing in the purchase and sale of rare and important books concerned with medicine and science, the firm has earned recognition as one of the world's foremost specialists in the field.

. . .

For the hundreds of artists and intellectuals who saw wisdom in leaving Germany in the 1930s, America was the logical place for many to seek refuge. "My parents, Bertha and Otto Heilbut, came from Berlin," Anthony Heilbut, a native of New York City, wrote in the preface to *Exiled in Paradise*, an aptly titled history of the migration. "Had there been no Hitler, I would have been born there." Focusing largely on the sciences and the arts, Heilbut described how extensively such towering figures as Theodor Adorno, Hannah Arendt, Hans Bethe, Peter F. Drucker, Albert Einstein, Hans Hofmann, Fritz Lang, Lotte Lenya, Otto Preminger, Max Reinhardt, Arnold Schoenberg, Igor Stravinsky, Bruno Walter, Billy Wilder, Kurt and Helen Wolff—the list goes on and on—influenced the tone and temper of American culture. "The range of their accomplishments is staggering," he enthused, and not without justification. For Otto L. Bettmann, the former rare-books librarian who would achieve international renown in America as "the Picture Man," coming to America in 1935 was "as if God himself had picked me up and set me down in Paradise." Bettmann had thought before leaving Germany about eventually becoming a publisher, plans he abandoned when he reached the New World.

The flight of Jewish booksellers from Nazi persecution was a phenomenon of similar magnitude, particularly in the way it enabled a resilient corps of scholar-dealers to channel great quantities of important research materials away from the continent and into North American collections. In a lecture given at Columbia University in 1986, Bernard M. Rosenthal, a third-generation bookseller who left Europe in 1935, called the emigrés who made their way across the Atlantic "the gentle invaders," and offered a concise summary of just how far-reaching an impact they had on the international book trade from their new base in America. "The antiquarian booksellers who made it to these shores were part of this much larger invasion of academics, artists, philosophers, scientists, doctors and other professionals, whose arrival profoundly affected the history and culture of this country," Rosenthal said in his remarks. "Without exception, they came because they had to, not because they wanted to." About thirty settled in the United States, most of them initially in New York City, although twenty or so others set up shop in Scandinavia, France, Holland, Switzerland, England, Canada, Latin America, and Palestine, which is now Israel. "But the most lasting influence of these booksellers is not in their sheer numbers," Rosenthal emphasized, "it's in their expertise, their craftsmanship and what one might call the bibliographical consciousness which all of them brought to their trade." While a few were able to bring some stock with them, most came equipped with little more than the knowledge they had amassed and the innate feel they had nurtured for books. Fully a third had earned their doctorates before leaving Europe.

Undoubtedly the most famous of the emigré booksellers was Hans P. Kraus, a bookseller with a name recognition exceeded in his time only by that of the acclaimed Philadelphia bookseller Dr. A. S. W. Rosenbach, and whose experiences were recorded in his 1978 volume of memoirs, *A Rare Book Saga*. The firm of Hans P. Kraus remains a leader in the trade, operated by his daughter, Maryanne Kraus Folter, and son-in-law, Roland Folter. The oldest of the emigré group was Emil Hirsch, at seventy-two already approaching the end of his career when he arrived on American shores; Lucien Goldschmidt, just twenty-five when he moved to New York in 1938, would play a significant role in the shaping of American book culture for half a century.

Two portraits hang on the wall of Bernard M. Rosenthal's second-floor bookstore in Berkeley, California, each the likeness of a bookseller. One pictures his paternal grandfather, Jacques Rosenthal, painted by the renowned Munich painter Franz von Lenbach, who had persuaded the German bookseller to sit for the painting. "Lenbach was a bibliophile, and when he was done with the portrait, my grandfather asked him, 'What is your fee?' This man had done portraits of such people as Franz Liszt, Richard Wagner, and Otto von Bismarck, so his fee for a painting usually was enormous. But in this case Lenbach said, 'No, no, no, just give me some books.' And that is what he took in payment." The other portrait does not have nearly as interesting a story, but it is important in that it pays homage to Leo S. Olschki, Rosenthal's maternal grandfather, and a notable bookseller in his own right who moved to Italy in 1883 in search of a milder climate, and made his mark in Verona. "The family tree," Rosenthal said with evident satisfaction.

Descended from a line of printers, Olschki became a bookseller by way of a curious circumstance, "and the story of how he acquired his stock is a story worth telling," Rosenthal wrote in a 1977 essay for the *Harvard Library Bulletin*. It happened that Olschki was the only person to appear at the court-ordered estate sale of a huge library, and being the only bidder present, he proceeded to acquire the entire stock—all of it bundled into a heap of canvas bags—for the outrageously minuscule price of 500 lire. Olschki's first catalog, issued three days later, described 340 fifteenth- and sixteenth-century books, "a measure of Olschki's inexhaustible energies, and perhaps also a measure of the cubic content of those sacks, that in the same year ten more catalogs followed in succession."

Rosenthal likes to tell the story of how Leo Olschki's firstborn son, Leonardo, responded when asked by a professor after he received a doctorate in romance philology from the University of Heidelberg if he now intended to enter his father's business. "No, Herr Professor, I don't think I am smart enough for that, and I have decided to devote my life to scholarship," the youngster replied. Leonardo Olschki went on to write respected monographs on French medieval literature, Dante, Marco Polo, and Galileo. At the age of sixty he began studying Chinese, and when he was in his seventies he published a volume of Oriental lyrics and epigrams.

When Ludwig Rosenthal, the elder brother of Bernard's grandfather, Jakob Rosenthal, died in 1929, the German poet and bibliophile Karl Wolfskehl wrote an obituary, in which he paid tribute to the man then renowned as one of the most influential booksellers in all of Europe:

I carry with me the unforgettable picture of Ludwig Rosenthal at the Munich Flea Market, now held in this city twice a year. Yes, the Flea Market! There too, he searched, and there, too, he found. There he stood, the head of a world-renowned firm, before the bookstalls at 8 AM on opening day, his gaze searching, powerful, grasping, darting over the disorderly piled-up masses and over row upon hazardous row of books, while his alert and industrious hands were feverishly digging into freshly opened crates—selecting here a volume, there a print, here again a manuscript, all finding their way to the ever-growing pile of his booty.

Ludwig and Jakob—a devoted Francophile who took the name Jacques during an extended book-buying trip to Paris—and a third bookseller brother, Nathan, separated in 1895 and formed their own businesses. The individual firms of Ludwig and Jacques contributed significantly to making Munich the capital of the antiquarian book world. "I didn't want to be a book person at all," Bernard Rosenthal told me. "I tell people it wasn't until I was twenty-nine years old that I decided to enter the trade after trying several other careers. They say, 'But you've got books in your blood,' and I suppose that's true. And I must say that I liked being a bookseller from the first day on." Bernard Rosenthal's father, Erwin Rosenthal, had earned a doctorate in art history, a specialty he brought to bear when he moved to the United States. Bernard was thirteen years old when he left Germany with his parents in 1933. They lived first in Italy before arriving in New York in 1941, where his father wrote his first catalog, a description of thirty books offered for sale by fellow emigré Emil Offenbacher. In a prefatory note, the elder Rosenthal described his approach to the task as one of offering "commentaries, or I might say talks," on each of the entries that had been selected for inclusion. "In these commentaries the effort has been made to introduce each book as a living personality—in each case a pleasant one, I hope!— describing its typographical importance and its historical and cultural associations."

In the mid-1940s the Rosenthals set up shop in Berkeley, California. Bernard's older brother, Albi, went to London and established the firm of A. Rosenthal Ltd. in 1936; he was twenty-one at the time, and remains in business eight decades later. "We never said the United States, by the way," Bernard Rosenthal told me. "We always said *America*—Ahmerrrica—it wasn't a country, it was almost looked upon as heaven, and Roosevelt was God."

A good deal of the transatlantic movement of books these expatriates negotiated was expedited in large measure by the sudden arrival of trained academics from Europe, people who became historians and teachers of the humanities and sciences in American universities. "They brought with them a greater consciousness of the continental book, so there was a great parallel movement," Rosenthal said. "These booksellers had connections in Europe, and when the war was over, they knew where to go and how to make the necessary arrangements."

On November 21, 1986, John Russell, the esteemed art critic for the *New York Times*, noted the closing of an Upper East Side cultural landmark at the end of his weekly column in two paragraphs that succinctly summed up a lifetime of achievement:

> Final Exhibition *(Lucien Goldschmidt, Inc., 1117 Madison Avenue, at 84th Street): The worst news of the season to date is that after 50 years in business, Lucien Goldschmidt has decided to close down at the end of this year. His gallery has been a combination—unique in New York, though still common in Europe—of bookshop, printshop and drawing room. The printed word, the illustrated page, the association copy, the architectural drawing, the working proof of a print by Daumier or Favarni, Jacques Villon or Matisse, the perfection of French 18th-century mapmaking, the drawing that was all the more tempting for being unattributed—all have abounded in his shop, spilling over onto tables, chairs and evocative heaps somewhere in the back room.*

All times and all places have been represented, and Lucien Gold-schmidt has had a way of making every one of us feel that he had been living for our visit and thought it the crown of his career. His final show includes the first polyglot Psalter ever printed (Genoa, 1516), the first complete set of Aristophanes in the original (Basel, 1532), the Cranach Press edition of "Hamlet" with designs by Gordon Craig (Weimer, 1930) and D. R. Wakefield's "Sporting Fishes of the British Isles" (Tiverton, 1985). It has prints by Rembrandt, Piranesi, Delacroix and Toulouse-Lautrec, a set of 120 lithographic presentations of the alphabet (Strasbourg, 1834–35), and drawings that run from Luca Cambiaso in the 16th century to Manolo, the friend of Braque and Picasso, in the 1920's. All these things are there for one reason—that they caught Lucien Goldschmidt's fancy. New York will be a duller place without him.

Six years later Lucien Goldschmidt's obituary appeared as a short item noting the soft-spoken bookman's death at the age of eighty. The article noted that Goldschmidt had been the first dealer in the United States to exhibit Matisse's portfolio *Jazz* in 1949, and that he had organized numerous important exhibitions at the Grolier Club on East Sixtieth Street. Paradoxically, his passing was noted with far greater depth in England, where Nicolas Barker, at that time the Head of Preservation at the British Library, wrote in the lead sentence of his obituary for the *Independent* that Goldschmidt "was a citizen of the world" whose life was divided between books and art. "Booksellers and art dealers normally lead rather separate careers, but Goldschmidt combined both, giving to each his own individual, highly independent taste. Words and images combined to form an outlook on the world that was, in one word, civilized."

Born in Brussels in 1912, Goldschmidt was educated at the College Royal Français in Berlin where his father was a lawyer, and learned the basics of the book business from Pierre Berès in Paris. "What Lucien actually wanted early in life was to be a publisher," his widow and partner in the business, Marguerite Studer Goldschmidt, told me. "He wanted to know everything, and he thought bookselling was a good place to begin." When the political situation began to deteriorate in Paris, it was Berès who suggested that Goldschmidt consider leaving the country. "People had their ears open and they heard certain things," Mrs. Goldschmidt said. "Lucien was told very simply, 'If I were you, I would not come back to work on Monday.' Berès told him it was better if he just left now, before things really get sticky. So he left." Goldschmidt took the advice and with the help of friends, made his way to the United States in 1937 and promptly set up shop in New York as the American representative of Pierre Berès.

Born in England to Swiss parents and trained in Geneva as a librarian, Marguerite Studer met Goldschmidt in London during World War II when he was serving as an intelligence specialist with the U.S. Army. "Lucien was introduced to some very interesting people at that time, curators, professors, people with lots of knowledge. I was in charge of the Bush Library at the time, where everyone in London went who wanted foreign books, and we met there. We corresponded for two years and got married in 1946. His first words to me were: 'Marguerite, now you work for me.' It has been my pleasure to play second fiddle to Lucien all my life. I did a good deal of research for him, I wrote all the descriptions for our catalogs; I did what was necessary. I became a bibliographer."

In 1953 the couple opened Lucien Goldschmidt, Inc. on Madison Avenue, and from the beginning their stock showcased fine prints and master drawings on equal terms with rare books. "Lucien made many trips to Europe in search of material. We had things from the Renaissance right up to the time of Picasso. It was amazing. We had German books, Italian books, Spanish books, and all the illustrated books, what you call the *livres d'artistes*, which were a specialty of Berès, but very few things in English." Goldschmidt's catalogs for master prints, original photographs, and drawings, usually illustrated with reproductions, were equally incisive and informative. "He became an expert in art because so many early books have illustrations in them," Mrs. Goldschmidt said. "The art really interested him. We had a huge library of reference books which I sold after he died. But he was amazing. He really had a very good eye. He could see in an instant what century it was, what country it was from. Now I am making a list of all the prints that are left over. Look around you at the furniture he bought. This huge table here is from Austria. And then he was interested in old keys—look at the *keys* there on the walls."

The Goldschmidt apartment in Upper Manhattan is precisely appointed with paintings, engravings, prints, and fine antiques. "Since Lucien died, you have no idea all the slips of paper he left here and there, it's dreadful," his wife said in mock frustration. "Look, these are his notes stuffed in this notebook here; every time he saw something that interested him, he would keep it. He was like a magpie. All of his auction catalogs are filled with notes. He worked all the time, and he never bought with a certain customer in mind, he always bought for stock. There was an aesthetic side to him which was very, very polished. Nothing was miscellaneous, everything had its place. He would put books aside and do them in sections. Every catalog was a performance, like a production, a play."

Between 1950 and 1986, Lucien Goldschmidt produced 64 catalogs, 111 special lists, and descriptions of many museum exhibitions. Everything he wrote, according to his wife, followed a specific logic, and everything reflected the depth of his research. In 1974 he and Weston J. Naef curated and installed a groundbreaking exhibition of photographically illustrated books from 1844 to 1914 at the Grolier Club. The handsomely produced monograph that emerged from this presentation, *The Truthful Lens*, remains one of the most coveted publications to be issued by the organization, and is regarded by many as the most authoritative reference in the field. Goldschmidt's best-known catalog, *The Good Citizen: A Collection of Books Written to Further or to Undertake the Improvement of Mankind*, was issued in 1981. In the preface, Nicolas Barker compared the 263 items Goldschmidt chose for the list with the landmark exhibition mounted in London in 1963, *Printing and the Mind of Man*, which had displayed 500 of the most influential works to have been issued over the previous five centuries and was the brainchild of the London bookseller Percy Muir.

"It is strange that, given the frequency and variety of this class of speculation, and the degree to which it has, from the beginning of time, permeated all other human intellectual activities, no other bookseller before Mr. Goldschmidt has, so far as I know, made it the subject of a catalogue," Barker wrote. "Yet, now that he has done it, what an obvious idea it seems. Like all new notions, it tempts the reader to further speculation: can one trace the concept of the social contract? How far is this or that utopian fable a fantasy or a tract for the times? What part has religion had in modifying men's behaviour towards each other? One could go on indefinitely."

A sampling of the entries demonstrates why institutional librarians considered Goldschmidt's catalogs such essential tools, and how he became a principal supplier of materials for their collections. Every work, however obscure, was fully referenced and described, its historical pertinence clarified. Goldschmidt selected apposite excerpts from the books, translated them into English, and printed them in the outer margins of the catalog alongside the main entries. If a census was available for a particular title, it was cited. For a "rare and little known early edition" of the *Nicomachean Ethics* in the Latin version of Joannes Argyropoulos, published in Cologne in 1508, Goldschmidt noted that neither the British Library nor the Bibliothèque Nationale had a copy, but that Harvard did. For Dr. Isaac Kerlin's *Mind Unveiled; or, A Brief History of Twenty-Two Imbecile Children* (Philadelphia, 1858), with original albumin photographs by Frederik Gutekunst, Goldschmidt pointed out that the monograph was the first photographically illustrated medical book published in the United States, and "was ahead of its time in the faith it placed in redeeming backward children."

Just as appealing to institutional librarians were the affordable prices of Goldschmidt's inventory. An analysis of the *Good Citizen* catalog, appearing as it did in a decade known for the robust activity of the rare-book market, bears this out quite tellingly. Of the 263 entries offered for sale, 125 of them were priced between $50 and $250, with another 105 priced between $250 and $1,000, together accounting for about 90 percent of the list. Of those that remained, 32 books were priced between $1,000 and $6,000, 16 of them in the $1,000 to $2,000 range. The highest priced was $9,000 for a first edition of the first printed work of Baruch Spinoza, in a contemporary binding. For $30, a curator could have acquired a 1908 pamphlet in which Leo Tolstoy declared, "I cannot keep silent," on the issue of capital punishment. A research librarian intent on building a collection of women's history might well have been tempted to spend $225 for a book in which Theodor Gottlieb von Hippel, a German teacher and lawyer, argued in favor of granting equal opportunity to both sexes; published in 1792, the tract contains this statement: "Adam is an animal without Eve, and Eve without Adam is a nun in a cloister." Goldschmidt's catalog, Barker concluded in his preface, "makes a notable enlargement of the horizons of the sociologist and the bibliographer alike. It will inspire new reflections on the history of one of the most central, perhaps the most central, of all human preoccupations, mankind itself."

Goldschmidt spent twelve years gathering the books for that catalog, all the while working on others that pursued different themes. "We had a number of private collectors—Lessing J. Rosenwald was one of our customers, Philip Hofer used to visit the shop all the time—but most of our business was with institutions," Mrs. Goldschmidt said. "I believe we made the foundation of several college collections because my husband was able to explain to librarians why they should have the books. We sold a great deal of material to Harvard, the University of California, the University of Texas, the Newberry Library, places like that." Among the materials Goldschmidt found during his many trips to Europe were numerous unpublished letters written by Henri de Toulouse-Lautrec

(1864–1901), the French artist and lithographer famous for his pictures of barmaids, clowns, prostitutes, and actors of Montmarte. In 1969, with Herbert Schimmel, the collector who bought the material from him, Goldschmidt edited a volume of the correspondence he had located.

Goldschmidt received very little public attention in his lifetime, and he chose not to write his memoirs. "He never said much about his experiences in Europe before the war," his wife said. "He saw the way things were going when he left, and he undoubtedly would have disappeared had he stayed. He very much enjoyed being an American. He retired when he turned seventy-five, and the reason he gave was that he didn't want to come out of the shop on a stretcher."

In a lecture he gave at Columbia University in 1989, Goldschmidt addressed himself to the state of his profession with words that serve, in a prophetic way, as a kind of eulogy for what he called "the loss of the scholarly bookseller." The most important change, he said of his fifty years in the business, "is the striking devaluation of literature and reading," a sentiment expressed by many others of his generation. "I can recall the time when a substantial public expected to find in their favorite authors answers to perennial questions of humanity. They were credited with a depth of understanding not available in texts on sociology, psychology, or philosophy. But by the early 1930s, we were witnessing the fall of earlier stable attitudes and a radical dismantling of high culture well under way."

The essential problem, Goldschmidt felt, was not one of supply, "but rather how to continue buying with the expectation of placing the materials among credit-worthy customers who would pay their bills." With the end of World War II, "it was clear that material was still abundant" in Europe, and with it came an insatiable demand in the United States. "The most immediate change was the entry as a major force into the market of the college and university libraries, some of them recently established. From Texas to California, from Florida to Massachusetts, from coast to coast, the search for books and periodicals took on novel proportions."

He cited statistics: Harvard's collections more than doubled from 4.2 million books in 1940 to 9.6 million in 1977; from 1940 to 1977, the University of California at Berkeley went from 1.1 million volumes to 4.9 million, while UCLA, invigorated during the stewardship of Lawrence Clark Powell, increased its holdings tenfold, going from 347,000 volumes in 1940 to 3.9 million in 1977.

"Nothing like that had been known before, nor is it likely to be seen again," he said, and with the increasing influence of electronic sources in university libraries more evident now than when he gave the lecture in 1989, his words are more prescient than ever. "The many ways of photocopying have had an essential role in the loss of the scholarly bookseller. Professors do not have private libraries any longer. Once upon a time, I saw collections of that sort running to 40,000 volumes. How could anyone now form such a library? As for dealers, how could they fill a building, say of five floors, with books worth owning and allowing a profit when sold? Where could they find trained help? There used to be accumulations of the books of past generations. They came from castles and country houses, inherited dwellings with inherited reading matter, or from families squeezed by financial trouble, as was very evident in the 1930s and '40s. One gentleman not noted for kindness said of another collector, 'Sure, he is forced to disgorge some of his library. He is down to a mere 50 meters.' "

When he was closing the store in 1986, Goldschmidt received a letter from Roger E. Stoddard at Harvard University. "I think that only librarians understand the debt their institutions owe to booksellers, as the great fuss of labels and bookplates and exhibitions concerns only those who have *given* their books or their funds," Stoddard wrote in words that undoubtedly expressed the sentiments of his colleagues. "Few people understand what a very great gift a bookseller can make to an institution and you have made literally thousands of them over the years. God bless Lucien Goldschmidt." In an interview with me, Stoddard credited the emigré booksellers with creating many of the great research collections among American universities in the years immediately following World War II. "Booksellers in general have been among my greatest teachers," he said, "and these booksellers in particular were among the very best. They knew what was important. They showed you why it was important, and why it was essential for a great research library to have what they were offering in your collection. And they knew where to get the material."

In their dual lives as scholar-booksellers, Leona Rostenberg and Madeleine B. Stern have written or edited forty-six works on a wide variety of literary and bibliographic subjects. Of these, ten have been published under both their names, two of them appearing within a year of each other when both were in their mid-eighties. As the women approached their ninetieth birthdays in the late 1990s, the firm of Rostenberg & Stern continued to issue erudite catalogs and offer choice selections from their stock at the New York Antiquarian Book Fair, held each spring in the Seventh Regiment Armory on Park Avenue in Manhattan.

"We're pretty old-fashioned, but we're thinking about getting a computer and getting our books out on the Web," Rostenberg, the older of the two, said one morning during an interview at their book-lined apartment on East Eighty-eighth Street in Upper Manhattan. "Oh, I don't know about that," Stern said, demonstrating a penchant the two have for finishing each other's sentences. "It's a little late in the day for us to start learning about computers; I'm still pretty comfortable working on my typewriter."

Trained as a scholar in the 1930s with the intention of being a teacher, Leona Rostenberg found part-time work while attending Columbia University cataloging books for Herbert Reichner, a noted bibliophile, writer, and editor of the periodical *Philobiblon* in Austria, who moved to New York in 1938 with the intention of being a publisher. From 1939 to 1944, Rostenberg worked as typist, cataloger, and customs agent in Reichner's shop at 34 East Sixty-second Street. Despite the man's demanding regimen, Rostenberg credits the experience with persuading her to become a bookseller. "How amazing that you know anything about books," he said to her early on. "Nobody in America really does."

Seated comfortably on a silk sofa with their aging dachshund, Bettina, napping contentedly between them, Rostenberg and Stern used a German expression, *Fingerspitzengefühl*, to help explain what keeps their enthusiasm for the hunt vibrant and alive after so many years. As Rostenberg translated the word into English, she raised both hands from her lap and rubbed her thumbs against her forefingers. "This is how you know a rare book when you see one," she said. "You feel an electric tingling running through your fingertips. It comes from experience, but it's instinctive too; you have to have a feel for them. *Fingerspitzengefühl* was Reichner's word, and he passed it on to me when I left my apprenticeship with him to start my own business in 1944. He said you will not find rare books any other way. It is the one piece of advice I have always considered indispensable."

Rostenberg began working with Reichner after she learned that the doctoral dissertation she had spent six years preparing at Columbia University had been rejected. Her subject, the role of sixteenth-century humanist printers in the dissemination of learning and reform throughout Europe, had been deemed too arcane by an obdurate faculty adviser, although other scholars thought it brilliant. Thirty years later, Columbia recognized the enduring value of Rostenberg's many published works and voted to award her a Ph.D. The earlier snub turned out to be a blessing, since it persuaded the young graduate student to pursue a career among rare books, not as an academician locked on a tenure track at a university.

"Reichner was not a pleasant man by any means; he treated me like a serf," Rostenberg said of the period she calls her "five years in Siberia." Nonetheless, she learned a great deal about the business. "My horizons were expanding with every book I handled, as I became familiar with his

stock I gradually learned to dismiss the uncontrolled ravings of my frenetic employer." Rostenberg also began to write professional articles for
various journals, and before returning home from work at night, she
paused to sift through her employer's wastepaper basket. "Every time he
threw a foreign catalog away, I retrieved it, thus accumulating records of
European dealers' stocks. Although I may not have been conscious of it,
I was preparing and being prepared for the life of an antiquarian bookseller."

Her intention at the time, like that of her friend Madeleine Stern, was
to devote her life to literary research. Both were the daughters of prominent New York City families; Rostenberg's father was a respected physician, Stern's a prosperous businessman. The two women met in 1930 at
the Temple Emanu-El Sabbath School in New York City, where each
worked as a part-time teacher. Stern was a freshman at Barnard College
and Rostenberg a senior at New York University. Both aspired to careers
in scholarship, dreams they would fulfill in meaningful ways, but neither
had the slightest thought during those bleak days of the Great Depression that a shared love for learning would lead to a long and fulfilling
enterprise in the dealing of rare books.

After finishing her first book, a biography of Margaret Fuller, the
nineteenth-century literary critic, social reformer, and colleague of
Ralph Waldo Emerson, Stern was awarded a John Simon Guggenheim
Memorial Fellowship to conduct research into the life of Louisa May
Alcott. For Christmas in 1943, Stern gave her friend five boxes of sta-
tionery, shipping labels, and business cards, all handsomely engraved
with the words LEONA ROSTENBERG—RARE BOOKS. In the upper left-hand
corner of each was embossed the picture of a Renaissance printer and his
apprentice taken from Jost Amman's *Book of Trades,* a device the firm of
Rostenberg & Stern still uses in its catalogs. As further incentive Stern
lent Rostenberg one thousand dollars to help her establish the business.
The following year, Rostenberg set up shop in her family's home in the
Bronx, and was in the book business to stay. On April 9, 1945, Stern

called Rostenberg with more good news: "You have a junior partner. I'll be up tomorrow."

After operating for twenty-five years out of Rostenberg's house on East 179th Street, it was time, they wrote in *Old Books, Rare Friends,* a charming memoir of half a century in the antiquarian book trade, "for the two book ladies of the Bronx to change their address." In 1969, they moved into a handsome East Side apartment between Madison and Park Avenues, where they have lived and worked ever since. "We still buy books because we enjoy the detective work that goes along with it," Stern said. "We may not get around as much as we used to, but we continue to cerebrate as much as we ever did. The idea is to have fun." Indeed, Rostenberg and Stern have so much fun with their literary sleuthing that they often call each other "Holmes and Watson," affectionate references to Arthur Conan Doyle's unflappable detective Sherlock Holmes and his sidekick, Dr. Watson.

Their most spectacular coup was the discovery in 1942 of a pseudonym used by Louisa May Alcott (1832–1888) to write a series of "blood and thunder" stories on such sensational subjects as transvestitism, mesmerism, sadomasochism, hashish smoking, and fetishism. Alcott surreptitiously published these stories in *Frank Leslie's Illustrated Newspaper* and *Frank Leslie's Chimney Corner,* the leading tabloid journals of the mid-nineteenth century in the United States. That exciting find, uncovered among the Alcott journals, papers, and letters preserved in the Houghton Library of Harvard University, persuaded Stern to write *Louisa May Alcott,* published in 1950 and still regarded as the definitive biography of the renowned author of *Little Women.*

Once Rostenberg and Stern had established Alcott's use of the pen name A. M. Barnard for some of those early pieces, they began to search for the stories themselves. These efforts led to the publication of half a dozen volumes edited and coedited by Stern, among them *Behind a Mask: Unknown Thrillers of Louisa May Alcott* (1975), *A Double Life: Newly Discovered Thrillers of Louisa May Alcott* (1988), and *Freaks of Genius:*

Unknown Thrillers of Louisa May Alcott (1991). The recent renaissance of interest in all things involving Louisa May Alcott has been attributed in no small measure to the indomitable digging of Rostenberg and Stern. While the Alcott discoveries remain their most renowned accomplishments as literary detectives, there have been others equally impressive. Their personal favorite involves the identification and acquisition of books published in the early seventeenth century by what they call the Pilgrim Press. These were tracts written against the Church of England and published in Leiden between 1617 and 1619 by the religious dissenters who sailed to America on the *Mayflower* in 1620. "We regard these books as a kind of American incunabula, because they represent the earliest writings of the first European settlers in America," Rostenberg said. She recalled an occasion when she and her partner found one of these items in a dealer's booth at a book fair in New York.

"When Madeleine finds something, she uses a different voice," Rostenberg said. "So I heard her say, 'Leona, come over here,' in *that* voice, and I knew something was brewing. I went over and she had found one of the Pilgrim Press books. We tried to show no emotion at all, so we said, 'We will take this thing and a couple of other things,' calling it a 'thing.' It was thirty dollars for everything. This dealer wrote down on the invoice, 'one old book.' That was a wonderful find." Stern nodded in agreement, but quickly added how it was her partner "who got us started on the Pilgrim Press books" in the first place. "Leona found out about them by studying a catalog she got from Reichner. She read up on it, researched it, ate it up. And when the opportunity came, we were ready."

Because they are proven scholars, Rostenberg and Stern have taken steps over the years to prepare catalogs that are centered around various intellectual themes and disciplines. Their first list, issued in 1945, remains their favorite to this day. They called it *A Catalogue for the Easter Term Containing Divers Matters Relating to the History of the Book*. Within a week, they sold more than half of the items in the catalog. They received eight orders for an ephemeral article published in 1787 on "The Art of the Paper War," including calls from Harvard University and the Newberry Library in Chicago. Another catalog, *The Man of the Renaissance,* featured 425 items, each devoted to different professions. There was Machiavelli's *Prince* and Vasari's *Lives of the Artists,* Petrarch's *Sonnets* and Rabelais's *Letters.* Yet another offered one or two books published in each year of Shakespeare's life, 1564 to 1616.

In 1956 Stern was elected chair of the Middle Atlantic Chapter of the Antiquarian Booksellers Association of America (ABAA) and promptly proposed that the group organize the first ABAA book fair to be held in the United States, which was mounted in 1960. In 1957 the New York Public Library engaged the partners to act as their official agents at New York auctions; later they served the Library of Congress in the same capacity. In 1972 Rostenberg was elected president of the ABAA, the second woman to hold that position. (The late Frances Hamill of Chicago was the first.) While all this was going on, universities throughout the country were contacting Rostenberg & Stern with the idea of strengthening their holdings. On many occasions, the entire contents of their catalogs were purchased en bloc by such institutions as the University of Buffalo, the University of Texas, and Brigham Young University.

In the epilogue to their memoir, Rostenberg and Stern commented on recent trends in the trade: "Every age is critical of the next, and we are no exceptions. Although we admire and befriend many young dealers who do not confuse value with price, we deplore the all-too-popular conception entertained by many dealers that books are to be regarded primarily as investments. Such booksellers go in for dollarship, not scholarship." With advancing age, the women began to acknowledge, in varying degrees, diminished eyesight and diminished hearing. "We have become each other's eyes and ears to survive," they wrote. "We do more than survive—we experience the passion that has dominated our lives; we continue our hunt for books, practice our Sherlockian exploits, and, living our double lives, write and cowrite books. It is true we may be stepping back. We are not stepping out." In their concluding chapter,

Rostenberg and Stern detailed the unending joy they have experienced as lifelong friends and business associates, and in helping so many individuals and institutions build important collections. The dedications of the book are to each other, "with love and gratitude."

M ost of the emigré booksellers concentrated on specialties not pursued by their American colleagues, and for the most part they stayed away from Americana, American and English literature, and autograph material, concentrating instead on medieval manuscripts, early continental printed books, art books, fine bindings, history of medicine and science, bibliography, and out-of-print scholarly books in the humanities. Their work was enthusiastically welcomed on college campuses, where academic libraries were just beginning to build collections in many of these areas. "The books they wanted were no longer out of reach somewhere in Europe, or confined to the shelves of a few rather intimidating, or seemingly intimidating establishments; and the expert dealers one previously visited in Munich, Frankfurt, Vienna or Berlin were now in mid-Manhattan or Los Angeles," Bernard Rosenthal wrote.

Not all Jewish booksellers who left Europe, as Rosenthal made clear, ended up in the United States. Some found other countries happy to offer sanctuary. Bernard Amtmann, the founding president of the Antiquarian Booksellers Association of Canada and regarded in his time as the dean of Canadian booksellers, was a native of Vienna who fled Austria in 1938, making his way to North America in 1947. During the war he served heroically with the French Resistance, at one point leading a commando unit engaged in sabotage operations. Before moving to Ottawa at the age of forty, he began to develop an attraction toward old books, and within days of his arrival he was gathering inventory for what he had determined would be his life's work. Although Amtmann never attended college, he had a hunger for knowledge and spent hours in the Public Archives and the Library of Parliament learning the history of Canada and honing his bibliographic skills. In 1951 he moved to Montreal and opened a shop on Greene Avenue. Granted citizenship in 1954, he spent the remaining twenty-six years of his life devoted to preserving the documentary artifacts of his new country. A particular interest of his was gathering political ephemera, much of it polemical tracts dashed off in the heat of debate. "There have been thousands of these items printed throughout the years, almost all thrown away or used to light fires," two Canadian booksellers, John Mappin and John Archer, wrote in a privately printed appreciation of their colleague's career. "He learned the importance of agrarian radicals in Western Canada, the role both religious and secular of the church in French Canada, and the influence of the Loyalist tradition throughout English Eastern Canada, and he continued to find books, pamphlets, and ephemera that were not recorded."

When he learned on one occasion that a certain "religious institution" in Montreal had already sent half of the old books in its library to a landfill and was about to discard the rest, Amtmann called the local bishop and offered a thousand dollars, sight unseen, for all that remained. A deal was struck, and some two hundred cartons of material were diverted to his office in short order. Most of the books were of little value, although there were enough items of interest to fill six boxes, including a first edition of *Règlement de la confrérie*, the first book printed in Montreal. In time the title would fetch $2,500 at auction; more importantly, it found a secure new home in the rare-books library of McGill University. But like so many good book stories, there is an amusing footnote to this one. Several weeks after the discards had been delivered to Amtmann's office—and a full year before the scarce Montreal imprint was put up for sale—another cleric from the "religious institution" called to complain about the price paid for so many books. Since the issue was one of volume, not content, Amtmann offered to return most of the titles he had bought—he would retain just six of the two hundred cartons— and allow church officials to keep the thousand dollars they had already received. The offer was promptly accepted, and the bookseller had found a convenient way to get rid of 194 boxes of books he did not want clogging up his inventory. "Most important," his colleagues wrote in tribute, "one of the most significant of Canadian books was recognized for what it was, and took its place of honour in the Rare Book Room of McGill University."

During the 1960s Amtmann became a major supplier to Canada's rapidly growing network of colleges and universities, to whom his fluency in English and French proved useful. When Queen's University wanted to document the history of French Canada, Amtmann found thousands of appropriate titles and passed them on at prices well below their cataloged values. "One of his delights was establishing historical significance, relating old material to the issues of the day and finding why it was important," Mappin and Archer wrote. "Which libraries had it? Which did not? How many copies were there in the country? How many copies were there anywhere? Finding why an item was important was as much part of the chase as finding it in the first place."

Between 1971 and 1973 Amtmann published *Contributions to a Short-Title Catalogue of Canadiana,* a four-volume compilation of thirty thousand items that had passed through his hands over the years, some ten thousand of which had never been recorded anywhere else. Amtmann was regarded in some circles as a haughty perfectionist; his most lasting contribution was his continuing effort to alert Canadians to the fragility of their cultural documents, even if sometimes it seemed that he was a bit too strident in making his point. A 1977 episode Mappin and Archer called their friend's "last public brawl" occurred two years before his death, and involved his disappointment at the government's unwillingness to purchase 2,500 letters and personal papers of Sir James Robert Gowan (1815–1885), a wealthy Irishman who immigrated to Canada in 1832, served for forty years on the bench of Ontario, and was an influential member of the Canadian Senate. The archive included substantive correspondence with numerous people prominent in the country's formative years, including Sir John A. Macdonald (1815–1891), the Scottish-born statesman who formed the first government in 1867. Amtmann had appraised the papers, which he had received on consignment, for $250,000; the Ontario Archives offered him $25,000. Deeply insulted, he issued a pamphlet that characterized the archive as "a splendid manifestation of real national heritage."

The far more salient purpose of the tract, though—it was titled *A Conspiracy against the Canadian Identity*—was to condemn the "ongoing" actions of a certain unnamed "academic establishment" that he asserted had mindfully "retarded and delayed the discovery of the Canadian identity." While some critics considered the polemic arrogant and self-serving, it energized serious debate on the issue, and burnished Amtmann's stature as a guardian of Canadian heritage. Today, the bibliographical archive Amtmann painstakingly assembled during his thirty-two-year career is installed in the National Library of Canada, and his business files are at McGill University. Amtmann's efforts on behalf of his adopted country's heritage were acknowledged by the University of Saskatchewan when it presented him with an honorary Doctor of Laws degree toward the end of his life. The citation singled out his "indomitable will to find and record the printed and written sources of our national literature."

B y far the most prominent American bookseller of the twentieth century was Dr. A. S. W. Rosenbach of Philadelphia, known to his colleagues, customers, and admiring public as "the Doctor," a title he earned the hard way, having received a Ph.D. in English literature from the University of Pennsylvania in 1901. Rosenbach's dealings with the great collectors of the period, most notably Henry E. Huntington, Mr. and Mrs. Henry Clay Folger, Countess Estelle Doheny, Lessing J. Rosenwald, and John H. Scheide, along with his flamboyant triumphs in the auction galleries, brought him a degree of renown that extended far beyond the cozy world of bibliophiles. When the Washington lawyer

Frank J. Hogan decided in 1931 at the age of fifty-one to satisfy a lifelong hunger for rare books, he entrusted himself entirely to the care of Rosenbach. "I would be willing to blindfold my eyes, stop up my ears, have my mouth gagged and follow *your* judgment," he wrote on one occasion. "I am as proud of your collection as you are," the Doctor replied, and there is little doubt that the Philadelphia bookman, an enthusiastic collector in his own right, meant every word of the compliment.

For all the recognition some dealers may occasionally achieve, their fundamental reason for being is to purvey a particular kind of merchandise. Even with that standard as a base, however, the very best, as we have seen, are also scholars who often rescue precious objects from certain oblivion, sometimes fulfilling the far more significant role of discerning value "where others see only piles of rubbish," as John Hill Burton blithely observed in the mid-nineteenth century. A good deal of this can be attributed to a kind of fervor that for the most part is undefinable, but constantly in play nonetheless. No standard curriculum teaches anyone how to become a bookseller; there are no minimum scores to achieve on a professional proficiency test. A bookseller's name and reputation stand for a great deal, and skills, for the most part, are learned in the field. The reasons dealers have for entering the trade in the first place can be revealing.

"The bookseller, too, is a collector, even though his collections do not remain in his hands," Archibald Hanna, a former librarian at the Beinecke Rare Books and Manuscripts Library at Yale, wrote in the foreword to a collection of erudite catalogs compiled by Peter Decker, a specialist in Americana who helped build the university's collections. "It has often been said that a bookseller enters the trade because he is otherwise unemployable," Decker confided in an autobiographical essay he prepared for the occasion.

Stephen Weissman, respected on both sides of the Atlantic for his facility for turning up fascinating books in the unlikeliest of places, graduated from Harvard College in 1959 as a mathematics major, turned to

English in graduate school, and opted to become a bookseller after sitting in on a few sessions of the seminar conducted in the Houghton Library by the legendary bibliographer and rare-books librarian William L. Jackson. "It was technically a bibliography course, but it was the most genteel course I ever took," Weissman told me in an interview in his London flat shortly after moving his business, Ximenes Rare Books, to England from New York in the late 1990s. "It met once a week on Wednesday afternoons in the Keats Room, and we sort of passed around Shakespeare quartos and discussed them. Jackson used to talk about where they came from, how much they were worth, who bought them, who sold them, things like that. I think at that point the treasure-hunt side of the trade appealed to me most of all. To be honest, I wasn't that keen a graduate student, and the notion of becoming an English professor had little appeal. Most of my time then was spent playing poker, going to the racetrack, various forms of gambling, actually, and although I didn't quite realize it at the time, this business I was drifting into turned into a respectable form of playing cards and betting on horses. It is a kind of gambling business, and ever since I have been doing it full time, my card playing has pretty much vanished."

Librarians everywhere acknowledge the debt they owe to dealers. "There has probably never been a great bookseller who was not also a great book buyer," Lawrence Clark Powell, the renowned librarian of the University of California at Los Angeles, believed. "If and when I have the opportunity of planning a library school curriculum, I shall require a course in the buying and selling of books, on the economics and the diplomacy of book collecting, shaped around the trinity of book collector, bookseller, and librarian." And Powell had no compunctions about giving credit where it was due. "My own apprenticeship in the book trade was every bit as valuable a preparation for librarianship as was the graduate year I spent in studying for a professional degree," he wrote, and his apprenticeship was with Jake Zeitlin of Los Angeles, considered by some to have been the West Coast counterpart to Dr. Rosenbach.

There have been a few instances where booksellers have gone on to become librarians at major institutions, most notably David A. Randall (1905–1975), a graduate of Lehigh University who dropped out of Harvard Law School in 1929 to become an apprentice bookseller after auditing George Parker Winship's justly celebrated Fine Arts 5E course in bibliography. In time he became manager of the rare-books department at Charles Scribner's on Fifth Avenue, helping a variety of famous collectors build wonderful libraries. When one of his more influential clients, Josiah K. Lilly Jr., was making plans to give his books to Indiana University in the 1950s, he persuaded Randall to become the founding librarian of the Lilly Library, a position he held from 1956 to 1975. "Randall was a bookman at heart, rather than an administrator, and he never lost his touch or his enthusiasm for finding books or collections," Joel Silver, a librarian at the Lilly Library and the author of numerous works of book history, wrote in an appreciative essay. "As a longtime bookseller, he knew good books when he saw them, and his acquisitions during his early years at Indiana could not be duplicated today at any price." The key to Randall's success as a university librarian, Silver believed, "came from not only reading about books, but from constantly handling the books themselves."

The same could be said for Wilberforce Eames (1855–1937), a young bookseller and bibliographer who left the trade in 1883 to work at the Lenox Library, and later as bibliographer and head of the American History Division of the New York Public Library. "At an age when most small boys shy away from books, he chose them as the companions of his life," Deoch Fulton wrote in a brief sketch of Eames for the Grolier Club. Another former bookseller to make the switch to librarian was Edwin Wolf 2d (1911–1991), a well-born Philadelphian who as a prep school graduate disdained the option of a college education, choosing instead to work with his uncle, Dr. A. S. W. Rosenbach. Wolf later gained international distinction as head of the Library Company of Philadelphia, the famed lending library founded by Benjamin Franklin, and as the author of numerous important monographs, including a standard biography of his famous mentor.

Nowhere is the depth of scholarship more apparent than in the catalogs booksellers prepare to detail the items they are offering for sale, ostensibly to explain why they are important and justify their prices. The arrival of the Internet and the ubiquitous use of online listings are recent innovations that have reduced the number of printed catalogs being issued, but the most respected dealers continue to prepare them, and the most astute collectors continue to pore over their contents with unbridled enthusiasm. The most profound impact the World Wide Web has had on catalogs is that lower-end books now tend to be listed exclusively online, with far greater effort expended on describing the choicest books.

Fred Schreiber, with his wife Ellen the owner of E. K. Schreiber Books in New York City, enjoys the respect of his colleagues for the research and erudition he devotes to the writing of his catalogs, and for the remarkable lengths he will go to determine the significance of the material he offers for sale. Because his specialty subjects—incunabula, early printed books, Renaissance humanism, early illustrated books, Greek printing, early editions of the Greek and Latin classics—more often than not involve works that few modern readers have ever heard of, much less know intimately, the challenge for Schreiber is to determine exactly what he is dealing with, and why a prospective buyer would consider it essential.

"The ancient Greeks had a word, *aretē*," Schreiber explained to me over lunch one summer afternoon in a pleasant Italian restaurant on Columbus Avenue, not far from the apartment on Central Park West where he operates his business. "This word is not easily translated into English, but it is commonly interpreted to mean something akin to virtue, or excellence. The term refers to the quality that makes a thing or person a good instance of what it is. Thus, for example, speed is the *aretē* of the thoroughbred racing horse, sharpness the *aretē* of a knife, courage the *aretē* of a soldier. But what is the *aretē* of a bookseller's catalog? My answer is, The ability it has to sell books. That is its reason for being. So a catalog should not say more than it has to say, nor say less; it should say just what it needs to say to sell the book."

Though the concept may sound disarmingly straightforward, it is not as simple as it sounds. "It is often tempting to show off one's knowledge in a catalog, or to wax didactic, but this just clouds the issue," Schreiber continued. "When I first started writing catalog descriptions, I used to say too much, but I have gradually learned to trim down my descriptions to their essentials. What is this book about? What is there about it that justifies the price I have determined it should command? There is another crucially important point: Everything you say about a book must be true. Any claim you make about it should be supported by evidence. This also sounds much simpler than it actually is. It is often an almost unsurmountable task to remove the layers of misconceptions about a given edition that have accumulated over the centuries and are now universally accepted as truths."

With 80 percent of his customers librarians and curators who are buying for institutional collections, Schreiber has learned that he has to be a salesman as much as a scholar, and that the people he is dealing with are more often than not specialists in their fields. Schreiber was born in 1935 in Berlin. Three years later, the day after Kristallnacht, his family fled to France. After the war, at the age of seventeen, he moved to the United States. "I came to America with no education, I spoke no English, I didn't have a trade," he told me. From 1953 to 1960 he worked as a shipping clerk on Forty-seventh Street in the diamond district, and began attending high school at night when he was twenty-two. Three years later he went on to Queens College, graduated Phi Beta Kappa, and won a Woodrow Wilson scholarship to attend Harvard Graduate School, earning a Ph.D. in classics in 1970. After receiving his doctorate, he began teaching at Herbert Lehman College at City University in New York (CUNY), becoming an associate professor. "I was granted tenure, and then, in 1978, when I was forty-three years old, I quit to go into the rare-book business," he said.

Before committing themselves entirely to bookselling, Schreiber and his wife agreed that they would try their hands at the trade first. "I took a leave of absence from teaching for one year. I played it safe. We put all our savings into buying inventory. Everything we had. It was a big gamble. But I figured if it doesn't work out, I'll go back to teaching. So we put all our money into our first catalog." Having bought shrewdly from other booksellers and at auction, Schreiber sold about 60 percent of his first offering in short order; after much agonizing deliberation he told the chairman of his department at CUNY that he was giving up his tenured position. "I had a child, I had a mortgage, so it wasn't easy to reach that life-changing decision. But, with Ellen's encouragement, this is what I decided." Since he had no client list, Schreiber sent the catalog out "to every library and bookseller I could think of" to drum up business. When I asked Schreiber to reflect on what the "defining moments" in his development as a scholar-bookseller were, he immediately cited two episodes from his earliest days, when he was weighing the security of a university position against the uncertainty of the antiquarian book business.

The first epiphany came after he had distributed his premiere catalog. To his great surprise, he immediately got an order for an eighteenth-century edition of the treatise *Education of an Orator* by the first-century Roman writer Quintilian, with a commentary by Johann Matthias Gesner. Schreiber had it priced at $50. When he learned that the person buying it was Emil Offenbacher, a respected bookseller in Queens, he decided to deliver the book in person. "I guess I was looking for some pointers in the business," Schreiber said. "I also was curious to know why a bookseller who had earned a reputation for knowing what he was doing was interested in an old edition of a Latin classic with content that had no relevance whatsoever to the subjects he specialized in as a dealer."

A self-educated man who came to the United States as a Jewish emigré after Hitler took power in Germany, Offenbacher sensed Schreiber's curiosity immediately. "Are you wondering why I ordered this book from you?" he asked straightaway. Schreiber replied shyly how that indeed was the case. "Mr. Offenbacher proceeded to leaf through the volume looking for a specific passage. After finding the page, he handed the open book back to me, asking me to translate a certain Latin passage of Gesner's commentary. When I had finished translating the passage, in which Gesner compared the laws of oratory to those of musical structure, and described a certain 'Bacchius' playing some kind of wind instrument, Emil said, 'What you have just read happens to be the earliest published biographic reference to Johann Sebastian Bach, and as such it is of the greatest importance in the history of musicology.' " Schreiber's recollection of this encounter is of such import to him that he has posted a summary of it on his website, and it includes an instructive moral: "Behind the smile with which he accompanied this piece of information I could almost hear Emil's unspoken thought: 'And therefore this book is worth many times more than what you sold it to me for, you *Dummkopf!*' "

The lesson Emil Offenbacher taught Schreiber that day was that there are many facets to an antiquarian book, some of them concealed below the surface. That was "big lesson number one" in Schreiber's apprenticeship as a bookseller. "Big lesson number two" came shortly thereafter, when he issued a catalog with his detailed description of a fifteenth-century book by Michael de Hungaria (Michael of Hungary) that he had recently acquired. This is a collection of sermons in Latin; embedded in the edition were three verses printed in Middle English. "I saw this copy being offered by another dealer, and something told me it was important, and there may be more here than meets the eye. I paid twenty-five hundred dollars for it. I am telling you the price because it is important in this context. Remember, I was making about fifteen thousand dollars a year at the time as a teacher, and twenty-five hundred was big money for me. What had intrigued me were the three lines in Middle English. The book was printed in 1480 in Louvain, and I wondered, could these possibly be quotations from the New Testament? The context was students at Cambridge or Oxford swearing 'by Christ's blood,' and these were printed in Middle English. So I researched the question, and sure enough I found that the first verse was a quotation from 1 John 1:7. So the question then arises, When was the earliest printing of any portion of the Bible in English? Well, turns out, this just might be it. So my heading in the catalog was, 'Possibly the Earliest Biblical Quotation Printed in English.' I wrote a detailed description of the book and offered it at $4,200. Well, I began to get orders from everywhere, from all over the world. I couldn't believe it. The first order came in from a bookseller in Connecticut, Laurence Witten, who is now passed away, and I sold it to him."

Shortly thereafter, the book was featured in Witten's catalog with Schreiber's description printed virtually verbatim, and offered for sale at $16,500; it promptly was bought at that price by a major private institutional library. From this experience, Schreiber learned several other important lessons, the first being that research is just half the challenges, with knowledge of the market the other. "I didn't know the business yet. I knew the book just fine, and it was my description that persuaded the library to buy it, otherwise it would have been just another incunable. So even though I knew *what* I had, I didn't know what kinds of things *sold*, and to whom, or what their actual value was in the marketplace. Once these veteran booksellers out there saw what I had discovered, they instantly recognized that a book like this sells very easily. Larry Witten knew that market, and I did not. He had knowledge, and knowledge is power in this business. So this reinforced my conviction. I knew how to do my research, but I did not yet know the business. It's good to be a scholar, but that's not going to put food on your table. The rest comes with experience."

Although he learned the craft of bookselling in the United States, Schreiber agreed with my suggestion that he is in the tradition of the European bookseller. "Very definitely. The Europeans brought with them not only knowledge of where the old books were, but what was *in* them. I read a lot, and I learned the business by reading the catalogs of people like Emil Offenbacher, William Salloch, and Bernard Rosenthal." Like the booksellers whose work he admires, Schreiber takes a great deal of pride in his catalogs. "It is fair to say that when I left teaching I had become disenchanted with academic life. I came to realize that I had driven myself to scholarship not because I wanted to teach—even though, I must say, I was a very good teacher—but because I wanted to *learn*. I left teaching at a time when interest in the classics was in decline, and the real possibility arose that I would some day soon be teaching remedial English. That is not something I wanted to be doing with a doctorate in classical philology. I also found myself having to water down my lectures, and that was not fair to the best students in class. As a professor I published several academic papers on specialized classical subjects that I doubt any of my colleagues ever read. Now, when I issue catalogs, I know people read them, because I have the sales to prove it."

Schreiber said that shortly after he published his first catalog, he was pleasantly surprised to receive a complimentary letter from a world-renowned classicist who congratulated him on his description of a particular Greek book. "The irony is that a few years before, I had published an article in a classical journal on the very same topic and got absolutely no feedback from anyone. But here, with my first catalog, I received a response from a prominent scholar, and it made me feel that I was doing something right."

The ultimate goal in writing a catalog, Schreiber concluded, is the same ambition that drives every conscientious writer. "I hope this doesn't sound self-serving, I don't mean it that way. But what I strive after most of all is to be able to discover the truth about a book, not distort the facts, not exaggerate its importance, but still make it very appealing. And that I find very challenging."

Most successful booksellers, and many astute collectors for that matter, will readily admit that having the candid advice of a mentor at crucial points along the way was crucial in their development. For Priscilla Juvelis, one of the preeminent dealers in twentieth-century book arts and the women's rights movement in the United States, and president of the Antiquarian Booksellers Association of America from 1998 to 2000, guidance and encouragement at the start of her career came from the late John F. Fleming, generally acknowledged to be the dominant American bookseller of his generation, and among the greatest of all time.

"I didn't know anything about the rare-book field before I met John," Juvelis told me one chilly April morning in her tastefully appointed shop at 1166 Massachusetts Avenue in Cambridge, a five-minute walk from Widener Library at Harvard University. Indeed, before Juvelis met the eminent bookseller for lunch one day in 1979, she had only the vaguest idea that she might enter the antiquarian trade at all, let alone become a savvy professional who would earn recognition as an authority in her chosen specialty within five years of becoming a major player. Juvelis had worked at a variety of jobs in New York publishing, starting in 1970 as secretary to William Jovanovich, the former publisher of Harcourt Brace Jovanovich, and then serving as director of HBJ International Corp. She later worked as director of subsidiary rights for the Franklin Library. A native of Marblehead, Massachusetts, and a 1967 graduate of Boston University in political science, she met Fleming through a mutual friend, Jack Tanzer, who directed the purchase and sale of master paintings at the Knoedler Gallery in Manhattan. "I had reached a point where I wanted to go into business for myself," Juvelis said. "I wasn't entirely clear on what I should do, just that I wanted to be my own boss. Jack knew that I had worked in publishing and that I knew about buying and selling. He said he had a friend who sold rare books, and that friend happened to be John Fleming."

An introduction was arranged and a lunch scheduled, where the two became "pretty fast friends," Juvelis recalled. "I told him about my background and my interests. My father was a buyer of art and antiques, so I knew something about collecting. He finally said, 'Gee, I don't understand why you don't become a rare-book dealer.' I said, 'How would I learn about it?' And he said, 'Well, come and work for me, dear, and we'll see what happens.' " For the next year, Juvelis worked in Fleming's shop at 322 East Fifty-seventh Street between First and Second Avenues, a massive apartment built originally for a lawyer with a practice in music and musicians, and formerly the New York office of Dr. A. S. W. Rosenbach, who had given Fleming his first job in the business in 1925. The suite featured a sixty-foot room with twenty-foot ceilings designed to function as a concert hall, and was decorated with tapestries and paintings, including a life-size portrait of the great British actor David Garrick. Fleming conducted his business at a huge Renaissance table set dramatically on a platform.

Following Fleming's death on December 20, 1987, at the age of seventy-seven, the *New York Times* declared him to have been the "rarebook dealer and collector who for 30 years dominated the antiquarian market." In England, the *Independent* of London echoed those remarks, noting that his passing brought to an end "a legendary period in the history of bookselling that stretches back almost a century." Born in New York City, Fleming began his career in 1925 at the age of fifteen as a clerk for Dr. Rosenbach. "In his first week on the job, Mr. Fleming demonstrated that a book for which Mr. Rosenbach paid $3,000 was worthless, and thus cemented a lifelong friendship," the *Times* wrote. In time Fleming became manager and vice president of the Rosenbach company; three years after Rosenbach's death in 1952, Fleming paid $2 million for his stock and set up shop in the Doctor's East Fifty-seventh Street apartment.

Over the years, Fleming helped build collections for a veritable who's who of twentieth-century collectors, Clifton Waller Barrett, Abel Berland, Countess Estelle Doheny, the Viscountess Eccles, Jane Engelhard, Arthur A. Houghton, Mrs. Paul Mellon, Lessing J. Rosenwald, William H. Scheide, Louis Silver, and Alice Tully among them. Working with Belle da Costa Greene, founding librarian of the Pierpont Morgan Library in New York, and her successors, he served for many years as an adviser to the library in the development of its collections.

Fleming's obituary in the *Independent*, reprinted in the spring 1988 issue of the *Book Collector,* identified his strengths: "He was completely discreet: his judgment of prices, the condition of books, the extent of his customers' purses and determination, was faultless." It also described his character: "He was generous of his time to the young and the poor, as well as the rich and famous, and was particularly good to beginning booksellers." Fleming's willingness to give a year of apprenticeship to Priscilla Juvelis was in keeping with his reputation of helping out the next generation. "After spending a year with him, I moved back to Boston and started out on my own. But we remained very close. He invited me to parties, where I met some very important people, we traveled to Europe together, we attended auctions together. Watching John work an auction, at the preview and in the gallery, was worth its weight in gold. He was the master." She said that she has appropriated for herself Fleming's oft-stated axiom, which cites three qualities in fixing the value of a rare book: "Condition, condition, and condition."

As we spoke, Juvelis pasted labels on her latest catalog, *The Legacy of Seneca Falls: Some Key Documents and Books in the American Women's Rights Movement,* an impressive effort featuring sixty-six items, most of them from the nineteenth century. A week later, Juvelis would proudly report that almost every item listed had been sold, most of them in one fell swoop to a single collector before copies of the catalog had been received by everyone else on the mailing list. "This happens every so often in the trade, and I offer it as a tip to collectors who are looking for a competitive edge," Juvelis said. "I sent an advance copy out to one of my very best customers, a person who is a major collector of women's history and women's literature. If you as a collector have a good working relationship with a dealer, that dealer more often than not will quote you choice material in your specialty before listing it generally to everyone else, or at least send you a copy of a new catalog before sending it to everyone else. Some people might be uncomfortable with that arrangement, but as a bookseller, you learn very quickly how important it is to accommodate your most valued customers."

It was a similar experience in 1983—three years after setting out on her own—that Juvelis believes established her credentials in the antiquarian field and helped her earn early recognition as a leading authority in *livres d'artistes*, books illustrated by the great masters of the late nineteenth and twentieth centuries with original graphics, many of them housed in hand-crafted bindings, exquisite works of art in their own right. A quick look at the title page of that catalog, *The Book Beautiful and the Binding as Art*, indicates that the 219 books were being offered for sale by two booksellers in a joint venture, John F. Fleming and Priscilla Juvelis. Artists represented in the catalog included Pierre Bonnard, Georges Braque, Marc Chagall, Aristide Maillol, Henri Matisse, Pablo Picasso, Georges Rouault, and Jacques Villon, illustrating the literature of such writers as Guillaume Apollinaire, Charles Baudelaire, Honoré de Balzac, Georges Duhamel, Paul Eluard, Gustave Flaubert, Anatole France, André Gide, and Paul Verlaine.

"There is an added dimension in this extraordinary collection," Juvelis and Fleming wrote in their preface, and that was the custom-made bindings produced by the world's finest practitioners of this venerable decorative art, names that included Rose Adler, Paul Bonet, Georges Cretté, Henri Creuzevault, and Pierre Legrain. The initial collector of the books was a Buenos Aires businessman named Carlos Scherrer who spent considerable time in France in the early years of the twentieth century, and who died in 1941. A second collector, also an Argentine, and the person from whom Juvelis acquired the books in 1983, chose to remain anonymous, a wish that Juvelis continues to honor. "I heard about the books from a friend in the art world who was buying this collector's paintings," Juvelis said. "The American market for *livres d'artistes* was not particularly strong at the time, and only French dealers were bidding on the books. Some of the biggest dealers in Paris were involved. So I went down to Argentina, I offered what I thought it would take to get the collection, and I came in with the highest bid. There were about a thousand books, all of extraordinary quality, with all the big names represented. I had to borrow the money to close the deal, but it was a once-in-a-lifetime opportunity, and I couldn't pass it up."

As soon as the books arrived in Massachusetts, the first order of business was a telephone call to Fleming. "I talked to John in the morning, and he was on the next plane up to Boston from New York; he was here that afternoon. He would go anywhere, at the drop of a hat, at the chance of seeing a great book. He had a deep passion for books that went beyond buying them and selling them." Fleming's first reaction at what he saw was total silence. "I showed him one book, a magnificent volume that I took from its *chemise* and *étui* [sleeve and case], and he said nothing," Juvelis recalled. "I got the next one down, same response. This went on for about half a dozen books, by which time I was getting very nervous. Finally, he said, 'Well, it's clear that the English can't hold a candle to the French when it comes to making beautiful books, isn't it. Now, dear, what was it you paid for this collection?' I told him what I paid, and he said, 'Right. Then we're partners.' "

These were precisely the words Juvelis wanted to hear, but she had a small qualification of her own. "I agreed immediately that we would do it together, but it was important for me to make clear that we were partners, as I remember putting it then, 'on everything that has to do with this collection.' What I was saying was that any new customers that came our way through this project, we would share completely. This was the entrée I needed to truly establish my bona fides as a bookseller at this level." Beyond adding his formidable reputation and financial backing to the enterprise, Fleming contributed his sage advice, and together they selected the finest items to include in the list. "I deferred completely to John on the pricing," Juvelis said. "The market in *livres d'artistes* may have been unfamiliar to him, but he had an innate sense of books." Individual prices were not included in the catalog but printed on separate sheets and furnished to potential buyers on request. The final sentence in the preface proved prophetic: "The collection will be offered for sale en bloc until November 1, 1983."

Before the catalogs had come back from the printer, one of Fleming's customers asked to see the books. "This man came in and bought the books en bloc, and then decided he would build on the collection. I had the very good fortune to help him do that. In this case, I have to say that the customer, as much as John, taught me about the field of twentieth-century book arts, because to satisfy this customer, I had to build on my knowledge of art, artists, and the art world. It mattered to him that I knew the field better than anyone else. We're talking about an extremely intelligent man with an aesthetic sense that enables him to see in a moment whether you know what you're talking about. By having all these books go through my hands, it was the education of a lifetime. I managed in a few years to handle the most beautiful books in the finest bindings imaginable. It was really beyond anything I hoped would happen."

Juvelis cited her work with another client, Iola S. Haverstick of New York, with helping her develop strength in women's history and women's literature. "She bought a Sarah Orne Jewett item and an Edith Wharton item from my very first catalog in 1980, and has strongly impressed upon me over the years the importance of exploring the works of other women writers." With Jean W. Ashton, Caroline F. Schimmel, and Mary C. Schlosser, Haverstick curated a 1998 exhibition at the Grolier Club in New York, *Emerging Voices: American Women Writers, 1650–1920.*

In his 1985 interview with *Forbes* magazine, Fleming said that one lesson he learned from Dr. Rosenbach was to be willing to pay top dollar for the best books. "If you want to make money, you've got to have the guts to buy them," he said. "You've also got to buy the great books." Just as Rosenbach passed invaluable knowledge on to Fleming, so too did Fleming pass on a good deal of what he knew to Juvelis. "What he taught me most of all was to really love books," she said. "And he always insisted on total honesty. 'I believe in the divine law of retribution,' he used to say. The truth is that I couldn't have done it without him. He was my mentor, my teacher, my friend."

I n 1973 William S. Reese, a bright young man with a variety of exciting options to choose from, found himself torn between going to Harvard or Yale, each of which had accepted his application for admission to the class of 1977. Both Ivy League schools enjoy outstanding reputations, so the soft-spoken bookseller who grew up on a farm outside Baltimore in rural Maryland could hardly go wrong in either case. "Yale is a place where I have a big family legacy, so in that sense if I had gone somewhere else it would have annoyed a lot of people," Reese confided in a wide-ranging interview in his New Haven, Connecticut, office, and indeed his pedigree includes the names of several distinguished alumni of the university. He is descended on his father's side from William Tecumseh Sherman's older sister, who married a man named William Reese—the bookseller's middle name, in fact, is Sherman—and his mother traces her lineage back to Oliver Wolcott, a Yale graduate, onetime governor of Connecticut, and a signer of the Declaration of Independence. "Yale figures prominently in my personal history, but the real reason I picked Yale over Harvard, believe it or not, had nothing to do with my family's expectations, and everything to do with the Beinecke Rare Book Library and its collection of Americana. Harvard has wonderful Americana, but nothing like they have at Yale. So it was the rare-book library, and what it offered, that carried the day for me."

When he arrived in New Haven in the fall of 1973, Reese checked in at the Beinecke Rare Books and Manuscript Library, a beautiful marble building with a glassed-in stack of rare books six stories high occupying the center core, and operated apart from the general collections maintained in Sterling Library. He promptly introduced himself to Archibald Hanna, curator of the Yale Collection of Western Americana. Hanna, who held that position from 1952 to 1981, has a clear memory of his first meeting with the lanky Reese, at six feet, three inches someone easily mistaken for a member of the basketball team.

"Freshmen as a rule don't come into the rare-book library at all, never mind the first day of school," Hanna told me one afternoon over a leisurely lunch at Mory's in New Haven (the house, of *Wiffenpoof Song* fame, where Louie dwells). "We hit it off right away, and I am not exaggerating when I say I came to regard Bill as my unofficial junior partner.

The thing about him is that he has an astounding memory, and he just devours knowledge. I supervised his senior essay, which he wrote on the evolution of the American book trade in the nineteenth century. He was one of twelve outstanding students the university allowed to spend their entire senior year on a project without taking any classes. My mentoring on the project consisted of reading the chapters as he brought them in for me to read, and I never found anything to add or subtract. After he graduated, he stayed on for six months and worked as my unpaid part-time assistant." As Hanna's deputy in the stacks, Reese's responsibilities involved culling the circulating collections in Sterling Memorial Library for books that more properly belonged in Beinecke.

Hanna recalled that when he was appointed curator of Yale's Western Americana collection in 1951, he was given one piece of advice by James Babb, the university librarian, and a serious bibliophile in his own right. "Jim Babb said to me, 'Archie, how well you do in this job will depend entirely on your relationship with the booksellers.' Yale has always made it a point to develop close friendships with the booksellers, and I have to say that everything I learned about the book trade I learned from them myself. We invited a group up here for dinner from time to time, and it really paid off, because so many librarians regarded booksellers as their antagonists. Before long a lot of these people were sending us advance copies of their catalogs, or they would call me on something important before letting anybody else know about it. We respected the booksellers, and they treated us admirably in return."

Hanna credited two New York dealers, Edward E. Eberstadt (1883–1958) and Peter Decker (1893–1988), with helping Yale assemble the preeminent collection of Western Americana in the United States. Eberstadt was instrumental in counseling a wealthy private collector, William R. Coe, to build an extraordinary holding of the material, which ultimately went to the university as a gift. "Ed had this exquisite ability to make a book sound irresistible," Hanna said. "I can remember him offering me an item, and saying something like, 'I don't need to point out to a scholar of your knowledge and background the importance of this pamphlet,' but he would anyway. And then he would say, 'Look, I had to pay thirty dollars for this, and I am going to let you have it for ninety-five dollars,' and by the time he left, I was thanking him for the privilege of letting me buy it. But you know what? Ten years would go by, and I would never see another copy of that pamphlet come on the market at any price. So he had been absolutely right about our having to have it."

Hanna enjoyed a close relationship with Decker, who remained active in the business until his death, and introduced him to Bill Reese. A former journalist in New York and New Jersey, Decker became a bookseller in 1920, when he was asked by William Abbatt, his former employer at the *Magazine of History,* to dispose of his private library. Decker found that he enjoyed the ambience of the book world, and in time he became an authority in American history, travel, discovery, railroading, and Indian culture, specialties that put him in good stead with Frederick W. Beinecke, an owner of the Sperry and Hutchinson S&H Green Stamp Company who was determined to build a great collection of western Americana for Yale, his alma mater. The Beinecke family would later underwrite construction of the great rare-book library that now bears their name.

Decker was pleased to pass on useful tricks of the trade to Reese, and took him along occasionally on scouting trips. "It was through Peter that I actually ended up in the book business," Reese said, recalling what turned out to be the most pivotal career decision of his life. "I was just a collector at the time—I won the Van Sinderen Book Collecting Prize at Yale my sophomore year—but that was all in fun. It was right about that time that an old customer of Peter's in Summit, New Jersey, named Melvin Nichols died and left this huge collection to his cousin, who was his nearest relative. This woman wanted nothing to do with the books, and arbitrarily put a price of $40,000 on them. I went to the house with Peter and it was plainly obvious, even with the very little I knew then, that this was fabulous stuff. It was George Armstrong Custer material,

Americana, Civil War material, American Indians, a whole lot of western Americana, just wonderful. So what happened is this. Peter looked at me and said, 'This is an incredible deal, but I'm eighty-two years old, and I don't want to mess with it. You should buy it.' Peter lived to be ninety-five, and he was hale and hearty to the very end, but it was at his behest that I went and borrowed the $40,000 from my parents to buy the collection, and that is how in 1975 at the age of nineteen I became a professional bookseller."

Once the books had been removed from the New Jersey house by a crew of Yale students recruited to help, Reese found himself with twenty tons of general stock on his hands. Despite the size of the purchase, there was no anxiety about what he had just done. "I was not nervous at all because I earned my investment back within six months. This had happened in the spring; by the end of that summer I had paid my parents back, and I still had most of the stock left. So this was an unparalleled learning experience. One of the hardest things to do in the book business is to buy right. It's relatively easy to figure out what the best books are, and it's relatively easy to figure out what is in great condition and what is not in great condition. What is not easy to figure out is how to buy something at a price that you can make a profit on it."

Today, with a staff of eight people working for him, Reese has delegated a good deal of responsibility around. The computer has enabled him to build a database of 60,000 records, 25,000 of them in Americana, the rest in literature. "I've only got about eleven thousand live ones in Americana, meaning that we've got copies of those items for sale; the remaining fourteen thousand represent items that have passed through our hands. When certain books come back into our hands we don't have to write a new description. As a result, we only have to catalog the new books."

For all the tasks he assigns to his staff, Reese does not allow anyone else to authorize purchases. "I buy everything, and I catalog the most important things myself. It goes back to what I said before. Buying books is the key to the book business. Once you have good books, these days especially, it's not hard to sell them. It's buying them and knowing how to price them, and therefore knowing what you can pay for them, that matters. That's the key to the book business. I devote a lot more time to buying books than I do to selling books. And I think that if you pose that question to any of my peers, they will all say the same thing."

I have known Reese for a number of years, and talk with him about a great variety of subjects, and have always found him to be a font of fascinating information. There is no doubt in my mind that he is, in the words of Lou Weinstein, owner of Heritage Books in Los Angeles, "without question the American bookseller of his generation," a sentiment shared throughout the trade, and among many librarians as well. The lengthy interview we had for this book took place just two weeks before the concluding session of what was being described as the last big book auction of the twentieth century, the sale at Sotheby's in New York of the Frank T. Siebert Library of the North American Indian and the American Frontier. Given the general obscurity of Dr. Frank T. Siebert (1912–1998), whose name was unknown to all but a few booksellers and scholars at the time of his death, the sudden availability of so many remarkable treasures at one time triggered a flurry of news articles about the odd physician who had spent the better part of seventy years amassing a collection that was second to none in its area of specialty.

The character of the library was described by Bailey Bishop, a veteran Massachusetts bookseller with whom Siebert had done a lot of business, in the introduction to the two-volume sale catalog: "Rarity after rarity in remarkable condition, numbering about fifteen hundred books, pamphlets, broadsides, maps, manuscripts, prints, photographs, and newspapers, some famously elusive or the nicest copies in existence, crammed into a nondescript cottage in the middle of Maine, leaving little room for living—this collection was known to rare book librarians and dealers, and noted by bibliographers, but never seen by other bookmen until Dr. Siebert's death last year at the age of eighty-five."

Had I known about Dr. Siebert when I was researching my book about bibliomania, I would have moved heaven and earth to profile him as an archetypal victim of the "gentle madness," though given his reputation for reclusiveness, he would likely have spurned every entreaty. But if anyone was ever afflicted with advanced symptoms of the condition, it was this onetime Pennsylvania pathologist who gave up a promising medical practice, divorced his wife of eight years, abandoned his two daughters, lived for a while in his car while casting about, then moved to rural Maine to devote himself to his twin passions, books and the study of Indian linguistics.

For all his obvious eccentricity, what elevated Siebert's narrative above the commonplace was the fact that he was much more than a collector of artifacts. He also was an independent scholar of Indian customs and language, a fascination that began when he was a child. "I never had any training or education in either linguistics of anthropology of any sort, and am entirely self educated in this regard," he wrote in a letter to Ives Goddard, chief linguist of language studies for the Smithsonian Institution. When Siebert wrote that letter in 1965, he was embarked on a program of gathering whatever information he could of various remnant Indian groups, and meticulously compiling data that he had gathered on their languages. His book collecting began as a teenager. "Unable to find any decent books on Indians or their history and languages (other than junk) in local Philadelphia libraries, in 1928 I started my own search and purchase campaign," he explained in another letter to Goddard, this one posted ten years later. Siebert's first acquisition—at a cost of twenty-five cents—was a copy of the 1904 reprint of the Reverend John Eliot's *Logick Primer* of 1672, printed in a Native American dialect known as the Massachusett language. When working as an unpaid medical intern in 1939, Siebert raised the $6.50 he needed to buy a copy of the exceedingly rare second edition of David Zeisberger's *Delaware Indian and English Spelling* by selling bottles of his own blood. He bought his books with money he had from a small inheritance, and from whatever income he generated from his writings. "The heart of Siebert's collecting was from the late 1930s when he was a medical student into the 1950s," Reese said. "Most of the books he bought when he was a well-paid professional, and they cost him just a fraction of what they were ultimately worth."

Once settled in Maine, Siebert committed himself to his studies on endangered Indian languages, and wrote numerous learned essays. "His work was doggedly independent, and he preferred not to rely on other scholars, of whose work he was often highly critical," a predilection that drove him to acquire primary source material, Goddard wrote, and the final decades of his life were marked by periods of intensively productive scholarship. During the final thirty years of his life, Dr. Siebert worked closely with the Penobscot Indians of Maine on their reservation in Old Town, Maine, compiling a dictionary of their threatened language, which remained unpublished at his death. "Though he ran out of time at the end, he left behind the most important documentation of two key languages of eastern North America, Eastern Abenaki and Catawba, as well as extensive primary ethnographic data, and a total body of work the immense value of which largely remains to be appreciated," Goddard wrote.

Toward the end of his life, Siebert had reconciled with his daughters, Stephanie M. Finger and Kathleen L. Davis, both of Pennsylvania, but neither had ever seen his library, and neither had any idea of its worth while he was alive. Siebert named them as beneficiaries of his estate but left the manuscripts for his dictionary to the American Philosophical Society of Philadelphia for completion and publication. "My sister and I ended up caring about him, proud to have a father who was so unusual," Finger said a few days before the first sale in May 1999. "He thought he was indestructible, would live forever and keep the collection forever."

Reese talked with the doctor often about the ultimate disposition of the collection, but his attitude was clear. "I had developed a friendship with Frank, and he was quite wary about what the institutions would do with his books," he said. "There were some librarians that he liked individually, but he felt that as a class they had prevented him from getting a lot of things that he wanted back in the 1950s and '60s when libraries were building their special collections. He viewed them as his enemies, and he would get sputtering mad to even think of it. This was a touchy topic with him because he quite clearly was not going to part with anything until he died. So discussing the future of his collection with him, which I dared to do a couple of times, was done at your peril. He hated the thought of other people getting their hands on his books. At one point he talked to me about setting up an independent library, but I told him that was crazy because he would need a serious endowment to support it. I told him, 'You have a great collection, but it is what it is, it's a rare-book collection. You need resources to back up a library.' I urged him to think about placing his books with the American Antiquarian Society, where they would have made a perfect fit, but he put it off and put it off, and in the end he did nothing."

As heirs to the estate, Siebert's daughters consigned the books to Sotheby's. The presale estimate was $5.5 million, a figure Reese said he would have happily paid for the entire collection, if given the opportunity to buy it. "Like everyone else, I had never seen the books when Frank was alive, and I wanted to get in and see them. But I knew what he had, and what he had was absolutely fabulous." Reese tried to persuade Bailey Bishop, who was acting as an adviser to Siebert's daughters, to sell the collection to him en bloc, "but he chose to go to the auction route, and I can't say that I blame him."

When Reese was offering that recollection to me, the results of the first Siebert sale were already in. Of the 548 lots that had been sold, Reese had prepared bids on every one, and was successful in 246 instances, accounting for 50 percent of the $5.9 million spent at that session. "I was the underbidder on another hundred lots, so I essentially was the price maker for two-thirds of the sale, because as the auction houses will tell you, underbidders are just as important as the bidders, since they deter-mine the final outcome." Reese continued his determined pace in the concluding session of the Siebert sale. Of the 531 lots sold, Reese bought another 275, and was underbidder on 61. "On the whole sale combined, I ended up with just about half the sale exactly, by both lot and value," he calculated. "I was buyer or underbidder on seventy-five percent of value." Of the $12.1 million spent in both sessions, Reese accounted for $6 million of the action.

"I was bidding for about twenty different people and institutions, ranging from a single inexpensive book for one customer to the most expensive lot in the sale for someone else. So I worked with my customers to determine what they were interested in, and how they would like to build their collections. I also bought a good deal of material for my general stock. When you are buying for stock, obviously you are working on a thinner margin, and you have to be a bit more conservative in your approach."

Causing the biggest stir was Reese's purchase of a first edition of Samuel de Champlain's account of his voyages to the New World, published in Paris in 1613, and including the first "modern map" of the east coast of Canada, decorated with images of foxes, beavers, and verdant woods; projected to bring anywhere from $80,000 to $120,000, it went to Reese in behalf of a private collector for $398,500, more than three times the estimate. He paid another $134,500 for a 1632 edition of Champlain's *Voyages*, and $96,000 for the 1675 presentation copy of Thomas Church's account of King Philip's War, the only copy offered for sale at auction in eighty years.

Coming as it did in the waning months of 1999, the Siebert sale gave Reese the opportunity to make his name synonymous with the last great book sale of the twentieth century, recalling the aplomb with which the bookseller George D. Smith dominated the Robert Hoe sale in 1911–12 on behalf of Henry E. Huntington, the way Rosenbach bought at will at the Jerome Kern sale in 1929, or how the flamboyant New York dealer Lew D. Feldman bought twentieth-century literary manuscripts for the University of Texas in the 1960s with what seemed to be wild abandon, in one memorable instance arriving late for a London session dressed in pajamas, a robe, and a raincoat, and bidding aggressively on fifty-six successive items, and sweeping away everything in sight. On November 29, 2000, Reese continued his dominance in Americana at the Sotheby's sale in New York of the Library of Laird U. Park Jr., a collection of books, manuscripts, and letters incorporating all aspects of American history, with specific emphasis on Philadelphia, the home of the collector. Of the $5.2 million spent on 394 lots, Reese accounted for $2.4 million, or 45 percent of the total.

"I am constantly amazed at his ability to know books," Ellen S. Dunlap, president of the American Antiquarian Society, marveled about Reese, who was elected to the elite society in 1981 when he was twenty-six, the youngest person to be so honored, and serves on the institution's governing council, the youngest person ever entrusted with that responsibility. Similar circumstances apply at the Grolier Club in New York, one of the world's most exclusive bibliophilic organizations. Reese's grasp of his material is clearly evident not only in the catalogs he issues but in the various monographs and essays he has published, including commentary for a number of important exhibitions mounted at the Grolier Club in New York, and at the Beinecke Library, just two blocks from his shop on Temple Street.

Reese also is one of the few booksellers who admit to being collectors in their own right, making no bones about the fact that his collection of Herman Melville material may well be the finest in private hands, or that his interest in color-plate books printed in the United States during the nineteenth century is personal. To observe the one-hundredth anniversary of Melville's death in 1991, the Beinecke Library exhibited fifty-one titles from Reese's collection, including several annotated books from the author's own library. In 1999 the Grolier Club displayed 113 of Reese's color-plate books, including seven titles showcasing the artworks of John James Audubon, most notably the exceedingly rare chromolithographic edition of *Birds of America* published in 1858 by the famed outdoor artist's son, John Woodhouse Audubon. A hardcover catalog of the exhibition, *Stamped with a National Character,* featured a lengthy essay Reese wrote on the history and development of color illustration in the United States in the nineteenth century.

A constant in everything Reese undertakes, be it scouting books for clients, collecting for himself, writing learned essays, or making plans for auctions, is careful preparation. For the Siebert sale, he researched the history of every item put on the block and spent a week in the Sotheby's showrooms examining each title, often with the clients he was planning to represent.

"I have people who say to me, 'Look, I'm willing to spend a half a million bucks at this sale, what can I buy that I am never going to get another chance at?' What I bring to the table is an idea of what is important for their collections, and what it is probably going to cost. So I bring the context of the market to the process. I'm not just saying, 'Well, it's a pretty book,' I'm saying, 'Look, this is the auction record for this book, but the market has changed radically since then, so if you really want it, you are going to have to be thinking in terms of spending fifty thousand dollars instead of fifteen or twenty.' And that is why I was able to do so well at the Siebert sale. I gave my clients what turned out to be a very accurate idea of what they were going to have to spend, and where they would have to concentrate their fire. And I was right most of the time."

7.

MANY YEARS

In a word, literature is my Utopia. Here I am not disfranchised. No barrier of the senses shuts me out from the sweet, gracious discourse of my book friends. They talk to me without embarrassment or awkwardness.

—Helen Keller, The Story of My Life

Mrs. Calloway made her own rules about books. You could not take back a book to the Library on the same day you'd taken it out; it made no difference to her that you'd read every word in it and needed another to start. You could take out two books at a time and two only; this applied as long as you were a child and also for the rest of your life, to my mother as severely as to me. So two by two, I read library books as fast as I could go, rushing them home in the basket of my bicycle. From the minute I reached our house, I started to read. Every book I seized on, from Bunny Brown and His Sister Sue at Camp Rest-a-While *to* Twenty Thousand Leagues under the Sea, *stood for the devouring wish to read being instantly granted. I knew this was bliss, knew it at the time. Taste isn't nearly so important; it comes in its own time. I wanted to read immediately. The only other fear was that of books coming to an end.*

—Eudora Welty, One Writer's Beginnings

L loyd E. Cotsen is a man of myriad curiosities, chief among them a passion for acquiring Noah's Ark toys and sculptures, colorful Navajo tapestries, delicately crafted bamboo baskets from Japan, and flawless examples of traditional folk art gathered during his many trips to exotic places throughout the world. On the day that I arrived for my first interview with the Los Angeles philanthropist and amateur archaeologist, 23,000 illustrated children's books in thirty-two different languages had just been trucked across the continent to Princeton University in New Jersey, the first shipment of primary source material to stock a new research collection there. Some academics were not overly thrilled to be getting this shipment, much less to accommodate it in a time of shrinking storage space and stretched operational budgets, but Lloyd Cotsen is a persuasive man, and the books he had gathered during a decade of frenetic collecting were accorded a hearty welcome when they began to arrive on campus toward the end of 1995. Formally dedicated the following fall, the Cotsen Children's Library now occupies its own wing in the Firestone Library, maintained by its own staff and supported by its own endowment. Just as important, programs intended to foster reading among schoolchildren who might otherwise never set foot in a university library are now being developed, hardly the mission of an elite Ivy League college more accustomed to enriching the intellects of highly motivated undergraduates, but one that Princeton has begun to develop nonetheless under the prodding of a dynamic alumnus, along with other extracurricular considerations, including the sponsoring of international conferences.

In the months leading up to the opening of the Cotsen Children's Library, some members of the Princeton faculty had been complaining privately about the willingness of university officials to allow an influential donor to impose unprecedented demands on them as a condition of accepting his largesse. In its agreement with the former president, principal owner, and chief operating officer of the Neutrogena Corp., Princeton agreed to establish a separate library on campus, and to maintain an enormous collection of books that at the time did not support any major course of study in its curriculum. There were other considerations to be taken into account as well, of course, as Cotsen—pronounced *coat-zin*—stressed with a few carefully chosen words. "We're talking about eight figures here," he explained, giving the matter some candid context. When I suggested that eight figures could mean anything between $10 million and $99 million, he agreed to narrow the parameters a bit, but not by very much. "Okay, it's not ninety-nine million," he said. "But it's not ten million either."

What Cotsen was suggesting by these numbers was a measure of munificence that goes well beyond the reach of his pet project. His generosity to Princeton over the years has by no means been limited to illustrated books for children, and if the university had any misgivings about accepting his terms for the library, they were never aired in public. The matter was resolved, to the apparent satisfaction of all parties, which is a credit, perhaps, to the delicate way college officials chose to appease a man they had already accorded the rare honor of designating a "Charter Trustee of the University." Cotsen's gifts to his alma mater are ongoing, and have included the endowment of a professorship in the humanities and creation of numerous fellowships that support the work of teachers and students alike. And given his philanthropic nature, there is the expectation of much more to come.

Princeton's agreement with Cotsen came at a time when administrators at other colleges and universities around the United States were finding themselves forced to tiptoe a very fine line in deciding how far well-heeled benefactors could determine precisely how their money could be spent. Some institutions faced with similar predicaments have not been as fortunate as Princeton. In 1989, the University of Utah returned $15 million in stock it received from a businessman who had insisted on having the institution's medical center named after him. At the University of California, Los Angeles, a $1 million grant from the Turkish government to establish a chair in Ottoman studies was first accepted, but returned when it was learned that scholars using archives in Istanbul would be refused access to any material that might document the Armenian massacres of 1915. News leaked to the press that UCLA had accepted Turkey's offer had prompted a flurry of petitions in protest, including one signed by fifty-seven scholars and writers, Susan Sontag, Arthur Miller, and Kurt Vonnegut Jr. among them. The Turkish government, the petition alleged, "prohibits intellectual freedom, outlaws enquiry about its country and its history, incarcerates its intellectuals and has one of the worst human rights records in the world today." In January 1998 UCLA regents voted to rescind the agreement and return the $250,000 deposit they already had received from the Turkish ambassador.

Perhaps the most controversial conflict of all involving an American college and a wealthy donor came in 1995 when Yale University sent back a $20 million gift it had received from Lee M. Bass, a Texas financier and a member of the class of 1979 who had tendered his substantial gift with the proviso that it be used to promote the study of Western civilization, and that it endow up to eleven professorships to teach the courses. The main sticking point was not the proposed program but the young benefactor's insistence that he be allowed to approve the faculty appointments funded with his money. The Yale Corporation found this to be an unacceptable intrusion on its academic freedom and, to the vocal displeasure of many alumni, returned the money. It was reported at the time to be the largest gift ever returned by any American institution to a donor.

Yale once again found itself in an embarrassing situation two years later when the New York playwright Larry Kramer, class of 1957 and founder of the AIDS activist group Act Up, proposed endowing a chair in gay studies. Arguing that the subject was too narrow a field to justify a permanent professorship, Yale offered to bring visiting lecturers to campus, but Kramer refused the compromise, and the university declined his gift, which the dramatist estimated to be worth more than $5 million once his papers, which he had planned on giving to Yale as part of the package, were factored into the bequest. A few months later Kramer announced that he was having discussions with the Harry Ransom Research Center at the University of Texas at Austin and the University of Southern California, but nothing ever came out of the talks, and the disposition of the papers remained unresolved. "It shouldn't be such a problem to give away your money," he said in exasperation. It was also in 1997 that Harvard University, America's oldest, most prestigious, and wealthiest academic institution, turned down a $3.2 million gift from Ken Lipper, a former deputy mayor of New York City, to establish a chair in Holocaust studies, not because of the focus but because the donor insisted on naming an untenured associate professor of government, Daniel J. Goldhagen, the best-selling author of *Hitler's Willing Executioners,* to the post, a demand perceived in some quarters as "intolerable interference."

At Princeton, the situation with Cotsen was never regarded as "intolerable," but the gift-bearer was demanding the formation of programs that did not support any academic majors, although one survey course in children's literature was taught periodically in the English Department. "You could say it's sort of like the tail wagging the dog," was the way one prominent Princeton educator described the situation for me, and he left it at that. "I don't have to be told that a lot of people see me as a loose cannon, and that particular comment doesn't surprise me at all," Cotsen said when I asked his reaction. "What some of these people would like is for me to sit back, keep quiet, and be Daddy Warbucks. Well, guess what? That's not going to happen."

And indeed it never did. Cotsen established a library at Princeton in every sense of the word, and thousands of children's books, many of them hundreds of years old and some of them quite rare, were just the beginning of what he envisioned. For starters, there was the $8 million he put up to cover renovation of the wing that once had housed the microfilms reading room in the Firestone Library, to start an endowment that would sustain the operation, and to fund the programs that he expected would be developed. Then there were the books that cost him many millions more, just how many millions he would not say. "It doesn't matter," he said when I asked what he had invested in the collections. He also made long-term provisions to underwrite the salaries of a professional staff, and to ensure that the holdings would be constantly strengthened, he retained New York bookseller Justin Schiller, widely regarded as one of the world's leading authorities in children's literature as a consultant. Meanwhile, a full-time staff remained on duty in California to see that accurate bibliographical information was entered into the computers, that duplication of newly acquired titles was kept at a minimum, and that booksellers were paid expeditiously. With all those details in place, additional funding was provided to organize and support outreach programs.

Cotsen told me that at one time he had seriously considered establishing the library at the University of California, Los Angeles, where he has supported other programs, but that he decided in the end to set it up at Princeton when assured that his intentions would be accommodated. "My credo is to be creative," he said with the self-assurance of a man who has built a personal fortune worth many millions of dollars, and who made clear in his conversations with me that he plans on giving a good deal of it away to worthwhile causes while he is still alive to oversee the dispersal. "I said if this is going to be a children's library, then I want children in there. I am paying for it, so the challenge for Princeton is not about raising the money. The question for them is, How do you put the two together?"

Cotsen would not give me a copy of the agreement he signed with the university, but he did let me read the document, and he was happy to discuss its contents. "I've given them four years," he said, leaving no doubt that his generosity had some very tight strings attached. "If they haven't made progress in the areas that are important to me, then what happens is that I reserve the right to pull the collection out of Princeton and turn it over to UCLA, and if it doesn't work out at UCLA, believe me, then I'll pull it out of there and send it to a third place. This is a very specific legal document we're talking about here." Whether or not Cotsen would actually go so far as to uproot the collection and return it to

California was anyone's guess, but through the first four years of its residence in New Jersey, the point was moot, since good-faith efforts were made to develop programs for children, and work was progressing on preparation of a five-volume catalog for the collection, another critical stipulation Cotsen had imposed; the first volume, its 6,695 entries covering the letters *A* to *L* and restricted to the twentieth century, appeared in 2000; volume 2, expected in 2001, will complete that sequence, and volumes 3 and 4 will describe the books published between 1486 and 1899.

"This is a clarification of what the Cotsen Library is aiming to do, and who is doing what, that's all it is," Cotsen had said when we first got together in 1996, tapping his finger on the "memorandum of understanding" he had reached with Princeton as he spoke. "What I am trying to provide is guidelines, not rules. Guidelines are guidelines, that's all. I set them up. These are the goals. As for the books I give, I have every intention of adding more things as time goes on, and I will have no reservations at all about bothering the librarian occasionally with my thoughts."

When we spoke again in the summer of 2000, Cotsen said that he was satisfied with the way things were going, and he was pleased to tell me that he was no longer thinking about exercising the bail-out clause he had reserved for himself to bring the library back to California. "It's staying at Princeton," he said. "The effort they have put into this is real, and I am delighted with what I have seen. We've succeeded in bringing kids into the room, and they're on the other side of the glass wall, not on the outside looking in." Academic programs were under way as well, moreover, and the publications were being produced. As further proof of Princeton's good intentions, Cotsen noted that a tenured chair in children's literature would be established at the university, which he would fund.

In his earlier discussions with me, Cotsen dismissed a suggestion that the library had become "the driving focus" of his life, pointing out that his plate was filled with many other philanthropic interests that demand his attention, but he did not deny that this undertaking was special. "There are a couple of projects I want to see through before I pack it all in, and education is at the heart of them all," he said. "I guess you could say that I am at a point where my life is sort of focusing itself, shrinking down really to the concept of relationships. I want to give some things away, and I'm not interested in pedagogical material, because there's enough of that stuff around already. For the library, I want things there that were in the child's hands, things that the child was exposed to. Not the teacher, but the child."

When Cotsen showed me around the Los Angeles suites in 1996, it was hard to believe that 23,000 volumes had just been removed, since the six rooms I saw were anything but empty. Four years later, his staff would tell me that the premises were once again bursting with newly acquired books, manuscripts, original artwork, antique board games, and old toys, some 80,000 objects all told that before long would be headed for New Jersey when sufficient space was available to receive them. "What I have over in this area is a subcollection of famous artists who did children's books," Cotsen said during our walking tour, indicating a metal shelf secured to an exterior wall, pointing out some first editions by Maurice Sendak, who designed the logo for the library. "I like Sendak a lot, and I hope to have him do something at the library. Now these here are all Scandinavian; over on that shelf are German counting books. Those across the way are recent acquisitions. Here, look at this; this is a Jewish Hagaddah by Japanese converts who wanted to go to Israel after the nuclear attack on their country. This other stuff reflects my interest in how the perception of American Indians in children's books has changed from a century ago, from sixty years ago to today, and how romanticized and unromanticized it's all become. I have some material that is prejudicial to blacks too, a few of them really terrible things, but somebody has to preserve that stuff, and it has to be available for scholars. I set up a fund to buy books for a foundation in Greece. I'm also looking at how children's stuff always managed to fall through the cracks. Here, these are manuscripts, and here are some incunabula. Edward Lear is another specialty of mine, I have some of his manuscripts. Children's cookbooks is another subspecialty, because all of my children like to cook. Look, here's another ark."

When I made my first visit to the Cotsen Children's Library at Princeton several months later, the curator, Andrea Immel, showed me some of the great rarities in the collection, books that include all of the great names in children's literature, encompassing six centuries. "The singular strength of the collection is that it is international," Immel said. "Most of the other important children's books collections—the Iona and Peter Opie at Oxford, the Betsy Beinecke Shirley at Yale, the Ruth Baldwin in Florida, the Elizabeth Ball at Indiana—focus for the most part on one national tradition. Well, we have more than thirty different languages in here, which makes it a nightmare for cataloging, but Lloyd has gone for depth in a really big way. I mean we have the things you would expect us to have—English, French, German, Italian, and the like—but we also have Turkish, Latvian, Russian, Swedish, Czech, Hungarian, Greek, Japanese, Chinese, Hebrew, Farsi, Urdu, Arabic, you name it. This is a tremendous mass of primary source material, more than enough to keep a lot of scholars busy for a very long time."

As much as Cotsen intends that the collection be used by researchers, he is adamant that the library—and by that, of course, he means Princeton University itself—reach out to youngsters in ways that will entice them into the world of books and reading. "Everybody tells me they like the books, but what everybody really wants of course is the money, and they all want the money on their terms," he said. "So the challenge I set out for Princeton was that they will get the money, but I want children in there, and it has to be more than a token gesture. They know me well enough to realize that I will not compromise my position on that."

In response to this demand, the library hired another staffer in 1999, and gave her the title of Outreach and Programs Coordinator. Among Bonnie Bernstein's first projects was a Young Curators program that opened in April 2000, and invited students from various elementary and middle schools to participate in organized projects at the library. A second-grade class looked into the different ways children have learned about the sea from ancient times to now. A group of fifth-graders examined what a typical school day would have been like during Colonial times, including the subjects they would have studied and the kinds of materials that would have been used as teaching tools. An eighth-grade class researched school fads and fashions from 1900 to the present time, concentrating on what young teens wore, the jargon they used, the activities that amused them. Online exhibits were produced, and links established through the Cotsen Children's Library Web page. Meanwhile a student theater troupe, the Cotsen Players, was established to develop shows based on children's literature for presentation in the library; the premiere performance, described as a "modern fairy tale that combines characters from several children's stories featuring twelve undergraduate actors," was titled *The Fairyland Detective Agency*.

A native of Boston, Cotsen received a bachelor's degree in history from Princeton University in 1950 and met his future wife, JoAnne Stolaroff, while serving in the Navy and stationed in southern California. After their marriage, Cotsen returned to Princeton with the idea of becoming an architect. "I dropped out of that program when I discovered I didn't have the discipline or the talent to be the next Frank Lloyd Wright," he quipped. Before enrolling in Harvard Business School, he spent a summer in Greece on a dig in the Peloponnesus, an awakening experience that began a lifelong fascination with archaeology. "I feel something extraordinary when I touch these things, something that I can't really describe," he said. "It may be mute, this artifact that you pick up and hold in your hands, but I have the feeling that I can listen to the voices. When I pick up a pot fresh out of the ground, I say to myself, 'Somebody made this.' To think here I am, a thousand years later, two thousand years later, whatever, and I wonder what these people were thinking, and what their lives were like. This resonates with me in a very profound way."

After receiving a master's degree from Harvard Business School in

1958, Cotsen returned to California and went to work for his father-in-law, Emanuel Stolaroff. "He was a super salesperson, and he had a small business at the time called Natone. They made lip brushes, sold women's cosmetic accessories from Europe. It was a business probably doing about $500,000 a year at the most. He brought me in and gave me responsibility for this product he had just bought the rights to, a soap bar made in Belgium called Neutrogena. The name means 'neutralizing' in Flemish or in French. If I had been there in California at the time he made the deal, I probably would have said, 'Don't take it,' but I was in Greece when he did it. He gave me responsibility for the product, which was doing about $80,000 a year at the time, to do with it what I could. So the first thing I did was go over to Belgium and spend six weeks learning how to make the product."

Once set up in Los Angeles, Cotsen directed his sales force to furnish dermatologists with free samples of the amber-colored translucent soap that they could pass on to their patients. He also sold at cost small bars of the product to various luxury hotels with the understanding that they would be placed in the bathrooms of their suites. "We're a marketing company, not a manufacturing one," he told a writer for *Forbes* magazine in 1981, explaining his basic strategy. "What people think they're getting is what's important." William H. Gates III, the billionaire software phenomenon who markets everything Microsoft makes under one name, is on record as saying that it was Cotsen's shrewd decision to market everything his company made—shampoo, hand lotion, soap, body cream, moisturizers—under the Neutrogena name that persuaded him to adopt a similar tactic with his own company.

"I didn't want to sell soap, I wanted to sell something else—health, well-being—and I wanted a brand name," Cotsen told me. "My overall goal was to take that one brick and make it into a wall. And that's what I did. I took this one product and made another product and made other products, all with the same name." Before long there were thirty or forty different products, all called Neutrogena. "All the other stuff we made, I got rid of the different names, even the ones named after my mother-in-law. She was very good about that. I really believed in focusing and doing one thing well, with everything and everybody." When Cotsen sold Neutrogena to Johnson & Johnson in 1994 for just under $1 billion, the company was reporting annual sales of $300 million.

Cotsen laughed heartily when he recalled returning from Belgium with the recipe and installing the equipment to make his first bars of Neutrogena. "I had set up a little place downtown, smaller than this apartment we're in right here. Well, there I was, making my first batch, and something was wrong. The timing was off, something wasn't working right, and out came whipped potatoes instead of mixed soap. So I had to take a wooden shovel and go into the tank and scoop out this stuff because the whipped potatoes just wouldn't flow through. I'm chuckling now because I can see that old cartoon drawing of the guy in a barrel with no clothes on. That was me. I went in the tank with no clothes on. The blades I had designed for the mixer were rectangular paddles of stainless steel, and every time I bent over to clear out the mix, I poked my ass on one of these sharp blades. Even today in our huge plant, with all the fancy machinery we have down there, all the blades have rounded corners. Nobody knows why that is until they hear this story."

When Cotsen sold the company shortly after observing his sixty-fifth birthday in 1994, he found himself confronted with an exquisite dilemma, one he described for me with a few colorful words: "What in the hell am I going to do with a couple hundred million dollars?" For openers, he decided that he would build a research library devoted entirely to children at an eminent university. He began buying up books from all over the world, many of them unquestioned rarities, others acquired for the information they contain. "I am fortunate that I have the resources to do this," he said. "Also—and just as important—I am not dumb." Cotsen said he probably selected 80 percent of the titles himself, and relied on the advice of Justin Schiller to recommend the rest. "When I am making a seven-figure purchase, I will consult with Justin." Although he does not like to discuss specific numbers, Cotsen acknowledged that he has, in fact, paid seven figures for an acquisition. "One book? A million dollars?" I replied, asking him to identify which one. "It doesn't make any difference," he said. "One book?" I pressed. "A seven-figure collection," he conceded. "This must be the Perrault we're talking about," I countered, and he confirmed, with a thin smile, that he was indeed talking about a marvelous collection of 130 books, many of them exceedingly rare first editions, he had bought through Schiller representing first appearances of the fairy tales of the French aristocrat Charles Perrault (1628–1703).

Cotsen said his passion for artifacts was nourished by the archaeological digs he began participating in regularly in the 1950s. "I'm not really a collector, I'm an accumulator," he told a reporter for the *Denver Post* who interviewed him in 1998 about a major collection of folk art he had recently given away, once again with clearly defined restrictions being imposed on the terms of the gift. "I buy things because they strike an emotional bell, they appeal to my curiosity, to the thrill of discovery of the extraordinary in the ordinary. They appeal to my sense of humor, and to my search for the beauty in simplicity. I decided I had a collection when there was no more space to put anything." The occasion for that article was the grand opening of the Neutrogena Wing of the Cotsen Gallery at the Museum of International Folk Art in Sante Fe, with a debut exhibition called "The Extraordinary in the Ordinary."

Cotsen chose the New Mexico museum for this particular gift not only because of its specialty in folk art, but because of assurances that 80 percent of the 2,500 pieces he committed in 1995 would be displayed within the first five years of its opening. He allowed museum officials to choose whatever they wished from a collection of 6,000 textiles, ceramics, and carvings he had assembled over four decades and had displayed in the Los Angeles offices of Neutrogena. In addition to the artworks, he provided money to add a wing to the museum. "I endowed enough support for staff so that they will never need to go into their operating budget to pay salaries, but that endowment cannot be used for anything else," he told me when the rooms in New Mexico were still under construction. Materials kept on permanent display are exhibited in the Cotsen Gallery, and items on revolving display are shown in the 8,775-square-foot Neutrogena Wing, and include such objects as Alaskan parkas made of walrus gut, puffin beaks and feathers lit from within to show their translucency, a nineteenth-century Chinese jacket made from bamboo stems threaded on cotton netting, and a Japanese ceremonial rain cape made from grass and seaweed that has been knotted and twined.

"There is no doubt that Lloyd wants things done in a grand way," Andrea Immel, the Cotsen Library curator, explained while showing me through the handsome wing attached to the Firestone Library that she supervises. "So yes, right now, there is a big-picture mentality that he has, and just how clear that is in his mind I honestly don't know, to tell you the truth. On the one hand he wants to have children coming in here on a regular basis. On the other hand he wants the book collection to evolve into an international research center. I know that he also envisions this as being a resource for historians, which I think, given the climate right now, probably means cultural history more than literature, at least until the mania for theory has passed, and interest in literary history returns. Of course let it be said that Lloyd does not have a scholar's temperament at all. I suppose that's why he has me. I'm the scholar on the team."

Even though she worked for Cotsen for nine years before moving to Princeton in 1995, Immel said she was surprised all the same when university officials invited her to apply for the curatorship of the new children's library. She agreed that Cotsen's stature as a major benefactor undoubtedly was a factor. "Oh, there is no question about that. I knew beforehand how important a donor Lloyd has been to Princeton University. But I also knew that Princeton did not really have programs that would naturally gravitate to the collection, and that there were some faculty members who were actively opposed to having it come here. The prevailing thought out there was that children's books were not befitting a research library of this stature." As an additional inducement, the university offered to hire Immel's husband, John Bidwell, also a professional librarian, as head of visual materials and curator of graphic arts at Princeton. "We were the first joint library appointments at Princeton, and this all came at Princeton's initiative." In 1999 Bidwell left Princeton to become Astor Curator of Printed Books and Bindings at the Pierpont Morgan Library in New York City, where Immel had worked as assistant curator of historical children's books from 1980 to 1982. She became Cotsen's personal librarian while pursuing her doctorate at UCLA.

Asked to describe how she sees her role, Immel emphasized that she is a "scholar for better or for worse, and not in any way a political creature. I am an old-fashioned enough kind of a curator to believe that part of my mission is to take care of my books as if they are my family. That is part of my cultural role. That is a very nineteenth-century view of librarianship, and is not a view that is much in fashion among library professionals today. Now you are supposed to think of yourself as an information specialist or a broker. I don't think the two are necessarily incompatible, but that is just the way things have gone in recent years."

A number of delightful stuffed animals decorate the Cotsen Library, a few seated in beanbag chairs, others perched on top of a glass barrier peeking over shelves. Small reading areas are set aside for children, with bins of books plainly in evidence. In the middle of the main room is a permanent exhibit called the Giant Book, with a series of inner chambers that celebrate three children's classics: Lewis Carroll's *Alice in Wonderland*, C. S. Lewis's *Chronicles of Narnia*, and E. B. White's *Charlotte's Web*. Fourteen feet high and fetchingly shaped like an open book, it has interactive displays, puzzles, appealing signs, everything that might entice a child to go inside and explore. Designed to entertain children who visit the library, it does very little to engage them directly in reading, although everyone involved makes clear that they consider it little more than a tangible first step. "These are the kinds of things that Princeton is finding out," Immel said. "Part of the problem, of course, is that you have rare books behind glass on the western wall over there that are not immediately accessible to kids. We don't have the advantage that a science museum has. They design things to be punched, touched, hit. We've got a little bit of that here, but you'll notice it's not necessarily tied in any significant way to the collection itself. What you see out there could be anywhere." Immel gave that some thought for a moment, then put Cotsen's continuing adventure into perspective. "I don't know if Lloyd has a clear idea of what he wants just yet," she said finally. "But it's a big challenge, and he's a bright guy; he'll know it when he sees it."

A phrase Cotsen uses again and again is his hope that the center will be recognized as a "living library," and liberal access to its treasures is part of what he means, although the books, like all rare-book collections, do not circulate. "I have always felt that education was at the center of everything, and that books are the primary tool. I still feel that way." One reason Cotsen decided against installing the library at the University of California, Los Angeles, just a few minutes away from his home in Bel Air, was his concern that the books would "stay in a shoe box for fifteen years" before anybody got around to doing something with them. "There are librarians who say to me, 'Why do you want to be in books anyway? Everything is going to go electronic?' I say nobody cuddles you like your mother in bed with a book. You don't do that with a computer. And it just isn't the reading, it's the emotional arm around you that gives such an emotional feel to that early reading experience." How all this relates to literacy and reading, Cotsen said he has no idea. "I can't tell you that. My goal, as an individual, is, what can I do. I can't change pre-motherhood, I can't change early motherhood, those are issues I can't change. But if I can have a kid walk into a place and come back home and say, 'Gee, I would like to read something,' if I can just stimulate this kid to want to read a book or just pick up a book, that's as much as I can do. Where it goes from there I have no idea."

In remarks delivered at the dedication ceremony in 1997 and printed later in a commemorative brochure, Princeton President Harold T. Shapiro marveled that Cotsen had given the university "an ageless treasure—a wonderful ark of learning that invites both scholars and children to set sail." Running along the bottom of the pamphlet is a sequence of illustrated panels painted by the German artist Lothar Meggendorfer, and reproduced from the publisher's proofs of *Arche Noah: Ein Bilderbuch*, published in Munich in 1903, a rare and colorful book from the collection dealing with the biblical episode of Noah and his Ark. During my two days of interviews with Cotsen in Los Angeles, the one image that stood out above all others was the flotilla of 350 model ships that decorated the two suites, which was not included in the gift to Princeton. A few of the pieces were crafted by skilled European artisans; some of them are several hundred years old, others are contemporary, but what they all have in common is that each is a vessel loaded with figures of wild animals. Each is a Noah's Ark, and the collection is of sufficient interest that the University of California, Los Angeles, has indicated its desire to organize a selective exhibition of the pieces in its art museum; in 2000, Cotsen told me he had decided to give the collection to the Skirball Cultural Center in Los Angeles. There also are an equal number of books on the general subject of Noah's Ark in the Cotsen Library, with more undoubtedly to be added in the years to come.

This wide variety of Noah's Ark material, each example an uplifting metaphor for rescuing what is precious and delivering it to safe haven, is central to understanding the forces that transformed what was once a pleasant family diversion into a major research collection now installed at one of the world's most respected universities. It is a painful episode of Cotsen's life, but one that is essential to understanding what moved him to create "a wonderful ark of learning" at Princeton.

On May 23, 1979, while Cotsen was away in New York on a business trip, a masked man bent on committing unspeakable mayhem broke into his house in Beverly Hills. Cotsen's wife JoAnne, their fourteen-year-old son Noah, and a sixteen-year-old houseguest, Christopher Doering, were bound and fatally shot with a .22-caliber pistol. Police were given a detailed description of the killer by a man who had been renting a guest cottage on the Cotsen property; he and his girlfriend had been subdued at gunpoint when they entered the house unannounced to pick up some mail, but the tenant managed to flee while the intruder was distracted by the woman. She then jumped through a glass door at the rear of the house to safety, suffering minor cuts in the process. A bulletin was issued for a slender man with an athletic build dressed in black, wearing a ski mask and gloves, and speaking in a foreign accent. A massive search was conducted, but no arrests were ever made. "I'd first like to know why," a distraught Cotsen said six months later as the investigation continued with no resolution. "I don't know if we'll ever know who. But I have to know the why."

The memory of getting the shocking news was a nightmare that could never go away. Cotsen heard a fragmentary report of the shootings on a car radio while driving to the airport in New York, anxiously called home, and had his worst fears confirmed by a police officer. He offered a $50,000 reward for information leading to the arrest of a suspect, but the trail had gone cold. At first police believed the crimes were the work of a prowler who had panicked. One nagging concern was evidence to suggest that the killer had remained in the house for about five hours, apparently waiting for someone to return, and as further details were gathered, a shocking scenario began to emerge. On February 26, 1980, Beverly Hills Police Chief Lee Tracy held a news conference to announce that after a lengthy investigation, detectives had concluded that the murderer was Erich Arnold Tali, a Belgian businessman who committed suicide on October 15, 1979, a few hours before he was to meet with police detectives who had traveled to Europe to interview him. The motive for the murders, Chief Tracy said, was business rivalry, and the intended target of the violence was Lloyd Cotsen, whose father-in-law had bought manufacturing and distribution rights to Neutrogena in the 1950s from a Brussels company. When the founder of the company died, he left the business to his mistress; she in turn married Tali, who unsuccessfully filed a series of lawsuits to reclaim the Neutrogena trademark. "He had developed a deep hate for Cotsen," Chief Tracy said, and told how his officers were led to Belgium by a brown chloroform bottle found at the murder scene bearing writing in Flemish and French. Christopher Doering had been chloroformed prior to his death. Forensic tests also showed that hair found in a ski mask and sweater left in an abandoned van determined to have been used by the murderer belonged to Tali as well, and investigators found credit card records indicating that the Belgian had been in the United States when the murders were committed, and that he flew from New York City to Brussels the following day.

For years Cotsen found talking about the loss impossible, and it remains an excruciatingly difficult subject for him to this day. But when I visited the adjoining apartments in Los Angeles, the Noah's Ark toys and sculptures were everywhere to be seen, prompting a gently phrased query from me as to their relevance. "I had a son named Noah—he was killed—he and my wife, in 1979," Cotsen replied simply. We had not discussed the matter at all to that point, yet those few words were more than sufficient an answer. "We used to buy books that had the names of our children in them somewhere, usually the titles," he said later. "After Noah died, I began concentrating more and more on the ones with his name, and then on collecting the actual arks themselves."

When I asked Cotsen to summarize for me what had set him on the path to establishing a "living library" for children at Princeton, he cited a family ritual that began when his two sons and two daughters were babies. "The genesis of the library is simple enough; my wife and I had four children, and in the course of having four children we would read to them every night—let me refine that and say my *wife* would read to them every night—and from that start we began a modest collection of books. My wife had been a docent at a museum, and she came out of an art background, so illustration was central to the collection, and because I was deeply involved in archaeology, I would sort of tell the kids Greek myths. I travel a lot, and wherever I was in the world, I would always bring home books for the children."

When JoAnne and Noah died, the dynamic changed dramatically. "I sort of moved from being the treasurer of the collection to the president," Cotsen said. "I had more means at that time, so the price I was willing to spend for a book went from five dollars or ten dollars to one hundred dollars a book. Before long it went a lot higher than that. This went on for fifteen years or so, but over time it became more purposeful and larger in scope. I developed a sense of wanting to do something that was more lasting, and it was that impulse that made me a more serious collector. The idea of having a library—an educational library—was the next step, although I can't say that I came to that right away. I don't think I started thinking about this on a grand scale until the late eighties."

But once the idea began to take shape, Cotsen wasted no time in his quest to acquire material in great volume. Alerted to the fact that a major player with unlimited resources had suddenly entered the arena, well-connected booksellers around the world began offering material to him, and once he started buying in earnest, "all kinds of fabulous stuff—books, original artwork, everything you can imagine—suddenly came out of the woodwork," he said. "I didn't have the time to put the collection together one book at a time, so I looked for entire collections. When I buy a whole collection, I am buying the intelligence that went into creating it. That is worth something, and I am happy to pay that premium." This method has a few drawbacks, not least of which is that Cotsen no longer had the time to spend with the books he was acquiring. "Before my wife died, I used to read almost every book that came into the house. Then it went down to one out of every three books. Today, I don't read one out of a thousand, but I do thumb through them. Right now, I'm interested in creating a collection that is comprehensive. I want a library with a kind of magical vitality to it, one that I like to say connects the headlands of scholarship with the heartlands of youth."

As we continued our walk through the Los Angeles apartments, we came to a shelf that held three stacks of books with the names of Cotsen's surviving children, Corinna, Tobey, and Eric, taped above them on separate pieces of paper. "These are books that were special to my kids when they were young," Cotsen said. "I told each of them they could take whatever they wanted out of what was in the library up to the time their mother and their brother died. Everything else goes over to Princeton. I'm also building up new collections for my grandchildren. What I usually do is walk into a bookstore about three or four times a year and wipe the place out."

Books from the Cotsen family personal collection occupy a special place in the Princeton library, Andrea Immel pointed out in the introduction to volume 1 of the catalog, and are

> *readily identifiable by their blue bookplates illustrated with the image of a faun playing pan pipes, which Mrs. Cotsen selected from the third volume of* Joy Street, *the 1920s British annual for children. Many of the family bookplates have been annotated by Mrs. Cotsen in her own hand, and her jottings constitute an informal history of a family reading together—the kind of evidence that historians are always longing to discover. Her notes frequently record when the book was added to the family collection, or if it had been a gift from someone to one of the children on a special occasion.*

Sometimes, Mrs. Cotsen recorded the children's response to a text they read aloud together; in other instances—such as when her daughters were studying French—she wrote messages of encouragement on the bookplates.

In 1998 Cotsen published a gorgeous large-format facsimile edition of a photo album he had acquired at auction two years earlier in England containing an extraordinary suite of family photographs representing a "pictorial biography" of Beatrix Potter (1866–1943), the great children's book author-illustrator who created Peter Rabbit, Jemima Puddle-Duck, Mrs. Tiggy-Winkle, and other classic characters. A detailed evaluation of the contents, written by Ivy Trent, Cotsen's personal librarian in Los

Angeles, is inserted in a pocket on the rear pastedown of the book, titled *Marseilles, Genoa and Pisa*. Cotsen's dedication page reads as follows: "This facsimile edition is dedicated to my Children: Corinna, Tobey, Eric and Noah and to their mother, JoAnne, who had the wisdom to introduce them to Beatrix Potter's world as young children." In 2000 the first volume of the general catalog of the collection was dedicated to "my late wife, who started it all with her desire and energy reading to our children and encouraging their imagination and creativity through exploration of the words and pictures of children's stories."

Cotsen does not use the word *memorial* to describe the library itself; he does not use the word *tribute* either, but chose instead to name it for his entire family, and let what it is, and what he hopes it becomes, speak for itself. "Something you develop very early on in archaeology is a sense of loss, of learning to appreciate what once was there and now is gone forever, and this passes over into the way you approach your life," he said. "If you have never lost anything, it seems to me you will be forever oblivious to the world around you." That is as close as Cotsen comes to explaining the impulse he had to form a bequest that will reach out to children and help shape them as human beings.

Of the many places Cotsen has visited all over the world, he confesses a special affection for Greece, where he spent so many rewarding summers on archaeological digs. At one point during my visit with him, he took note of my surname and offered a few pleasantries in the language of my Greek ancestors. When we were finishing our second afternoon of conversation, he gave me a handsome card with the words "Cotsen Children's Library" embossed on the front in bold capital letters. I asked him to inscribe it as a memento of my visit. Underneath his signature he wrote κρονια πολλα, a traditional expression of friendship pronounced "chronia polla," a welcome sentiment, indeed, to receive from the architect of a "living library" for children. It means "many years."

PART THREE

BOOK PLACES

8.

THE PEOPLE'S PALACE

It is, no doubt, possible that my own personal experience may have led me to value a free library beyond all other forms of beneficence. When I was a boy in Pittsburgh, Colonel Anderson of Allegheny—a name I can never speak without feelings of devotional gratitude—opened his little library of four hundred books to boys. Every Saturday afternoon he was in attendance himself to exchange books. No one but he who has felt it can know the intense longing with which the arrival of Saturday was awaited, that a new book might be had.
—Andrew Carnegie, The Gospel of Wealth

A few months after observing its one hundred and fiftieth birthday with a series of gala events, the Boston Public Library suffered the worst calamity in its illustrious history, reminding us in a most elemental way how indispensable books are to the intellectual vitality of a modern community. Disaster struck shortly after 1 A.M. on August 16, 1998, when a 103-year-old cast-iron water main buried deep beneath Copley Square burst its seams and sent thousands of gallons surging through the basement of the McKim Building, the most admired architectural landmark in the Back Bay section of the city, and the focus of a $65 million restoration that had brought renewed attention to its magnificent murals by Edwin A. Abbey, John Elliot, Pierre Puvis de Chavannes, and John Singer Sargent. As the alarm went out for help, staff members began converging on the scene, many of them arriving well before sunrise to offer assistance. By that time row after row of metal shelving had already buckled under the force of coarse gray silt oozing up through the seams, leaving thousands of bloated books floating in three feet of frigid water. To help curators deal with the loss of so much precious material at one time, a team of grief counselors was called in to offer emotional support.

This was by no means the worst catastrophe to strike a book repository over the previous decade—it was not even the most severe recorded in the United States—but it came at a time when librarians everywhere were discussing the future of printed books, and debating whether aging materials like these were worth keeping at all, let alone making heroic attempts to save. The heaviest losses recorded to date by an American library came on April 30, 1986, when an arsonist's match ignited Central Library in downtown Los Angeles, destroying 375,000 books in the sixty-year-old structure and setting in motion one of the largest book-salvaging operations ever undertaken in North America. Although 80 percent of the library's 2.3 million volumes were saved, 700,000 were soaked during the massive attempt to douse the flames, and 600,000 others were damaged by smoke. Fearful that mildew and mold would render all preservation efforts moot, and with a deadline of forty-eight hours imposing a growing sense of urgency on the hastily improvised salvage operation, some fifteen hundred citizen volunteers joined weary staff members in a frantic race against the clock to get the soggy books packed in boxes and sent off to every available freeze-drying facility located in the metropolitan area. As storage space began to fill up, officials from McDonnell Douglas Co. in Huntington Beach offered use of their Space Simulation Center for the rescue effort, and the United Growers of California cleared out a refrigerated warehouse to make room for truckloads of saturated volumes.

"As we mourn the old Central Library, we must also recognize that library buildings as such don't really matter," Lawrence Clark Powell, a Los Angeles native and head librarian at the University of California,

Los Angeles, from 1944 until 1961, wrote a month after the inferno. "Saving most of the books matters more." Powell fondly reminisced about his first job as an apprentice librarian at the old building in 1937, and he praised the professionals he worked with then for having given him a "new education" that helped shape his life's work. But what Powell lamented most about the disaster was not the loss of the "zigurat-style" edifice that had been gutted by fire, but "the hurt inflicted on the heart and soul of the Central Library: the useful materials that suffered damage or loss." Powell's response was shared by thousands of other library patrons. The sudden void in the educational, cultural, and intellectual life of Los Angeles was devastating, and seven years would pass before an expanded, handsomely refurbished, and fully restocked replacement was opened on the site to the public; total cost to taxpayers and private donors came to $223 million, a lot of money by any measurement, but dollar for dollar still one of the most economical investments any community can make, especially when the number of people affected by the operations of a municipal activity is factored in.

On February 14, 1988, a fire of even greater magnitude roared through the National Academy of Sciences Library in Leningrad, a national research institute built around a collection donated by Peter the Great in 1714, and one of the most important academic resources in what was then the Soviet Union. More than 400,000 books were incinerated in the disaster, many of them rare works dating from the seventeenth, eighteenth, and nineteenth centuries, and 3.6 million others were damaged. Six weeks after the fire, a group of conservators who had worked to save the Los Angeles collections were flown in to advise their Russian counterparts on tactics that had proven successful in the California catastrophe. By then some 250,000 volumes had been frozen at various fish-processing plants located around the city of Leningrad, since 1991 known once again as Saint Petersburg. As those facilities filled up, officials broadcast a public appeal for assistance. Thousands of Russian citizens brought books home and air-dried them in their kitchens, dens, and dining rooms, doing whatever was necessary to help save a portion of their national patrimony; about 600,000 volumes were cared for in this touching demonstration of bibliophilia at its most fundamental level.

In the aftermath of the Boston Public Library flood ten years later, barely thirty-six hours had passed before forklifts were loading pallets of books onto refrigerated trailer trucks that had been rushed to the scene. When I arrived to observe the rescue efforts, exhausted librarians and curators were still wading through mounds of wet paper. No people had been injured, yet there was the unmistakable sensation of being among a team of emergency medical technicians at the site of a bloody accident. The mood was particularly grim in an area of the basement used to store a million pieces of microfilm. "I don't have any idea yet of the actual losses," Henry Scannell, the department librarian, said, shaking his head in disbelief. "All I can say right now is that it's in the tens of thousands." He picked up a reel of sodden film that had moored itself on a mound of gray silt and quickly determined its content. "Now this is a set of Canadian patents. We can replace this if we have to. Microfilm, by its nature, you can usually get a new copy, assuming you can afford to buy one." The formula for determining whether a reel of film is irreplaceable is fairly straightforward, he added. "If somebody else out there has a copy, then you should be able to get one." The short-term tactic was not nearly so discerning, however. "I am removing these reels in blocks, not one at a time, and like the books, they will be frozen and dried, and then we will have an idea how much of it is going to be recovered."

The refrigerated books were driven to Disaster Recovery Services, a vacuum freeze-drying facility in Fort Worth, Texas. Other items that had absorbed ambient moisture were shipped to the company's Amesbury, Massachusetts, facility for dehumidification. Some seventy thousand plastic crates normally used to transport milk and bread, most of them donated by area vendors, were packed with books and microfilm. Stuart Walker, the library conservator, took me into the southeast corner of the basement, one of the sections hardest hit by the flooding. "Until a few years ago, all of the area we are in now was a deep, dark, scary, nineteenth-century basement," he said. In 1993, $20 million was spent to convert the space into a modern research and storage facility for government documents, microfilm, and science reference materials. The basement of the newer building next door, opened in 1972 and known informally as the Johnson Building for the architect Philip Johnson, who designed it, is used to store various sound archives, supplies, and a sixteen-millimeter film collection. "All of the appointments you see around you are new," Walker said. "There was nice carpeting here, nice lighting, nice furniture. One of the first things we did yesterday was take the carpets out to lower the relative humidity."

In an emergency situation like this, the immediate responsibility of the conservator is to establish priorities. "You have to determine exactly what it is you're going to salvage," Walker said. "Before you can do that, you must acknowledge that you cannot save everything. Once you have done that, you begin to triage, and essentially you are deciding as quickly as you can what is going to live and what is going to die." More than anything else, the freezing buys time, he said. "The books are already wet, and you can always re-wet them if you have to. Once you have frozen the material, you remove the water vapor directly from ice, you don't pass back to the water phase, you go through a chemical process called sublimation, which is drawing a vacuum and adding a slight amount of heat. I think in this case it is about fifteen degrees Fahrenheit. At that atmospheric pressure, with that heat, water boils. So you have boiling water but you don't have boiling liquid water, because it is too cold."

Once the water main had been closed, the leak sealed, and the basement pumped out, flexible yellow tubes were threaded along the floor to pump chilled air in from portable cooling units set up outside. Fans and dehumidifiers were installed and set to run at full throttle. "Those are the three elements," Walker said. "You lower the temperature, you circulate the air, you dehumidify. What you have basically with a flood is a forty-eight-hour window of opportunity. The critical thing is to get the material up off the ground before mold begins to grow. When the collection begins to get moldy, you are faced with a catastrophic loss, an irreplaceable loss. This stuff you see here, you can send it out to be freeze-dried, and it will come back looking oddly enough as if nothing had happened to it. The freeze-drying actually sucks dirt that has embedded itself in the material up to the top of the pages. There will be dirt on the outer edges, but you can brush that right off."

By the time I arrived to observe the rescue efforts, the library staff was proceeding according to plans that had been formulated years earlier in anticipation of just such a crisis. "We are prioritizing by things that cannot be replaced. These things down here on the floor are all Priority One. What's on the top shelf is dry; that's Priority Two. Priority One is what is wet," Walker said. With a collection of more than 8 million books, the Boston Public Library uses every available corner of storage area in the two-building complex, and in several off-site storehouses maintained away from Copley Square. Books kept in the basement are not among the rarest in a collection that is regarded as one of the strongest among the world's public libraries, but some exceedingly scarce items are there nonetheless, especially a huge archive of patents and genealogical documents, which are among the most consulted materials in the library.

"Down in the corner there are some old science-project books," Marilyn McLean, the science department curator, told me. "You can take them with you when you leave if you want because they are replaceable, they are not worth that much money, and I am not concerned about them. You want them, they're yours, be my guest, nobody cares. We can go in the stacks and replace that material in a matter of minutes. So those aren't on anybody's priority list, and they are not going to be sent to Fort Worth either. The stuff that was all over the floor here, that's a different matter altogether, and we're working on that right now. We've got some book jackets with no books anymore, and we are doing an inventory so we can at least know what is gone. The shelf list to this department is now being microfilmed because at least we will have a record of what we used to have."

A year after the flood, a detailed inventory of the damages was calculated and released. Some 105,000 print items, including books, maps, and close to 3 million microfiche images and films, had been sent out for treatment. About 60 percent of the printed materials were returned to the shelves, although most of the original microfiche and film reels, about 315,000 objects, were damaged beyond salvage. Duplicates for most of the filmed materials were located at other libraries, and copies were made. Most of the computer terminals, microfilm readers, metal shelving, and furniture in the basement were replaced. The total cost of the disaster was estimated at $18 million, with most of the money to cover the losses coming from insurance and private donations. "There was never any question that we should make the effort, and to make it as quickly as we could," Bernard A. Margolis, president of the library, told me. "Our books are our most precious resource."

Alexandre Vattemare had fame beyond his wildest dreams, but what the nineteenth-century French ventriloquist and impersonator wanted most of all was immortality. Known professionally as Monsieur Alexandre, Vattemare had the gift to make people smile and shake their heads at his tricks of mimicry. When the showman traveled to the United States in 1839 to launch a series of stage performances, he brought along a kind of scrapbook called the *Album Cosmopolite* that contained tributes from admirers all over Europe, with Queen Victoria, Ludwig van Beethoven, Victor Hugo, the emperors of Austria and Russia, the sultan of Turkey, and the painter Sir Edwin Henry Landseer leading his list of admirers. Monsier Alexandre's advance notices, apparently, were not exaggerated; after winning over a packed Park Theatre audience in New York City, he set out on a triumphant tour of major North American cities.

Although the response undoubtedly pleased Vattemare, his agenda during these travels was a desire not so much to spread his celebrity, since he already had international approbation in abundance, but to advance a proposal that would allow for "the intellectual treasures of the cultivated world" to enjoy the "same dissemination and equalization which commerce has already given to the material ones." What he was advocating, specifically, was the "establishment in every quarter of the world" of a network of "free libraries and museums" to be open for the perusal and enjoyment of everyone. Vattemare was something of an eccentric, to say the least, but he did have an agreeable way of getting people's attention. During a subsequent trip to the United States in 1847, he was granted an audience before the U. S. House of Representatives in Washington, D.C. With the blessing of John Quincy Adams, a former president of the United States and the ranking elder citizen of the Commonwealth of Massachusetts, the curious French crusader carried his mission to the blue-blooded aristocrats of Boston. The historian Walter Muir Whitehill called this "little man" who "descended" on New England a "whirlwind" of energy.

Addressing Mayor Josiah Quincy and the Boston City Council, Vattemare urged the consolidation of sixty small special-interest libraries already functioning in the metropolitan area into a single public institution. That was not likely to happen any time soon, but he did make friends all the same with a gift of one hundred books furnished by the Municipal Council of Paris, a modest contribution in pursuit of cultural détente, but one now regarded as "the incipient collection" for what in a few years would become the core of America's first major public library. On March 18, 1848, the legislature of the Commonwealth passed a bill authorizing the city "to establish and maintain" such a "municipal institution" in Boston. Approved promptly by the governor, the act became law on April 3, 1848, the date accepted as the birthday of the library. Justin Winsor (1831–1897), the founding president of the American Library Association and one of the true pioneers in the modern library movement in the United States, gave the French ventriloquist his due: "Whatever we think of Vattemare, whether we call him an enthusiast, or something worse or better, we must recognize his contagious energy, which induced

State after State to succumb to his representations, so that by 1853 he had brought one hundred and thirty libraries and institutions within his operations." Between 1847 and 1851 Vattemare arranged for the transfer of 30,655 books from France to North America.

Today, there are more public library buildings in the United States than McDonald's restaurants—16,090 according to the most recent inventory, with about 750 million books now in their collections, or 2.7 volumes per capita. When Vattemare began his project, there was only one public library operating in the country—Peterborough, New Hampshire, the idyllic community Thornton Wilder used as a model for Grovers Corners in the play *Our Town*, claims the distinction of having authorized the nation's first tax-supported public collection in 1833—but important book collections had been established all the same. According to one detailed inventory, 694 private libraries, with an aggregate of 2,201,632 books on their shelves, were operating throughout the country by mid-century. Census figures show that at about the time Vattemare was making his rounds in America, Massachusetts had seventy-eight of these collections, containing a total of 200,000 volumes, with "no other State approaching" those holdings.

On June 30, 1852, Mayor Benjamin Seaver asked a blue-ribbon committee of Bostonians to outline in specific detail what "objects" they felt would be "attained by the establishment of a Public Library," and to clarify "the best mode of affecting them." The report they returned a month later is regarded today as the generative document of the public library movement in the United States. Most of the elegant prose was written by George Ticknor, a Harvard historian and bibliophile who "threw himself heartily into the movement, with a spirit of progress and liberality much in advance of what some of his associates" thought desirable, Winsor wrote. The trustees took pointed note of a municipality's obligation to provide "munificent appropriations" for the intellectual well-being of its citizens, declaring that "a large public library is of the utmost importance as the means of completing our system of public education."

Enthusiastically received by city officials, the final report was included as a last-minute enclosure in a prospectus of materials circulated abroad to encourage foreign investment in Boston. In a classic case of good luck, the package was sent to the London banking house of Baring Brothers and forwarded to the desk of Joshua Bates, a Massachusetts native who had navigated a reverse variation of the American dream by moving to England as a young man in search of fame and fortune, not the other way around. Bates worked at a number of jobs on his path to success, rising eventually to a partnership in the premier financial house of its day. On October 1, 1852, Bates wrote a letter to the Boston city fathers offering to give them $50,000 for their dream project with the stipulation that the money be used to purchase books, and it was tendered with the explicit understanding that before it could get the money, the city had to build a suitable structure to contain them. Bates also insisted that the library would have to be "perfectly free to all, with no other restrictions than may be necessary for the preservation of the books." The gift was being given, he explained, as "a small return for the many acts of confidence and kindness which I have received from my many friends in your City." In the letter of transmittal, Bates explained that his own "experience as a poor boy" growing up in Boston had given him the idea for making such a gift. "Having no money to spend and no place to go, not being able to pay for a fire in my own room, I could not pay for books, and the best way I could pass my evenings was to sit in Hastings, Ethedridge & Bliss's bookstore, and read what they kindly permitted me to; and I am confident that had there been good, warm, and well-lighted rooms to which we could have resorted, with proper books, nearly all the youth of my acquaintance would have spent their evenings there, to the improvement of their minds and morals."

In a centennial history of the Boston Public Library, Walter Muir Whitehill computed the buying power of the gift at $1 million in 1956 dollars; today, of course, it would be considerably more than that. By stipulating that the $50,000 could be used only for the purchase of books—salaries, improvements, and miscellaneous expenses would have to come from other accounts—Bates had guaranteed that the collection would grow rapidly. Titles that could not be acquired domestically were located in England and France, bought by none other than Joshua Bates himself. Before long, affluent Bostonians were responding with generous gifts of their own, many of them following the example of the British benefactor by dedicating their funds exclusively toward the acquisition of books.

When the first Boston Public Library building on Boylston Street formally opened its doors on New Year's Day, 1858, 78,000 volumes were available to readers. Capacity for the new building had been pegged at 250,000 volumes, more than enough room, everyone agreed, to allow for measured growth of the collections in the years ahead. To mark the occasion, the illustrious orator, statesman, and clergyman Edward Everett (1794–1865) spoke extemporaneously for forty-six minutes. Everett's impromptu remarks were considerably more succinct than the formal presentation he would spend two hours delivering at ceremonies consecrating the Civil War battlefield of Gettysburg on November 19, 1863— he was the "other" prominent dignitary to make a memorial address that day—but the former president of Harvard University offered one point that he surely would have found amusing had he been alive two decades later. Glancing around the glittering new building, Everett declared the facilities to be more than sufficient to accommodate the reading needs of the citizenry for the next century.

By 1878, however, it had been necessary to double storage space in the cramped building, and there still was not nearly enough room to contain the burgeoning collections. In just twenty years the holdings had quadrupled to 320,000 volumes, and they were being used; loans of 4,000 books were being recorded every day, some 1.2 million volumes circulating a year. By 1895, the first building was abandoned as totally inadequate—the original site on Boylston Street facing Boston Common is occupied today by the famed Colonial Theater—and the collections were moved into the grand edifice in Copley Square designed by Charles Follin McKim of McKim, Mead and White of New York City.

Using a palazzo he had seen during a trip to Italy as a model, McKim created a rectangular granite building with an elegant courtyard at the center. It was sited in the Back Bay section of the city, an aptly named neighborhood then being reclaimed from the Charles River Basin with fill hauled in from neighboring communities. Like the graceful structures built in Venice many centuries earlier, the Boston Public Library was designed to float on a foundation of wooden pilings sunk into the soft soil. For the main entryways, six bronze doors featuring personified images of Music, Poetry, Knowledge, Wisdom, Truth, and Romance were crafted by the sculptor Daniel Chester French. A floor of white Georgia marble, inlaid in the center aisle with brass intarsia, dominates the entrance hall. Henry James praised the "high and luxurious beauty" of the sweeping main stairway for "its amplitude of wing and its splendour of tawny marble." On either side of the landing were placed two lions couchant cleaved from solid blocks of unpolished Siena marble by Louis Saint-Gaudens, whose brother, Augustus Saint-Gaudens, carved the sculpted head of Minerva, the goddess of wisdom, that adorns the keystone above the main entrance. "Let in the light," Oliver Wendell Holmes had declared in a declamatory poem read at the laying of the cornerstone on September 28, 1888: "This palace is the people's own!"

And the people's palace it became; the Boston Public Library was the first library in the United States to allow patrons the privilege of taking books home, and the first to establish a branch system. In 1895 it opened the first room intended for the exclusive use of children. Although most of its funding comes from taxpayers, the library continues to have generous benefactors. Major support for the McKim Building restoration was provided by the BPL Foundation, a nonprofit "friends" organization that also has underwritten improvements at the branches, and supports the purchase of special collections, a holding of rare books and manuscripts that is among the strongest in the country, second in depth and importance among public libraries only to its giant sibling on Fifth Avenue and Forty-second Street in New York City.

For Bernard A. Margolis, a native New Englander who had worked at a variety of library jobs in Michigan and Colorado before being selected in 1997 for the "dream" assignment in Boston, as he described it to me, the appointment came at a crucial time in the life of the institution. Not only was the hundred and fiftieth anniversary hard on the horizon, but there also was a huge restoration to be seen through to completion, and a campaign to build a $100 million endowment by the end of the twentieth century that needed to be shepherded along. Twenty-five branch operations required attention as well, and then, from out of nowhere, there were the consequences of a devastating flood to deal with. "I am a manager, I am an administrator, sometimes I have to be a politician, then I have to be a salesman," he said. "I also am an orator and a fund-raiser and a huckster. I am one million different things, and I am hustling all the time. But more than anything I like to think of myself as someone who embodies the principles of equal access, someone who promotes the idea that you get rich at the library, the idea that it doesn't matter who you are, it doesn't matter the color of your skin, your name, the language you speak, the nation of your ancestry, the clothes you wear—this is a place where you can come and get rich."

With more than 8 million items in the library's collection, Margolis said the lasting lesson of the 1998 flood was a renewed appreciation of how important everything is to the vitality of the institution. "We are professional collectors here, and we throw very little out. This is something, institutionally, that we firmly believe in, and I am the guardian of that principle. Part of our mission is shaped by the reality that Boston, in terms of its diversity, is a world city, and we are now buying books in forty languages. Let me give you an example of our attitude. We have the largest collection of city directories in the world, about fifty thousand of them. These are spectacular tools, invaluable resources. Sure, they are out of date, and indeed some people do laugh, they say, 'City directories, who cares?' Well, when you have cultures being destroyed, as you saw in Bosnia, where do people go to reestablish their culture? Where do they make a start? We have directories here, and we also have some newspapers that you will never find in the countries of their origin. What we do is capture all the evidence of culture, in not just our own extended community but as much of this huge world out there as we can, a world that is shrinking all the time. We could very well be the only big-city American library that still keeps all of the local newspapers. The others rely on microfilm as their preservation copy. We keep the originals."

Margolis picked up a copy of the first trustees' report issued in 1852, and turned to the founding principles that outlined four "classes" of books that should be acquired by a public library. One category, predictably enough, was material "that will be often asked for," and by that George Ticknor and his colleagues meant "the more respectable of the popular books of the time," gathered in sufficient numbers so that "*many* persons, if they desire it, can be reading the work at the same moment." But it was the second category that Margolis said was his favorite, and was the one he read aloud for me: "*Books that few persons will wish to read, and of which, therefore, only one copy will be kept, but which should be permitted to circulate freely, and if this copy should, contrary to expectation, be so often asked for, as to be rarely on the shelves, another copy should then be bought.*" The concept of buying books that "*few persons will wish to read*"—and the italics were provided by the framers of the mission statement—is central to the mission of a modern librarian, Margolis said, and "it was a stroke of wisdom on the part of the founders to place it right there alongside the things that everybody wants to read. And why is that important? Because these are materials that document a community, and speak to an interest that may be there fifty years, a hundred years, from now. We encourage people to give us old books, and not many libraries do this, as you know, because it's labor intensive and most of the stuff you get you probably already have and probably don't need more of. But gifts very often bring us things that we missed the first time around, the more obscure things, the things that nobody else wants to read. And sometimes you get lucky. Just a few months ago, to cite one recent example, we found a land grant signed and sealed by John Adams buried in a box of gifts."

In April 1998, on the occasion of the Boston Public Library's hundred and fiftieth birthday, Kevin Starr, the state librarian of California and a former director of the San Francisco Public Library, offered some words of recognition. "Right from the start, the Boston Public Library signaled a movement that said, 'Where do you find the city? You find it here.' In city after city, the public library becomes the shared public space, the area in which the poetry, the history, the identity of a particular community is expressed, and the Boston Public Library does this gloriously—in terms of its siting in Copley Square, in terms of its grand architecture, in terms of its intellectual identity. It says, 'Here is something fine and enduring about Boston.' "

With several model operations thriving in the United States by the late 1800s, the stage was set for the unprecedented philanthropic activity of Andrew Carnegie (1835–1919), the Scottish-born industrialist who funded the construction of 1,689 libraries in 1,419 communities throughout the United States between 1893 and 1919. Like Joshua Bates, Carnegie required that something substantive be given in return for his largesse. In contrast to Bates—who offered to buy books, providing the people of Boston construct and maintain a building to contain them—Carnegie committed himself to donating the buildings only if the recipients agreed to furnish the land, acquire the books, and provide sufficient funds for staff and general operations. Carnegie explained his attitude toward philanthropy in an 1889 essay published for the *North American Review*: "The main consideration should be to help those who will help themselves; to provide the means by which those who desire to improve do so; to give those who desire to rise the aids by which they may rise; to assist, but rarely or never to do all."

Carnegie was not the first wealthy benefactor of public libraries in the United States—George Peabody in Danvers, Massachusetts, Walter L. Newberry in Chicago, Charles Bower Winn in Woburn, Massachusetts, and Enoch Pratt in Baltimore, preceded him by a few years—but he was the first to undertake the exercise on a sweeping scale that stretched from coast to coast, and included gifts in Canada and his native Scotland. Years before there was a public library operating anywhere in America, important book collections had been formed for limited general use. From 1848 to 1895 the Astor Library in New York City enjoyed renown as one of the most judiciously assembled resources available anywhere on the continent, but because no books could leave the premises, its usefulness was limited. Access to the reading room was granted at first to everyone over fourteen years of age, but when it became apparent that "crowds of school boys" were coming in "more for amusement than improvement," the restriction was raised to sixteen. Founded by the millionaire fur trader and financier John Jacob Astor (1763–1848), the collections were assembled with exquisite taste and discrimination by Joseph Green Cogswell (1786–1871), a former lawyer and teacher from Massachusetts who was invited to New York in 1838 with the idea of developing a suitable library gift to the city, and given an initial stipend of $400,000 to make it happen. The original plan called for assembling a collection of about 100,000 volumes, a nice round number that Cogswell believed would allow for creation of "a well digested, systematic library." Given free rein by Astor to travel, Cogswell followed a carefully planned itinerary through Europe in pursuit of material. During his first trip abroad in 1848–49, he spent $35,000 for 28,364 books. In 1851 he scouted out titles in England, France, Italy, the Netherlands, Scandinavia, and Germany, buying 28,000 volumes for $30,000. This activity did not go unnoticed among the cognoscenti on the Continent, and it attracted the attention of the Scottish scholar John Hill Burton:

Dr. Cogswell, the first librarian of the Astorian library, spent some time in Europe with his princely endowment in his pocket, and showed himself a judicious, active, and formidable sportsman in the book-hunting world. Whenever, from private collections, or the breaking-up of public institutions, rarities got abroad into the open market, the collectors of the old country found that they had a resolute competitor to deal with—almost, it might be said, a desperate one—since he was in a manner the representative of a nation using powerful efforts to get possession of a share of the literary treasures of the Old World.

When the Astor Library opened in 1854, the collection stood at about eighty thousand volumes. The *Evening Post* expressed pleasure that "a library so large, and so complete in all its parts, has never before been put in order within anything like the same time," but its editors were nonetheless critical of the rules prohibiting use of any books outside the building's walls, and the limited hours of operation. Still, the collection was enormous for its time, constantly prompting people to ask Cogswell to confide the precise number of titles he had acquired. In a semi-official account written for the *Home Journal*, which was reprinted in many newspapers and appeared as the fifth annual report to the trustees of the Astor Library, Cogswell addressed himself to the size issue with a hint of exasperation. "I trust I shall not be understood as implying that the real worth of a library is to be estimated by its number of volumes, which is very like estimating a farm by its number of acres," he wrote. "Use and time are the only certain tests of the value of a library."

Cogswell's most lasting contribution to the development of public libraries in the United States, it turned out, was not the specific titles he gathered for John Jacob Astor but the sense of functionality and purpose he embodied in his acquisitions policy. Long after Astor's books were combined with those of James Lenox (1800–1880) in 1895 to form the core collection of the New York Public Library, the estimable Boston bookseller George Goodspeed declared the institution at Fifth Avenue and Forty-second Street to be not only "great," but also "one of the most useful" intellectual resources in the world, an attribute it retains with great panache and purpose to this day. The two private collections were joined when Samuel Jones Tilden (1814–1886), a former governor of New York and an unsuccessful Democratic candidate for president of the United States in 1876, died and left a $2 million trust to establish a free library in Manhattan for the use of the public. City officials put up the $9 million to build the library, but the contents and operating costs were borne by the private trust.

After an open competition in which numerous proposals were submitted—including one from McKim, Mead and White, which placed third—the architectural firm of Carrère and Hastings was awarded the contract to design a worthy repository on what was once the site of a municipal reservoir in Midtown Manhattan. President William Howard Taft attended dedication ceremonies on May 23, 1911, twelve years after work had begun. The next day, thirty thousand people streamed through the front door to take in the splendor of the Beaux Arts building, which radiated opulence on every visible surface. Some 530,000 cubic feet of Vermont white marble had been used, more marble than for any other structure built in the United States up to that time; the New York Stock Exchange, by contrast, used 50,000 cubic feet of the stone.

When the first readers were admitted in the spring of 1911, a million books were on the shelves to serve them, all selected in the tradition established by Joseph Cogswell, with great care and discernment. Continually augmented over the years through purchases and bequests, the holdings today number about 50 million items, which grow at the rate of ten thousand objects a week. Claiming depth in a plentitude of areas— there are materials in three thousand languages and dialects—the New York Public Library ranks on a level with the finest research collections in the world. That it is a treasure house open to everyone—no identification of any sort is required to access materials in any of the four research libraries—is underscored by the countless ways in which the riches have been used.

When the esteemed literary critic Alfred Kazin died on June 5, 1998, his eighty-third birthday, the novelist Philip Roth, renowned as a tireless consumer of books in his own right, offered the ultimate compliment: "He was America's best reader of American literature in this century." Six months earlier, I had met with Kazin in his apartment on the Upper West Side of Manhattan to discuss his eventful life as author and critic for the literary column I wrote for more than twenty years; of immediate interest was release of what would turn out to be Kazin's final effort, *God and the American Writer*. All of Kazin's books were free of jargon and notable for their accessibility, a quality that he attributed to having respect for his audience. "My books come out of deep personal urgency, which has nothing to do with anything except my own problems and my own interests. So I am not trying to impress anyone. You will find that a lot of people in academe write for each other to the point that they are impenetrable to the larger world around them. I write for what Virginia Woolf called 'the common reader,' since I am a common reader myself. I never aim at my audience. My intention simply is to express what I myself most deeply feel. If you do that successfully, then the reader will receive your message."

Kazin had dedicated *God and the American Writer* to the memory of the historian Richard Hofstadter, a lifelong friend he got to know during the late 1930s when both were spending days on end doing research at the New York Public Library. In *New York Jew,* an intellectual autobiography of the 1940s, 1950s, and 1960s, Kazin described how he spent close to five years engaged in "great all-day bouts of reading" in Room 315, preparing himself to write what would be the first serious study of the "new" American literature that had recently emerged, a landmark work he would title *On Native Grounds,* and still in print after the passage of more than half a century. "Year after year I seemed to have nothing more delightful to do than to sit much of the day and many an evening at one of those great golden tables and acquainting myself with every side of my subject," he wrote. "Whenever I was free to read, the great Library seemed free to receive me. Anything I had heard of and wanted to see, the blessed place owned."

The literary critic Harold Bloom, author of such best-sellers as *The Book of "J," The Western Canon,* and *Inventing Shakespeare,* and recognized as one of the most astute readers of his generation, has credited the New York Public Library with energizing a passion for literature that astounded Alfred Kazin, his older contemporary. In one of four interviews we have had over the years, Bloom told me that his exhaustive regimen was such that several years earlier he had exacerbated a severe case of bleeding ulcers and aggravated a heart condition that required him to undergo major surgery from having read for great periods without pausing for rest. "I have done nothing but read all my life," he said, pointing to a pile of volumes stacked high beside the well-worn leather chair in his New Haven, Connecticut, living room, where he spends much of his day when not teaching or writing. "And I go on reading, and I reread things all the time. I reread Shakespeare daily. I recite poems to myself all the time as I walk around. After you leave today, I will go on the constitutional required by my doctor, and I will just recite poems to myself as I go." Bloom is, in fact, the only thinker of consequence I have ever met who could not name a book that he had wanted to read that remains unread. "I think I have, in fact, read all the books," he said with a laugh, and quoted the French poet Stéphane Mallarmé: "The flesh is sad, alas, and I have read all the books."

When his thirty-fifth book, *How to Read and Why,* was published in the fall of 2000, Bloom was interviewed on the C-SPAN cable television network program *Booknotes* by Brian Lamb. Tracing his development as an intellectual, Bloom recalled his youth as the child of immigrant parents in the 1930s and 1940s in the East Bronx, when only Yiddish was spoken in the household. He taught himself to read that language when he was three, and mastered Hebrew and English by the time he was five. "I would have been nowhere in this life without the various branches of the New York Public Library when I grew up," he said. "I started reading at the Melrose branch of the Bronx Public Library when I was so small I couldn't carry the books home. My three sisters, much older, kindly carried them for me. And I went from the Melrose branch of the Bronx Public Library, and I'd read through it, to the Fordham branch of the Bronx library, which is its research branch, and I used that up. And I descended, at fifteen, clutching my nickels in hand for the subway, to the Forty-second Street Library, determined to read through that in the main reading room. And, of course, I would never have succeeded. But soon enough, I was a Cornell undergraduate, having won a fellowship, and spent four years trying to read out that library, and, for the last forty-six years, have been trying to read out the Yale Library, which no human being can read through, though I've done what I could."

During the early years of the twentieth century, the New York Public Library was a refuge for many immigrant scholars. Isaac Bashevis Singer found the Yiddish and Hebrew books he needed to research his weekly column for the *Jewish Daily Forward* there, and told a young woman he had met that if she ever wanted to see him again, she should look in the library. "She came and found me," the future Nobel Laureate would relate, and they became husband and wife a year later. "Name a writer who has lived in New York, and he or she has surely spent countless days and evenings there," Sara Rimer wrote as the main branch approached its seventy-fifth birthday in 1986. In 1995 Robert A. Caro, the Pulitzer Prize–winning biographer of the legendary New York City public works czar Robert Moses, recalled the critical moment of his professional life as the day he was given a key to work in the Frederick Lewis Allen Memorial Room on the first floor of the library. Named for a journalist, social historian, and former editor in chief of *Harper's Magazine* whose own work was informed by access to the institution's vast holdings, the Allen Room provides space for up to eleven authors at a time who have no place of their own to write. The only requirement for eligibility is a signed contract for a work in progress.

Of particular interest to Caro was the privilege accorded resident writers to keep noncirculating materials at their desks and not return them at the end of the day like everyone else. Other writers in residence at the time included Joseph Lash, the author of *Eleanor and Franklin,* James Thomas Flexner, the author of a four-volume life of George Washington, Nancy Milford, the biographer of Zelda Fitzgerald and Edna St. Vincent Millay, and Susan Brownmiller, who was working on *Against Our Will.* Before long Caro was having lunch in the employees' cafeteria with his colleagues, talking more often than not about the mysteries of their shared craft. "Suddenly, just by being given a desk in the Allen Room, I had been made to feel a part of the community of writers." A row of bookshelves in what Caro called the "sanctum sanctorum for writers" is devoted to works produced by "alumni" of the room, and in the spring of 1975 he returned one night after everyone had gone, hoping to see if his newly released life of Moses, *The Power Broker,* stood alongside the others. To his great relief, it was there, flanked by such titles as Theodore H. White's *Making of the President: 1964* and Betty Friedan's *Feminine Mystique.* "That was the place, of all places," Caro concluded, "where it belonged."

At a Literary Lions fund-raiser in 1998, the essayist Cynthia Ozick told how her job as a part-time assistant page in the Periodicals Room fifty years earlier made her feel "part of the heartbeat of that place." It was in that same room that DeWitt Wallace, the resourceful son of a Minnesota clergyman, worked out his idea for founding a magazine that would gather excerpts of articles of "enduring value and interest" from previously published journals. Wallace spent endless hours poring over thousands of magazines and journals, condensing the pieces that had caught his fancy and writing them out on sheets of yellow paper in longhand. The first issue of *Reader's Digest* was mailed out by his wife and partner, Lila Acheson Wallace, in February 1922 in a premiere press run of five thousand copies. At its height in the 1990s, the magazine appeared in forty-one editions around the world in seventeen languages, with a total monthly circulation of 30.5 million. During the first year of operation, Mrs. Wallace worked out of a basement cubicle in Greenwich Village, while her husband continued to find the content they needed in his makeshift "office" at the library. In later years, one of the couple's many benefactions was a gift of $2 million to rehabilitate the chamber where their magazine took shape, now known as the DeWitt and Lila Wallace Periodicals Room.

A younger contemporary of Wallace, the inventor Chester Carlson (1906–1968), spent every spare minute he could muster in the late 1930s making full use of the library's treasures. A graduate of the California Institute of Technology, Carlson began thinking of ways to make his job as a patents officer in an electronics firm easier. "I frequently had need for copies of patent specifications and drawings, and there was no really convenient way of getting them at the time," he recalled toward the end of his life. Carlson's idea was to develop a process that would enable him to use "light to affect matter in some way" other than photography to make an image on paper, and he began by scrutinizing the enormous collection of technical materials in the New York Public Library's science collections. Eventually he came across references to a property called photoconductivity, and learned that the electrical conductivity of certain materials can be affected by the exposure to light. In time, his experiments with what he called electrophotography would be christened xerography—a combination of the Greek words for "dry" and "writing"—leading ultimately to the introduction in 1959 of the Xerox 914, the world's first photocopying machine (the numbers represented the size of a nine-by-fourteen sheet of paper). The original notebooks documenting Carlson's research were given by his widow to the New York Public Library, the one place above all others where she felt they belonged; microfilm copies are in the Rochester Institute of Technology and the University of Rochester, the hometown of Xerox.

In 1926 Edwin H. Land (1909–1991), a privileged young man from Massachusetts, dropped out of Harvard College during his freshman year, moved to New York City, and immersed himself in what he regarded as more meaningful study in Reading Room 315 of the great research library on Fifth Avenue. There, according to a former colleague, he "intensified his education" in the fields of optics, light, and electricity. Land would later say that he found primary inspiration to develop an inexpensive and efficient method for instant photography in the writings of William Bird Heraputh, an obscure English physician who in 1852 had determined through microscopic analysis that dogs treated with quinine had crystalline needles in their urine. From Land's standpoint, the key finding was evidence that overlapping perpendicular needles were black when they crossed, while those that were parallel were clear. From this curious piece of nineteenth-century arcania, Land went on to develop the first sheet polarizer, a leap of inductive perception that led ultimately to formation of the Polaroid Corporation and production of a camera celebrated for its power to treat its owners with immediate visual gratification; it made him a millionaire many times over. In due course, Harvard University awarded its distinguished dropout an honorary degree, giving the inventor the right to be known forever after as Dr. Land.

People who wonder how 420,000 maps and atlases might be used profitably in a public library need look no further than the probings of Juan Trippe (1899–1981), a brazen entrepreneur with a fancy for adventure and a flair for innovation who came of age during a time of golden opportunities. An early champion of commercial aviation, Trippe dreamed of opening travel routes between the United States and the Far East with a small fleet of amphibious aircraft known as flying clippers, but before he could launch the operation, he needed a chain of staging posts to service his planes on the sixty-hour flights across the Pacific Ocean. Hawaii was available for the first leg, Midway and Guam were nicely positioned for stops in the home stretch, but three thousand miles of open water were left uncovered in the middle. Reading through the library's superb collection of nineteenth-century clipper logs and nautical charts in the Map Division, he found repeated mention of a barren atoll in the northwest Pacific known as Wake Island. Digging deeper into its history, he learned that the 3.5-square-mile coral islet had been discovered in 1568 by the Spanish explorer Alvaro de Mendaña de Neira, and visited in 1796 by William Wake, an English sea captain, for whom it was named, then largely forgotten. Navy Lieutenant Charles Wilkes, the explorer of Antarctica, fixed its location in 1851, but the uninhabited island was not included on official maps, even after its annexation by the United States following the Spanish-American War. After securing long-term leases to operate seaplane bases on the island, Trippe's fledgling company, Pan American Airways, began regular flights to the Orient in 1935; the service was immortalized the following year by Humphrey Bogart and Pat O'Brien in the film *China Clipper*.

With close to half a million cataloged books in its inventory, the Slavic and Baltic Division on the second floor is larger than most public library collections in the United States in its own right, and its holdings are of such richness that scholars from abroad routinely travel to the United States to study the history of their own countries. This paradox was particularly apparent during the repressive years of the Soviet Union, according to Edward S. Kasinec, chief librarian of the division. "Why do you suppose the Soviets approached us in the 1920s when they wanted to sell the Romanov material?" he asked while giving me a tour of a 1998 exhibition that showcased a selection of books, manuscripts, watercolors, and original photographs that once belonged in the libraries of twenty-six members of the imperial dynasty that ruled Russia from 1613 to 1917. The New York Public Library bought three thousand of these materials from a cash-starved Soviet government in 1923. "The Slavic and Baltic Division was established in 1898," Kasinec said. "Once the Communists decided to sell the books of the czars, this was the logical place for them to go." The reputation of the library's Slavic collections was such that Leon Trotsky went there on his first day in New York in 1917, and visited regularly during the two months of his stay while writing for Nicolai Bukharin's Leninist newspaper, *Novy mir* ("New World").

When Robert Ripley, creator of the fabulously successful *Ripley's Believe It or Not* illustrated newspaper column, died in 1949 at the age of fifty-five, it was widely reported that the master of the incredible-but-true anecdote had traveled to 198 countries in search of his material, leaving no stone unturned to prove that truth indeed is stranger than fiction. The traveling part of the story was accurate enough, but the bulk of Ripley's information, it turned out, had been mined in the New York Public Library by an indefatigable researcher from Brooklyn who had an uncanny capacity for digesting and remembering everything he examined. A native of Poland who moved to the United States as a child, Norbert Pearlroth was an obsessive reader who was fluent in fourteen languages. When Ripley hired him to translate foreign publications in 1923, he was working at a bank in Manhattan, but his extraordinary facility for research was immediately recognized, and he remained with the column through 1975, long after it had been acquired by King Features Syndicate. When Pearlroth died in 1983 at the age of eighty-nine, it was reported that he had spent seven days a week over a fifty-two-year span in Room 315, "unearthing at least 62,192 facts and anecdotes" for the feature. "Everyone has always believed that all of this information was found wandering the world," Pearlroth's son Arthur said of his father's five-decade quest for obscure details. "But it was really found on Forty-second Street and Fifth Avenue at the Main Library."

As little known as Pearlroth was outside his immediate circle—Robert Ripley was presented to the public as the omniscient genius, after all—his name was known among the staff of the New York Public Library where he did his research. The same cannot be said for Martin Radtke, a native of Lithuania who had found a new life in the United States in 1913, first as a gardener, later as a shrewd investor. After learning English, he began to educate himself on the niceties of business and finance in the library's Economics Division, later broadening his reach to include art, literature, science, and history. A lifelong bachelor accustomed to living simply in a small Queens apartment and taking the subway into Manhattan, Radtke saved most of his wages, and as he became more comfortable with the nuances of Wall Street, he began dabbling in the stock market, steadily building up an admirable portfolio. Though hurt by the Great Crash of 1929, he was not wiped out, and set about rebuilding his modest fortune, supplementing his income by caring for a greenhouse in Rye, New York, drawing on horticultural material he researched at the library to perfect his skills. By 1946 he had recouped his fortune and was spending more and more time in Reading Room 315, continuing his lifelong program of self-improvement, according to the broker at Merrill Lynch, Pierce, Fenner & Smith who had handled his account, and who regarded him as a friend.

When Radtke died in March 1973 at eighty-nine years of age, the New York Public Library found out how much he had valued its free and open resources when his will was probated. "Nobody here had a clue as to who this man was until we received a telephone call from his lawyer," Catherine Carver Dunn, senior vice president in charge of the Development Office, told me, and Radtke's file at the library confirms this void by including only the few biographical odds and ends that were pieced together after his death by close friends and associates. The pertinent clause in Radtke's will reads as follows:

> *I had little opportunity for formal education as a young man in Lithuania, and I am deeply indebted to the New York Public Library for the opportunity to educate myself. In appreciation, I have given the Library my estate with the wish that it be used so that others can have the same opportunity made available to me.*

Radtke's bequest amounted to $368,000, by no means the largest gift ever presented to the library, but unquestionably one of the most heartfelt. Six months after he died, the library honored his generosity by placing an engraved marble plaque quoting the relevant words from his will in the floor between the twin staircases at the main doorway in the lobby;

the names of all other donors are inscribed on the interior walls of the building. "Martin Radtke was typical of his generation in that the library was his university," Richard W. Couper, at that time president of the library, said at unveiling ceremonies attended by 250 people.

Beyond the welcome infusion of funds brought in by the Radtke gift was the fortuitous timing of its arrival. "Go thou and do likewise," Couper told the audience with a sense of muted urgency that was not lost on one reporter, who noted in a concluding paragraph how the library "in recent years has had serious economic difficulties." In point of fact, the fiscal condition of the institution, paralleling that of the city itself at the time of the gift in 1973, was perilously grave, and it would get considerably worse before it got much better. When the decade ended seven years later, the New York Public Library found itself in the worst financial shape of its entire existence, a situation exacerbated by the unique organizational nature of the institution as a privately held foundation, its formal designation as a "public" institution notwithstanding. Unlike most other municipal libraries that receive primary support from taxpayers, the New York Public Library was established in 1895 through the creation of a nonprofit corporation that depended on private support for its operations. The city of New York agreed to build the building and to furnish funds for the branches, but the flagship building on Fifth Avenue, known today as the Humanities and Social Sciences Library, and three other research components, the Arthur Alfonso Schomburg Center for Research in Black Culture in Harlem, the Performing Arts Research Center at Lincoln Center, and the Science, Industry and Business Library on Madison Avenue and Thirty-fourth Street, rely preponderantly on private funds. Nowhere is this distinction made more evident than by the full-page advertisement the New York Public Library takes out each December in the *New York Times* to salute and list by name its "Corporate Partners," emphasizing in the annual holiday greeting that even though it may be the "largest publicly accessible library system in the world," it remains a "private institution with a public mission."

This unusual management structure—private funding for the research libraries, public money for the lending libraries—has been in place since 1901 when Andrew Carnegie offered to underwrite construction of sixty-seven satellite libraries throughout the city, providing they were managed by the same board of trustees. Because the proposal was tendered while construction of the new Central Research Library was under way, the burden was eased by limiting the New York City network to Manhattan, the Bronx, and Staten Island, which now operates eighty-five branches. Separate boards were established to oversee the boroughs of Brooklyn and Queens, and they continue to operate their own systems today. The Brooklyn Public Library operates fifty-eight branches, and maintains the only public bookmobile in New York City. With sixty-three locations, Queens Borough Public Library serves a population of 2 million residents, 840,000 of whom are registered borrowers, fully a third of them immigrants from other countries fluent in tongues other than English. In 2000 the Queens Borough Public Library reported lending 17.2 million items in sixty-five languages, the highest circulation of any municipal library system in the United States.

When Couper stepped down as president and chief executive officer at the New York Public Library in 1981, he took some solace in having submitted the first balanced budget in half a century, but confided "the absolute pain" he felt in having had to terminate 225 people from a staff of 1,309, and to have reduced operations at the Central Research Library from eighty-seven hours a week to forty-six in order to do it. Conditions were substantially worse at the branches, where operations had been cut back to three days a week. Couper was succeeded by Dr. Vartan Gregorian, a historian and former provost of the University of Pennsylvania who arrived with a clear understanding of what lay ahead, beginning with a simple conviction about the function libraries play in a modern society. "They are not a luxury," he proclaimed, "they are a necessity, especially in poor areas, where they are the only intellectual or cultural influence in the community." Gregorian began his new job in New York armed with a grim report that projected a deficit of $52 million by 1985, unless new strategies were developed.

Hiring Vartan "Greg" Gregorian to guide the resurgence proved to be a stroke of genius. Philip Hamburger would later describe the compact man with a neatly trimmed salt-and-pepper beard in a *New Yorker* profile as a phenomenon seemingly born to destiny. "I was immediately struck by his benign resemblance to the two sculptured lions, Patience and Fortitude, that guard the main steps of the library," Hamburger wrote of their first meeting, but admitted after several interviews that looks can be deceiving. "One must approach him as one would an extraordinary force of nature, a tornado, perhaps, or a hurricane." The Pulitzer Prize—winning historian Arthur Schlesinger Jr., who researched *The Age of Jackson* in Reading Room 315, would describe Gregorian as a "a great cultural impresario" blessed with uncommon vision, a man combining "the talents of a missionary and a showman." Born in Tabriz, Iran, into an Armenian family, Gregorian grew up in Beirut. He moved to the United States in 1956 and earned his bachelor's and doctoral degrees in history and the humanities from Stanford University. When he was appointed president of the New York Public Library in 1981, he had been teaching at the University of Pennsylvania for nine years, and had been a finalist in the search for a new president there.

Widely respected as an expert in Middle Eastern and Armenian studies, Gregorian did not feel he was abandoning academe by becoming the custodian of a public library, however challenging an opportunity it may have been. "The library is essential for higher education," he said when his appointment was announced. "I will be dealing with students and scholars. In a sense I am only changing my focus, not my interest. I was urged to take the position because of what I have been doing." Beyond the immediate need to raise money for continued operations was the physical state of the building and the fragile collections, which were deteriorating at an alarming pace. Cutbacks in staff had resulted in books not being shelved, and the grand old facility itself showed accelerating signs of neglect and decay. Reading Room 315 in particular had been subdivided in recent years; its seventeen-foot arched windows overlooking Bryant Park had been painted black during World War II as a precaution against German air raids, and layers of grime and dust had obscured the hand-carved wooden fixtures and the painted panels on the ceiling. The fiscal crisis that afflicted the city was of such severity that the trustees had considered charging user fees at the central research library, and selling off rarities from its collections.

Money was the immediate priority, and the library was headed onto the right track by the able assistance of Andrew Heiskell, a retired chairman of Time, Inc., who was named chairman of the board of trustees on the same day Gregorian was appointed president. Not only did Heiskell support Gregorian every step of the way, he recruited dynamic new people of means to serve on the board and identified potential benefactors to lobby for support. What is now regarded as the most pivotal development of all was securing the unqualified backing of Brooke Astor, the widow of Vincent Astor, and benefactor of numerous New York City causes. Mrs. Astor had been a trustee for the previous twenty-seven years, but in 1982 she informed the boards of her numerous philanthropic interests that she was devoting her attention exclusively to the welfare of the New York Public Library, which had been partly founded, after all, with a bequest from her late husband's great-great-grandfather, John Jacob Astor. As honorary chairwoman of the board, she worked wonders, not only with her own generous gifts from the Vincent Astor Foundation but in persuading others to emulate her efforts. A typical consequence of Mrs. Astor's involvement came in 1985, when David Rockefeller gave $2.5 million to relocate and restore the reading room of the Rare Books and Manuscripts Division, and made the gift in her name. "I have never done anything like this before," he said of the unusual gesture, one way of paying tribute to "a remarkable woman who is largely responsible for getting the library revitalized."

Gregorian told me that when he arrived for his first meeting of the board of trustees in 1981, the agenda included discussion of plans to sell off valuable pieces of the research collection—there was talk, for instance, about putting the library's copy of John James Audubon's *Birds of America* on the auction block—along with calls for curtailing hours of operation and closing some of the branches. Gregorian recalled listening politely to the suggestions, and then asserting his view of the situation. "My notion was that people with means will not assist a dying institution. They will pay for a funeral for old time's sake, but they will not assist a dying institution. So when I came to New York I maintained that death is not an option, so don't even think about it. New York Public Library must survive, and our first job was to stress how central it is, how crucial it is, how wonderful it is, to the entire community. It was built with marble, it was built to last, because culture has to last, knowledge has to last. My attitude was that the cause was so valuable that if I succeed, it would be a miracle, if I fail, I would be a great martyr. Either way, I could not lose. Let me say that the timing was perfect for me. The combination of forces was right, and it was good that I did not know the limitations beforehand. Had I been there from the beginning, I would have seen constraints everywhere. Coming from the outside, I only saw possibilities."

Within a year of Gregorian's arrival, major exhibitions were being organized, drawn from the library's special collections. Literary luncheons and dinners were sponsored by the Friends of the Library, featuring major authors, and a lively series of talks was scheduled in the spruced-up Celeste Bartos Forum Room, which in recent years had been used for storage. "My idea was to bring the rich and the mighty into an alliance with educators and intelligentsia, and there once again Mrs. Astor was very influential," Gregorian said. "Then you have to bring the mayor and other politicians in, City Council and so forth. And the branches could not be neglected, since that is where the political muscle resides. So we built tremendous political, intellectual, and social power on behalf of New York Public Library."

Just before he left in 1989 to assume duties as president of Brown

University in Rhode Island, Gregorian announced that a four-year campaign to raise $307 million—half of it for the permanent endowment, the rest to satisfy immediate needs—had reached its goal. When I interviewed him in 1997, he was winding up his eight-year tenure at Brown and looking forward to another new challenge, this time as president of the Carnegie Corporation in New York. He had been replaced at the New York Public Library by another educator, the Reverend Timothy S. Healy, a native New Yorker and for thirteen years the president of Georgetown University in Washington, D.C. Like Gregorian before him, Father Healy saw an essential continuity between the two jobs. "A university is a place of teaching, a library is a place of learning," he said. A proven fund-raiser, he also saw wisdom in continuing Gregorian's vigorous example. Three months before his unexpected death from heart failure in 1993, Father Healy gave a status report on his activity. "The endowment was $170 million when I got here. It's $220 million now. I'd love to see it at $300 million or $400 million."

For Father Healy's successor, the board of trustees chose Paul LeClerc (pronounced *luh-CLAIR*), a respected Voltaire scholar, professor of French, and, for the five years prior to his appointment at the New York Public Library, president of Hunter College in Manhattan. "Mr. LeClerc takes over at a hopeful time for the library, which has fought its way back in the last decade from decrepitude, penury and decline to a state of financial well-being that is the envy of many other cultural institutions," William Grimes wrote in the *New York Times*. With consolidation, reflection, and planning the order of the day, no major shakeups were in the offing, though LeClerc would make his own mark on the institution nonetheless. "For this place to remain viable, I have to raise, on average, six hundred thousand dollars a week," more than $30 million a year, he told me in one of several conversations we have had since 1996. Sometimes there are donors like the fashion designer Bill Blass, whose $10 million gift in 1994 was used to install new technology services in the catalog room, and the real estate developer Frederick P. Rose and his wife, Sandra Priest Rose, whose $15 million gift made possible the eight-een-month restoration of Reading Room 315 that was completed in November 1998, the room being renamed in their honor. "If this is to be my legacy, I will be a happy man," LeClerc said, pointing out how the cavernous room—which at 297 feet long, 78 feet wide, and 51 feet high is almost large enough to accommodate a football game—had been restored to its original brilliance as a luxurious haven for readers, reaffirming the library's commitment to its print heritage. "Restoring and modernizing this room symbolizes in a much broader sense what we hope to accomplish throughout the library system. We want to transform a hundred-year-old library into a great twenty-first-century library."

Other large gifts have included $20 million from Dorothy and Lewis B. Cullman to renovate the Library for the Performing Arts at Lincoln Center, and to help underwrite the $100 million needed to transform the old B. Altman department store on Madison Avenue and Thirty-fourth Street into the Science, Industry and Business Library, a high-tech research unit known by the acronym SIBL—called "Sybil"—which opened in 1995. Under LeClerc's stewardship, a Center for Scholars and Writers was established, with Peter Gay, Sterling Professor of History Emeritus at Yale University, appointed director. The center offers nine-month fellowships to scholars, nonacademic research professionals, and creative writers to work in residence at the library on projects that benefit from use of its collections. And in 2001, the board announced that a campaign to fatten the endowment to $500 million had exceeded its goal by $30 million.

"We now have four classrooms at SIBL," LeClerc said in April of 2000, four years after we had sat down in his office for our first interview. "When you and I first met we didn't even have a website. Last month alone we had seventeen million hits on the library's website, with readers coming in from 161 countries, and getting bigger all the time. Places like Easter Island and Andorra are logging on, we can track things like that. We are putting in a new training center in the library for the performing arts, and we are now building classrooms in this building, and a whole new orientation center in which to train readers, to help people who read in traditional ways. The larger point of all this is that as we make these places more sophisticated in terms of information technology, we realize increasingly that we have a responsibility to the public to help them use these libraries skillfully, effectively, efficiently. What we are doing is converting librarians into teachers. This is for everybody."

ONCE AND FUTURE
LIBRARY

Do not
abandon hope, all who enter here,
the land of home-made hells;
resume the joyful bundle.
Take it up. It's light.
It blows in the wind,
is sometimes hard to hang onto
as it twists in the gusts.
But hang on hang on.
Remember how it was before,
in the pit of forgotten dreams . . .
          —Deetje Boler, *"When the Moon Fell Out of the Sky"*

As a slickly produced videotape buoyantly titled *The Library of the Future* opens, a young urban professional returns to his tastefully appointed apartment in San Francisco after a long day at the office, eager to enjoy some leisure time in the fabled City by the Bay. Inside the doorway of the imaginary character's home, the man, "Mr. Taylor," is greeted by the holographic image of an attentive woman. "All appliances are stable, dinner is prepared," the virtual housekeeper reports in an evenly modulated voice: "Today is Monday, November 8, 2001."

Before partaking of his evening meal, Mr. Taylor makes himself comfortable in front of a personal computer and logs on to the website of the San Francisco Public Library. A digitized voice comes online and asks if any help is needed to choose from the lengthy menu of tempting selections on the screen. Mr. Taylor answers in the affirmative, and presses the Enter button on his keyboard. At that point an electronic fireball comes shooting out of the terminal, executes several spectacular loops in the living room, and streaks out an open window into the twinkling night sky like a heat-seeking missile. Micro-moments later, the bolt of energy arrives in a purple flash over what the viewer presently learns is the city's New Main Library, "a magnificent structure of glass, steel, and stone," a voice in the background intones, "a building designed to last well into the twenty-first century."

Because the videotape was produced in 1988, not 2001, the gleaming building we see in *The Library of the Future* is nothing more than a dream in progress, an architect's model of a "state-of-the-art" information emporium then being designed to the exacting specifications of Kenneth E. Dowlin, the San Francisco city librarian from 1987 to 1997, and the author in 1984 of a book titled *The Electronic Library*, which laid out in hopeful detail the conceptual blueprint for just such a facility. To lead viewers around this confident stride into the future is a robotic-looking man whose form-fitting jumpsuit would do justice to Captain James T. Kirk of the Starship *Enterprise*. For this eventful mission across the time line, the cyborg has one basic message to impart, and he summarizes it succinctly toward the end of his presentation: "The San Francisco Public Library provides the resources demanded by the Information Age. It is the nucleus of an information delivery system dedicated to serving the public. The primary source of knowledge and achievement at the center of this modern metropolis." The video concludes with a final pitch delivered basso profundo by an actor identified in the credits as Hugo Napier: "How well we answer the challenge ahead depends on what we do today. The steps we take now will ensure that we are prepared to meet those challenges. For while we are firmly rooted in the present, we must always keep an eye on the future."

Although the gleaming building touted in the video is called a library, alert viewers will have noted by now the incidental presence of books in this illusory nerve center of the third millennium. Indeed, the word *book* itself is mentioned just twice, the first time when some vintage hardcovers are pictured in a tight close-up as curiosities from the past. What we are looking at in this scene, the narrator informs us, is "the Center for the Book, where rare and priceless collections are protected in environmentally controlled rooms and displayed for public appreciation." The other reference comes about a minute later with the unambiguous assertion that "over three million" volumes will be stored in the new library, a figure that would cause considerable consternation in 1996 when city officials conceded that nothing approaching that capacity was ever provided for in the final plans, even though the building itself, with 375,000 square feet of interior space, contained more than enough room for sufficient shelving, had shelving been a top priority of the planners. Instead, a vaulted atrium with a glass roof was placed in the center of the building, with acoustics that seemed more suited to a concert hall than a reading room, and intimate alcoves were situated off the main floors that proved ideal for private cocktail parties but not nearly sufficient to support the city's substantial book collection. Another vignette in the videotape pictured an antiquated wooden cabinet with drawers extended and three-by-five cards strewn about like so many shards of pottery in an underwater debris field; the voice-over triumphantly reports the long-awaited transition to an electronic catalog system.

All told, the discussion of print culture consumes a scant ten seconds in the twelve-minute production. Everything else in this glossy fantasy is about computers, the exciting era of instant communication that is about to dawn, and unlimited access to electronic sources of knowledge. Other than the assertion that shelving for 3 million books would be available in the new building—and the project's champions would argue years later that cutbacks in funding forced them to eliminate an entire floor from the original design—there is nothing egregiously misleading about the videotape. In point of fact, it can be argued that for all its silliness, *The Library of the Future* is a realistic representation of what Dowlin and his colleagues had in mind for the 800,000 residents of San Francisco in the first place. And when placed alongside the controversy that attended the grand opening of the New Main in April 1996, most spectacularly reports that books in large number had been secretly carted off to a landfill, the message of the videotape was unmistakable, in many ways prophetic.

Underwritten with funds provided jointly by Pacific Bell and the U.S. Department of Health, Education and Welfare, *The Library of the Future* was produced at a time when San Francisco voters were being asked to approve a special referendum authorizing construction of a new library. The issue was not unpopular by any means, since just about everyone agreed that the facility built seventy-five years earlier with support from the Carnegie Corporation and known as the Old Main had become obsolete, run-down, and inadequate. To nobody's great surprise, Proposition A authorizing the appropriation of $105 million for the new project passed with 78 percent of the vote. Another $35 million would be raised through a variety of creative strategies that included private funding for a number of "affinity centers" that promoted ethnic, racial, gender, and social diversity with various "feel-good" spaces set aside in the library.

When I arrived in the San Francisco Bay Area in the fall of 1997 to begin research on what already was being called the library scandal of the 1990s, the New Main had been open for eighteen months, and a lot of water, as an old Navy skipper of mine used to say, had already passed under the keel. I would meet with every major player in the melodrama, with two notable exceptions: Marjorie G. Stern, the greatly admired president of the Friends of the Library and a driving force in galvanizing private support for its projects, declined my request to be interviewed, and several calls to the office of Cathy Simon, lead architect on the New Main, were never returned. Simon was defending a lawsuit brought by the city against her firm, Simon Martin-Vegue Wilkelstein Moris of San Francisco, and its associate in the library undertaking, Pei Cobb Freed & Partners of New York, at the time of my visit, and not likely to comment publicly on the criticism involving her design in any case. A $2 million settlement on the claims was reached in 1998.

Though Simon was not available for my questions, she did write an essay in 1993 for a scholarly journal published by the University of California Press that addressed in general terms her aesthetic sense of the project. "A five-story skylit court, sixty feet in diameter, catches the light like a gigantic lantern," she wrote of the building's center. "Here the order of the building is revealed and the architecture of movement begins and ends. A grand stair moves through the space vertically, turning in and out of the illuminated central space." Further on in the essay, she described the "choreography of this kinetic architecture" as not only a "means of access" but a way of defining her "perception" of the whole plan of the building. "In this sense, the central court can be seen as the table of contents of a book, in which chapter headings outline the complexity contained within. Only upon immersion in the text, however, does the true depth or richness of the work unfold." Nowhere in the article did she indicate what percentage of the building's total space would be committed to the shelving of library materials.

In a special supplement published by the *San Francisco Chronicle* in the spring of 1996 to mark the grand opening of the New Main—and, like the promotional videotape produced eight years earlier, also titled *Library of the Future*—Simon told a reporter that her design was influenced by a recurring image she had of bridges. "Bridges are the central metaphor for the library," she said. "You're taking a journey, going from darkness into light, ignorance to knowledge. You cross the linear atrium that separates the open stacks of books from the electronic library in the center. You go through these layers of activity, from very busy to more contemplative; you can be in a collective situation or at the window, sitting and reading." Though ever mindful of the Beaux Arts tradition prevailing in the Civic Center complex, Simon said she felt obligated all the same "to respond to the future" in her plans. "While the library is set in an early twentieth-century context, it's also a building meant for the next millennium." To achieve that goal, Simon said that she and her staff "worked with the librarians to make sure everything they wanted was included."

Exactly what kind of accoutrements the senior library staff wanted in the new building was suggested in another *Chronicle* article that profiled Kenneth Dowlin as a "technological visionary" who "packs a big stack of high-tech gadgets and futuristic ideas." The New Main, Dowlin asserted, "is good for books, but it is designed first and foremost for people," and to that end, three hundred computer terminals had been installed for public use, just the beginning of things to come. "More and more serials will go electronic," the city librarian explained, "and, eventually, so will books, so the print collections will probably start shrinking."

Barely a year after making that portentous statement, Dowlin resigned his position under fire to become the most prominent victim of the infighting, but his opponents did not go unscathed. "Politics is a contact sport," Steven A. Coulter, the president of the Library Commission during the key years of planning, construction, and dedication, told me during a three-hour interview. "If you want to dish it out, you better be prepared to get a good dose of it back in return." Coulter did not shy away from attacking his critics during our interview, and he minced no words when accusing some mid-level librarians and book handlers, with no substantiation other than a "gut feeling," of having deliberately undermined daily operations to make the commission and the administration look bad in the eyes of the public. In his day job, Coulter was vice president in charge of public affairs for Pacific Bell, a major donor of private funds to the library and a significant provider of communications services to its operations. We met in his office on the thirty-third floor of the Pacific Telesis Building in the heart of the financial district, where the company has its headquarters.

A former state representative in Nevada with a background in journalism, Coulter moved to San Francisco in the 1970s. To prove that he could absorb political hits as well as dish them out, Coulter showed me a Wanted poster tied the week of my visit to utility poles throughout the city by a citizen's group that had been severely critical of his tenure on the Library Commission. The poster bore Coulter's likeness. "Goes with the territory," he said. I later shared his "contact sport" remark with John N. Berry III, editor in chief of *Library Journal* and a keen observer of the San Francisco quagmire from the time it began making news in 1996. "Running a library is not about bloodletting," Berry said simply. "Running a library is about running a library."

For all the no-quarter combat that went on in the trenches, the one event above all others that thrust the San Francisco Public Library into the national limelight was the sudden involvement of a best-selling novelist and respected magazine journalist who in 1992 moved his family to Berkeley, six miles across the Oakland–Alameda Bay Bridge from the city the late *San Francisco Chronicle* columnist Herb Caen delighted in calling "Baghdad by the Bay." A tall, bearded, soft-spoken native of New York City who is almost professorial in speech and demeanor, Nicholson Baker arrived on the West Coast a few months before *Vox*, his best known and most controversial work, began attracting the attention of readers worldwide. A review in *Time* magazine had described the 196-page novel as "1-900-AURAL SEX," a clever reference to the titillating way the two protagonists who never meet give pleasure to each other over the telephone. The book enjoyed an unexpected resurgence of notoriety in 1998 when Kenneth W. Starr, the independent federal prosecutor in the Whitewater investigation, subpoenaed the records of two Washington, D.C., booksellers, hoping to prove that a former White House intern might have bought a copy of the book and passed it on to William Jefferson Clinton. The subsequent disclosure of a blue dress laden with the president's DNA rendered the *Vox* purchase an irrelevant detail in the Monica S. Lewinsky story, but Starr's ploy did cause a firestorm of protest among people who feel they have the right to read what they want without fear of invasive government scrutiny.

Hard on the release of *Vox* came publication in 1994 of *The Fermata,* another racy novel featuring a young man whose ability to freeze time by snapping his fingers enables him to remove the clothes of attractive women. This book, even more piquant than its predecessor, prompted some critics, including a number of people in San Francisco who became his sworn adversaries, to cast Baker as a person obsessed with fantasies of the flesh. On April 4, 1994, the *New Yorker* published "Discards," Baker's 17,000-word essay bemoaning the widespread disappearance of card catalogs in libraries throughout the United States. Baker did not single out San Francisco in that piece, but he did attract the attention of people eager to have such a prominent figure as their ally, including Gray Brechin, an instructor at Berkeley and a columnist for several alternative publications who had joined the fray with pointed criticisms of his own. Brechin's publishing credits include two books from the University of California Press, *Farewell, Promised Land: Waking from the California Dream* (1998) and *Imperial San Francisco: Urban Power, Earthly Ruin* (2000).

The concern of these "library activists," as they described themselves to me, went well beyond the fate of the 3.5 million three-by-five cards in the San Francisco catalog, thousands of which were already being baked into ceramic tiles to be used as wall decorations in the new library; their overriding interest focused on the changing mission of the institution itself, and the fear that books had become irrelevant distractions in Kenneth Dowlin's vision of the future. By enlisting a best-selling novelist and respected essayist, the activists were able to transform a down-and-dirty local skirmish into a national story that continues to have profound implications, as many other cities try to determine the composition and direction of their public libraries.

On May 30, 1996, at the invitation of the Librarian's Guild, Local 790 of the Service Employees International Union, Baker gave a talk in the

Koret Auditorium of the public library titled "The Library of the Present: Books, Catalogues, and the Destruction of Knowledge," in which he formally cast his lot with the activists. In what he called his "warm-up act for the main event," Brechin talked generally about the "destruction of knowledge in the information age," noting how people like Baker and himself were identified as "Luddites" for their reluctance to sign on totally to the computer revolution. In his remarks, Baker threw down the gauntlet and admitted his deepening disquiet: "I am apprehensive about the City Librarian, Mr. Dowlin, who came here in 1987, and who has been responsible, since the earthquake, I believe, for the destruction of— not twenty thousand books, not fifty thousand books, not a hundred thousand books, not a hundred and fifty thousand books, but the destruction of, the systematic removal to a landfill of—at least *two hundred thousand library books*, more library books than were destroyed in the so-called Ham and Eggs fire that burned nearly everything in the collection in 1906."

Baker's involvement in San Francisco library politics led ultimately to a court action in which he successfully sued the city to gain access to the card catalog, and to save the huge archive from destruction by having it designated a municipal record. The cards, Baker argued, represented a collection of "historical artifacts" that possess important bibliographical information not contained in its electronic counterpart, a central thesis of his "Discards" essay. As word spread that Baker was working on yet another *New Yorker* article—this one dealing directly with the dumping of books at the San Francisco Public Library—accusations began to get personal. Baker was called an "opportunistic pornographer," an "antediluvian nutbag," a "shameless carpetbagger," a "card-carrying fetishist." Steve Coulter wrote a letter to Tina Brown, at that time the *New Yorker*'s editor, in an attempt to discredit Baker, impugn his motives, and kill his piece before it ever got into print. Coulter readily acknowledged to me that he made such an effort—Baker had already given me copies of the letters exchanged—and offered no apologies for his actions. "My only regret is that they went ahead and published the damn thing," Coulter said. The article, titled "The Author vs. the Library," appeared on October 14, 1996, six months after the New Main opened to the public, and centered around the allegation that Dowlin had allowed thousands of books to be secretly shipped off to a local landfill in city dump trucks, ostensibly because there was not enough room in the new building to house them, but more likely because they did not fit into his concept of a twenty-first-century library. The dumping charge ultimately was proven to be true, although serious disagreement remains to this day over just how many books were carted away, and which library official actually ordered their removal.

"There is no doubt that thousands of books were thrown away," Baker told me in the first of several interviews we had. "It was a wasteful, possibly a criminal act. What bothers me above all else is that a public institution will vandalize itself and decide it will spend, if not waste, huge amounts of money for technology, and at the same time dispose of an existing book collection that is irreplaceable. As far as I am concerned, it is a hate crime directed at the past."

The immediate reaction to Baker's essay among senior library officials was anger. Coulter was particularly blunt about the "troublemaker with a word processor" who had arrived in the Bay Area "charging in on a white steed" from the East Coast on a mission to cause trouble. "He is an outsider, he is only after a story," he said dismissively. That Baker's interest in preserving the primary records of history went well beyond nailing down a "good story" in San Francisco would become clear in the summer of 2000, when yet another *New Yorker* essay, this one titled "Deadline," disclosed what he had been up to since moving his family to South Berwick, Maine, in 1998. In that article, Baker reported on his successful effort to preserve seven thousand bound volumes of original American newspapers that had been deaccessioned by the British Library in England—some of the very last examples to be found anywhere of early issues of the *New York Times*, the *Chicago Tribune*, the *New York*

Herald Tribune, and the *New York World*—and his establishment of a nonprofit corporation in New Hampshire, the American Newspaper Repository, to maintain them. At one point in the piece Baker noted the absurdity of paying $63,000 for a lengthy archive of the *Chicago Tribune* when the equivalent run on microfilm would have cost him $177,000. "We're at a bizarre moment in history, when you can have the real thing for considerably less than it would cost to buy a set of crummy black-and-white snapshots of it which you can't look at without the help of a machine."

Baker's indignation with the systematic disposal of microfilmed artifacts did not end with newspapers. In the spring of 2001, *Double Fold: Libraries and the Assault on Paper,* a greatly expanded version of his *New Yorker* essay, challenged the entire premise of using inferior copies as surrogates for all printed material. Writing in what he openly acknowledged was a "prosecutorial" tone, Baker alleged that the federally funded campaign to cope with the "brittle book" crisis had been overstated by conservators for close to fifty years, and that along with the vast runs of newspapers, which were his primary concern, close to a million volumes owned by American libraries had also gone off to landfills and incinerators after being "guillotined" and filmed. He characterized conservation programs that sanctioned the destruction of original materials as a misguided effort bent on "destroying to preserve." The publication of *Double Fold*—the title is derived from a controversial test that purportedly determines the brittleness of books—set off a flurry of discussion in professional circles that did nothing to diminish Baker's image as a "library activist."

However upset city residents may have been about the clandestine dumping of books, an even greater shock was in store when word began leaking out that storage space in the new library was so scarce that something in the neighborhood of a million volumes from the Old Main

Library were being stored in a cavernous basement garage known as Brooks Hall, a dark subterranean place off-limits to public scrutiny. Just as distressing was the seemingly disorganized and chaotic way that business was being conducted in the new facility. As 1996 became 1997, it had become harder to get a book out of the library, and there were cascading complaints about the inadequacy of the software installed for the electronic catalog.

An in-house survey of library users showed that in its first year of operation, only 38 percent of patrons searching for books by title at the New Main could actually find them. Four years earlier, when the library was still operating out of the Old Main, this factor, known as the "title fill rate," had been 71 percent. In its final full year at the old facility, the rate had fallen to 51 percent. The national average, according to figures compiled by the American Library Association, was 70 percent. Further inflaming an already ugly situation was a painfully slow process of getting returned books back onto the shelves. A higher-than-expected report of red ink stirred passions even further, and as the first anniversary of business in the New Main arrived, Dowlin's job was in great jeopardy. For his part, Dowlin cited the nature of San Francisco politics as the underlying cause of the problems, suggesting in his interview with me that he had been the scapegoat for the folly of others.

Coulter was appointed head of the Library Commission in 1988 at a time when a vote on the bond issue was imminent, and his purpose from the outset was one of persuasion, particularly of potential donors. Coulter, who is himself gay, said he was encouraged to go ahead with the "affinity center" concept after seeing for the first time the Arthur Alfonso Schomburg Library in New York City, a unit of the New York Public Library located in Harlem, and arguably the finest and most comprehensive collection of African-American material maintained anywhere in the world. As one of his Library Commission responsibilities, Coulter had visited some of the best-known libraries in the United States looking for ideas he and his colleagues could appropriate for their new facility.

"When I saw what had been done for African-American culture in New York City, I knew instantly that what we should do was create its equivalent in San Francisco, only for gay culture," he said. "I envisioned making this the gay Schomburg Library."

Among the most widely publicized "affinity centers" in the New Main is the James C. Hormel Gay and Lesbian Center, named in honor of its principal benefactor, a San Francisco resident and heir to the Hormel meatpacking fortune who gave $500,000 to build and appoint the room. Hormel made national news in 1998 when President Clinton named him ambassador to Luxembourg, sparking criticism from conservative Republicans in the Senate concerned over the propriety of appointing an openly gay person to such a high government position. But as attractive as the center is—and it is quite beautiful—very little has been committed toward the building of research-level collections. A notable opportunity was missed in 1994, when the massive archive of the poet Allen Ginsberg, an openly gay man who had been active in the Beat culture of San Francisco, was bought by Stanford University for $1 million. One critic of the concept suggested that the "affinity centers" might have been more accurately called a "naming opportunity for corporations."

As head of public affairs at Pacific Bell, Coulter said, he persuaded his employer to finance production of *The Library of the Future* videotape as a tool to recruit donors. A local firm, Advanced Entertainment Associates of San Francisco, was hired to make the film. "I told Ken, 'Here is the money, go do it,' and then I saw the damn thing, and I looked at it, and I said, 'This is terrible.' I asked Ken, 'What in the hell did we do here?' I got him the money, and I told the people in charge, 'Do a good job, project his vision.' I had hoped it would be something we could use in our fund-raising efforts, but it was the coldest, most insensitive, most undesirable picture of the future that I had ever seen. I told Ken all of this. I told him, 'Ken, a videotape of libraries ought to be filled with kids, you have kids in there as a sidelight.' So we never really used it for fund-raising."

Whether the video accurately reflected Dowlin's vision, however, is another matter entirely, as Coulter readily acknowledged. "Ken saw himself as a prophet 'way out there,' but the difference between being a prophet who does not have to produce, and being a prophet who does, I think is a lot," he said. "And so when he went from a theoretical place to actually having to do it, then I think he ran into a lot of problems." Another difficulty Dowlin encountered, Coulter added, was that "he was not very good politically. I think a lot of his ideas were intriguing, and I thought he was a nice guy to deal with personally." But once the library opened in 1996, Coulter said he perceived a "disconnect from reality" in Dowlin, and the commission members "had some strong discussions" about the direction the library was taking. "The book-shelving problem, for example. The commission had an entirely different view than Ken on how we had to handle that. He wanted to go to war with the union over staffing, and we wanted him to work it out."

When Coulter showed me the Wanted poster with his picture on it, he said it was the work of a loose-knit group of private citizens he called "the gadflies," the same people, it turned out, who had described themselves to me as "library activists." He described them as frustrated people—"a lot of them are leftovers from the Vietnam War protests"—who had nothing better to do with their lives than criticize any form of bureaucracy. As far as Coulter was concerned, the staff librarians who condemned the discarding of books and the consolidation of subject categories into one general department were nothing more than a "bunch of frustrated middle-aged white women" insensitive to the needs of minorities, and bent on wresting control of the library for themselves. He suggested, among other charges, that delays were the result of "sabotage" on the part of staff pages fearful of losing their $15-an-hour jobs to the $7-dollar-an-hour shelvers Dowlin proposed to replace them with.

"I can't prove it, but I believe they were doing this intentionally, and that they wanted to maximize the pain on Dowlin in order to get rid of him," Coulter said. "I say that in Ken's defense. But I've already told you on the other side that he was his own worst enemy on a lot of other stuff, and he would not listen to the commission. Up until the very end I absolutely ordered him to meet with the union on these issues. He had an obligation to sit down with them, and he wouldn't do it. He refused to deal with the union most of his last year here, and as far as I am concerned it was the kiss of death for him."

Of all the statements attributed during his ten-year tenure to the embattled librarian whose vision of an electronic library impelled him to establish a "library of the future," the most damaging came in the aftermath of the 1989 San Francisco earthquake that left half a million books strewn about the Old Main. Surveying the disarray, Dowlin was quoted as saying that the catastrophe offered a rare opportunity to purge "the Augean Stables" of unwanted books. Those who had to consult their encyclopedias soon learned that he was referring to one of the Twelve Labors of Hercules, in which the resourceful son of Zeus was required to clean out an enormous complex of putrid oxen stables owned by King Augeas of Elis in a single day. Hercules accomplished this distasteful assignment by diverting the path of the river Alpheus so that it gushed directly through the torpid stalls, flushing, in one cleansing rush of water, the smelly accretion of many decades. For better or for worse, Dowlin had equated the books entrusted to his care to cow manure, and the decisive means by which he felt their removal could be expedited did nothing to soften the reputation he had fashioned, wittingly or unwittingly, for pursuing "anti-intellectual" policies in the San Francisco Public Library. When I asked Dowlin, he acknowledged that he had indeed made that remark, but had only been passing on what somebody else said about the chaotic state of the Old Main. "It was not original with me. It was used years earlier by a local columnist with regard to the library; I merely repeated it." The matter of who made the statement first aside, the more pertinent issue involved the sentiment it implied, that a golden opportunity to free up precious space had presented itself in the garb of a natural disaster, and that the moment was to be seized without hesitation. There was a precedent, in other words, for dumping books, and just how many were discarded, in both instances, remains a mystery.

Dowlin and I met on a weeknight in his suburban apartment south of San Francisco, with a glorious sunset filling the sky over the Pacific Ocean a few miles to the west. As a professional librarian with a profound interest in the electronic age, Dowlin came to San Francisco having already built a library along the high-tech guidelines he espoused in his book. In his prior assignment, Dowlin presided over the construction and management of the Pikes Peak Library District in Colorado Springs, Colorado, and he made it clear that he came to San Francisco with an explicit mandate. "I was hired to build a modern library, and that's what I did," he said. "When I was being interviewed for the job of city librarian, the mayor at the time, Diane Feinstein, said to me, point-blank, 'Can you build a new library?' And I said, 'Yes, I can.' She had only three months left in her term. She wanted the library built, and she was starting to think about her legacy. Then I was interviewed by the Library Commission, and it was more of the same. So there was no question in my mind, I was hired to do this project."

As to the charge that as many as 200,000 books—perhaps even as many as 500,000, according to an interview I had with California state librarian Kevin Starr in 1999—may have been sent off to the landfill, Dowlin said, "Those numbers stink," and stated his belief that "they are a figment of Mr. Baker's imagination." The reason for the disparity, he maintained, was that "there was never any inventory conducted, and any semblance of an inventory was based on a three-by-five-card system that had essentially broken down twenty years earlier. Nobody at the time knew how many books the library had." So how many books, then, actually went to the landfill? "I don't know, okay? Because I didn't count the books, and there are no records of what was discarded."

Dowlin and I spoke briefly about the *Library of the Future* videotape and discussed whether or not it accurately expressed his vision. Dowlin said that he looked at the tape the night before our interview, expecting that the matter might come up in our conversation, and he dismissed a suggestion that it had downplayed the relevance of print. "It's got a rare-book room in there, doesn't it? It's got books and magazines. I just don't understand this mono view people have of the world. I think that the San Francisco Public Library is a multidimensional institution, and that I am a multidimensional person." Books, he insisted, were always meant to be an integral part of the scheme, and he hired professional consultants and pollsters to find out precisely what services the people of San Francisco wanted in their new library. "We put together something like forty community focus groups, and over the process of design, we testified at the Arts Commission, the Library Commission, the Board of Supervisors, we probably had fifty different public hearings. What I am telling you is that I built that building based on what the people of San Francisco wanted, not what the press wanted, not what the literary world wanted. In fact I am starting to sense that a lot of the backlash here is coming from the 'literary world,' not the citizens of the city."

The reference there was not only to Nicholson Baker, but also to the noted poet, essayist, and short story writer Tillie Olsen, a longtime resident of San Francisco whose heartfelt words of support had been used prominently when the library was being planned. A prime example of her early endorsement appeared in the library's 1994–95 annual report, where these words were printed in large type above her name: "The library—my refuge, my shelter, my source, resource, joy—where I browsed hungrily through the stacks, finding my teachers, my inspiration, my companions." When the full extent of book discards began to be reported, however, and when Olsen discovered "wide open spaces" in the new building "where books are supposed to be shelved," she became increasingly critical of the New Main, and went public with her misgivings.

"Those words were from the heart," Olsen told me in the course of a four-hour interview that took in the full sweep of her life, but never strayed far from her passion for reading. Born in Meade, Nebraska, in 1912, Olsen said she considers it a badge of honor that her keen intellect and knowledge of the world were formed through a lifelong regimen of self-education. "I could not begin to compute the number of hours I spent in the Old Main Library," she told me. Several hundred books line the walls of her apartment, many of them with fraying bindings as evidence of constant handling, most of them studded with yellow paper slips marking pages that contain favorite passages. Olsen has spent most of her life since 1930 living in the San Francisco Bay Area, leaving periodically to teach writing and to give lectures at various colleges around the country; one of her students at Amherst College in the 1970s, she told me, was the novelist Scott Turow. "My college is the college of literature," she said, proudly tapping a copy of *Silences,* which notes in the biographical summary on the back of the dustjacket that she regards public libraries as her secondary education. She then quoted for me, verbatim and from memory, the text of the inscription that appears on the façade of the Old Main Library: "May this structure throned on imperishable books be maintained and cherished from generation to generation for the improvement and delight of mankind."

Olsen's first published book, a collection of stories titled *Tell Me a Riddle,* was released in 1962 when she was fifty and remains her best-known work of fiction. Her 1978 collection of essays, *Silences,* is a detailed examination of voids in the creative process, particularly among women, poor people, and the uneducated. Olsen's own experience provided many of the insights for that book, but the factual background came from her reading. Although she has a dozen honorary degrees, Olsen never finished high school, and experienced protracted "silences" of her own while raising two children largely by herself. "I did a good deal of the research for the book in the Old Main, and it was such a magnificent place to work in, with wonderful facilities for children," she said. "I have to say I was absolutely thrilled about the idea of getting a new library. But I was totally unprepared for what I saw after they opened it up. The first thing I thought when I went inside was, 'What a waste of space.' That was followed by, 'Are you going to have any quiet in here?' One of the things that has always distinguished a great library is that you go in and people can talk, but you are quiet. Quiet has to do with concentration. All the noise and traffic was part of my horror, and that was before I even started asking for certain books. Not one book that I wanted was there. Even worse, there was no satisfactory answer forthcoming of where any of these books I was looking for might have gone."

When news stories began to appear in the local newspapers about discards and severely reduced space for shelving, Olsen said she threw her support to "this marvelous organization" of library activists informally known as the Edith Cedar Group. "The New Main is a betrayal of what a public library is all about," she said. "And those of us who were raising these questions—wondering where all the books were, wondering where all the money had gone, wondering why they were cutting back on staff, wondering why they had consolidated the collections—we were made out to be the villains."

In October 1998 the famed Beat Generation poet Lawrence Ferlinghetti added another view to the mix on the very day he was anointed San Francisco's first poet laureate by Mayor Willie Brown. In a speech given in the New Main Library, Ferlinghetti—the cofounder in 1953 of the celebrated City Lights bookstore and an outspoken activist in support of literary causes everywhere—called for a number of municipal improvements: the banning of automobiles in the inner city, a commitment to paint the Golden Gate Bridge golden, and earmarking $10 million a year for the purchase of new books for the public library. "All that made this city so unique in the first place seems to be going down the tube at an alarming rate," he said to thunderous applause, and he specifically cited his beloved North Beach neighborhood, which he felt was becoming a "theme park, literally overrun by tourists," a place where kitsch had become king.

Not all the reviews for the New Main have been derisive, however. The novelist Isabel Allende wrote an enthusiastic foreword to Peter

Booth Wiley's authorized history of the library, calling the facility a "gift to the city of San Francisco and an homage to the spirits that live in the public library." Other contributions to Wiley's book came from the authors Ethan Canin, Anne Lamott, and Martin Cruz Smith. The internationally respected Berkeley bookseller Bernard Rosenthal was unequivocal in his praise. "I think they built a beautiful facility over there," he told me, and that view was echoed by Philip D. Leighton, the noted consultant on library design and, with the late Keyes Metcalf of Harvard University, author of two editions of *Planning Academic and Research Library Buildings*. He was not an adviser on the San Francisco project, but he told me that he has genuine respect for the results.

And there are other supporters, many of them people in the computer field who feel that Dowlin was unfairly vilified by his opponents for an admirable job done under adverse political conditions. "The paradox in libraries, particularly public ones, is that there are some people who grew up thinking books were sacred," Michael Schuyler wrote in *Computers in Libraries*, a trade publication. "They don't want to throw any away, no matter how dated they are." Schuyler was convinced that Ken Dowlin, whose resignation occasioned his writing of the story, had "created a masterpiece of a library that attracted so many people that use skyrocketed," and that he fell out of favor because of budget shortfalls, nothing else. At the end of the essay Schuyler was identified as an electronic systems librarian in Washington State, a job description that may put in perspective his concluding thought, which he called the "bottom line" of the whole unfortunate episode: "Technology, including its ugly side, is going to win anyway." In *The Electronic Library*, Dowlin devoted some attention to "messages of our past and those of today," suggesting that the principal difference between the two is length; modern communication uses far fewer words than ever before.

Information has reached the stage where a significant proportion of what is produced is throw-away. Scientific theories have a much shorter period of relevance than they once did. The bumper sticker is the epitome of communication today. A premium is placed on one's ability to communicate in short bursts. Celebrities rise to prominence and then disappear very quickly. In sports it is difficult to remember the teams, let alone the players. The disposable syndrome has moved from paper plates, diapers, and clothes to information.

The major contributor to this new tendency "to throw away images of information," Dowlin continued, is technology, and while allowing that "some information that is not volatile and is perhaps more permanent in nature will still be published and distributed in a traditional mode," he underscored his belief that "greater amounts of transient" information, not fewer, would become the norm. "The Polaroid camera is to permanent photography as the copying machine is to publishing. Audio and visual information are easily copied, and just as easily discarded." The future librarian, he argued, will focus more on being a "guide," a kind of "information transfer agent," a "gatekeeper" blessed with "value added" skills. "Whereas the current criterion for success of a librarian is to find the container of the information, the new criterion must be based on finding the information."

Following up on Dowlin's assertion that he came to San Francisco hard on the heels of having built a new library in Colorado Springs, I found it prudent to inquire how his work was regarded by his successors there. It happened that the person who succeeded Dowlin had moved east in 1997 to become president of the Boston Public Library, and was only too pleased to talk with me about his seven years at the Pikes Peak Library District. "I am a librarian by profession, but I consider myself a bookman first," Bernard A. Margolis told me eighteen months after he had taken over his new job in Massachusetts. "I like books. I collect books. I am passionate about books. I have thousands of books in my home, several hundred of them still waiting to be removed from their shipping crates and properly shelved. And this is how I went to Colorado in 1990, as a bookman." Margolis said his first reaction there was grim. "I found a library serving a major urban center that was so deficient in its collections that even the most sophisticated of technologies couldn't make up for the lack of substance. I found an institution that had a grand reputation for technology, but actually with not nearly as much application as I had hoped to find. We put a phenomenal amount of work into correcting what I thought was a major deficiency. We were able to build the collection from half a million items to over one million items in seven years. I think that what Ken should have done was divide the resources between investing in new technologies—which I absolutely believe have an important place in libraries—but at the same time maintaining this important and relevant perspective around books and traditional library materials."

The essential question for Margolis, of course, was how the residents of Colorado Springs felt about the public library under Dowlin's stewardship. "The number of complaints that I received about the lack of books was simply overwhelming," he replied. "I remember the first time I gave a dinner speech, an elderly man came up to me and said, 'Mr. Margolis, if you do nothing else, buy a few books.' From what I could see, Ken had seriously neglected the collections, and the allotted resources had been refocused on technology. I think the thrust and expectation was that a library is a connection to information, which I see as a narrower purview than the world of knowledge and culture. I think, frankly, that the technology did a fair job—but only a fair job—as an information tool and as an information resource. I believe that in Ken's hell-bent lunge forward toward what he earnestly believed was the future, he had sacrificed the librarian's stock-in-trade, this enormously important human connection between people and books, something that is still very much at the core of what a library is supposed to be. People are enriched by books. They may be enriched by computers as well. But a book is an instrument of creation."

The flamboyant mayor of San Francisco, Willie Brown, for the most part, managed to keep his distance on the library issue. He did not demand that Dowlin resign, and if urgent hints came from City Hall that it might be an opportune time for him to step aside, they were passed on in confidence. Dowlin, in any case, insisted that the departure was his idea entirely. "It was time for me to move on," he said. "What I do is build libraries. The library is now operating; the job I was hired to do was accomplished." While that may well be the case, his decision to leave could not have come at a less propitious moment, since at the time of his resignation Dowlin had already thrown his hat in the ring to be the next president of the American Library Association. When the balloting was held a few months later, he was, in effect, a librarian without a library, and he lost the election decisively.

The library activists Coulter dismissed as "troublemakers" and "gad-flies" called themselves the Edith Cedar Group, a name derived from two intersecting streets where strategy sessions were held in the home of a member. Within the organization was a self-described political action cell of three operatives charged with keeping the issue on the front burner: Jim Kirwan, Timothy Gillespie, and Walter Biller, known among their colleagues as the KGB for the first initials of their sur-names, among themselves as the "war council." A trained historian who worked with the Smithsonian Institution for seven years before moving to California in 1987, Biller compiled an impressive archive of documen-tation that includes every public record he could get his hands on. The suggestion, for instance, that an electronic library was in the long-range interests of Pacific Bell, the employer of the president of the Library Commission and a major corporate donor to the project, was backed up with figures showing precisely how much the company receives from the city each year for costs related to the delivery of infor-mation services. A commercial artist, Kirwan prepared the graphics and "raised a lot of hell," according to one member, as a political activist who wrote a lot of letters to the local newspapers. Gillespie, a freelance public relations specialist, was the "go-to guy" on media relations, according to Biller.

The group was joined in its efforts by a small cadre of other operatives, including Deetje Boler, a dedicated social activist who stockpiled hundreds of library discards, keeping them safe for the day when officials might "regain their senses" and welcome them back with open arms. I met with Boler one night in the offices of the Gray Panthers at 1182 Market Street, just around the corner from the Civic Center complex and the New Main Library. The Gray Panthers is an advocacy group with a particular interest in the welfare of older citizens, but one that regards itself as intergenerational in its approach. "One of our sayings in the Gray Panthers is that we are working to make a world that everybody wants to grow old in," Boler said by way of introduction. "As far as the issue of the books goes, a connection for my group is that the books in our library collection were put there over a span of four generations by people with the expectation that they would come down to later generations."

A veteran of numerous causes going back to the early 1960s, Boler described herself first and foremost as a "multi-issue" person whose professional background is in social research. She is also a poet; her book *Psyche in the Mouth of the Dragon* was published in 1978 with support from the National Endowment for the Arts. "I have been working on nuclear issues, tenants issues, animal rights, I have been involved in a variety of different things. In this case, it was like some invisible button got pushed. You just don't throw away our books." She joined in the opposition when the dumping became front-page news throughout the Bay Area, prompting the library to institute a short-lived policy in which citizens could browse through the mass of discards and take what they wanted, free of charge. "I went over right then and there, and because I am an activist, I made a sign that said 'Giving Away Books Is Censorship, Stop the Discards.' I sat outside the basement door where they had the books on tables, and I was ignored. My feeling in the matter was that this

Adopt-a-Book program of theirs did not solve the problem because the public was still losing its collection. When my sign didn't put a stop to what was going on, I decided to take as many books as I could."

Boler gathered up 1,370 books during the giveaway, and persuaded a number of her Gray Panther colleagues to do the same. In a "discard report" she prepared in 1997, Boler cited library figures indicating that 57,000 books were rescued in this manner, with another 20,000 remaining when the Adopt-a-Book program ended in October 1996. "I took as many books as I could get my hands on," she told me. "I went over there four or five times. I took books off the shelves as quickly as I could. I made the most of every minute I was allowed to be in there trying to pick out worthwhile titles. I can tell you that certain books would come my way and my heart would just leap. It is a kind of irrational lust that comes upon you. I was coming upon little fragments of our culture that I was saving, and I became more and more outraged at the library for giving them away. This is when I came up with the idea of hanging on to the books and shaming these people by saying that I will happily give them back to you as soon as you have a policy in place that assures me you will take care of them." Once she had the books in hand, Boler wrote out white index cards for each title, indicating the locations in any of the thirty-nine boxes she finally wound up filling, and entered all the information in a database. "I checked out every book in the library computer, and there was no record at all that any of these books had been removed from the collection. I did a little more checking and determined that a good number of them represented last copies in the city system. The oldest book I have is from 1872, but there really weren't that many nineteenth-century books, just seven all together, but of course the reason for that is that most of the older books were destroyed in the 1906 earthquake, and the bulk of the collection came afterward."

Boler gave me printouts of the compilations she prepared for the books. One of the reports, filling fifty-four single-spaced pages, lists every title alphabetically by author, and includes the year of publication, call number, and "discard status" reported by the city. The inventory begins with Raoul Abdul, author of *Black Entertainers of Today* (1974), and concludes with William K. Zinsser and *Pop Goes America* (1966). The second list, comprising twenty-three pages, represents "last copies" in the city collection; similarly arranged, it identifies 604 works brought in from the branches. A number are works of fiction, but most titles represent a variety of disciplines—history, geography, politics, economics, science, yoga, gardening, international relations, psychology, biology, marine ecology, genetics, travel, astronomy, medicine, evolution, biography, sports, city management, literary criticism, archaeology, theology, linguistics, race relations, and oral histories—exactly the subjects typically found in public libraries. Boler's "last copy" list begins with Sir Thomas Barclay and *The Wisdom of Lang-sin* (1927) and concludes with C. G. Jung, *Memories, Dreams, Reflections* (1965).

"It is a varied, richly diverse collection, covering interesting and relevant subjects treated by many fine authors, which really needs to be seen to be appreciated," Boler wrote in her detailed report of the 1,370 books she had gathered in her Adopt-a-Book forays. She estimated the replacement cost at somewhere between $35,000 and $61,650, and that was just for the 1,370 books she had gathered. Replacing the unknown number of books sent off to the landfill—assuming they could all be found on the open market—would take millions. Five years after Boler had gathered the books, they still remained in her custody, packed carefully in the original thirty-nine cardboard boxes, still being held against the day they might return to the public collection. "They are a difficult responsibility," she told me in a telephone conversation we had in the summer of 2000. With Albert Gore Jr. seeking the Democratic presidential nomination at the time of that talk, she said she had entertained thoughts of taking *Let the Glory Out: My South and Its Politics,* a book written in 1972 by the candidate's father, the late Senator Albert Gore Sr., and giving it back to the library "as something they might find useful in the months ahead, since it was the only copy they ever had," but she thought better of it. "I have written a number of letters and have received no answers in all this time. I thought about going in there and making a scene and insisting that they at least take back the last copies, but I think now I will wait until there is a permanent replacement for the city librarian and deal anew with whoever that might be. But do I think they will ever take the books back? Who knows. All I can say is that hope springs eternal."

In his interview with me, Steve Coulter did not mention Boler by name, but clearly she represented the "gadfly element" he chose to single out, one of the people on the fringe, as he put it, who enjoy making life difficult for the establishment. Boler's unabashed credentials as an activist—she was wearing a Stop Truth Decay button on her T-shirt when we met—make her an easy target for that kind of characterization. During my stay in San Francisco, I also spoke with six librarians active in the library workers union—the "middle-aged white women" denounced by Coulter—and with two library pages who told me how they saw books being loaded by the hundreds onto sanitation trucks and removed for disposal. "The humanist outlook is gradually being squelched here," Annette G. MacNair, a reference librarian in the General Collection Division since 1968, said. "I think people like me are being crowded out. We are being hounded out of our jobs because we refuse to go along with the party line. We are being treated with disdain and contempt by the Library Commission and by the library director. What you are seeing is the takeover of a cultural institution. This is not a humanistic library any longer, it is a technocratic library. The scholarly nature of what we had has been dumbed down. It is no longer an homage to culture, to history, even to the history of San Francisco. Do we have a labor collection? Do we have a poetry collection? The answer to both is no. What we have now is a mishmash."

Andrea V. Grimes, whose job description includes responsibility for special collections, expressed amusement with "all the talk we hear about the 'library of the future,' when our immediate concern as professional librarians has always been the 'library of the present.' What we are being forced to deal with right now is the consequences of having dumped so many books, and the outright elimination of subject categories." During the darkest days of the discards, a tag system was used to identify the fate of various books, Melissa Riley, another librarian, said. "A green tag meant the book is dead; a yellow tag meant it stayed in the stacks." There is validity, they all agreed, to reports that some staff members were substituting yellow tags for green tags to save them from the landfill. "We called that place on the third floor the 'de-selection chamber,' " Catherine M. Bremer said. Other reports that people assigned to Arts and Music flatly refused to weed books out of the collection are true as well, they all confirmed.

As to who ordered the dumping of the books, nobody I talked to was willing to take any credit for the decision. "You have the Augean stables quote," Annette MacNair said. "What more do you need than that? When it became clear that there was not nearly enough room here for all the books, we were told that we had to do 'massive weeding,' and we had to do it immediately. The public was never told that there was not going to be enough room for their collections. Close to sixty percent of our bound periodical collections are now in Brooks Hall as a testimony to their bad planning. And you know what? Nobody cares. Look, a library is not Barnes & Noble, and it is not Blockbuster video. The uniqueness of a library is the joy of discovery. You go in and you find something that will be nowhere else that is open to the public. You find material that you were never even looking for." And how do these librarians respond to being characterized as angry middle-aged white women? "Well, he's got that right," MacNair said. "I am angry. It happens that I am middle-aged as well, and okay, for whatever it may be worth, I'm white. But the angry part is the part that matters. I'm not just angry, I'm pissed, because a great old library has been jerked around. And what really makes me angry is when people come in here and say, 'Where are the books?' "

Regardless of who ordered it, the disposal proceeded on a massive scale for at least nine months, according to two library pages who not only agreed to talk with me but consented to the use of their names. The three of us met in the cafeteria of the New Main Library on a weekday, on their own time, during a lunch break. "They were loading books in the back of Department of Public Works trucks, and they were hauling them away on a daily basis," Alan D'Souza said. "I actually have some photographs of this," Claire LaVaute, the other page, added. "I felt like such a fool. I couldn't help myself. I cried. Alan was there, he'll tell you, I cried. I just couldn't believe what they were doing."

LaVaute said that her job as a technical assistant placed her in a position where she could see the removal over an extended period. "I had to be down there on the fourth stack probably six hours of every day, and right there in the well were all the books. I was assembling magazines so that they could be sent out to be bound, and that was what brought me close to what was going on. I would walk back and forth during the course of the day, and there in the well were all the books to be dumped. It was absolutely horrifying." LaVaute said she brought her concerns to several members of the administration. "There was all this finger-pointing, and nobody wanted to take responsibility. But I can tell you, it was a mountain of books they had down there." D'Souza said he was assigned the task of preparing discarded books for removal by city sanitation crews. "There would be stacks of books on the shelves; my job was to make sure they were tied up in tidy bundles so the DPW guys wouldn't hurt their backs, and so the books wouldn't fall out when they were tossing them in the trucks. I would take the bundles and stack them neatly inside this room downstairs; it was only after the story began to hit the press that the place was put under lock and key."

I asked D'Souza and LaVaute what they thought about Coulter's allegation that sabotage may have been the cause of the reshelving problems that maimed library efficiency. "I can't believe he said that," LaVaute said. "This is so infuriating, so insulting. You just got my blood boiling. I can tell you this—that once I approached Ken Dowlin after a staff meeting, and I asked him, 'Why haven't you hired any pages when it is so obvious that we need them?' He said to me that he wanted to free up the staff, and to use the money to hire three or four times more people at less money, and that high school students could do the job just as well, and that he didn't need people who were preparing for professional library careers for this kind of work. That's the reason the books were not shelved. They didn't have enough people to do the job."

Both Dowlin and his immediate successor, Regina Minudri, told me that the San Francisco Public Library is not a research library, even though public libraries in other large American cities—most notably those in Boston, New York, Philadelphia, Chicago, and Cleveland—perform such a function admirably, even maintaining in some cases materials not found in any depth in nearby university libraries. "We are probably the strongest public library in northern California in terms of collection size, breadth, and depth," Minudri said. "But we are not a research library. We have excellent material on the history of San Francisco, and we have an excellent collection of Californiana. We are a very good reference library; we serve a lot of children, we have wonderful branches, and we provide a lot of quick information. I would say that we are a middle-of-the-road urban library, with all of the urban library problems that all North American libraries face. But we are not a research library for scholars. We don't have the money, the resources, or the space for that, and even more disturbing, we have no room here for growth."

Selected by the Library Commission to succeed Dowlin, Minudri was praised by both sides after assuming responsibility in what everyone recognized as unusually stressful times. A former president of the American Library Association, she had served as librarian of the Berkeley Public Library for seventeen years and was on the short list of finalists for the San Francisco position in 1987. She suffered a stroke in 1999 and was replaced by Susan Hildreth, a deputy, on an interim basis at first, and permanently in May 2001. "A friend of mine said, 'It's kind of ironic, don't you think, that you're coming in to clean up the mess they wouldn't have had if they had hired you in the first place,' " Minudri said in our 1997 interview, though she was careful not to be overly critical of Dowlin in her conversation with me. She nevertheless did concede that the New Main was not the design she would have pushed for had she been in charge when it was being planned. "This library is brand spanking new, and we don't have enough room for our collections," she said. "This building was full when it opened. We have a lot of very pretty spaces, architecturally they're very pleasing to look at, but we just don't have enough room for what we have. There might be many reasons for that, and I don't want to cast any aspersions on people, but we have tons of material in Brooks Hall that in all likelihood will stay down there for the immediate future."

Minudri said she did not want to denigrate the role architects play in the design of libraries, "but as a librarian I look at things with a different viewpoint. Here I probably would have gone for a more mundane approach, with floors straight across. The truth is that I wish that we had another thirty thousand linear feet of shelving in here, but I don't see how that's possible right now, so the next best step is to renovate Brooks Hall. When you build a building like this, you build for at least twenty years of growth. What happened here I think is that they found all kinds of material squirreled away that they didn't realize they had. I do like the exterior of the building, and I do like the atrium, but I don't think it needs to be six stories high. We have this beautiful-looking building here that isn't holding the collections, so one could argue that the architect won. That's kind of a catchphrase that librarians use; if the building doesn't come out the way you wanted it, you say the architect won." A continuing paradox has been that even though the New Main library is a larger building than the Old Main, it holds fewer books. One course of action advocated by some factions was to keep both buildings operating, but that was impossible, since the Old Main had already been designated for renovation as an Asian arts museum.

Before we met for our interview, Minudri had allowed me to make a walking tour through Brooks Hall, and I had seen the flip side of the library of the future in the company of Susan Goldstein, the city archivist, whose materials were being stored there for lack of space in the New Main among other elements of the collection, about a million items all told. "They never thought about archival space in the new building," Goldstein said. Puddles of water lay on the concrete floor outside the chain-link fences that had been set up to close off the overflowing collections stacked high on a hodgepodge assembly of industrial shelving; some 75,000 square feet of space was occupied by books. In a separate space were the old card catalogs that the library had been required to keep by court order. A number of nonlibrary artifacts—former mayor Diane Feinstein's wedding dress stood out—were in there with the books.

In an attractively illustrated history published to coincide with the opening of the New Main Library in 1996, Peter Booth Wiley, the San Francisco author commissioned to write the book, described William R. Holman as a dynamic man who was hired in 1960 to create "a first-class institution." A native of Oklahoma, Holman began his career as a librarian in the Southwest and made a name for himself in Texas by directing a "successful effort to transform the San Antonio Public Library into an award-winning institution with a reputation for public outreach." When Holman arrived in San Francisco, he "blew into town like a breath of fresh air," impressing everyone with his "rapid-fire straight-from-the-shoulder answers" and his poise and self-confidence, "to the point of brashness." One of his first comments to reporters was an observation that "San Francisco is a bookish, unique city, and certainly doesn't deserve a third-rate library."

Constantly fighting for more money, Holman managed to win small increases in the budget, working all the while to reorganize the catalog system and add new books. By 1962 he had established a new Literature, Philosophy, and Religion Department, with 100,000 books available directly to the public in a revamped room on the second floor. Two months later the Library Commission approved his reorganization plan, which added departments for art and music, history, travel, and biography; the following year, a Business and Science Department joined their ranks. Meanwhile, he brought in new staff, strengthened programs for children, minorities, and the handicapped, and required that all new librarians have master's degrees in library science.

Holman added many important books to the collections during his seven-year tenure in San Francisco, and worked with Warren Howell, David Magee, and William P. Wreden, three prestigious local booksellers, to acquire many scarce materials. In 1964 he established a special archive of local interest that became the San Francisco History Room. A printer in his own right, Holman was attracted to San Francisco partly by the prospect of meeting such local craftsmen as Robert Grabhorn, Andrew Hoyem, and Adrian Wilson, and one of his early priorities was to form a strong collection of fine-press publications featuring examples of their work.

For all his accomplishments in San Francisco, Holman admitted frustration over his inability to build a new main library, and he soon grew weary of all the political infighting. He left in 1967 while still in his forties and accepted a position at the University of Texas in Austin. Although he had been away from San Francisco for many years by the time a new library finally was built, Holman's efforts did not go unappreciated, as an appraisal of his tenure in the specially commissioned history of the library makes clear. In that work, Peter Booth Wiley offered this assessment of him: "He had reorganized and professionalized the staff, attracted well-known librarians from outside the city, started to rebuild the book collections, secured much larger budgets, and built a Rare Book and Special Collections Department. Above all he made the library, for the first time in its history, a significant cultural center."

Wiley's characterization of Holman as a person who spoke "straight from the shoulder" made him someone whose views seemed worth seeking out. When I contacted him one morning by telephone at his home in Texas, he was pleased to share his thoughts, especially since he had returned to San Francisco just a year before we spoke to see the Old Main once more before it closed for good, and to take a look at the "library of the future" he had been hearing so much about.

"Let me begin by saying that I think a library is like an individual, that it has a distinct personality," he offered before allowing me to ask a single question. "You never want to be like a bird with a single note. You don't have much range or influence in your little world. Nobody knew who I was when I walked in last year, it had been a long time away for me. I have to say that I was aghast with what I saw. First of all, they had closed all the departments, which was quite disconcerting. My feeling is that you have to have well-trained, well-read, articulate people at every desk. I always have a lot of questions when I go into a library. It happens that I'm writing a memoir now, and I want knowledgeable people who can give me half a dozen references. What you want is somebody who can synthesize all of this for you. I left the Old Main that day and walked down those long stairs I knew so well, and I got a visitor's permit to go into the new library. I walked in there, and I was taken profoundly, I must say, by the beauty and intensity of the building. It definitely occupied the same amount of space as the old building, but the problem is that there was no room for books. You build a new building today, you should have at least forty percent stack space set aside in your plan. Well, they don't have anything close to that. There's an old saying, 'If you want to destroy a library, hire an architect,' and I'm afraid that's what has happened there. At the very time that they were cutting back on space, they were doing away with the literature and the philosophy and the humanities, all the other departments that are so important in the life of a sophisticated city."

Holman said that the thirty years he had been away from San Francisco had given him distance and perspective. "Looking at it now, I think what happened is that they got so caught up in raising money they forgot about the fundamentals," he said, summing it up. "Ken Dowlin came to San Francisco with a certain mind-set about what a library is supposed to do. The problem is that this is not a lazy population they have out there.

You've got to have real concern for book collections, and for readers who don't necessarily read the same things you want to read. If you're going to have a metropolitan center, you have to have a metropolitan library. Giving the man his due, he did get the budget, and he got the library built. There is a cautionary tale in all this, I think, and I don't see any absolute horror in it. I do see a future, and that is part of the challenge, which is also part of the fun. The challenge is not the arrival, it's the journey. And the journey is to fulfill the aspirations of a finer library."

On July 16, 1999, more than three years after the New Main opened its doors to the general public, a "post-occupancy evaluation," known by the acronym POE, was completed by an independent oversight committee and submitted to the Library Commission. If the opponents were seeking vindication, they found some satisfaction in the pages of this report, prepared by a team of outside architects, engineers, and librarians at a cost to the city of $240,000, and issued in two volumes. The consultants were asked to provide "an objective, empirical assessment of the performance" of the New Main Library, "identify problems," "propose solutions," and if all went well, "contribute to the published literature on library design guidelines to help San Francisco as well as other cities when they plan new libraries." Put in less delicate terms, the idea was to provide the necessary documentation for how not to go about building a "library of the future."

In its final report issued in January 2000, the committee computed that it would take $28.3 million to repair the library in accordance with the POE, and the figure did not include provisions for increased staffing or the cost of renting off-site space. The lion's share, some $17.7 million, would be used to renovate Brooks Hall and provide it with a public access point and a reading room for the city archives and government documents now being stored there. Other expenditures would go toward increasing shelving capacity in the New Main by 2.7 percent, from 150,054 linear feet to 165,242 linear feet, about 232 linear feet per million dollars. Among their conclusions, the consultants found that while the building is a "significant piece of architecture with attractive interior spaces," considerable renovations would be necessary to increase services on the first and second floors, and "increase the density of use" on all floors.

The state librarian of California, Kevin Starr, wears several hats, chief among them historian, educator, and columnist. A former professor of history at the University of San Francisco, he has written a number of books on western American history, six of them as part of a series published by Oxford University Press known as Americans and the California Dream. Among his university degrees are a master of arts and a doctorate of philosophy from Harvard in history, and a master of library sciences degree from the University of California at Berkeley. He also has taught at the University of Southern California, and since his appointment as state librarian in 1994, has also held the title of university professor at the University of California, Los Angeles. A fourth-generation San Franciscan, Starr is proud of his curriculum vitae, since it demonstrates that he is a librarian who maintains his standing as a working scholar.

As a person who grew up, lived, and worked many years in San Francisco, Starr is in a unique position to comment on the library controversies in the city, not only as a professional charged with supervising the way the state spends $113 million on its libraries each year but as someone who from 1974 to 1976 served as city librarian. "That was my first job as a librarian," he told me. "I was made acting librarian of the city the first year, and when I got my master's of library science degree at Berkeley, they made me city librarian. I insisted on getting the library degree, by the way; it was a condition I imposed on myself. The fact that I was a productive scholar and that I loved books did not compensate for the fact that I did not have my union card, which I was very proud to get."

Starr said he decided it was time to step down from the San Francisco job in 1976 when his proposal to renovate the Old Main was rejected by the Library Commission. "I thought that for about $18 million or $20 million, I could have recycled that building for a couple hundred years. I advanced plans that would have taken about 37 percent of our space on the Hyde Street side that was literally dirt earth, and develop that with closed shelving. I then would have finished off the wing on the Hyde Street side, and sunk a great geodesic dome in the center. The Library Board said the idea was unworthy. They wanted a new building."

While plans were being advanced for a replacement facility, Starr said that he was never once asked for any recommendations based on his own experience, and that when the New Main was finally completed he decided to keep his counsel. "It was a done deal at that point, and anything I might have said would have accomplished nothing." When the first complaints began to emerge, he still maintained a respectful distance. He agreed to talk with me in late 1999, shortly after the $240,000 post-occupancy evaluation report was released in preliminary form, and the criticisms that had been disclosed were part of an official report. "It's on the record now, and I guess my first response is that I was right," he told me. "On the other hand, let me also say that I am thrilled that the Old Main will find a new life as the Asian Art Museum. It is a beautiful building that was built for the long haul, and the fact that it has many productive years ahead of it is gratifying to me, because I felt that way about it all along. That is another validation of sorts."

On the more pressing issue of the New Main, Starr voiced particular disappointment that city officials committed themselves to building "what amounts to a reverse paradigm of what a great public library should be." He elaborated on what he meant by describing the project in these terms: "It is a building that was mongered by notions. It got mongered by an architectural notion such as that great light well that sweeps up through the center of the building and makes it impossible to store books. It got mongered by the notion that the new building should be a sort of mall for computers rather than a great public library. It also lost sight of the fact that the San Francisco Public Library, despite all its difficulties, and its underfunding, was a distinguished collection."

I asked Starr to explain his use of the past tense, and he repeated the word *was* for emphasis. "I say it *was* a distinguished collection because the very act of going into that new building meant they had to deaccession about half a million books, and as we know in librarianship, you never move and deaccession at the same time, because that just winds up in bulk dumping. Every title on your shelf has a constituency. There is only one way to deaccession books, and that is title by title by title." It was because of this critical decision, he continued, that no detailed record of discards was ever kept. "They didn't do this because they were not going through the process of professional deaccession, where you take each book, you look up its records, and you examine it and say, 'What is the constituency of this book in terms of its circulation?' But more importantly, 'What is the constituency of this book in the architecture of academic knowledge?' "

Asked why he thought the process had been conducted in such secrecy, Starr said the reason is obvious. "Do you think the taxpayer, the book-buying public, would cooperate with the dismantlement of a collection which had been developed since 1906, and even before 1906, if you take into account the retroactive buying of titles? I researched a good part of my Americans and the California Dream series at the San Francisco Public, and I found superb collections there in show business, in the history of Hollywood. They had some spectacular collections in California fiction. These were not serious novels that anyone had read in fifty years, mind you, but they were important in that they chronicled the life of California. Books like that should be kept on the shelves regardless of how little used they are." Reminded that his figure of 500,000 books is at considerable variance from the 200,000 estimated by some critics to have been discarded, and measurably more still than that claimed by Dowlin, Starr cited "the other couple hundred thousand sitting in storage that they're trying to give away. There's a million books in storage, and I know for a fact that they are actively trying to give away a hundred thousand of them. And we don't have any records for any of this, do we?"

Regarding the "affinity" rooms in the new library, Starr would not dismiss the concept out of hand, "provided they are tied to collections. If they are just making public meeting rooms, then they could be done in less expensive spaces. I am not against these theme rooms because San Francisco is a city of great tolerance and inclusiveness, but if you're going to do it in a library, you should do it in a library way, with books, manuscripts, and archives attached. They can't build any collections there now because there is no room; the library as entertainment mall can not support these kinds of things. You have to have a traditional library for that, a classic library, and you need space for collection development. It saddens me to hear you say you were told the San Francisco Public Library no longer considers itself a research library, that if you want to do work in any kind of depth, you now have to go over to Stanford or Berkeley. That's the same as saying if you want to write a book in Boston, go over to Harvard, you don't need the Boston Public Library anymore, get rid of the special collections."

Given the fact that he is a state official who probably should remain above the controversy, Starr allowed that he was "probably being indiscreet" in talking so frankly with me. "But I am also a librarian, and the things we are discussing here are much too important. These people disestablished a distinguished collection. To say that the San Francisco Public Library, the largest public library at the center—at ground zero—of the fourth largest urban population mass in the nation should divest itself of a collection that was moving toward a hundred years old, to disestablish that collection without any mandate or public discussion, is shocking."

10.

IN THE STACKS

You promise, and solemnly engage before God, Best and Greatest, that whenever you shall enter the public library of the University, you will frame your mind to study in modesty and silence, and will use the books and furniture in such manner that they may last as long as possible. Also that you will neither in your own person steal, change, make erasures, deform, tear, cut, write notes in, interline, wilfully spoil, obliterate, defile, or in any other way retrench, ill-use, wear away, or deteriorate any book or books, nor authorise any other person to commit the like; but, so far as in you lies, will stop any other delinquent or delinquents, and will make known their ill-conduct to the Vice-Chancellor or his deputy within three days after you are made aware of it yourself: so help you God, as you touch the Holy Gospels of Christ.

—*Bodleian Statutes, 1610*

For all the seismic changes that computer technology has brought to the way information is gathered, stored, and disseminated, the finest colleges and universities continue to be judged by the strength of their libraries and the depth of their research collections. The stature of faculty, the awarding of prestigious grants, and the generosity of donors are critical factors as well, but a superior library still guarantees respectability and is one of several yardsticks by which academic excellence is measured. In his penetrating essay "In Defense of the

Book," written at century's end, the critic William H. Gass offered a "fundamental formula for excellence" often "ignored if not forgotten" in academe: "A great library will attract a great faculty, and a great faculty will lure good students to its log; good students will go forth and win renown, endowments will increase, and so will the quality of the football team, until original aims are lost sight of, academic efforts slacken, the library stands neglected, the finer faculty slip away, good students no longer seek such an environment, and the team gets even better."

In the years immediately following World War II, Lawrence Clark Powell made a determined effort to elevate the reputation of the University of California at Los Angeles by applying a simple credo. "I have been in many of the world's great bookshops, and have removed thousands of books, leaving dollars in their stead," the West Coast librarian wrote. Between 1945 and 1958 Powell more than tripled UCLA's collections, increasing its holdings by more than a million volumes. He boasted of his willingness to go anywhere and do pretty much what was necessary to strengthen the library:

> *I have hunted books on the main floor and on the mezzanine, up in the attic and down in the cellar. I have crawled on dusty floors and climbed up shaky ladders. I have paid too much for books, too little for others. I have worked in overheated American shops and under-heated British ones, oblivious to both heat and cold. I have competed with pigs and chickens in one shop. The joy that I experience in book-shops has nothing to do with their size. I like them all.*

The impassioned, some might say obsessive, quest undertaken by Harry Huntt Ransom in the late 1950s, 1960s, and early 1970s to establish a comprehensive repository of twentieth-century literary documents created a vital resource for the University of Texas that today draws scholars to the Austin campus from all over the world. Not content to rest on its laurels and absorb what it acquired during its formative years, the

Humanities Research Center—since 1976 formally named for Harry Ransom—has continued adding to collections that now include some 38 million pages of manuscript. An exhibition presented early in 2000, *Islands of Order,* focused on materials gathered during the 1990s and reaffirmed the university's "sustained commitment to collection development and our vigorous pursuit of major archives," according to Thomas F. Staley, director there since 1988. Featured were examples from the papers of the writers Isaac Bashevis Singer, Bernard Malamud, Anthony Burgess, Peter Matthiessen, Doris Lessing, Adrienne Kennedy, Penelope Fitzgerald, Penelope Lively, Elizabeth Olds, and the playwright Tom Stoppard, including his screenplay for the 1998 hit film *Shakespeare in Love.* In addition to manuscripts, letters, and books, a few telling artifacts—Malamud's portable Royal typewriter and the Underwood with Hebrew characters used by Singer among them—were on display, along with original portraits of authors that the Ransom Center collects.

A more recent contender in the high-stakes paper chase has been Emory University in Atlanta, Georgia. Buoyed by generous gifts of Coca-Cola stock from the late Robert W. Woodruff that are now worth well over $1 billion, Emory gathers choice material in a number of academic disciplines and uses it, along with generous financial inducements, to lure prestigious scholars away from other institutions to its burgeoning campus. The university's purchase in 1997 of a 2.5-ton Ted Hughes archive, Britain's poet laureate from 1984 to 1998, for an undisclosed sum—but reported by the *Sunday Times* of London to be "about" £500,000—was added to other recently acquired collections that include important manuscripts of William Butler Yeats, Seamus Heaney, Thomas Kinsella, and Frank Ormsby. The transfer prompted a number of British critics to renew their oft-expressed lament over seeing so much literary material cross the Atlantic for sums that cannot be matched at home. "Why do the American universities want the papers?" the *Times* arts correspondent asked in bewilderment. "It is a feeding frenzy," he was told by an unidentified American curator.

Before assuming the presidency of Brown University in 1989, Vartan Gregorian spent eight eventful years directing the fortunes of the New York Public Library. He is credited with reviving and restoring to greatness an institution that had fallen on hard times. "Never have libraries been needed so desperately," he said at the time, "and never have they been falling so steeply into neglect." When Gregorian set up shop in Providence, Rhode Island, as the president of a fashionable Ivy League university, his first order of business was to invigorate fund-raising, strengthen the faculty, and initiate an aggressive acquisitions program in the library that would increase holdings by a third, making a respectable academic collection even stronger. When Gregorian left Brown in July 1997, he had more than tripled the endowment, bringing it from $264 million to $965 million; by the time his successor was installed that fall, the figure had eclipsed the $1 billion mark. Just as impressively, Gregorian had created eleven new academic departments, added 270 faculty members, and expanded the library's collections from a little more than 2 million volumes to just under 3 million. During this remarkable period of growth, the number of secondary-school students applying for admission surged, making Brown one of the most selective undergraduate programs in the country.

"No university in the world has ever risen to greatness without a great library, and no university is greater than its library," Gregorian told me one Saturday morning a few months before he was scheduled to assume his new position in New York City as chairman of the Carnegie Corporation, a philanthropic organization that distinguished itself for the 1,689 public libraries it built throughout the United States between 1886 and 1917. Gregorian wasted little time in establishing priorities, authorizing sizable grants in support of library programs, returning the organization full circle to its founding principles in support of reading and literacy. "Libraries are not centers of information—they are centers of learning," he stressed in his interview with me. Gregorian said that whenever he talks about the fundamental role libraries play in shaping society, he makes it a point to quote John Naisbitt, author of the book *Megatrends,* who saw around him a world that is "wallowing in detail, drowning in information, but is starved for knowledge." The goal of every library, Gregorian asserted, "is to transform information into knowledge; what we must provide is not just information, but its distillation into knowledge."

With that caveat as a premise, Gregorian then cited a study prepared by a Brown University colleague in 1996 that confirmed in specific detail what so many other academic administrators and librarians already knew from hard experience, that escalating prices and dwindling budgets had resulted in the purchase of fewer and fewer library materials, and that this trend was likely to continue for the foreseeable future. The report's findings, researched and written by Brian L. Hawkins, at that time vice president for academic planning and administration at Brown, were summarized by its gloomy title: "The Unsustainability of the Traditional Library and the Threat to Higher Education." The basic conclusion Hawkins drew—and one which Gregorian quoted to me almost verbatim—is that the explosive growth in "available information," combined with a continued reduction in buying power, means that academic libraries are now able to preserve a minuscule and constantly dwindling portion of the scholarly record, and the share they are able to acquire in the future will get smaller and smaller every year. Among Hawkins's projections was a forecast that by the year 2001, academic libraries would be able to buy just 2 percent of the research materials they could acquire two decades earlier, and that by the year 2026, "the acquisitions budgets of our finest libraries will have only 20 percent of the buying power they had forty-five years earlier."

One solution put forth by Hawkins—that universities continue to develop a "new and revolutionary paradigm" in which electronic access be promoted as a major goal—has already been embraced by cost-conscious institutions everywhere, with increasing amounts of money being committed toward the purchase of computer equipment, software, and online services, and less for books and journals. Two years after writing the report, Hawkins left Brown to begin developing plans for a "national electronic library" under the auspices of EDUCAUSE, a nonprofit computing organization established by a consortium of American universities.

For Gregorian, one reality underscored by the Hawkins report was that the task of choosing which printed materials will be bought and preserved has become more demanding a responsibility than ever before. "The printed materials universities choose to select for their permanent collections, and how they go about selecting them, is going to be the key issue," he said. "There are thousands of scientific titles that come up every year for purchase, thousands and thousands of them. These are tremendously expensive items—some of them can cost as much as $20,000 a year for a single subscription—and they become antiquated in a couple of years, some in a matter of months. Well, what people are now realizing is that you don't have to have all of these journals in your library, and even if you had the money to buy them, you don't have enough space for all of them anyway. What matters is that you have access for your students and your faculty for everything they need, and the access to the scientific journals increasingly has become electronic. So what I am sure will happen is that most scientific publications will be published primarily in electronic forms. That seems quite inevitable to me right now. As for the humanities, the social sciences, and the history of science, those are the areas where having copies will continue to be relevant, and in those fields, the dilemma will be how you make the appropriate choices from all that is available."

Karen A. Schmidt, the director of collections at the University of Illinois at Urbana-Champaign, considers the cancellation of subscriptions to serial journals a disquieting trend that she, at least, has tried to stem by maintaining a steady budget for acquisitions, although she harbors no illusions that she can reverse what is happening elsewhere. Schmidt and a colleague conducted detailed studies that document serial cancellations at five midwestern academic libraries between 1987 and 1996. Their overall conclusion: "Serial collections are getting leaner, monograph collections are suffering in relative silence, and the depth and richness of library collections are disappearing," in many cases being replaced by online services such as JSTOR that offer access to full-text versions of scholarly articles at a fraction of what it costs to maintain journal subscriptions.

Those findings were supported on a much broader level by the Association of Research Libraries (ARL), a consortium of 122 institutions in the United States and Canada that annually ranks its members by their total holdings and for the number of items they have added over the previous year. The figures are broken down further not only to reflect the purchase of books, serial publications, reels of microfilm, and monographs but to indicate how much material has been loaned and borrowed through reciprocal agreements, and record the amount of money spent on acquisitions, salaries, and general operations. The ARL takes special pains to point out that the "quantitative rank order" it compiles is "not indicative of performance and outcomes *should not* be used as measures of library quality," yet the numbers command close attention among educators intent on keeping ahead of the competition. Although ARL institutions comprise a small subset of all academic libraries in North America, they are reliable indicators of what is going on throughout the world of higher education. Total holdings among ARL institutions in 2000 hovered just above 474 million titles, or about half of the 900 million books estimated to be maintained by the 3,408 American colleges and universities that report their holdings to the U.S. Department of Education. Of this total, about 450 million represent "unduplicated titles," meaning that only one of these items is available in the nation's academic collections.

Harvard University, custodian of the oldest library in North America, stands alone at the top in every major category, and its staff works assiduously to maintain that dominance. With 14.4 million volumes on hand at the start of the twenty-first century, Harvard's numbers placed it

3.9 million ahead of Yale University, its closest competitor, and 4.9 million ahead of the University of Illinois at Urbana, an unheralded but surprisingly steady third. "This was the vision of the first president of the university back in 1868," Karen Schmidt said. "Our founders knew that we could never have a great university out here in the middle of a cornfield unless we had a great library. Let's face it, nobody of stature would want to come here unless we had the books to lure them. So we have always been a collection-oriented library."

As impressive as the University of Illinois program is—and it maintains the largest library of any public university in the world—it is not likely to approach the numbers posted by Harvard, which not only has more books but spends more money each year and acquires more materials than all the others to retain that position, adding 289,322 volumes in 2000 alone and allotting $80.8 million to total library expenditures, an all-time high and an increase of $3.8 million over the previous year.

Thirty-three other institutional libraries added anywhere from 100,118 to 267,068 volumes to their general collections during the same twelve-month period. But as robust as these figures may appear, they belie what is still the most dramatic trend in the way many academic libraries are now doing business, placing a greater reliance on electronic sources, which result in what the compilers of the data call a steady "decline of ownership," particularly in the addition of new monographs and serial journals. Between 1986 and 1996, a ten-year period notable for the widespread application of the Internet as a learning device, the number of serials purchased dipped by 17 percent, while monographs fell an astonishing 35 percent. Most tellingly, perhaps, the median number of books added reached a low of 3.81 volumes per student in 1996, compared to 4.18 volumes per student added ten years earlier, resulting in significant "resources per student" reductions at most academic libraries. Because fewer new printed materials were available on most campuses—and because they were still very much in demand—faculty and students were borrowing 2.7 times as many items through interlibrary loan during that period.

The statistics, moreover, do not state directly how many books may have been deaccessioned by any of these institutions, a process that very few librarians like to acknowledge, let alone discuss, although there are separate listings for "volumes added, gross" and "volumes added, net," with the latter category, needless to say, always being lower. In 1998, for example, Harvard acquired 310,016 new volumes but reported a net gain of 285,193, meaning that 24,823 items were removed from the collections. The most commonly cited reasons given are wear, tear, and the elimination of infrequently used materials that exist in duplicate copies, although some Harvard librarians prefer the word *grooming* to *weeding*, pointing out that systematic withdrawals are part of the process. Their counterparts at the University of Michigan like to say that books on the margins are not discarded, but "decanted," meaning they are moved, like vintage wine, from one vessel to another—in this case, poured into a huge depository maintained in Chicago by a nonprofit consortium of institutions known as the Center for Research Libraries.

At Princeton University, librarians and instructors take special pride in pointing out that their students and faculty borrow more books than at any other college or university in the United States. During the 1996–97 academic year, 555,328 titles were charged out, an average of 86 books for every student and faculty member. Anthony Grafton, one of the leading proponents of an academic discipline known as history of the book, teaches two courses on the subject at Princeton.

"Our library likes to boast that we circulate more books per capita than anyone else, although I think one reason Harvard is lower than us is because Widener Library allows readers to take books and copy them without checking them out," Grafton told me when I asked about the special place books have in the Princeton curriculum. "But our numbers are still quite striking to me because the factor that usually makes for high circulation in a university library is a preponderance of graduate programs, and Princeton is primarily an undergraduate institution, which is not to say that we do not have any outstanding graduate programs here, because we do, but the emphasis of the institution is on undergraduate learning. What I am saying in essence is that the library is the essential core of academic life here."

Grafton said that he expects all of his students to work with primary sources, undergraduate and graduate alike. "One of the great things about teaching at a place like this is that your best students are so much abler than you are. I try to get my undergraduates to use special collections as much as possible. That's one of the reasons I am here—to try to tempt and seduce the students to be book people. I insist, when I have a senior, that he or she is in here once a week to show his or her face and say, 'This is what I have been doing.' And I want to see it. I do answer e-mail, and at the height of a term I might get five or six a week from each of my students, but e-mail is something you add on to enrich and to make better the contact that you have day to day. My students love, they don't just like, they *love* their books. Every student that I work with, every student that I have any kind of relationship with, is a book lover. They love books, they read books, we swap fiction recommendations, they go to bookstores, they find wonderful things and bring them in to show me. They're book lovers, and the ones who are most skilled are most often the ones who are lovers of traditional books."

The suggestion that a university could possibly function without books is "extremely sinister" to Grafton, and he finds any kind of systematic deaccessioning of collections a "criminal" act; "You are foreclosing the future, and we don't know what's going to look interesting in five or ten or thirty years." The computer is essential on campuses today, Grafton agreed, and he finds it an invaluable tool for tracking down material at other libraries. "We can plan students' research trips right here in this office, and it's fantastic. Twenty years ago, something like this was well nigh impossible, we had only the National Union Catalog to consult, and you couldn't get fully reliable information. The computer has just transformed this kind of teaching. I had a senior who just went to Europe to do archival work for her thesis, and she arrived at my door two weeks before leaving with e-mail permissions from every archivist she contacted and appointments confirmed for using their collections, all without ever setting a foot out of the country."

Another Princeton professor widely recognized for his attention to the history of the book, Robert Darnton, pointed out that as important as traditional materials are at Princeton, the budget for computer technology now rivals the budget for the entire library system. "Acquisitions budgets everywhere are under siege and have been squeezed and reduced. I served for a while as head of the faculty library committee at the university, and I argued very strongly that computer information technology, if that's going to expand, great, but it must not be at the expense of acquisitions."

One of the most vocal advocates of a balanced approach in library services during the 1990s—and probably one of the least understood—was Peter Lyman, professor and associate dean at the School of Information Management and Systems at the University of California at Berkeley, and from 1994 to 1998 the university librarian. Prior to accepting that position, Lyman served for three years as university librarian and dean of libraries at the University of Southern California in Los Angeles. We met in his office on the Berkeley campus in September 1997 six months before the latest ARL compilation would reflect a dip in the university's ranking, its second drop in two years, and spark a renewed attack from some faculty members who had been protesting what they maintained was a steady erosion of support for the humanities. Three months after we spoke—and three months before the new figures were released—Lyman resigned as university librarian, and though his departure may have come as a surprise to some, he made clear in his interview with me that he was getting weary of waging battles that he could not hope to win, and that such a move was imminent. "You've caught me on a day that I'm pretty ticked off," he said, and part of the reason for his displeasure that day was the continuing refusal of the administration to increase funding for the purchase of new books. "I'm not going to stay in this job, it makes me too angry," he said flatly. "I am a faculty member, and I'm going to teach. The reason for this is the issue that you and I are talking about right now. It just infuriates me."

The issue we were talking about was the issue everyone in library circles had been discussing over the previous decade, but in Berkeley's case it was clear that choices had been made at the highest levels to moderate the importance of books in the overall scheme, and the numbers were starting to have an impact. In 1997 the budget for library acquisitions at Berkeley stood at $8 million, a lot of money at any institution, but the figure was fixed, with no allowance for inflation, and there was no indication that the policy was about to change any time soon. The first of what would be eight consecutive budget cuts had been imposed on the library in 1989, and with the cost of scholarly journals reaching unprecedented highs—a 150 percent increase in a little more than a decade—the squeeze was felt most profoundly in the stacks of Bancroft Library. "I think it is a horrendous and appalling mistake that this university is not supporting the buying of books," Lyman told me. "We are supposed to be the collection of record for the state of California. If we don't collect something here, it probably means that it does not exist in a research collection in this state, perhaps in the West. Historically, we have been the repository for all of higher education in the West. And they've just abandoned that. We are buying fewer and fewer books every year."

Lyman blamed a single factor above all others for creating the situation, one, he said, that is prevalent throughout American research libraries. "It is apparent to me that technology is the drug of choice among administrators. Science, technology, medicine, and business have become the cash crops of the universities. The sciences bring in income, they bring in big grants, and so caring for their needs is very important." Lyman said recent ARL statistics validate his belief that the gulf separating private institutions with independent sources of income from publicly funded state universities will get wider and wider. "Harvard is the only academic library in the country that I know of that has kept up with inflation.

Everybody else is buying less than they used to." And the reduction in book purchases has progressed in tandem with the extraordinary increase in the price of scientific journals. "I worry about this not just in terms of the situation here at Berkeley, but in the larger sense that we are destroying the tradition of the book as the repository of scholarship by killing the market. If the traditional marketplace for a product disappears, before long the product itself will disappear. That is a legitimate concern I have over the fate of the academic monograph."

Because the shelf life of new research in the sciences is short, and because immediate access to the latest articles is essential, the transmission medium of choice is rapidly becoming electronic. At schools like Berkeley, where support for the sciences drives the allocation of resources, the far deeper concern for Lyman is that "there is a tacit devaluation of the humanities and the social sciences. Digital libraries really serve the sciences, technology, medicine, business—those are the areas of knowledge that map to this form of communication pretty well, so issues like preservation are not as important because the real value of the information dies out in three to five years anyway. That information is in very short formats. I have nothing at all against that, by the way. I think it is wonderful. But when you choose digital libraries as a replacement for books and print, what you are doing is choosing the sciences over the humanities. And what I think we are seeing—this is what many people in the faculty here feel the battle for the library budget is really all about—what we are seeing is an academic priority being played out. It is not about books per se, and it's not about libraries per se. In my opinion, it is about the role of the humanities in the university."

Given this position, people unfamiliar with Lyman's background could be excused for thinking he is hostile to technology, when the facts suggest otherwise. "I am one of the few academics who has done a lot of research on computers and the university," he said. "I know a lot about technology, but I am a social scientist and I come out of the humanities. I am very interested in the new kinds of genres that could emerge from network information, but I don't see them replacing print. Oddly enough, my reputation at Berkeley is of being a 'techie,' when in fact I am someone who is very skeptical, in a good sense, about technology. I think it is very promising, but I would call it experimental. I am on record, in fact, as saying precisely that." Indeed, an address Lyman gave at a conference sponsored by the Andrew W. Mellon Foundation in 1997 on the subject of "scholarly communication and technology" began with those very words, and he emphasized the point a year earlier in an article he wrote about the emerging concept of the digital library for a landmark issue of the journal *Daedalus* devoted entirely to the subject, and published under the general rubric of "Bricks, Books, and Bytes."

A 1962 graduate of Stanford University, Lyman holds a master's degree from Berkeley and a doctorate from Stanford, both in political science. He became a librarian, oddly enough, after establishing what he called the Center for Scholarly Technology at the University of Southern California. "It was a computer center for the humanities, and it sort of blew everyone's mind away, and then they asked me to be the university librarian. It was all quite a surprise to me. I wouldn't have had the chutzpah to do this on my own. I think that both USC and Berkeley thought that with libraries changing so profoundly, they needed an academic perspective on things. The net result is that I am one of the few academics who has done a lot of research on computers and the university."

The Association of Research Libraries also assembles what some library professionals regard as an even more telling compilation than raw totals, one it calls the "index score rank," which applies specific values for "volumes added," "volumes held," "current serials," "total staff," and "total expenditures" and computes a qualitative list that more accurately reflects activity in the library. In 1989 Berkeley vaulted into second place in these rankings for the first time, topped only by Harvard. For the next six years Berkeley bounced back and forth between second and third, but dipped dramatically to fourth in 1996, and to fifth three months after Lyman announced he was stepping down as university librarian.

When Lyman submitted his resignation, he made no public comment about his reasons for leaving. In January 1998 the ARL rankings showed that Berkeley had an index score rank of fifth for the previous year, and eighth in volumes added, a trend that suggested further slippage. With a collection of 9.1 million volumes and an inventory of 80,000 current serials and 110,000 government documents, Berkeley is still a major repository, but the university supports more graduate programs than any other institution in the United States—104 as it entered the twenty-first century—and awards more doctorates; in light of these figures, a prevailing attitude among many faculty is that the university needs every resource it can get. A few weeks after Lyman's resignation was announced, the point was hammered home in an essay published in *California Monthly,* the alumni magazine. Titled "Has the Library Lost Its Soul?" the article was written by Leon F. Litwack, a historian with an international reputation and at that time the outgoing chair of the Academic Senate's library committee. The recipient in 1980 of a Pulitzer Prize for *Been in the Storm So Long: The Aftermath of Slavery,* Litwack has distinguished himself for his painstaking use of primary material, a good deal of it researched at Berkeley, where he earned three academic degrees in the 1950s, including a doctorate in history.

"The future of the library will no doubt lie in some form of digital technology, with technocrats deciding how library funds will be spent and what faculty and students at the University will see," he wrote. "Digital access will come to be viewed as a cost-saving substitute for the expertise of professional librarians. But these changes will exact a heavy price. Our students will be deprived of some invaluable learning opportunities and experiences, and our standing as a major research library will suffer enormously, as will the ability to retain and hire faculty." In the rush to implement new technology, he charged, "there is no sense of the need for balance, little or no awareness that different academic disciplines may have different needs, not all of them fulfilled by the new technology." And with more and more books being kept in an off-site warehouse thirty miles away in Richmond, "nearly empty shelves confront the browser," making chance discoveries next to impossible. "During my more than thirty years at Berkeley, as a student and as a faculty member, the University's library has been the backbone of my research and teaching. Now I find myself relying almost exclusively on my private library for research and lecture materials."

On April 24, 1998, Robert Berdahl became the eighth chancellor of the University of California at Berkeley, succeeding Chang-Lin Tien, whose tenure was striking for a reluctance to support the library and its programs. Berdahl confronted the issue directly in his inaugural remarks, pledging to reverse the decline. "Our library has fallen seriously behind where it needs to be," he said. "We cannot allow this to continue. We need to catch up." Significantly, the infusion of new library funds he announced shortly thereafter—$5.2 million—was $2 million more than requested by Litwack's committee earlier in the month. When we spoke again two years later, Lyman expressed no regrets about his decision to step down from the library; he was "so glad to be out of administration and into teaching once again." He was pleased to report that the appointment of Berdahl in 1998 had brought about a change in attitude about the library. "The new chancellor has shown an awareness and a willingness to talk about the problem at the highest level, and that is a hopeful sign. When the chancellor now states publicly that this is a problem for the whole university, the librarian is no longer the target."

As most universities in the United States were cutting back on book purchases, the University of Toronto in Ontario—a publicly supported institution that serves Canada as a kind of de facto national library in several key areas—continued to enjoy the luxury of having a dedicated budget for book purchases that is adjusted annually for inflation, regardless of what other expenses are run up on the purchase of new technology. The result, according to Carole Moore, university librarian, is that "we are getting more of everything, and using more of everything." Another pleasant consequence of Toronto's enlightened acquisitions policy is that the university's ARL ranking has been steadily rising; by the beginning of the twenty-first century, only Harvard and Yale could claim ownership of more books.

Just as members of the Berkeley faculty were quick to equate declining ARL numbers with a deterioration in stature, universities that made strides climbing up the list were ecstatically trumpeting their higher standings. In 1997 the University of New Mexico played host to the ARL annual meeting, using the occasion to report that in the previous ten years it had "raced up the association's university-library rankings, climbing from 102 on a list of 105 to 47 on a list of 109," its 2-million-volume collection placing it "ahead of the luminary likes of Georgetown, Notre Dame, Purdue, Dartmouth and Syracuse." When the University of South Carolina moved into forty-ninth position in 1999, the institution's public affairs office issued an ebullient press release: "The ranking by the Association of Research Libraries puts USC ahead of Brown, Syracuse and Tulane universities and the universities of Notre Dame, Nebraska and Missouri." John M. Palms, the university president, was quoted as being delighted at having fulfilled a long-range vision of building a library "considered one of the top fifty in America." In February 2000 the University of North Carolina in Chapel Hill announced that the acquisition of a 1,200-volume William Butler Yeats collection had made the library "the first in the Southeast, and one of only 20 in North America, to reach the five-million volume milestone."

Toward the end of 2000, Duke University, just seven miles away from Chapel Hill in Durham, North Carolina, observed the acquisition of its five-millionth book, a noteworthy achievement made particularly extraordinary in that it was accomplished within seventy-six years of the institution's opening as a private university on the campus of Trinity College, which it absorbed in 1924. Established with the financial backing of James B. Duke, the founding president of the American Tobacco Company and owner of a huge hydroelectric company that provided power throughout the Carolinas, the university pursued an aggressive program of book acquisition from the outset, and for a time during the years of the Great Depression was able to outspend every other academic library in the United States, with the notable exception of Harvard. "Essential for the growth of graduate work in the arts and sciences at Duke was the strengthening of the library," Robert F. Durden wrote in a penetrating history of the university's emergence into an internationally recognized institution, and the quest for books was unswerving. While competing programs felt the continuing economic pinch of the 1930s, Duke had the means to acquire important material that suddenly had become available all over the world, and at bargain-basement prices to boot. As the university grew, other bequests were earmarked for the specific purpose of building the collections, so that by 1933 the three-year-old university library building was reported to be "approaching the saturation point." Three years after that, the burgeoning repository was declared to be "the heart of the university." By 1940 the rare books and manuscript room alone housed more than 600,000 items, "and the collection had become one of the major repositories for the study of American and especially southern history."

A five-year plan for strategic growth of the Perkins Library at Duke released in August 2000 took special pains to compare Duke's holdings with sister institutions in the Association of Research Libraries, and another organization "of the most selective private colleges and universities" in the country, the Consortium on Financing Higher Education (COFHE). Of the thirty-one COFHE institutions, eighteen are universities, and it is these, the writers of the report acknowledged, that Duke uses for "benchmarking in a wide array of areas of institutional life," most notably in assessing the strength of their library. Of singular concern to the authors of the report was a desire to determine what it would take for Duke to move up from ninth place in the rankings.

For example, for Duke to "catch up" with the University of Pennsylvania (ranked 7th), Duke would not need to increase total hold-

ings on current serials, but would need to increase the number of volumes added each year by 19,000 and the total expenditures by nearly $6 million. For Duke to take a position between Columbia and Cornell (from 9 to 5) would require an increase in total volumes of close to 2 million, an increase in volumes added of over 70,000, an increase in total expenditures of $8.5 million, and an increase in staff of 120. While it is not realistic to expect such dramatic increases overall, these comparisons indicate two clear facts: (1) Duke's collections, although large at close to 5 million volumes, are not growing as rapidly as those of peer libraries; and (2) total library expenditures are also lower, by a range of between $6 million (Pennsylvania, Princeton) through $8.5 million (Columbia), $19 million (Yale), to $53 million (Harvard). Duke is closest in total expenditures to Johns Hopkins, a library that is smaller by 1.5 million volumes and ranked 40 within ARL.

In the extensive plan that followed, the group outlined in specific detail suggestions the members felt will "help significantly to improve our standing vis-à-vis other institutions and to strengthen Duke's libraries at a critical juncture." Electronic resources are an essential part of the mix, but an aggressive approach to augmenting the "physical collections" continues apace, a decision reinforced by student demand for hard copies. "Circulation figures for books have increased an average of 10.8 percent in each of the past ten years, from 139,480 in 1988/89 to 248,008 in 1998/99."

For newly created institutions that have severely limited resources and nothing in the way of precedent to guide their acquisitions policies, the issue of how to initiate a comprehensive program of collection development becomes more complex, and can sometimes be quite creative. By far the most dramatic example of an institution forming a major research library in one decisive transaction, and achieving international respect in the process, was accomplished by the University of Chicago in 1891, before a single building had been erected on the newly established campus. The acquisition was made possible by the sudden availability of a huge inventory of books assembled over the previous forty years by S. Calvary and Company of Berlin, one of Europe's most respected antiquarian booksellers.

The original agreement called for the newly chartered university to purchase a quarter million items from Calvary, but a nasty disagreement that developed after the first materials were shipped clouded the deal for years, and the actual number of titles that changed hands totaled 57,630 books and 39,020 German doctoral dissertations, still a major coup, but not nearly as great as it should have been. The university's behavior was less than admirable in the matter, as the late Robert Rosenthal, the esteemed curator of special collections at the University of Chicago for many years, acknowledged in an essay written in 1979 for an exhibition of some of the more spectacular books acquired in the purchase.

Before agreeing to buy the books, which became known as the Berlin Collection, the university's founding president, William Rainey Harper, hired several librarians to evaluate the contents. In their report, they described the collection as one that would normally require "many years, incalculable pains, and many thousands of dollars" to create, and concluded that its availability presented a "once in a century" opportunity. Among the high points Harper cited in his subsequent report to John D. Rockefeller, the founder and chief benefactor of the university—and the italics are his—were "one of the largest and most complete collections of periodicals to be found anywhere in Europe," an "extraordinarily rich and valuable collection in classical philology including *some very rare copies,*" and "one of the richest collections in classical archaeology to be found anywhere, including some works *not found even in the Royal Library of Berlin and the British Museum.*" The material, he promised, would bring to the university "an acquisition of inestimable value," one that would make "a profound impression on the literary world." Harper's prediction proved accurate. In a front-page article reporting the purchase, the *New York Times* called the agreement "one of the largest book deals ever consummated in America," assuring the university of international stature at the very outset of its existence, an eminence it has never lost.

A catalog value of the books was computed at $700,000, and the press reported a sales figure of $300,000; the actual amount paid was $45,000. For that embarrassingly low figure—which, in fact, was the cause of the hard feelings that followed—the university became the proud custodian of the largest library in Chicago. "The combination of great treasures and row upon row of standard texts of the sixteenth and seventeenth centuries placed the University Library in the noble company of the great seats of European learning" overnight, Rosenthal wrote, and the "rigor with which the University pursued the past made it an immediate part of the working 'apparatus' of the institution."

While the University of Chicago purchase of the Berlin Collection is probably the most dramatic example of a single bookstore making a serious impression on the holdings of an academic library, it is by no means unique. In an unpublished memoir of his life as a respected New York bookseller, the late Louis Cohen, founder of the Argosy Book Store, noted in passing that he "purchased the entire stock of many booksellers over the years," in some instances turning them over "intact to college libraries." He cited two transactions specifically, both en bloc purchases made in the 1960s from a pair of Fourth Avenue booksellers that had recently closed down. "The entire stock of about 100,000 volumes of the Aberdeen Bookshop," and the "entire stock of O'Malley Bookshop, consisting of about 35,000 volumes," were both sold to Pennsylvania State University.

An explosive period of growth and prosperity in Canada during the 1960s created an unprecedented pressure for expansion of the national network of publicly funded colleges and universities. A temporary solution was to hire more faculty and expand programs at existing institutions, but the long-term requirements were such that several new institutions were created from scratch, all having to be equipped with libraries that needed books, and quickly. To fill the empty shelves, newly appointed librarians bought recently published titles from conventional suppliers, but it was the obscure, out-of-print materials so necessary for the support of ambitious research programs that inspired the pursuit of other strategies. Some were quite inventive, none more so than those improvised at York University in Toronto by Thomas F. O'Connell, a career librarian enticed into leaving a comfortable position at a premier Ivy League institution with an offer to become the director of a fledgling program.

Today, York University has an enrollment of forty thousand students, and its library of 2.3 million volumes enjoys the stature of full ARL membership, but when the institution began admitting its first students in 1967, there was a paucity of material available for their use, and very little time afforded to correct the situation, O'Connell, now retired, told me in an interview, "What I needed right away was three things—books, books, books." A native of Boston who had spent twelve years as a Harvard librarian, O'Connell was eager to take on the challenge offered to him in Canada. "I went from a library that had everything to a library that had nothing. I knew I could never duplicate what I had left behind in Cambridge—I couldn't duplicate what was sitting across town at the University of Toronto—but I had to start somewhere. Thankfully, money was not the problem, we had plenty of funds to work with. The problem was how to go about getting a credible collection in operation right away."

O'Connell decided to focus on categories where his immediate competition, the University of Toronto, was weak. "They were very strong on British history, but they didn't have an awful lot on American history, and they had nothing on French Canada, which was a major shortcoming in my view, so we concentrated on those two areas at first." To find material, he began scouting every secondhand bookstore that specialized in nonfiction, and was fortunate to "strike gold" during a trip to his home turf in Boston. After negotiating a deal with Ernest D. Starr, the owner of

Starr Book Company, to buy out virtually every book in his shop, then located at 37 Kingston Street in the Downtown Crossing section of the city, O'Connell dispatched several tractor-trailer trucks to pick up the material. O'Connell could not remember precisely how many books he acquired, although Starr's widow, Lillian Starr, and Norman B. Starr, his son and successor, both estimated the load to have numbered about 100,000 volumes, perhaps even a bit more. "All they left behind were the cookbooks and the paperbacks," Norman Starr recalled. "What I remember is that a couple of people came down here from Canada looking to buy a whole lot of books in a big hurry. They were telling my father the kinds of things that were on their want list, and he said, 'Why don't you just buy the whole thing?' The idea appealed to them in a big way, he quoted them a good price, they shook hands on the spot, and then came in the following Sunday morning to pick it all up." The story is celebrated among booksellers for the fact that within days of the sale, another 100,000 books had been moved into the store to replace the ones just carted off to Toronto, all drawn from a large supply Starr maintained nearby in storage. "I still have two warehouses filled with books," said his son, who now operates the family business in Cambridge, across Massachusetts Avenue from Harvard University. "Our particular madness as booksellers has always been that we buy a lot more books than we can ever possibly sell."

O'Connell told me he made the deal with Starr for a number of compelling reasons. "I am from Boston, and I knew his reputation was that of a very good bookman. He also had very clean stock. The books were sound, and they weren't falling apart. They weren't junk, and the price was right. We paid something like thirty cents a volume, and there was no way I could pass up a deal like that." Pleased with what he accomplished at Starr, O'Connell sent another truck to Montreal and cleaned out the stock at Librarie Ducharme, then a leading dealer of Canadiana printed in French, an essential consideration in a country that has two official languages. "That was a case of our showing up at the right place at the right time," O'Connell said. "Our dean of arts and sciences gave me a call one day when I was on vacation on Cape Cod. 'Tom,' he said, 'Ducharme has closed, they're looking to liquidate everything, and they have some really wonderful stuff. We've got to get it.' I don't remember how many books exactly we pulled out of there, but it was fabulous material."

Making the books from Boston and Montreal especially fabulous was the fact that most of them were out of print, and largely unavailable on the open market. To secure copies of titles that were still in print—and thus procurable through conventional channels—O'Connell worked out an arrangement with officials in California who were stocking a string of new state universities being built to support a rapidly growing population. "We piggy-backed ourselves on everything they bought in California. If they ordered eight or ten copies of a particular title, we had them get another one or two for us. We took advantage of all the good work they did identifying what they needed for a core collection, and by buying in greater volume, we both got a better deal on the price."

O'Connell left York University in 1975 to take another library program, his alma mater, to new heights. At that time Boston College was a small Jesuit school with a solid but limited regional reputation. "I am proud to say that I doubled the collections at BC in ten years. When I left BC I had brought in close to a million volumes. I built two libraries in my time, and the key element in both instances was money. You can't do anything without it; that was the story thirty years ago, it's the story now. And just as important is a dedicated staff. Whenever I was interviewing people for jobs, I would always ask them, 'What interests you in libraries?' If they said 'books,' I hired them on the spot."

O'Connell's retirement from Boston College in 1985 came at the very time that electronic sources of information were about to usher in a new era of library management. Instead of signing on entirely to the "paradigm shift," however, the agenda at BC has been to continue gathering books. "We've added close to another million volumes altogether since Tom O'Connell left," Robert K. O'Neill, the director of special collections at the John J. Burns Library of Rare Books and Manuscripts since 1987, said. "When a lot of university libraries were cutting back in the 1980s and 1990s, we maintained, and even increased, the volume of books and journals we acquired each year. We add about 36,000 volumes regularly, and we buy large collections en bloc when we have the opportunity." In 1998 O'Neill arranged the transfer of 35,000 volumes of Jesuit material from the Bibliothèque des Fontaines in Chantilly, France, a library north of Paris that began building its collection in the nineteenth century. "They used to have a school there, and they closed it down. They also compiled a Jesuit dictionary, so we knew it was a great reference library. The bulk of their books went to the municipal library in Lyon, but we got a terrific break on what we wanted, sort of one Jesuit institution helping out another." O'Neill concurred with O'Connell that aggressive library growth depends on the ready availability of money. "We have a $900 million endowment," O'Neill said late in 1999, and the figure was moving purposefully toward the billion-dollar mark The current chief librarian at Boston College, Jerome Yavarkovsky, readily agreed that gaining recognition as a premier research institution demands a strong library. "Numbers provide a threshold for respectability," he said, "but the quality still has to be there. Size is a reflection of quality, and that applies to print and electronic materials." What gave Yavarkovsky's words particular pertinence was the fact that when we spoke, Boston College was being considered for membership in the ARL, an accomplishment that would bring the institution additional esteem among its peers.

Duane E. Webster, a career librarian and executive director of the ARL since 1989, told me in the fall of 1999 that the Boston College application for admission to ARL membership would likely be approved the following year, and in fact it was. What the ARL found especially attractive about Boston College's application, Webster said, was the distinctive character of its collections. "Every library worth its salt is built on selectivity and organized around a set of solid intellectual principles. A research library collection is a composite of curatorial decisions over decades, sometimes over centuries. Part of what we look at in determining membership is that you are making a distinctive contribution to what we call the 'knowledge commons' as opposed to the 'intellectual commons.' That is because the American approach to knowledge is unique. We have this unique distributed collection of independent autonomous research libraries, whereas in other countries there are frequently government-supported research libraries. We don't really have a national library in this country. What we do have is a group of autonomous research libraries, which independently, by themselves, probably have richer collections than most countries have in the aggregate."

The availability of 474 million books among 122 research libraries assumes some duplication in the holdings, a factor that is not in dispute, particularly with regard to materials published in the United States. One of the traditional goals of the ARL has been to encourage the development of specialties, and from 1948 to 1972 an arrangement in force among members of the organization amounted to a portioning of the world outside North America along geographical lines, tailored to suit the strengths of individual institutions. Drafted in 1942 as a *Proposal for a Division of Responsibility among American Libraries in the Acquisition and Recording of Library Materials,* the agreement became known as the Farmington Plan, named for the town in Connecticut where the organizers gathered to adopt the guidelines. They met, in fact, at the Colonial home of the noted bibliophile and library benefactor Wilmarth S. Lewis, whose efforts to assemble and publish the enormous archive of the eighteenth-century writer Horace Walpole were chronicled in *Collector's Progress* and *One Man's Education.* Today Lewis's house is maintained as a special collections library by Yale University.

The Farmington Plan got its impetus in 1939 when the outbreak of war in Europe impeded access to important research materials by American scholars, and threatened numerous collections with destruction. At the urging of Archibald MacLeish, then the Librarian of Congress, suggestions for ways to fill gaps in American collections were formulated. An early version called *A Plan for Preserving the Records of Civilization Through the Instrumentality of the Library of Congress as a Trustee of the Nation* recommended the drafting of a "want list of all the valuable books and other documents not found in any of the great American libraries," and for acquiring "copies or microphotographs of this entire body of record for the Library of Congress so as to make it available to the nation."

As envisioned by its founders, the great American research libraries would select sections of the world, collecting intensively in those areas while "promoting agreements of specialization among libraries to the end that at least one copy of each such title might be placed in an appropriate library in this country," and avoiding needless replication. By 1947 the plan was refined to include "one copy of every work which might reasonably be expected to have interest to a research work in America," and by the following year it was in operation, allocating responsibilities to sixty institutions. Cornell University, which already had major Southeast Asia holdings, opted for Burma, Cambodia, Malaya, and Vietnam. Brandeis University, determinedly preeminent in Near Eastern and Judaic studies, laid claim to Israel, Saudi Arabia, Syria, Yemen, Oman, Egypt, Kuwait, Iraq, and Aden. The University of Florida, meanwhile, staked out the Caribbean, gathering material from Haiti, Guadeloupe, Jamaica, Netherlands Antilles, Leeward Islands, Barbados, Martinique, the Bahamas, Bermuda, the Dominican Republic, and Cuba. Northwestern University keyed on Africa; the University of California at Berkeley assumed responsibility for all publications issued in Korea, the Philippines, and Yugoslavia, with selected interest in Borneo, China, Hong Kong, and Tibet, and various Ural-Altaic, Far Eastern, and Oceanic languages and literatures.

Rivalries were inevitable, and frictions developed, but for twenty-four years the program worked with varying degrees of success. The reliance on a network of dealers caused some universities to grumble. "The immediate consequence was a limitation on the freedom of the individual library to select its books and its book agents," Robert Vosper wrote in a 1965 evaluation of the plan after asking members for their unfiltered views. His findings revealed widespread dissatisfaction with the program as conceived, and reductions in acquisitions budgets at many institutions made the continued authorization of blanket orders increasingly difficult. On December 31, 1972, the Farmington Plan was terminated, and institutions once again were on their own. Since then, research libraries have pretty much followed their own programs, but established specialties have in most instances been strengthened, and for more than twenty years, a spirit of cooperation was evident among independent libraries that leads some observers to believe a new kind of Farmington Plan tailored to the electronic age is possible.

Duane Webster cited an Andrew W. Mellon Foundation study published in 1992 that related the number of doctoral degrees granted during the twentieth century to the number of books added to research collections during the same period. The report—a composite of all ARL institutions—showed quite persuasively that when the number of books acquired in a given year went down, the number of Ph.D.'s awarded went down at a comparable rate, and when acquisitions began to pick up again, the number of doctorates granted increased right along with them. "It is hardly a coincidence that universities with large numbers of active doctoral programs are the same universities that have large—and growing—collections," the authors of the report argued. An examination of recent ARL statistics for Berkeley indicates that this finding remains relevant in the age of the Internet. In 1994, the university awarded 896 doctorates, more than any other institution in the United States, but as the print collections were cut back, the Ph.D.'s declined noticeably as well, reaching a low of 785 in 1999. In 2000—a year when expenditures for library monographs were $6 million, surpassed only by Harvard and Stanford—the number of doctorate degrees awarded by Berkeley rose to 804.

"These figures, while they are input measures, are the best description data for any institution," Webster said. "So numbers do matter. I really think they do. Our 122 libraries own close to 50 percent of the information resources in the United States. In 1998 we spent an aggregate of $727 million for acquisitions, of which 9 percent was invested in electronic resources. So for all the talk you hear, we are still primarily buying print. In any collection there will always be duplications, but what we are looking for among our members is breadth and depth. There has to be more than bulk."

In 1957 Paul H. Buck, the librarian of Harvard College and a prominent exponent of strength in numbers, put the institution's massive holdings in perspective. "The library does not collect books for the sake of collecting," he made clear. "It is not engaged in a statistical race with other libraries. Its great size would be a mere curiosity, not a source of pride, if a smaller collection could equally well meet the needs of Harvard and the scholarly world." Buck—a trained historian who won a Pulitzer Prize in 1938 for *The Road to Reunion*—offered further justification for gathering so many books by making a few pertinent comparisons: "The great foreign libraries, during the present century, at least, have been unable to acquire publications of countries other than their own on the scale that has been possible at Harvard. As a result, Harvard's collection on the French Revolution probably can be equalled only at the Bibliothèque Nationale. Its holdings on the Italian Risorgimento are stronger than those of any library outside of Italy, if not of any in the world. It is believed that Harvard's collection on German history surpasses any in Germany." As to what this superiority meant in terms of stature, Buck—who would later serve as provost of the university— offered this: "So long as its Library is outstanding, Harvard will have an extremely valuable advantage over other institutions in attracting and holding the best scholars and teachers." And central to maintaining dominance, he felt, was to continue buying more books than any other college or university year after year, a policy that has never wavered. "A library does not remain static when it stops growing—it rapidly decays. A collection that does not contain the results of the most recent research is a dying collection." When Dr. Buck offered that observation in the pages of the library's *Annual Report*, Harvard's collection was calculated at 6,085,761 volumes; forty-five years later, the number had more than doubled to 14,437,361.

I n 1965 the U.S. Congress passed the Higher Education Act as part of Lyndon Johnson's Great Society. Title II of that bill authorized an immediate infusion of federal funds to colleges and universities throughout the country to add heft to their programs. For the next seventeen years—until Ronald Reagan pulled the plug in 1982—billions of dollars were distributed for the purpose of building libraries, implementing new programs, and beefing up collections. The consequences were enormous, particularly among librarians at smaller schools who suddenly found themselves in a position to acquire materials they never dreamed they would be able to own. "What happened was that they went a little bit crazy," recalled Michael Ginsberg, a Massachusetts dealer who sold entire collections of secondhand, out-of-print, and antiquarian books to a number of institutions throughout the country during the heyday of Title II. "I did a lot of work with start-up institutions, and a lot of work with existing institutions that suddenly found themselves with large amounts of money that they had to use for books. I have estimated I handled something like a million books over a ten-year period, 1965 to 1975, and there were twenty-five or thirty other people around the country who were doing the same thing. It was a wonderful time to be a bookseller. No matter what I bought I could sell. I was selling between 85 and 90 percent of everything I bought, and the markups were anywhere from three, four, five to one."

Ginsberg handled institutional sales for the J. S. Canner Co. of Boston, which specialized in periodicals before the passage of Title II. "I went to work for Canner full-time in 1961, and it was my job to develop that end of the business. I have always had an instinct for going into a bookstore and pulling the good books off the shelves and leaving the others behind. I discovered when I was thirteen or fourteen years old that I could go into the Brattle Book Store down on Washington Street and buy a book for two dollars, then take it up to Goodspeed's on Beacon Hill and sell it for twenty-five dollars. We're talking about a four-block difference here, a five-minute walk at most. I was intrigued by the discovery that the same book was priced differently in different bookshops. When I was supplying books to institutions, I went scouting all over North America to find stock. I developed certain skills. I would go into a bookshop and I would go through the place in an hour, leaving piles on the floor with my business card. They would ship it on to us, and we would pay our bills on receipt of the material. I made about a dozen trips to Japan over the years, and I opened up a number of universities there. In one deal I sold fifty thousand books to Simon Fraser University in Canada."

When Ginsberg took over the book department for Canner in 1961, total sales were $40,000 a year. "By 1965 I had it up to $450,000 a year, and it rose up in the early 1970s to where it was about three-quarters of a million a year. It was a golden era for eight to ten years, when librarians really were the people who counted. You didn't think in terms of private collectors, you didn't think in terms of museums, you didn't think in terms of historical societies, you geared your business to the university libraries who had the money to spend."

Content matters to institutions, of course, but in their frantic efforts to establish credibility quickly, quantity can be even more crucial than quality. "There was a time in the not-so-distant past when some academic libraries bought a lot of things in order to spike their numbers," David H. Stam, the retired librarian at Syracuse University, acknowledged in an interview. "That is one reason why I am not overly concerned about a lot of the books that are quietly being eased out of large library collections now. The truth is that so many of them were worthless to begin with." Michael Winship, a noted bibliographer who teaches at the University of Texas at Austin and is a prominent exponent of the academic discipline called history of the book, addresses the issue from another tack. "I am a great believer in benign neglect as a conservation technique," he said, agreeing in principle with policies being practiced at a number of large libraries—Cornell University, to name just one—that allow thousands of brittle books of minimal scholarly value to die of natural causes without attempting any heroic measures to save them.

The examples of two recently established state universities, each opened at a time when the full implications of the Internet and the World Wide Web were beginning to take hold throughout America, suggest the attitude that some educators will be adopting in the years ahead, especially those not constrained by existing library policies. Each of these institutions—California State University at Monterey Bay and Florida Gulf Coast University at Fort Myers—issued mission statements that underscored their reliance on technology to implement programs of "distance education," an emerging version of the correspondence courses so popular in the United States during the 1800s.

The decision to open the twenty-second campus in the California State University system—the next rung down from the nine "UC" campuses, which include UCLA and Berkeley—on a beautiful site overlooking the Pacific Ocean was made shortly after the Department of Defense announced it would be closing Fort Ord in Monterey, an Army base since 1917, and for many years the home of the Seventh Light Infantry Division. "We see this as a campus of opportunity," John C. Ittelson, director of distributed and online learning, told me in an interview. "We were given 1,385 acres of a forty-six-square-mile base, and we were informed that we had a year to make a university out of it. It was never in the state's master plan to have a campus here."

It was never in the state's master plan to have a library there either, although one was worked into the scheme when word leaked out that books were not a part of the equation. A former ammunition dump was selected as the site and hastily converted into a book repository. "You simply don't have to build a traditional library these days," was the explanation offered by Barry Munitz, chancellor of the California State University system at the time. He made that comment to a writer for *News-week* magazine for quotation in an article titled "Wiring the Ivory Tower."

Even with a building on campus known as a library, the primary purpose of Cal State Monterey Bay has never been one of supplying printed books to students. In the spring of 2001, the university's total holdings numbered just forty thousand volumes, twenty-five thousand of which were bought in 1995, the first year students attended classes, meaning that only fifteen thousand books were added in the first six years of operation. "The issue here is access to information, and how we get the materials our students need," Ittelson told me. Getting people to do things differently "is a process of seduction," he made clear. "If we had all the money in the world, we couldn't create this humongous library that everybody seems to think we need."

In a curious extension of logic, one factor that argues against forming a comprehensive library of printed books is what Ittelson described as "our toilet-flushing problem," a severe lack of water that limits the number of students the university can accommodate at any one time. "We have less than 4 percent of the old Fort Ord camp site, which means that our water allocation is limited to 4 percent of what is available. The net effect is that we will never be able to serve more than ten thousand students here on campus, yet the state of California has gone on record as saying that this university needs to serve twenty-five thousand students. So what do you do to reach this goal? We have put in place a very aggressive plan for what we call 'distributive learning,' which means that by the year 2005, most of our students will be off campus." Most students, as a consequence, will take their courses by computer, do their research online, and turn their papers in by e-mail. For those attending classes in person, the library remains more of a "learning center" than a repository of books. "It's a philosophical change partly brought about because of confined resources, but it also is a way of identifying the problems that we are trying to solve." Any further doubts about how incidental printed books are to the curriculum are dispelled by a "collection policy" the university posts on its website:

To the extent possible and economically feasible, the CSUMB Library uses electronic resources instead of print. Therefore, what would usually be termed library collections has been redefined at CSUMB to broadly incorporate access to materials as well as ownership of them; to license and/or acquire relevant electronic publications for onsite use; and to put in place a core collection of important print materials not available in other formats.

Prospective students who are uncomfortable with this policy are bluntly encouraged to apply someplace else. "In a traditional institution, change is a marginalized activity," Peter P. Smith, the university's founding president, told a writer for the *Chronicle of Higher Education* shortly after the college opened. "In this institution, change is at the core." And the direction, he emphasized, is clearly plotted. "If you think that technology is the worst thing in the world, then you really shouldn't come here."

At Florida Gulf Coast University in Fort Myers, a 760-acre campus built on what was once a tract of pine uplands and cypress swamps on the edge of the Everglades, the mission statement strikes a familiar tone: "The virtual space characteristics of the 21st Century library will provide an electronic environment or process for teaching, learning, and accessing information wherever it is located or needed." The university's announcement that it had spent $750,000 outfitting twenty-three classrooms with their own "teaching podiums," each unit described as a "multimedia lectern" that enables teachers to display images from every imaginable electronic source, prompted the *St. Petersburg Times* to give Florida's tenth state university the nickname "Virtual U."

Unlike California State University Monterey Bay, which was forced to improvise an academic program in little more than twelve months, Fort Myers was a deliberately planned operation six years in the making. At one point in the early stages of development, Roy E. McTarnaghan, the newly appointed president of the university, declared his intention to create a library that would "be no larger than a telephone booth." When

Dr. Carolyn M. Gray accepted an offer in 1994 to leave Brandeis University in Waltham, Massachusetts, to become dean of library services at Florida Gulf Coast University, she was aware of McTarnaghan's remark, but knew it was an impossible goal to implement, at least in the short run.

"Dr. McTarnaghan made that statement, but he had quickly been persuaded that such a library was not yet possible," she said. When Gray learned about the Florida institution's plan to be a "different kind of university," she was attracted by the opportunity it offered a librarian with her particular background and temperament. "I have worked in technology since I got into the library field in 1976," she said. "My job at Brandeis was to bring the first full-fledged electronic library online. Now I had an opportunity to apply the values and the vision that I had been developing all those years toward the creation of a new kind of library." But with all the technological wonders that were envisioned, Gray never doubted that she still needed books. "I worked very closely with the planners and the architects, and I made it pretty clear that we needed space for at least two hundred thousand volumes. Even if our ultimate goal is to develop a total virtual library, that is something which is impossible to achieve right now, so that was never my interest or intent. At one time our president may have thought, as part of his vision for the university, that it was achievable. But the fact remains that if we wanted to function as a university, we had to have books."

So instead of supervising the installation of a building the size of a telephone booth, Gray set about the more mundane task of assembling a conventional print collection. On the day that FGSU welcomed its first 2,700 students on campus in 1997, she had put together a core collection of 130,000 volumes, many of them highly desirable academic titles long out of print, and normally unobtainable on such short notice. How Gray managed to get the books is a testament to good timing and decisive action, those two fortuitous qualities, combined with the unfortunate demise of a small liberal arts college a thousand miles away in East Orange, New Jersey.

In May 1995, after 102 years of continuous service, Upsala College granted bachelor's degrees to its last class of graduates. Faced with $12.5 million in debt and declining enrollment, the school declared bankruptcy and turned all of its assets, including a 125,000-volume library, over to a trustee for liquidation. "When I heard that those books were available, I went immediately to Dr. McTarnaghan and got his authorization to put in a bid for the liberal arts portion of the collection, which came to about 65,000 volumes," Gray said. "I didn't want the social science and science books they were offering because that was all badly outdated material. But the general materials were exactly what we were looking for. We paid about $450,000."

Had she tried to get the same books on the open market—assuming all of the out-of-print titles were available at any one time—Gray believes she would have had to spend as much as $4 million, based on the going rate for other books. "The current average cost of a new library book right now is $51 a volume; that is the average cost of academic books in print," she explained. "If we were going to buy 55,000 volumes at $51 a book, we would be committing $3 million right there." To supplement the Upsala acquisition, the university in fact did spend another $5 million, bringing its core collection up to 130,000 volumes, a respectable number for any first-year institution, and prompting the fiscally minded university president to nominate Gray for a state efficiency award.

To get the library functioning as quickly as possible, Gray "outsourced" every bibliographical task, including the cataloging of all the books, which was done by the Online Computer Library Center, Inc. of Columbus, Ohio, known as OCLC. "Upsala used the old Dewey decimal system, and we were going over to Library of Congress," she said. "OCLC sent a crew of fourteen people down here for six weeks, and did the whole thing for about $6 a volume." Meanwhile she hired the Academic Book Center of Portland, Oregon, which specializes in building institutional libraries, to coordinate the purchase of new titles. "We knew what programs we would be offering, but we had no faculty in place yet to suggest the titles they wanted for the courses they would be teaching. So what the Academic Book Center did was take the program areas we knew we would be teaching, and then analyzed the holdings of libraries at peer institutions. Because everyone's books are listed in the OCLC data base, we could compare the titles they have with the ones we had acquired from Upsala. We planned to teach criminal justice, for instance, so we examined the collections at John Jay School of Criminal Justice in New York. We then put together what we called a 'gap title list' to tell us what we still needed to acquire."

Any parent who has ever taken a son or a daughter off on a tour of prospective colleges learns after a while to anticipate the introductory drill by rote. A campus visit usually includes a stroll through the dining hall, a look at typical dormitory rooms, a peek at the athletic facilities, and an admiring walk through the library, where an estimate of the institution's total holdings is always given, particularly among the prestigious liberal arts colleges of the Northeast—places like Amherst, Bard, Bates, Bowdoin, Bryn Mawr, Colby, Connecticut College, Hamilton, Middlebury, Trinity, Smith, Swarthmore, Mount Holyoke, Vassar, Wellesley, Wesleyan, Williams—which pride themselves in the strength of their print collections. The idea of having a library the size of a telephone booth would not be greeted with much enthusiasm by many alumni who contribute generously to their endowments, or for that matter by bright young high school graduates intent on securing the finest possible educations in an excruciatingly competitive world, and access to the most appealing research materials, electronic as well as print.

For institutions that direct their energy and resources to educating undergraduates, a library of 200,000 volumes is considered a respectable collection. Four hundred thousand is above average, and half a million or more is excellent. Liberal arts colleges that approach the million mark represent an elite handful, and it is no coincidence that institutions reporting holdings in that area are usually esteemed among the very best in the nation. A typical example is Oberlin College, a five-star institution twenty-five miles southwest of Cleveland, Ohio, with 2,900 full-time students, 2,300 of them undergraduates enrolled in the College of Arts and Sciences, the others in the internationally renowned Conservatory of Music. Total holdings, according to Ray English, the director of libraries, number 2 million items representing all media, including uncataloged government documents. "Books are very much a part of the calculus here," he said. "We assume that very strong local collections are essential for good undergraduate work." By "local," English means books that are "in-house and immediately available to our students and faculty." On average, Oberlin acquires 24,000 new books a year—more than half of the total holdings considered adequate at California State University at Monterey Bay after six full years of operation—and does very little in the way of discarding.

"We do some deaccessioning, but largely in the area of duplicates, things that are superseded and no longer meet the needs of the curriculum or research interests of faculty. And we keep a substantial portion of our collection in storage. The issues go well beyond usage, they go to questions of whether or not the need that the book was addressing when it was originally purchased still exists. We have in some instances withdrawn print copies of material when a different format, microform or electronic, was suitable, or when the print volumes were no longer usable." English said his annual budget for acquisitions is $1.8 million.

"The driving force in the finer liberal arts colleges is to sustain an intense academic environment, and that requires libraries to have superb collections. But it is not a question of purchasing everything. You need to carve out your own niche, which means you also need to draw on shared resources." So even with access to a superb collection on their campus, Oberlin faculty and students still borrow heavily from other institutions, mostly through a consortial arrangement known as OhioLINK, which facilitates rapid borrowing among all academic libraries in the state.

Oberlin's spacious central library, built at the center of an attractive campus, is the hub of the academic community. Founded in 1833, the college prides itself in having always been at the forefront of change in higher education, a trendsetter in a number of key areas. "We were the first coeducational college in the United States, the first to admit African Americans on a regular basis, we have been among the first to explore interdisciplinary academic programs," English said. But the college has never tinkered with the traditional concept of the library, or minimized the role books serve in the curriculum. A former library director at the college, the late William A. Moffett Jr., was the driving force in organizing an informal consortium of academic librarians known as the Oberlin Group of Liberal Arts College Libraries, consisting of seventy-five institutions throughout the United States. Combined holdings of the member schools approached 37 million volumes at the beginning of the twenty-first century. Among the charter members of the group, Oberlin College and Smith College in Northampton, Massachusetts, each with about 1.2 million cataloged volumes, have the largest collections.

"There has been an argument going on for some time among librarians that what is important today is not ownership, but access," English said. Access, he explained, has several layers of meaning. On one level it assumes that books from other institutions are available through interlibrary loan; on another, it supposes that information can be obtained electronically over the Internet. "There are some people who argue that the building of what have been called 'just-in-case collections'—meaning that you acquire books that aren't in demand now, but might be in demand at some vague point in the future—is 'no longer supportable,' to use an economic term, in view of the costs involved. The counter argument to that is the traditional argument, that it is important for a high-quality institution to have a really good library, period. What we see developing now is an attitude that supports ownership *and* access, not one against the other. But there is still a great deal of debate going on in the profession."

Hampshire College in Amherst, Massachusetts, offers the interesting example of a prestigious liberal arts college that was established in 1970 with the stated goal of creating an "academic library in transition," one that would place a tacit value on printed books but at the same time aggressively pursue the new technologies that were about to arrive with an impact that even its founders were unable to predict. Built on five hundred acres of Connecticut River Valley farmland in the late 1960s with $6 million in seed money donated by Harold F. Johnson of Southampton, Long Island, Hampshire began as an experiment in modern education. A wealthy alumnus of Amherst College, Johnson put up the money after being favorably impressed by a "New College Plan" prepared by the faculties and administrators of his alma mater and their colleagues at Smith, Mount Holyoke College, and the University of Massachusetts at Amherst, all located within a few miles of the proposed campus. As jointly articulated by its founders, the idea was to explore new approaches to teaching that did not rely on traditional methods.

The first class of 250 men and women who arrived in the fall of 1970 were greeted with the hopeful motto *Non satis scire*—"To know is not enough." It was in that spirit that Hampshire introduced what was called a "design-your-own-degree curriculum" in which undergraduates had free rein to develop their own courses of study. As envisioned by its creators, students would advance through divisional examinations that required them to prepare individual research projects. No Scholastic Aptitude Tests were required for admission, no grades were given, and professors enjoyed the uncommon luxury of deciding what they wanted to teach. There were no departments in any traditional sense either, although disciplinary boundaries were divided into four general areas, Humanities and Arts, Natural Science, Social Science, and Communications and Cognitive Science.

In *The Making of a College*, published in 1966 and designated by the Hampshire archivist as the institution's Working Paper Number One, Franklin Patterson, the founding president, declared that his mandate was to establish "a laboratory for experimenting with the ways the private liberal arts college can be a more effective intellectual and moral force in a changing culture." An essential element in the mix would be creation of an "experimenting and extended library," and to accomplish that goal, Patterson appointed Robert S. Taylor, founding director of the Center for the Information Sciences at Lehigh University to be director of the Library Center at Hampshire College. Taylor spent three years formulating a "prototype design" for what he termed "the academic library in transition." His findings, designated as Working Paper Number Two of the college, was published in 1967 as a book titled *The Making of a Library*.

"It is important to see the computer not only as an instrument which solves problems but also as a cultural and social artifact," Taylor declared in its pages. He made several predictions, a few of which were uncannily prescient: "The computer and related information technology, we believe, will be a pervasive influence in the culture of the latter part of this century" was one of the more obvious. Hampshire would quickly earn a reputation for being different, but books were not entirely eliminated from the plan. "The Library Center should be communications-oriented rather than book-object oriented," he determined, yet it also should "portray the range of media from print to sound to image, without destroying the book as a crucial cultural symbol," particularly since it represented "the creation of several millennia of civilized development."

Of paramount importance, Taylor believed, was to empower the library to "exploit all available channels and media of communication." With compact discs and the Internet still two decades away, he defined the additional "media of communication" to include "discs, tapes, slides, video tapes, and films," although he clearly anticipated the advent of undefined "electronic means." A "base point" in the strategy, Taylor maintained, was that the college "be bold in exploring the potential educational and economic advantages of new technologies for the support of learning." The idea at Hampshire, he proclaimed, was "to explore and test to see if the library can become something more than a sophisticated warehouse," a "step toward a deeper and more interactive learning process in the institution." Repeatedly, he called his model "a successor to the traditional book library."

Yet for all these bold pronouncements, there still had to be books, albeit the fewer the better, as far as Taylor was concerned. On opening day in 1970, he wanted no more than 30,000 volumes on hand, and his projections for growth extended thirty years into the future. "The book collection should never exceed 150,000 volumes for approximately 1500 students. A more likely figure is 100,000." Microforms, he advised, "should be used extensively for periodicals and serials," and fully one-third of the collection should always be "nonprint" media. "There are moments, and this is one of them, when we wish we did not have to use the word 'library,' " he wrote in a concluding chapter:

> The word carries too many connotations which, partially truth and partially myth, may not let the library get to tomorrow, may inhibit its adaptability. The term exaggerates the difference between print and other media. It emphasizes the warehouse rather than the dynamic process. It focuses on the physical objects rather than people. It impedes communication. It provokes a dichotomy between people who should be working together. All of these disadvantages have implications for operations and effectiveness, both now and in the future. We will, however, continue to use the word, but the reader should flag it in some way—perhaps quotation marks—so that he will stumble over it and begin to encase it in other contexts.

In the end, the central "communications" facility on campus was christened the Library Center. It was designed to house 200,000 volumes, although that number has never been reached, and all of the excess space has been allocated over the years to other functions. In 2001, thirty-one years after Hampshire admitted its first students, total library holdings were reported at 115,000 volumes, but a revealing compilation of statistics strongly indicated that usage of books among students and faculty was in no danger of becoming obsolete. The reason for this was the success of yet another founding premise of the college, the ready availability of books at Amherst, Smith, and Mount Holyoke colleges, and the University of Massachusetts, its older siblings in the Pioneer Valley. While Hampshire was free to "innovate completely," it retained the luxury of remaining "dependent on the other libraries for traditional sources."

Books, in other words, were in plentiful supply at the other colleges nearby, and under terms of what is known as the Five College Consortium, students from any of the five schools could take selected courses at any of the others, and use whatever "traditional sources" are held in their inventories. When Hampshire admitted its first students, a mere 18,000 volumes had been acquired, but with 2.5 million others available within a ten-mile radius at that time, ample materials were never more than thirty minutes away. By the year 2000, total holdings in the consortium had increased by 6 million volumes, reaching 5 million at the University of Massachusetts alone.

Circulation figures compiled by the Five College Consortium show that however free of conventional encumbrances Hampshire students may be in the way they design their curricula, they still get a great deal of use out of printed books. In the fiscal year ending June 30, 2000, they borrowed 84,891 titles from the other four schools, while loaning out 74,503, a fairly good indication that they need more material than they have immediately available to them. On the plus side, the numbers indicate that even though Hampshire borrows more books than it lends, it has built a collection that has proven useful to students and faculty at the other institutions in the valley. Indeed, the figures for all five of the schools show a healthy interchange of material—a total of 928,448 volumes shared among the colleges in a single year—persuasive evidence that individual collections have been built that do not overly replicate each other's strengths.

Looking back on his plan for the "experimenting library" from a remove of three decades, Taylor told me in a telephone interview that he was "amused" to think he had the audacity to make predictions that looked twenty-five years into the future. "Anything beyond five years these days is an exercise in science fiction. But I did not feel then, and I most definitely do not feel now, that the book is a dead species. One of the problems we had back then was trying to define where Hampshire College could really participate and provide some quid pro quo to the other colleges. I say this after the fact, of course, with the knowledge that more books are being bought at the college now than ever before, and I think this is a very heartening development."

Taylor conceded that his proposal to abandon use of the word *library* may have been "silly," but he reminded me that the era in which the proposal was being made encouraged departures from the norm. "You have to realize we were living at the end of the 1960s and there was a very real adolescent rebellion going on against tradition. And the book was immersed in that tradition. This is part of what Hampshire grew out of. We also made the mistake of having a pretty wide open library in the beginning, and we lost something like 15 or 20 percent of the books in our very first year. Let's be charitable and say they were borrowed and never returned, but the fact of the matter is that somebody was taking them out and not returning them. The kids wanted books, and given the lax attitude we permitted at the beginning, they were helping themselves."

Gregory Smith Prince Jr., the current president of Hampshire College, told me that the library has "moved into the second generation, and we are preparing for the third generation." A good deal of that, he added, involves an "aggressive approach" of having all five institutions in the consortium coordinate book acquisitions more carefully, "and become even more of a collective" in their holdings. "Here at Hampshire, we will move away from the preoccupation with technology and on to developing a policy of collections management, of who buys what. Historically, the dynamic in most book purchases is that the library responds to the needs of the faculty, and that is done as a single institution. What is coming is the need to balance that consideration with what the other four history departments are buying out here in the valley, to cite just one example. We really need to find a way to be effective and efficient in using scarce resources, and the library is one of the ways where it can be done effectively."

Significantly, a major element in Hampshire's plans for the next phase of its development is the design and construction of a new library wing that will allow for expansion of the printed collections, provide more reading space for students, and allow for a thorough reconsideration of the function of the library in academic life. As a college, Hampshire continues to be a work in progress, Prince stressed, and the renewed interest in printed books does not equate with a reconsideration of original values. "Conceptually, what happened thirty years ago is that this had to be a different kind of library if we were going to run a different kind of curriculum. We have a library that supports inquiry, but it does not attempt to provide *all* of the material that will support that inquiry. It works very hard to support all the processes that will make the necessary knowledge available to complete the active inquiry that is taking place. What becomes more critical, I believe, is the ability of the librarians and the staff to coach the students and faculty on ways to find the materials they need for the work they are doing. The book remains front and center in the process, but the guides to help our students find the books matter too. We are a very process-oriented educational institution that does not try in four years to provide all the content. We were created to be an alternative institution. But the truth of the matter is that none of this would work if we did not have the support of the four other schools."

The collective approach to building comprehensive book collections among a number of independent institutions is not unique to the Five College Consortium in western Massachusetts, and is best represented, perhaps, by the arrangement developed over the last seventy-five years in Claremont, California, where five undergraduate colleges and two graduate schools maintain separate faculties, administrations, and stylistically distinctive buildings on adjoining property, but share one "great central library" system of 2 million volumes for the use of all students and teachers, along with a special collections unit that contains 150,000 rare books and manuscripts.

Known as the Claremont Colleges, the cluster of small liberal arts institutions located thirty-five miles east of downtown Los Angeles in the San Gabriel Valley project an atmosphere that is more appropriate to the northeastern United States than it is to southern California, and the resemblance is not by happenstance. The town was founded as a resort by real estate speculators in 1884; when that venture failed three years later, a group of Congregationalist educators from Massachusetts and Connecticut bought up much of the land and opened Pomona College. Their intention from the outset was to establish a small, rigorous school in the "New England style," and the community that developed around them reflected their Yankee heritage. Once they cleared away the sagebrush and settled the dust, they planted thousands of oak and ash trees along the neighborhood streets to remind them of the countryside they left behind. At the center of the new community they installed a downtown district called the Village, a picturesque area with rustic touches that would not be out of place in rural Maine or Vermont, and for local government, they set up a town-meeting format. An initiative to become a city was approved by voters in 1907, but the residents still pride themselves in retaining a tradition of volunteer involvement in community affairs; the move to incorporation, in fact, was undertaken to avoid reliance on Los Angeles County for municipal services. Resident population in the city is now about 35,000 people, making the colleges by far the most important "industry" in the area. Many of the citrus farms that flourished in the foothill communities nearby prior to World War II have since been converted into housing developments.

In 1925 Pomona College president James A. Blaisdell decided to expand in a way that would retain the "richer intimacies" of a small liberal arts school but serve the growing number of young people who were interested in acquiring a high-quality private education on the West

Coast. Inspired by the example of Oxford University in England, Blaisdell created the first American college consortium by establishing the Claremont University Center, and made provisions for expansion by acquiring more land that would accommodate additional institutions, each independent from one another but sharing a nucleus of essential services, the library most prominent among them.

Scripps College—an all-women's school strong in the fine arts and sciences—was founded in 1926, followed by Claremont McKenna College in 1946, which emphasizes economics and government. The college of engineering and sciences, Harvey Mudd College, opened in 1955, followed eight years later by Pitzer College with its emphasis on social and behavioral sciences. The Claremont Graduate School began operations in 1926 and now offers master's and doctoral degrees in eighteen fields; the Keck Graduate Institute, specializing in biotechnology, opened in 1997. Each school has its own endowment and board of trustees, and the college presidents meet as a council to manage the consortium. Together, the seven institutions account for about 6,600 students, all but a thousand of them undergraduates, and like the Five College Consortium in the Pioneer Valley of Massachusetts, students enrolled in any of the Claremont Colleges can take courses offered in any of the others.

The group's librarians feel they have the best of both possible worlds. They have a collection of great scholarly breadth with holdings comparable to those of major research universities, yet each school maintains a small liberal arts college identity. Bonnie Clemens, director of the Claremont libraries, said that new books are added at the rate of 45,000 titles a year, 15,000 of which are individually purchased monographs. "Each college tells us what they want us to get, and they contribute financially on a formula basis to the operating budget and the acquisitions budget. The colleges are very strong and quite different from one another, which gives us a library that it would be quite impossible for any one of them to put together individually. We have a nice sort of balance here between cutting-edge technology and the book, but there is tremendous respect for the book, and undergraduates are encouraged to use the special collections."

Judy Harvey Sahak, the director of special collections, pointed out that most rare books and manuscripts have come by way of gifts. By far the best known is a collection of one thousand fifteenth-, sixteenth-, and seventeenth-century books on engineering, early science, metallurgy, mathematics, alchemy, and philosophy gathered in the early 1900s by Herbert C. Hoover during his years as a mining engineer. Herbert Hoover III, grandson of the thirty-first president of the United States, gave the books to Honnold Library in 1970. William Lincoln Honnold, for whom the library was named, had been a close friend of the bibliophile president. "The nature of the gifts we have received reflects the decision Pomona College officials made in the late teens that they did not want to become a large research university, they wanted to be esteemed among the very best liberal arts colleges in the country," Sahak said. "People who have been close to the program have understood that all along, and they have understood that when they give these wonderful collections to us, they are giving materials that will be used for the most part by undergraduate students in this kind of setting."

When Minor Myers Jr. was appointed president of Illinois Wesleyan University in Bloomington, Illinois, in 1989, he arrived on a mission to raise the school into the top tier of private liberal arts colleges in the United States. "The first thing I saw when I arrived was a library with well under 200,000 books, and I started complaining immediately," he told me in an interview that included a discussion of his own activity as a bibliophile (see chapter 3). "In many ways there is a minimal collection that you have to have, and we already had that, but there are other liberal arts colleges out there that have half a million books, a couple of them with a million, and if we had any thoughts at all of elevating ourselves into their company, one thing we needed was to get more titles on the shelves."

Myers committed himself to this strategy after receiving a report from an independent consultant who had been hired to evaluate the school's holdings. "This fellow was a big gun in the field of library science, and I suspect that what he thought we wanted was advice on how to get the most bang for our buck. I remember his words precisely. He said, 'You don't need any more books; what you need is more computers and a basic collection of *good* books.' My answer to that was, 'We all may agree readily on what a good book is, but tell me, sir, what is a *bad* book we should not have?' " To make sure everyone understood his attitude on the matter, Myers ordered that the rubber stamp bearing the word *discard* be removed from the library and sent to his office. "I have it on the shelf behind my desk," he said, "and that's where it stays; if any book has to go, for whatever reason—perhaps it's had its final breath of life and has to be replaced with a fresh working copy—I want to be informed." And instead of thinning the collection back as the consultant had recommended, he initiated a program of broadened acquisitions, announced his intention to double holdings by the year 2007 to 400,000 volumes, and undertook a campaign to raise $23 million for construction of a new library.

"We get suggestions from the faculty, and we are adding generally in the areas of history and literature. We got a great buy on sixteen hundred volumes of nineteenth- and twentieth-century poetry from the Argosy Book Store in New York for three dollars each. We are doing a lot of retrospective buying, which is a way of saying we are buying things we missed when they were brand-new. Indian history is another example; twenty years ago we didn't teach it at all, ten years ago we couldn't afford to buy the books. So we're getting them now, but we are shopping around." Buying books that are not "brand-new" is a skill, Myers said, one that behooves people who buy for institutions to master. "These books follow a funny pattern. They are a certain price when they are new, and they vary as they go to slightly out of print, and then on over to the remainder category, when they are at their cheapest. But then they reach a point where all of a sudden they are scarce, and then they start swinging over to rare, where the price suddenly starts to go up dramatically."

Two years after we had our first conversation, Myers called me at home one afternoon with some exciting news. "The board of trustees has just approved the new library," he said ebulliently. "We break ground in November." Most of the $23 million had been raised, he added, and the Boston architectural firm of Shepley Bulfinch Richardson and Abbott had designed a five-story structure centered around a circular core on the upper two floors, to be known as the Great Reading Room. Computer work stations will be present in abundance, but there also will be space available to shelve 400,000 books. "Great universities cluster around great libraries," Myers said. "If you want to be a great college, you need a great library. It's as simple as that."

Myers emphasized that he is not building up Illinois Wesleyan's infrastructure and print collections simply to achieve higher recognition among peer institutions. "It's not just a matter of status, it's a question of teaching, research, and imagination. The things you have available at hand for students on an immediate basis are just as important as teaching or research. What I want is something gloriously useful that offers a dazzling source of information for students. Rather than wait two or three weeks for something to come in on interlibrary loan, I want a lot of real live books, and I want them here. Serendipity is the imagination factor I am talking about. It is the material you find in the stacks when you aren't prepared to find anything. This may sound increasingly quaint in this day and age, but my idea of a college is a collection of students and faculty gathered around a great library, and here we will have a great reading room at the center of it all to make it happen."

11.

DEEP SLEEP

Books are faithful repositories, which may be awhile neglected or forgotten; but when they are opened again, will again impart their instruction; memory once interrupted, is not to be recalled. Written learning is a fixed luminary, which, after the cloud that had hidden it has passed away, is again bright in its proper station. Tradition is but a meteor, which if once it falls, cannot be rekindled.
—*Samuel Johnson*, A Journey to the Western Islands of Scotland

Thomas Carlyle's frequently quoted sentiment of the 1840s that a "true university" is "a collection of books" has been echoed by many professional educators over the years, though not always in the same crusty terms. For Archibald Cary Coolidge, a pioneering library director at Harvard College during the early years of the twentieth century, academic greatness was possible only if an "indispensable nucleus" of books was provided at the core. Coolidge's frequently stated credo—"There is no such thing as a dead book at Harvard"—is often credited with shaping what is now the strongest academic library in the world, and the largest library anywhere that allows authorized users the privilege of browsing through the stacks at will.

Unlike other institutions that see wisdom in constantly weeding their collections down to more manageable proportions, Harvard makes a determined attempt to keep everything it acquires, including material that has been lying around unused and gathering dust for decades.

Coolidge—who during times of budgetary restrictions was known to buy important material for the general collection with his own funds—believed that the best library combined quality with quantity. A wealthy bachelor who centered his life around Harvard, Coolidge was a "tireless exponent of the principle that every venture into a new area of university scholarship has to be backed with books," according to the historian William Bentinck-Smith. George Lane Kittredge, a member of the Faculty Library Council during Coolidge's tenure, once said of the Harry Elkins Widener Library stocked so admirably by his colleague that every other building in Harvard Yard "could burn to the ground and we would still have a university." Coolidge was warmly remembered by his friends for a speech defect that rendered him unable to pronounce the letter *R*. Asked once to identify the source of his extraordinary knowledge of the world, he is said to have replied, "Oh, I wead and I wewead and I bwowse awound."

As it entered the twenty-first century, Harvard reported 14.4 million books, magazines, journals, newspapers, and reels of microfilm among its holdings, making it a source of tremendous pride to faculty and students alike. "But even these amazing numbers do not measure the surpassing excellence of the collection," Michael McCormick wrote in the *Harvard Library Bulletin*. "For they are the best selected millions of volumes even the greatest scholar could imagine." Inevitably, McCormick made clear, a professor's perspective on the Widener Library centers on research and teaching and having the perception to make meaningful connections between the two. "To stand in Widener Library is to stand in one of the great achievements of civilization. To be a scholar and to stand in this place is an almost ineffable experience. I think it is the greatest research library in human history. This is the one place in the world where you can see almost any book that matters—any book, that is, any unit of knowledge, devised by man and preserved by man—usually within a matter of minutes, if not seconds."

Sometimes, if a title is unusually obscure and is stored off-site, a little more time is necessary, but the delay is rarely more than twenty-four hours. That is because a sizable portion of Harvard's books are kept not in Cambridge or Boston but on a satellite campus in the town of Southborough, Massachusetts, some thirty miles to the west in Worcester County. There, off a long narrow road in the middle of a 140-acre tract of dense woods, are two academic operations that go about their business with quiet efficiency, each functioning apart from the unending scurry of classroom activity in Cambridge, and each fully involved in the interests of teaching and the support of research.

The primary occupant of the property is the New England Regional Primate Research Center, operated by the Harvard Medical School in collaboration with a number of other Boston-area universities and teaching hospitals. Established with grants from the National Institutes of Health, it opened in 1966, and on any given day some two hundred scientists, support staff, and graduate students pursue various projects in comparative pathology and physiology, working with owl monkeys, squirrel monkeys, rhesus monkeys, and a dozen other species of nonhuman primates, about seventeen hundred animals in all. Work at the center has led to the discovery of a syndrome in monkeys that resembles AIDS; other findings have established that AIDS is caused by a virus, that nicotine is addictive, and that the herpes virus can cause leukemia. Because the center's work is criticized by activists who oppose medical research involving animals, it maintains a low profile, and no signs direct the way through the New England countryside to the Southborough Campus.

In 1986 another tenant, the Harvard Depository, took custody of six acres from the medical school, which has title to the land, and began shelving thousands of low-circulation volumes sent over from Cambridge inside an austere storage facility called a module, the first of six environmentally controlled buildings that would sprout up on the site over the next fifteen years, with plans afoot to erect another four at measured intervals. A tour of the immaculate, almost antiseptically clean complex, known by the acronym HD, evokes the halcyon experience of visiting the Valley of the Kings along the Nile River in Thebes, only here the resting place is for seldomly consulted books, not dead pharaohs. When ideas for the Southborough depository were being developed in the early 1980s, a small reading room was included in the blueprints at the behest of faculty members who were keen on retaining some bond, if only in spirit, with the volumes being sent off to deep sleep. Today the room is used for coffee breaks and conferences with visitors who come regularly to Southborough from around the world, most of them emissaries from other institutions eager to see at first hand the workings of what has become known in library circles as the Harvard Model.

Before moving out to Southborough, Harvard stored many of its low-circulation books at a poorly ventilated warehouse across the Charles River in Boston known as the New England Depository, which was established by a consortium of local institutions in the 1940s to free up shelf space in their primary facilities. In that arrangement, books were stored by size on conventional shelves. Widely referred to by library professionals as off-site storage, the practice of warehousing books has become increasingly attractive to universities reluctant to commit more and more space to shelving books on their central campuses. Yale University, Case Western Reserve University, Vanderbilt University, the Johns Hopkins University, the University of Missouri at Columbia, the University of Texas at Austin, and the University of California at Berkeley are among many American institutions with large research collections that have chosen to warehouse books that might otherwise be deaccessioned. In some instances, existing buildings have been acquired and modified. Ohio University converted a former car dealership into a book repository, and the University of Pennsylvania took over an old newspaper warehouse in Philadelphia. At Cornell University, a former apple orchard about a mile off campus became the site for its Harvard Model storage facility.

For its imaginative solution to the problem, the University of Minnesota looked no farther than the gently sloping bluffs that grace the west bank of its Twin Cities campus by the Mississippi River in downtown Minneapolis. On July 31, 1997, heavy earthmoving equipment began digging two parallel caverns underneath a 60-foot layer of limestone and topsoil, removing 2.5 million cubic feet of sandstone and shale over the next year. The completed shafts measure 600 feet in length by 65 feet wide, and each is 22 feet high. When the $46.3 million Minnesota Library Access Center opened in April 2000, it had a total storage capacity of 2.5 million volumes, with sufficient land reserved nearby for three additional tunnels as the need arises, a prospect officials feel will come sooner rather than later. The north cavern, set aside for university archives, was reported to be 85 percent filled within a year of operation; the south cavern opened with 15 percent of the storage capacity accounted for. A subterranean strategy of similar scope was undertaken in Stockholm by the Kungliga Biblioteket, or Royal Library of Sweden, between 1992 and 1997, when room for ten spacious *bokmagasiner,* or book chambers, was created by blasting 110,000 cubic feet of granite out of the ground, enough pulverized rock to fill 33,000 dump trucks; the rubble was hauled off for use in the construction of new railroad beds.

The Minnesota solution differs from its counterparts elsewhere in the United States in that it is not off-site at all, and its immediate proximity to campus allows for delivery of books by conveyer belt within an hour of receiving requests. Aboveground, another new facility, the four-story Elmer L. Andersen Library, houses eight special collections and archival units and the central offices for the subterranean center; the building is named for a former Minnesota governor and ardent bibliophile who donated an excellent collection of 12,500 volumes to the university and supported library development during his administration.

In a joint venture, officials of Columbia University, Princeton University, and the New York Public Library announced plans in 1999 to build a Harvard Model facility outside Princeton, New Jersey. "We will have the acreage for sixty years," Columbia's provost, Jonathan R. Cole, said, calling the agreement "a triumph of collaboration and cooperation."

Karin Trainer, university librarian at Princeton, made clear that printed books will remain integral to the school's mission. "We love acquiring," she said. "That's our job; to put our hands on as much material as we can. And then we have the responsibility to make sure that it is well preserved and accessible."

About the same time that Princeton, Columbia, and the New York Public Library were joining forces, four academic programs in Colorado were making plans for a collaboration of their own, one that added a new twist to the scenario by combining the books selected for off-site deposit by the four institutions into one centralized collection, creating in effect an entirely new library known as PASCAL, short for Preservation and Access Service Center for Colorado Academic Libraries. Joined in the venture are the University of Colorado, Boulder; the University of Colorado, Denver; and University of Colorado Health Services, each a publicly funded state institution; and the University of Denver, which is private. While such a strategy unquestionably will conserve space on the four campuses, a few eyebrows in the library community have been raised at a decision to avoid replication of titles by keeping just one copy of any particular book earmarked for storage, and discarding all the others.

"The whole point of this project is to free space in our libraries for new books and patron services," Scott H. Seaman, associate director for administrative services at the University of Colorado, Boulder, told me. Ideally, the copy that is in the best condition will be the one that is retained in the depository, but as a practical matter that will not always be possible, he conceded. "I expect that if we have one copy of a book, say, from the University of Denver already in PASCAL, and we are told a couple months later that we will be getting another from Boulder, my sense is that the first one is the one that will be the copy of record." The $4.4 million facility, a modified Harvard Model, was built on a parcel of land at the former Fitzsimons Army Medical Center in North Denver; the base was closed by the Department of Defense in 1998 and turned over to the state, which is using the site for a new $1.5 billion University of Colorado Health Sciences Center. Construction of the first PASCAL unit was completed in November 2000, and books began arriving in January 2001. "We have been assigned sufficient room on the property for four more modules," Seaman said. "This project does two things. The first is that it provides a long-term home for the scholarly record, and the second is that it accomplishes this very inexpensively."

In cases where seldom-used materials are no longer kept in central repositories, or where they are not even welcome in off-site storage facilities, one option has been to send books on the margins to an independent depository located on the campus of the University of Chicago known as the Center for Research Libraries. Established in 1949 by ten midwestern universities, the center's mission has evolved to the point where it is now regarded as a sanctuary of last resort for titles that might otherwise be headed for the shredder. Today, this "library for libraries," as it styles itself, receives material from several hundred institutions throughout North America, all of it "rarely used" and largely unwanted. "We have about five million items that we hold in common for our members," Beverly P. Lynch, the president of the consortium, known by the acronym CRL, told me.

"If we find that a title being offered to us is held in more than five institutions, we make a judgment on whether or not we will want to keep it here. Usually we will suggest that some provision for the book be arranged elsewhere, since scarcity is one of the components we work with. We have become a unique collection by virtue of the fact that everything we have is not, for the most part, retained in other research libraries. A curious sidelight to all this is that we are not a collection that was built by careful selection, but by what you might call careful deselection, since what we do is accept deposits of unwanted and superseded materials from our member institutions. But after fifty years, the collections have become collections of international importance, because nobody else has them."

During my visit to CRL, I saw thousands and thousands of books in long rows of compact shelving, large runs of obscure foreign newspapers wrapped in brown paper and stacked on wooden skids, mounds of government reports, hundreds of course catalogs from colleges and prep schools, many of them dating from the early nineteenth century. Maintained alphabetically on one floor alone are 750,000 printed dissertations, a good percentage of them in foreign languages, and the largest collection of its kind in the world. "There was an antiquarian bookseller who had the chutzpah to offer us a thousand dollars for our copy of Walter Benjamin's doctoral thesis," Lynch told me. "I have decided to keep that one in the vault where it will be safe." Once books are sent to Chicago by any of the three hundred participating institutions, they become the property of CRL and are available for use by scholars, either in a small reading room maintained in the building, or on temporary loan. Traffic averages about forty thousand requests a year, confirming the viability of the collection. "I think that all collections should be alive," Lynch said, "and this is one creative way to do it."

At the Harvard Depository in Southborough, books arrive daily by truck and are unloaded in a central processing unit where staff members prepare them for storage. The $3.3 million it now costs to build the modules—the first four storage units erected in the 1980s and early 1990s cost about $2 million each—remains a remarkably reasonable figure, given the fact that each is capable of storing between 2 and 3 million books, although some space is allotted to institutional archives, files, correspondence, and other records. By the beginning of 2001, six modules and one cold-storage vault for film and magnetic-based materials were in place, with space available to accommodate four more units in the initial six-acre complex, for a total capacity of 26 million books, or "book equivalents."

One reason the Harvard Model works so smoothly, the manager of the facility, Ronald A. Lane, told me during a tour, is because the approach is one of storage, not scholarship. "A basic underlying concept is that this is not a library," Lane said as he led the way through Module 1, a squat building of pure function laced with warrens of book-bearing bulkheads engineered to use every inch of available space, and the paradigm for all variations that have followed since its installation. "We don't deal with cubic feet here, we deal with what we call BSF, or book storage feet." The shelves rise to a height of forty feet, with the largest volumes stored in plastic trays on the bottom, and the smallest books, reachable only by a battery-powered forklift known as a "man-aboard," on top. "This module is fitted with nine thousand shelves, giving us a total of 150,000 BSF. Each shelf is thirty-six inches deep by fifty-three inches wide, and if you look closely, you will see very little open space on top of the books. That is because we shelve books strictly by size, not by subject. If you picture a normal library shelf, you have tall books and short books kept together because they deal with the same topics, and it's half air. Most libraries keep books together by subject matter. What we do is eliminate the air, and we do that very simply by sorting the books for size, not topic."

The environment in each module is cycled seasonally by computer to maintain precise levels of temperature and humidity, then scrubbed through charcoal filters to remove impurities; all lighting is by sodium vapor lamps. "We're not just a storage facility, we're also a preservation facility. The controls we have in place here increase the life of paper-based media considerably," he said, though exactly by how much remains to be determined. Lane's background is in industrial warehousing, not education, an important distinction to emphasize in the context of his assigned responsibilities. He refers to each of Harvard's libraries as "customers," and the books entrusted to his care as "inventory," which he manages in individual "accounts." Law school books are kept with law school books, medical school books with medical school books, divinity school books with divinity school books, and so forth down the line for the entire university. "We don't mix customers together when we sort, we don't mix them in trays, and we don't mix them on shelves. It keeps the customers and their media together; the customers are very edgy about having their books mixed in with anyone else's."

If Lane is asked to locate a book by title or author, he maintains that he "wouldn't have a clue" on how to find it. "That is because every book that comes in here is identified by the different customers with their own bar codes. We unpack books as they come off the loading dock, we take them to that processing area you see over there, and we use a very simple template to determine what size tray we are going to put them in. Then we put our own bar code on the tray to identify the location." Every day, Lane's crew follows a carefully structured timetable. Books sent in from Cambridge are processed for storage in the morning, books requested for return the next day are retrieved starting at three-thirty in the afternoon. "Let's say someone from Widener calls up and says they want 'Harvard Widener FTX9,' " Lane said, reading an item off that day's work schedule. "All they give us is their own bar code number. The computer is going to tell me it's in Aisle 2 on the left, Ladder 2, Shelf 6, TA10357 on the front." About 2,000 books are retrieved each week in this manner, some 100,000 titles a year, and in the first fifteen years of operation, every book that has been requested has been located. "We are not allowed to lose books," Lane said. "We maintain an unblemished retrieval record, knock on wood."

Because the Houghton Rare Books and Manuscript Library is one of his "customers," Lane assumes that some books of value are sent to him. "We have no idea what they are because we don't deal with selection, and all the cataloging is done on the customer's end. I could have the Gutenberg Bible here, and I wouldn't know I had it. All I know is the bar code, and what kind of tray I'm going to put it in." While the likelihood of any uncommonly rare book being stored in Southborough is not particularly high, what Lane does know is that books sent to the depository usually go there because they are "low-retrieval" items, meaning they are books, journals, periodicals, and rolls of microfilm that nobody has asked to see in years, and are not likely to want any time soon. Harvard has chosen to keep these items rather than deaccession them as so many other libraries in the United States have been doing with increasing regularity. The policy at some libraries pressed for space has been to discard books that have not been used by students or faculty, in some cases for as few as five years. For his part, Lane has nothing to do with deciding whether any of the volumes sent to him are candidates for deacidification and rebinding, or for conversion to microfilm or electronic format. "That is not my job or my concern; we just store."

Barbara Graham, the associate director of the university library in charge of administration and programs, whose responsibilities include preservation, supervision of university archives, and oversight of the Harvard Depository, cited the human factor as being critical in the success of HD. "We have a wonderful staff, which is absolutely essential, because this is a labor-intensive operation. One of the ways that technology will assist the scholar is to provide enhanced intellectual access to material that might not be close at hand. We're talking about really robust, persistent, and enduring metadata here." Graham has been involved with HD since its inception, and has noted several significant changes over the past two decades.

"Book storage is very much an evolving science," she emphasized, particularly in areas involving HVAC—"heat, ventilation, and air-conditioning"—systems designed to extend the life spans of books by centuries. "Basically these modules are huge environmental boxes. This complex of buildings looks like a sophisticated warehouse, but it really is a laboratory, and the zero-defects rule is taken very seriously here. I think we are constructively reflective about our responsibilities. Our concern is that we are doing the right thing in the right way with regard to the materials."

One tangible modification to the original Harvard scheme was the recent adoption of a design that allows for greater storage capacity. The concept was pioneered at Yale University, where two units 50 percent larger than the first four Harvard modules went on line in 1999; Modules 5 and 6 in Southborough followed a similar pattern, enlarging available space in the new units from 8,500 to 13,500 square feet, increasing capacity from 2 million items to substantially more than 3 million per unit.

A future innovation in remote storage could involve the use of robotics for retrieval, an approach being developed at a facility operated by the University of California at Northbridge. As seductive a solution as automation may be, however, it has been tried before in the library world with varying degrees of success. In one infamous instance at the Health Sciences Library at Ohio State University, a huge machine designed to shelve and retrieve up to 200,000 volumes was dismantled and removed after twenty years of sputtering operation. Known as the Randtriever, the device was designed by engineers at the Sperry-Rand Corporation and marketed in the late 1960s and early 1970s as a first-generation compact storage-and-retrieval system. Five were sold altogether, the first installed in the Netherlands at Erasmus University in Rotterdam, the second at a new Health Sciences Library built by Ohio State University in Columbus in 1972 specifically to accommodate it. The three others were placed in smaller libraries in Bloomington, Indiana; Logansport, Indiana; and Ankeny, Iowa. Each system housed a tower of metal shelving, two floors in height. Books were stored in random order in colored plastic baskets that could be mechanically stacked and retrieved via conveyor tracks. When a title was requested at the circulation desk by call number, an attendant would enter a corresponding number into the Randtriever, initiating the process.

At Ohio State, a 120,000-volume collection was placed in random order in the $812,000 system, code-named RT. From the very beginning, according to one university report, "it was apparent that the RT could not handle the mechanical stress of retrieving items," and heavily used materials were removed from the system and placed on conventional shelves. The university made every attempt to make the machine work efficiently over the twenty years it was in operation, but finally gave up in frustration. Maintenance costs averaged $300,000 a year, while books were damaged or lost altogether. On August 23, 1992, the RT was shut down for good, and the bulk of the collection was moved to remote storage. "The very last book removed from the RT was *Orthoptics: A Discussion of Binocular Anomalies,*" the university reported with obvious relief, its ill-fated adventure in automated book storage mercifully ended. For the next four years the unwieldy contraption remained immobile behind a glass wall, a monument to mechanical folly. Its removal in 1996 was celebrated with a total rehabilitation of the building and the installation of compact shelving. The other four Randtriever systems, meanwhile, were abandoned as well.

Sidney Verba, the Carl H. Pforzheimer University Professor at Harvard, and director of the Harvard University Library, agrees that there is no "single, simple solution" to the dilemma facing research libraries, noting that collections "continue to grow," at accelerating rates, "but facilities do not." The HD concept, he said, is "designed to provide a safe environment for the secure preservation of materials, and with a mandate to be responsive to libraries and researchers, is our best possible solution." Depending on whose count you accept, Harvard University has anywhere from ninety to one hundred "libraries" in its system, a number that is very hard to pin down because of varying definitions of what constitutes a formal library. Factors involve such considerations as whether or not a specific collection is maintained by its own staff, whether it is part of a particular college or department, or whether it is a distinct element of a larger collection. The university also has a library in Italy that serves medieval scholars, and another at Dunbarton Oaks in Washington, D.C., specializing in Byzantine history. "What I do know is that we have millions of books, and it is the policy of the university to keep them, not dispose of them," stressed Kenneth E. Carpenter, assistant director for research resources and the person responsible for deciding which books will stay in the university's largest book sanctuary, Widener Library, and which ones must go off to the depository in Southborough.

While Lane's job is to "just store," the far more delicate task of deciding which books are removed from general circulation in the Widener Library belongs to Carpenter. "Let me say first of all that Harvard *has* done some weeding over the years, but very, very little, and it tends to have been done in outlying libraries of the system. I know, for instance, that we used to have a copy of the proceedings of the Royal Academy of Sciences in Stockholm, a huge set of books that went back to the eighteenth century and was the journal of one of the leading scientific societies of Europe. At some point, someone in a science library or some-place like that, I don't know who because there is no paper trail, decided, 'Who reads this, we need the space,' and got rid of it. And now we don't have it anymore. We do have the German translation of the eighteenth-century edition, but we don't have that Swedish edition. And that bothers me a lot, because Harvard is a place where there are going to be people who will be interested in those books. As a matter of fact, I read Swedish, and I wanted to consult those journals. That's how I discovered they were gone."

Prior to moving over to Widener in 1980, Carpenter was for twelve years curator of the Kress Library of Business and Economics at the Harvard Business School, one of the finest collections of books on economics maintained anywhere in the world, and notably strong on materials published before 1850. "I used to buy eighteenth-century books on economics that were uncut, meaning that they had never been used in the two hundred years since they had been printed, and could very easily go another two hundred years before someone wanted them, which was just fine with me. I figured that a day will come along when someone needs them, and they will be there. Some books have not been used because of their rarity, and adding them to a great library increases the chances of their being discovered. When you begin to have a significant percentage of all the economic literature that has been published in the world, which happens to be the case at Kress, it becomes all the more useful when you continue to increase the quantity. I have the view that it matters very much where a book is located. If a given book is outside the major research libraries, of which there are not all that many, then it can very well remain outside the body of literature that gets cited in footnotes and is used repeatedly by scholars. When it gets into one of the great libraries, that increases its chances of becoming part of the body of literature in a particular field."

Because a library, as Vartan Gregorian maintained, is the soul of a university, scholars take very seriously the suggestion that any books, regardless of how infrequently they are used, should be removed from campus and sent to a warehouse where they are not going to be discovered by students and researchers poking their way through the stacks. At least one prominent librarian, David C. Weber, the director emeritus of libraries at Stanford University in Palo Alto, California, feels that "just because books are 'retired' is no reason to strip them of their intellectual associations." At the Stanford Auxiliary Library, an off-site facility that opened during his stewardship, "access to the shelves is routine and browsing continues to help the scholar pursue his or her reasoning. Not keeping most books in classified order will sooner or later be realized as deplorable." Weber's adamant belief is grounded in the conviction that "book collections are and will remain the primary treasures in which scholars in humanistic disciplines mine intellectual ores."

Harvard's position on the wisdom of maintaining a preeminent research collection is clear, and the university's librarians are confident they have enacted procedures that will assure access to its most obscure items. "We have developed specific guidelines for choosing the books that go out to the depository," Carpenter said as he led me to Room D-N91 in the basement level of Widener, a transit area where books recently culled from the stacks had been loaded onto metal book trucks and were being readied for transit to Southborough. A random look at some of the spines disclosed such titles as *Economics of Agriculture Production, Beef Cattle, Land Use, Part-Time Farming,* all of them undoubtedly pertinent to their respective subjects at some distant point in time, but none of them recent titles. Another metal truck was filled with several dozen books in the Ukrainian language and printed in Cyrillic, which had also been selected for some reason other than their language.

"It takes me about an hour and a half to fill up one of these dollies here," Carpenter said. "With specific regard to literature, when I first started doing this, I wanted to make sure that the best books were staying, and not leaving. So I would go to encyclopedias and draw up lists of authors who were important, making sure they remained in the library. Then one day it dawned on me that what I was really doing was reinforcing the established canon, and that I was shaping scholarship in a very traditional and conservative way. I realized that I needed to develop some very flexible guidelines that would not get in the way of serendipity. I have a daughter who was working on her Ph.D in French literature here at the time, researching French women authors of the eighteenth century, authors she found here in these stacks, but authors you will never find mentioned in any encyclopedia. This was one of those epiphanies you hear so much about, and it made a huge impression on me. What I had been doing was reinforcing traditional canons. By removing some of these books, I was preventing any possibility of a student discovering new authors of importance, and this has always been a part of the process of scholarship."

After consulting with faculty, Carpenter developed a policy that seemed fair to everyone. "What finally made sense is that even these canonical authors often were on the shelves with lots of their books unused, or editions of their books unused, so that instead of bypassing them, I should send out some of the books of the people who are not going to be forgotten. The point is that we know who they are, and if we need additional copies, we can always bring them in from the depository—and also keep on the shelves at least one book of every single author."

Books sent out to the depository are on twenty-four-hour recall, but a student or teacher first has to know they exist. Removing an obscure author entirely from Cambridge reduces the possibility of a chance discovery. "Harriet Beecher Stowe is not an obscure author, but she is a good example of what I am talking about. We will without question keep

Uncle Tom's Cabin in Widener, for instance, but we probably will send her first book, a totally outdated volume on world geography that nobody ever asks to see, out to the depository. And we are following this policy now with all our literature collections, Danish, Finnish, Latvian, Estonian, Greek, Arabic, the whole works." Because some academic departments are smaller than others, anxious faculty sometimes will be opposed to any move that might be seen as a threat to their continued existence. "A recent example was Celtic," Carpenter said. "The people there are already edgy because it is a small department. They fear that sending their books off to exile could be perceived as a first step to eliminating the department. So you have to talk to them and reassure them that they are not being picked on. I don't happen to read the Celtic languages, but a graduate student who does is using the guidelines that the faculty members and I agreed on, and that student is pulling the stuff and listing it for storage."

Included among the books Carpenter chose for deposit in Southborough were some recently purchased titles, a circumstance that in most institutions would raise questions about why they had been acquired in the first place. "I was terribly worried about drawing up guidelines for sending *new* material off to the depository, because I thought someone might say, 'Well, if we are sending these books out there right from the beginning, maybe we shouldn't even be buying them at all.' For some blessed reason, nobody has ever said that to me; this is Harvard, after all. These are things we feel we should have, and they are there for the future." According to the guidelines drawn up by Carpenter and reviewed by the faculty, the kinds of new books Harvard buys and sends straight off to the depository include institutional histories, amateur local histories, books printed on acidic paper that are "clearly going to self-destruct," works written about recent events in foreign languages, and books "that are likely to be stolen from Widener, books, let's say, like histories of erotic art."

Other candidates for storage are even easier to select. "Do we need five hundred volumes of philatelic material here?" Carpenter asked. "We had twenty-six shelves of technical and training manuals produced by the U.S. War Department, a collection that was not kept up, and is rarely consulted, if at all; that was an easy choice. Certain reference books that are no longer current are strong candidates as well, but I make sure that biographical dictionaries and anthologies stay here." While duplicate copies of certain books would seem to be suitable prospects for transfer, Carpenter said that for some authors the library's policy is to keep in Widener every copy that has some form of variant text. "Regardless of which books we send out for storage, they are never more than twenty-four hours away. We guarantee intellectual access to all of our books."

Carpenter's figures bear that out. There were 1,369,144 items in storage at the Harvard Depository occupying 92,296 book storage feet in fiscal year 1997. Of those, 54,845 titles, or 4.01 percent of the total holdings in Southborough, were retrieved at some point and brought back to Cambridge. Books are being transferred to the depository, meanwhile, at an orderly rate of about 200,000 volumes a year. Capacity at Widener is fixed at 3.2 million, about a third of all the books on campus. Carpenter's workload increased early in 1999, when Harvard began a major renovation of the building, which opened in 1912, requiring the removal of 750,000 books during the construction. "We have to send out enough so that we can begin to get large chunks of empty shelves here," Carpenter said. "It can't be just one or two titles at a time. And once we can get large chunks, then we can begin to reorganize the stacks in a way that makes more sense. Up until the last ten years or so, all of the moves we made in the stacks had to do with ways to squeeze in more books. We need to open up a fair chunk of space here to make room for new books."

Several weeks after we had that conversation, Carpenter invited me to tag along with him as he made volume-by-volume evaluations of material being considered for storage in Southborough. Before we went on our sortie into the stacks, he showed me the results of an experiment with a program designed by a university computer scientist that uses circulation records to identify likely candidates for storage. For this day's drill, Carpenter suggested that the program concentrate on economics. About two hundred books pulled by staff members were lying on a metal book truck, awaiting his inspection. "What I find is that I can look at these books very quickly and determine whether or not the program is on target," he said as he leafed quickly through the volumes. "Now here is something that caught my eye immediately. This is one book I feel ought not to go out to the depository. It is about German economics during the Weimar Republic, and even though it hasn't been signed out in a good while, I feel it probably belongs here, so it will stay." Of the books on the truck earmarked for off-site storage, Carpenter ended up approving all but seven. Many were volumes of essays known as *Festschriften*, anthologies of commissioned pieces usually published in honor of an eminent figure, and he unhesitatingly signed off on all of them. A five-volume set dealing with such arcane subjects as interest fluctuations in Basel and the history of the Levant paper trade during the early 1500s, though obviously "a hard-core scholarly work and covering all kinds of topics that historians and medievalists are going to be interested in," went into storage as well. "It's my sense that this is the kind of book that will be used only because someone has a particular reference to it, and if that's the case, they'll find it easily enough. So the program has some promise, and since I spent only about ten minutes on this truck, I have to conclude that the computer didn't do such a bad job."

A demonstration of more traditional selection methods came next, and we set out with an empty metal truck in tow for a quadrant on the first level known as 1 West to look at various works of Baltic literature; Carpenter had little difficulty consigning twenty volumes of fiction, drama, and poetry to storage, applying his rule that at least one title by each author remain on the shelves. "One of these books I just left behind has been charged out twice, so that was relevant to my deliberations," he said. "Here we're into Soviet stuff," he announced when we arrived at 1 South. "Look at that book there." He was pointing to a volume with a pictorial cloth cover featuring a group of children gazing with patriotic fervor into the sky as a formation of Russian war planes passes overhead. "You can tell right away that this is pretty lightweight stuff and not a scholarly work. I don't need to spend very much time at all with that one." Moving along to 1 East and German literature, Carpenter found three copies of one obscure novel; he kept one in Widener and sent the other two out. He then spent about thirty seconds deciding whether or not to dispatch a Czech translation of some verse by a German author named Robert Hamerling that had been inscribed to a former Harvard professor. "What I see here is that it came into the library in 1935, it was borrowed once in 1960, and hasn't been touched since. Since we have two German editions here of the same work, I'm going to send the translation to HD, and keep one of the original editions here."

Taking a tiny elevator up to the fifth floor, we went to 5 East, where a massive collection of American literature is kept. Once again, duplicate copies of little-used books made for easy choices. When Carpenter came to *The Spartan*, a 1922 novel by a woman named Caroline Dale Snedekar, he paused. "We can see the book hasn't been borrowed since 1992, but it has been rebacked, which means that it has gotten some use over the years, so I'm not so sure that I would want to send this book out to the depository. I have to be very cautious about possibly diminishing the utility of the collections." Nearby were two copies of *The Inverted Pyramid* (1924) by Bertrand W. Sinclar; Carpenter determined that only one should stay in Cambridge. On a good day, Carpenter figures he can pull a thousand books from the stacks, which puts him well on the way to processing 250,000 a year. "I try to pick books from all the sections in the library because I want everyone to know that it is being done in an even-handed fashion," Carpenter said as we headed back with a full truck. "When I get going, I can move along at a pretty good clip, and I work in all areas. Everyone has to give some—but no one is going to be decimated."

In the fall of 1996, Cornell University librarians—custodians of the tenth largest academic research library in the United States—were given four years to remove about 2 million books from their central repository in Ithaca, New York, and place them off campus in a new storage facility then being built on an old apple orchard about a mile away. "Our board of trustees has made it very clear," Ross Atkinson, deputy university librarian for collection development, told me one crisp autumn evening in his office overlooking the scenic campus. "We have been adding two and a half to three miles of shelving a year here, and we are just a normal research library. The trustees have now come back and told us there will be no more new shelves on Central Campus beyond the year 2000, that five million volumes on Central Campus is enough. 'If you want any more books than that,' they told us, 'you are going to have to put them out in the orchard.' "

Cornell's collections in 1996 totaled 6.8 million volumes, which meant that 1.8 million books, at the bare minimum, would have to go into storage, and that did not account for any new acquisitions. Because of restrictions on tampering with the open space that still remains on the historic grounds overlooking Cayuga Lake in south-central New York, the most recent Cornell library, a striking three-level repository for rare books and manuscripts in the humanities and social sciences, was built entirely underground. Named for its principal donor, Carl A. Kroch, class of 1935 and former chairman of the Kroch & Brentano's bookstore chain, the 97,000-square-foot facility was designed to house 2.5 million books, more than 167,000 maps, several million rolls of microfilm, and a constantly growing complex of electronic paraphernalia. From the surface, the only hint that a cavernous library has been sunk into the earth below are the two skylights that poke up through the soil like a pair of periscopes on the conning tower of a submarine.

The university's complaint of constantly dwindling shelf space is one echoed at universities throughout the United States, and many officials admit that concessions are being made. "I may be crucified for saying this, but I honestly can imagine a library of the future without books," Charles B. Faulhaber, director of the Bancroft Library at the University of California, Berkeley, said when I asked him to comment on the dilemma and speculate on the future. At Cornell there is no question that books are a part of the overall plan, but they are also part of a larger concept, and are being treated accordingly.

"We have reached a point where we can't go on adding shelves indefinitely," Atkinson insisted, even though the university is one of the largest property owners in the region, and availability of land is not a major problem. Neither, for that matter, is money; in January 1996 the university announced completion of what at that time was the largest fund-raising campaign in the history of higher education, raising $1.5 billion in five years, $250 million more than its original goal. If storing more than 5 million books on the Central Campus were a crying priority, there is no doubt that it could have been funded.

One option, of course, would be to deaccession low-use books outright, a course of action that the university "does very little of," according to Atkinson, although such a strategy is by no means out of the question, and is done periodically, albeit with very little fanfare. "When we describe a quality library, I think that we need to articulate the intelligence and the care that goes not just into growing that library, but pruning it when necessary as well," explained Sarah E. Thomas, the Cornell University librarian. "We have to be selective. We are not a vacuum cleaner gobbling things up. We are looking for materials that either supplement our existing collection, or fill in gaps where we are not as strong."

Before assuming the Cornell librarianship in 1996, Thomas was the head of cataloging at the Library of Congress. Among her first chores in Ithaca was to hear what people throughout the university's nineteen libraries had to say about dealing with unwieldy collections. "We are looking into electronic deposit of dissertations," she said, citing just one example that remains under review. "From the student's perspective, it might be cheaper to have a dissertation that has already been typed on a word processor deposited on disc. They would not be required to have so many bound copies on acid-free paper, and at the same time it would solve some of the library's storage problem for these materials. We are looking into that."

Another proposal Thomas briefly considered involved the far more drastic measure of making computer copies of the fifteen-thousand-volume Nestlé collection at the university's School of Hospitality and Hotel Management, and then selling the printed books. "Some people over there are saying, 'Why don't we just digitize everything in this collection, why don't we make ourselves the electronic research center in the world for this area?' I'll be honest with you, I got excited about the proposal when I first heard about it, because this is a very small discipline, hotel management and the literature of hospitality, and I thought it would be an excellent test case of what it would be like to be a totally electronic library; it could be a world resource on the subject. It's an intriguing idea to consider, but it just seems a little too simple for me to sign off on right now."

An inherent danger in this approach, Thomas agreed, would be the temptation for people to say, "Today hotel management, tomorrow Shakespeare." Other, more immediate, problems would involve copyright issues that digitally scanning books that are not in the public domain might provoke, and whether or not one library should assume such a heavy responsibility on its own. "I straddle the fence as someone who is an administrator, one who is always looking at the cost-effective ways to do things, and trying to be in a leadership position where I have to keep my eyes five to ten years out. Then there are people down there on the front lines who have to do the job for today. I come out of that world, and I still have a great allegiance to it. I still feel it is my responsibility to be evaluating all of these ideas that come up—those that are practical, those that are harebrained."

While getting rid of an entire collection of books on food preparation and hotel management may not be a viable option for the immediate future, Cornell has been involved in other programs that are among the most innovative in the world, attracting the attention of some observers worried that the university has embarked on a path that will lead inevitably toward total reliance on computer-generated material. Of particular moment has been a Cornell program that makes new copies of decaying materials known as "brittle books" through computer imaging.

Begun in 1989 with the backing of the Xerox Corp., which has headquarters in nearby Rochester, Cornell technicians scanned more than 2.5 million pages from ten thousand books and journals during the first ten years of the project. Every item copied had to be free of all copyright restrictions and be in the public domain. Using the digital images, new copies were then made, some printed on acid-free paper, others preserved on what are known as computer-output microfilms. The disbound originals were then discarded.

The person who has supervised the Cornell University Library Digital Conversion Project from its inception is Anne R. Kenney, associate director for preservation and conservation and codirector of the Cornell Institute for Digital Collections, and recognized as one of the most knowledgeable library professionals working in the conversion of printed material to digital images. She oversees Cornell's role in developing, with the University of Michigan, the Making of America digital library, a database of material that documents nineteenth-century life in the United States. Kenney has written widely and lectures often on her specialty, and with a prior background as an archivist—a "dedicated book person," she made clear while we were making our introductions— she speaks with authority about the technological changes that are taking place in research libraries throughout the world. Since 2000 she has also served as director of programs for the Council on Library and Information Resources.

"We estimate that about one million volumes here at Cornell are endangered by their having been printed on acidic paper, and that for them to be preserved, they will have to be reformatted," she said. For the vast majority of books that fall within this threatened category—about a third of Cornell's holdings, by Kenney's calculation—mass deacidification is not an option. Most of these books will continue their inexorable descent into decay without any steps taken to save them. If any of them are "preserved" at all—and they would represent only a fraction of the holdings—it is the information that will be retained, not the artifacts themselves.

The problem with such an approach is that once original paper copies are gone, they are gone forever, and even the most ardent advocates of digital imaging acknowledge that rapid degradation is an unsolved problem. "In all of our projects undertaken in the name of preservation, we have created either paper replacements or computer-output microfilm copies that meet nationally recognized standards for quality and longevity," Kenney said.

Anyone whose first computer used five-inch floppy disks, then upgraded to three-and-a-half-inch disks, and is now getting comfortable with Zip drives has some sense of the complex problems posed by this situation. Information that was once thought safely stored in one medium is no longer easily accessible in another. If digitized information is to be available indefinitely, steps have to be taken to transform it from one format to the next when software changes, or when operating systems change. Kenney agreed that thousands of perforated cards are undoubtedly stored somewhere on the Cornell campus that people would be hard-pressed to read today because the equipment no longer exists to process them.

"Had they been rigorous at the time of creation, we would have migrated that stuff as we went along," she said. "It's a matter of being vigilant about putting safeguards in place to do it. I don't know of any institution that has really fully committed the kind of resources to make that happen. We do it all the time in a paper-and-film-base world by maintaining proper humidity and temperature controls. If we didn't do that, we'd lose those collections as well. But somebody has to be there to do it. Somebody has to be alert. It doesn't take a genius to migrate that stuff. It's a matter of being vigilant about putting safeguards in there. It's not so much a technical problem as it is an institutional problem to create the mechanisms that will assure that it happens. We are going to have to do that anyway, because an increasing amount of the information that comes to us now comes in electronically."

With the benefit of having spent ten years scanning books, old magazines, periodicals, graphic arts, rare books, manuscripts, maps, and university archives, Kenney said she still feels that digital imaging is not yet the answer to long-term preservation, although research toward that end continues. "This is still nothing more than a way of capturing images, not preserving them," she said. "Let's be clear about that. Digital imaging is not digital preservation. What it offers is a means for capturing with good fidelity the informational content of hard-copy sources. It is used as a reformatting technique, but then an analog version is always produced. I don't know of any institution that has developed an effective digital preservation solution."

For all the work Cornell is doing in the area of digital reformatting, the program remains experimental. Three million digitized pages is a lot of pages, but that number represents only about twenty thousand titles, a mere fraction of the 1.2 million books that Cornell librarians have estimated are "brittle," and which they believe are certain to disintegrate. "We tackle it at the point of circulation through our brittle-books program, and with outside support to reformat the really strong holdings we have, such as in agriculture, Southeast Asian history, mathematics," Kenney said. For all that oversight, the vast majority of brittle books at Cornell are not likely to survive, either as objects or reproduced in other copies. "That is why we rely on consortial activities here," Kenney said. "If Columbia University microfilms a cache of brittle books, we are not going to do the same books. The fact is that we cannot do them all."

When a decision is made not to preserve a particular book, it is impossible to save the volume once it passes a certain degree of decay. Cornell calls this process "phased deterioration," an innocuous way of saying that books determined to be of lesser intellectual value than others will be allowed to die a slow death, with no heroic lifesaving attempts and no digital copies likely, either. "The medical analogy is fair," Atkinson said. "Let's say we will try to make these books as comfortable as we can; we will give them a nice place to rest, make sure the temperature and the humidity are ideal, but allow the natural process to take its course."

For the fortunate few chosen for rescue at Cornell, deacidification is the answer in only some cases. To preserve by "reformatting" means, essentially, that the information is transferred to some other surface, either on photographic film, or on a new paper version. Since the 1970s, when the "brittle book" crisis was becoming increasingly apparent, major preservation grants, principally from the National Endowment for the Humanities, have been directed largely toward the microfilming of decaying volumes. Because microfilm is proven to last—the process has been in general use since the 1930s, and copies have not deteriorated appreciably—it remains the method of choice among many librarians and archivists. Given the costs and the storage space that microfilms consume, making a digital image of a printed page with a scanning device is an especially attractive option, but it does have its drawbacks, the most pressing being that nobody can say for certain how long digital images will last.

"The fact is that they're not very permanent at all," Kenney readily acknowledged. "And it's not the technology that's the problem. I sleep at night as a preservation administrator knowing that I have an analog backup. This very much remains a period of transition, and I don't know how long it will last. Right now I don't trust Cornell or any other institution to ensure that what we scanned last week will be available to my children's children."

The idea of converting material from paper copies to electronic versions also presents philosophical difficulties, as G. Thomas Tanselle, a noted bibliographer, educator, and editor, argued out in a 1996 essay, "The Future of Primary Records: Technology's Impact on Publishing and the Printed Record." Even though he is an outspoken advocate of keeping all primary records in their original form, Tanselle makes clear

that he embraces the promises of new technology: "The electronic handling of texts offers so many advantages that it is hard to see why anyone
would not welcome it." But that position, he maintained, "has nothing to
do with recognizing the importance of all primary records and understanding that the preservation of individual surviving electronic forms of
texts will be just as imperative in the future as the preservation of handwritten and printed forms is at present." Of immediate concern to Tanselle "is the question whether old texts should be repackaged in new
forms," and to reaffirm the notion "that a converted form can replace the
original is to disregard the role of primary evidence in pursuing the past."

In 1999 the Council on Library and Information Resources (CLIR),
a nonprofit foundation based in Washington, D.C., formed a seventeen-
member commission to study what factors argue for retaining works in
their original form, and to advise on the kinds of strategies that might be
used to preserve them. Named to chair the Task Force on the Artifact in
the Library of the Future was Stephen G. Nichols, the James H. Beall
Professor of French and Humanities and chair of the Romance Languages Department at Johns Hopkins University, and also director of the
School of Criticism and Theory at Cornell. An admitted conservative
when it comes to keeping original materials, Nichols told me shortly after
his appointment was announced that the group was formed in response to
"a serious argument that has been brewing among preservationists as to
what constitutes preservation. That is the issue, really, and it goes all the
way back to Plato, who was greatly concerned about the context of articulated thought, because he felt that if you did not know what the occasion
was when a thought was uttered, you would not be able to understand it.
When you photograph a book, you have a microfilm, but the microfilm
does not preserve the historical materiality of that manuscript. It doesn't
have the binding, the other things that you would look at. So what is the
definition of an artifact? You start with the materiality of the object.
Anything that destroys the materiality of the object is going to destroy
the historical specificity of the object."

Nichols said his task force would concentrate on developing a protocol to preserve not only physical objects but visual materials such as film and prints, and newer materials that exist only in digital formats. "The good news is that our task force is very much a task force geared toward trying to figure out ways to preserve as much as we can." In the area of printed books, the group is concentrating on material that has appeared in the last two centuries. "Where we come in is what happens after 1800, since anything printed before that date, by general scholarly convention, has been established to be important, and worthy of preservation for that fact in and of itself." Early in 2001, a preliminary draft of the group's findings, *The Evidence in Hand: The Report of the Task Force on the Artifact in Library Collections*, was posted on the World Wide Web at the clir.org site.

During my first visit to the Ithaca campus, Kenney took me to a room in Olin Library where half a dozen "scanning technicians" were making digital copies of brittle books. Several shelves were filled with material, and every volume had been "disassembled" for the procedure. The spines had been sliced from the bindings—"guillotined," in the jargon of librarians—and every page was now a single sheet of paper ready to be placed on a flat surface that looks for all the world like a sophisticated xerographic copying machine. "Each page will be scanned, a quality-control check will be made, the electronic data will be stored, a hard copy will be printed and sent out to be bound, and the original discarded," Kenney said.

At one work station, a technician was making digital copies of handwritten pages bound in a volume of nineteenth-century letters. I asked what the material was, and learned that this was one of seven volumes of outgoing correspondence kept by the secretary to Ezra Cornell, the prosperous financier who founded the Ivy League university in 1868, and for whom the institution was named. Some of the letters were in Ezra Cornell's hand, and amounted to early versions of carbon copies, reproductions made by a process that used water pressure to elicit an image.

The young man making the digital copies demonstrated how he could remove stains and smudges that had discolored the sheets over the years. Kenney said she believed the originals would be discarded once the copies were made, but that the decision remained with the university archivist. Some time later, I asked Elaine D. Engst, director of the university archives, for a status report, and was relieved to learn that the seven letterpress books for Ezra Cornell had been scanned into a database, but that the originals remained part of the collection.

"Most of those letterpress books are in terrible condition, but the Ezra Cornell papers are a very special case," Engst said. "This is a nineteenth-century copying technique that involved a process whereby the original letter was somehow set on top of a damp piece of paper, and there was a press that somehow make a copy. You had to be very careful about how wet you got the paper, but good images have lasted just fine. The process was used for well over a century until carbon paper came along and is now regarded as a dead technology. Thomas Jefferson had a portable letterpress device that he used for his correspondence. For most of this material, it is the information that is important to us, and we do make decisions on whether to keep the originals on a case by case basis. We are keeping these books as artifacts of the technology. This is Ezra Cornell, after all. The idea that you are destroying a book associated in some way with the founder has the potential to upset a lot of people."

When we spoke again in the fall of 1999, Kenney reported that Cornell was now "outsourcing" all books and journals designated for scanning to private vendors, and that a study had been undertaken to determine if they can "capture the imagery" without having to guillotine the books at the spine. "We're testing some prototype equipment," she said. "The big question now is whether you can get the kind of quality you want, and whether you can get it at an affordable price."

She also said that the university had been funded to "explore issues associated with digital preservation, not just digital conversion," and that an "archiving strategy" was being developed to catalog the university's image collections. "We are running the entire digital collection through what are called optical character-recognition programs, which turn an image file into a searchable text file."

In a much broader context—one that drifted into the tools of scholarship—Kenney asserted her belief that the first stage of research "isn't a matter of looking at what you want," but of "getting rid of the stuff" that is irrelevant and in the way of what has to be done. "I am interested in winnowing out the six million volumes I don't want, and I am interested in finding the ten volumes I need. When you get to the text itself, you are bound to make similar decisions. And what these tools do is provide you with a way of extending the process you do now to looking at the text itself."

12.

AS IN A VIAL

There are certain types of building over which there hovers an aura of myth. The most transcendent of all, the cathedral, is grounded in the sacred so that both form and pattern of use are fused in the language of ritual. But there is one type of building which is profane yet in fulfilling its proper role touches the hem of the sacred: the great library.

—*Sir Colin St. John Wilson,* The Design and Construction of the British Library

A few hours after Japanese warplanes attacked Pearl Harbor on December 7, 1941, Librarian of Congress Archibald MacLeish ordered the immediate evacuation of irreplaceable books and documents to secret storage depots situated well outside Washington, D.C. Packed in hermetically sealed containers, the most precious materials of all were shipped under heavy military escort to Fort Knox in Kentucky, to be kept alongside the nation's reserve supply of gold bullion until the threat of enemy attack had passed. Another seventy thousand books and manuscripts were packed into twenty-nine trailer trucks and driven to secure sites in Virginia and Ohio. While all this complicated maneuvering was going on, a full bibliographic record of the massive collection that remained behind was microfilmed for safe deposit in a fireproof building, so that if the unthinkable had happened—if the library was destroyed as it had been in the War of 1812—the nation's most valuable holdings, and a documentary listing of everything that had been lost, would have survived.

Once the removal had been completed, MacLeish disclosed that seven hundred staff members and five hundred volunteers had spent two weeks working nonstop on the carefully synchronized project that had been developed nine months earlier in anticipation of just such an emergency. "I am happy to be able to report that our principal treasures are already in places of security," he wrote in the official publication of the American Library Association. Though he chose not to identify the remote storage locations at the time, MacLeish reassured everyone that these "materials beyond value" were in the safety of an "inland repository many miles from Washington, under maximum security against any dangers now anticipated." And while the core holdings of books and papers would be inaccessible for most of the war, their essential spirit, he reminded everyone, would remain fresh and clear. "I believe all librarians will join me in declaring that although libraries may be driven underground by the enemies of freedom, they will never be driven out of action. Indeed 'One-Book' Hitler and his friends may find in time that libraries are weapons more dangerous to their hopes than planes or guns or submarines."

Today, America's primary repository for books, the James Madison Memorial Building, occupies a full city block on Capitol Hill and serves as the official monument to the fourth president of the United States. Opened in 1980, it is a place where the notion of rarity takes on an almost metaphysical relevance, with abstractions like "worth" and "value" measured in terms of collective pride and national heritage, not in how many dollars some cherished article might fetch on the open market. Two other structures located nearby complete the Library of Congress complex: the ornate building begun in 1886 and now named after Thomas Jefferson and the John Adams Annex, a utilitarian storehouse of pure function that opened in 1938.

For most Americans who visit Washington, the Jefferson Building is synonymous with the Library of Congress, as well it should be, since it was the third president of the United States who imbued the institution with his vision of the world and directed its growth into a collection that is truly universal. When the Library of Congress was established in 1800, the mission—defined quite accurately by its name—was to provide the members of the House and the Senate with the reference materials they needed to write legislation and to conduct the country's business. The move toward a comprehensive storehouse of knowledge took hold in the aftermath of misfortune. To replace the mundane holdings that went up in flames when soldiers put much of the capital to the torch in 1814, Thomas Jefferson offered to sell the nation his personal library, a proposal that was accepted after much debate in the House of Representatives. The 6,487 volumes hauled by wagon train from Monticello to Washington reflected Jefferson's broad intellectual interests, and shaped the grand strategy that now drives the library's acquisitions policy. In an address delivered before the American Historical Society in 1836, Secretary of War Lewis Cass stated for the record just what kind of literary resource the United States of America should have. The Library of Congress, he said, needed to grow "in *all* the departments of human learning, as it will render it worthy of the age and country and elevate it to an equality with those great repositories of knowledge which are among the proudest ornaments of modern Europe."

As an edifice, the Jefferson Building is one of the grandest architectural achievements of nineteenth-century America. Completed in 1897 and gloriously refurbished in an $81.5 million renovation project a hundred years later, it asserts the vitality of the American people through a lively mélange of sculpture and murals. With exquisite façades and bold interiors that are acknowledged to be among the most detailed in the country, the landmark is an apt showpiece for an institution that culls the cultural DNA of the nation and preserves it "as in a vial," in the words of John Milton, for future generations.

In striking contrast to the Jefferson Building is the cavernous Madison repository. With 2.1 million square feet of floor space contained within its white marble walls, it is the largest building ever erected for the storage of books. On the bottom floor is a compact crypt ten feet wide, ten feet deep, and eight feet high known among staff members as the Top Treasures Vault. To enter this highly restricted area, approved visitors must first pass through an unmarked vestibule rigged with an impressive array of security devices, an anteroom where lights blink purposefully on a side wall, where air-cleansing machines hum efficiently in the background. "This is a chamber for storing some of our nation's most precious possessions," Thomas C. Albro II, at the time of my visit chief of the library's conservation division, said over his shoulder while working through a complicated sequence of codes and commands. Directly in front of him stood a thick metal door painted battleship gray. On the other side of this steel barrier was a small grouping of sealed plastic boxes, each filled with argon gas, each lying flat on a shelf and sheltering an object of extraordinary historical significance.

"Around the time of the Japanese attack on Pearl Harbor, the items you see here were designated as the top treasures of this library," Albro said once we were inside. "These were among the materials that were removed immediately from Washington and stored for the duration of the war in Fort Knox." Not kept in this vault are the holy trinity of American documents, the Declaration of Independence, the Constitution, and the Bill of Rights, which are on public view seven blocks down Pennsylvania Avenue in the National Archives, and enjoy a level of protection that is apparent to the thousands of visitors who view them every year. Before the National Archives and Records Administration (NARA) was established as an independent federal agency in 1937, those national icons also were in the care of the Library of Congress. Why they were transferred to the new federal agency, and why various other materials, including those now kept in the Top Treasures Vault, remained behind at the library, is central to understanding the missions of the two institutions. Every piece of paper and electronic record sent to the National Archives is an *official* document of the United States government, a finished product, and as the twentieth century drew to a close, more than 5 billion of these items were being maintained in NARA storage facilities located around the country. In addition to its collection of printed books, magazines, almanacs, motion pictures, photographic negatives, sound recordings, digital images, and maps, the Library of Congress stockpiles an immense cache of what is regarded as primary material—letters, manuscripts, journals, diaries—that animates a constantly unfolding saga known as the United States of America. As the Library of Congress observed its bicentennial in 2000, just under 121 million artifacts were entrusted to its care, but only eighteen items of "incalculable symbolic value" have been chosen for storage in the Top Treasures Vault.

Although the existence of the vault has never been publicized, anyone with a modest grasp of American history should be able to figure out what some of the materials safeguarded inside are. "You could probably make a strong case for putting 350 or so other things in here as well," Albro said. The earliest document relating to American nationhood stored in the vault is General George Washington's commission to serve as commander in chief of the newly formed army of the United Colonies, signed by John Hancock and Charles Thomson, and dated June 19, 1775, but without doubt the most resonant treasure is a four-page sketch of the Declaration of Independence written in longhand by Thomas Jefferson, the rough draft of what would be the first public paper issued by the new republic. This working version of Jefferson's soaring prose includes emendations suggested by Benjamin Franklin, John Adams, and the full Congress as the debate for separation from England was argued in Philadelphia during the hot summer of 1776. Lying near this document is the holographic copy of Jefferson's first inaugural address, dated March 4, 1801. Next to that is a lengthy letter Jefferson wrote to Dr. Benjamin Rush on September 23, 1800, containing this credo: "I have sworn upon the altar of God eternal hostility against every form of tyranny over the mind of man."

Of the 42,100 items in the Abraham Lincoln Collection, six are kept in the Top Treasures Vault. They include drafts of the sixteenth president's first and second inaugural addresses, the Emancipation Proclamation as proposed to the cabinet in 1862, and the creased handwritten copy of the Gettysburg Address he read at the dedication ceremony of the Civil War battlefield in 1863. There also is a letter that Lincoln wrote on December 20, 1859, to Jesse W. Fell, a Bloomington, Illinois, friend who was assisting his run for the presidency. In the letter, the hopeful candidate succinctly summarized his background and qualifications for high office, presumably for use in the campaign. "If any personal description of me is thought desirable," he noted of his physical appearance, "it may be said, I am, in height, six feet, four inches, nearly; lean in flesh, weighing, on an average, one hundred and eighty pounds; dark complexion, with coarse black hair, and grey eyes—no other marks or brand recollected." Lincoln considered this sketch of himself crude at best, and noted as much in a scrawled aside to Fell with words of such unparalleled modesty that they may well constitute the most understated self-appraisal in the history of American politics: "There is not much of it, for the reason, I suppose, that there is not much of me."

In two volumes of manuscript on another shelf is James Madison's "Notes of Debates in the Federation Convention," along with his "Draft on the Committee of Detail," the most accurate records in existence of the proceedings undertaken to create the U.S. Constitution in 1787. Significantly, there is one item kept in the steel vault that is not unique—it is not even American in origin—yet it would be hard to argue against including the St. Blasius copy of the Holy Bible among the Top Treasures of the library. This is one of three known perfect copies of the Bible printed on vellum by Johannes Gutenberg about 1455 in Mainz, Germany, and like the Declaration of Independence, another instance of the prototype of a particular innovation—in this case printing by means of movable metal type—being the outstanding example of its genre, and the standard by which all that follow must be measured. There are three volumes in the Library of Congress set, which is named for the Benedictine monastery in Germany that owned it for more than three hundred years; one of them is always on permanent display in the main exhibition hall.

After allowing me some time to consider these artifacts—no touching was permitted in here—Albro led the way to a large room where a staff of twenty-five conservators give intimate attention to an unending succession of reclamation projects. On the day of this visit, one of the treasures from the steel vault, George Washington's letter accepting his appointment as commander in chief of the Continental Army, was being measured for a new frame. "We have a stabilizing program that we call phased conservation," Albro said. "Basically, what you see in this room are individual items selected from the national collections through a process of negotiation between the conservators and the curators based on their importance to the library, and based upon their condition. Ideally, the equation reads 'most valuable, worst condition.' That is where we start, in theory at least, and then we work our way down through 121 million objects."

In a typical year, the Preservation Division treats about 4,000 volumes that require careful attention, along with another 300,000 "unbound paper-based items" such as letters and broadsides that can be processed as individual sheets. Books in need of new bindings are outsourced to private vendors at the fixed price of $12 a volume. "That sort of thing has been going on for years," Albro said. "Here, in the Conservation Division, most of the items we work on are going to consume anywhere from fifty hours to five hundred hours of staff time, depending on the need. What you're talking about are the tip-top items, things in many cases where monetary value is unassignable."

One example of a five-hundred-hour project was a scrapbook kept by Harry Houdini, and filled with close to four hundred "incredible" objects, "newspaper clippings, posters, all of them folded up and jammed into one album" by the legendary magician. "What had to happen in this instance was that these items could not all go back into the album, because once they had been unfolded and treated, they couldn't fit back in." The strategy taken in this instance was to photograph each page and create a facsimile of the album as it originally appeared, and then treat the items individually and reassign them, in different order, to other containers. "The average kind of job we do probably is hitting right on a hundred hours. Obviously, this is not a production-oriented operation, it's a place that is very high in symbolic content. The goal of taking care of the library's entire collection with this degree of attention is not humanly possible. But we are obliged, at least, to make an effort at the highest possible level."

In 1801, a year after John Adams approved an act of Congress providing for the "accommodation of the Government of the United States" in the new federal city of Washington, D.C., the Library of Congress received its first acquisitions, a shipment of 740 books and three maps from London. By the time British troops used the collection as kindling to set the capital on fire thirteen years later, the numbers had grown to about a thousand volumes. Today, 24,000 items arrive at the library each day, many of them coming by way of agreements worked out with fifteen thousand research institutions and foreign governments for the reciprocal exchange of materials. Unlike some other national collections, the library does not keep everything it receives, not even the copies of every book published in the United States that are deposited there by law, although that practice may change in the near future with construction of an off-site depository that is being considered specifically for that purpose.

The Library of Congress is unique among the world's major repositories in that its acquisition policy imposes no geographic, historical, or political limitations. Along with an ambitious mandate to document the entire American experience, it gathers everything of merit that it can find anywhere in the world, and it maintains agents and offices in foreign countries for this specific purpose. The energy of this approach lies not so much in the vast array of individual objects that have been accumulated but in the entirety of holdings known as the critical mass. "The growth of the collections is relentless," the library asserts on its website, and the statistics bear that claim out.

Some 450 languages are represented, set down in more than thirty-five writing scripts, and they appear in all kinds of media, from cuneiform tablets produced in Babylonia four thousand years ago to the latest CD-ROMs. "We have more books in Arabic than any other library in the world," Dr. James H. Billington, the Librarian of Congress, told me one gorgeous fall afternoon during an interview in his office overlooking the Capitol dome. When the Kuwait National Library was left in ruins by retreating Iraqi forces in 1991, the Library of Congress was able to stock a replacement collection with duplicate copies of books in Arabic from its Cairo field office. "We have similar strength in a multitude of areas," he added, a factor, curiously enough, that has not gone unnoticed by a corps of cost-conscious domestic critics.

In December 1995 the General Accounting Office (GAO) commissioned a $1.3 million review of operational practices at the library with an eye toward streamlining the way the book custodians do their business, which would have imposed drastic limitations on the kinds of things they collect. Conducted jointly by Booz-Allen & Hamilton, Inc., an international management consulting firm, and Price Waterhouse, auditors, the report—endorsed by the GAO and recommended to a congressional oversight committee for implementation—proposed that the library abandon the practice of building and maintaining "a universal collection of knowledge and creativity" available to all Americans, and confine itself to a more "functional" posture that concentrates predominantly on the "Congress and the nation." Had it been adopted, the proposal also would have imposed drastic restrictions on outside access to the materials as well, making it exceedingly difficult for citizens who are not public officials to use their national library.

The efficiency experts also thought it a good idea for the library to create programs that "focus on increasing revenue." To this end, the accountants unwittingly offered a telling case study of why they are referred to so often as "bean-counters" more comfortable with their calculators than they are with the rules of syntax. Written in the kind of fractured language typically used to justify million-dollar consultant fees, their sweeping proposal, stripped to its essentials, would have reduced the library's $350 million annual budget radically and eliminated its traditional responsibility as a purveyor of information. Here is one of their findings: "The Library lacks a clear technology vision to support processes within the Library and the creation of networks of institutions that enable the world's knowledge resources to be shared." Once that sobering nugget had been digested, there was this to ponder: "Unclear roles and responsibilities and the lack of accountability for performance negatively affect the Library's implementation of an integrated planning and program execution process." And this: "The primary institutional mechanism for feedback or evaluation of program efforts is the tracking of the annual budget, which is not an effective mechanism for assessing the achievement of a strategic plan."

To its credit, the joint committee of Congress that considered the recommendations dismissed them summarily. "We need many other components to maintain our national security besides hardware," Senator Mark Hatfield said at the close of the hearing over which he presided, citing the library's fundamental mission as one of furthering "knowledge, ideas, concepts, matters of the mind, matters of the spirit." The *Washington Post* published two brief stories on the proposal, treating it in both instances as a local item to appear well inside the newspaper, and ran a short editorial in opposition to the plan, which was quoted in the Senate hearing and read into the *Congressional Record*. The matter was not otherwise reported by the major media.

"The absence of national coverage doesn't surprise me at all, because what happens in the library is rarely considered big news in the District of Columbia, let alone in the rest of the country," Billington told me a month after the proposal had been rejected. "The Messiah could make a personal appearance in the main reading room, and the chances are fifty-fifty that it would get any attention from the press." Billington characterized the

GAO report as a "totally gratuitous recommendation that we cease being a universal collection, that we should be an entirely electronic operation, and that we work exclusively for the Congress. My reaction to that was totally negative and confrontational, and we went after it tooth and nail. The library community was very good on this, and I must say we got total support from the Congress. They completely rejected the study. But I do wish there had been more of an alarm raised about the ramifications of all this throughout the country, because it was a cautionary issue of no small significance."

Billington is a scholar trained in the humanities, not a career librarian. His appointment in 1987 by President Ronald Reagan continued a practice of going outside the library profession for top-level direction that began with the elevation of the poet Archibald MacLeish (1892–1982) to the position in 1939. A few examples from the recent past at other institutions have included the educators Dr. Vartan Gregorian, the Reverend Timothy S. Healy, and Dr. Paul LeClerc at the New York Public Library; the Reverend Leonard E. Boyle, an internationally renowned paleographer, as head of the Vatican Library in Rome from 1984 to 1998; and Jorge Luis Borges, the great South American fantasist, as director of the National Library of Argentina from 1955 to 1971. The willingness to select someone whose background is in the humanities to direct the fortunes of a major library is not without its detractors, however. Franklin D. Roosevelt's announcement in 1938 that he intended to name MacLeish Librarian of Congress ignited a firestorm of opposition among members of the American Library Association, who urged the president to consider an appointee of their choosing. For advice on the matter, Roosevelt turned to his close friend and political adviser, U.S. Supreme Court justice Felix Frankfurter (1865–1965), a former president of Harvard Law School, the author of numerous learned books, and a founder of the American Civil Liberties Union. "What is wanted in the directing head of a great library," the jurist promptly replied in a letter to Roosevelt, is "imaginative energy and vision." The new librarian, he believed—and there was no doubt that Frankfurter favored the selection of his former Harvard colleague—should be a person "who knows books, loves books, and makes books." Armed with these essential virtues, Frankfurter believed, "the craftsmanship of the library calling" was a skill that could be nurtured while on the job. The exigencies of the times, he believed, demanded above all else that a person of great moral character—a person with an unbending reverence for free expression—be appointed to the position. "In the world in which we live it is no longer agreed that the common culture is a common treasure. In the world in which we live it is no longer agreed that the greatest glory and final justification of human history is the life of the human mind." Frankfurter then clarified for Roosevelt what he believed was ultimately at issue:

> *To many men and many governments the life of the human mind is a danger to be feared more than any other danger, and the Word which cannot be purchased, cannot be falsified, and cannot be killed is the enemy most hunted for and hated. It is not necessary to speak of the burning of the books in Germany, or of the victorious lie in Spain, or of the terror of the creative spirit in Russia, or of the hunting and hounding of those in this country who insist that certain truths be told and who will not be silent. These things are commonplaces. They are commonplaces to such a point that they no longer shock us into anger. Indeed it is the essential character of our time that the triumph of the lie, the mutilation of culture, and the persecution of the Word no longer shock us into anger.*

In time, MacLeish would earn praise from all quarters for the sureness of voice and strength of will that he brought to bear during the seven years of his tenure as head of his country's national library, and the practice of going outside the profession for the top position has been continued since then. Billington's immediate predecessor, Daniel J. Boorstin, is internationally known as a scholar, teacher, and author of numerous books that have won the Pulitzer Prize, Bancroft Prize, and Francis Parkman Prize, among many other honors. He was Librarian of Congress from 1975 to 1987. As a historian and a teacher himself, Billington has firm beliefs about the direction that print culture will be taking in the years ahead. "There is no question in my mind that there has been a general degradation of the book in the last thirty or forty years by the academic monograph, and that is largely due to hyperspecialization and bureaucratization," he said. "With the move to electronic formats, what I believe you will now see is that books containing data will be online, and the serious kind of traditional literature that has always been in book form will continue to appear in book form. The book, in my view, will be freed from a very heavy burden that it has had to bear all these years. It will be allowed to flourish anew."

This change will be particularly apparent, Billington continued, in academic publishing. "Book publishing now plays a role in the certification of the academic guilds by struggling into publication things with very limited interest that are written in jargon for a narrow audience. They are not written in a language that enriches and improves and extends the human condition, but are merely written in a kind of bad functional form of communication among experts. That stuff should all go online because that's where it belongs. And I believe that is going to help the scholarly world, because right now there is a real divide in academia between those who get their books published, and those who don't. It is a very unfair sorting-out process. By that I mean there are a lot of wonderful Ph.D. theses that never get published, and a lot of truly lousy ones that do, and that's a totally irrational mechanism for functionality. But in terms of enriching the general culture of the country, and appealing to a broader audience that never reads any of these academic monographs, published or unpublished, that material will be available online. You will have much less artificial gradations on the basis of what gets published and who is fashionable within these academic guilds. You will get much less pomposity, and much more democracy among these specialized guilds. And you will then free up the publishing world to become entities that they have not on the whole been, entities that are truly synthetic—entities that put things together rather than just take them apart."

As custodian of the world's largest library, whose tenure coincides with the explosive growth of the Internet—and since he has actively supported the development of electronic programs at the Library of Congress—Billington is constantly asked his views about the role the Library of Congress will play in preserving the sanctity of the printed book. "We are not digitizing books," he made clear, although he has vigorously supported the massive scanning of various other collections in the library. "We want to use digitization to bring special materials into the world of books, the kind of materials that have always been kept in libraries. These are what we call nonbook materials, and they are not restricted to rarities but include documentary photographs, maps, posters, cartoons, broadsides, recorded sound movies—all the materials that are not books but are part of the traditional library. The important point here is that we are not trying to replace the traditional print culture with a new culture at the Library of Congress. That is not going to happen. This is the national library of the United States of America, and we have to stockpile information and knowledge however it's packaged for the government, and for the scholarly community. So we couldn't avoid that even if we wanted to, because we will soon be getting deposits in digital form anyway. What we are creating is an extension of the basic library principle of providing access. We are extending our unique materials available to the whole world."

The concept becomes especially useful when dealing with "special materials" like manuscripts, notebooks, or letters that exist in single copies, he added. "We are making it possible so that unique and rare items can be searched, played with, and browsed. You bring them into the world of books in the sense that you bring them into the world of interactivity, where an investment of a person's active thinking is involved, just as it is involved in reading. It transports these materials into the world of books."

Billington has not been without his critics, and a number of them are professional librarians from within his own ranks who have questioned a proposal to abandon the traditional method of shelving books by subject categories, and to begin storing by volume size, a method used in all off-site book warehouses to maximize space, and one used for about 40 percent of the books kept in the New York Public Library. The major objection to shelving by size and not by category is that the possibility of chance discovery through browsing vanishes, a circumstance that is not likely to affect the scholarly community at the Library of Congress, since the stacks are closed to everyone except researchers for members of the House and Senate. A decision to make such a change, in any event, was put on indefinite hold in the spring of 1999 when the library began moving 4 million books to a new off-site storage facility in Fort Meade, Maryland, relieving the pressure, if only temporarily, on Capitol Hill.

When I arrived at the old British Library in Bloomsbury early one weekday morning for an interview with David Bradbury, the director general in charge of collections and services, a long column of moving vans was queued up to a platform just outside his window, each vehicle engaged in a steady transfer of books to a new building a mile away that had been thirty-six years in the making. Hanging on a far wall in the cramped quarters—overseeing, in a sense, all of the commotion going on at the loading dock nearby—was a portrait in oil of Sir Anthony Panizzi (1797–1879), the Italian emigré whose unprecedented efforts on behalf of the British Museum Library during the early years of the nineteenth century earned him acclaim as an "administrator of genius" and the "prince of librarians." Indeed, this very suite of rooms once served as Panizzi's office; now, the mass of books he and his colleagues had stockpiled over two and a half centuries was leaving in color-coded boxes at the rate of twenty thousand volumes a day. All told, some 12 million books were being moved from seventeen warehouses scattered about the realm to the huge brick building on Easton Road in St. Pancras, while 6 million others would remain in remote storage.

To enter Bradbury's office on the first floor of the old building, it had been necessary to pass through a false door disguised to blend in with the surrounding bookshelves in the King's Library, a charming reminder of an eventful era that was about to end forever. On this particular day, Bradbury was wearing a bright red tie that featured a repeated image of Mickey Mouse, his arms piled high with books. It reminded me of a famous scene in Walt Disney's classic film *Fantasia* in which Mickey, playing the role of a naughty sorcerer's apprentice, unleashes an army of water-bearing broomsticks that run rampant and threaten to flood the kingdom; only the last-second intervention of the master wizard stops the pandemonium and prevents a deluge from taking place. Given the unending parade of trucks visible outside his window, Bradbury's sporty neckware seemed appropriate to the moment. Not long after witnessing this bibliographic exodus in action, I would see a similar rite of passage being performed on the other side of the English Channel in the heart of Paris, where millions of books from the old Bibliothèque Nationale on rue de Richelieu were being moved across the river Seine to a cluster of glass towers built in an old industrial district of the city known as Tolbiac.

Both of these high-profile projects were undertaken at a time toward the end of the twentieth century, when the function of libraries was being hotly debated around the world, and the contrast between the two—one betraying a decided touch of stodginess, the other making a bold statement about innovation and change—could not have been more profound. That the new British Library and the new Bibliothèque Nationale were approaching their completion dates at the same time made the differences between them all the more noteworthy. For my purposes, it seemed especially worthwhile to catch a passing glimpse as the "precious life-blood" of these two extraordinary national collections, to borrow another phrase from the *Areopagitica*, was being transferred from creaky old trappings into what were being proclaimed as exciting gateways to the future.

On the cool spring morning in 1997 that I met with David Bradbury, the sixty-thousand-volume library of rarities gathered by King George III and given to the nation by his son George IV in 1823 was still shelved in the old Exhibition Room, and would not be in its new setting until the following year. During a later trip to London, I would witness the unveiling of a six-tiered tower of bronze and glass that had been installed in the new building just off the main entrance hall to receive these remarkable books. A simple ceremony, accompanied by the playing of a bagpipe, marked the moment.

"I share the views of many colleagues, including my American colleagues, about national libraries being national memories, the repository of national thought, of our language, of our whole written history," Bradbury told me, and to that end the British Library continues to add close to three miles of new material a year to its shelves, including titles published in the United Kingdom that are received on legal deposit. But documenting the whole of British culture is only a part of the British Library's mission, and like the British Museum from which it emerged as an independent entity in 1973, it does not limit its curiosity to things that are homegrown. Bradbury pointed to the portrait of Sir Anthony near the window of his office to emphasize the point.

"Panizzi was the great librarian of Europe of the nineteenth century. He aspired that the British Museum Library should be the greatest French national library outside of France, the greatest Italian library outside of Italy, and so on down the line, and for many of them, we do have almost the best collections in the world for those countries, particularly for places like Italy, where they had those huge internal problems right up until after the last war. Many Italian scholars still come here to do their research on Italian history and Italian culture, because we actually collected materials systematically during the nineteenth century, which none of their libraries did at that pivotal time." In the years following World War II, the library strengthened its collection of Eastern European materials as well, filling a void created by widespread destruction of cultural material in those regions. "There were so many turmoils, and so many collections were being thrown out, vandalized, privatized, sold, given away, with the result that the repository for a good deal of that material now is here in the British Library," Bradbury said. Despite the ceaseless addition of books, however, the library now imposes limitations on the materials that it decides to keep. "It is not affordable in this day and age to collect everything from everywhere," Bradbury said. "Nobody can do that anymore."

When the new building at St. Pancras formally opened its doors in 1998, it marked the first time in 246 years that the British Library was not a tenant on somebody else's property. For the first 220 years of its existence, it was a division of the British Museum, which had been created in 1753 by an act of Parliament. Although important libraries and museums abound throughout the United Kingdom, London for the most part had no great gathering of artifactual curiosities or book collections accessible to the public until then. There were a few libraries in the capital at the time, but they were reserved for the use of certain professional groups— lawyers, clergymen, physicians, and the like. The acquisition by the government of a large collection of antiquities, books, and natural history specimens gathered by Sir Hans Sloane, physician and president of the Royal Society, along with the manuscript libraries of Edward Harley, earl of Oxford, and the legendary antiquarian Sir Robert Bruce Cotton, set in motion a process that led to the establishment of the splendidly eclectic institution that today remains unique in the world. From the very beginning of the museum's existence, its curators, archivists, and librarians chose to build on their strengths, and they cast what can only be described as a very wide net. "No other country provided an equivalent of the British Museum, which dealt not only with books, manuscripts, prints and drawings, coins and medals, antiquities and ethnography, but also with natural history specimens," P. H. Harris wrote in an exhaustive history of the library through 1973, the year it became independent of the museum.

When Panizzi announced his proposal to build the imposing Round Reading Room in 1845, he acknowledged that the expense for such a project would be great, but "so is the nation which is to bear it." His ambitious plan called for erecting the largest hemispherical dome in the world since the Roman emperor Hadrian rebuilt the Pantheon in the second century A.D., and twelve years passed before his dream became a reality. "Paris must be surpassed," Panizzi had insisted, a rallying cry that was repeated a century later when the British found themselves looking across the Channel once again at a parallel undertaking in France.

As the St. Pancras project edged slowly toward completion, the roll call of luminaries who had sharpened their intellects in the Round Reading Room was recited by sentimentalists who lamented the inevitable ending of a vibrant era. It was recalled widely in the press how Karl Marx spent thirty years toiling under the sky-blue, gold-ribbed dome, working away at *Das Kapital*. One of the great Bloomsbury dwellers of all time, Virginia Woolf, had expressed her debt to the institution eloquently: "If truth is not to be found on the shelves of the British Museum, where is truth?" The biographer and novelist Peter Ackroyd, a dedicated reader for three decades, set a good deal of his 1994 mystery thriller *Dan Leno and the Lighthouse Golem* (published in the United States as *The Trial of Elizabeth Tree: A Novel of the Limehouse Murders*) in the Round Reading Room, contriving to have Marx, Oscar Wilde, and the novelist George Gissing sitting in close proximity to one another at the same table day after day in the autumn of 1880. "This is a charmed place," Ackroyd wrote in tribute, "almost a holy place—it is possible to feel the presence of all the generations who have been inspired by it." Charles Dickens, Anthony Trollope, Thomas Hardy, Sir Walter Scott, Mahatma Gandhi, Rudyard Kipling, John Ruskin, Madame Blavatsky, Isadora Duncan, T. S. Eliot, E. M. Forster, and George Orwell are among the scores of notables who made full use of their reading privileges, but none more so than George Bernard Shaw (1856–1950), who made sure everyone knew just how great a debt he owed the library when it came time to read his will. Shaw's association with the institution began shortly after he moved to London from Ireland in 1876, determined to become a dominant man of letters. The aspiring writer spent so much time immersed in its limitless resources that he rented a plain flat near Bloomsbury just to be closer to the building. "It became his club, his university, a refuge, and the centre of his life," Michael Holroyd, Shaw's biographer, has written. "He felt closer to strangers in this place than to his own family." Shaw spent hours on end in the Round Reading Room, requesting on average one new book each day, all the while preparing lectures, working on articles, writing letters to the press, adding to his musical knowledge, and completing his long literary apprenticeship.

Shortly before observing his ninety-fourth birthday in 1950, the Nobel laureate stipulated how he wanted the royalties from his writings to be dispersed after his death. He made numerous provisions to pet causes, including the National Gallery of Ireland, "to which I owe much of the only real education I ever got as a boy in Eire," the Royal Academy of Dramatic Art, which he had served for thirty years as a councillor, and the British Museum, "in acknowledgement of the incalculable value to me of my daily resort to the Reading Room of that Institution at the beginning of my career." When Shaw died, his earnings were considerable, but they became unexpectedly lucrative by virtue of a project that he had absolutely forbidden to be undertaken during his lifetime. Despite repeated entreaties, Shaw had pointedly refused every offer to transform his play *Pygmalion* into a musical comedy. "Over my dead body," was one response, which is pretty much the way it turned out. Six years after his death, *My Fair Lady* opened on Broadway with Rex Harrison and Julie Andrews in the leading roles, turning out smashing performances that would lead to a hugely successful Hollywood film. The playwright may have had reason to turn in his grave, but the beneficiaries of his estate found themselves jumping with joy, as more than $20 million in additional royalties was generated by the windfall.

Invested shrewdly, the British Museum's share of the bequest was reported in 1999 to be worth more than £9 million, although the trustees of the institution were not required by law to disclose the figures. One major complication did get aired publicly, however, one that could not possibly have been foreseen when Shaw wrote out his will in 1950. Although he had specifically designated the parent institution—the British Museum—as a primary beneficiary of his estate, it was evident that his gratitude was meant to benefit the library, which did not become an independent institution until 1973, twenty-three years after his death. Despite repeated protests from the library to share equitably in the bequest, the museum trustees retained firm control of the bequest, doling out small portions for book acquisitions every now and then but keeping the lion's share for their own projects. Heated protests were raised in the House of Lords, prompting one government official to suggest that if the museum and the library were unable to agree on a fair solution, legislation would be forthcoming in Parliament to resolve the impasse once and for all. Finally, on December 21, 1999, the two parties agreed on a formula that would split the bequest's capital sum and royalties equally, and the embarrassing squabble came to a merciful end.

When Colin St. John Wilson was awarded the assignment to design a new national library in 1962, he was a forty-year-old lecturer in architecture at Cambridge University approaching the prime of his career. Although computers were beginning to make their mark in communications, nobody was suggesting the imminent demise of print or questioning the need for conventional storage facilities. The library was still a division of the British Museum, and the proposed site for its new home was next door in Bloomsbury. Approved by the government in 1964, Wilson's original design called for a granite building standing in a large piazza. A network of small streets behind Great Russell Street would have had to be demolished, a detail that resulted in the formation of a vocal "Save Bloomsbury" campaign, and led to abandonment of that plan in 1975. By then, an act of Parliament had already created a national library that was independent of the museum, giving support to a faction that favored a complete split and a new building at another location.

Of the many objections raised to the new design, the most frequently quoted came from Prince Charles, the person who had laid the cornerstone in 1982. In an offhand comment offered six years later, the Prince of Wales compared the building to a "dim collection of sheds, like an academy for secret policemen." Gerald Kaufman, an outspoken member of Parliament, said the squat "brick pile" looked to him like "a Babylonian ziggurat seen through a fun-fair distorting mirror." Proving himself a master of tasteless imagery, Kaufman offered yet another barb, judging the new Central London landmark to be "as glamorous as a public lavatory." Not to be outdone, the National Heritage Commission declared it to be "one of the ugliest buildings in the world."

To this day, Wilson enjoys telling interviewers that it took Sir Christopher Wren the same length of time to build St. Paul's Cathedral after the Great Fire of London in 1666 as he spent on St. Pancras, "and Wren was fired before the job was finished." By 1999 Wilson was calling the experience his personal version of the Thirty Years' War. "I liked the idea of a building that's dumb on the outside and rich on the inside," he wrote in a small monograph that detailed his approach to the undertaking. "To me, designing a library isn't about addressing a crowd. It's not a big rhetorical exercise like an opera house."

Built on a 9.5-acre site that was once home to a freight storage yard, the completed library projects an outward appearance of staying close to the surface, hunkered down, in a sense, and well beneath the line of fire. Book storage is on four levels, but it is all belowground, reaching a depth of 110 feet. Faced with a veneer of 10 million salmon-colored bricks fired by hand in British kilns, the library stands in stark contrast to the King's Cross railroad station next door, an eccentric building with Gothic spires built in the 1860s when Victorian exuberance was in full bloom. Now being restored and updated, King's Cross is intended to serve as terminus of the Channel Tunnel. "The new library will be the first building people lay their eyes on when they arrive in London from France," Wilson said. "Visiting scholars won't even have to take a taxi to get there. It will be a threshold to Britain. That's a fluke of circumstance, of course, but after everything we've been through, we deserve a break."

As luck would have it, Wilson got the ultimate break when readers from all over the world finally began to experience the amenities he had provided so painstakingly for their comfort. For all the postured snorting and dismissive insults the architect had been forced to endure over three decades, visitors found very little to deplore once they passed through the entrance hall of creamy Portland stone and began to make use of the cathedral to learning he had designed. The facilities were intelligently laid out and attractively appointed. The eleven reading rooms were spacious and quiet, the solid wooden desks of American oak were comfortably designed and fitted for computer outlets, the lighting, by individual lamps, was excellent, the banisters on stairways were padded with leather. The staff, moreover, was knowledgeable and eager to help, and books arrived with a minimum of disquietude, available for perusal, on average, within thirty minutes. And the most basic of considerations—an excellent restaurant and spotless rest rooms—did not go unnoticed either.

"It is clear that despite its prolonged gestation, this is a building of genuine quality," a historian from Glasgow wrote with profound relief in the *Scotsman*. "This is almost certainly the last great hand-built building we shall ever see," the architecture critic for the *Guardian* predicted. "It fought for its site in the Sixties, its existence in the Seventies, its budget in the Eighties and its reputation in the Nineties," Simon Jenkins wrote a few days before Queen Elizabeth II formally opened the building in June 1998, giving it at long last a royal blessing, declaring the library "remarkable." A few months earlier, in her annual New Year's Honors listing, she conferred a knighthood on St. John Wilson, entitling him to be called Sir Colin. The Prince of Wales, meanwhile, paid a visit of his own, seeing the inside for the first time. "His Royal Highness was delighted to have been asked to see round the library and was impressed with the quality of the materials, the craftsmanship inside and the peaceful atmosphere created for users," a Buckingham Palace spokesman said afterward. "He seemed to be perfectly happy," Sir Colin remarked. "We shook hands. He very much liked the courtyard when he arrived."

When all was said and done, the new British Library had cost £511 million to see through to completion, three times more than first projected, although the original estimates were calculated in the early 1960s. It was the costliest building constructed in Britain in the twentieth century, and by far the most controversial. The most candid assessment to come from within the institution was written in 1994 by Sir Anthony Kenny, at that time chairman of the British Library Board. "The Library is aware that there are those who do not share its faith in the promise which St. Pancras holds out," he noted with model British reserve. Resistance had been mobilized on two fronts, he continued, making a concerted defense all the more difficult to mobilize. "Traditionalist opposition is motivated primarily by the desire to retain in its present function the Round Reading Room in Bloomsbury. Futurist opposition is inspired by a vision that the printed book is being superseded by the computerized database." The "traditionalists," he continued, were committed to maintaining the status quo, while the "futurists" dismissed the St. Pancras building outright as "a white elephant of a construction whose miles of shelving will stand empty once the Library's holdings have all been microfilmed or digitized to bring them into the twenty-first century."

The drastically scaled-down building eventually built—the first design would have accommodated up to 25 million books—included 340 kilometers of shelving, although ample land remains available at the site for future expansion, should that become necessary. "Those who believe in the death of the book think of it as a waste of space; their opponents regard it as an inadequate repository for the national printed archive," Kenny wrote. He then speculated on what might happen to the inventory should all 18 million volumes in the national collection ultimately be digitized. "Even if we imagine this gigantic operation successfully completed, it would be the act of a barbarian then to destroy all the scanned volumes in order to be relieved of the need to store them." Showing a savvy sense of the still unresolved dilemmas inherent in computer technology, Kenny took note of "the rapid obsolescence of information technology," a condition that would require "the electronic replicas" of printed books to "constantly need costly retranscription," a daunting task. "Otherwise, superannuated platforms would have to be specially maintained by computer antiquarians in order to make sure that the texts remained accessible. Old fashioned books may fade and decay; but the technology for human access to their contents, so long as they survive, has not changed since the invention of the spectacles."

During my interview with David Bradbury, the conversation inevitably turned to this very issue, the fate that modern technology holds in store for the massive print collections it threatens to displace. "We did a basic calculation of what it would cost to digitize our whole library collection," he said. "It is somewhere in the range of five billion pounds, and those projections are not likely to ameliorate appreciably in the years ahead, since the cost of labor will always be a constant factor to consider. That is something like ten St. Pancras buildings that we are talking about, so you can be certain that is not going to happen any time soon, quite likely not ever. There is no way, in my opinion, that books are in any immediate jeopardy of dying out, at least not as far as we are concerned. I can assure you that the British Library is about books."

At Waterloo Station in London, my wife and I boarded a sleek Eurostar passenger train for France, making the trip to Gare du Nord in downtown Paris in three hours flat, the same amount of time it takes me to drive from my home in central Massachusetts to midtown Manhattan. The contrasting nature of the ride on either side of the Channel Tunnel suggested a double metaphor that struck me as appropriate to the sagas of the two new national libraries we were viewing side by side, or tête-à-tête, as the case may be. In southeastern England, where older railbeds prevent the frisky locomotives from exploiting their aerodynamic marvels to full advantage, the somnambulant crawl through the suburban countryside recalled the sluggish pace of the St. Pancras project over the previous thirty-five years. But once through the blackness of the thirty-one-mile tube, a modern marvel of technology if ever there was one, the gleaming yellow train flashed through northern France at speeds that reached 186 miles an hour, a hard charge that paralleled the swiftness with which François Mitterrand's pride and joy became a reality on the banks of the river Seine. Even the nickname the French gave their new library—TGB, for *"Très Grande Bibliothèque"*—was a not-so-subtle reference to TGV, a popular acronym for the *train à grande vitesse,* "high-speed train," developed by their engineers to worldwide acclaim.

France is the proud possessor of the oldest national collection in the world, with roots that extend back to the fourteenth century, but up until the day ground was broken for the new glass-and-steel towers at Tolbiac in 1991, the country had never constructed a building for the specific purpose of housing it. Unlike the seemingly interminable effort to plan and build the new British Library, the Tolbiac project swept toward completion with few hindrances. Voices were raised in opposition, but none so severe as to derail the project. "The building of a library for the twenty-first century has been a response to certain practical necessities," President Mitterrand said of his decision to have the high-profile project serve as the capstone to his fourteen-year tenure as president of the republic. "But in addition to answering these necessities it was deemed right that France should make clear, in the form of an exemplary monument, both her sense of the value of her intellectual heritage and her confidence in the future of books and the act of reading."

On March 30, 1995—just three years after the cornerstone was laid—Mitterrand presided over the formal dedication of the building, which by then had been named in his honor. Two years after that, all the books were finally in place, and the new French National Library was declared operational. Eight billion francs, about $1.2 billion, were reported to have been spent, an enormous amount of public money committed to one project at a time when unemployment in France never went below 10 percent, all the more reason why British observers were astounded by the decisiveness of the process. "Whereas the construction of the new French library has been a model of speed and efficiency, the St. Pancras project has been a farce beyond the reach of satire," Andrew Martin wrote in the *Sunday Telegraph* for his readers in England.

Dominique Perrault was thirty-six years old in 1989 when an international jury of architects headed by I. M. Pei and Joseph Belmont recommended him as one of two finalists to design the most ambitious public works project undertaken by the French government in the twentieth century. Largely unknown outside professional circles, Perrault enjoyed the respect of his colleagues, but his most compelling attribute was that he had captured the imagination of the president of the republic. For his formal presentation, Perrault had placed four L-shaped wooden blocks on a slab of wood, each facing inward to form the corners of a rectangle, each suggesting the contours of an open book. Laid subtly in the center were a few sprigs of spruce, the merest suggestion of a pine-tree garden. The runner-up design featured a scheme of two scallop shells clipped together around a bridge that extended outward across the Seine. Both proposals were rich in symbolism, but it was the four towers shaped like open books that carried the day.

One of the judges, Sir Richard Rogers of England, was mightily impressed by the "will to act" evident in the French project. "The speed at which it has all happened is incredible, especially compared with the endless bureaucratic fiddlings that have bogged down the British Library," he added, unwilling to resist an opportunity to take yet another swipe at what so many of his countrymen had perceived to be the folly of the century. For Perrault, the "kernel of the project" grew from a "vision" he had of a garden surrounded by four towers, a wooded sanctuary he likened to the inner cloister of a medieval monastery, a solemn place suited for quiet contemplation. "The presence of nature, of trees, of a piece of woodland, make the library a place outside time, whose references are universal."

Working for the most part by himself, Perrault was oblivious to the concerns being raised by some professional librarians, conservationists, and architectural critics who felt that the last thing in the world fragile books needed was constant exposure to bright sunshine. Perrault's intention was to have a massive gathering of the nation's literary patrimony—a core collection of 12 million books—visible behind glass windows in four rising towers, on display, as in a shrine, for everyone to see. Persuaded finally that this would cause irreparable damage to the books, Perrault allowed for wooden shutters to block out the light, but eliminating the 264-foot-high spires was never considered, and his plans included costly provisions to keep temperature and humidity constant behind the glass façades.

This approach was not entirely uncharted territory; there was precedent for putting large numbers of books in tall buildings, most notably at the University of Texas in Austin, where the famed Texas Tower—the most recognizable landmark on the campus—had been used for that purpose for about forty years before conventional quarters were built in the late 1970s. "Our experience is that having a tower for books is not a good idea," Richard W. Oram, librarian at the Harry Ransom Humanities Research Center, told me during a visit to the campus early in 2000. "It never worked out here, and one of the reasons was that so much depended on the constant use of a single elevator to reach the books. Any librarian could have told the French that stacking books high in a tower was not a prudent way for them to go, if only they had bothered to ask."

Perrault, for the most part, remained indifferent to what he saw as irrelevant sniping from the perimeter. "You are a bit like a nuclear submarine, deeply submerged in the thick of the action, emerging only on rare occasions," he told an interviewer at one crucial point, and as inauguration of the complex approached, he maintained his distance. "The architect should not allow his art to be sullied by petty quarrels," he wrote in a book published to mark the dedication. "The library is as alive as I always imagined it would be; behind its transparent envelope, it is entering a new period in its existence as a building."

Perrault asserted in the book—commissioned by his firm, as a notation on the copyright page makes clear—that what he visualized from the outset, four towers "inter-connected by a network of circulation services," a totally modern facility that incorporated "every type of technology, every type of specific circulation for users, and every type of security arrangement," had been triumphantly realized. When he offered that observation, occupancy was still three years away, and the judgment of staff and readers remained to be formed. In the meantime, there was unflagging support from the one person whose approval mattered most, François Mitterrand, who by then was fighting what would prove to be a fatal battle with cancer, and in no mood to delay completion of the public monument that would bear his name. "The building he has designed is lucid in its symmetry," the president declared of Perrault's masterwork, "its lines are restrained, and its spaces and functions are laid out with simplicity. It is hollowed into the ground as if in quest of silence and peace, yet its towers stand four square to assert its presence in the heart of the city."

Mitterrand—who died nine months after presiding over the dedication—emphasized that beyond erecting a worthy repository for the nation's books, what he wanted most of all was to set in motion a revitalization of the Thirteenth Arrondissement. In the past, he noted, urban planners had placed such "elements of prestige" as the Louvre, the Eiffel Tower, Notre Dame Cathedral, and the Tuileries on the western side of the city. By raising a key cultural monument in Tolbiac, "a mighty readjustment of Paris toward the east" would be set in motion. When seen in this context, what mattered most of all was not functionality but economic development and a sense of national destiny.

What is not immediately apparent in a walk through the lower levels of the new Bibliothèque Nationale is obvious in a cross-sectional sketch of the design: the basement sections are below the waterline of the river Seine. Even Perrault appreciated the severe limitations that had been imposed on him, writing that the Tolbiac site occupied "a stretch of industrial waste land on the banks of the Seine in the East End of Paris," seventeen acres just upriver from the Austerlitz train station that allowed him only one direction to go—up.

Early in 1991 Philip D. Leighton, a retired Stanford University professor who is one of the world's leading consultants on library design, was asked by the editors of *Le Debat,* a Paris journal, to write an evaluation of the Tolbiac facility for its May 1991 issue. Though respectful of the country's ambitious commitment, Leighton identified a number of problems he found peculiar to the design and likely to cause problems in the years to come. "There can be no doubt that the proposed facility is a grand scheme," he wrote, citing the estimated price tag of more than $1 billion as ample proof of serious intent; he congratulated the French government "for the will to undertake such an effort" at a time when the long-term mission of huge libraries was being examined worldwide.

Leighton compared the "general form" of Perrault's building to "four legs punctuating the air," with a large flattened "well" in the middle that made it look very much like a "table placed upside-down at the edge of the Seine." The symbolism of four open books is a striking concept to behold, he allowed, but there were considerable tradeoffs in the bargain. To create this visual effect, it was necessary to accommodate twenty-four corners within the L-shaped towers and another twenty in the five wells, forty more than would have been necessary in a simple cube. "Generally, the closer a building comes to being a simple cube, the lower the construction cost," he explained. Even more disturbing was Perrault's plan to store books in towers that would constantly be exposed to sunlight, an idea later modified by masking the windows with wooden shades. The architect's subsequent "realization that the environment surrounding the books is of critical importance for their very survival" was a decided improvement, but by no means did it provide a solution to the larger problem. Leighton did not compare the Tolbiac design with the new British Library in London directly, but he did discuss the basic storage strategies employed in both projects:

It is interesting to consider that the naturally most stable environment in a typical building is the basement, and the least stable is at the edge of the building envelope, above the ground. A cave will maintain the same temperature and humidity year round while a mast will fluctuate the temperature of the breeze. A glass box will capture the heat of the sun, and once captured, it will take considerable energy to remove the heat by mechanical means. Shades inside the glass walls will do little to prevent the entrance of solar heat. Should the mechanical systems fail, the books will be cooked, and cooking definitely reduces their life. For each 10 degrees C the average temperature is raised, the life expectancy of the books will be cut in half. For a collection that is to be preserved for many future generations, this is indeed a very serious business.

The optimal solution, Leighton wrote, would have been to place the books underground in a manner not unlike the one employed by Colin St. John Wilson in the new British Library. At Tolbiac, the use of a huge "well" for a forest garden precluded that option, but there also was the matter of the river Seine a few yards away, to consider: "One serious concern about storing books in a cave or underground, especially next to a river, is the prospect of flooding." Leighton's practical suggestion was to install an "outer envelope" in the towers "designed to provide the best possible insulation from heat."

Most new libraries built today have the storage of printed books as a principal goal, and usually allow for continued growth of the collections. What Leighton found at Tolbiac were facilities that would be full by 2030, possibly a lot earlier than that. He saw a design scheme "so symmetrical and crystal-like" that it permitted few possibilities for future adaptations. Some 400 kilometers of shelf space—about 248 miles—are available for storage, but nothing beyond that. An option, he wrote, "would be to fill in the central hole" where the garden is, "but one suspects that future expansion is not part of the great well's purpose." Leighton also found fault with the idea of placing the eleven reading rooms at such great distance from the books, and with having the collections spread out among sixty "discrete stack floors" in the four towers, making timely delivery of material more burdensome, and the reliance on technology so much greater. "It is all too common to find systems of dumb-waiters, house phones, and vacuum tubes abandoned simply because they did not work as anticipated, they were too costly to maintain, they were too noisy, they caused damage to the books, they were not reliable, or the function of the library changed sufficiently to make the system out-dated," he wrote in what would prove to be a most prophetic observation when readers were admitted seven years later. But with "enough money, space, staff, and patience, this scheme can be made to work," he concluded hopefully. "However, given that there are so many requirements to make this building work well, it appears almost certain that it is destined not to work well."

Leighton did not limit his comments to the science of book storage and the location of reading rooms. He also had thoughts on a design that would require arriving visitors to walk up a large flight of wooden stairs, only to descend once again by escalator to the main entryway. "The issue I raised was pretty straightforward," he told me in the first of several telephone conversations we had several years later, and after he had furnished me with an English version of his published evaluation. "The concept that the glass towers could be an emblem of the nation's patrimony was interesting, but the books, in my view, as I stated in my essay, would be cooked. This was to be a significant portion of the French national collections stored in those towers, and what they wanted for it was a complete exterior exposure."

Leighton made clear that he is not an architect and that he does not design libraries, he evaluates them, but he does have a clear sense of priorities. "Books are for reading and computers are for research," he explained. "I don't get into collection development at all, but I do contend that a large collection, whatever the nature of its content, is going to grow at a measured rate. There is nothing I can see to indicate that the flow of printed materials will stop in the immediate future. And it is in this regard that I am interested in issues related to preservation of materials, and I am interested in a rational relationship of the functional parts of libraries."

Attitudes on the role of libraries work in cycles, Leighton has determined. "Over the last forty or fifty years a pragmatic approach has been in vogue that argues that you ought to be able to do anything with the given space. I believe this generation is moving toward a greater interest in a design that tells a story, and I think the whole concept of storytelling has to do with generating a logic that goes beyond the technology." At Tolbiac, the storyline developed by Dominique Perrault is clearly expressed, with a gathered expression of the nation's literary heritage contained within four glass towers that embrace a garden of Norway pines transplanted fully grown from Rouen. "My general approach to the process is pragmatic," Leighton continued. "It is the art of the architect to bring out the story, but it has to be in a manner that is efficient and functional." What disturbed him most of all about Perrault's design was that such a "massive expenditure of human energy" should have been applied to creating a library that is "influenced so little by the nature of the book, the nature of man, and the nature of accessing, the using and storing of information."

Given Leighton's unquestioned qualifications—he is the author of two editions of *Planning Academic and Research Library Buildings*, the standard text in the field pioneered by the late Keyes D. Metcalf, a former librarian of Harvard College, and published by the American Library Association—French authorities could not possibly ignore his critique. Their response was to retain him as a consultant. "I was brought to France for a week and given a desk and a computer," he said. "By that time, the project was pretty well along. I can tell you that I made some recommendations, and that a number of them were implemented, and that I was sworn to secrecy. My sense is that I was probably hired with the idea that I wouldn't write any more articles critical of the library, although they did publish a selectively edited version of my official report."

Because librarians at the Bibliothèque Nationale were left out of the design process, they were presented with a fait accompli. What began as an effort to create a new Bibliothèque Nationale de France quickly became Tres Grande Bibliothèque, an institution that would make the sum of human knowledge available to everyone, and do it in a hurry. Books would be moved to the new site, but most of them would be there as a visible symbol of French accomplishment. For readers outside Paris, the real business would be conducted by computer hookups. Jean Favier, appointed president of the Bibliothèque Nationale de France in 1996, acknowledged as much in an essay called "The History of the French National Library," written for a special issue of *Daedalus*, a publication of the American Academy of Arts and Sciences, that was devoted entirely to the future of libraries. To understand the special needs of all the French people, he argued, it is necessary first to understand the distinctive nature of their beloved City of Light, and the national library that evolved at its core:

> *Paris is one of the few capital cities that is at the same time the political headquarters of a still heavily centralized country, a metropolis of ten million people, and the most important university city in the country. With three hundred foreign diplomatic missions, 360,000 students in twenty universities, and some one hundred grandes écoles; hundreds of thousands of professionals in middle and senior management involved in politics, public service, liberal professions, or business management; and millions of individuals in the general public—all potential library patrons—it is clear that to find a reasonably comparable match of the community's needs, one would have to combine London with Cambridge and Oxford, Frankfurt with Heidelberg, Rome with Florence and Milan, or Washington with*

*New York and Cambridge. Of course, this does not mean that one is
superior to the other; it is merely stating a fact.*

Formed by scholars who directed the library from the sixteenth to the
twentieth centuries, the Bibliothèque Nationale progressively lost what
Favier called its "encyclopedic character," an approach to learning epito-
mized by Denis Diderot at the height of the Enlightenment in the
eighteenth century with publication of his monumental work, the *Ency-
clopédie.* Based entirely on reason, encyclopedism holds that all knowledge comes from the senses. "While writers, researchers in the social
sciences, or university professors in literature can often be found in the
reading rooms, this is not true of doctors, physicists, or mathematicians,"
Favier continued. "With time, erudition withdrew into itself. Restoring
encyclopedism is a necessary step towards the creation of a system
encompassing universal knowledge." To accomplish that goal in the
modern age, he reasoned, "a conciliation between the older and newer
forms of thought memorization" is necessary. "It is important not to
repeat the mistake made in the sixteenth century when manuscripts were
still preferred to prints, which they considered a less noble product; or
when the manuscript or correspondence of a contemporary historian had
less claim to shelf space at the French National Library than medieval
manuscripts and collections of copies from scholars or ancient original
pieces, a mistake made well into the twentieth century."

To achieve these goals, "a new building was needed," one that would
be a national symbol for France, but one that would also contribute to the
spirit of "decentralization" of the nation's resources and make them
available to all citizens. "The capital city needed, and still needs, to win
forgiveness for its national library," Favier allowed. "It is therefore
important that non-Parisians have equal access to the library." So Tolbiac, with its 12 million books, its gleaming glass towers and verdant
Norway pines, was designed with the idea of "interfacing" with the third
millennium. A double mandate was assumed by the Bibliothèque

Nationale de France, one that would serve accredited scholars in the *rez-de-jardin*, or garden level, and "all adult readers" at the higher, or *haut-de-jardin* level. Most of the entire print collection—supplemented each year by the addition of fifty thousand new periodicals and fifty thousand new monographs—is now housed in the new facility. Of parallel importance, Favier stressed, was the need to "take into consideration the new types of documents, currently found under two categories—audiovisual and computerized—that involve digital technology."

When I interviewed Jacqueline Sanson, adjoint director general and head of the printed books and audiovisual departments for the Bibliothèque Nationale de France, she made sure I got examples of her two business cards, one giving the address of her office at rue de Richelieu, the other indicating her new quarters at Tolbiac. The point to be made was that she conducts her business in both buildings, and that she will continue to do so under the new system. "Richelieu does not close," she said pointedly at the outset of our talk. We met in her second-floor office overlooking an elegant courtyard, La Cour d'Honneur, built in the eighteenth century, one of several additions made over the years to the crowded complex of buildings in the heart of the city, just a ten-minute walk from the Louvre. The oldest structure in the crowded Bibliothèque Nationale complex, facing the rue des Petits-Champs to the south, was once the opulent residence of Giulio Mazarini (1602–1661), a onetime papal diplomat from Italy who became a naturalized Frenchman, was made a cardinal in 1641 without ever having been ordained a priest, and was handpicked by Cardinal Richelieu to succeed him as chief minister the following year. Cardinal Mazarin amassed a great personal fortune during his eighteen years in this position, one of the largest of the ancien régime, and with the sage counsel of Gabriel Naudé, author of *Advis pour dresser une Bibliothèque* (Advice on Building a Library), he assembled a magnificent private collection of forty thousand volumes; the forty-two-line Bible known today as the Gutenberg Bible—the Western world's first printed book—was for many years referred to as the Mazarine Bible after a detailed examination of the splendid example housed in the Bibliothèque Mazarine established its early history.

A candid woman of few words, Sanson said she had no time to be happy or unhappy about the presumed shortcomings of the new building, and had no opinion to share on what she thought about Perrault's radical design. "I do not think anything about that matter at all," she said. "I decided at the beginning of all this not to complain. The new Bibliothèque represents progress for us because now we have more space for our collections, more comfort for the readers, and more money for the acquisitions. So what more do you want? My position is that I have no problems whatsoever with any of this." This realistic sentiment—an attitude of sanguine acceptance coupled with sincere gratitude for the massive government commitment to the national collections—was apparent the next day at Tolbiac when I interviewed a number of her colleagues, several of whom, like herself, were department heads.

After we had finished our conversation, Sanson took us on a walking tour of the Richelieu buildings, going first through the Louis XV room in the Cabinet des Médailles, where a statue of Voltaire by Jean-Antoine Houdon—a resident of the Bibliothèque Nationale for many years—is the primary focus of attention. A matter of continuing embarrassment to preservers of France's literary heritage is the knowledge that Voltaire's seven-thousand-volume library is in Russia, not in Paris, brought to St. Petersburg by Catherine the Great in 1765. There is some solace, however, in the knowledge that Voltaire's heart, given to the library in 1864, is enclosed in the pedestal of Houdon's statue, which portrays the writer in old age, smiling, and seated. In addition to being one of the world's great libraries, the Bibliothèque Nationale is also a splendid storehouse of treasures, and quite possibly the oldest museum in France. There is only one permanent exhibition on view, but it may be the earliest surviving formal display in the world. The Cabinet des Médailles, successor to the Cabinet du Roi, is a direct descendant of the "treasure houses" of the Middle Ages.

For most of its existence, the Bibliothèque Nationale has been known mostly by scholars. Of all the libraries in the world, this was the first to be designated a legal depository, a place where a copy of all works published within the nation's borders must be sent. That act was decreed in 1537. Designed by the architect Henri Labrouste between 1857 and 1873, the reading room is celebrated for the elevation of its soaring vaults, the arching elegance of their supports, and the sunlight that streams in through the overhead windows. Cast-iron columns, a triumph of nineteenth-century technology, support nine wrought-iron cupolas to form three bays. Sanson pointed out the murals painted inside the openings of the bays by the artist Alexandre Desgoffe. The motif—a forest of trees—is repeated in real life at the Tolbiac garden. Labrouste's hall has accommodations for 344 seated readers, and standing space for anther seventy; the Tolbiac facility made provisions for two thousand. In a section of the old reading room known as the hemicycle, the ceiling is decorated with stucco medallions of ground gold illustrating the arts and sciences, designed by Oudiné. Five levels of openwork iron floors are visible behind a glazed opening at the back, where the collections were stacked. On the day of my visit, books were arriving at Tolbiac at the rate of fifty thousand volumes a day, many of them coming in from Richelieu, as well as various other storehouses located throughout France, three as far away as Versailles; *Le Monde* anointed the ambitious exercise "*la grande migration de la Bibliothèque nationale de France.*" But not everything from Richelieu was making the trip across the Seine to the Left Bank, as Sanson had been quick to point out. "Everything after Gutenberg," for the most part, would be moving, but the rich collection of manuscripts, corrected proofs, maps, globes, prints, bindings, photographs, musical scores—one of the strongest in the world—was staying downtown, along with the coins, the musical instruments, and the fabulous artworks.

Within days of admitting its first readers, the grumblings about services grew into an ominous roar. Angry workers staged work stoppages, fistfights broke out among frustrated patrons, and wails of protest from visiting scholars over interminable delays in getting books down from the stacks were reported in the daily press. Further complicating matters was a computer system that did not work properly. In January 1998 a pregnant employee lost her baby when jostled by a researcher outraged by continued failures of the system. Technical problems were of such severity that readers were unable to activate the turnstiles with their magnetic cards and enter the building. When the book-retrieval system did find the titles it was looking for, oftentimes they were sent in the wrong direction. Writing in *Le Figaro,* three French professors—Marie-Madeleine Fontaine, Anne-Marie Lecoq, and Michel Crouzet—denounced the new setup as a "sinister farce" that impugned the integrity of academic research, and compared the new building to the ill-fated steamship *Titanic.* "It was in the face of this Kafkaesque situation that the personnel said: 'We can't continue to work like this,' " the head of the library workers union told Jennifer Ludden of National Public Radio. In response to changes demanded by the nine unions representing the 2,500 workers, management agreed to shut the library on Mondays and remain open only five days a week.

Early predictions had been that four thousand people a day would visit the new building, and when those numbers fell well short, library managers blamed the difficult location and a sparsity of parking. The opening of a new subway station at Tolbiac in 1998 improved access considerably, and the number of visitors began to increase in the weeks that followed. Early in 2000, a report prepared by the Conseil Supérieur des Bibliothèques—the French High Council of Libraries—on library activity throughout the nation was issued for the years 1998 and 1999, including a lengthy examination of the first two years of operation of the new Bibliothèque Nationale de France. An official English translation was posted on the Internet in the spring of 2000.

In the area of the "national digitizing programs," the council reported expenditures of 25 million francs a year, and was pleased to report that the "patrimonialisation" of the World Wide Web was continuing apace. By the beginning of 2000, 80,000 public domain books and 300,000 documentary images from the national collection were available for access on the Gallica website. While acknowledging the problems that beset the first months of operation, the council suggested that the news media "has made excessive use of the sensational and shown that some journalists must have been struck by amnesia," principally in ignoring the dual function that had been assumed, namely the role of a national library for researchers, and a public library for everyone else.

It would be worthwhile to recall here a few points on the progress of the project: the initial idea in 1988 was born of a new library concept that was to incarnate the connection of multiple networks. This library, which could very well have settled to exist in the virtual, eventually materialized, in a manner which we are tempted to qualify as traditional, into a very real building. The architectural project by Dominique Perrault selected on August 16, 1989, planned for a capacity of approximately 5 million volumes on the basis of the collections officially divided up back in 1945. On August 21st, the government decided to abandon this organizational criteria and announced that all of the printed collections of the Bibliothèque Nationale (around 13 million volumes) would be transferred to the new Tolbiac site, without the architectural choice that had been made ever being questioned.

The current situation of the Bibliothèque Nationale de France cannot be assessed properly without keeping in mind these successive diversions from the initial concept and the impact this has had. Moreover, the profound changes of the digital age and the new issues raised by these changes have affected personnel practices and public usage. The conditions under which the missions of such an institution may be carried out consequently need to be rethought.

Of primary importance, the council members concluded—and the emphasis is theirs—is not to "*minimize the profound reasons for discontent,* in which operational problems with new equipment during start-up, however important these may have been, were symptomatic of an underlying unrest."

After a brief period of relative calm, problems returned to the Bibliothèque Nationale late in 2000. A fire in an underground corridor was followed by a staff walkout after sixteen employees reported "violent headaches and burning sensation in the throat and eyes," a situation considered serious enough that scientists were called in to investigate the source. "The building is just not safe," the library workers' union charged in a statement. "Staff and public who stay there face a real danger."

On the other side of the English Channel, meanwhile, the British Library was basking in the glow of positive reviews, and Colin St. John Wilson suddenly found himself in demand as a public speaker. During one trip to the United States in the spring of 2000, he gave a number of lectures at American universities. I caught up with him in Brunswick, Maine, where he addressed a gathering at Bowdoin College; a few weeks later he spoke at Harvard. Enough time had passed at this point that he was able to look back on the long experience with some perspective, even some flashes of good humor. Wilson found comparisons between the British Library and the French Bibliothèque Nationale a matter of some amusement, "a tale of two cultures, really," he offered. "You could write a comic little piece and call it 'A Tale of Two Libraries,' where almost every design decision and political decision that was made was the exact opposite of the other." He offered what he felt was one salient example: "We put the books down in the cellar, where a Frenchman would put his wine. The point is that books are like wine, they belong in the basement. The French turned the whole scheme upside down; they put the readers down in the cellar, and the books up in the sunlight, which is the one thing you do not do to wine, or to books."

We both had a small chuckle over that one, prompting Sir Colin to muse that like the French national library, the new British Library also has a glass tower—the King's Library at the core of the building—"but we had the good sense to put ours indoors." He agreed that his design lacked the "charisma" of other buildings, but he dismissed any suggestion that it lacks excitement. "The thing I like is this: it is simultaneously a monument, a holy of holies if you like, a kind of sculpture to celebrate the book. It's a bit like that flat box of a building at Mecca, the Muslim shrine, where people walk around in reverence. It's not a pretty face. It's a library. For me, that is something truly symbolic, and a far sight better than the other kind of empty rhetoric you might see elsewhere in your international travels. I think one of the things in particular we have got right is that in thinking of the readers, we have taken aboard the concept that each person has a very different and highly personalized spatial conception of what makes them feel comfortable."

Wilson said he was ever mindful of the trauma many patrons felt at the prospect of giving up the Round Reading Room, which is why he took extra pains to indulge their comforts in the new library. "It was always fascinating for me to watch where some people would sit—the same people always at the same places—and it always rather encouraged me that most of the people who used the Big Round were not particularly comfortable. So in terms of enclosure, what was important was to create a whole range of options, to give people choices of how they might sit. People do have different hangouts. They appropriate their spots. For me, it is the whole architectural theory at work here, the psychology of spatial perception. It's to do with touch, which is terribly important."

A perfectionist who believes in getting it right, Wilson had a hand in everything, including the choice of artworks to decorate the library. For a wall by the marble staircase in the main entrance hall, he commissioned the weaving of the largest tapestry made in the twentieth century, a postmodernist collage based on the painting *If Not, Not,* by R. B. Kitaj. Outside, at the Euston Road entrance, a huge gate framed by monumental brick portals spells out "British Library" in iron letters designed by David Kindersley, a pupil of Eric Gill. Just beyond the doorway, overlooking the enormous piazza studded with slabs of Portland stone, is a bronze statue of Sir Isaac Newton crouched over a divider, measuring the universe. Sculpted by Sir Eduardo Paolozzi, the statue stands twelve feet high on a twelve-foot brick plinth, and was inspired by an image of the

English physicist made by the poet and artist William Blake. Wilson said he chose the subject as a way of embodying the purpose of a great library, which is to search for truth in sciences and the humanities. "I see in this work an exciting union of two British geniuses," he said at the unveiling of the sculpture.

In a lengthy interview given to the *Independent* a month before he was knighted by the queen, Wilson looked back on the previous thirty-five years with grim satisfaction, noting that the chorus of insults led by the Prince of Wales had cost him dearly, seriously damaging his reputation and forcing him to close his firm for lack of business. But he refused to let being maligned as the "architect of the Great British Disaster" defeat his will to see the project through. "What keeps me going?" he asked his interviewer. "A sense of history and a sense of purpose, which is partly classical, partly religious. I believe with the Greeks that it is the nature of everything to fulfill itself. And I do believe with William Blake that everything that lives is holy and has a purpose. We are here to contribute—which doesn't mean you mustn't expect a fight."

EPILOGUE

P rofessor Dr. Mohsen Zahran, project director of the international effort to build a new library in Alexandria near the hallowed grounds of the great repository from antiquity, looked over the top of his horn-rimmed glasses directly into my eyes before answering what clearly was the most sensitive question I had posed to him on the morning we sat in his office for an interview. When we met in the fall of 1998, the new library, grandly christened Bibliotheca Alexandrina at a formal cornerstone-laying ceremony a decade earlier but beset since then by numerous delays, would not be completed for another three years, but already some critics were grumbling that anything approaching a focused research collection remained to be built, and wondering why no professional librarian had been appointed to supervise its development. I had asked Zahran, an architect and urban planner trained at the Massachusetts Institute of Technology and formerly head of the architecture department at the University of Alexandria, to give me an update on acquisitions, which at the time were relying for the most part on gifts, although a modest budget of $1.5 million was being spent on book purchases.

"We are just a baby," he said, pronouncing each word deliberately to make sure I got the point of what was taking place less than a mile from where we were speaking. "As you have seen for yourself, we are still in the process of shaping our destiny, of determining what we will be. So what I say to people who question our will is this: Please do not judge us by what is pledged in the dawn of life, judge us by what we accomplish in full maturity. This library is not for today, it is not for this week; it is for the twenty-first century." For the moment, at least, Zahran's principal concern was to get the building built, furnished, and appointed; the shelves would fill up with marvelous material, he assured me, and the books already assembled would be kept in a conference center that adjoins the library, and transferred over when appropriate.

The day before my meeting with Zahran, I was given a walking tour of the Bibliotheca Alexandrina by an engineer for the consortium of Snøhetta, the Norwegian firm that won an international competition in 1989 to design the new building, and Hamza Associates of Cairo, its Egyptian colleague. Built on an 11.5-acre site facing the Eastern Harbor of the city, and set behind a circular wall of 4,600 Aswan granite slabs inscribed with examples of every known writing script, the library has the aspect of a giant white cylinder emerging from the seabed and, with its oval roof tilted 16 degrees toward the horizon, suggests the outline of a rising sun on the shore of the Mediterranean. Baffled glass panels set in place on the roof in 1999 direct sunbeams over the outstretched waters, a shimmering reminder of the Pharos lighthouse that stood across the harbor for centuries.

Fully a third of the building was designed to lie belowground, with seven terraced floors cascading downward from the rear facing the harbor to provide space for 3,000 readers, and ample accommodations for the ten thousand visitors its governing body, known as the General Organization of the Alexandria Library (GOAL), hope in time will come each day to marvel at its modernist beauty. About half of the $200 million needed to make the project a reality has come from the United Nations Educational, Scientific, and Cultural Organization (UNESCO), with additional support provided by the Egyptian government, Saudi Arabia, the United Arab Emirates, Iraq, and the Sultan of Oman. From outside the region, the French government, meanwhile, has donated computers; Norway has provided furnishings; Japan has given audio-visual equipment; Italy has underwritten a conservation laboratory; Germany is installing a mechanized book-delivery system; and a network of "friends" groups around the world, including several in the United

States, has coordinated fund drives and book donations. Given Egypt's limited economic resources, the continued participation of outsiders is essential, as Suzanne Mubarak, wife of the country's president, Hosni Mubarak, made clear in a speech at the Library of Congress on March 27, 2000. "I am confident that we can meet this challenge," she said. "Our forefathers did, and I have no doubt that, with the support of the rest of the world, we can do it again."

First broached in the 1970s as a way of helping Egypt regain the glory that it enjoyed in ancient times, the idea for a revival of the great library gained UNESCO support in the 1980s, when it was decided to separate the original proposal from the University of Alexandria, which adjoins the site and donated the land, and make it an independent research center. To attract scholars from outside the region, of course, there has to be an abundance of primary material that cannot be located elsewhere, and to that end the library needs considerably more than the donations it has received thus far. "I expect the library to be a lighthouse for the intellect," Zahran said, "a beacon of wisdom and knowledge for this entire region," but he was quick to point out that the target collection of 8 million books will take at least twenty years to acquire, probably a lot longer than that, and he knows that the period of expansion comes at a time when people are questioning the wisdom of storehousing printed material in the first place.

Named for a picturesque mountain in central Norway used as a setting by Henrik Ibsen in the play *Peer Gynt*, Snøhetta was formed in 1989 by a group of young architects, a number of them from the United States, for the specific purpose of entering the Alexandria competition. In an interview with me, a founding partner of the firm, Craig Dykers, stressed the collaborative nature of the project, noting that the library was "not a manifestation of a single person," but an "architecture created by many people to be used and enjoyed by many people." Though the company has its headquarters in Oslo, a good deal of the design was developed in Los Angeles, a city chosen as a base of operations for the similarity of climates in Southern California and Egypt. Born in Germany to American and British parents, Dykers studied architecture at the University of Texas, Austin, and now lives in Oslo.

Unlike the Pharos lighthouse from antiquity, for which numerous likenesses and physical descriptions survive, nothing has come down through the centuries to indicate what the original library might have looked like, a factor that liberated the architects to explore a variety of exciting options. Dykers cited the shape of the Eastern Harbor as inspiring the "architectural response" he and his colleagues ultimately chose. "The geometry of the harbor opened up a study into the nature of the circular form itself. It became quickly apparent to us that so many cultural, religious, and symbolic parallels relate to the circle. It is a shape that gives us a sense of continuity and eternity, it is a reflection of human knowledge."

Once the architects had determined that an "idea of time" must be present in the "ultimate expression of the building" as well, they were certain that they had chosen the correct path. "In order to understand the abstract notion of timelessness, it was necessary to reexamine some very basic human characteristics that have remained unchanged throughout our history," Dykers explained. "Basic notions of life are often taken for granted despite their importance in determining how we perceive the world we live in. For example, how do we understand the earth we walk upon? What happens when we tilt or remove the edges from the things we ordinarily see quite readily? The tilted circular form of the library does not respond to forms we ordinarily think of when we think of buildings, yet it does quite readily correspond to forms we would be comfortable with in nature, such as with the tilting cliffs along the Nile, terraced landscapes and valleys, or distant planets and stars."

For the interior, the architects took their cue from other great repositories, although the visual effect is still strikingly original, with fourteen terraced half-levels that resemble a spacious amphitheater. With a diameter of 160 meters, the reading room will be one of the largest in the world, providing space for 500,000 open-access volumes. "Libraries of the past have been meditative spaces as well as places of research," Dykers said. "The Alexandria Library is predominantly a research institution associated with the Alexandria University. For this reason the main reading room has retained some sobriety associated with libraries of previous centuries." Because the roof tilts toward the northwest, the natural sunlight that flows inside the building is indirect, and will not strike any of the books. Column capitals that support the upper beams are fluted to diffuse light about the room.

Though undeniably rich in symbolism, there has remained the vexing matter of content, and as formal completion dates came and went, and as more and more journalists wrote stories about the impending revival, the issues that had been circulating quietly among academics and librarians finally found their way into print. On March 12, 2000, two reporters for the *Sunday Telegraph* wrote that the "sole purpose" of the new building "will be to house objects that the Internet threatens to make obsolete," leading them to ask this question: "So what are the citizens of Egypt, one of the world's more impoverished countries, doing spending £112 million on building it?" On April 8, 2000, a correspondent for another London newspaper, the *Economist*, quoted one unnamed critic of the project as proposing "Elephantina Albina"—white elephant—as an appropriate name for the new building, a wisecrack that echoed in many respects the caustic barbs aimed at the British Library during its long years of development. Like the writers of the *Sunday Telegraph* article, the issue of central concern to the author of this unsigned piece was whether or not Egypt could afford the $30 million a year it is estimated will be necessary to maintain the operation and build a major research collection. "These are hefty burdens in a country where twelve state universities pack in close to a million students, and whose existing national library—a dusty hulk in Cairo—suffers from leaky plumbing, spotty cataloging and a woeful lack of trained staff." Writing in the May 16, 2000, issue of the *New Yorker*, Alexander Stille framed the quickening debate with another brace of questions:

*What does it mean to "revive" an ancient library whose exact loca-
tion and contents are unknown? Can a library that will start with
about two hundred and fifty thousand books—far fewer than the
number in the library of a small four-year college in the United
States—hope to live up to its grand claims? Does it make sense to
build a library designed to hold eight million books at a moment
when so much information is moving from printed to digital form? In
the age of the Internet, does it even make sense to conceive of a universal library in terms of glass, aluminum, and concrete?*

A month after that lengthy essay appeared, the *Wall Street Journal*
brought attention to the library's meager holdings in a front-page story of
its own, one made noteworthy not so much for its disclosures, since the
same ground had been covered rather thoroughly in Stille's *New Yorker* article, but for the mocking tone of its headline: "Check This Out: A Global
Library Grovels for Books." In a cursory examination of the materials being
stored in the conference center, the journalist, G. Pascal Zachary, mentioned
various lightweight books he saw during his visit, "a tribute to Princess
Di, the Guinness Book of Records, a tome on marine-insurance law, a
reference work on building standards and a self-help text promising '101
ways to improve business performance' " most dubiously present among
them. "Surely," he huffed, "this isn't how the ancient library of Alexandria, famous for containing the whole of human knowledge in the time of
Christ, operated."

Early in 2001 I contacted Dr. Mohammed M. Aman, dean of the
School of Information Studies at the University of Wisconsin in Milwaukee, and a native of Egypt, for an update on the inaugural preparations.
Before assuming his current position in 1979, Aman directed the School
of Library and Information Service at Long Island University, and was
head of the division of Library and Information Science at St. John's
University in New York. Aman has been closely involved with the Bibliotheca Alexandrina throughout its development, having served on the

selection board that awarded the design contract to Snøhetta, and retained by UNESCO in 1991 to draft a collection development policy for the library, a copy of which he forwarded on to me. In the document, Aman identified the library's scope of interest to include anything dealing with the cultural heritage of Egypt, the Mediterranean region, Africa, and the twenty-one countries of the Middle East whose national language is Arabic. "It is hoped that the Library will gradually emerge as the repository of all valuable materials on the history and culture of the region," he wrote, and gifts do play a critical role in developing special collections, as some early holdings of books and manuscripts relating to the history of Alexandria and the construction of the Suez Canal already demonstrate. "But in the long run, the library cannot rely on the magnanimity of others, and however well intentioned the acquisitions policy I drafted may be, it will not take shape until there is a director in place who is blessed with a strong sense of the humanities," Aman told me.

A few weeks after we had that conversation, Egyptian officials announced the appointment of Dr. Ismail Serageldin, a Harvard-educated economist, author, teacher, and former vice president for development of the World Bank as director general of the Bibliotheca Alexandrina. Answering questions I posed to him by e-mail, Serageldin asserted that the library has sufficient books on hand to meet immediate needs, but that his long-range goal is to "create a unique collection for scholars worldwide," and to do that he must move quickly to provide depth in art, culture, and the humanities. "One area we will concentrate on is the ethics of science and technology, which has not really been addressed fully anywhere else until now." The Internet, meanwhile, will allow the new center to establish "strong links" with major libraries such as the Bibliothèque Nationale and the Library of Congress, presenting "possibilities of cross-cooperation" that will be "a first for this part of the world." Serageldin made clear his belief that "printed books will always have a role in education, as well as in our personal lives," and that within ten years, "the Bibliotheca Alexandrina will have made a significant name for itself. I think the BA will begin to build itself as an institution that will demand its own presence to be recognized throughout the world." The ultimate objective, Serageldin concluded, is to create "a center of excellence for learning, research, and dialogue between scholars, institutions, organizations, and governments in the spirit of the ancient library."

In his 1998 interview with me, Mohsen Zahran regarded the project that had occupied his full attention over the previous decade in the carefully calibrated language of an architect. "Alexandria is a city that was planned from the very beginning of its existence, and it is one of the oldest planned cities in the world that is still functioning," he said. "It has suffered a great deal through many civilizations, and has gone through many phases—the process of birth, growth, maturity—but not death. It is that fine curve that is represented in the design of the library, and in its mission. What gives the design a sense of timelessness is its emphasis on the circle. As long as there is the sun, as long as there is the earth, this symbol of the human will to prosper from intellectual inquiry will remain fresh and alive. We can never restore what once was, but we can revive the soul and the purpose of the ancient library. The Bibliotheca Alexandrina is just a baby now, and like all babies, it has the promise of genius."

The words of John Hill Burton (1809–1881), at one time the historiographer-royal of Scotland and a bibliophile of the first rank, seem particularly pertinent in this regard, and have weighed heavily in my willingness to give the Bibliotheca Alexandrina the full benefit of the doubt in its endeavor to reclaim national greatness through creation of a magnificent library, particularly as it approached its formal opening on April 23, 2002. "You may buy books at any time with money, but you cannot make a library like one that has been a century or two a-growing, though you had the whole national debt to do it with," Burton wrote in *The Book-Hunter*, and reinforced his conviction with words that embody the twin virtues of patience and fortitude: "A great library cannot be constructed—it is the growth of ages."

NOTES

Sources cited in the notes by the author's last name or by a short form of the title are to be found in the General Bibliography.

PROLOGUE

The prologue draws on the author's interview with Otto L. Bettmann.

2   "Huge Photo Archive Bought": Steve Lohr, *New York Times*, October 11, 1995. Six years after acquiring the Bettmann Archive, Corbis announced that it was burying the pictures 220 feet belowground in a subzero storage area fashioned from a limestone mine 60 miles northeast of Pittsburgh, Pennsylvania, to protect them against the ravages of deterioration. "The objective is to preserve the originals for thousands of years," a company official said, noting that only 225,000 images—less than 2 percent of the whole collection—had been digitally scanned since 1995, and that it will take at least twenty-five more years to complete the job, probably longer. See Sarah Boxer, "A Century's Photo History Destined for Life in a Mine," *New York Times*, April 15, 2001.

4   "treasure house": Robert D. McFadden, "Otto L. Bettmann, 94, Dies; Founded Archive of Photos," *New York Times*, May 4, 1998.

5   "the heavenly food": Quoted in Basbanes, 83.

5   Mayor Fiorello La Guardia: For an excellent profile of the "Little Flower" of New York City, see the biography by William Manners, like this book—but for different reasons—also titled *Patience and Fortitude* (New York: Harcourt Brace Jovanovich, 1976).

6   "There are two meanings": MacLeish, in Eva Goldschmidt, 45–46.

6   "What's past is prologue": William Shakespeare, *The Tempest*, 2.1.253.

CHAPTER 1: ETERNAL LIFE

This chapter draws on the author's interview with Roger C. Norris.

13   For detail on the jeweled casket of Darius, see Peter Green, *Alexander of Macedon*, 244–245.

14   "An island lies": Plutarch, *The Lives of the Noble Grecians and Romans* (New York: Modern Library, n.d.), 819. Pharos also is the island where Menelaus was becalmed for twenty days while returning home from Troy with Helen after angering Proteus, a son of Poseidon known as the Old Man of the Sea. In the poem, Homer gives a kind of navigational fix for its location: "an island out in the ocean's heavy surge, well off the Egyptian coast—they call it Pharos—far as a deep-sea ship can go in one day's sail with a whistling wind astern to drive her on." Robert Fagles translation of *The Odyssey* (New York: Viking, 1996), 135.

14   "snug harbor": Fagles, trans., *Odyssey*, 135.

14   Eastern Harbor: See Peter Green, *Alexander of Macedon*, 276.

14   eight hundred gold talents: Pliny the Elder, 6.18; Strabo, 7.4. All quotations from Pliny's *Natural History* are drawn from the translation in 10 volumes by H. Rackham, Loeb Classical Library (1938–62); all quotations from *The Geography of Strabo* are drawn from the translation in 8 volumes by Horace Leonard Jones, Loeb Classical Library (1917–32).

15   Lighthouse coins, souvenir models, and "Sostratus of Knidos": Empereur, 84.

17   Work nurtured at Alexandria: See Peter Green, *Alexander to Actium*, 90–91; Canfora, passim; Basbanes, 62–68.

18   "What seems indisputable": Jon Thiem, "The Great Library of Alexandria Burnt: Towards the History of a Symbol," *Journal of the History of Ideas* 40 (October–December 1979): 507–26.

17   two stone relics: Delia, 1454–56.

20   French explorer Franck Goddio: For a full discussion of sculptures recovered from the Eastern Harbor and accounts of the two competing French marine archaeological efforts conducted there, see Foreman; Empereur.

20   "It has a colonnade": Quoted in Clark, *The Care of Books*, 6.

21   world traveler Louis Szathmary: See Basbanes, 357–62, for profile, and preface to the Owl paperback edition of *A Gentle Madness* (1999) for an update.

22   "What I may call the personal element": Clark, *Libraries,* 6–7; "It is unnecessary": Ibid., 10; "I will next shew": ibid., 26; "bird's eye view": ibid., 28.

23–24   "I personally examined": *The Care of Books,* viii; "position" and "arrangement": ibid., 4–6; "The enclosure, paved": ibid., 10. Pliny discusses the decoration of libraries in his *Natural History,* bk. 7, chap. 30, and bk. 35, chap. 2.

24   cluster of white marble temples: For an illustrated assessment of archaeological excavations conducted at Pergamum, see Akurgal, 69–111.

26   "inner citadel": See J. V. Luce, *Celebrating Homer's Landscape: Troy and Ithaca Revisited* (New Haven, Conn.: Yale University Press, 1998), 55.

27   Great Altar of Zeus: An exhibition featuring marbles from Pergamum was shown at the Metropolitan Museum of Art in New York and the Fine Arts Museums of San Francisco in 1996; see Renee Dreyfus and Ellen Schraudolph, eds., *Pergamon: The Telephos Frieze from the Great Altar* (San Francisco: Fine Arts Museums of San Francisco, 1996).

27   "reflects a certain megalomania": Quoted in Stephen Kinzer, "Seeing Pergamon Whole," *New York Times,* September 14, 1997.

28   "delight of the world at large": Quoted in Clark, *Libraries,* 8.

29   Pliny the Elder: For an excellent biographical sketch, see introduction by H. Rackham to Pliny's *Natural History,* vol. 1 (1945), 1. xi–xii.

29   "the names of my authorities": Ibid., 13

30   "For, as the Roman Empire fell": Cahill, 3–4.

31   "written by the holy fingers": Henderson, 187; Dunlop, 6; Reeves, 22; photo of Cathach of Saint Columba in Henderson, 188.

32   "To every cow belongs her calf ": See Dunlop, 58; Reeves, 28–29.

33   Irish majuscule: Henderson, 24; Henry, 226.

33   Reilig Odhrain: Nicholas A. Ulanov, "Iona: Scotland's Isle of Saints," *New York Times,* June 28, 1981.

33   "whence savage clans": Samuel Johnson, *A Journey to the Western Islands of Scotland,* ed. Mary Lascelles (New Haven, Conn.: Yale University Press, 1971), 148.

34   "Its Gospel text": Henry, 149.

34   "By the known standards": Henderson, 179–80.

34   *polari:* See photo of an Irish book satchel in Savage, *Old English Libraries,* 13, and Lerner, 40.

35   inventory of library holdings: Clark, *Libraries,* 102.

35   Irish scribal craftsmanship: Henderson, 27; Reynolds and Wilson, 77.

35   Gallus remained behind and built a hermitage: Factual material for Saint Gall segment drawn from: King and Vogler; Duft; Hobson, 24–35. Detail on the Plan of Saint Gall from Price.

35   "If then it seems to you": Quoted in Hobson, 25.

36   the oldest building plan: In 1980, the University of California Press published a monumental study of the Saint Gall building plan in three volumes, including 1,073 original illustrations. An exhibition featuring models of the reconstruction toured the United States that year. See Price.

37   Alcuin personally knew everyone . . . who could read: Arnold Beichman, "Is Higher Education in the Dark Ages?" *New York Times Magazine,* November 6, 1983.

37   Charlemagne's biographer Einhard: Susanna Checketts, *New Straits Times,* May 2, 1995.

38   "Thus a liturgically significant": King and Vogler, 93.

38   *Casus Sancti Galli:* Ibid., 134.

39   "For thee": Price, quoted on title page.

40   "Saint Gall together": King and Vogler, 93.

41   "nowhere else": Ibid., 145.

42   "work of art of the highest order": Duft, 10. For a learned discussion of the origin of "House of Healing for the Soul," see Cora E. Lutz, *The Oldest Library Motto and Other Literary Essays* (Hamden, Conn.: Archon Books, 1979), an elegant rumination of "detours that were motivated by accidental encounters in libraries."

43   "Form follows function": Quoted in Wiegand and Davis, 348.

43–44   From Clark, *The Care of Books:* "Adopted by man," 1; "Each carrel," 97–98; "The uniformity," 90; "A document setting forth," 66; "let each brother," 68. In 1999, Henry Petroski, the noted civil engineer and author of numerous books on technology, offered an updated evaluation of the development of book storage, and cited his gratitude to John Willis Clark, lauding *The Care of Books* as the "seminal work on the subject." See Petroski, 9.

45   "The main appeal": Wall, 13.

46   "I straightaway": Wood, 112.

46   "myrmidons": Savage, *Old English Libraries,* 68.

47   "It is impossible": Cram, 33.

49   triumph of medieval engineering: Architectural detail of Durham Cathedral described in Wall.

49   Cuthbert's cult: Bonner. For a detailed overview of the cathedral library's collections, Hobson, 54–65; Thompson, 381–86.

49   "mountain, marsh, and moor": Sir Walter Scott, *Marmion,* canto II, stanza XIV.

50   Lindesfarne Gospels: See Henderson, chap. 4.

50–51   "pewes or carrells": *The Rites of Durham,* cited in Clark, *The Care of Books,* 91.

51   "In 1391": Quoted in Hughes, 2.

51   armaria and aumbry: Savage, *Old English Libraries,* 91; Thompson, 619.

52   decorated wooden casket: For Saint Cuthbert's casket, see Henderson, 115–16.

54   "He was the first English historian": Wall, 126, 129–32.

54   "Grey towers of Durham": Quoted in Hughes, x.

54   "public libraries": Clark, *The Care of Books,* 74.

54   "In some abbeys": Savage, *Old English Libraries* 86–87.

55   Richard de Bury: For a discussion of the writing of *The Philobiblon,* see Basbanes 83–87.

55   Librarians began to chain: Chained libraries are treated fully in Streeter.

55   "In the Middle Ages books were rare": Streeter, 3.

57   Cathedral Library at Hereford: See Morgan; Joan Williams; Jancey.

59   Knighted in 1998: See Mark Henderson, "British Citizen Getty Likely to Become Sir Paul," *Times* (London), December 29, 1997.

60   "the most important . . . medieval map": Quoted in Richard Savill, "£2.5m Map for Sale to Help Save Cathedral," *Daily Telegraph* (London), November 17, 1988.

62   "I therefore submit": Clark, *The Care of Books,* 170.

62   Factual detail on the Leiden University Library drawn principally from Scheurleer et al.

65   "seems too plentiful": Bachrach, 106.

65   "by scholars for scholars": Ibid., 110.

66   Factual detail on Bodleian Library drawn from Macray; David Rogers; Hobson.

66–67   "I concluded at the last": Quoted in Macray, 15.

67 "There hath bin heretofore a publike library in Oxford": Quoted in Macray, 15.

68 "bookes in the Syriacke": Ibid., 42; "All new books," 44–47; "Sir Thomas Godly," 31–33; "So drunk" and "having been acquainted," 47–48.

69–70 "Heere in this goodly Magazine of witte": Samuel Daniel, quoted in Macray, 27.

70 "You, having built an ark": Quoted in Macray, 35.

70 "On all sides": Clark, *The Care of Books*, 318.

Chapter 2: Godspeed

This chapter draws on the author's interviews with Abbot Ephraim of Vatopedi, Robert Allison, Father Isidore, Marino Zorzi, the Reverend Leonard E. Boyle, Fabrizio Massimo, Werner Arnold, and Paul LeClerc.

72 *Treasures of Mount Athos:* For factual information and scholarly insight on the book and artistic traditions of Mount Athos, the best source in English by far is Karakatsanis.

72 100,000 square meters of wall surface: Karakatsanis, 20.

72 icons: For a detailed description of Greek icons and their heritage, see Evans and Wixom; Mathews.

73 "the only one": Quoted in Evans and Wixom, 22.

73 "every stone": Quoted in Kallistos of Diokleia [Timothy Ware], "Wolves and Monks: Life on the Holy Mountain Today," *Sobornost* 5, no. 2 (1983): 1–12.

74 "if someone were to set up a colony": Vitruvius, *On Architecture* 2: 1–4, quoted in Romer, 56.

75 "pray without ceasing": Quoted in *The Holy and Great*, A: 23.

75–76 "When the Turks breached the walls": Mathews, 7.

79 "Much of the difficulty": Hasluck, 3.

79 "a mule is provided": Ibid., 6.

80 "Huge monastic complexes": Georgios I. Mantzaridis in Karakatsanis, 16–19.

80–81 "Young Orthodox today": Kallistos, "Wolves and Monks"; for a perceptive profile of Timothy Ware/Bishop Kallistos of Diokleia, see "Private View: The Bishop with a Different Easter," *Financial Times* (London), April 2, 1994.

81 "Like some negligent . . . parent": Deuel, 272.

81   Codex Sinaiticus: See Bentley.

82   "venerable game": Curzon, iv;"pounded down": ibid., 371; "I did not attempt": ibid., 375.

84   Vatopedi: For collections, history, and architectural detail of the monastery, see *The Holy and Great*.

86   "After a first glance": Symonds, *The Age of the Despots*, 32; "Democracies, oligarchies": ibid., 34.

89   "the richest collection": Grafton, *Rome Reborn*, 5.

89   "passionate desire": Symonds, *The Age of the Despots*, 20–21; "The ultimate effect": ibid., 25.

90   "The Biblioteca Laurenziana": Wittkower, 123.

90   "history of the Laurenziana": Austin, 73; "We were to be received": ibid., 115.

91   Leonard E. Boyle: At his death in 1999 at seventy-five, the Reverend Leonard E. Boyle was serving as director of the Leonine Commission, which since 1880 has been producing a critical edition of the writings of Saint Thomas Aquinas from all available manuscript sources. That monumental undertaking is about halfway finished, and may well take another hundred years to complete (see Murphy). A world-renowned paleographer (a scholar who reads ancient manuscripts), Father Boyle had served as chief librarian and keeper of manuscripts at the Vatican Library from 1984 to 1997, and was responsible for initiating digitization programs of the holdings to make them more accessible to scholars. He was forced to leave his position in the wake of a lawsuit stemming from the sale of world rights to reproduce images in the library, a move intended to raise money for modernization. Father Boyle awarded the contract to a California woman on the recommendation of his superior, a cardinal, but never spoke publicly about the scandal that developed when the agreement broke down, and he took the brunt of the criticism in "Library Privileges," an essay written by Alexander Stille for the *New Yorker* (September 28, 1998, 43–59). In the obituary he wrote of Father Boyle for the *Independent* (November 2, 1999), Nicolas Barker noted that Boyle's "rigid silence" was an ultimate act of loyalty that inevitably made him the "scapegoat" for the folly of others, but his "integrity was above suspicion" all the same. Barker's final words expressed the views of anyone who ever had the privilege of meeting this gentle bookman: "Open-handed and open-hearted in life and in scholarship, as humble as generous, he had, like Pius XI, an inner reserve of sanctity."

92   Palazzo Massimo: See Carlo Cresti and Claudio Rendina, *Palazzi of Rome* (Rome: Könemann,1998), 92–101.

93   "Though it was not part": G. Cyprian Alston, "The Rule of St. Benedict," in *The Catholic Encyclopedia* (New York: Robert Appleton, 1923), and New Advent online version.

93   "For a period of more than six centuries": Putnam, 1: 11–12.

94   Rebuilt and reconsecrated: For a balanced history of Monte Cassino, see Leccisotti; for more on the Allied bombardment of the abbey, see Hapgood and Richardson.

95   report released by the Vatican: David Colvin and Richard Hodges, "Tempting Providence: The Bombing of Monte Cassino; Italy, 1944," *History Today* 44 (February 1994): 13.

95   "If we have to choose": Quoted in Hapgood and Richardson, 158–59.

96   "I have worked in many libraries": Orcutt, 37–38.

97   "a knack of surviving": De Hamel, 7.

98   "Any investigation": Newton, 5–7.

98   abbey's own copy of the Rule of Benedict: See Reynolds and Wilson, 96–97, and G. Cyprian Alston in the *Catholic Encyclopedia*. For more on the "manuscript tradition" of the rule, see Joel Chamberlain in *The Rule of St. Benedict: The Abingdon Copy* (Toronto: Pontifical Institute of Medieval Studies, 1982), 1–15. Though made in the tenth century, the Monte Cassino copy is by no means the oldest extant. A copy at Oxford University (Bodleian ms. Hatton 48) in uncial script with insular capitals was produced about 720 in Northumbria, and a copy at Saint Gall (ms. 914), was made by two scribes from the monastery of Reichenau about 815. The Saint Gall copy is believed to have been made from the Charlemagne copy, which descended from Benedict's original.

99   world's oldest library building: The key distinction to be considered here is "in its original form." Merton College, the first fully self-governing college at Oxford University, opened in 1264, with records surviving that document the storage of books there as early as 1276. Between 1371 and 1378 a formal library was erected on the south and west sides of the central quadrangle, and although that building has remained in constant use since then, improvements and modifications have been ongoing since the early 1500s, with major work taking place between 1589 and 1623, including the introduction of the first stalled presses in England. In 1792, chains were removed from all but two of the books, and additional shelves were built below the reading desks. The Merton College Library

now contains 350 medieval manuscripts and 70,000 printed books. See Thompson, 393–96, and http://www.merton.ox.ac.uk/college/library-description.html.

100 Petrarch visited Verona: Reynolds and Wilson, 116.

100 "queen of ecclesiastical libraries": E. A. Lowe, ed., *Codices Latini Antiquiores: A Paleographical Guide to Latin Manuscripts Prior to the Ninth Century* (1934–1966; reprint, Osnabrück: Otto Zeller, 1982), 4: xix.

100 "With a ladder Maffei examined": Thompson, 153.

101 "one of those exceptionally able . . . men": see Hobson, 19.

101–3 The history and collections of the Biblioteca Malatestiana: Hobson, 66–75; Staikos, 304–19.

104 Cardinal Bessarion: Staikos, 321–37.

105 "the most splendid": Grafton, *Rome Reborn*, 22.

105 to acquire manuscripts: For more on Bessarion's collecting, see Jardine, 62; Staikos, 325; Reynolds and Wilson, 133.

105 "I tried": Quoted in Jardine, 62.

106 "Throughout his life": Ibid., 196, 198.

107 "I could not select": Quoted in ibid., 63.

107 "free access": Lowry, 230.

107 "most magnificent and ornate": Quoted in Bruce Boucher, *Andrea Palladio: The Architect in His Time* (Abbeville Press: New York, 1994), 31.

108 headquarters for Greek printing: Lowry, 229–34.

108 "Venice may not have been": Ibid., 8.

109 "I answered that to buy": Quoted in Symonds, *Revival of Learning*, 175.

110 plans for the new library: For details on design and construction of the Laurenziana, see Wallace; Wittkower.

111 "Spare no expense": Quoted in Wallace, 136.

111 "At the back of the library": Argan and Contardi, 186–87.

112 "A secondary problem": Wallace, 136, 141.

113 "In this corner": Quoted in Quint, 15–16.

113 "Good books do not waste": Quoted in Paredi, 13.

114 library of Gian Vincenzo Pinelli: For more on Cardinal Borromeo's acquisition of the library, see Marcella Grendler, "A Greek Collection in Padua: The Library of Gian Vincenzo Pinelli (1535–1601)," *Renaissance Quarterly* 33, no. 3 (autumn 1980): 386–416.

114 Biblioteca Ambrosiana: For architectural detail and early acquisitions, see Paredi, 13–16; Quint, 14–22; Jones, 41–44.

115 "one of the best libraries": Quoted in Paredi, 16.

116 "There is nothing": Quoted in Jones, 44.

116–17   library of Duke August Brunswick-Wolfenbüttel: Details from Schmidt-Glintzer; Hobson, 202–12; Staikos, 392–407.

119   censorship rules "were so extraordinary": quoted in Frame, 73.

120   "There are a large number": Quoted in ibid., 85.

123   *Index Librorum Prohibitorum*: Burke.

124   "when scribes, illuminators": Grafton, *Rome Reborn*, 5; "are not primarily theological": ibid., ix; "In number alone": ibid., 5.

124   "little volume": Niccolò Machiavelli, *The Prince*, tr. and ed. W. K. Marriott (New York: E. P. Dutton, 1908), 1–2.

126   "When evening comes": Niccolò Machiavelli, *Machiavelli and his Friends*, tr. and ed. James B. Atkinson and David Sices (Dekalb: Northern Illinois University Press, 1996), 263–65 (Letter 224).

126   Nuremberg Chronicle: For a meticulous examination of the technical achievement involved in the 1493 production of the Nuremberg Chronicle, see Adrian Wilson; the monograph is based on an examination of the page-by-page layouts that were discovered in 1973 in the binding of a Bible printed by Anton Koberger, a unique artifact to survive from the first fifty years of printing in the fifteenth century, known as the incunabula period.

127   "all happenings": Febvre and Martin, 124.

127–29   "Several pages have been left": Quoted in Adrian Wilson, 189; "Schedel's library reveals": ibid., 25–26; "I venture to promise": ibid., 207; "Speed now, Book": ibid., 209.

130   "Since I know": *The Journal of Christopher Columbus,* translated by Cecil Jane (New York: Clarkson N. Potter, 1960), 191.

130   "government by paper": J. H. Elliott, ed., *The Spanish World* (New York: Harry N. Abrams, 1991), 4.

130   Archive of the Indies: See García.

131   "widely scattered": García, 12.

132   "The Catholic Kings": Ibid., 11.

132   Biblioteca Columbina: Morrison, 46–50; Hobson, 104–10.

133   *Historie:* For publishing history of Ferdinand Columbus's *Historie,* see Morrison, 50–53.

133   "invaluable document": Washington Irving, *The Life and Voyages of Christopher Columbus* (New York: G. P. Putnam's, 1868), vol. 3, 375.

133   "Don Ferdinand was no less": Quoted in Keen, xxiv.

133–34   "Here were gathered": Ibid., viii–ix.

135   national library: Ferdinand's proposal for the library in Seville, and details of his will: Wagner, 1–7.

135   Samuel Pepys: For a profile and a description of Pepys's library, see Hobson, 212–21; Basbanes, 99–107.

136   "It is impossible": Quoted in Wagner, 5.

136   "suffered a shameful neglect": Morrison, 50.

136   "unique among early library founders": Hobson, 107.

137   "The age will come": Quoted in Hobson, 108; original Latin and variant translation in Morison, 54.

137   "This prophecy was fulfilled": *Haec profetia impleta est per patrem meum almirantem anno 1492*: Quoted in Morrison, 59.

CHAPTER 3: MADNESS REDUX

This chapter draws principally on the author's interviews with Jay Fliegelman, Carol Fitzgerald, Abel E. Berland, Diana Korzenik, Alan Jutzi, Amy Myers, Rolland Comstock, and Minor Myers Jr.

152   "There are several reasons": Constance Lindsay Skinner, "Rivers and American Folk," an undated promotional essay believed to have been written in 1935 for the Rivers of America series and issued by the first publisher, Farrar and Rinehart, and reproduced in many of the early editions.(See Cecile Hulse Matschat, *Suwannee River: Strange Green Land* [1938], following page 296.) For a detailed checklist of the books in the series and concise biographies of the authors, illustrators, and editors, see Carol Fitzgerald, *The Rivers of America: A Descriptive Bibliography* (New Castle, Del.: Oak Knoll Press, 2001).

161   "one of the true jewels in our crown": Copy of letter from William Cagle, furnished to the author by Abel Berland, and used with permission.

161   Robert Hoe: For profile and description of the great sale of his books, see Basbanes, 173–84.

167   Drawing Act of 1870: See Diana Korzenik, *Drawn to Art: A Nineteenth Century American Dream* (Hanover, N.H.: University Press of New England, 1985). For transfer of Korzenik Collection, see Suzanne Muchnic, "Educational Tools That Can Teach Us a Lesson: Huntington Receives a Collector's Array of Historical Art Supplies," *Los Angeles Times*, April 5, 1998. Among Korzenik's other publications is *Art Making and Education: Disciplines in Art Education, Contexts of Understanding* (Urbana: University of Illinois Press; 1993), which she wrote with Maurice Brown, professor of painting at State University of New York–New Paltz.

168 "It cannot be stated too often": Quoted in Basbanes, 194–95.

169 "One for the Books": David Streitfeld, *Washington Post*, August 19, 1996.

174 catalog of a Grolier Club exhibition: *Yours Very Sincerely C. L. Dodgson (Alias "Lewis Carroll"): An Exhibition from the Collection of Jon A. Lindseth* (New York: Grolier Club, 1998), dedicated to "William Self, who knows great books."

176 David Kirschenbaum: Profiled in Basbanes, 331–34.

CHAPTER 4: SPLENDID ANACHRONISMS

This chapter draws principally on the author's interviews with Fred Bass, Nancy Bass, Sheldon M. Wool, Marvin Mondlin, Judith Lowry, Naomi Hample, Adina Cohen, Peter B. Howard, Alan Bell, and Elisabeth Westin Berg, and from an unpublished memoir written by Louis Cohen (1904–1991), furnished by his daughters to the author, and used with their permission.

183 "a Communist uncle": John Nielsen, "Old Bookstores: A Chapter Ends," *New York Times*, May 31, 1981; see also Dickinson, 78.

183 "exhaustive, definitive listing": Obituary of Eleanor Lowenstein, *New York Times*, December 2, 1980; see also Dickinson, 132.

183 Obituary of Walter Goldwater: *New York Times*, June 28, 1985.

189 "To the uninitiated, entering the Strand": *Wall Street Journal*, August 21, 1986.

190 "the last bookstore of its kind": Nicolas Barker, *Independent* (London), January 16, 1991.

190 "an oasis of calm and mustiness": Dinitia Smith, *New York Times*, October 13, 1997.

199 "of that kind which I call Serendipity": Anecdote used in the *Oxford English Dictionary* for the seminal citation of the word.

200 "Puzzled customer": Ian Jackson, *The Key to Serendipity*, vol. 1, *How to Find Books in Spite of Peter B. Howard* (Berkeley, Calif.: privately published, 2000), [4].

202 "Mr. Howard's 'Logic' ": Ibid., 42. See also Ian Jackson, *The Key to Serendipity*, vol. 2, *How to Buy Books from Peter B. Howard* (Berkeley, Calif.: privately published, 1999).

203 "The Ninth Row's Happy Fan": Jane Vandenburgh, *Wall Street Journal*, August 8, 1993.

206   Carl Petersen collection of William Faulkner material: Basbanes, 295–300.

207   London Library: For an anecdotal history of the library, see Wells; for its formative years, see Harrison.

208   "A good friend": Quoted in Mary Blume, "Shh! Wafts of Change at London Library," *International Herald Tribune*, August 30, 1993.

208   "Nothing has changed": Quoted in Wells, 224.

209   "The London Library": A. S. Byatt, *Possession* (New York: Random House, 1900), 3–4.

210   "We've lost our 'Religion' ": Wells, 179.

214   Skokloster Slott: For background on Skokloster and its collections, and a description of the Bernadotte Library and the Nobel Library, see Nicholas A. Basbanes, "A Swedish Library Tour," *Biblio* 3 (January 1998): 10–13.

215   "Send me the library and the curiosities": Charles Eaton, "Christina of Sweden and Her Books," in *Bibliographica*, vol. 1, 5–30.

CHAPTER 5: PROFILES IN BIBLIOPHAGIA

This chapter draws on the author's interviews with Umberto Eco, Carlo Alberto Chiesa, Barry Moser, Maurice Sendak, Penelope Fitzgerald, and Robert Coover, and from the personal journal Barry Moser maintained while preparing the Pennyroyal-Caxton Bible.

219   Bibliophagia: The *Oxford English Dictionary* defines a *bibliophagist* as a "devourer of books"; the *Random House Dictionary* describes a *bibliophage* as "an ardent reader; a bookworm."

222   "prodded by a single idea:" Eco, *Postscript*, 13.

222   "turns on the theft and possession of a book": Eco, *The Name of the Rose*, 446.

222   "almost worn away": Ibid., 467.

226   "more reasonable picture": Eco, *The Role of the Reader*, 5; "According to the principles": Ibid., 176.

228   "I find something uncanny": Quoted in Lanes, 120. Sendak discussed the role of music in his work in his Caldecott Medal acceptance address of 1964; see Sendak, 145–55. For a comprehensive survey of Sendak's book illustration, see Lanes; John Lahr, "The Playful Art of Maurice Sendak," *New York Times Magazine*, October 12, 1980, 44.

229   "one of the most powerful men": Quoted in Jane P. Marshall, "Opera

Music Lures Sendak's Creative Muse," *Houston Chronicle*, October 19, 1997.

229 "His books have helped": Quoted in Jacqueline Trescott, "Medaling in the Arts," *Washington Post*, January 10, 1997.

233 Ursula Nordstrom: For an excellent biographical profile of Nordstrom and a representative selection of her letters, including many to Sendak, see Leonard S. Marcus, ed., *Dear Genius: The Letters of Ursula Nordstrom* (New York: HarperCollins, 1998).

234 a discriminating collector: For an incisive description of Sendak's collection of books, letters, and pertinent artworks, with insight on how these objects have influenced his work, see Giroud and Sendak.

235 "it is our hope that the visitor": Ibid., 7.

236 "the majestic mountain": Herman Melville, *Pierre; or, The Ambiguities: The Kraken Edition*, ed. Hershel Parker, pictures by Maurice Sendak (New York: HarperCollins, 1995), 1.

238 Death of Penelope Fitzgerald: Richard Ollard, *Independent* (London), May 9, 2000; Dinitia Smith, *New York Times*, May 3, 2000.

239 Three months before Fitzgerald's death, *The Knox Brothers* (Washington, D.C.: Counterpoint, 2000) was issued in a new edition.

241 "the highest standards": A. N. Wilson, "Obituary of Penelope Fitzgerald, Novelist," *Daily Telegraph*, May 3, 2000.

241 "of all the postmodernist writers": Michiko Kakutani review of Coover's novel *A Night at the Movies*, *New York Times*, Jaunary 7, 1987.

242 "What I write tends to be controversial": Quoted in Mel Gussow, "A Writer Who Delights in Layers of Complexity," *New York Times*, June 1, 1996.

242 "The End of Books": *New York Times Book Review*, June 21, 1992.

242 "promises (or threatens)": Landau, 19.

243 *Hamlet on the Holodeck*: See Murray, passim.

243 "utterly essential": Robert Coover, "Hyperfiction; And Now, Boot Up the Reviews," *New York Times*, August 29, 1993.

245 "unreadable": Diane Greco quoted in Lisa Guernsey, "New Kind of Convergence: Writers and Programmers," in *New York Times*, April 9, 1999. An owner of Eastgate Systems and a pioneer in "experimental storytelling," Greco was quoted a year later by Linton Weeks in the *Washington Post* (April 26, 2000) as saying that books are destined to "become objects of nostalgia." Her partner, Mark Bernstein, expressed his conviction that the "future of literature lies on the screen." On the matter of "linearity" in creative writing—and

whether or not "nonsequential writing" is an innovation, or if it has echoes in the work of such authors as Laurence Sterne, William Faulkner, Don DeLillo, and Salman Rushdie—see Michiko Kakutani, "Culture Zone: Never-Ending Saga," in *New York Times Magazine,* September 28, 1997, 40.

245 "throwback": Nicholas A. Basbanes, in "Barry Moser: A Noted Artist and Illustrator Plans to Enter the Twentieth Century," *Sunday Telegram* (Worcester, Mass.), November 16, 1986.

247 Andrew Hoyem: For more on Hoyem and the Arion Press Lectern Bible see Carol Grossman, "Arion Press: A Legacy of Literary Artistry," *Biblio* 2 (September 1997): 30–37; Carl Nolte, "The Good Book in Good Hands," *San Francisco Chronicle,* December 27, 1998; and David Holmstrom, "Making a New Bible the Old Way," *Christian Science Monitor,* November 10, 1999. For more on Donald Jackson and the Saint John's Bible project, see Per Ola and Emily D'Aulaire, "Inscribing the Word," *Smithsonian* (December 2000): 79–88.

250 Pioneer Valley: The Mortimer Rare Book Room at Smith College, under the direction of Martin Antonetti, has initiated a major research project to document the rich book arts tradition in western Massachusetts.

252 "I saw a printing press operated by a master": Quoted in Jon Anderson, *Chicago Tribune,* March 24, 1988. Moser discussed the influence of McGrath in his development as a bookman in 1998 in a talk called "There Was a Time" and printed in Moser, 39–52. There he describes his first meeting with the master printer as "the great epiphany" of his life: "I had, that day—unknown and unexpectedly—come home. Come home to my future life and to my artistic form: The Book."

252 "The focus of a private press": Colin Franklin, in Lisa Baskin, *The Gehenna Press: The Works of Fifty Years* (Dallas: Bridwell Library and Gehenna Press, 1992), 7–8. See profile of Leonard Baskin in Basbanes, 285–92. For a particularly sensitive Baskin obituary, see Albert H. Friedlander in the *Independent* (London), June 8, 2000; also Roberta Smith, *New York Times,* June 6, 2000.

254 "woodiness": Bliss, 245–46.

255 "It is generally agreed": Ibid.

260 "gargantuan bricoleur": Robert Hughes, "Iron Was His Name," *Time,* January 13, 1983, 70.

CHAPTER 6: HUNTERS AND GATHERERS

This chapter draws principally on the author's interviews with Pierre Berès, Roger E. Stoddard, Heribert Tenschert, Nico Israel, Max Israel, Otto Bettmann, Marguerite Goldschmidt, Bernard Rosenthal, Fred Schreiber, Leona Rostenberg, Madeleine B. Stern, Stephen Weissman, Priscilla Juvelis, Archibald Hanna, William S. Reese, and Ellen S. Dunlap.

262   Bernard Quaritch Ltd.: See the *Book Collector,* special number, 1997.

263   "need the assistance of a professional": Pierre Berès, *Book Collector,* summer 1997, 248–51.

265   "Dealers took note": Dalya Alberge, "Art Market: Odd Books Achieve a High Turnover," *Independent* (London), October 23, 1990.

265   "All works": Associated Press wire service dispatch, April 21, 1998.

267   "One of the richest manuscript Books of Hours known": Tenschert, *Leuchtendes Mittelalter, Neue Folge III*, Catalog 45 (Ramsun, Switzerland: Heribert Tenschert, 2000), 480.

269   "Tenschert quality" books: See *Fünfzig Unica/Fifty Unique Books/ Livres Uniques*, Catalog 40 (Ramsun, Switzerland: Heribert Tenschert, 1998).

276   "Nico Israel has earned": Sebastiaan S. Hesselink, in Croiset van Uchelen, van der Horst, and Schilder, ix.

276   "greatest asset": Lord Waddington, in ibid., 495–96.

276   *Adagia:* Associated Press, November 21, 1990.

278   "My parents . . . came from Berlin": Heilbut, ix–xi.

278   "The antiquarian booksellers": Bernard M. Rosenthal, *The Gentle Invasion*. In 1995 the Beinecke Rare Book and Manuscript Library at Yale University acquired from Rosenthal a collection of 242 books printed before 1600 that had been annotated by contemporary readers. In 1997 Yale published *The Rosenthal Collection of Printed Books with Manuscript Annotations,* a compilation that includes complete descriptions by Rosenthal. In the preface Robert G. Babcock, curator of early books and manuscripts at the Beinecke, noted that other than a few modifications, the book "would have been Catalog 34 of Bernard M. Rosenthal, Inc.," and he explained why a rare-books library decided to publish what amounted to a bookseller's catalog in an elegant hardcover edition: "The bibliographical and historical information Rosenthal supplies, as well as the sample transcriptions of annotations, should provide a sound basis for an appreciation of the books." Rosenthal's method, moreover, had an addi-

tional benefit: "Because the volumes described in this catalog combine features of both printed books and manuscripts, none of the standard methods of cataloguing brings out the full range of interest of these artifacts."

280   "story of how he acquired his stock": Bernard M. Rosenthal, "Cartel, Clan, or Dynasty?" 389–390.

281   "I carry with me": Ibid., 385.

282–83   "Final Exhibition": John Russell, *New York Times*, November 21, 1986.

283   "citizen of the world": Nicolas Barker, *Independent* (London), January 6, 1993.

285   *The Truthful Lens* (New York: Grolier Club, 1980).

286   "It is strange": Preface by Nicolas Barker to *The Good Citizen: A Collection of Books Written to Further or to Undertake the Improvement of Mankind*. Catalog no. 52, Lucien Goldschmidt, Inc., 1981, 5–6.

287   Toulouse-Lautrec: Lucien Goldschmidt and Herbert Schimmel, ed., *Unpublished Correspondence of Henri de Toulouse-Lautrec* (London: Phaidon, 1969).

288   "the loss of the scholarly bookseller": Lucien Goldschmidt, in *The Scenery Has Changed*, 9–21.

289   letter from Roger E. Stoddard: Quoted with permission.

290   Herbert Reichner: See Rostenberg and Stern, 104–15; 395–401.

291   *Fingerspitzengefühl*: Ibid., 171–73.

293   "You have a junior partner": Ibid., 148; "the two book ladies": ibid., 211.

295   "Every age is critical": Ibid., 254; "We are not stepping out": ibid., 254–57.

296   Bernard Amtmann: Factual detail and quotations drawn from Mappin and Archer.

299   A. S. W Rosenbach: The definitive biography of "the Doctor" is Edwin Wolf 2d and John Fleming, *Rosenbach* (Cleveland: World Publishing, 1960); for a more recent examination of his business correspondence, see Basbanes, chap. 5.

300   "I would be willing": Quoted in Basbanes, 217.

300   "The bookseller, too, is a collector": Archibald Hanna, in Decker, v.

300   "It has often been said": Ibid., xxiii.

301   Ximenes Rare Books: Stephen Weissman christened his book business Ximenes in 1965 as a tribute to Derrick Somerset Macnutt (1902–1971), a famous crossword setter for the *Observer* who used the name as his pseu-

donym; *The Penguin Book of Ximenes Crossword Puzzles,* published in 1982, contains 100 of his best creations.

301   "There has probably never": Powell, 73–74. For excellent primary material on Jake Zeitlin, see "Books and the Imagination: Fifty Years of Rare Books," 1980, two volumes in typescript, prepared by Joel Gardner in conjunction with the Oral History Program of University of California, Los Angeles. Also on deposit there is "Looking Back at Sixty: Recollections of Lawrence Clark Powell, Librarian, Teacher, and Writer," 1973, two volumes in typescript, prepared by James V. Mink. Powell died on March 14, 2001, at the age of ninety-four, in Tucson, Arizona. See Myrna Oliver, "Lawrence Clark Powell; Lifted UCLA Library to Prominence," *Los Angeles Times,* March 20, 2001; Hanna Miller, "L. C. Powell Dies, Known as Dean of U.S. Librarians," *Arizona Daily Star,* March 20, 2001.

302   "Randall was a bookman at heart": Silver, 5–10; for more on George Parker Winship and Fine Arts 5E at Harvard, see Basbanes, 191–93.

302   "At an age": Deoch Fulton, in *Grolier 75,* 75–77.

310   "rare-book dealer": *New York Times,* December 18, 1992.

310   "a legendary period": Reprinted in *Book Collector* 37 (spring 1988): 121–23.

311   "He was completely discreet": Ibid.

312   "There is an added dimension": John F. Fleming and Priscilla Juvelis, *The Book Beautiful and the Binding as Art* (joint catalog, 1983), 1.

314   "If you want to make money": Jeffrey A. Trachtenberg, "The Rare Book Game," *Forbes,* October 28, 1985, 336.

319   "Rarity after rarity": Bailey Bishop, in *Frank Siebert Library,* 1:6. For an excellent biography of Siebert and a full bibliography of his scholarship, see Ives Goddard, "Frank T. Siebert, Jr. (1912–1998)," *Anthropological Linguistics* 40 (1998), 481–98.

320   "I never had any training": Quoted in Goddard, 482.

321   "His work was doggedly independent": Ibid., 486.

321   "My sister and I ended up caring about him": Quoted in Rita Reif, "A Man Who Traded Everything for an Indian Trove," *New York Times,* May 16, 1999.

324   Laird U. Park Jr.: See *The Americana Library of Laird U. Park, Jr.* (New York: Sotheby's, 2000).

325   *Stamped with a National Character: Nineteenth Century American Color Plate Books* (New York: Grolier Club, 1999); see also *A Herman Melville*

Collection (New Haven, Conn.: Beinecke Rare Book and Manuscript Library, Yale University, 1991).

CHAPTER 7: MANY YEARS

This chapter draws principally on the author's interviews with Lloyd E. Cotsen and Andrea Immel.

328   University of Utah: See Jacques Steinberg, *New York Times*, March 15, 1995.

329   UCLA returns $1 million: Robert Fisk, "Middle East: Turkish Money Fails to Blot Out the Stain of Genocide," *Independent* (London), January 17, 1998.

329   Lee M. Bass: Dan Shine, "Yale OKs Return of Gift to Billionaire," *Dallas Morning News*, March 15, 1995.

329   Larry Kramer: Kim Strosnider, "After Snub, Yale Alumnus Considers Withholding Gift of Papers," *Chronicle of Higher Education*, September 26, 1997; Karen W. Arenson, "Playwright Is Denied a Final Act," *New York Times*, July 9, 1997. See also Glenn Hurowitz, "Still Fuming, Kramer Lashes Out at Yale Administrators," *Yale Daily News*, December 1, 1997.

330   Ken Lipper: Dinitia Smith, "Holocaust Studies Gift: A Headache for Harvard," *New York Times*, July 19, 1997.

336   "We're a marketing company": *Forbes*, March 30, 1981, 63; for the sale of Neutrogena Corp. to Johnson & Johnson, see *Cosmetics International* 18 (September 10, 1994): 1.

338   "I'm not really a collector": Quoted in Joanne Ditmer, *Denver Post*, October 19, 1998. See also MaLin Wilson, "Santa Fe's Folk Art Museum Adds an Elegant Angle to Its Abundance of Whimsy with the Opening of the Neutrogena Wing," *Los Angeles Times*, August 23, 1998; "Neutrogena Wing a Class Act," *Albuquerque Journal*, August 30, 1998.

341 –42 "an ageless treasure": Harold T. Shapiro, dedication remarks at Cotsen Library, printed by Princeton University in commemorative brochure.

342   Details of the deaths of JoAnne Cotsen, Noah Cotsen, and Christopher Doering, the investigation of the killings, and the resolution: Associated Press, May 24, 1979; May 25, 1979; September 3, 1979; February 26, 1980; February 27, 1980.

346   "readily identifiable": Andrea Immel, in *A Catalogue of the Cotsen*

Children's Library (Princeton, N.J.: Princeton University Library, 2000), xxiii.

347 "This facsimile edition": In *Marseilles, Genoa and Pisa: A Beatrix Potter Photograph Album Representing a Pictorial Biography* (Los Angeles: Cotsen Occasional Press, 1998).

Chapter 8: The People's Palace

This chapter draws on the author's interviews with Henry Scannell, Marilyn McLean, Stuart Walker, Bernard Margolis, Alfred Kazin, Harold Bloom, Edward Kasinec, Catherine Carver Dunn, Vartan Gregorian, and Paul LeClerc.

352 Los Angeles fire: See Bob Baker, "Library Races against Time to Save Books," *Los Angeles Times*, May 1, 1986; Bob Baker, "Engineer with Unusual Skills Faces His Biggest Challenge," *Los Angeles Times*, May 1, 1986.

352 citizen volunteers: William Nottingham and Edward J. Boyer, " 'Like Paying Interest on a Debt'; 1,500 Rally to Library's Need in Ashes of Disaster," *Los Angeles Times*, May 4, 1986; "Aerospace Firm to Defrost Wet, Frozen Library Books," *Los Angeles Times*, May 10, 1986.

352 "As we mourn the old Central Library": Lawrence Clark Powell, "Life Was Learned in Los Angeles' Library," *Los Angeles Times*, May 11, 1986. The impact of a public library on the town of Panajachel, Guatemala—and how gravely its loss was felt when a fire of unknown origin destroyed it on November 28, 2000—is detailed by David Gonzalezin "Once upon a Time, a Magical Room in Guatemala," *New York Times*, January 9, 2001. Though the collection of 8,002 volumes was modest by North American standards, the library, known as the Biblioteca Popular, may well have been "the finest community library in Guatemala and perhaps in all of Central America," and it held "a very real magic" for the community's 12,000 residents, a third of whom were enrolled in schools. The day after the fire, children "rooted through the mess in a vain search for any book that survived." An effort was undertaken by Ann Cameron, a New Yorker who moved to the village in 1983, to rebuild the collections through donations.

353 Leningrad fire: Katherine M. Griffin, "Americans Help Soviets Bind Wounds after Library Fire," *Los Angeles Times*, April 27, 1988; Dennis Kimmage, "Scholar in USSR Faults 'Upside-down Glasnost' after Library

Fire Destroying Half-Million Books," *American Libraries* 19 (May 1988): 332; Lance Morrow, "A Holocaust of Words," *Time,* May 2, 1988, 96.

357   Alexandre Vattemare: See Whitehill, 3–17; Winsor, 279–94.

358   "Whatever we may think of Vattemare": Winsor, 286.

359   694 private libraries: Ibid., 293. See also Shera; Farnum. For an excellent analysis of the American public library movement during the years of its formation from 1876 to 1920, and the role it played in the development of an industrialized society, see Garrison. For British library initiatives in the nineteenth century, see Ogle.

359   "attained by the establishment of a Public Library": *Report of the Trustees,* reprinted by the Boston Public Library. For a documented account of the first public library established in the United States, see George Abbot Morison, *The Story of the Peterborough Town Library* (Peterborough, N.H.: Peterborough Town Library, 1967), available through the library.

359   16,090 public library buildings: *Public Libraries in the United States* (NCES 2000-316), a compilation of figures reported to the National Center for Education Statistics in the Office of Educational Research and Improvement of the U.S. Department of Education.

359   written by George Ticknor: Whitehill, 27.

359   "A large public library is of the utmost importance": *Report of the Trustees,* 8–9.

360   forwarded to Joshua Bates: Winsor, 287.

360   "free to all": Text of the Bates letters, Whitehill, 34–36.

361   Edward Everett spoke: Whitehill, 56; Winsor, 290–92.

362   "high and luxurious beauty": Quoted in Wick, 27.

362   "Let in the light": Full text of Holmes's poem in Whitehill, 147–48.

365   "Right from the start": Quoted in Mark Feeney, "Splendor in the Stacks," *Boston Globe,* April 19, 1998.

365   "The main consideration": Quoted in Van Slyck, 10.

366   "a well digested, systematic library": 32–35.

366   Joseph Cogswell's book-buying trips abroad: Lydenberg, 13–21.

366–67   "Dr. Cogswell": Burton, 179–81.

367   "a library so large": Quoted in Lydenberg, 21.

367   "I trust I shall not": Ibid., 32–35.

367–68   "one of the most useful": Goodspeed, 81; for profile of James Lenox, see Basbanes, 160–66.

368   Samuel Jones Tilden: Tilden is remembered for outpolling Rutherford B.

Hayes in the 1876 presidential election by 250,000 votes but losing the office when a specially convened electoral commission ruled in favor of his opponent, giving him the election by one electoral vote. Tilden chose not to challenge the decision for fear there would be another civil war. The incident received renewed attention in November 2000 when vice president Al Gore outpolled George W. Bush by more than 500,000 votes, but lost the Electoral College when the U.S. Supreme Court refused to allow a recount in Florida to continue.

368   Vermont white marble: Lydenberg, 419; Reed, 16–17.

369   "He was America's best reader": Quoted in Wilborn Hampton, "Alfred Kazin, the Author Who Wrote of Literature and Himself, Is Dead at 83," *New York Times,* June 6, 1998.

370   "Year after year": Alfred Kazin, *New York Jew* (New York: Alfred A. Knopf, 1978), 1–8.

370–71   "I would have been nowhere": Transcript of Brian Lamb interview with Harold Bloom for *Booknotes,* broadcast September 3, 2000, on C-SPAN.

371   "She came and found me": Quoted in Sara Rimer, "The 'People's Library' to Celebrate as a Cathedral of Knowledge For All," *New York Times,* May 19, 1986.

371   "Name a writer": Ibid.

372   "Suddenly": Robert A. Caro, "Sanctum Sanctorum for Writers," *New York Times,* May 19, 1995.

372   "part of the heartbeat": Quoted in Sandee Brawarsky, "One Hundred Years of Solitude," *Jewish Week,* May 26, 1995.

372   DeWitt Wallace: See John Heidenry, *Theirs Was the Kingdom: Lila and DeWitt Wallace and the Story of the Reader's Digest* (New York: W. W. Norton, 1993).

373   Chester Carlson and the Xerox machine: See David Owen, "Copies in Seconds: The History of Xerography," *Atlantic Monthly* 257 (February 1986): 64; Gary Jacobson, "Carlson's Timeless Lessons on Innovation," *Management Review* 78 (February 1989): 13.

374   method for instant photography: See Victor K. McElheny, *Insisting on the Impossible: The Life of Edwin Land* (Reading, Mass.: Perseus, 1998).

374   Juan Trippe and *China Clipper:* Jack Fincher, "To Be Airborne on a Not-So-Slow Boat to China; Pan American Airways' 'China Clipper,' " *Smithsonian,* November 1985, 184.

375   1998 Romanov exhibition: See Nicholas A. Basbanes, "Fit for a Czar," *Biblio* 3 (March 1998): 8–11.

375   Leon Trotsky in New York: *My Life: An Attempt at Autobiography* (New York: Charles Scribner's Sons, 1930), 230–38. On arriving in 1917, Trotsky's host, Nicolai Bukharin, "insisted on dragging us off to the Public Library the very first day," where Trotsky proceeded to "study the economic history of the United States assiduously."

376   "unearthing at least 62,192 facts": Obituary of Norbert Pearlroth, *Time*, April 25, 1983, 119; "Everyone has always believed": Quoted in Dorothy J. Gaiter, Pearlroth obituary, *New York Times*, April 15, 1983.

376   Martin Radtke: "Grateful Man Wills Library $368,000," *New York Times*, October 2, 1974.

377   "I had little opportunity": Radtke inscription inlaid in floor at main entrance to New York Public Library. In December 2000 the Boston Public Library announced it had just received "a $6.8 million thank you" in the will of Thomas R. Drew Jr., a retired public schoolteacher and onetime guidance counselor who lived his entire life modestly in the Dorchester neighborhood of the city and used the resources of the library's business branch to study the stock market and make a fortune. "This was a simple individual who wanted to say thank you to a system that allowed him to be successful in life," Mayor Thomas M. Menino told Tatsha Robertson of the *Boston Globe* (December 7, 2000).

378   "Martin Radtke was typical": *New York Times*, October 2, 1974.

378   "Corporate Partners": *New York Times*, December 3, 1999.

379   Separate boards: For more on decision to operate the New York Public Library separately from Brooklyn and Queens, see Theodore Jones, 62; Van Slyck, 113–24. For an account of the Flushing branch of the Queens Borough Library, "the busiest branch in the nation's busiest library system," see Vivian S. Toy, "Bustling Queens Library Speaks in Many Tongues," *New York Times*, May 31, 1998.

379   "absolute pain" and "not a luxury": Christopher Swan, "Quiet Crisis in the Library," *Christian Science Monitor*, May 21, 1981.

380   "I was immediately struck": Hamburger, 66.

380   "a great cultural impresario": Quoted in Jane Gross, "With the Talents of a 'Missionary and a Showman,' He Revived the Library," *New York Times*, September 1, 1988,

380   "The library is essential": Richard F. Shepard, *New York Times*, April 14, 1981.

381   "I have never done anything": Quoted in David Bird, "David Rockefeller Donation to Library Honors Brooke Astor," *New York Times*, Sep-

tember 5, 1985. For excellent profiles of Astor, see Philip Herrera, "The Gift of Inspiration," *Town and Country* 147 (December 1993); Marilyn Berger, "Being Brooke Astor," *New York Times*, May 20, 1984.

383   "A university is a place of teaching": Frank J. Prial, "Timothy S. Healy, 69, Dies; President of Public Library," *New York Times*, January 1, 1993.

383   "Mr. LeClerc takes over": William Grimes, "Top Library Post Goes to Hunter President," *New York Times*, September 1, 1993.

384   Center for Scholars and Writers: The Providence, Rhode Island, novelist Allen Kurzweil used a fellowship at the center in 1999 and 2000 to research and write a sophisticated suspense novel that is narrated by an enterprising young reference librarian of recondite interests, and uses the New York Public Library as an endearing "character" in its own right. *The Grand Complication* was published in the summer of 2001 by Theia, a literary imprint of Hyperion Books of New York. An advance reading copy of the novel prepared from uncorrected proofs was furnished to the author prior to its official release.

CHAPTER 9: ONCE AND FUTURE LIBRARY

This chapter draws substantially on the author's interviews with Steven A. Coulter, Kenneth E. Dowlin, Nicholson Baker, Tillie Olsen, Philip Leighton, Bernard M. Rosenthal, Bernard A. Margolis, Walter Biller, Deetje Boler, Annette G. MacNair, Melissa Riley, Catherine M. Bremer, Andrea V. Grimes, Claire LaVaute, Alan D'Souza, Regina Minudri, Susan Goldstein, William R. Holman, and Kevin Starr.

390   "A five-story skylit court": Simon, 110–11.

390   "Bridges are the central metaphor": Quoted in Jesse Hamlin, "Building Design Bridges Past, Present and Future," *San Francisco Chronicle*, April 18, 1996.

391   "technological visionary": Laura Evenson, "S.F. Librarian Has Eye on the Future," Ibid.

394   "I am apprehensive": Text of speech delivered by Nicholson Baker on May 30, 1996; copy furnished to the author by Baker.

395   *New Yorker* essay: Baker, "Deadline."

396   "prosecutorial" tone: Baker, *Double Fold*, x; "destroying to preserve"; Ibid., 22–36.

404   "All that made this city": Quoted in *San Francisco Chronicle*, October 14, 1998.

405   "gift to the city": Isabel Allende, in Wiley, 8.

405   "The paradox in libraries": Michael Schuyler, "SFPL, Viewed from the Top Left Corner," *Computers in Libraries* 4 (April 1997): 32.

405   "messages of our past": Dowlin, from excerpt of *The Electronic Library* in Cole, 183–99.

406   Copies of the two "discard reports" compiled by Deetje Boler were furnished to the author.

417   "first-class institution": Wiley, 171–79.

420   "post-occupancy evaluation": San Francisco Public Library Post Occupancy Evaluation (POE), Final Report, 2 vols., January 4, 2000, prepared by Ripley Architects, 49 Stevenson St., San Francisco, Calif.

CHAPTER 10: IN THE STACKS

This chapter draws on the author's interviews with Vartan Gregorian, Karen A. Schmidt, Anthony Grafton, Robert Darnton, Peter Lyman, Carole Moore, Thomas F. O'Connell, Lillian Starr, Norman B. Starr, Robert K. O'Neill, Jerome Yavarkovsky, Duane E. Webster, Michael Ginsberg, David H. Stam, Michael Winship, John C. Ittelson, Carolyn M. Gray, Ray English, Robert S. Taylor, Gregory Smith Prince Jr., Judy Harvey Sahak, Bonnie Clemens, and Minor Myers Jr.

426   "a great library": William H. Gass, "In Defense of the Book: On the Enduring Pleasures of Paper, Type, Page, and Ink," *Harper's* 299 (November 1999): 45–51. Institutional prestige is achieved by more than books, of course; in April 2000 astronomers at Harvard University and the Massachusetts Institute of Technology announced a joint program to build the most powerful telescope in the Southern Hemisphere, eclipsing, as it were, the optical telescope owned by the California Institute of Technology by a factor of twenty-five. Within days Caltech officials were discussing the construction of a telescope twenty-five times again more powerful than the one planned by its East Coast rivals. "These days, at major universities at least, it's not the ability to stalk the cosmos that brings admiration and envy from colleagues, it's the size and power of your telescope," Tatsha Robertson wrote in the *Boston Globe* (April 4, 2000). "We learned that to keep the best faculty we better have the best resources necessary," Paul Schechter, a physics professor at MIT, told her.

426   "I have been": Powell, 61. Among Powell's larger acquisitions was the 80,000-volume library of C. K. Ogden, the originator of an 850-word artificial language known as Basic English that provided the model for Newspeak, the simplified lexicon used by George Orwell in *Nineteen Eighty-four*.

427   Ted Hughes archive: Bo Emerson, "In a New Light," *Atlanta Constitution*, March 19, 1999. See also Ronald Schuchard and Stephen Enniss, "The Growth of Emory's Modern Irish Collection," *Gazette of the Grolier Club*, n.s., no. 50 (1999): 35–55. Estimated purchase price: see John Harlow, *Sunday Times* (London), February 7, 1999.

428   "Never have libraries": Quoted in Judy Klemesrud, "A Rally of Literary Lions for Public Library," *New York Times*, October 23, 1981.

428   more than tripled the endowment: For Brown endowment, faculty, and size of library, see Judith Miller, "Carnegie Corp. Picks a Chief in Gregorian," *New York Times*, January 7, 1997; Karen W. Arenson, "Gregorian, Ending an 8-Year Tenure at Brown, Is Leaving 'a Hot College Even Hotter,' " *New York Times*, January 8, 1997. See also *Brown Daily Herald*, October 20, 1997

429   "The Unsustainability of the Traditional Library and the Threat to Higher Education": In Hawkins and Battin, 129–53.

431   ranks its members: ARL ranked lists are fully searchable in all categories at http://fisher.lib.virginia.edu/cgilocal/newarlbin/arllist.pl. Holdings statistics for all American libraries are searchable at http://www.ala.org/library/weblinks.html.

431   450 million "unduplicated titles": *Academic Libraries in the United States* (NECS 2000-326), a compilation of figures reported to the National Center for Education Statistics in the Office of Educational Research and Improvement of the U.S. Department of Educaton.

439   "The future of the library": Leon F. Litwack, "Has the Library Lost Its Soul?" *California Monthly* 108 (February 1998): For a comprehensive overview of the Bancroft Library controversy, including an interview with Litwack, see Dashka Slater, "The Fate of the Books," *East Bay Express*, August 21, 1998.

440   "Our library has fallen": Quoted in Henry K. Lee, "Chancellor Vows to Improve Library," *San Francisco Chronicle*, April 25, 1998. See also Dan Ostmann, "Library Falls in Rank Due to Cuts in Funding," *Daily Californian* (Berkeley student newspaper), April 13, 1998.

441   "raced up": Ollie Reed Jr., "A Rare Edition," *Albuquerque Tribune*, May 15, 1997.

441   "The ranking by": "USC Libraries Ranked 49th in Quality," *Post and Courier* (Charleston, S.C.), August 8, 1999.

441   "the first in the Southeast": *Chapel Hill Herald*, February 18, 2000.

442   "Essential for the growth": For the development of Duke library, see Durden, 169–77.

442   five-year plan: full text available at http://staff.lib.duke.edu/plan2kx/.

442   "for Duke to 'catch up' ": Ibid., 6–7.

443   "Circulation figures": Ibid., 18.

444   one decisive transaction: Background, detail, and quotations detailing the University of Chicago's acquisition of the Berlin Collection drawn from Robert Rosenthal.

450   Farmington Plan: See Edwin Williams.

451   "want list": Ibid., 10.

451–52   "The immediate consequence": Robert Vosper in *Occasional Papers*, no. 77, October 1965, 4.

452   Degrees awarded, books added: See Cummings, 16–18.

453   "The Library does not collect": Buck, 53.

453   "A library does not remain static": Ibid., 57.

456   "You simply don't have to build": Quoted in Kate Hafner with Jennifer Tanaka, "Wiring the Ivory Tower," *Newsweek*, January 30, 1995, 62. See also Kathleen Kluegel, "Redesigning Our Future: Collection Development of Libraries," *RQ* 36 (March 1997): 330.

458   "to the extent possible": For mission statement of CSUMB, see http://library.monterey.edu/services/collections.html.

458   "In a traditional institution": Quoted in David L. Wilson, "New California State Campus Has Ambitious Plans for Technology," *Chronicle of Higher Education*, October 18, 1996. See also James Richardson, "Campus at Fort Ord: Blessing or Blunder?" *Sacramento Bee*, July 4, 1994.

458   "virtual space characteristics": For FGCU mission statement, see http://library.fgcu.edu/AboutTheLibrary/mission.htm.

458   "Virtual U": Bill Maxwell, in *St. Petersburg Times*, November 30, 1997. See also Goldie Blumenstyk, "New University Tries to Be a Model in Use of Technology," *Chronicle of Higher Education*, December 12, 1997; James Roland, "New Era in Education Begins," *Sarasota Herald-Tribune*, August 24, 1997; Joni James, "Gulf Coast University Is Being Watched; The New School Is Tossing Out Traditions," *Orlando Sentinel*, August 3, 1997.

460   Upsala College: See Rachelle Garbarine, "For Abandoned Campuses, Recycled Lives," *New York Times*, September 8, 1996; Terry Pristin,

"Piece by Piece, Selling Upsala," *New York Times,* January 2, 1996; Susan Jo Keller, "College Being Sold Off in Parts," *New York Times,* November 1, 1995; Christina Pretto, "SEC Probes N.J. Agency Loan to Bankrupt Upsala College," *Bond Buyer,* October 26, 1995.

463   Oberlin Group: http://www.columbia.edu/~cf48/.

465–66   "It is important to see": Taylor, 174; "The computer and related": Ibid.; "The Library Center should be": Ibid., 56; "exploit all available channels": Ibid., 2; "media of communication": Ibid., 7; "base point": Ibid., 35; "There are moments": Ibid., 200.

467   borrowed 84,891 titles: "Five College Libraries Direct Borrowing Circulation Statistics for July 1, 1999–June 30, 2000," copy provided to the author.

469   renewed interest: As part of its born-again appreciation for print Hampshire College has established a Center for the Book on its Amherst campus, and has provided space for the headquarters of the National Yiddish Book Center (see Basbanes, chap. 11).

469–70   "great central library": See Bernard, 363–87.

Chapter 11: Deep Sleep

This chapter draws on the author's interviews with Scott H. Seaman, Beverly P. Lynch, Ronald A. Lane, Barbara Graham, Kenneth E. Carpenter, Ross Atkinson, Charles B. Faulhaber, Sarah E. Thomas, Anne R. Kenney, Stephen G. Nichols, and Elaine Engst.

475–76   "indispensable nucleus": Bentick-Smith, 170; "tireless exponent": Ibid., 10; "Oh, I wead and I wewead": Ibid., 183.

476   "But even these amazing numbers": Michael McCormick, "Research and Teaching: Making Connections in Widener Library," *Harvard Library Bulletin,* n.s., 6 (fall 1995): 7–11.

477   Primate Research Center: See Karen Hsu, "Primate Research Defended," *Boston Globe,* November 6, 1999.

478   off-site storage: See Jeffrey R. Young, "In the New Model of the Research Library, Unused Books Are Out, Computers Are In," *Chronicle of Higher Education,* October 17, 1997.

478   University of Minnesota: Mary Jane Smetanka, "A Giant Hole in the Ground Will Hold University's Library Treasures," *Star Tribune* (Minneapolis), August 2, 1998.

479   "We will have the acreage": Quoted in Karen W. Arenson, "Three Packed Libraries Seek Storage Space in New Jersey," *New York Times,* March 22, 1999.

486   Randtriever: See Barbara VanBrimmer and Elizabeth Sawyers, "The Randtriever: Its Use at Ohio State University," *Library Hi Tech* 31, no. 3 (1990): 71–81. For an excellent overview of automated attempts in book storage, see Lynn M. Fortney, "Cybernetics and Librarianship: A Fifty-Year Perspective on Where We've Been and Where We're Going," a paper read at Auckland '99, an international conference sponsored by the Library and Information Association of New Zealand (LIANZA), and accessible at http://www.auckland.ac.nz/lbr/conf99/fortney.htm.

487   "single, simple solution": Sidney Verba, in Danuta A. Nitecki and Curtis L. Kendrick, *Library Off-Site Shelving: Guide for High Density Facilities* (Englewood, Col.: Libraries Unlimited, 2001), 11.

489   "just because books are 'retired' ": David C. Weber, letter to the editor, *Chronicle of Higher Education,* December 5, 1997.

501–2   "The electronic handling of texts": G. Thomas Tanselle, "The Future of Primary Records: Technology's Impact on Publishing and the Printed Record," in *Literature and Artifacts* (Charlottesville: Bibliographical Society of the University of Virginia, 1998), 96–123.

CHAPTER 12: AS IN A VIAL

This chapter draws on the author's interviews with Thomas C. Albro II, James H. Billington, Diane N. Kresh, David Bradbury, Colin St. John Wilson, Richard W. Oram, Philip D. Leighton, and Jacqueline Sanson.

506   shipped . . . to Fort Knox: See Donaldson, 348–53. It bears noting in this context that the federal installation chosen to safeguard the nation's Top Treasures during World War II was named for Major General Henry Knox (1750–1806), one of the truly great heroes of the American Revolution, and for several years before becoming commander of artillery and skilled tactician on the staff of George Washington, a resourceful bookseller in Boston who credited his insatiable appetite for reading as key to teaching him what he knew about weapons and military strategy. He later served as the nation's first secretary of war.

507   "I am happy": Quoted in Eva Goldschmidt, 66–67.

508   ornate building: For more on the character of Thomas Jefferson's

library, see Basbanes, 148–53. For more on the development of collections at the Library of Congress, see Goodrum; Conaway. For more on the architecture and decorations of the Jefferson Building, see Small.

508   "in *all* the departments": Quoted in Conaway, 40.

509   Top Treasures Vault: The Library of Congress offers descriptions of these artifacts at www.loc.gov.

510   "I have sworn upon the altar": See Goodrum, 285.

511   "If any personal description of me": See Merrill D. Peterson, *Lincoln in American Memory* (New York: Oxford University Press, 1994), 232–33; David Herbert Donald, *Lincoln* (New York: Simon and Schuster, 1995), 237.

513   acquisition policy: See *Library of Congress Collections Policy Statement*.

515   "The Library lacks": Management Review of the Library of Congress, Booz-Allen & Hamilton Inc.; Financial Statement Audit for the Library of Congress for Fiscal Year 1995, Price Waterhouse LLP (Washington, D.C., May 7, 1996.)

515   "We need many other components": Bill Holland, "Senate Protests Library of Congress Downsizing Recommended in Government Review," *Washington Post*, May 18, 1996; *Washington Post* editorial, "Library Futures," May 12, 1996. On the matter of keeping step with technological changes, the library came in for a measure of criticism in the fall of 2000 when a committee formed by Billington and chaired by James J. O'Donnell of the University of Pennsylvania issued a 266-page report, *LC21: A Digital Strategy for the Library of Congress,* that underscored the urgency of capturing, archiving, preserving, and making accessible digital materials before they vanish from the Internet. "It is really shocking how much digital information, in the ten years it has become a medium of communication, is disappearing because no one is archiving it, setting it aside," O'Donnell said in a statement. "Where we see the need in the next few years is to concentrate on born-digital information, information that doesn't come, ever, in printed form, which only exists electronically." The 266-page report contained 55 recommendations. It is fully accessible at http://www.nap.edu/books/0309071445/html/.

516–17   "What is wanted": Quoted by David C. Mearns, "The Brush of the Comet: Archibald MacLeish at the Library of Congress," *Atlantic Monthly* 215 (May 1965): 90–92; for more on Roosevelt's appointment of MacLeish as Librarian of Congress, and the opposition gathered against him, see Eva Goldschmidt, 1–6; Donaldson, 290–305.

520   proposal to . . . begin storing by size: See Grace Palladino, "Out of Sight, Out of Mind: Shelving by Height at the Library of Congress," *Chronicle of Higher Education,* June 11, 1999; Linton Weeks, "A Question of Shelf Sufficiency; Library of Congress Sizes Up a Tight Fit," *Washington Post,* February 17, 1997; Joel Achenbach, "The Too-Much Information Age; Today's Data Glut Jams Libraries and Lives. But Is Anyone Getting Wiser?" *Washington Post,* March 12, 1999; and David M. Shribman, "Booked Solid," *Boston Globe,* July 18, 1999.

520   Sir Antonio Panizzi: See Miller.

523   "No other country provided": Harris, 1.

523   "so is the nation": Quoted in Simon Jenkins, "The Spirit of St. Pancras," *Times* (London), June 20, 1998.

524   "If truth": Quoted in Angeline Goreau, "The Round Room Comes to an End," *New York Times,* November 9, 1997.

524   "This is a charmed place": Peter Ackroyd, "A Room with So Many Views," *Evening Standard* (London), July 28, 1994.

525   "It became his club": Holroyd, 51.

525   "to which I owe": Quoted in ibid., 782.

526   two parties agreed: Nigel Reynolds, "Deal Ends Fight over Shaw's Millions," *Daily Telegraph* (London), December 22, 1999.

526   new national library: For a thorough overview of the design and construction of the British Library at St. Pancras, see St. John Wilson.

527   "dim collection of sheds": Fiona Maccarthy, "Written in Stone," *Guardian* (London), August 26, 1995.

527   "brick pile": *Times* (London), November 24, 1997.

527   "one of the ugliest": *Times,* March 31, 1995.

528   "It is clear": Deyan Sudjic, "Reading between New Lines," *Scotsman,* October 27, 1997.

528   "This is almost certainly": Maccarthy, "Written in Stone." See also Carolyn J. Mooney, "Efficiency, Not Charm, Helps New British Library Win Scholars' Affection," *Chronicle of Higher Education,* July 16, 1999; John Lanchester, "Millions Well Spent: The New British Library," *Daily Telegraph,* July 13, 1998.

528   "It fought": Simon Jenkins, "The Spirits of St. Pancras," *Times* (London), January 20, 1998.

528   "His Royal Highness was delighted": Press Association, Ltd. dispatch, March 5, 1998.

529   "The Library is aware": Kenny, 17–18.

529   "Even if we imagine": Ibid., 23.

531   *Très Grande Bibliothèque:* Marcus Binney, "Books, Yes," *Times* (London), March 11, 1996.

531   "The building of a library": Mitterrand, in Perrault, 12.

532   "Whereas the construction": Andrew Martin, "A Library That Speaks Volumes," *Sunday Telegraph*, March 26, 1995.

532   Dominique Perrault: For the architect's account of the design and construction of the French National Library at Tolbiac, see Perrault.

532   "will to act": Ibid., 42.

532   "kernel of the project": Ibid.

533   "The architect should not allow": Ibid., 50, 54.

534   "The building he has designed": Ibid., 12.

535   evaluation of the Tolbiac facility: An English text of "Tolbiac: An Analytical Look at La Bibliothèque de France," Philip Leighton's evaluation prepared for the Paris journal *Le Debat* and published in May 1991, is used here with Leighton's permission.

539–40 "The History of the French National Library": Jean Favier, *Daedalus* 125 (September 1996): 283–88. See also Gérald Grunberg and Alain Giffard, "New Orders of Knowledge, New Technologies of Reading," *Representations* (Berkeley, Calif.), no. 42 (1993): 80–93.

541   Giulio Mazarini: See Richard Wilkinson, "Cardinal Mazarin," *History Today* 46 (April 1996).

542   For more on Bibliothèque Nationale, see Tesnière and Gifford; Pastoureau.

543   *"la grande migration"*: *Le Monde*, March 20, 1998.

544   "sinister farce": Transcript, "French National Library's Woes," *NPR Morning Edition*, December 9, 1998. See also Adam Sage, "Pounds 830m Library Where You Can't Find a Book," *Times* (London), April 28, 1999.

544   Conseil Supérieur des Bibliothèques: Text of report for 1998 and 1999, with an English version, posted at http://www.enssib.fr/autres-sites/csb/report98-99/csb-report98-99.html.

546   "The building is just not safe": Harry de Quetteville, "France's Library Malaise Returns as Bug Hits Staff," *Daily Telegraph* (London), November 4, 2000.

548   "I see in this work": Quoted in Nonie Niesewand, "Opening Chapter," *Independent*, July 4, 1997.

548   "What keeps me going?" Quoted in Paul Vallely, *Independent*, November 3, 1997.

Epilogue

The epilogue draws principally on the author's interviews with Mohsen Zahran, Craig Dykers, Mohammed M. Aman, and Ismail Serageldin.

551   "I am confident that we can meet": Quoted in Nevine Khali, "Suzanne Mubarak at the Library of Congress," *El-Ahram Weekly* (Cairo), March 30, 2000.

551   Revival of the library: See Michael Knipe, "Library Links Past and Present," *Times* (London), September 19, 2000; Michel Arseneault, "Alexandria, From Papyrus to the Internet, *UNESCO Courier*, April 1999, 40.

553   "will be to house objects": Alan Philips and Alasdair Palmer, "Reliving Lost Glories," *Sunday Telegraph* (London), March 12, 2000.

553   White elephant: "Runes Among the Ruins," *Economist*, April 8, 2000. See also Douglas Jehl, "Ancient World's Great Database to Get a Successor," *New York Times*, November 6, 1999.

554   "What does it mean to 'revive' an ancient library": Alexander Stille, "Resurrecting Alexandria," *New Yorker*, May 8, 2000, 90–99.

554   Paucity of holdings: G. Pascal Zachary, "Check This Out: A Global Library Grovels for Books," *Wall Street Journal*, June 1, 2000. See also: Elizabeth Bryant, "Alexandria Revives Ancient Library Amid Controversy," *St. Petersburg Times*, January 2, 1999; Ron Chepesiuk, "Dream in the Desert: Alexandria's Library Rises Again," *American Libraries* 31, no. 4 (April 1, 2000), 70; Jonathan Glancey, "Architecture: The Sequel," *Guardian* (London), January 29, 2001.

556   "You may buy books": Burton, 171. For more on the Bibliotheca Alexandrina, including photographs that document every phase of the construction, see http://www.snoarc.no/ and http://www.unesco.org/webworld/alexandria new/.

BIBLIOGRAPHY

Akurgal, Ekrem. *Ancient Civilizations and Ruins of Turkey*. Translated from the Turkish by John Whybrow and Mollie Emre. 4th ed. Istanbul: Haset Kitabevi, 1978.

Alexander, Jonathan J. G., ed. *The Painted Page: Italian Renaissance Book Illumination, 1450–1550*. Munich: Prestel-Verlag, 1994.

Argan, Giulio Carlo, and Bruno Contardi. *Michelangelo, Architect*. Translated from the Italian by Marion L. Grayson. New York: Harry N. Abrams, 1990.

Armstrong, Carol. *Scenes in a Library: Reading the Photograph in the Book, 1843–1875*. Cambridge, Mass.: MIT Press, 1998.

Austin, Gabriel, ed. *The Grolier Club Iter Italicum*. New York: Grolier Club, 1963.

Avrin, Leila. *Scribes, Script and Books: The Book Arts from Antiquity to the Renaissance*. Chicago: American Library Association, 1991.

Bachrach, G. H. "The Foundation of the Bodleian Library and XVIIth Century Holland." *Neophilologus* 36 (1952): 101–14.

Baker, Nicholson. "The Author vs. the Librarian." *New Yorker* 72 (October 14, 1996): 50–62.

———. "Deadline: The Author's Desperate Bid to Save America's Past." *New Yorker* 76 (July 24, 2000): 42–61.

———. "Discards." *New Yorker* 70 (April 4, 1994): 64–86.

———. *Double Fold: Libraries and the Assault on Paper*. New York: Random House, 2001.

Barwick, G. F. *The Reading Room of the British Museum*, London: Ernest Benn Ltd., 1929.

Basbanes, Nicholas A. *A Gentle Madness: Bibliophiles, Bibliomanes, and the Eternal Passion for Books*. New York: Henry Holt, 1995.

Bentinck-Smith, William. *Building a Great Library: The Coolidge Years at Harvard*. Cambridge, Mass.: Harvard University Press, 1976.

Bentley, James. *Secrets of Mount Sinai: The Story of Finding the World's Oldest Bible—Codex Sinaiticus*. Garden City, N.Y.: Doubleday, 1986.

Bernard, Robert J. *An Unfinished Dream: A Chronicle of the Group Plan of the Claremont Colleges*. Claremont, Calif.: Claremont University Center, 1982.

Bibliographica: Papers on Books, Their History and Art. 3 vols. London: Kegan Paul, Trench, Trübner, 1895–1897.

Biblioteca Capitolare Verona. Florence: Nardini Editore, 1994.

Bliss, Douglas Percy. *A History of Wood Engraving*. 1928. Reprint, London: Spring Books, 1964.

Bonner, Gerald, David W. Rollason, and Clare Stancliffe, eds. *St. Cuthbert, His Cult and His Community to AD 1200*. Woodbridge, England: Boydell Press, 1989.

Boorstin, Daniel J. *The Republic of Letters*. Edited by John Y. Cole. Washington: Library of Congress, 1989.

Bostwick, Arthur E. *The American Public Library*. New York: D. Appleton, 1917.

Brownrigg, Linda L., ed. *Medieval Book Production: Assessing the Evidence*. Proceedings of the Second Conference of the Seminar in the History of the Book to 1500, Oxford, July 1988. Los Altos Hills, Calif.: Anderson-Lovelace, 1990.

Brucker, Gene. *Florence: The Golden Age, 1138–1737*. Berkeley and Los Angeles: University of California Press, 1998.

Buck, Paul. *Libraries and Universities: Addresses and Reports*. Edited by Edwin E. Williams. Cambridge, Mass.: Harvard University Press, Belknap Press, 1964.

Burke, Redmond A. *What Is the Index?* Milwaukee, Wis.: Bruce Publishing, 1952.

Burton, John Hill. *The Book-Hunter*. New York: Sheldon, 1862.

Cahill, Thomas. *How the Irish Saved Civilization: The Untold Story of Ireland's Heroic Role from the Fall of Rome to the Rise of Medieval Europe*. New York: Doubleday, 1995.

Canfora, Luciano. *The Vanished Library: A Wonder of the Ancient World*. Translated from the Italian by Martin Ryle. London: Hutchinson Radius, 1989.

Carpenter, Kenneth E., ed. *Books and Society in History*. Papers of the Association of College and Research Libraries Rare Books and Manuscripts Preconference, June 24–28, 1980, Boston. New York: R. R. Bowker, 1983.

Carpenter, Kenneth E., and Richard F. Thomas, eds. "Widener Library: Voices from the Stacks." A special issue of *Harvard Library Bulletin*, n.s. 6 (fall 1995).

Castillo, Debra A. *The Translated Word: A Postmodern Tour of Libraries in Literature*. Tallahassee: Florida State University Press, 1984.

A Catalogue of the Cotsen Children's Library: The Twentieth Century, A–L. Introduction by Andrea Immel. Princeton, N.J.: Princeton University Library, 2000.

Chandler, John. *John Leland's Itinerary: Travels in Tudor England*. Gloucestershire, England: Sutton Publishing, 1998.

Clark, John Willis. *The Care of Books: An Essay on the Development of Libraries and Their Fittings, from the Earliest Times to the End of the Eighteenth Century*. Cambridge, England: University Press, 1901.

———. *Libraries in the Medieval and Renaissance Periods: The Rede Lecture, Delivered June 13, 1894*. Cambridge: Macmillan and Bowes, 1894.

Cole, John Y., ed. *Books in Our Future: Perspectives and Proposals*. Washington, D.C.: Library of Congress, 1987.

———. *For Congress and the Nation: A Chronological History of the Library of Congress*. Washington, D.C. Library of Congress, 1979.

Colón, Fernando [Ferdinand Columbus]. *The Life of the Admiral Christopher Columbus by His Son, Ferdinand*. Translated and annotated by Benjamin Keen. New Brunswick, N.J.: Rutgers University Press, 1959.

Conaway, James. *America's Library: The Story of the Library of Congress, 1800–2000*. New Haven, Conn.: Yale University Press, 2000.

Cowdry, H. E. J. *The Age of the Abbot Desiderius: Montecassino, the Papacy, and the Normans in the Eleventh and Early Twelfth Centuries*. Oxford, England: Oxford University Press, 1983.

Coxe, Henry O. *Report to Her Majesty's Government, on the Greek Manuscripts Yet Remaining in Libraries of the Levant*. London: George E. Eyre and William Spottiswoode, 1858.

Cram, Ralph Adams. *The Ruined Abbeys of Great Britain*. Boston: Marshall Jones Company, 1927.

Cramer, C. H. *Open Shelves and Open Minds: A History of the Cleveland Public Library*. Cleveland: Press of Case Western Reserve University, 1972.

Crinelli, Lorenzo, ed. *Treasures from Italy's Great Libraries*. New York: Vendome Press, 1997.

Croiset van Uchelen, Ton, Koert van der Horst, and Günter Schilder, eds. *Theatrum Orbis Librorum: Liber Amicorum Presented to Nico Israel on the Occasion of his Seventieth Birthday*. Utrecht: HES, 1989.

Cummings, Anthony M., et al. *University Libraries and Scholarly Communication: A Study Prepared for the Andrew W. Mellon Foundation*. Washington, D.C.: Association of Research Libraries, 1992.

Curwen, Henry. *A History of Booksellers, the Old and the New*. 1873. Reprint, Detroit: Gale Research, 1968.

Dain, Phyllis. *The New York Public Library: A Universe of Knowledge*. New York: New York Public Library/Scala Publishers, 2000.

Dain, Phyllis, and John Y. Cole. *Libraries and Scholarly Communication in the United States*. Westport, Conn.: Greenwood Press, 1990.

Dalrymple, William. *From the Holy Mountain: A Journey among the Christians of the Middle East*. New York: Henry Holt, 1998.

Dankey, James P., and Wayne A. Wigand, eds. *Print Culture in a Diverse America*. Urbana: University of Illinois Press, 1998.

Davenport, Cyril. *The Book: Its History and Development*. New York: D. Van Nostrand, 1908.

Davidson, Miles H. *Columbus Then and Now: A Life Reexamined*. Norman: University of Oklahoma Press, 1997.

Decker, Peter. Preface to volume 1 of *Peter Decker's Catalogues of Americana*. With a foreword by Archibald Hanna. Austin, Tex.: Jenkins Publishing 1979.

De Hamel, Christopher. *A History of Illuminated Manuscripts*. Boston: David R. Godine, 1986.

Delia, Diana. "From Romance to Rhetoric: The Alexandrian Library in Classical and Islamic Traditions." *American Historical Review* 97 (December 1992): 1449–67.

Deuel, Leo. *Testaments of Time: The Search for Lost Manuscripts and Records*. New York: Alfred A. Knopf, 1965.

Dickinson, Donald C. *Dictionary of American Antiquarian Booksellers*. Westport, Conn.: Greenwood Press, 1998.

Disraeli, Isaac. *Curiosities of Literature*. 9th ed., rev., 6 vols. London: E. Moxon, 1834.

Donaldson, Scott. *Archibald MacLeish: An American Life*. Boston: Houghton Mifflin, 1992.

Duffus, R. L. *Our Starving Libraries: Studies in Ten American Communities during the Depression Years*. Boston: Houghton Mifflin, 1933.

Dunlop, Eileen. *Tales of St. Columba*. Dublin: Poolbeg Press, 1992.

Durden, Robert F. *The Launching of Duke University, 1924–1949*. Durham, N.C.: Duke University Press, 1993.

Eco, Umberto. *The Name of the Rose*. Translated from the Italian by William Weaver. San Diego: Harcourt Brace Jovanovich, 1983.

———. *Postscript to "The Name of the Rose."* San Diego: Harcourt Brace Jovanovich, 1983.

———. *The Role of the Reader: Explorations in the Semiotics of Texts*. Bloomington: Indiana University Press, 1984.

Edwards, George, ed. *The Grolier Club Iter Hibernicum*. New York: Grolier Club, 1998.

Eisenstein, Elizabeth L. *The Printing Press as an Agent of Change: Communications and Cultural Transformations in Early-Modern Europe, Volumes I and II*. 1979. Reprint, 2 vols. in 1, Cambridge, England: Cambridge University Press, 1980.

Elsner, John, and Roger Cardinal, eds. *The Cultures of Collecting*. Cambridge, Mass.: Harvard University Press, 1994.

Empereur, Jean-Yves. *Alexandria Rediscovered*. New York: George Braziller, 1998.

Evans, Helen C., and William D. Wixom, eds. *The Glory of Byzantium: Art and Culture of the Middle Byzantine Era, A.D.* 843–1261. New York: Metropolitan Museum of Art, 1997.

Fletcher, H. George, ed. *The Wormsley Library: A Personal Selection by Sir Paul Getty, KBE*. London: Maggs Bros. Ltd./Pierpont Morgan Library, 1999.

Foreman, Laura. *Cleopatra's Palace: In Search of a Legend*. New York: Random House/Discovery Communications, 1999.

Frame, Donald M., ed. *Montaigne's Travel Journal*. San Francisco: North Point Press, 1983.

García, Pedro González, ed. *Discovering the Americas: The Archive of the Indies*. New York: Vendome Press, 1997.

Garrison, Dee. *Apostles of Culture: The Public Librarian and American Society 1876–1920*. New York: Free Press, 1979.

Giroud, Vincent, and Maurice Sendak. *Sendak at the Rosenbach: An Exhibition at the Rosenbach Museum and Library, April 18–October 30, 1995*. Philadelphia: Rosenbach Museum and Library, 1995.

Goldschmidt, Eva M., ed. *Champion of a Cause: Essays and Addresses on Librarianship by Archibald MacLeish*. Chicago: American Library Association, 1971.

Goldschmidt, Lucien. *The Scenery Has Changed: The Purpose and Potential of the Rare Book Trade*. The Fifth Sol. M. Malkin Lecture in Bibliography at the School of Library Service of Columbia University. New York: Book Arts Press/Columbia University, 1990.

Goodspeed, Charles. *Yankee Bookseller*. Boston: Houghton Mifflin, 1937.

Grafton, Anthony, with April Shelford and Nancy Sirasi. *New Worlds, Ancient Texts: The Power of Tradition and the Shock of Discovery*. Cambridge, Mass.: Harvard University Press, Belknap Press, 1992.

———, ed. *Rome Reborn: The Vatican Library and Renaissance Culture*. Washington, D.C.: Library of Congress, 1993.

Graham, Hugh Davis, and Nancy Diamond. *The Rise of American Research Universities: Elites and Challengers in the Postwar Era*. Baltimore: Johns Hopkins University Press, 1997.

Grant, Michael. *The Visible Past: Recent Archaeological Discoveries of Greek and Roman History*. New York: Charles Scribner's Sons, 1990.

Graubard, Stephen R., ed. "Books, Bricks, and Bytes." *Daedalus, Journal of the American Academy of Arts and Sciences* 125 (fall 1996).

Green, Peter. *Alexander to Actium: The Historical Evolution of the Hellenistic Age.* Berkeley and Los Angeles: University of California Press, 1990.

————. *Alexander of Macedon, 356–323 B.C.: A Historical Biography.* Berkeley and Los Angeles: University of California Press, 1991.

Green, Samuel Swett. *The Public Library Movement in the United States, 1853–1893.* 1913. Facsimile reprint, Boston: Gregg Press, 1972.

Grolier 75: A Biographical Retrospective to Celebrate the Seventy-fifth Anniversary of the Grolier Club in New York. New York: Grolier Club, 1959.

Grolier 2000: A Further Grolier Club Biographical Retrospective in Celebration of the Millennium. New York: Grolier Club, 2000.

Hansen, Esther V. *The Attalids of Pergamon.* Ithaca, N.Y.: Cornell University Press, 1947.

Hamburger, Philip. "Searching for Gregorian." In *Curious World: A New Yorker at Large.* San Francisco: North Point Press, 1987.

Hapgood, David, and David Richardson. *Monte Cassino.* New York: Congdon & Weed, 1984.

Harris, P. R. *A History of the British Museum Library, 1753–1973.* London: The British Library, 1998.

Harrison, Frederic, ed. *Carlyle and the London Library.* London: Chapman & Hall, 1907.

Haskell, Francis. *History and Its Images: Art and the Interpretation of the Past.* New Haven, Conn.: Yale University Press, 1993.

Hasluck, F. W. [Frederick William]. *Athos and Its Monasteries.* London: K. Paul, Trench, Trubner, 1924.

Hassall, A. G., and W. O. Hassall. *Treasures from the Bodleian Library.* New York: Columbia University Press, 1976.

Hawkins, Brian L., and Patricia Battin, eds. *The Mirage of Continuity: Reconfiguring Academic Information Resources for the Twenty-first Century.* Washington, D.C.: Council on Library and Information Resources and Association of American Universities, 1998.

Headlam, Cecil. *Oxford and Its Story.* London: J. M. Dent & Co., 1904.

Henderson, George. *From Durrow to Kells: The Insular Gospel-books, 650–800.* London: Thames and Hudson, 1987.

Henry, Françoise. "The Book and Its Decoration." In *The Book of Kells: Reproductions from the Manuscript in Trinity College, Dublin.* New York: Alfred A. Knopf, 1988.

Hibbert, Christopher. *Venice: The Biography of a City.* New York: W. W. Norton, 1989.

Holy and Great Monastery of Vatopaidi. 2 vols. Mount Athos: Holy and Great Monastery of Vatopaidi, 1998.

Honan, William H. *Treasure Hunt: A New York Times Reporter Tracks the Quedlinburg Hoard.* New York: Fromm International, 1997.

Hughes, H. D. *A History of Durham Cathedral Library.* Durham, England: Durham County Advertiser, 1925.

Irwin, Raymond. *The Origins of the English Library.* London: Allen and Unwin, 1958.

The Influence and History of the Boston Athenæum from 1807 to 1907. Boston: Boston Athenæum, 1907.

Jancey, Meryl. *Mappa Mundi: The Map of the World at Hereford Cathedral.* Rev. ed. Hereford, England: Hereford Cathedral Enterprises, 1995.

Jardine, Lisa. *Worldly Goods: A New History of the Renaissance.* London: Macmillan, 1996.

Johnson, Elmer D., and Michael H. Harris. *History of Libraries in the Western World.* 3d ed., rev. Metuchen, N.J.: Scarecrow Press, 1976.

Jones, Pamela M. *Federico Borromeo and the Ambrosiana: Art Patronage and Reform in Seventeenth-century Milan.* Cambridge, England: Cambridge University Press, 1992.

Jones, Theodore. *Carnegie Libraries across America: A Public Legacy.* New York: John Wiley and Sons, 1997. Appendix 2 includes statistical data of all Carnegie libraries.

Karakatsanis, Athanasios A., ed. *Treasures of Mount Athos.* Thessaloniki, Greece: Ministry of Culture/Museum of Byzantine Culture, 1997.

Keep, Austin Baxter. *History of the New York Society Library: With an Introductory Chapter on Libraries in Colonial New York, 1698–1776.* 1908. Fascsimile reprint, Boston: Gregg Press, 1972.

Kenney, Sir Anthony. *The British Library and the St. Pancras Building.* London: British Library, 1994.

Kent, Dale. *Cosimo de'Medici and the Florentine Renaissance.* New Haven, Conn.: Yale University Press, 2000.

Kinane, Vincent, and Anne Walsh, eds. *Essays on the History of Trinity College, Dublin.* Dublin: Four Courts Press, 2000.

Labowsky, Lotte. *Bessarion's Library and the Biblioteca Marciana: Six Early Inventories.* Rome: Edizioni di Storia e Letteratura, 1979.

Lackington, James. *Memoirs of the Forty-five First Years of the Life of James Lackington, Bookseller, Written by Himself, in Forty-seven Letters to a Friend.* London: Whitaker, Treacher, and Arnot, 1830.

Lamb, Charles. "Oxford in the Vacation" and "Detatched Thoughts on Books and Readers." In *The Works of Charles Lamb.* Edited by Sir Thomas Noon Talfourd. Vol. 3. New York: A. C. Armstrong & Son, 1880.

Landow, George P. *Hypertext: The Convergence of Contemporary Critical Theory and Technology*. Baltimore: The Johns Hopkins University Press, 1992.

Lanes, Selma G. *The Art of Maurice Sendak*. New York: Harry N. Abrams, 1984.

Leccisotti, Tomasso. *Monte Cassino*. Edited and translated into English from the 10th Italian ed. by Armand O. Citarella. Monte Cassino, Italy: Abbey of Monte Cassino, 1987.

Leigh, Robert D. *The Public Library in the United States: The General Report of the Public Library Inquiry*. New York: Columbia University Press, 1950.

Library of Congress. *Library of Congress Collections Policy Statement*. Compiled by the Collections Policy Office of the Library of Congress. Washington, D.C.: Library of Congress, 1994.

Liebaers, Herman. *Mostly in the Line of Duty: Thirty Years with Books*. The Hague: Martinus Nijhoff Publishers, 1980.

Lowry, Martin. *The World of Aldus Manutius: Business and Scholarship in Renaissance Venice*. Ithaca, N.Y.: Cornell University Press, 1979.

Lydenberg, Harry Miller. *History of the New York Public Library: Astor, Lenox and Tilden Foundations*. New York: New York Public Library, 1923.

Macray, William Dunn. *Annals of the Bodleian Library*. 2d ed. Oxford: Oxford University Press, Clarendon Press, 1890.

Mappin, John, and John Archer. *Bernard Amtmann, 1907–1979: A Personal Memoir*. Printed in an edition of 500 copies. Montreal: Amtmann Circle, 1987.

Melot, Michel, ed. *Nouvelles Alexandrines: Les Grands Chantiers de bibliothèques dans le monde*. Paris: Éditions du Cercle de la Librairie, 1996.

Metcalf, Keyes DeWitt. *Random Recollections of an Anachronism; or, Seventy-five Years of Library Work*. New York: Readex Books, 1980.

Miller, Edward. *Prince of Librarians: The Life and Times of Antonio Panizzi of the British Museum*. London: Andre Deutsch, 1967.

———. *That Noble Cabinet: A History of the British Museum*. London: Andre Deutsch, 1973.

Monfasani, John. *Byzantine Scholars in Renaissance Italy: Cardinal Bessarion and Other Emigrés*. Aldershot, England: Variorum, 1994.

Morgan, F. C., and Penelope E. Morgan. *Hereford Cathedral Libraries and Muniments*. Hereford, England: Hereford Cathedral Library, 1975.

Morison, Samuel Eliot. *Admiral of the Ocean Sea*. Boston: Little, Brown and Company, 1942.

Moser, Barry. *In the Face of Presumption: Essays, Speeches, and Incidental Writings*. Boston: David R. Godine, 2000.

Munby, Frank A. *The Romance of Book Selling: A History from the Earliest Times to the*

Twentieth Century. London: Chapman and Hall, 1910. Includes an excellent bibliography on the book trade compiled by W. H. Peet.

Murphy, Cullen. "All the Pope's Men." *Harper's* 258 (June 1979): 45–64.

Murray, Janet H. *Hamlet on the Holodeck: The Future of Narrative in Hyperspace.* New York: Free Press, 1997.

Naudé, Gabriel. *Instructions Concerning Erecting of a Library.* Translated by John Evelyn, with an introduction by John Cotton Dana. Cambridge, Mass.: Riverside Press, 1903.

Needham, Paul. *Twelve Centuries of Bookbindings, 400–1600.* New York: Pierpont Morgan Library/Oxford University Press, 1979.

Newton, Francis. *The Scriptorium and Library at Monte Cassino, 1058–1105.* Cambridge, England: Cambridge University Press, 1999.

Ogle, John J. *The Free Library: Its History and Present Condition.* London: George Allen, 1898.

On Research Libraries: Statement and Recommendations of the Committee on Research Libraries of the American Council of Learned Societies, Submitted to the National Advisory Commission on Libraries. Cambridge, Mass.: MIT Press, 1967.

Orcutt, William Dana. *From My Library Walls: A Kaleidoscope of Memories.* New York: Longmans, Green, 1945.

Paredi, Angelo. *A History of the Ambrosiana.* Translated by Constance and Ralph McInerny. South Bend, Ind.: University of Notre Dame Press, 1983.

Pastoureau, Mireille. *Bibliothèque Nationale, Paris.* Translated by Margaret Curran. Paris: Musées et Monuments de France/Bibliothèque Nationale, 1992.

Perrault, Dominique. *Bibliothèque nationale de France, 1989–1995.* Basel/Bordeaux: Birkhäuser/Arc en Rêve Centre d'Architecture, 1995.

Petroski, Henry. *The Book on the Book Shelf.* New York: Alfred A. Knopf, 1999.

Price, Lorna. *The Plan of St. Gall in Brief.* Based on the work by Walter Horn and Ernest Born. Berkeley and Los Angeles: University of California Press, 1982.

Promey, Sally M. *Painting Religion in Public: John Singer Sargent's "Triumph of Religion" at the Boston Public Library.* Princeton, N.J.: Princeton University Press, 1999.

Quint, Arlene. *Cardinal Federico Borromeo as a Patron and a Critic of the Arts and His Musaeum of 1625.* New York: Garland, 1986.

Reed, Henry Hope. *The New York Public Library: Its Architecture and Decoration.* New York: W. W. Norton, 1986.

Reeves, William, ed. *Life of Saint Columba, Founder of Hy, Written by Adamnan, Ninth Abbot of That Monastery.* 1874. Facsimile reprint from *Historians of Scotland,* Felinfach, Wales: Llanerch Publishers, 1988.

Rogers, David. *The Bodleian Library and Its Treasures, 1320–1700.* Henley-on-Thames, England: Aidan Ellis, 1991.

Romer, John, and Elizabeth Romer. *The Seven Wonders of the World: A History of the Modern Imagination.* New York: Henry Holt, 1995.

Rosenthal, Bernard M. *The Gentle Invasion: Continental Emigré Booksellers of the Thirties and Forties and Their Impact on the Antiquarian Booktrade in the United States.* The Second Annual Sol. M. Malkin Lecture in Bibliography at the Columbia University School of Library Science. Book Arts Press Occasional Publication no. 4. New York: Book Arts Press, 1987.

———. "Cartel, Clan, or Dynasty? The Olschkis and the Rosenthals 1859–1976." *Harvard Library Bulletin* 25 (October 1977): pp. 381–98.

Rosenthal, Robert. *The Berlin Collection: Being a History and Exhibition of the Books and Manuscripts Purchased in Berlin in 1891 for the University of Chicago by William Rainey Harper with the Support of Nine Citizens of Chicago.* Chicago: Joseph Regenstein Library, 1979.

Rostenberg, Leona. *Literary, Political, Scientific, Religious and Legal Publishing, Printing and Bookselling in England, 1551–1700: Twelve Studies.* 2 vols. New York: Burt Franklin, 1965.

Rostenberg, Leona, and Madeleine Stern. *Old Books, Rare Friends: Two Literary Sleuths and Their Shared Passion.* New York: Doubleday, 1997.

Savage, Ernest A. *The Story of Libraries and Book Collecting.* 1909. Facsimile reprint, New York: Burt Franklin, 1969.

———. *Old English Libraries: The Making, Collection, and Use of Books During the Middle Ages.* London: Methuen, 1911.

Schama, Simon. *The Embarrassment of Riches: An Interpretation of Dutch Culture in the Golden Age.* New York: Alfred A. Knopf, 1987.

Scheurleer, Th. H. Lunsingh, and G. M. Posthumus Meyjes, eds. *Leiden University in the Seventeenth Century: An Exchange of Learning.* Leiden: Universitaire Pers Leiden/E. J. Brill, 1975.

Schmidt-Glintzer, Helwig, ed. *A Treasure House of Books: The Library of Duke August of Brunswick-Wolfenbüttel.* Hannover: Herzog August Bibliothek Wolfenbüttel, 1998.

Schreyer, Alice D. *The History of Books: A Guide to Selected Resources in the Library of Congress.* Washington: Center for the Book/Library of Congress, 1987.

Schwartz, Charles A., ed. *Restructuring Academic Libraries: Organizational Development in the Wake of Technological Change.* Chicago: Association of College and Research Libraries, 1997.

Sendak, Maurice. *Caldecott and Co.: Notes on Books and Pictures.* New York: Farrar, Straus and Giroux, 1988.

Shera, Jess H. *Foundations of the Public Library: The Origins of the Public Library Movement in New England, 1629–1855*. Chicago: University of Chicago Press, 1949.

Silver, Joel. "David A. Randall: Bookseller, Bibliographer, Librarian." *AB Bookman's Weekly* 95 (Jan. 2, 1995): 5–10.

Simon, Cathy. "A Civic Library for San Francisco." *Representations* 42, *Special Issue: Future Libraries* (spring 1993): 107–13.

Small, Herbert. *The Library of Congress: Its Architecture and Decoration*. New York: W. W. Norton, 1982.

Sotheby's. *The Frank T. Siebert Library of the North American Indian and the American Frontier*. 2 vols. New York: Sotheby's, 1999.

St. John Wilson, Colin. *The Design and Construction of the British Library*. London: British Library, 1998.

Staikos, Konstantinos Sp. *The Great Libraries: From Antiquity to the Renaissance*. New Castle, Del.: Oak Knoll Press, 2000.

Stam, David H. " 'A Glutton for Books': Leigh Hunt and the London Library, 1844–46." *Biblion: The Bulletin of the New York Public Library* 6 (spring 1998): 149–89.

Streeter, Burnett Hillman. *The Chained Library: A Survey of Four Centuries in the Evolution of the English Library*. 1931. Facsimile reprint, New York: Burt Franklin, 1970.

Symonds, John Addington. *Renaissance in Italy: The Age of the Despots*. New York: Henry Holt, 1883.

———. *Renaissance in Italy: The Revival of Learning*. New York: Henry Holt, 1883.

Taylor, Robert S. *The Making of a Library: The Academic Library in Transition*. New York: John Wiley and Sons, 1972.

Tesnière, Marie-Hélène, and Prosser Gifford, eds. *Creating French Culture: Treasures from the Bibliothèque Nationale de France*. New Haven, Conn.: Yale University Press, 1995.

Thompson, James Westfall. *The Medieval Library*. Chicago: University of Chicago Press, 1939.

Thornton, Dora. *The Scholar in His Study: Ownership and Experience in Renaissance Italy*. New Haven, Conn.: Yale University Press, 1997.

Upon the Objects to be Attained by the Establishment of a Public Library: Report of the Trustees of the Public Library of the City of Boston 1852. Boston: Trustees of the Public Library of the City of Boston, 1852.

Van Brimmer, Barbara Ann, and Elizabeth J. Sawyers. "The Randtriever: Its Use at the Ohio State University." *Library Hi Tech* 31, no. 3 (1990): 71–81.

Van Slyck, Abigail A. *Free to All: Carnegie Libraries and American Culture, 1890–1920.* Chicago: University of Chicago Press, 1995.

Vervliet, Hendrik D. L., ed. *The Book through Five Thousand Years.* London: Phaidon Press, 1972.

Virga, Vincent, and curators of the Library of Congress, with historical commentary by Alan Brinkley. *Eyes of the Nation: A Visual History of the United States.* New York: Alfred A. Knopf, 1997.

Vogler, Werner, ed. *The Culture of the Abbey of St. Gaul: An Overview.* Translated from the German by James C. King. Stuttgart/Zurich: Besler Verlag, 1991.

Wagner, Henry R. *The Library of Fernando Colon.* Los Angeles: Fine Arts Press, 1934. Excerpt from an address delivered before the Zamorano Club, September 26, 1934.

Walker, Susan, and Peter Higgs, eds. *Cleopatra of Egypt: From History to Myth.* Princeton, N.J.: Princeton University Press, 2001.

Wall, James. *Durham Cathedral.* London: J. M. Dent and Sons., n.d.

Wallace, William E. *Michelangelo at San Lorenzo: The Genius as Entrepreneur.* Cambridge: Cambridge University Press, 1994.

Welch, Evelyn S. *Art and Authority in Renaissance Milan.* New Haven, Conn.: Yale University Press, 1995.

Wells, John. *Rude Words: A Discursive History of the London Library.* London: Macmillan, 1991.

Wheatley, H. B. *How to Form a Library.* New York: A. C. Armstrong and Son, 1887.

Whitehill, Walter Muir. *Boston Public Library: A Centennial History.* Cambridge, Mass.: Harvard University Press, 1956.

Wick, Peter Arms. *A Handbook to the Art and Architecture of the Boston Public Library.* Boston: Associates of the Boston Public Library, 1978.

Wiegand, Wayne A. *Irrepressible Reformer: A Biography of Melvil Dewey.* Chicago: American Library Association, 1996.

Wiegand, Wayne A., and Donald G. Davis Jr. *Encyclopedia of Library History.* New York: Garland Publishing, Inc., 1994.

Wiley, Peter Booth. *A Free Library in This City: The Illustrated History of the San Francisco Public Library.* San Francisco: Weldon Owen, 1996.

Williams, Edwin E. *Farmington Plan Handbook.* [Bloomington, Ind.]: Association of Research Libraries, 1953.

Williams, Joan. *The Chained Library at Hereford Cathedral.* Hereford, England: Hereford Cathedral Enterprises for the Dean and Chapter of Hereford, 1996.

Wilson, Adrian, assisted by Joyce Lancaster Wilson. Introduction by Peter Zahn. *The Making of the Nuremberg Chronicle.* Amsterdam: Nico Israel, 1976.

Wilson, Douglas L., and Rodney O. Davis, eds. *Herndon's Informants: Letters, Interviews and Statements about Abraham Lincoln*. Urbana: University of Illinois Press, 1998.

Wilson, N. G. *Scholars of Byzantium*. Baltimore, Md.: Johns Hopkins University Press, 1983.

Winsor, Justin. "Libraries in Boston." In *The Memorial History of Boston, 1630–1880*, 4: 279–94. Boston: James R. Osgood, 1881.

Wittkower, R. "Michelangelo's Biblioteca Laurenziana." *Art Bulletin* 16 (1934): 123–218.

Wood, Michael. *In Search of England: Journeys into the English Past*. Berkeley and Los Angeles: University of California Press, 1999.

Wormald, Francis, and C. E. Wright. *The English Library before 1700*. London: University of London/Athlone Press, 1958.

AUTHOR'S INTERVIEWS

People interviewed are fully identified in the text, and can be located by consulting the General Index.

Thomas C. Albro II	Adina Cohen
Robert W. Allison	Rolland Comstock
Mohammed M. Aman	Robert Coover
Werner Arnold	Lloyd E. Cotsen
Ross Atkinson	Steven A. Coulter
Nicholson Baker	John F. Dean
Fred Bass	Kenneth E. Dowlin
Nancy Bass	Alan D'Souza
Terry Belanger	Ellen S. Dunlap
Alan E. Bell	Catherine Carver Dunn
Pierre Berès	Craig Dykers
Elisabeth Westin Berg	Umberto Eco
Abel E. Berland	Ray English
Otto Bettmann	Elaine D. Engst
Walter Biller	Abbott Ephraim of Vatopedi
James H. Billington	Charles B. Faulhaber
Harold Bloom	Carol Fitzgerald
Deetje Boler	Penelope Fitzgerald
The Reverend Leonard E. Boyle	Jay Fliegelman
David Bradbury	Michael Ginsberg
Catherine M. Bremer	Marguerite Studer Goldschmidt
Kenneth E. Carpenter	Susan Goldstein
Carlo Alberto Chiesa	Anthony Grafton
Bonnie Clemens	Barbara Graham

603

Carolyn M. Gray

Vartan Gregorian

Andrea V. Grimes

Naomi Hample

Archibald Hanna

Kenneth Harris

James Herbert

William R. Holman

Peter B. Howard

Andrea Immel

Father Isidore

Max Israel

Nico Israel

John C. Ittelson

Alan Jutzi

Priscilla Juvelis

Edward Kasinec

Alfred Kazin

Anne R. Kenney

Diana Korzenik

Jill Beute Koverman

Diane N. Kresh

Ronald A. Lane

Claire LaVaute

Paul LeClerc

Philip D. Leighton

Judith Lowry

Peter Lyman

Beverly P. Lynch

Annette G. MacNair

Bernard Margolis

Fabrizio Massimo

Marilyn McLean

Regina Minudri

William A. Moffett Jr.

Marvin Mondlin

Carole Moore

Barry Moser

Amy Myers

Minor E. Myers Jr.

Stephen G. Nichols

Roger Norris

Thomas F. O'Connell

Tillie Olsen

Robert K. O'Neill

Richard W. Oram

Gregory Smith Prince Jr.

William S. Reese

Melissa Riley

Bernard M. Rosenthal

Leona Rostenberg

Judy Harvey Sahak

Jacqueline Sanson

Henry Scannell

Karen A. Schmidt

Fred Schreiber

Scott H. Seaman

Maurice Sendak

Ismail Serageldin

Colin St. John Wilson

David H. Stam

Kevin Starr

Lillian Starr

Norman B. Starr

Madeleine B. Stern

Winston Tabb

Robert S. Taylor

Heribert Tenschert

Sarah E. Thomas

William M. Voelkle

Stuart Walker

Duane E. Webster

Stephen Weissman

Michael Winship

Sheldon M. Wool

Jerome Yavarkovsky

Mohsen Zahran

Marino Zorzi

INDEX